Que

The Que Special Edition

Thank you for purchasing *Using MS-DOS 6,* Special Edition, the latest addition to Que's Special Edition series. The Special Edition line is the best-selling line of tutorial-references on popular computer software, from the world's leading publisher of computer books.

Since the introduction of the IBM PC more than 10 years ago, the Using series of computer books from Que has been the favorite tool of PC users wanting to quickly learn how to become productive with their computers. In 1987, we realized that the growing complexity of the most popular software products had generated the need for even more comprehensive coverage than our Using books provided. In response to this need, we published the first *Using 1-2-3,* Special Edition. Since then we have published Special Editions on each of the most important software products in the industry.

From its inception, Que's Special Edition line has offered the clearest and most comprehensive coverage of the personal computer industry's flagship products. In every Special Edition from Que you can expect to find the following features:

- The most complete single-volume reference to your software

- Many step-by-step tutorials, examples and screen shots

- Functional use of color to bring to your attention helpful tips, notes, and warnings about use of your software

- Unique *For Related Information* cross-references at the end of major sections of each chapter, complete with page numbers, to help you quickly and easily find the information you need

- Handy keystroke and command quick references printed on the inside covers

Whenever you need the best book on personal computer software, look for the Special Edition from Que.

Lloyd Short
Publisher

Using MS-DOS 6
Special Edition

JONATHAN KAMIN

DAVE ANGEL

ERIC BAATZ

DOUG BIERER

MATTHEW HARRIS

ROBERT P. KING

MARK SCHULMAN

Using MS-DOS 6, Special Edition.

Copyright © 1993 by Que® Corporation.

Library of Congress Catalog No.: 93-83296

ISBN: 1-56529-020-8

95   94   93   4   3

Interpretation of the printing code: the rightmost double-digit number is the year of the book's printing; the rightmost single-digit number, the number of the book's printing. For example, a printing code of 93-1 shows that the first printing of the book occurred in 1993.

Some of the art in this book was created by Hartman Publishing. Screens reproduced in this book were created using Collage Plus from Inner Media, Inc., Hollis, NH.

This book is based on MS-DOS Version 6.0 and earlier versions.

Publisher: Lloyd J. Short

Associate Publisher: Rick Ranucci

Operations Manager: Sheila Cunningham

Publishing Plan Manager: Thomas H. Bennett

Acquisitions Editors: Chris Katsaropoulos and Sarah Browning

CREDITS

Title Manager
Walter R. Bruce III

Product Directors
Timothy S. Stanley
Brian Underdahl

Production Editors
Tracy L. Barr
Joy M. Preacher
Kathy Simpson

Editors
Elsa M. Bell
Barb Colter
Kelly Currie
Gregory R. Robertson

Technical Editors
Matthew Harris
Dave Knispel
Eric P. Bloom
Horace E. Shelton
Jerry Ellis

Book Designer
Scott Cook

Production Team
Jeff Baker
Claudia Bell
Jodie Cantwell
Paula Carroll
Laurie Casey
Brad Chinn
Brook Farling
Carla Hall-Batton
Heather Kaufman
Bob LaRoche
Jay Lesandrini
Linda Seifert
Tina Trettin
Phil Worthington

Formatter
Jill L. Stanley

Composed in *Cheltenham* and *MCPdigital*
by Que Corporation

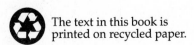
The text in this book is
printed on recycled paper.

Dave Angel has been programming mainframe, minicomputers, and PCs since 1968. He's been involved in MS-DOS since early 1982. Currently working for Software Emancipation Technology in Waltham, MA, Dave works with UNIX, Windows NT, Windows, and MS-DOS. When not programming or writing, he's active on CompuServe's IBMNET forums.

Eric Baatz has been a long-time programmer and manager in New England. He has worked on a wide variety of personal computers and workstations from the PDP-8 and Intel 8086 to Sun SPARCstations. He has also been a beta tester for a variety of PC applications and operating systems. His current software interests are centered around words and information.

Doug Bierer wrote his first computer program on a PDP-8 in 1970, his first contact with PCs was with a Tandy TRS-80 Model I, and he has since worked with a variety of programming languages and is familiar with several operating systems. He has contributed to a number of Que books, including *Using Windows 3.1*, Special Edition, *Windows 3.1 QuickStart*, and *Tuning Windows 3.1*. He is the author of *Connecting Windows for Workgroups 3.1*, also published by Que. Doug works for Vitek Systems Education in San Jose, CA, training network administrators and systems integrators how to install and maintain Novell's NetWare and Univel's UnixWare.

Matthew Harris is a coauthor of *Using Paradox 4.0*, Special Edition, *The Paradox Developer's Guide*, and *Using FileMaker Pro 2.0 for Windows*, published by Que. A consultant living in Oakland, California, Mr. Harris has been involved with the microcomputer industry since 1980 and has written commercially distributed applications, as well as applications used in-house by several clients. Matthew has provided technical support, training, and database consulting services to a variety of companies, large and small.

Robert P. King is an independent computer consultant who services and provides custom software to his small business clients with a specialty in multiuser systems. He was the founder of Mighty Byte Computer Centers, Inc., and served as its president from 1979 to 1980. In addition to providing *ad hoc* support to his own business clients, he provides support as an independent sysop of Novell's DR support forum, NDSG, on CompuServe. He also is a coauthor of *Using DR DOS 6*, published by Que Corporation.

Jonathan Kamin is a freelance writer and microcomputer consultant in Lake Oswego, Oregon. He is the author of the two-volume *MS-DOS Power User's Guide, Expert Advisor: DOS*, and over 20 other computer titles on DOS, environments, utilities, and applications. He served as editor and staff writer at Sybex Computer books for four years. He holds a Ph.D. from Princeton University, has taught sociology and music, and has written professionally for over 20 years.

Mark Schulman is a computer programmer and instructor with Cincinnati Bell Information Systems, the computer subsidiary of Cincinnati Bell. He has worked with a wide range of computer hardware and operating systems from micros to mainframes. He has taught as a visiting instructor at a number of major companies, including AT&T Bell Labs and many of the Bell operating companies, in topics that include DOS, UNIX, OS/2, and the C and C++ programming languages. He lives near Orlando, Florida.

TRADEMARK ACKNOWLEDGMENTS

All terms mentioned in this book that are known to be trademarks or service marks have been appropriately capitalized. Que cannot attest to the accuracy of this information. Use of a term in this book should not be regarded as affecting the validity of any trademark or service mark.

MS-DOS 6 is a registered trademark of Microsoft Corporation.

CONTENTS AT A GLANCE

IV Advancing Your DOS Capabilities

TABLE OF CONTENTS

I Understanding DOS Fundamentals

8 Understanding and Managing Directories 221

III Getting the Most from DOS

IV Advancing Your DOS Capabilities

Introduction

Since its introduction in 1981, MS-DOS has grown to be the most widely used operating system in the world. Thousands of applications programs have been written for MS-DOS operating systems. With more than 40 million users worldwide, DOS affects more people than any software product ever written.

As DOS has evolved, Que Corporation has helped hundreds of thousands of personal computer users get the most from MS-DOS. *Using MS-DOS 6*, Special Edition, represents Que's continuing commitment to provide the best microcomputer books in the industry. This book is a comprehensive learning tool and reference volume for users of MS-DOS and PC DOS. This Special Edition reflects the maturity of DOS and the far-reaching impact that DOS-based microcomputing has had on the way people work.

DOS is the operating system of choice for the majority of personal computer users. *Using MS-DOS 6*, Special Edition, offers DOS users a source of information so that they can organize their work with the PC more effectively and make their hardware respond more efficiently.

Who Should Read This Book?

This book is written and organized to meet the needs of a large group of readers. This book is suited for readers who are new to DOS, providing easy-to-follow tutorial information for learning how to use DOS. *Using MS-DOS 6*, Special Edition, is also a comprehensive reference on DOS for the more advanced user.

Maybe you are just beginning to use a PC and want to get up to speed quickly. Perhaps you have upgraded your hardware to a more powerful PC with more memory and disk capacity. Or maybe you have upgraded your version of DOS and want to take advantage of its new or expanded features. If you find that you fit into any of these categories, this comprehensive edition is a "must have" volume.

What Hardware Is Needed?

This book applies to the family of IBM personal computers and their close compatibles—those that operate using the Intel family of microprocessors—including the IBM PS/1 and PS/2 series, COMPAQ, Hewlett-Packard, Gateway, Zeos International, Packard Bell, Tandy, Dell, Northgate, CompuAdd, EPSON, Leading Edge, Zenith Data Systems, and others. If your computer runs the MS-DOS operating system, you have the necessary hardware.

What Versions Are Covered?

Although this book includes information regarding DOS 3.0 and later versions, special attention is given to features new to DOS Version 6.0. (Users of DOS between Versions 2.0 and 3.0 also can benefit from this book, but many useful DOS features and commands discussed in this book are not included in these versions of DOS.)

What Is Not Covered?

This book does not include the DEBUG or LINK commands, nor does it include a technical reference to the applications programming interface that DOS provides programmers. If you are interested in programming at the operating system level, Que offers a complete line of books that cover DOS programming: *DOS Programmer's Reference*, 3rd Edition; *Using Assembly Language*, 3rd Edition; and *Advanced Assembly Language*.

Also not included in this book are computer-specific setup or configuration commands, such as IBM's SETUP for the PS/2 and Toshiba's CHAD for laptop displays. Although these commands often are distributed with the same disks as DOS, they are too variable to be covered adequately here. Your computer-supplied manual and your PC dealer are the best sources of information about these machine-specific features.

How Is This Book Organized?

You can flip quickly through this book to get a feeling for its organization. *Using MS-DOS 6*, Special Edition, approaches DOS in a logical, functionally defined way. The material in this book is arranged into four main parts, a Command Reference, and a set of appendixes.

Part I: Understanding DOS Fundamentals

Part I, "Understanding DOS Fundamentals," is devoted to explaining the fundamental role of DOS in a working PC.

Chapter 1, "Understanding the Personal Computer," takes a look at today's PCs. The chapter explores the major components of the PC and addresses the use of system and peripheral hardware. In this chapter, you get a feel not only for your system but also for systems with different keyboards, displays, and peripherals.

Chapter 2, "Understanding the Role of DOS," introduces DOS as the PC's operating system. This chapter examines DOS from both a product-oriented and a software oriented point of view. Chapter 2's explanations of the parts of DOS and how they interact clears up any confusion about what DOS does on your PC.

Chapter 3, "Starting DOS," steps through the process of booting DOS and explains important concepts along the way. You also are introduced to the DOS Shell, the visually oriented user interface provided with DOS 6.0, and DOS 6.0 alternate booting methods.

Chapter 4, "Using the DOS Shell," gets you up and running with the DOS Shell. This chapter explores the DOS Shell screen and discusses the aspects of the Shell common to all its commands.

Chapter 5, "Using DOS Commands," introduces and explains how to use DOS commands. You learn the concepts behind issuing commands at the DOS command line. The chapter explains syntax, parameters, and switches in an easy-to-learn fashion. Important keys and various examples of the DOS command also are covered.

Chapter 6, "Understanding Disks and Files," recognizes the important job DOS performs in managing disks and files. This chapter defines files and clearly explains file-naming conventions. Also explored are the uses of hard disks and floppy disks and the common disk capacities available with DOS, as well as the disk-level DOS commands that copy and compare floppy disks and analyze disks for damage.

Part II: Putting DOS to Work

Part II, "Putting DOS to Work," covers the DOS commands and concepts that make up the core of DOS's utility. The information covered in Part II enables you to use DOS effectively to manage your PC work.

Chapter 7, "Preparing and Maintaining Disks," examines the process of formatting disks. You learn what formatting does and how DOS uses formatted disks to store your files. You also learn how to partition a hard disk into sections that DOS can use as logical disks. Also presented is the disk level DOS command, CHKDSK, which analyzes disks for damage.

Chapter 8, "Understanding and Managing Directories," explains fully the important concept of DOS tree-structured directories. This inside look at DOS's file-management strategy prepares you to manage the DOS file system. Additionally, you use the DOS Shell and DOS command line directory-level commands to customize a multilevel file system on your PC. You learn how to create, change, and remove DOS directories. Included are commands that enable you to view your directory structure.

Chapter 9, "Managing Your Files," illuminates the file-level DOS commands. Because you probably will spend most of your time with DOS working with files, this chapter offers an in-depth view of the file-level commands. Each command includes examples that help you appreciate the full power of these important commands. In this chapter, you also learn about DOS 6.0's new capability, Interlink, which enables you to easily share files and printers among computers.

Chapter 10, "Understanding and Using Workgroups," describes and then walks you through using Workgroup Connections, which enables a computer to connect to a Windows for Workgroups 3.1 or LAN Manager network. In this chapter, you learn how to install a network adapter card in your computer, install the Workgroup Connections software, connect to the network, use electronic mail, and share directories and printers that are available on a network.

Chapter 11, "Working with System Information," covers the commands that set and retrieve system information in your DOS-based computer. These commands often are neglected, but they key you into the control panel of DOS. These commands are helpful whether you oversee one PC or help other users with their PCs.

Chapter 12, "Controlling Devices," explains the DOS commands that control the behavior of logical DOS devices. By using these commands, you can control the way DOS sees your system's drives and directories. You learn how to use your printer while doing other computer work, and you see how to use DOS pipes and filters effectively.

Chapter 13, "Understanding Backups and the Care of Data," offers important considerations for protecting your data. DOS provides two important utilities that enable users to maintain disk backup sets of a hard disk's contents. This chapter covers both Microsoft Backup for DOS and Windows backup utilities for protecting your hard disk information.

Part III: Getting the Most from DOS

Part III, "Getting the Most From DOS," provides the information you need to tap the expanded power available with DOS. This part of the book helps you use the many features provided with DOS and helps you customize your computer system.

Chapter 14, "Using the DOS Editor," provides a tutorial approach to DOS's built-in text-file editor. The examples developed in this chapter show you how to use the DOS Editor as a day-to-day utility. With the careful attention given to the Editor's practical use, you learn the skills needed to quickly compose a text file. Practical examples of using the DOS Editor to create memos and batch files also are presented.

Chapter 15, "Understanding Batch Files, DOSKey, and Macros," guides you through the process of creating batch files and keystroke macros. The commands related to batch files are explained in a tutorial style. Useful examples make mastering the basics of batch files easier. The important concept of the AUTOEXEC.BAT file also is explored. The keystroke recording utility DOSKey is introduced. You learn how to use DOSKey to make entering DOS commands easier and faster, as well as how to record commonly used commands as macros.

Chapter 16, "Configuring the DOS Shell," discusses how you can customize your use of the DOS Shell. In this chapter, you learn how to set various options that determine how you interact with the Shell. You also learn how to add and remove program items and program groups from the program list area of the DOS Shell window and how to associate particular file names extension with a specific application program listed in the program list.

Chapter 17, "Configuring Your Computer," is a comprehensive collection of DOS commands and directives that can help you get the best performance from your PC. In this chapter, you learn how to control the way your PC boots, using alternate boot options now available in DOS 6.0. Additionally, you learn how to use Microsoft MemMaker, a DOS 6.0 utility that automatically and optimally configures the way your PC uses RAM. And you learn how to protect your files from viruses by using both the DOS and Windows versions of Microsoft Anti-Virus.

6

Chapter 18, "Getting the Most from Your Hard Disks," describes how you can keep your hard disk at its most efficient level. This chapter describes SMARTDrive, a disk cache that increases the speed with which you can access data on your hard disk. You also learn about Microsoft Defrag, a utility that keeps your files in proper order. Additionally, you explore the subject of disk compression—the ability to store more information on your hard disk than ever before—using the new DOS 6.0 DoubleSpace utility.

Part IV: Advancing Your DOS Capabilities

Part IV, "Advancing Your DOS Capabilities," tops off your understanding of DOS. In this part, you learn about controlling and programming your screen and keyboard, how to use international character sets, and how to program using QBasic, an interpretive BASIC programming language.

Chapter 19, "Understanding ANSI.SYS," shows you how to make DOS screens look colorful and controlled. The details of the ANSI.SYS driver are presented in workshop fashion. You learn how to reassign keys, control the cursor's position on-screen, display the date and time, and more.

Chapter 20, "Understanding the International Features of DOS," steps you through the complicated but sometimes necessary configuration of a PC to various international language standards.

Command Reference

In the Command Reference, you find all DOS commands arranged in three groups—DOS Utilities, Batch Commands, and Configuration Commands. The commands, arranged alphabetically within each group, are shown with syntax, applicable notes, and possible screen messages. You can use this section as a reference and as a source of practical advice and tips. The command reference is a complete, easy-to-use, quickly accessed resource on the proper use of DOS commands.

Appendixes

Using MS-DOS 6, Special Edition, also includes six appendixes containing useful information.

Appendix A, "Installing DOS 6," explains how to install DOS 6.0, whether you are upgrading from a previous version of DOS or installing a new copy of DOS to a hard disk or to diskettes.

Appendix B, "DOS Messages," lists and explains screen messages that you may see while using DOS.

Appendix C, "Changes between Versions of DOS," shows changes between versions of DOS.

Appendix D, "DOS Control and Editing Keys," lists the DOS control and editing keys.

Appendix E, "ASCII and Extended ASCII Codes," provides the ANSI control sequences supported by DOS through ANSI.SYS.

Conventions Used in This Book

Certain conventions are followed in this edition to help you more easily understand the discussions.

UPPERCASE letters are used to distinguish file names and DOS commands. *Note:* Although uppercase letters are used in the example for what you type, you can type commands in either upper- or lowercase letters.

In most cases, the keys on the keyboard are represented as the appear on your keyboard. Key combinations are connected by hyphens. For example, Ctrl-Break indicates that you press and hold down the Ctrl key while you press the Break key. Other hyphenated key combinations, such as Ctrl-Z or Alt-F1, are performed in the same manner.

Words or phrases defined for the first time appear in *italic*. Words or phrases that you type (when following the tutorials and examples) appear in **boldface** characters. Screen displays and on-screen messages appear in a `special typeface`.

The notation for issuing commands and running programs appears, in fullest form, in lines like the following:

*dc:pathc***CHKDSK** *filename.ext /V /F /?*

In any syntax line, not all elements of the syntax can be represented in a literal manner. For example, *filename.ext* can represent any file name with any extension. It also can represent any file name with no extension at all. However, command names (such as CHKDSK) and switches (like /V, /F and /?) are represented in a literal way. To activate the command CHKDSK.EXE, you must type the word **CHKDSK**. Any *literal* text (text you must type letter for letter) in a syntax line appears in uppercase letters. Any *variable* text (text you replace with other text) is shown in lower case letters.

Not all parts of a syntax line are essential. Any portion of a syntax line that appears in **boldface** is mandatory; you must always give this part of a command. In a previous example, to issue the CHKDSK command, you must type the word **CHKDSK** as it appears.

Portions of a syntax line that you see in *italic characters* are optional; you supply these items only when needed. If you do not type an optional item, DOS uses the item's default value or setting for the item.

Understanding DOS Fundamentals

PART

1

OUTLINE

Understanding the Personal Computer

Your personal computer is a convenient tool that can increase your productivity. When you use it in an informed manner, the personal computer can provide indispensable benefits. You're not alone in relying on this revolutionary machine. Just read the Sunday paper—the ads offer an array of personal computers. Yet the proliferation of personal computers is a relatively new phenomenon.

Little more than a decade ago, computers were large, expensive machines that were not available to individual users. Early computers were room-sized cabinets filled with thousands of tubes and transistors. The few users who knew anything about computers had to share with other users the resources of these early machines.

As recently as the early 1970s, computers were filled with thousands of discrete electronic parts and integrated circuits called *chips*. Circuitry based on thousands of chips is expensive to manufacture and maintain.

During that decade, however, advances in computer technology produced complex chips that incorporated the jobs of hundreds of these discrete components. Most of the essential electronic building blocks a computer needs now can be contained on one of these miniature chips, or *microprocessors*.

Computers that use microprocessors are called *microcomputers*. By the end of the 1970s, several companies had begun to sell microcomputers. Microcomputers were small enough and inexpensive enough for individual users to purchase for use in their businesses or homes. And through the notion of having a microcomputer dedicated to a single user, the term *personal computer* developed.

Reading about those old personal computers now is like reading about the first automobiles. By today's standards, both were slow and temperamental. To maintain these early automobiles, the owner needed to be somewhat of a scientist. Without those pioneering automobiles, however, your driving experience might be far less routine today. Likewise, without the early microcomputers, you might still be doing all your automated work by hand. While automobiles took nearly 40 years to become practical personal transportation, microcomputers have taken less than 10 years to revolutionize the way people approach their work.

In the early 1980s, International Business Machines (IBM) introduced the IBM Personal Computer, which was an immediate success. Before long, the IBM PC captured the infant microcomputer industry and shaped its formative years. The IBM microcomputer was so popular that it became a de facto standard for personal computers.

Today, many manufacturers sell computers that are functionally equivalent to the IBM Personal Computer. Nearly all programs developed for the IBM microcomputers also run on these *compatible* personal computers offered by other manufacturers. For many years, the primary software that IBM's personal computers and the compatibles had in common is the MS-DOS disk operating system introduced by Microsoft for the original IBM PC.

In this chapter, you learn about system elements that can be generalized to any IBM PC or compatible. If you have never used a personal computer, reading this chapter can give you a good start. If you're an old hand at using computers, you may want to skim the chapter to refresh your basic knowledge.

Key Terms Used in This Chapter

Display	The screen or monitor.
DOS	An acronym for Disk Operating System. In IBM PC, XT, AT, PS/2, and functional compatibles, DOS refers to both IBM DOS and MS-DOS.
Peripheral	Any device (aside from the main components) that is connected to the computer to help it perform tasks.
Disk	A plastic or metal platter coated with magnetic material and used to store files. A disk drive records and plays back information on disks.
CD ROM Disk	A plastic platter coated with a metal foil used to store files optically rather than magnetically. Unlike magnetic disks, CD ROM disks usually can only play back information—ROM stands for Read-Only Memory.
Modem	A device for exchanging data between computers through telephone lines.
Input	Any data a computer reads.
Output	Any data a computer produces.
Bit	A binary digit; the smallest discrete representation of a value that a computer can manipulate.
Byte	A collection of eight bits that a computer usually stores and manipulates as a unit.
K (kilobyte)	1,024 bytes, used to show size or capacity in computer systems.
M (megabyte)	1,024 kilobytes, used to measure values or capacities of millions of bytes.
Data	A catch-all term that refers to words, numbers, symbols, graphics, photos, sounds—any information stored in bytes in computer form.
File	A named group of data in electronic form—in particular, a named group of data recorded on a disk.

Exploring the Components of Computer Systems

 NOTE To read this chapter, you don't need to switch on your PC. Having your PC nearby, however, may be handy. The topics covered here discuss what the computer is all about.

Personal computer systems based on the IBM PC come in a wide variety of configurations. For example, you can find equally powerful machines in the traditional desktop configuration, in portable laptop models, in compact lunchbox-sized computers, and even in hand-held models.

Hardware and software are the two main segments of a computer system. Both components must be present for a computer to do useful work for its operator. Hardware and software work together in a manner similar to a VCR and a videocassette. The VCR unit is like the hardware because it is electro-mechanical. The videocassette is like the software because it contains the information and control signals necessary for the VCR to display pictures on the TV screen.

Understanding Computer Software

At one time, you may use your VCR to view a videocassette that contains cartoons. At another time, you may watch a taped public television special on the crisis in education. Although you use the same hardware (VCR) at both viewing sessions, the software (the videocassettes) stores different pictures and sounds. Likewise, the PC can be a word processor during one work session and a database manager during the next. The software program you use is designed to work in a specific way.

Your computer has the potential to do useful work. By using different software packages, or applications programs, you determine what kind of utility you get from your computer. Software enables a PC to be a flexible tool. You can *program* (instruct) a computer to perform a wide variety of operations. Almost anything you can reduce to calculations can be made into a program and then entered into the computer.

You probably use many small "computers" that have been programmed. Calculators, telephones with number memories, VCRs that automatically record television programs, and arcade games are examples of small computer-assisted devices that use a form of software. Because these devices have built-in software, their usefulness is limited to their built-in capabilities. Because personal computers are designed to accept outside software, they are far more versatile than programmed devices.

You can teach your computer to perform chores much as these everyday devices do. With the proper software, the computer can serve as a word processor, a spreadsheet, a project manager, a mailing-list generator, or even a wily chess opponent. Table 1.1 illustrates the variety of software you can buy for your computer.

Table 1.1 Computer Software

Type of Software	Example
Operating systems	MS-DOS, UNIX, OS/2, Windows NT
Databases	dBASE IV, Alpha 4, Q&A, Paradox 4.0
Spreadsheets	Lotus 1-2-3, Quattro Pro, Excel
Word processors	WordPerfect, WordStar, Microsoft Word
Sales management	Act!
Utilities	PC Tools for DOS, Norton Utilities, Fastback
Graphics	AutoCAD, AutoSketch, CorelDRAW!, Harvard Graphics
Integrated programs	Microsoft Works
Games	Flight Simulator, Jeopardy!
Home finance	Managing Your Money, Quicken
Desktop publishing	First Publisher, Ventura Publisher, Aldus PageMaker, Picture Publisher
Communications	ProCOMM Plus, Frecom FAX96

The operating system, such as MS-DOS, is the most important type of software for the PC. Operating systems provide a foundation of services for other programs. These services provide a uniform means for programs to gain access to the full resources of the hardware. Operating systems that help programs access disk resources are called *disk operating systems.* (Chapter 2, "Understanding the Role of DOS," introduces you to disk operating systems.)

This book shows you how to use the most common operating system for the IBM PC and compatibles. The IBM versions of DOS (also called PC DOS) and the different versions of Microsoft Corporation's DOS (MS-DOS) are highly compatible. For this reason, the generic term *DOS* is used to refer to both.

FROM HERE...

For Related Information

▶▶ "Understanding the Parts of DOS," p. 52.

▶▶ "Understanding the Functions of DOS," p. 59.

▶▶ "Viewing DOS" p. 73.

Understanding Computer Hardware

A PC's *configuration* is based on the PC's components and its overall outward appearance. The PC on your desk is a configuration of components, or hardware.

Hardware is the collection of electro-mechanical components that make up the PC. In general, the term *hardware* refers to the system unit, the keyboard, the screen display, the disk drives, and the printers. The components exist in a wide variety of configurations, but the computers all operate in essentially the same manner. Figure 1.1 presents four common PC configurations. Notice that in all four cases, the PCs have system units, keyboards, displays, and disk drives. Internally, the PCs have many common components that make up the microprocessor support circuits.

Hardware falls into two main categories: system hardware and peripheral hardware. *System hardware* is directly associated with processing or computing activity. The microprocessor is the system hardware component that is central to the computer's capability to function. Because of the microprocessor's central role, it is also called the *central processing unit*, or *CPU.*

Technically, any device used by a computer for input or output of data is a *peripheral.* Displays, printers, modems, keyboards, and disk drives are all items of peripheral hardware. Peripheral hardware supports the system hardware's computing activity.

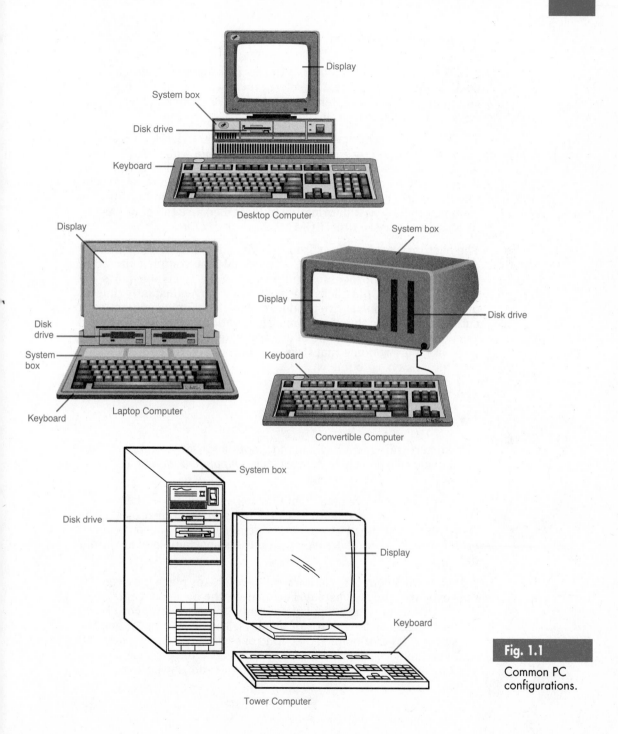

Fig. 1.1

Common PC configurations.

System Hardware

A PC's system hardware consists of the microprocessor and its support components and circuits. The microprocessor is a chip that does the computing in the computer. System hardware is often soldered or socketed to circuit boards in the computer.

The computer's random-access memory, or RAM, performs a system-hardware function by storing programs and data while the PC is turned on. System read-only memory, or ROM, also is considered system-level hardware. ROM contains program pieces that are stored permanently. The PC's microprocessor can retrieve information from ROM but cannot store any new information in ROM. Because the contents of ROM are not very flexible, ROM is often called *firmware*.

The microprocessor steps through each instruction in a program in order to execute the program. To coordinate the complex interactions between the microprocessor and the rest of the electronic parts, such as RAM and ROM, the microprocessor relies on a constantly timed set of pulses. These pulses are produced by a clock-timing generating circuit. Don't confuse this clock-timing generating circuit with the clock-calendar that keeps the time of day and date. The timing generator is more like a metronome that ticks at a determined speed to provide a beat for musicians to follow.

Peripheral Hardware

System hardware must have outside input in order to compute. The input comes from various devices called *input devices*. The keyboard is an example of an input device.

In order for your work on a computer to be useful, when the system hardware has completed some aspect of its work, it must output the result for you to see or store. The system hardware's output goes to *output devices*. Your PC's display monitor is an example of an output device.

A great deal of your interaction with the PC takes place between you, the keyboard, and the display. Fortunately, the basic concepts of using a keyboard or viewing a display are simple. Some differences do exist, however, between keyboards or displays. The next two sections discuss some of the principles that control keyboards and displays. Understanding these principles may help you avoid confusion when working with this book, DOS, and your applications programs.

Exploring the Computer Display

The *display*, also called the *monitor* or the *screen*, is the part of the computer's peripheral hardware that produces visual output. The display is the normal, or *default*, location for output for the PC; the display is the PC's primary output device.

Most displays offered with PCs work on the same principle as a television set. Like televisions, most PC displays use a *cathode ray tube* (CRT) as the means to display output. (Some PC users refer to the PC's display as the CRT.) Manufacturers also incorporate other types of technology into computer displays. To produce flatter (and thinner) displays, for example, manufacturers use a technology known as a *gas plasma* display. Gas plasma displays produce an orange color against a dark background.

Another technology adapted to computer displays is liquid crystal. *Liquid crystal displays* (LCDs) work on the same principle as many digital watch displays. Most LCDs produce dark characters against a lighter background. Older LCD screens work well only in brightly lighted rooms because the light striking the display increases the contrast of the display output. Most newer LCDs employ a backlight that increases display contrast.

Regardless of the display type, all displays have one function in common. They take electrical signals and translate them into patterns of tiny picture-element dots, or *pixels*, that you can recognize as characters or figures. Not all displays produce the same total number of pixels. Some displays are noticeably sharper than others. The more pixels available with a display, the sharper the visual image. The sharpness, or *resolution*, of the visual image is a function of both the display and the display adapter.

The *display adapter* is a collection of circuits that interface with the system hardware. The display adapter controls the computer display. In some PCs, the display circuitry can be part of the *motherboard*, which is the main circuit board that contains the majority of the PC's system components. The display circuitry also can be on a separate board, which fits into a slot in the computer. The display adapter can be a Monochrome Display Adapter (MDA), Monochrome (Hercules) Graphics Adapter (MGA or HGA), Color Graphics Adapter (CGA), Enhanced Graphics Adapter (EGA), Video Graphics Array Adapter (VGA), Super Video Graphics Array Adapter (SVGA), Extended Graphics Array Adapter (XGA), or some less-common type of special display adapter. These display adapters fall into one of two main categories: adapters that display text only or adapters that display text and graphics.

Text Displays

The letters, numbers, and punctuation that appear on-screen are produced as patterns of dots, or *pixels*. Each pattern is stored in the computer's memory in a code known as the American Standard Code for Information Interchange (ASCII).

Most DOS programs use a display operating mode called *text mode*. In text mode, ASCII-coded characters compose the visual display. Each ASCII code represents a letter or a symbol. When a program instructs the display adapter to display a letter or symbol, the adapter "consults" an electronic table containing ASCII codes. The display adapter uses the electronic table like a set of stencils.

The principle is similar to the principle used to display scores on a lighted sports scoreboard. Instead of lighting a pattern of bulbs, the display adapter illuminates a pattern of pixels. Each number on the scoreboard is a different arrangement of illuminated bulbs. Each letter on your screen is a different arrangement of pixels.

The standard ASCII character set contains 128 characters—a sufficient number to represent all the letters, numbers, and punctuation commonly used in English. When IBM introduced the PC, however, the company added another 128 codes to the standard ASCII set. The additional codes, referred to as *extended ASCII codes*, represent pixel patterns that display lines, corners, and special images such as musical notes.

Programs can use combinations of these extended ASCII characters to produce boxes and other graphics-like characters. In text mode, display adapters can produce only predetermined characters and special shapes. The extended codes enable a text display to incorporate a wide variety of borders, boxes, and icons. The original IBM PC had a display adapter—the Monochrome Display Adapter—that could operate only in text mode. Nearly all currently available monochrome adapters also operate in graphics mode, using a standard developed by the Hercules company.

Graphics Displays

In graphics mode, the display adapter can control and light up any pixel on-screen. Thus, complex figures with curves and fine details can be displayed. Graphics-based screens are perhaps the most pleasing to view. Charts, drawings, digitized pictures, animated game characters, and what-you-see-is-what-you-get (WYSIWYG) word processing text are all graphics-based outputs.

Usually, the computer must work harder—and, therefore, take longer—to create a graphics image than to create a text image. A graphics screen does not have an electronic stencil. To light the correct pixels on the display, the display adapter must find the screen-coordinate points for each pixel. No table of pixel patterns exists, as in text mode.

Not all monitors and display adapters have the same number of pixels available. The greater the number of pixels, the finer the detail (and, usually, the greater the cost) of the display. Each computed pixel has characteristics that tell the graphics adapter what the color or intensity of the pixel should be. The greater the number of colors and intensities, the more storage space in memory is required. Graphics adapters offer varying combinations of pixel densities, colors, and intensities. Table 1.2 lists the most common display types, including the colors available and the pixel resolution.

Table 1.2 Resolution and Colors for Display Adapters

Adapter Type	Graphics Mode	Pixel Resolution	Colors Available
CGA	Medium resolution	320×200	4
CGA	High resolution	640×200	2
EGA	All CGA modes		
EGA	CGA high resolution	640×200	16
EGA	EGA high resolution	640×350	16
MGA	HGA Monochrome graphics	720×348	2
MDA	Text only	N/A	N/A
VGA	All CGA and EGA modes		
VGA	Monochrome	640×480	2
VGA	VGA high resolution	640×480	16
VGA	VGA medium resolution	320×200	256
SVGA	Super VGA resolution	800×600	16 or 256
SVGA	Super VGA resolution	1024×768	4, 16, or 256
UVGA	Ultra VGA resolution	1280×1024	16
XGA	Extended graphics	800×600	256

Figure 1.2 demonstrates the principle of resolution that affects the quality of a graphics display. The higher-resolution image (left) uses four times as many pixels as the low-resolution image (right).

Fig. 1.2

Resolution in a
graphics display.

NOTE Each pixel in a graphics display must be placed on the
screen individually. The greater the number of pixels and
colors on the display, the more time required for the computer to "paint" the complete graphics screen. For some
software programs—like Microsoft Windows—the length of
time needed to repaint a high-resolution screen display may
be inconveniently slow.

If slow screen painting is a problem, you can speed up some
screen displays with a special video display adapter. Called
video accelerators, these special display adapters are designed to drastically reduce the amount of time that the
computer takes to paint the graphics screen. Video accel-
erator cards are usually tailored for specific software programs, such as Microsoft Windows. Let your dealer help you
determine whether you will benefit from using a video accel-
erator card.

Your applications programs may use text mode or one of the graphics
modes. Before you decide to buy software that uses a graphics mode,
let your dealer help you determine whether the package is suitable for
your display.

T I P Many CGA or EGA display-system users can upgrade their display
adapters and display monitors to the newer VGA, SVGA, or XGA display system by installing new hardware. Check with your dealer to
determine whether you can take advantage of the higher-resolution
VGA display system.

Exploring the Computer Keyboard

Keyboards, like displays, can vary from PC to PC. The effect of one
keyboard's variation from others is not as critical as the differences
among displays and display adapters. Programs normally don't require

that you use a specific type of keyboard, but you need to understand how DOS and other programs use the keys on your keyboard. Like displays, keyboards have certain common characteristics. This section familiarizes you with the keyboard.

The computer keyboard has the familiar QWERTY layout. (The name QWERTY comes from the letters found on the left side of the top row of letters on a standard typewriter.) But a computer keyboard is different from a typewriter keyboard in several important ways.

The most notable difference is the presence of the extra keys—the keys that do not appear on a typewriter. These special keys are described in table 1.3. The keyboard also includes 10 or 12 special function keys.

Table 1.3 Special Keys on the Computer Keyboard

Key	Function
Enter	Signals the computer to respond to the commands you type; also functions as a carriage return in programs that simulate the operation of a typewriter.
Cursor keys	Changes the on-screen location of the cursor; includes the left-arrow ($\leftarrow$), right-arrow ($\rightarrow$), up-arrow ($\uparrow$), and down-arrow ($\downarrow$) keys. A few keyboards also have diagonal arrow keys.
PgUp/PgDn	Scrolls the screen display up or down one page.
Home/End	Home moves the cursor to the screen's upper left corner; End moves the cursor to the lower right corner.
Backspace	Moves the cursor backward one space at a time, deleting any character in that space.
Del	Deletes, or erases, any character at the location of the cursor.
Insert (Ins)	Inserts any character at the location of the cursor.
Shift	Creates uppercase letters and other special characters; when pressed in combination with another key, can change the standard function of that key.
Caps Lock	When pressed to the lock position, causes all letters to be typed in uppercase. To release, press the key again.
Ctrl	Control key; when pressed in combination with another key, changes the standard function of that key.

continues

Table 1.3 Continued

Key	Function
Alt	Alternate key; when pressed in combination with another key, changes the standard function of that key. Not all programs use Alt.
Esc	In some situations, pressing Esc enables you to "escape" from the current operation to an earlier one. Sometimes Esc has no effect on the current operation. Not all programs respond to Esc.
Num Lock	Changes the numeric keypad from cursor-movement to numeric-function mode.
PrtSc	Used with Shift to send the characters on the display to the printer.
Print Screen	Found on Enhanced Keyboards; same as Shift-PrtSc.
Scroll Lock	Locks the scrolling function to the cursor-control keys. Instead of the cursor moving, the screen scrolls.
Pause	Suspends display output until another key is pressed (not provided with standard keyboards).
Break	Stops some programs in progress.
Numeric keypad	A cluster of keys to the right of the standard keyboard. The keypad includes numbered keys from 0 through 9 as well as cursor-control keys and other special keys.

Many of the special keys are designed to be used in combination with other keys. Pressing Shift and PrtSc in combination, for example, causes DOS to print the contents of the current screen through an attached printer. Simultaneously pressing Ctrl and PrtSc causes DOS to print continuously what you type. Pressing Ctrl and PrtSc a second time turns off the continuous printing. Table 1.4 describes the more common key combinations used in DOS.

Table 1.4 DOS Key Combinations

Keys	Function
Ctrl-Num Lock	Freezes the display; pressing Ctrl-S or any other key restarts the display.

Keys	Function
Shift-PrtSc	Prints the contents of the video display (print-screen feature).
Print Screen	Found on Enhanced Keyboards, same as Shift-PrtSc.
Ctrl-PrtSc	Sends lines to both the screen and the printer; giving this sequence a second time turns off this function.
Ctrl-C or Ctrl-Break	Stops execution of most programs.
Ctrl-Alt-Del	Restarts MS-DOS (system reboot).

CAUTION: If you use the Ctrl-Alt-Del keystroke combination to restart MS-DOS indiscriminately, you may lose data. In general, only restart DOS when you are at the MS-DOS prompt. The DOS prompt is described in Chapter 3, "Starting DOS."

The function keys are shortcuts. Not all programs use these keys, and some programs use only a few of the function keys. When used, however, the function keys automatically carry out repetitious operations for you. F1, for example, is often used to access on-line help, which displays instructions from the computer's memory to help you understand a particular operation. The DOS 6.0 Shell uses F3 to back out of one operation and move into another. In a DOS Shell session, F10 moves the cursor to the menu line, where you select actions. The action provided by a function key is determined by the program you are using. Always check the program's documentation to determine the result of pressing any particular function key.

These and other keys recognized by DOS 6.0's Shell are explained in detail later in the book. Information about configuring the DOS Shell is covered in Chapter 16, "Configuring the DOS Shell."

You use the keyboard to put information into the computer. Each character you type is converted into a code the computer can process. The keyboard, therefore, is considered an *input device*. DOS expects commands to be input through the keyboard as you work at the DOS level.

AT Keyboards and Enhanced Keyboards

Many early PC-compatible computers used a keyboard similar to the IBM PC keyboard. Other machines use keyboards patterned after IBM's Personal Computer AT keyboards. IBM's PS/2 computers use the 101-key Enhanced Keyboard. Some users prefer the keyboard arrangement of the original PC keyboard, whereas others prefer the AT-style keyboard or the Enhanced Keyboard, which is the only keyboard that has the Print Screen and Pause keys.

You can determine whether your computer has a PC-style keyboard, a Personal Computer AT-style keyboard, or an enhanced-style keyboard.

The 102-Key Keyboard

Some keyboards enable you to change key caps and switch key definitions for the Caps Lock, Ctrl, Esc, and ~ (tilde) keys. Northgate Computer Systems, for example, offers these options as well as an enhanced-style keyboard.

Northgate's enhanced-style keyboard locates the first 10 function keys to the left instead of across the top of the alphabet and number keys. Because this arrangement requires one more key than the 101-key Enhanced Keyboards, this type of keyboard is called the 102-key keyboard.

Nonstandard Keyboards

Small computers, such as laptop, notebook, and palmtop computers, use nonstandard keyboards, usually to conserve space. On some computers, space is so restricted that you need an external numeric keypad for use with software that performs advanced calculations. Most laptop and notebook computers, for example, don't have room for a dedicated numeric keypad. A group of the letter keys also serve as numeric keys when you press a special function key (often labeled *Fn*) on the laptop's keyboard.

Your computer manuals explain how to use the special functions of the nonstandard keyboard. Usually, the "missing" keys are functionally available to you through multiple-key sequences. Normally, however, a nonstandard keyboard does not affect your work with DOS.

For Related Information

▶▶ "Changing File Attributes with the DOS Shell," p. 229.

▶▶ "Working with Directories through the DOS Shell," p. 243.

▶▶ "Selecting Files in the DOS Shell," p. 282.

▶▶ "Using the DOS Shell To Search for Files," p. 288.

▶▶ "Printing Files from the DOS Shell," p. 304.

FROM HERE...

Exploring the System Unit

In a typical desktop PC, a box-shaped cabinet contains all other parts of the PC. This box is called the *system unit*. The devices connected to it are the *peripherals*. The system unit and peripherals make up the complete computer system. Peripherals such as the display and the keyboard are connected to the system unit.

The system unit houses all but a few parts of a PC. Included in the system unit are circuit boards, a power supply, and a small speaker. System units vary in appearance, but a horizontal box shape is the most common. A vertical "tower" shape is also popular because it frees desk or table space.

The system unit houses the computer's main circuit board, called the *motherboard*. The motherboard contains the microprocessor and the circuits and chips that support it. Normally, the motherboard has electrical sockets into which users can plug various adapter circuit boards for additional peripherals. The electrical sockets are often referred to as *expansion slots* because of their slot-like appearance.

Electronic components known as chips provide the computer with its memory and are located on the motherboard. In some cases, an additional memory adapter is plugged into an expansion slot to increase the system's memory. The number of expansion slots available varies from model to model. Most motherboards have a socket for a math coprocessor. Math coprocessors improve the speed and precision of calculations in number-intensive programs.

In addition to standard system-level components, most system units house other hardware devices or their associated adapter boards. A great variety of devices can be included in a PC, but a few types are common. Figure 1.3 shows some of the common peripheral devices; the following sections discuss these parts in more detail.

Hard disk platters are sealed inside the hard disk drive.

Floppy disks are encased in either a flexible 5¼-inch jacket or a rigid 3½-inch jacket.

Fig. 1.3

Some typical peripheral devices for a computer.

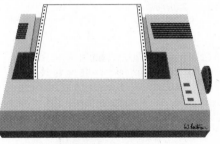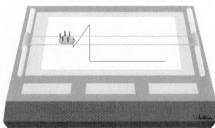

A printer, which is like a typewriter without a keyboard, accepts input from the computer and renders the input as characters on paper.

A plotter produces drawings from the computer. Like a printer, a plotter accepts input from the computer and renders it as a line drawing on paper.

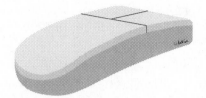

A mouse is a computer input device whose shape is vaguely reminiscent of a real mouse.

A modem enables you to transfer signals between computers by using telephone lines.

A digitizer tablet provides a work surface that many users find more natural than using a mouse. The "puck" display shows the position of the puck on the tablet.

Fig. 1.3

Continued.

Understanding Disk Drives and Disks

Disks and disk drives work together to store and retrieve information and programs. Disk drives are complex mechanisms, but they carry out a basically simple function. They read and write information from and to disks. You don't have to know about the mechanical aspects of disk drives to use them, but some insight into drive mechanics may help you appreciate the drives' role.

Disks are circular platters or pieces of plastic that have magnetized surfaces. The disk drive rotates the disk in much the same way a phonograph rotates a record. Within the drive, one or more read/write heads convert electrical signals (computer data) into magnetic fields on the disk's magnetic surface. This process is called *writing data to the disk*. Disk-drive heads also recover, or *read*, the magnetically stored data and present it to the computer as electrical signals that the PC can use.

Computers don't store data on disks in a disorganized fashion. Computers rely on the operating system (MS-DOS, for example) to provide a template for disk organization. When a computer writes to a disk, DOS ensures that the data is stored as a named collection of information called a *file*. You (or the program) refer to files by name. DOS supervises the translation of the file's name into a set of physical coordinates, which the disk drive uses to read the correct data. A disk's primary job, therefore, is to act as a storage medium for files, much as a VCR tape stores a movie or television program. Unlike data stored in silicon memory chips, magnetically stored disk data is not lost when the computer's power is turned off.

You know that a drive is reading from or writing to the disk when the small light on the front of the disk drive or on a front panel of your computer is on. The light is the drive's signal that the drive is in use. Generally, do not open a floppy disk drive door or eject a disk until the light goes out. If you open the door or eject a disk while the light is on, an error message may appear. In rare cases, the program may stall, or you may lose disk data.

Three types of disk drives are currently available. The two most common types of disks (and their drives) are available in a variety of sizes; these disks store information as patterns of magnetic fields. The third type of disk drive—called *CD ROM* (Compact Disk Read Only Memory)—is becoming increasingly common. CD ROM disks store information optically, using microscopically tiny patterns of light and dark spots.

Magnetic disks are either *floppy* or *hard*. Floppy disks, also called *diskettes*, are removable and flexible and store less data than hard disks. A floppy disk's primary advantage is that it is portable. You can use floppy disks to move data from one computer to another. DOS, as well as other software, is supplied on floppy disks.

Hard disks, also called *fixed disks*, are nonremovable, high-capacity, rigid platters. To increase storage capacity, several platters can be stacked within a single hard disk drive. Both sides of each platter are available for data storage. Most DOS-based disk drives, whether floppy or hard, operate in this two-sided manner and are called *double-sided* disk drives.

CD ROM optical disks come in only one size, a 4 1/2-inch plastic platter coated with a metal foil. Most CD ROM drives can only read from a CD ROM disk; you cannot add new information to the information recorded on a CD ROM disk. Although read/write CD ROM disks and drives are available, they are very expensive and not very common. CD ROM disks are removable and can store large quantities of information. Currently, CD ROM disks are used mostly for electronic encyclopedias and similar applications that include sound, complex graphics, and video information, as well as the more usual text information.

Whether a disk is magnetic or optical, the components of a disk drive are roughly similar to those of a phonograph. The disk, like a record, rotates. A *positioner arm*, like a phonograph's tone arm, moves across the radius of the disk. A *head*, like a pickup cartridge, translates the encoded information to electrical signals. Unlike phonographs, however, disk drives do not have spiral tracks on the disk's surface.

The disk's surface is recorded in concentric rings or *tracks*. Track arrangement on each platter surface resembles a rings-within-rings geometry. The closer the adjacent tracks are packed on the disk, the greater the storage capacity of the disk. Chapter 7, "Preparing and Maintaining Disks," explains in more detail how DOS uses the drives and disks on a PC.

Floppy Disks

Floppy disks store from 360K to 2.88M of data and come in two standard sizes. (Other sizes of floppy disks are available but are not widely used.) *Minifloppies* are 5 1/4-inch disks, and *microfloppies* are 3 1/2-inch disks. The mini- or micro- prefix refers to a floppy's physical size, the size of the disk's jacket. Floppy disks generally are referred to as *floppies* or *diskettes*. In this book, the term *floppy disk* refers to both 5 1/4-inch and 3 1/2-inch disks.

Although floppies come in two sizes, each size has more than one storage capacity. The 5 1/4-inch floppies generally are 360K double-sided, double-density or 1.2M double-sided, high-density. The 3 1/2-inch disks are 720K double-sided, double-density, 1.44M double-sided, high-density, or 2.88M double-sided, ultra-high-density. Make sure that you know your drive's specification before you buy or interchange floppies. Floppies of the same size but with different capacities can be incompatible with a particular disk drive.

Fixed Disks

In 1973, IBM developed a hard-disk technology and code-named it *Winchester*, a term that is sometimes used to refer to any hard disk.

Hard disks often consist of multiple, rigid-disk platters. The platters spin at approximately 3,600 RPM, which is much faster than a floppy disk drive spins. As the platters spin in the drive, the head positioners make small, precise movements above the tracks of the disk. Because of this precision, hard disks can store enormous quantities of data— from 10M to more than 100M.

Despite their precision, hard disks are reasonably rugged devices. Factory sealing prevents contamination from entering the housing. With proper care, hard disks can give years of service.

Hard disk platters for personal computers may range from 1.2 to 8 inches in diameter. The most common platter sizes, 3 1/2 inch and 5 1/4 inch, hold between 2.5M and 25M of information per platter side; most hard disk drives contain two to four platters. Over the past few years the manufacturing technology for hard disk drives has steadily improved, resulting in increasingly smaller drives with increasingly greater capacities. A physical limit does exist, however, to how much information can be recorded on a given amount of magnetic material. This limit is the ultimate governing factor in the capacity of a hard disk relative to the size and number of its platters.

Until recently, a hard disk capacity of 40M to 65M was typical. Contemporary computers are more likely to have hard disk capacities of 80M to 120M. If you have a laptop or notebook computer, you may have a slightly smaller capacity hard disk than an equivalent desktop system. Because physical space is severely limited in a laptop or notebook computer, manufacturers tend to equip these computers with the physically smallest hard disk drives possible. In choosing a hard disk, the manufacturer may make a trade-off between physical size and the hard disk's capacity, choosing a lower capacity hard disk in order to conserve space.

FROM HERE...

For Related Information

▶▶ "Formatting Floppy Disks," p. 181.

▶▶ "Formatting a Hard Disk," p. 197.

Understanding Peripheral Devices

In addition to the display and the keyboard, several other peripherals can be useful. Many state-of-the-art computer programs require that you use a mouse (or similar input device) to take the greatest advantage of the program's features. Other peripherals, such as printers and modems, enable you to use your computer's output as you want.

The Mouse and Other Pointing Devices

The mouse is a device you move on the surface of your desk. The computer correlates the movement of the mouse to the movement of some object—usually referred to as the *mouse pointer*—on the display. The mouse pointer usually appears as a solid block when the display screen is in a text-only mode and as an arrow-head shape when the display screen is in a graphics mode.

The mouse is contoured to fit comfortably under your hand. (Many manufacturers make models that are specifically contoured for left- or right-handed users.) The contoured shape and the cable tailing from the unit give the vague appearance of a mouse sitting on the table. The mouse's switch buttons (it has two or three) are positioned so that they lie beneath your fingers.

Not all software supports mouse input, but many popular programs do. Generally, mouse-based programs enable you to use the mouse to point to options on-screen and click one of the buttons on the mouse to carry out a task. Because you use a mouse by pointing at elements displayed on-screen, the mouse is often referred to as a *pointing device*.

In the years since the mouse was originally introduced, several variations of this pointing device have appeared. One of the most common alternatives to a mouse is the *trackball*, sometimes called a *palmball*. The trackball has a movable ball on top of the unit; you rotate this ball with the palm of your hand (or fingertips) to move the mouse pointer on the display screen. The trackball has push-button switches similar to those on a mouse; the trackball's switches also lie under your fingers when your palm is over the ball. Because you do not move a trackball over the surface of your desk, a trackball requires less desk space to use. Many trackball users also feel that the trackball gives them a more delicate control over the mouse pointer—an advantage when using painting or drawing software.

Another alternative to the mouse is the *mouse pen*. You hold a mouse pen like a regular writing pen and move the pen over the surface of your desk to move the mouse pointer on the display—just like a regular mouse. The switches on a mouse pen are located on the barrel of the pen.

Digitizer tablets, like the one shown in figure 1.3, are also sometimes used as an alternative to a mouse. The *digitizer tablet* consists of a large rectangular work surface, called the *tablet*, and a movable positioning device, called a *puck*. The position of the mouse pointer on-screen corresponds to the position of the digitizer puck relative to the edges of the tablet. Digitizer tablets are usually used only with computer-aided drafting and design (CADD), where existing drawings must be traced and absolute precision is required.

Printers

Printers accept signals (input) from the CPU and convert those signals to characters (output), which usually are imprinted on paper. You can classify printers in two ways: by the manner in which they receive input from the computer and by the manner in which they produce output.

The way a printer receives input from the PC is important in determining the type of printer assignments you make with DOS and other software. The way a printer actually produces the output determines the print quality, graphics capability, and speed of the printed output.

The terms *parallel* and *serial* describe the two methods by which printers receive input from personal computers. The terms *dot-matrix*, *daisy-wheel*, *laser*, and *inkjet* name the generic categories of the ways that printers produce output.

T I P

Parallel printers usually print faster than serial printers, but serial printers operate at longer cable lengths than parallel printers. A serial printer can be 50 feet or more from the PC, whereas a parallel printer may have trouble getting its input from a cable more than 15 feet long. Having a printer nearby is convenient but can be noisy. When buying a printer, ask your dealer to demonstrate both serial and parallel printers before you decide.

Printers usually are rated by their printing speed and the quality of the finished print. Some printers print by using all the addressable points on the screen, much as a graphics display adapter does. Some printers offer color printing.

Parallel and Serial Printers

You connect printers to the system unit through a *port*, a connector on the back of the system unit. A port is an electrical doorway through which data can flow between the system unit and an outside peripheral. A port can be part of the computer's main system board—called the motherboard—or have its own expansion adapter or share an expansion adapter with other ports or circuits.

Computers that have ports built into the motherboard usually have at least one parallel port and at least one serial port. Many contemporary expansion adapters have two parallel ports and two serial ports on each adapter. Often, the serial and parallel ports are also combined with some other circuit, such as a disk drive controller. Older computers that use Color Graphics Adapters (CGA) or Monochrome Graphics Adapters (MGA) for the display screen often include a parallel port for connecting a printer on the video display card.

The terms *parallel* and *serial* relate to the way the electrical data is delivered from the port to the printer. A serial port delivers the bits of the data byte one after another in a single-file manner. Sending one complete byte (character) using serial communications takes longer, but communications require fewer wires in the cable. Serial printers can communicate with the port over longer distances than parallel printers. (In other words, you can put a serial printer farther away from the computer.)

With a parallel port, all the bits of a data byte are sent at the same time through separate wires in the parallel cable one complete byte (character) at a time. Parallel printer connections are more common than serial connections.

Dot-Matrix, Daisywheel, Laser, and Inkjet Printers

All printers have the job of putting their output on paper. Most of the time, this output is text, but output also may be a graphics image. The four classifications of printers are distinguished by the mechanical method of getting output on the page.

The most common printer is the *dot matrix*. Dot-matrix printers use a print head that contains a row of pins, or wires, which produce the characters. A motor moves the print head horizontally across the paper. As the print head moves, a vertical slice of each character forms as the printer's controlling circuits fire the proper pins. The pins press corresponding small dots of the ribbon against the paper, leaving an inked-dot impression. After several tiny horizontal steps, the print head leaves the dot image of a complete character. The process continues for each character on the line.

The *daisywheel printer* also steps the print head across the page but strikes the page with a complete character for each step. All the characters of the alphabet are arranged at the ends of holders that resemble spokes on a wheel. The visual effect of this wheel is similar to a daisy's petals arranged around the flower head. Because the characters are fully formed, rather than made of dots, the quality of daisywheel printing is high.

Laser printers use a technology similar to photocopying. Instead of a light-sensitive drum picking up the image of a photocopied document, the drum is painted with the light of a laser diode. The image from the drum is coated with toner (usually a black powder), and the toner is then transferred to the paper in a high dot-density output. The output characters look fully formed. Laser printers can also produce graphics image output. The combination of high-quality text and graphics can be extremely useful for desktop publishing.

Inkjet printers are similar to dot-matrix printers in that a head mechanism moves horizontally across the paper and produces a line of characters. The inkjet head shoots fine jets of ink onto the paper to form characters. The quality and speed of inkjet printer output approach those of laser printers, although inkjet characters are not quite as crisp.

Modems

Modems are peripherals that enable a PC to communicate over standard telephone lines. Modems are serial-communications peripherals that send or receive characters or data one bit at a time. Modems require communications software to coordinate their communications with other modems.

Modems differ in the speed with which they communicate information. Modem speed is indicated by the modem's *baud rate*, the number of bits per second that the modem can send or receive. A modem transmitting or receiving at 300 baud (bits per second) is transmitting or receiving approximately 30 bytes per second. In the early days of computers, 300 baud was considered quite fast, but this is no longer true. Typically, modems now communicate with other modems at speeds of 2400 or 9600 baud; a baud rate of 1200 is usually considered the lowest acceptable modem speed. As a rule of thumb, faster modems cost more than slower ones.

Some modems can be installed within the system unit in an expansion slot. A modem that is installed inside the system unit is called an *internal* modem. Many modems attach to the system unit through a serial-communications connector. The modem is contained in its own stand-alone case. This stand-alone type of modem is called an *external* modem.

Some modems incorporate facsimile (FAX) circuitry so that they can be used for FAX transmission and reception. Modems that communicate

9600 baud—the typical FAX transmission speed—or more are becoming increasingly popular. As FAX use becomes more widespread, FAX-modem combinations are becoming more prevalent.

Understanding How Computers Work with Data

Now that you have been introduced to the essential parts of a computer system, you are ready for a general overview of how these parts carry out the job of computing. Fortunately, you do not have to know the details of a computer's operation to use a computer effectively in your work. But if you do undertake some exploration, you may adjust more quickly to using a computer. The fundamentals of computing are easier to understand than many people think.

Computers perform many useful tasks by accepting data as input, processing it, and releasing it as output. Data is any information—a set of numbers, a memo, a FAX transmission, sound, or an arrow key to move a game symbol, for example. Input comes from you and is translated into electrical signals that move through a set of electronic controls. Output can be grouped into three categories:

- Characters or graphics the computer displays on-screen or printed in some fashion. Printed output is often called hard copy.

- Signals the computer holds in its memory.

- Signals stored magnetically on disk.

Computers receive and send output in the form of electrical signals. These signals are stable in two states: on and off. Think of these states as you think of the power in the wire from a light switch you can turn on and off. Computers contain millions of electronic switches that can be either on or off. All forms of input and output follow this two-state principle.

The term used to describe the two-state principle is *binary*, which refers to something made of two parts. Computers represent data with binary digits, or *bits*—0 and 1. For convenience, computers group eight bits together. This eight-bit grouping is called a *byte*. Bytes are sometimes packaged in two-, four-, or eight-byte packages when the computer moves information internally.

Computers move bits and bytes across electrical highways called *buses*. Normally, the computer contains three buses. The *control bus* manages the devices attached to the PC. The *data bus* is the highway for information transfer. The *address bus* routes signals so that data goes to the correct location within the computer. The microprocessor is connected to all three buses and supervises their activity.

The microprocessor can address certain portions of its memory in any order. This portion of the computer's memory is called *random-access memory*, or *RAM*. Some portions of a computer's memory are permanent. This portion of memory is called *read-only memory*, or *ROM*. ROM is useful for holding unalterable instructions in the computer system.

The microprocessor relies on you to provide instructions in the form of a program. A *program* is a set of binary-coded instructions that produce a desired result. The microprocessor decodes the binary information and carries out the instruction from the program.

You can begin from scratch and type programs or data into the computer each time you turn on the power. But of course, you don't want to do that if you don't have to. Luckily, the computer can store both instructions and start-up data, usually on a disk. Disks store data in binary form in files.

As far as the computer is concerned, a file is just a collection of bytes identified by a unique name. These bytes can be a memo, a word processing program, or some other program. The job of the file is to hold binary data or programs safely until the microprocessor calls for that data or program. When the call comes, the drive reads the file and writes the contents into RAM.

Displaying a word on a computer screen seems to be a simple matter of pressing keys on the keyboard. But each time you press a key to enter a character, the computer carries out a series of complex steps.

A personal computer is busy on the inside. Program instructions held in RAM are called up and executed by the CPU. Resulting computations are stored in RAM. The CPU uses the data bus to determine *what* the data should be, the control bus to determine *how* the electrical operations should proceed, and the address bus to determine *where* the data or instructions are located in RAM.

Chapter Summary

DOS is much easier to learn when you are familiar with the PC and its components, and this chapter provided a quick overview of personal computers. In this chapter, you learned the following important points:

- IBM and compatible computers operate basically in the same way.

- A computer's hardware works with software to do useful work.

■ System hardware does the "computing" in the PC.

■ Peripheral hardware provides the PC with input and output capability so that the PC can work with you.

■ PCs have text displays or graphics displays. Text displays cannot show the output of many graphics-based software programs. Graphics displays can show both text and graphics.

■ The PC's keyboard offers standard typewriter keys as well as special keys, such as the function keys. Programs like DOS and the DOS Shell determine how the special keys work.

■ The PC's main box is the system unit. The system unit houses the disk drive(s) and the motherboard, where the system hardware resides.

■ Disk drives are either hard disk drives, floppy disk drives, or a CD ROM drive.

■ Hard disk drives and floppy disk drives record information with magnetic patterns and can be both written on as well as read from.

■ CD ROM disks can only be read from, and not written to.

■ Many PC systems include a printer, modem, or mouse. PCs accommodate these outside peripherals as well as other attachments.

■ Computers "compute" by operating on binary representations of information. The source of the information is called input. The destination of the resulting computational result is called output. PCs store information in eight-bit bytes.

You gain insight into computers as you progress through this book. Chapter 2, "Understanding the Role of DOS," introduces the role of DOS in the personal computer. Because DOS was designed around the system hardware and peripherals discussed in this chapter, you may want to move directly to Chapter 2 while the information in this chapter is fresh in your mind.

Understanding the Role of DOS

C hapter 1, "Understanding the Personal Computer," introduced you to personal computer systems and their components. That chapter describes software and shows how data moves in the computer. This chapter introduces DOS, the disk operating system, which serves as an important link between the hardware, the software, and you. (*Note:* As with Chapter 1, you can read this chapter without being at your computer.)

An *operating system* is a collection of computer programs that provides recurring services to other programs or to computer users. These services include disk and file management, memory management, and device—such as keyboard, display, or printer—management. Computers need software to provide these services. If the computer's operating system software did not provide these services, you or the applications program you use would have to deal directly with the details of the PC's hardware, file system, and memory use.

Without a disk operating system, every computer program would have to contain instructions telling the hardware each step required to do its job—giving step-by-step instructions for storing a file on a disk, for example. Because an operating system already contains these instructions, any program can call on the operating system when a service is needed. The operating systems are called *disk operating systems* because most of the commands are kept on the disk (floppy or hard) rather than in memory. As a result, the operating system requires less memory to run.

Originally, MS-DOS was developed by Microsoft Corporation for use with the first IBM PCs. IBM licensed the software from Microsoft, and for many years distributed their PC computers with a version of DOS called IBM DOS, also known as PC DOS.

The IBM PC became immensely popular, and many manufacturers began producing computers designed to be compatible with the IBM PC and, later, the IBM AT. To be truly IBM-compatible, the competing computers not only had to use the same type of hardware that IBM used but, more importantly, had to use the same type of operating system software that IBM used. Many of IBM's competitors, such as Compaq, licensed their own versions of MS-DOS from Microsoft; other companies simply distributed "generic" versions of MS-DOS.

Key Terms Used in This Chapter	
Program	Instructions that tell a computer how to carry out tasks
BIOS	An acronym for Basic Input/Output System; the software that provides the basic functional link between DOS and the peripheral hardware in a PC
Redirection	A change in the source or destination of a command's normal input or output
Application	A program; a set of instructions that tell the computer to perform a program-specific task, such as word processing
Interface	A connection between parts of the computer, especially between hardware devices; also refers to the interaction between a user and an applications program
Batch file	A series of DOS commands placed in a disk file; DOS executes batch-file commands one at a time

As the IBM PC hardware became an informal standard for most of the microcomputers on the market, so did the IBM operating system software: MS-DOS. In fact, MS-DOS has outlived the IBM PC computer as a standard in the microcomputer marketplace. Most contemporary PCs are designed to be MS-DOS compatible, and most manufacturers or dealers supply MS-DOS with their computers. In a few cases, a manufacturer might provide a version of DOS specifically tailored to special hardware in their computer.

Hundreds of brands and models of PCs use some form of MS-DOS. The manufacturers may put their own names on the disks and include different manuals with the DOS packages they provide, but all types of DOS are similar when they operate on a PC. When you read about DOS in this book, you can safely assume that what you read applies to the version of DOS used by most manufacturers. In special cases, differences are noted.

What Is DOS?

DOS is an acronym for Disk Operating System. Nearly every computer has some sort of disk operating system. Computers that do not have disk operating systems are severely limited in reliable data storage. In addition to disk-file storage, disk operating systems manage many of the technical details of computers. From the user's perspective, however, disk management is perhaps the most important service these operating systems provide.

Many computers, including personal computers and large multiuser computers, use these three letters—DOS—as part of their operating system's name. Microsoft's MS-DOS and IBM's version of MS-DOS, IBM DOS, are examples, as are Apple's DOS 3.3, DR DOS, and ProDOS.

Although various operating systems are all called DOS, more people associate the term *DOS* with MS-DOS than with any other disk operating system. In this book, the term *DOS* refers to MS-DOS, a single-user, single-tasking disk operating system that provides the framework of operation for millions of today's personal computers.

Examining the Variations of MS-DOS

MS-DOS is an operating system that accommodates variation in its exact makeup while retaining its core characteristics. Just as a car model can have differences in style, color, and standard equipment, DOS can have variations. The basic framework for the car (and DOS) enables differences to be introduced as the final tailoring of the finished product. This capability for variation enables various computer manufacturers to adapt MS-DOS to their computers. Both IBM DOS and COMPAQ

DOS, for example, are variations of MS-DOS. As DOS has matured as a product, it has been enhanced, and these enhancements have been released as new versions of DOS. Each new version has built on its predecessor while retaining the original version's primary design features.

Product-Specific Variations of DOS

Today, all commonly available variations of MS-DOS are similar in design and operation—with good reason. MS-DOS works with computers designed around Intel's 8086 microprocessor family. This family includes the 8088, 8086, 80286, 80386, and 80486 microprocessors. When conceiving the original IBM Personal Computer, IBM designers selected the Intel 8088 microprocessor to be the "brains" of their computer.

IBM's Personal Computer was a grand success. The enormity of the original IBM PC's influence on the PC market convinced other PC manufacturers using the 8086 family to follow closely IBM's personal computer design. Because IBM used an open approach to designing the IBM PC, other companies could configure their computers to use programs and hardware designed for the IBM PC. From a DOS perspective, these computers are virtually alike, even though the PCs may be more advanced than the original IBM PC.

The closeness of a PC's design to the IBM PC and to other IBM personal computers, such as the IBM PC/AT, determines to what degree a PC is said to be *IBM-compatible*. No industry standard concerning compatibility has been established formally. Instead, a de facto standard has emerged through the principle of supply and demand. Consumers have demanded a high degree of IBM compatibility in PCs. Most PCs (and their respective variations of MS-DOS) that were not designed to be compatible with the IBM PC have been discontinued, sell in specialty markets, or are available only in countries other than the United States. Because of this "shaking out" of the market, most PCs can operate successfully by using a version of IBM DOS, even though most compatible manufacturers offer their own variation of MS-DOS.

Users see the variations in MS-DOS implementations among PC manufacturers as subtle differences, usually limited to the names of a few commands or the manner in which parameters are given. Some manufacturers include in their MS-DOS packages additional utilities that work with a feature of that manufacturer's PC model. As a general rule, if you are proficient at using one variation of MS-DOS, you are proficient with all variations of MS-DOS. In a practical sense, the terms MS-DOS, IBM DOS, and DOS are interchangeable. You can use just about any compatible computer that runs DOS as its operating system by applying what you have learned about DOS from working with another PC.

Changes among Versions of DOS

Another type of variation involves the evolution of the product itself. As MS-DOS has evolved, the core product has been enhanced several times. Each release of enhancements is a distinct version of the program. Since its appearance in the summer of 1981, DOS has evolved through six major versions. Table 2.1 lists the important differences among versions of DOS, beginning in 1981. Appendix C, "Changes between Versions of DOS," provides more detailed coverage of these changes.

Table 2.1 Quick Reference to Versions of DOS

MS-DOS Version	Significant Change
1.0	Original version of DOS.
1.25	Accommodates double-sided disks.
2.0	Includes multiple directories needed to organize hard disks.
3.0	Uses high-capacity floppy disks, the RAM disk, volume names, and the ATTRIB command.
3.1	Includes provisions for networking.
3.2	Accommodates 3 1/2-inch drives.
3.3	Accommodates high-capacity 3 1/2-inch drives; includes new commands.
4.0	Introduces the DOS Shell and the MEM command; accommodates larger files and disk capacities.
5.0	Includes enhanced memory management, task swapping, an improved DOS Shell, a full-screen text editor, and support for even larger disk capacities.
6.0	Introduces multiple start-up configurations, support for workgroups, anti-virus scanning, disk compression and optimization, enhanced support for MS Windows users, and power saving and file transfer support for laptop computers. Includes enhanced file backups, enhanced recovery of deleted files, and an enhanced on-line help system.

Even with the introduction of Microsoft's OS/2 and the presence of several versions of the UNIX operating system, DOS remains strong. You can expect your investment in learning DOS to continue paying dividends; most industry experts predict that DOS will have a presence in the PC picture for years to come.

T   I   P

Operating systems such as OS/2 and UNIX are getting a great deal of media attention. One of these systems eventually may emerge as the replacement for DOS in everyday personal computing. Even if you move to OS/2 or UNIX at some point, however, you will find that you can use much of your DOS expertise with these operating systems.

FROM HERE...

For Related Information

▶▶ "Determining Your DOS Version with VER," p. 166.

Examining the DOS Package

Your purchase of a computer probably included a DOS package. You may have purchased DOS as a separate item if your computer did not include DOS. Most dealers and manufacturers either supply DOS with each new PC or sell DOS as an accessory package to a PC. Most often, the DOS package includes one or more manuals and two or more disks. The DOS software itself is on the disks.

MS-DOS Version 6.0, for example, comes packaged with four to six disks, depending on the computer model for which the software is intended. DOS packages supplied by particular computer manufacturers may have more or fewer disks. The disks may contain supplemental programs for the PC, such as programs that control unique hardware features in particular PC models. These supplemental programs often are considered part of DOS because the manufacturer includes them in the physical DOS package. Depending on the context, supplemental programs may be associated with the term *DOS package*, but for the purpose of this book, consider such supplemental programs to be outside of DOS.

Normally, the DOS package contains a DOS reference manual, which is an important supplement because it contains specific information about your version of DOS. The DOS reference manual included in the

DOS package must attempt to supply an accurate description of that version of DOS for new and advanced users alike. Therefore, many PC users prefer to consult another book, such as this book or other books about DOS published by Que Corporation. DOS users can select a book that fits their needs closely, whether they are beginning, intermediate, or advanced DOS users.

Many manufacturers include in the package other manuals that look similar to the DOS reference manual and contain information specific to the computer model or its auxiliary software. Compaq, for example, supplies a manual describing the operation of the tape unit included in some Compaq models. Although the discussion of the tape unit includes references to DOS, this manual is not considered a standard part of DOS for all PCs. The topics in these specialty manuals are not covered in this book, so keep such additional manuals at hand for reference.

Understanding the Purpose of DOS Disks

DOS disks that come in the DOS package are special disks because they contain DOS files—the files needed to start your PC and subsequently support your commands and applications. These DOS files contain the computer-level instructions that provide the functional aspects of DOS. The PC doesn't have these computer-level functions built in. The DOS disks serve as the key that unlocks the potential of the computer. When the operating system information stored on these disks is loaded into your PC, programs can take advantage of the PC's computing potential.

NOTE If you are fairly new to DOS, here's a word of wisdom. Don't use the master DOS disks that come in your DOS package for everyday work. The manufacturers intend for you to make copies of these master DOS disks and use the copies when you need to use DOS. (Indeed, with DOS 6.0, you have to install the operating system on your hard disk or on other floppy disks before you can use it.) Be sure to store your masters in a safe place. Make sure you have at least one good (tested) set of working DOS floppies even if your computer has a hard disk that contains the DOS files.

Even after you install DOS on your hard disk, keep floppy disk copies of your DOS package disks. You may need them if your hardware experiences problems or some software holds your hard disk hostage.

You can hold the DOS disks in your hand because the disks are *physical*. The instructions that the disks contain, however, are *logical*—not physical. In the world of computers, you view something in a logical way by understanding the concept of its operation.

This conceptual view includes the steps that make the computer "compute." Each time you turn on your PC, it must refresh itself by reading the DOS instructions from the DOS system files on the PC's start-up disk into the PC's working memory before the computer is ready to run your favorite software. DOS, your PC, and your favorite software work together to produce the computing result. If you remove any ingredient, you cannot compute.

In a similar way, when you mow your lawn, you count on the operation of the mower and the application of your mowing technique to get the job done. Mowing the lawn is conceptually the interplay between you, the mower, and the lawn. If you simply push a dead mower over the grass, you are going through the motions, but the grass is not mowed. If you start your mower but let it sit in one spot, the potential of the spinning blades is available, but the grass is still not mowed. Only when you start the mower and push it correctly across your lawn is the lawn mowed.

Likewise, you can start DOS on your computer and let it sit, but you are not doing any useful computing. You can attempt to use your computer without starting DOS, but nothing happens. Conceptually, DOS is the go-between that links you with the computer's capability of doing useful work. You have to know how to start DOS from the files on the DOS disks or on a hard disk. After DOS is started, you can mow through a memo or a spreadsheet.

T I P   You must prepare—or *format*—each disk with DOS before DOS can use the disk; only formatted disks that also include the DOS *system files* can start your PC. Disks that contain the DOS system files are called DOS *boot disks*. System files are briefly discussed later in this chapter and again in Chapter 3 "Starting DOS"; disk preparation and formatting is discussed in Chapter 7, "Preparing and Maintaining Disks."

NOTE   Some laptop computers include the DOS system files and command interpreter in permanent read-only memory (ROM). If your laptop PC is configured in this way, you can turn on your computer and start DOS without inserting a disk.

Examining the Files on the DOS Disks

Like the files on other disks, the files on the DOS disks have specific purposes. Every file available to DOS has a *file name*. The file name can have two parts, with a period separating the parts. The first part, called the *root file name*, can include up to eight characters. The optional second part of the file name, called the *file name extension*, can be up to three characters long. On the DOS disks, a file name extension helps describe the general purpose of the file. Each version or variation of DOS has an individual assortment of file names on the DOS disks. Even with the variations, you can benefit by looking at the file names of one particular DOS disk. The following list shows the names of the DOS files on the MS-DOS Version 6.0 disks.

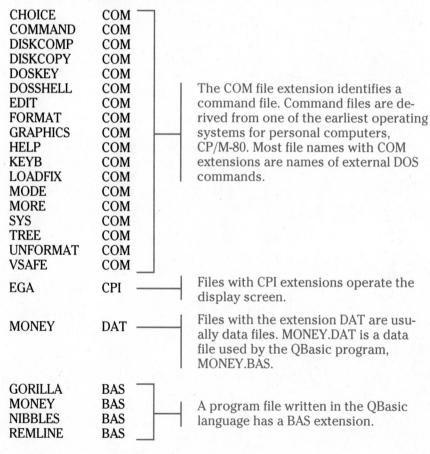

CHOICE	COM	
COMMAND	COM	
DISKCOMP	COM	
DISKCOPY	COM	
DOSKEY	COM	
DOSSHELL	COM	The COM file extension identifies a command file. Command files are de-
EDIT	COM	rived from one of the earliest operating
FORMAT	COM	systems for personal computers,
GRAPHICS	COM	CP/M-80. Most file names with COM
HELP	COM	extensions are names of external DOS
KEYB	COM	commands.
LOADFIX	COM	
MODE	COM	
MORE	COM	
SYS	COM	
TREE	COM	
UNFORMAT	COM	
VSAFE	COM	
EGA	CPI	Files with CPI extensions operate the display screen.
MONEY	DAT	Files with the extension DAT are usu-ally data files. MONEY.DAT is a data file used by the QBasic program, MONEY.BAS.
GORILLA	BAS	
MONEY	BAS	A program file written in the QBasic
NIBBLES	BAS	language has a BAS extension.
REMLINE	BAS	

DOSSHELL	INI	
MSAV	INI	
QBASIC	INI	

Files that store initialization parameters often have the extension INI.

DOSSHELL	GRB	
DOSSHELL	VID	

DOSSHELL.GRB and DOSSHELL.VID are display configuration files, which tell the DOS Shell what type of display adapter is installed in your system.

APPNOTES	TXT	
README	TXT	

Files with the TXT extension are text files that contain supplemental information. The README.TXT file, for example, provides special instructions for installing DOS 6.0.

APPEND	EXE
ATTRIB	EXE
CHKDSK	EXE
DBLSPACE	EXE
DEBUG	EXE
DEFRAG	EXE
DELTREE	EXE
DELOLDOS	EXE
DOSHELP	EXE
DOSSHELL	EXE
DOSSWAP	EXE
EMM386	EXE
EXPAND	EXE
FASTOPEN	EXE
FC	EXE
FDISK	EXE
FIND	EXE
INTERLNK	EXE
INTERSVR	EXE
LABEL	EXE
MEM	EXE
MEMMAKER	EXE
MOVE	EXE
MSAV	EXE
MSBACKUP	EXE
MSCDEX	EXE
MSD	EXE
MWAV	EXE
MWAVTSR	EXE
MWBACKUP	EXE
MWUNDEL	EXE
NLSFUNC	EXE
POWER	EXE
PRINT	EXE
QBASIC	EXE

EXE files are executable program files. Except for technical details of their internal structure, they are much like COM files. By entering the root name of an EXE file, you cause a program to run.

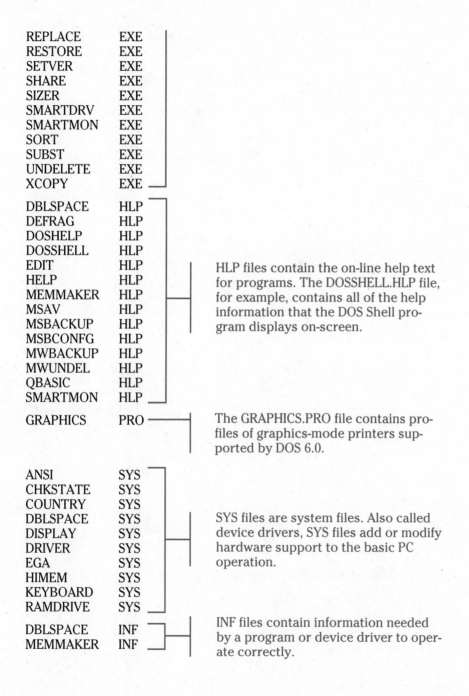

REPLACE	EXE
RESTORE	EXE
SETVER	EXE
SHARE	EXE
SIZER	EXE
SMARTDRV	EXE
SMARTMON	EXE
SORT	EXE
SUBST	EXE
UNDELETE	EXE
XCOPY	EXE

DBLSPACE	HLP
DEFRAG	HLP
DOSHELP	HLP
DOSSHELL	HLP
EDIT	HLP
HELP	HLP
MEMMAKER	HLP
MSAV	HLP
MSBACKUP	HLP
MSBCONFG	HLP
MWBACKUP	HLP
MWUNDEL	HLP
QBASIC	HLP
SMARTMON	HLP

HLP files contain the on-line help text for programs. The DOSSHELL.HLP file, for example, contains all of the help information that the DOS Shell program displays on-screen.

GRAPHICS	PRO

The GRAPHICS.PRO file contains profiles of graphics-mode printers supported by DOS 6.0.

ANSI	SYS
CHKSTATE	SYS
COUNTRY	SYS
DBLSPACE	SYS
DISPLAY	SYS
DRIVER	SYS
EGA	SYS
HIMEM	SYS
KEYBOARD	SYS
RAMDRIVE	SYS

SYS files are system files. Also called device drivers, SYS files add or modify hardware support to the basic PC operation.

DBLSPACE	INF
MEMMAKER	INF

INF files contain information needed by a program or device driver to operate correctly.

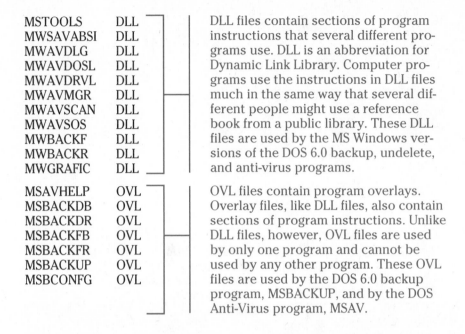

MSTOOLS	DLL
MWSAVABSI	DLL
MWAVDLG	DLL
MWAVDOSL	DLL
MWAVDRVL	DLL
MWAVMGR	DLL
MWAVSCAN	DLL
MWAVSOS	DLL
MWBACKF	DLL
MWBACKR	DLL
MWGRAFIC	DLL

DLL files contain sections of program instructions that several different programs use. DLL is an abbreviation for Dynamic Link Library. Computer programs use the instructions in DLL files much in the same way that several different people might use a reference book from a public library. These DLL files are used by the MS Windows versions of the DOS 6.0 backup, undelete, and anti-virus programs.

MSAVHELP	OVL
MSBACKDB	OVL
MSBACKDR	OVL
MSBACKFB	OVL
MSBACKFR	OVL
MSBACKUP	OVL
MSBCONFG	OVL

OVL files contain program overlays. Overlay files, like DLL files, also contain sections of program instructions. Unlike DLL files, however, OVL files are used by only one program and cannot be used by any other program. These OVL files are used by the DOS 6.0 backup program, MSBACKUP, and by the DOS Anti-Virus program, MSAV.

Understanding the Parts of DOS

Remember that the DOS disks contain the files necessary for DOS to do its job. When DOS is loaded, it acts as a go-between so that you and the PC can do useful computing. You also can look at DOS as an entity divided into modules. This modularity enables DOS to "divide and conquer" the various operating system requirements placed on DOS by users and programs.

DOS has four main functional components:

- The command interpreter (COMMAND.COM)
- The DOS Shell
- The basic input/output system (BIOS)
- The DOS utilities

These components are contained in files that come with the disks in your DOS package. In the following sections, you learn about these components and their duties.

NOTE Don't worry if you haven't completely grasped the significance of a computer's operating system at this point. An operating system is a multifaceted software creation, and some facets are easier to master than others. You may benefit from reading this chapter again after you have read through the rest of the chapters in Part I. Many ideas presented in this chapter are touched on again in later chapters. Rest assured that after you start using DOS, you will quickly develop your own personal definition for this versatile operating system.

The Command Interpreter

The command interpreter, which is DOS's "friendly host," interacts with you through the keyboard and screen when you operate your computer. The command interpreter is also known as the *command processor* and often is referred to simply as COMMAND.COM (pronounced "command dot com" or just "command com"). COMMAND.COM accepts your DOS commands and sees that they are carried out.

COMMAND.COM displays the *DOS prompt* (C>, A>, and so on), also known as the *command prompt* or the *command line*. The DOS command prompt is a request for input. When you enter a command, you are communicating with COMMAND.COM, which then interprets what you type and processes your input so that DOS can take the appropriate action. COMMAND.COM, through DOS commands, handles the technical details of such common tasks as displaying a list of the contents of a disk, copying files, and starting your programs.

You can compare COMMAND.COM to a waiter. When you go to a restaurant, you may be attended by a waiter whose job is to see to your needs. You communicate your dining requests to the waiter as you communicate your command requests to COMMAND.COM. When you are ordering, for example, the waiter may inform you that an entree is not available or that a combination of additional side dishes isn't included with a certain dinner. Similarly, COMMAND.COM communicates to you when a command is not available or when an additional part of a command is not allowed.

Your waiter doesn't prepare your meal. The waiter communicates your instructions to the personnel in the kitchen in a way that the cooks understand. Likewise, COMMAND.COM doesn't carry out most DOS commands; instead, it communicates to other DOS modules that specialize in the requested service. Your waiter may provide some simple services, such as pouring more water or offering condiments. These simple services are built into the waiter's job. COMMAND.COM also has some simple DOS commands built in. These built-in commands are available whenever you are using DOS. COMMAND.COM does not have to rely on the presence of other DOS modules to carry out the work of these internal commands.

COMMAND.COM is an important part of DOS. Many PC users may think of COMMAND.COM's operation as being the essence of DOS because COMMAND.COM is so visible. DOS does many things behind the scenes, but COMMAND.COM is up front, as illustrated by figure 2.1. Thus, PC users equate issuing commands with performing DOS-level PC-management work because issuing DOS commands is the primary area of their DOS activities. Because you instruct COMMAND.COM rather than the hardware directly, you never need to know the details of how the hardware operates.

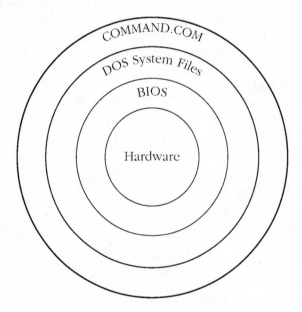

Fig. 2.1

The relationship of COMMAND.COM with other DOS modules and your hardware.

Chapter 5, "Using DOS Commands," discusses DOS commands more fully, and Part II of this book is devoted to the DOS commands users most often issue. Issuing commands, however, is only a part of using DOS to manage a PC. Many of the commands you issue at the DOS prompt work with the file system. Chapter 6, "Understanding Disks and Files," provides an inside view of the file system and makes using disk- and file-related DOS commands more meaningful.

The DOS Shell

The DOS Shell, first available in DOS 4.0 and much improved in MS-DOS Versions 5.0 and 6.0, is a visually oriented interface between you and the command interpreter. The DOS Shell provides an alternative to typing commands at the DOS command prompt. By using the DOS Shell, you can perform DOS functions without having to memorize all the available DOS commands. You can think of the DOS Shell as a protective layer between you and the command interpreter (COMMAND.COM), as depicted in figure 2.2. The DOS Shell is a final layer that insulates you from having to control details of the computer's hardware electronically.

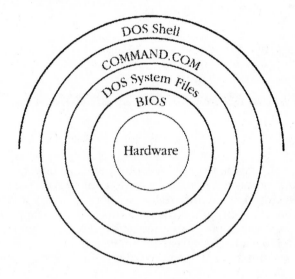

Fig. 2.2

The DOS Shell in relation to other DOS modules and hardware.

Instead of giving you the command prompt, the DOS Shell lists directories and file names on-screen, helping you keep track of the programs and data on your disks (see fig. 2.3). Through menus and helpful screen prompts, the Shell enables you to manipulate the listed file and directory names to perform disk- and file-related tasks easily.

Using the DOS Shell, you also are able to start applications programs by selecting from an on-screen list. When you first install MS-DOS 6.0, the DOS Shell lists four options in the program list, the lower half of the screen, as shown in figure 2.3. You can easily add more programs to the list, turning the DOS Shell into a command center from which you can control any session with your computer.

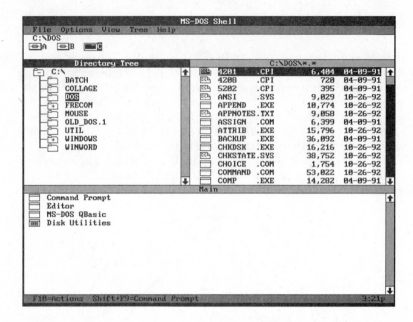

Fig. 2.3

The DOS Shell
list of directories
and files.

The Shell even enables you to switch quickly between several programs on your PC, a procedure sometimes referred to as *task swapping*. For example, you may be working on your monthly budget in a spreadsheet program and decide that you need to consult travel expense data, which is stored in a database file. Without forcing you first to leave the spreadsheet program, the DOS Shell's Task Swapper enables you to start the database program, retrieve the desired information, and then switch back to the spreadsheet. Indeed, with the Shell, you can switch back and forth among several programs at the touch of a keystroke.

Chapter 4, "Using the DOS Shell," introduces you to the DOS Shell and explains how to get around the DOS Shell screen and how to control the screen display. You also learn how to use the DOS Shell as a platform from which to run all other programs on your computer's hard disk. Specific capabilities of the DOS Shell are covered in Part II of this book. Chapter 16, "Configuring the DOS Shell," describes how to configure the DOS Shell to fit your needs.

The Basic Input/Output System

The *hidden*, or *system*, files are another part of the operating system. These special files define the hardware to the software. When you start a computer, the DOS system files are loaded into RAM. Combined, the files provide a unified set of routines for controlling and directing the computer's operations and are known as the *input/output system.*

The hidden files interact with special read-only memory (ROM) on the motherboard. The special ROM is called the *Basic Input Output System*, or simply *BIOS.* Responding to a program's request for service, the system files translate the request and pass it to the ROM BIOS. The BIOS provides a further translation of the request that links the request to the hardware, as illustrated by figure 2.4.

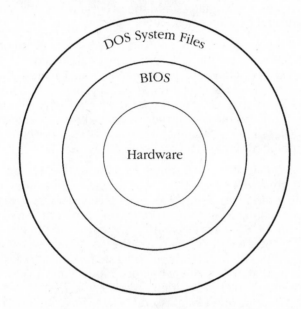

Fig. 2.4

The DOS system files as they relate to BIOS and the hardware.

DOS provides uniform service to the hardware by getting assistance from the permanent ROM BIOS in the computer. ROM BIOS can vary among computer makers, but the computers are highly compatible when the design of the ROM BIOS is integrated with DOS. In large part, the DOS input/output system, through the special BIOS, determines the degree to which a PC is compatible with other PCs.

The Hidden Core of DOS

Inside a working PC, DOS is the collection of services that DOS offers in the form of built-in groups of related instructions, or *software routines.*

These routines are the core of the services DOS provides to your applications programs. The extensive file-system management provided by DOS, for example, is made up of these routines. Programmers can access these software routines to perform a variety of internal operations with the PC. These functions are common repetitive actions that operating system designers have included in DOS to make life easier (and programs more uniform) for PC programmers. DOS commands rely on these service routines to do standard low-level computer work. By accessing the built-in DOS service routines, a program doesn't need the details of how DOS works with the PC. With the interface to DOS service built in, computer languages and the programs they produce can use DOS uniformly.

The internal file system and input/output aspects of DOS are often as invisible to DOS users as interaction with the DOS Shell or COMMAND.COM is obvious. When you order from a waiter, you don't need to know the details of how your meal is prepared. You just want timely service and satisfaction with your food. Similarly, you (or your program) want timely and appropriate services to be conducted by the internal parts of DOS. You don't care how DOS goes about doing its internal job, detailed though the procedure may be.

Fortunately, you do not have to know much about these internal DOS programming concerns to operate your PC. Having some idea of what goes on at the internal level, however, may give you more insight into how a DOS command or your word processing program works. Programming at the DOS level is fascinating and rewarding to many, but this book does not attempt to teach you the programming aspects of DOS. If you want to know more about programming at the DOS level for additional insight or to write actual programs, you can refer to books published by Que Corporation on this topic. *DOS Programmer's Reference,* 3rd Edition, and *Using Assembly Language,* 3rd Edition, are suggested.

If the programming aspects of DOS do not interest you, you are not alone. Most DOS users are generally uninformed about "what goes on in there," and they do just fine. As your DOS skills increase, however, you may find that having a general layman's notion of "what goes on in there" enables you to become a more self-reliant PC user. Throughout this book, you get simple explanations of internal operations, helping you learn about this invisible but essential part of DOS.

The DOS Utilities

The DOS utilities carry out useful housekeeping tasks, such as preparing disks, comparing files, finding the free space on a disk, and printing in the background. Some utilities provide statistics on disk size and available memory and compare disks and files. The utility programs are files that reside on disk and are loaded into memory by COMMAND.COM when you type the command name. They are called *external commands* because they are not loaded into memory with COMMAND.COM every time you turn on your computer. An example of an external command is the FORMAT command, which is used to prepare disks for use with DOS.

Disk operating systems insulate you and your programs from the need to know exactly how to make the hardware work. To list the contents of a disk in a disk drive, for example, you don't need to know the capacity or recording format of the disk or how to get the computer to direct the output to the screen. An applications program that needs to store data on disk does not have to reserve space on the disk, keep track of where the data is stored on disk, or know how the data was encoded. DOS takes care of all these tasks.

For Related Information

▶▶ "Understanding the DOS Shell Window," p. 84.

▶▶ "Using the DOS Shell Menus," p. 89.

FROM HERE...

Understanding the Functions of DOS

By now, you no doubt suspect that DOS does many "technical" tasks that are not easy to comprehend. Certainly, much of DOS's activity is technical. But most of the DOS activities you need to understand in order to make DOS work effectively are not difficult. This section briefly describes the common DOS functions you use again and again as your computing expertise grows. Later sections treat each topic in detail.

Managing Files

One of DOS's primary functions is to help you organize the files you store on your disks. Organized files are a sign of good computer housekeeping, and good housekeeping is crucial when you want to take advantage of the storage capacity available on today's disks.

Consider, for example, that the smallest capacity floppy disk can hold the equivalent of 100 letter-sized pages of information. Now imagine that each sheet of information makes up one file: you have 100 files to keep track of. If you use disks that can hold more information than a standard floppy disk (such as a hard disk), file organization becomes even more crucial.

Fortunately, DOS gives you the tools to be a good computer house-keeper. DOS lists files for you, tells you their names and sizes, and gives you the dates when they were created. You can use this information for many organizational purposes. In addition to organizing files, DOS can duplicate files, discard files that are no longer useful, and replace files with matching file names.

Managing Disks

Certain DOS functions are essential to all computer users. For example, all disks must be prepared before they can be used in your computer. This preparation, called *formatting*, includes checking disks for available space. Other DOS disk-management functions include the following:

■ Labeling disks electronically

■ Making restorable backup copies of files for security purposes

■ Compressing files to reduce the amount of disk space that the files use

■ Copying disks

■ Viewing the contents of files on a disk

Redirecting Input and Output

DOS expects its input to come from a standard place—the keyboard, for example. DOS sends its output to a standard place, such as the display screen. DOS designers recognized that sending output to another device, such as a printer, may sometimes be necessary; therefore, they provided DOS with the capability of *redirecting*, or sending in another direction, the output that normally goes to the standard output. Through redirection, a list of files that usually appears on-screen can be sent to the printer. You see useful examples of the redirection of common commands when these commands are discussed.

DOS also contains commands that enable you to tailor your PC's hardware environment to your specific needs. In fact, DOS provides much versatility in its configuration capabilities. Fortunately for users just starting with DOS, the standard configuration of the PC works fine. In this book, however, you learn how to make simple alterations to the PC's DOS configuration.

Adding configuration control to your DOS activities isn't an everyday activity. Usually, a user establishes a tailored configuration using the CONFIG.SYS file. When established, the CONFIG.SYS file remains relatively unchanged. Chapters 16, "Configuring the DOS Shell," and 17, "Configuring Your Computer," cover the topic of configuration. Don't worry about configuration for now. You will be ready to understand it later.

Running Applications Programs

Computers require complex and exact instructions—programs—to provide you with useful output. Computing would be impractical if you had to write a program every time you had a job to do. Happily, that condition is not the case. Programmers spend months doing the specialized work that enables a computer to function in many different ways: as a word processor, database manipulator, spreadsheet, or generator of graphics. Through a program, the computer's capabilities are applied to a task—thus the term *applications programs*.

Applications programs, like DOS, are distributed on disks. DOS is the go-between that gives you access to these programs through the computer. By simply inserting a disk into your computer's disk drive and pressing a few keys, you have an astonishingly wide variety of easy-to-use applications at your disposal.

Applications constantly need to read data from or write data to disk files because you need to see what you have typed by viewing text information sent to the screen or printer. The program you use requires that you enter information by typing from the keyboard or moving the mouse in a certain way. These input and output tasks, although common repetitive computer tasks, are not trivial. Thanks to DOS, however, you can take these repetitive tasks for granted. DOS takes responsibility for the technical details of input and output, providing applications with an easy-to-use connection, or program interface, that oversees the details of these repetitive activities. As a computer user, you want easy-to-understand information about disk files, memory size, and computer configuration. DOS provides these services.

You can compare DOS to a soft-drink dispenser. When you walk up to a soft-drink machine, you concern yourself with having the right coins and making a selection. You probably don't think of the wires, motors, refrigeration equipment, or the mechanism that calculates change. You know to put the coins into the slot, press the correct button, and pick up your drink from the dispenser. The maker of the soft-drink machine has provided you with an easy-to-use interface that has relatively simple input and provides straightforward output. You have a need, and through your actions, the machine carries out many detailed steps internally to provide you with a service that fills your need. DOS's service provisions are not unlike those of the soft-drink machine. DOS is perhaps a bit more complicated, but the concept of internal details you don't see is the same for DOS as it is for the soft-drink machine.

Running Macros and Batch Files

Most of your interaction with DOS takes place through the keyboard or with a mouse. You type commands for the DOS Shell or COMMAND.COM to carry out or use the mouse to select options from menus. Commands, however, also can be stored in memory as a *macro* or placed in a disk file called a *batch file* and "played back" to COMMAND.COM. Chapter 15, "Understanding Batch Files, DOSKey, and Macros," covers macros and batch files and explains how to create them.

COMMAND.COM responds to these batches of commands from the computer's memory or from a file, just as COMMAND.COM responds to commands typed from the keyboard. Macros and batch files can automate frequently used command sequences, making keyboard operation simpler.

Difficult-to-remember command sequences are ideal candidates for macro or batch-file treatment.

Handling Miscellaneous Tasks

Some DOS functions, such as setting the computer's clock and calendar so that files and applications programs can have access to dates and times, fall into a "miscellaneous" category. You also may need to use DOS's text editor to create text files such as memos, notes, or batch files. You can even see the amount of RAM available for applications programs through DOS.

For Related Information

▶▶ "Introducing the DOS File System," p. 140.

▶▶ "Examining Disks and Drives," p.151.

▶▶ "Understanding Disk Preparation," p. 178.

▶▶ "Formatting Floppy Disks," p. 181.

▶▶ "Understanding the Contents of Batch Files," p. 548.

▶▶ "Understanding the AUTOEXEC.BAT File," p. 551.

▶▶ "Using Batch-File Commands," p. 565.

▶▶ "Using DOSKey," p. 590.

▶▶ "Creating and Using Macros," p. 596.

FROM HERE...

Chapter Summary

Anyone who uses a personal computer can benefit from a working knowledge of DOS. You cannot use your computer to run most popular programs unless you start the program with DOS. Although someone you know may be willing to do DOS-related work for you, you will become more proficient at computing if you learn a little DOS. Besides, the results greatly exceed the effort you spend learning DOS.

In this chapter, you learned some facts about the role of DOS in personal computing. The following are some important points to remember:

■ The term *DOS* is an acronym for Disk Operating System. Many computer operating systems have the term DOS in their names.

■ MS-DOS is the name of an operating system originally developed in conjunction with the IBM PC and now used widely by many personal computers. To most PC users, DOS means MS-DOS.

■ When PC users use the term DOS, they may be referring to only one contextual part of DOS.

■ DOS works with the Intel 8086 family of microprocessors and its descendants: the 80286, 80386, and 80486.

- The DOS package includes a number of disks that contain the files necessary for DOS to do its job.

- The file names on the DOS disks include extensions that indicate the purpose of each file.

- The BIOS layer of a PC is contained in permanent ROM and works with the hardware to provide a foundation of services for DOS.

- COMMAND.COM is the DOS command processor that executes DOS commands.

- The DOS Shell program, available with DOS 4.0, 5.0, and 6.0, provides a visually oriented environment that enables the user to execute DOS commands by selecting them from a menu and to start and switch between several applications programs easily.

- DOS has many functions, including managing files and disks, redirecting input and output, running applications programs and batch files, and handling miscellaneous tasks such as setting the computer's date and time.

Now that you have an understanding of the fundamental relationships between the various parts of DOS and of how DOS interacts with the computer's hardware, you are ready to start your computer. The next chapter takes you through the steps of turning your computer on and loading DOS. You will learn how your computer loads DOS into memory and get a basic understanding of how DOS configures itself and your computer as it loads.

Starting DOS

Now that you have an overview of the PC and of DOS, you are ready to start your PC and to learn more about the practical operation of DOS. This chapter is an overview of the start-up process. The first time you start your computer, you may not know what to expect. After you learn a few computer terms and perform the basic start-up procedure, you will begin to feel at ease. Before you flip the switch on your PC, however, take time to understand some preliminary information about the start-up process.

The operators of early computers started their computers by entering a short binary program and then instructing the computer to run the program. This binary program was called the *bootstrap loader* because the computer, through the bootstrap program, figuratively pulled itself up by the bootstraps to perform tasks. The early computer operators shortened the name of the start-up process to *booting*. The term stuck. Today *booting the computer* still refers to the start-up procedure. Fortunately, the process of booting is now relatively automatic.

NOTE This chapter assumes that you don't know how to boot a computer or understand the process behind booting. A few commands are necessary to show you the complete boot process, but don't worry if you don't know them. Just type the examples; later chapters cover these commands in detail.

Key Terms Used in This Chapter

Cold boot	The process of starting a PC from a power-off condition.
Warm boot	The process of restarting a PC while the power is on.
Cursor	The blinking line or solid block that marks where the next keyboard entry will appear.
Pointer	The arrow- or block-shaped on-screen object that you can move by dragging a mouse across the surface of your desk or by rotating the ball of a track-ball.
Default	A condition or value that the computer, the program, or DOS assumes when you do not supply one.
Prompt	A symbol, character, or group of characters displayed by DOS or a program, indicating that you must enter information.
DOS prompt	The characters that COMMAND.COM displays to inform you that you can enter a DOS command. C> is an example of a DOS prompt.
Command	A directive you type at the DOS prompt that instructs DOS to provide a service, such as displaying a directory or copying a file.
Parameter	Additional instructions given with a command to let DOS know how to carry out the command.
Syntax	The way commands and parameters should be put together at the DOS prompt. COMMAND.COM interprets the syntax of your instructions to DOS.
Logged drive	The current default disk drive that DOS uses to carry out commands that involve disk services (such as displaying a directory). Unless you change the appearance of the DOS prompt with a command, the letter of the default drive is the DOS prompt.

Performing a Cold Boot

The term *cold boot* comes from the fact that the computer's power is off and that the unit is not yet warm. If the boot process is new to you, you should make checking your computer a part of your booting routine.

Making Preliminary Checks

If you travel by airplane, you may have noticed that before taking off, a pilot checks to make sure that all equipment is in working order. Just as this preliminary checking of the airplane is important, so is your checking of your computer's equipment. Your PC isn't as complicated as an aircraft, but a few preliminary checks help you avoid computer failures—often referred to as *crashes*.

Computers require clean, steady power sources. Choose a three-wire (grounded) electrical outlet that does not serve devices such as copy machines, coffee makers, refrigerators, hair dryers, portable heaters, or other electrical gadgets. Ask your computer dealer about a line conditioner, or surge suppressor, if you must share an outlet.

Make sure that the computer's power switch is off before you plug in your computer. Some computers have switches marked with 0 and 1. The side marked 0 is the off switch position. Many PCs keep themselves turned off after an electrical *drop out*—a momentary interruption in electrical power to the outlet—even when the PC's switch is in the on position. This feature ensures that the unsettled power conditions that caused the computer to switch off have passed before you can turn on the computer again.

Ventilation is important to computers. Make sure that your PC has enough space around it for proper ventilation. Computers must dissipate the heat generated by their internal electronic components. Keep paper, books, beverages, and other clutter away from the system unit's case. Also watch out for dust accumulation around the fan area and the base of the system unit—especially if your computer is placed on the floor. Don't set up the system unit on a rug or a cloth pad; these surfaces can obstruct the ventilation slots on the bottom of the computer. In general, always keep three or four inches of clear space behind the computer's system unit for correct ventilation. Keep this book, your DOS manual, DOS disks, and your PC system manual nearby for reference.

T I P If you stand your computer system unit on its end on the floor, make sure that the cooling fan is not obstructed by the back of a desk or some other furniture. Use one of the commercially available vertical floor stands to make the system unit more stable. Watch out for dust on the floor accumulating in the fan area.

T I P If you have a tower-type system unit on the floor, make sure that the cooling fan is not obstructed by the back of a desk or some other furniture, and avoid placing the unit on a rug or carpet. The system unit's feet may sink into the carpet, resulting in a blockage of the ventilation holes on the bottom of the system unit. Remove the rug or carpet, or place the system unit on a board, a chair mat, or some other hard, smooth surface on top of the carpet.

Understanding the Boot Disk

As you may remember from the discussion in Chapter 2, "Understanding the Role of DOS," DOS consists of various modular components working together. Although a part of your computer's BIOS is permanently stored in ROM, your computer must read the DOS system files and command interpreter from a hard disk or a floppy disk every time you boot your computer. In order to boot your computer, therefore, you must have a specially prepared disk containing the DOS system files and command interpreter.

You can boot your computer from a hard disk or from a floppy disk. You can use any disk containing the DOS system files and command interpreter to boot your computer. The disk from which the computer reads the DOS system files and command interpreter is called the *boot disk*, regardless of whether the disk is the hard disk or a floppy disk.

Today, most computers have a hard disk, and the standard practice is to install DOS on the hard disk so that it is bootable. Your dealer or the support person who set up your PC probably installed DOS on the hard disk and made the hard disk bootable.

You usually boot your computer from the hard disk. Occasionally, however, you may need to boot your computer from a floppy disk. This chapter describes how to boot your computer from your hard disk or from a floppy disk. Chapter 7, "Preparing and Maintaining Disks," describes how to add system files to a floppy disk.

NOTE Even if you have a hard disk with DOS installed on it, learn how to boot from a floppy disk in case your hard disk becomes unbootable. Booting from a prepared floppy disk is the same as booting from a hard disk, except that you must first insert the bootable floppy disk into the floppy drive. Chapter 7, "Preparing and Maintaining Disks," describes how to add system files to a floppy disk. Check your DOS manual or Appendix A, "Installing DOS 6," for information on using the DOS Setup program for installing DOS onto floppy disks.

Starting the Boot

If you have a key lock on the front of the system unit, unlock the unit. To boot from the hard disk, first make sure that floppy drive A is empty. Almost all computers automatically check for a disk in drive A during the boot process and then try to read the system files from the floppy disk in drive A. If the floppy disk in drive A is not bootable, DOS displays the following message:

```
Non-System Disk or Disk Error
```

If you ever receive the message Non-system Disk or Disk Error as a result of accidentally leaving a nonbootable disk in drive A, simply remove the disk from the drive and follow the procedure at the end of this chapter for performing a warm boot.　**T I P**

After you make sure that the disk drives are empty, you can boot from the hard disk by turning on the computer.

To boot your computer from a floppy disk, you first must insert a bootable floppy disk into drive A. Chapter 6, "Understanding Disks and Files," describes how to insert a disk and how to write-protect a floppy disk. Chapter 7, "Preparing and Maintaining Disks," describes how to add system files to a floppy disk so that it is bootable. Check your PC system manual for the location of drive A and for specific disk-insertion instructions.

Finally, turn on the video display switch, if necessary, and give your screen a few seconds to warm up. (Some video displays receive their power from the system unit and do not have a switch.) The computer's power switch is often on the right side toward the rear of the system unit. In tower system units, the power switch is usually on the front of the system unit. Snap on the switch; the cold boot has begun.

T I P   Always let the spring action of the PC's power switch snap the switch on or off. If you hold the switch arm between your fingers and ease the switch on, the switch doesn't make immediate and decisive electrical contact. Easing the switch on may cause fluttering power, and the PC may fail to turn on.

Watching the Progress of the Boot

The instant you snap on the switch, the computer's electronics do a *power-on reset* (POR). The *random-access memory* (RAM), the microprocessor, and other electronics are zeroed out, similar to cleaning the slate. The system then begins a *power-on self-test* (POST). The POST ensures that your PC can deal responsibly with your valuable data. The POST can take from a few seconds to a couple of minutes. During the POST, you may see a blinking cursor on the display or a description of the test, similar to the following message:

```
ABC Computer Co.

Turbo

RAM check

2048 KB 0K

OK
```

When the POST finishes, you hear one beep, and drive A starts activity. The bootstrap loader in most computers is programmed to first check for the DOS system files on a floppy disk in drive A. If drive A has no disk in it, the bootstrap loader is programmed to look for the DOS system files on the computer's hard disk. If you boot your computer from your hard disk and you do not have a disk in drive A, your hard disk begins activity after a few moments.

After the bootstrap loader finds the DOS system files—whether on your hard disk or on a floppy disk—it loads DOS from the disk into the computer's RAM. When the DOS 6.0 bootstrap loader begins loading the DOS system files (described in Chapter 2, "Understanding the Role of DOS"), the message Starting MS-DOS... appears.

When the DOS system files are loaded into memory, DOS checks for a special file named CONFIG.SYS. The CONFIG.SYS file contains specific configuration information for your computer and the applications programs you use. Chapter 17, "Configuring Your Computer," describes CONFIG.SYS.

A new feature in DOS 6.0 enables the CONFIG.SYS file to display menus so that users can choose different, preprogrammed configurations each time they boot the computer. If your computer has been set up with a menu, DOS displays the menu shortly after the Starting MS-DOS message appears. A typical menu follows:

```
MS-DOS 6 Startup Menu

    1.   Windows
    2.   MouseDOS
    3.   OnlyDOS
    4.   DTP

Enter a choice: 1
```

If DOS displays a start-up menu, type the number corresponding to the configuration you want, and then press the Enter key. DOS continues the boot process. See Chapter 17, "Configuring Your Computer," for more information on configuration menus.

As the boot continues, DOS loads various *device drivers*—special software programs for controlling parts of your computer, such as the software needed for a mouse or trackball. As DOS loads each device driver into memory, you may see additional on-screen messages identifying the device driver and reporting its condition or status.

Technical Note

The term *booting* comes from the old concept that with no external help, you can "pull yourself up by your bootstraps." In other words, you can start with nothing and turn it into something useful. Needless to say, the act of creating something from nothing requires some wide interpretation of what "nothing" is. When you boot your PC, the PC is nothing on a scale of computing output. The potential is there, but you cannot compute with it.

Much of this computing potential resides on the DOS boot disk in three disk files. The file that contains the core of DOS, the file that contains the basic input and output additions for ROM BIOS, and the COMMAND.COM file are on disk, ready to be loaded into the PC. Before the PC can load these files and make DOS available, the PC must test itself, initialize external hardware, and load the three DOS files from disk into random-access memory (RAM).

Special instructions built into the PC enable the PC to access a predetermined part of the boot disk and read the boot sector into RAM. The boot sector contains a short machine-language program that finds and loads two DOS hidden system files. The boot program then looks for the CONFIG.SYS file in the root directory of the boot disk. (Chapter 17, "Configuring Your Computer," discusses the CONFIG.SYS file.) If the boot program finds CONFIG.SYS, it opens the file and installs into memory any device drivers referred to in CONFIG.SYS.

By loading device drivers during the boot process, DOS is configured to meet specific hardware and running requirements for each individual PC. The device drivers for the standard DOS devices—such as the screen, the keyboard, floppy and hard disks—are built into DOS; other devices—such as sound cards and CD ROM drives—must have their device drivers loaded from disk. You select and control which device drivers are loaded with CONFIG.SYS.

The boot program locates the COMMAND.COM file and loads it into memory. The boot program then turns control of the PC's resources over to COMMAND.COM. COMMAND.COM searches the root directory of the boot disk for a file named AUTOEXEC.BAT. After COMMAND.COM finds the AUTOEXEC.BAT file, its contents are executed as a series of DOS commands. (Chapter 17, "Configuring Your Computer," and Chapter 15, "Understanding Batch Files, DOSKey, and Macros," discuss AUTOEXEC.BAT.) By arranging for this special batch file to be executed at boot time, DOS can tailor the startup of every PC to meet the specific needs of the user.

When COMMAND.COM has executed AUTOEXEC.BAT, you see the
DOS prompt described later in this chapter (assuming that none
of the AUTOEXEC.BAT commands starts a program such as
the DOS Shell). COMMAND.COM then is ready to receive your
command.

A new feature in DOS 6.0 enables you to completely bypass the
execution of the CONFIG.SYS and AUTOEXEC.BAT files or to program DOS to display each line of the CONFIG.SYS file and allow
you to choose whether or not to load that specific device
driver. Press the F5 key to completely skip CONFIG.SYS and
AUTOEXEC.BAT, or press the F8 key to display each line of
CONFIG.SYS and ask for confirmation before executing it. Refer to
Chapter 17, "Configuring Your Computer," for more information
on this feature.

For Related Information

▶▶ "Understanding CONFIG.SYS," p. 630.

▶▶ "Understanding DOS 6.0 Boot Options," p. 681.

▶▶ "Boot Menus," p. 683.

FROM HERE...

Viewing DOS

When the cold boot completes its preliminary loading of DOS, a DOS
screen appears, ready to accept your commands. The screen you see
depends on the version of DOS running on your computer and on the
view of DOS you have chosen. With DOS 4.0 and later versions, you
have two view options:

■ The command line (DOS's only view prior to 4.0)

■ The DOS Shell

The command line is the traditional look of DOS. The command line
appears on a plain screen with one letter of the alphabet representing
the current, or active, drive, followed by a greater-than symbol—A>, for
example.

The combination of this drive letter and the greater-than symbol is
referred to as the *command prompt* or *DOS prompt.* The most common

command prompts are A> for floppy disk systems and C> for hard disk systems. If you are using DOS 3.3 or an earlier version or if you or your dealer has enabled the command line view, the plain command prompt is your view.

NOTE The DOS 6.0 Setup program that installed the DOS system files on your Master disks probably created a special start-up file named AUTOEXEC.BAT. When your boot disk contains this file, DOS reads it every time you boot your computer. The Setup program places in AUTOEXEC.BAT a command that causes the command prompt to appear in one of the following forms (depending on whether you are booting from the floppy disk drive, drive A, or from the hard disk drive, drive C):

```
A:\>

C:\>
```

These command prompts are equivalent, respectively, to the prompts A> and C>, but they provide a bit more information. The colon (:) and backslash (\) represent the *directory path*, which is discussed fully in Chapter 8, "Understanding and Managing Directories."

NOTE If you are using DOS 6.0 and you boot from the SETUP disk (Disk #1), you may see the DOS 6.0 installation program, Setup. You can stop Setup by pressing F3; you then see the DOS prompt.

The DOS Shell is still a relatively new look for DOS, first available in DOS 4.0 and significantly enhanced in DOS 5.0. The DOS Shell provides a full-screen, visually oriented window with menus, screen areas, pop-up help screens, and graphic representation of directories and files (see fig. 3.1). You can issue many standard DOS commands by pointing to and selecting these items with a mouse.

Although the DOS Shell provides the friendliest way to use DOS, learn the basic commands from the command line. Working with the DOS prompt is the traditional way to use DOS. Although using the Shell is easy, you still need to know something about DOS commands and terminology because they remain substantially unchanged from previous versions of DOS. If you have DOS 5.0 or 6.0, refer to Chapter 4, "Using the DOS Shell," for details on using the DOS Shell. For now, press the F3 key to exit the DOS Shell. You see the DOS prompt appear. When the prompt appears, you are operating your computer from the DOS command line.

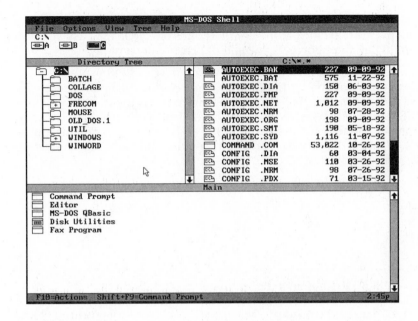

Fig. 3.1

The DOS Shell
window.

The DOS Shell that comes with DOS 6.0 isn't the only visually oriented
user interface for DOS. Many independent companies sell add-on software that performs many of the same functions as the DOS Shell. In
fact, the term *shell* often is used to describe any program that adds a
layer of user friendliness to an existing program.

Programs like PC Tools for DOS, XTree Gold, and Norton Desktop
for DOS give you a DOS user interface similar to that of the DOS Shell.
Many users find that shell programs enable them to use the features of
DOS more competently. Others discover that without some knowledge
of the DOS command line, they are at a disadvantage when they must
operate a PC other than their own. This book encourages you to learn
both the DOS Shell and command line.

Entering the Date and Time

DOS uses the date and time to *stamp*, or record, the time and date of a
file's creation or last change. Today, most computers come with a built-
in, battery-powered calendar and clock. The clock keeps correct time
even when the unit's power is off so that the correct time and date are
always the default values. Many older PCs, or PCs based on the original
IBM PC, do not have built-in clocks. These PCs keep time when the
power is on; to ensure proper time and date stamping, however, you
must set the correct time as a follow-up of the boot process.

When the computer boots, DOS automatically reads the time and date from the system clock, if the computer has one. DOS may ask you, however, to enter the correct time and date manually anyway.

If your computer's boot disk contains an AUTOEXEC.BAT file, DOS doesn't prompt you for the time and date during the boot process unless the AUTOEXEC.BAT file specifically contains the two commands, DATE and TIME. When no AUTOEXEC.BAT file is present, DOS always prompts you to enter the correct time and date. Some configurations of DOS offer the date prompt first and then the time prompt; others offer the time prompt first.

The prompt for the current date is as follows:

```
Current date is Thu 10-31-1991

Enter new date (mm-dd-yy):
```

Unless you have a battery-powered system clock, you need to enter the current date at the prompt. Even if you have a battery-powered clock, the date may be incorrect.

T I P

If having your files stamped with the correct date and time is important to you, put the DATE and TIME commands in your AUTOEXEC.BAT file so that you can check the date and time every time you boot your computer.

To accept the default (suggested) date, press Enter. If the date is not correct, change it. Look at the date template that DOS shows in parentheses. Enter the calendar month as a number (1 through 12) in place of *mm*. Likewise, enter the day between 1 and 31 in the place of *dd*. When you enter *yy*, you do not have to include the century. DOS assumes the twentieth century and accepts *93* for 1993, *94* for 1994, and so on.

NOTE

A *default* value is a suggested response that DOS or an application program uses unless you suggest another value. When you are working with the DOS Shell or the DOS command line, DOS uses the default if you don't specify a different value when the computer prompts you. You usually press Enter to accept the default. You learn more about defaults when you read about commands in later chapters.

If you enter a value that DOS is programmed to reject, DOS displays an error message. Don't worry about making a mistake; DOS prompts you again for the date, and you can reenter the date correctly.

> **NOTE** DOS is programmed to issue on-screen error messages when you provide an incorrect response. Different mistakes produce different error messages. Appendix B, "DOS Messages," is a useful guide to the error messages that DOS displays. Reviewing the various error messages helps you understand DOS's handling of the mistakes it detects.

The DOS prompt for the current time is as follows:

```
Current time is 11:17:00.75a

Enter new time:
```

When DOS prompts you, enter the current time. The template for time is *hh:mm:ss*. The hours are in 24-hour (military) clock format for DOS 3.3 and earlier versions. With these versions, you don't see the *a* or the *p* in the DOS time prompt. DOS 4.0 and later versions accept 12-hour time with a trailing *a* or *p* for AM or PM. You can include the seconds, but they aren't required. Again, if you enter a time format that DOS isn't programmed to accept, DOS prompts you again.

> **NOTE** Sometimes called *Return* or *New Line*, Enter is an important key to DOS. You press Enter to activate a command you type at the command line. You can type a command at the DOS prompt or a response to a command's prompt, but DOS does not act on your entry until you press Enter. In a sense, Enter is like a "Go" key, instructing DOS to execute a command or accept a response. You can always correct a line while you are typing by using Backspace. After you press Enter, however, you cannot correct the line. If you press Enter without a command at the prompt, DOS simply scrolls up a new command line.

If your PC prompts you for the time and date and you respond, the boot process is complete. If your AUTOEXEC.BAT file bypasses the time and date steps, the boot process is completed without a time and date step.

Using the Booted PC

After the boot is complete, the system prompt indicates the *logged drive*, the active drive that responds to commands. An A> prompt and a blinking cursor indicate that DOS is logged onto drive A, usually a floppy disk drive. A C> prompt and a blinking cursor indicate that DOS is logged onto drive C, usually a hard disk drive.

You can change the logged drive by entering the drive letter followed by a colon (:) and then pressing Enter. DOS reads the drive letter and colon as the disk drive's name. You can change from drive A to C, for example, by typing **C:** at the prompt and pressing Enter. (If you are using two floppy drives, substitute B: for C: in the example.) The sequence on-screen is as follows:

```
A>C:

C>
```

Understanding the Logged Drive

DOS remembers the logged drive as its *current* drive (also called the *default drive*). Many commands use the current drive and other current information without your having to specify the information in the command.

You don't need to specify the drive if you are requesting information from the logged drive. This special attention to the logged drive doesn't mean, however, that the other drives in your system are out of reach. You can use any drive on your system at any time by using a drive specifier in a command. You learn later how to include the drive name when you request information from a drive that is not current.

Stopping the Computer's Action

You occasionally may want to stop the computer from carrying out the action you requested through a DOS command. You may, for example, want to stop a command that produces long output or takes a long time to complete. You also may want to stop a command that you issued in error. In addition to the last resort of switching the power off, three key sequences, which you can think of as the "panic" buttons, are available to stop a DOS command:

Sequence	Action
Ctrl-C	Stops commands. The Ctrl-C keystroke takes effect whenever DOS pauses for you to type more information or while DOS is sending output to the screen or other output device (such as the printer or a disk file). DOS carries out many commands too quickly for you to intervene with Ctrl-C.
Ctrl-Break	Performs the equivalent of Ctrl-C. The Break key is located next to the Reset key on some keyboards; on other keyboards, Break shares the same key with Scroll Lock or Pause.
Ctrl-Alt-Del	The warm-boot key sequence. Ctrl-Alt-Del should not be your first choice to stop a command, but sometimes using Ctrl-C or Ctrl-Break does not stop the command. If Ctrl-Alt-Del fails, press the Reset button (if your computer has one) or turn off the power—your last resort.

Performing a Warm Boot

The *warm boot* is essentially the same process as the cold boot, but you perform a warm boot when the PC's power is on. A warm boot restarts DOS without your touching the power switch; the warm boot is easier on the electronic components of your computer than turning the power off and then on.

You may need to warm boot your PC for several reasons. If you change your system's start-up configuration (described in Chapter 17, "Configuring Your Computer"), you must restart the PC. If your system becomes unresponsive to keyboard or mouse input (also called *hung up*), you often can perform a warm boot to correct the problem. You even can start a different version of DOS from another disk by performing a warm boot.

To perform a warm boot from your hard disk, make sure that drive A is empty. To perform a warm boot from a floppy disk, insert the bootable floppy disk in drive A.

To start the warm boot, locate the Ctrl, Alt, and Del keys. Hold down both Ctrl and Alt and then press Del. The computer is reset, and the boot process begins.

When you warm boot the PC, the computer skips the preliminary POST operation, resets the CPU, and immediately loads DOS. The warm boot then follows the same process that the cold boot followed. Your PC is reset and ready for a computing session.

Warm booting a running computer is generally preferable to turning its power off and then back on. Each time you turn on your computer, electricity surges through its electronics, and your hard disk has to lurch into action. Although these events are normal, performing a cold boot when you could do a warm boot places an unnecessary strain on the system's components.

The Ctrl-Alt-Del keystroke usually is effective to perform a warm boot, but occasionally you may be forced to use the Reset button, if your computer has one. Sometimes your computer's keyboard may be so *frozen* that your PC doesn't recognize that you have pressed Ctrl-Alt-Del. In such a case, press the Reset button. Your computer restarts without actually being turned off, but otherwise acts as if you had performed a cold boot, performing the POST operation and then loading DOS.

Many PCs do not have a Reset button. If your computer doesn't have a Reset button and the Ctrl-Alt-Del command doesn't work, you must perform a cold boot. Turn off the power switch, count to 10 to give the hard disk time to stop completely, and then turn the power back on.

Chapter Summary

This chapter presented the boot process that starts your PC. As part of the boot process, you were introduced to the following key points:

- The boot process resets your computer for a fresh DOS session.

- You must boot your computer from a specially prepared disk called the boot disk.

- The boot disk is usually your hard disk; you also can boot the computer from a floppy disk in drive A.

- When you cold boot the computer, it performs a POST (Power-On Self-Test) before loading the DOS system files.

- Systems that don't have an AUTOEXEC.BAT file on the boot disk will prompt you to enter the time and date as part of the boot process.

- In the command line view, DOS shows a prompt that indicates the logged drive.

- In the DOS Shell view, DOS presents a visually oriented user interface through which you select actions you want to carry out.

The next chapter introduces the fundamentals of using the DOS Shell. Chapter 5, "Using DOS Commands," then discusses the concept of DOS commands. Now that you know how to boot your PC, you are ready to use the Shell and the command line to begin managing your computer through DOS.

Using the DOS Shell

T he DOS Shell program was first introduced in DOS 4.0 and was significantly enhanced in DOS 5.0. From a user's point of view, the DOS 6.0 Shell works in the same way as the Shell program in Version 5.0. The DOS Shell program is a visually oriented user interface which replaces the DOS command line with easy-to-use and easy-to-understand menus and enables you to use a mouse (or other pointing device) to perform many common DOS tasks. Managing your computer is easier from the DOS Shell because you select commands from a menu instead of typing the commands on the DOS command line.

More significantly, with the DOS Shell, you can easily perform operations that are impossible to perform simply through the command line. You can start one applications program, for example, and then switch to a second application without exiting from the first. You can search quickly through directories or an entire hard disk for a specific file name (or file names). Using a mouse, you can select and copy files between directories or between disks without having to type a file name. The Shell also enables you to view the contents of disk files in ASCII or *hexadecimal* (base 16, a numeric code in which ASCII or non-ASCII file contents can be represented). Using the DOS Shell, you can even associate specific file name extensions with a particular applications program so that selecting a file causes DOS to start the associated program.

This book presents the basics of DOS from the perspectives of both the DOS Shell and the command line. The Shell, however, may become your preferred interface to DOS. This chapter introduces you to the DOS Shell, guiding you around the DOS Shell screen and describing how to control the display. The text discusses the aspects of the Shell common to all the program's commands. The material also explains how to use the program list area to start a program.

After you become familiar with the information in this chapter, turn to Chapter 5, "Using DOS Commands," for a basic introduction to using the DOS command line. You will then be ready to examine the other chapters in the book. In particular, Part II, "Putting DOS to Work," explains how to perform DOS tasks from the DOS Shell or the command line.

When you understand the information presented here and in Part II of this book, you may want to learn how you can customize the Shell. Turn then to Chapter 16, "Configuring the DOS Shell," to learn how to fine-tune the DOS Shell to best fit your needs. Chapter 16 also explains how to use the Shell's impressive task-swapping capability.

Key Terms Used in This Chapter

Shell	A program that acts as a user interface to the features and capabilities of an operating system.
Mouse pointer	The block- or arrow-shaped screen icon that indicates where the mouse action occurs.
Selection cursor	An area of highlighted text that shows where selected action occurs.
Scroll bar	An area of the screen containing arrows and icons that serve to move the items through the window.
Pull-down menu	Additional selection items that drop down when an item from a horizontal list is selected.
Text mode	Screen mode available to all PC users. In text mode, all screen presentation is composed of ASCII characters.
Graphics mode	Screen mode available to users of PCs equipped with graphics adapters. In graphics mode, screen presentation uses bit-mapped graphics.

NOTE To reap the greatest benefit from the Shell's modern design, use a mouse. For the mouse to be available, the *mouse device driver* must be loaded into memory before you run the DOS Shell. This chapter and remaining chapters often recommend the mouse method of performing a task but also explain the equivalent keyboard methods.

DOS 6.0 includes a generic mouse device driver. This mouse driver is called MOUSE.COM, and the DOS 6.0 Setup program installs MOUSE.COM into the DOS directory. You can use this generic mouse driver by typing **MOUSE** at the DOS command line and then pressing Enter. Do not install the mouse driver if another mouse driver is already installed. If you want the mouse driver installed automatically every time your computer boots, put the following line in your AUTOEXEC.BAT batch file (the example assumes that DOS is installed on your hard disk):

    C:\DOS\MOUSE.COM

You may also use the INSTALL command in your CONFIG.SYS file to load MOUSE.COM every time your computer boots. Chapter 15, "Understanding Batch Files, DOSKey, and Macros," describes DOS batch files, and Chapter 17, "Configuring Your Computer," describes the CONFIG.SYS file.

Usually, the manufacturer of your mouse includes with the mouse a diskette containing mouse device drivers specifically written for your mouse. Whenever possible, use the manufacturer-supplied mouse device driver. Consult the documentation that came with your mouse or computer system for information on installing your mouse and mouse device driver. If the computer dealer or computer support personnel set up your computer for you, your mouse device driver is probably already set up correctly.

For Related Information

FROM HERE...

▶▶ "Using Batch-File Commands," p. 565.

▶▶ "Understanding the AUTOEXEC.BAT File," p. 551.

▶▶ "Examining AUTOEXEC.BAT Files," p. 558.

▶▶ "Fine-Tuning Your Computer with CONFIG.SYS and AUTOEXEC.BAT," p. 663.

▶▶ "Using the INSTALL Command," p. 672.

Getting Started with the DOS Shell

When you install DOS 6.0, you are asked whether you want the DOS Shell to start every time you turn on your computer. If you select this option, you need merely to turn on your computer to reach the DOS Shell screen.

If your computer does not display the DOS Shell automatically when you turn on your computer, type **DOSSHELL** at the DOS prompt to load the DOS Shell into memory. The DOS Shell first displays a copyright notice and then displays the full-screen DOS Shell window. When the Shell first loads, it also displays a smaller window in the center of the screen containing the message Reading Disk Information. After the Shell scans the file information on your boot disk, which may take a few seconds, the Shell removes the small window and displays a listing similar to the listing shown in figure 4.1.

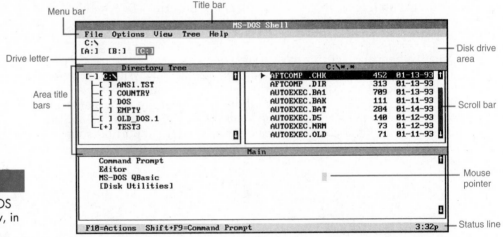

Fig. 4.1

The Initial DOS Shell window, in text mode.

Understanding the DOS Shell Window

When you start the DOS Shell for the first time, the DOS Shell window looks similar to the screen shown in figure 4.1. The top line of the screen, the *title bar*, displays the program name, MS-DOS Shell. The second line of the screen, called the *menu bar*, lists the names of available menus. You can select all DOS Shell commands from menus that pull down from the menu bar.

Just below the menu bar, the DOS Shell window lists the current drive and directory and the available disk drives. This book refers to this portion of the screen as the *disk drive area*. The first time you display the Shell, the drive area lists the current drive and directory and the available drives in the following manner:

```
C:\
[A:] [B:] [C:]
```

If your computer doesn't have a hard (fixed) disk drive, [C:] is not listed. If your system has more than one hard disk drive or you have DBLSPACE compressed drives, you also may see [D:], [E:], and so on (refer to Chapter 6, "Understanding Disks and Files," for a complete discussion of disk drives).

Initially, the DOS Shell window appears in text mode, as shown in figure 4.1. The section "Understanding the Shell Screen Modes" later in this chapter discusses how to switch the display to a graphics mode. Figure 4.2 shows the 34-line graphics mode available for VGA displays.

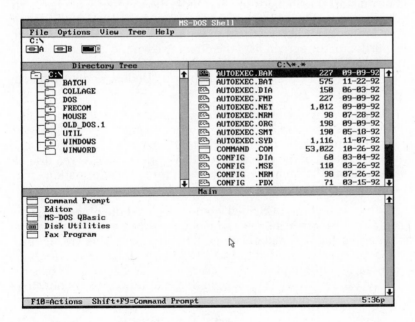

Fig. 4.2

The DOS Shell window displayed in graphics screen mode.

In graphics mode, the drive area depicts your disk drives area as follows:

Notice that the icons above differ slightly from each other. The icons that depict drives A and B represent floppy disk drives. The icon for drive C indicates that this drive is a hard disk drive. Refer to Chapter 6, "Understanding Disks and Files," for a full discussion of disks and drives.

The last line of the DOS Shell window is the *status line*. The status line usually displays two messages: F10=Actions and Shift+F9=Command Prompt. At the right end of the status line, the Shell displays the current time. Occasionally, the status line also displays other messages related to the command you are executing.

Between the drive area and the status line, the DOS Shell divides the window into rectangular *areas*, each of which is headed by an *area title bar*. On the right side of each area is a *scroll bar*, which you use to move around an area.

When you start the Shell for the first time, the window is divided into the drive area and three larger areas (refer to fig. 4.1). The *directory tree area* is in the upper left quadrant of the window—below the drive area. This portion of the screen lists the directories of the current disk drive in a tree-like format. Use of the directory tree area of the DOS Shell window is covered extensively in Chapter 8, "Understanding and Managing Directories."

The *file list area*, in the upper right quadrant of the Shell window, lists the names, file size, and file date (when last changed) of files in the current directory (refer to Chapter 8 for a complete discussion of directories). The name of the current directory appears in the area title bar. Refer to Chapter 9, "Managing Your Files," for more information on using the file list area.

The bottom half of the DOS Shell window is called the *program list area*. This area of the screen serves as a menu for starting DOS applications and for accessing DOS disk-related utility programs. This area lists a group of programs, referred to as a *program group*. The name of the currently listed program group appears in the area title bar. The section "Using the Program List" later in this chapter discusses how to use this portion of the DOS Shell screen.

Occasionally, you may want to remove one or more areas from the Shell screen to provide more room for the other areas. Refer to the section "Modifying the View" later in this chapter for more information about turning window areas on and off.

At times, a fourth area, the *active task list area*, also may be displayed in the DOS Shell window. The active task list area displays the names of DOS applications you have activated through the DOS 6.0 task swapper. Figure 4.3 shows the DOS Shell window with the active task list displayed.

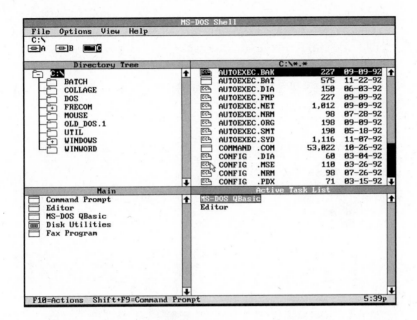

Fig. 4.3

The DOS Shell window with the active task list displayed.

Selecting an Area

Although you can have as many as five areas displayed in the DOS Shell window—disk drive, directory tree, file list, program list, and active task list—only one area is *selected* (active) at a time. The selected area is indicated by a highlighted area title bar. An area must be selected before you can perform any operation in that area.

When you first start a DOS Shell session, the drive letter of the current disk drive is highlighted, indicating that the disk drive area is selected. The area title bars shown in figures 4.1 and 4.2, for example, are not highlighted. Contrast these figures with figure 4.3, which shows a highlighted area title bar above the active task list.

You have two methods by which to select an area in the Shell window:

■ Move the mouse pointer into the area you want to activate and click the left button. The Shell highlights the area's title bar.

■ Press the Tab key to cycle through the areas that are currently displayed in the window.

Moving around an Area

After you select an area, the Shell highlights one of the items listed in the area. This highlight is called the *selection cursor*. To move the selection cursor within the selected area, use one of the following methods:

- Use the cursor-movement keys on the keyboard. Press the up- or down-arrow key to move up or down one item at a time. Press PgUp or PgDn to move up or down a page at a time. Press Home or End to go to the beginning or end of the list.

- Use the mouse and the scroll bar, shown in figure 4.4, to scroll up or down. Using the scroll bars is described in the following paragraphs.

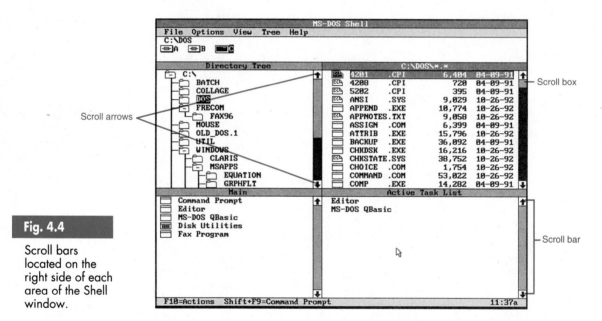

Scroll arrows

Scroll box

Scroll bar

Fig. 4.4

Scroll bars located on the right side of each area of the Shell window.

The scroll bar has the following components:

- A scroll arrow at the top and bottom of the bar. By clicking the scroll arrow, you scroll text up or down one line at a time. Click the scroll arrow and hold down the right mouse button to scroll continuously in the direction of the arrow.

- A scroll box, located on the scroll bar between the up-scroll arrow and the down-scroll arrow. The position of the box on the scroll bar indicates the relative position of the selection cursor with respect to the entire list of items in the selected area.

Click the scroll bar above the scroll box to move the selection cursor up one page at a time. Click below the scroll box to move down one page at a time.

You can scroll quickly through the list in either direction by clicking the scroll box, holding down the left mouse button, and dragging the box in the direction you want the selection cursor to move.

For Related Information

▶▶ "Expanding the File System through Subdirectories," p. 235.

▶▶ "Working with Directories through the DOS Shell," p. 243.

FROM HERE...

Using the DOS Shell Menus

You can initiate virtually every DOS Shell operation by choosing options from menus. These DOS Shell menus fall into two categories: the menu bar and pull-down menus.

Using the Menu Bar

When the disk drive area, directory tree area, or file list area is active, the menu bar lists five menu names: File, Options, View, Tree, and Help. The Tree menu name does not appear when the program list or active task list is the active area. Selecting a menu name displays a pull-down menu.

You can select a menu option from the menu bar in one of three ways:

■ Move the mouse pointer to an option and click the left button.

■ Press the F10 key or the Alt key to activate the menu bar. The Shell underlines one letter in each menu name and places a selection cursor on the menu name File at the left end of the menu bar. Press the key that corresponds to the underlined letter in the menu name you want to select. To select View from the menu bar, for example, press F10 or Alt and then press V.

■ Press F10 or Alt to activate the menu bar, use the right- or left-arrow key to move the selection cursor to your choice, and press Enter. This method is sometimes called the *point-and-shoot method*.

Even after you select a menu name, you can still select another menu name by clicking the name with the mouse or by using the left- or right-arrow key.

Using Pull-Down Menus

When you select a menu name from the menu bar, the Shell displays a pull-down menu, which displays a list of items below the menu bar. If you select File, for example, while the file list is the active area, the Shell displays the File pull-down menu shown in figure 4.5. The items listed in the menu depend on which area is active.

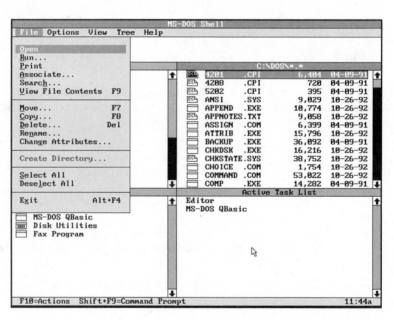

Fig. 4.5

The File pull-down menu displayed when the file list area is active.

To select an item from a pull-down menu, use one of the following methods:

- Move the mouse pointer to a menu item, and click the left button.

- The Shell underlines one letter in each menu item. Press the key that corresponds to the underlined letter in the item you want to select. To select View File Contents from the File menu in figure 4.5, for example, press V.

■ The Shell places the selection cursor on the first item at the top of the pull-down menu. Use the up- or down-arrow key to move the selection cursor to your choice, and then press Enter.

When a menu is pulled down, you can display an adjacent menu by pressing the left- or right-arrow key. To cancel a pulled-down menu without making a selection, click the menu name or an area outside the menu, or press Esc. The Shell returns to the preceding window display. You also can press Alt or F10 to cancel a pulled-down menu while maintaining an active menu bar so that you can select another menu name.

The DOS Shell uses the following conventions when it lists menu items:

■ A menu item that displays a dialog box, which is discussed later in this chapter, ends with an ellipsis (...).

■ A menu item that is dimmed, such as the Create Directory item shown in figure 4.5, is not a valid option in the current context.

■ Some menu items toggle between two states—on or off. A menu item that is toggled on displays a small diamond (♦) to the left of the item name. The diamond is absent when the item is turned off.

■ Some commands that can be selected through menu items have shortcuts in the form of key combinations or keystroke commands. When a keystroke command shortcut is available for a command, the Shell lists the keystroke in the menu, to the right of the command. Five of the commands in the File menu, for example, list shortcut keystroke commands (refer to fig. 4.5).

Using Keystroke Commands

The DOS Shell provides many keystroke command shortcuts. Many of these commands are listed in pull-down menus. Two such commands, F10 and Shift-F9, are listed in the Shell window status line.

Table 4.1 lists all DOS Shell keystroke commands for DOS 6.0. After you learn these keystroke commands, you may find them quicker to use than any equivalent menu items. Using menus always requires that you use multiple keystrokes or that you take one hand from the keyboard to use the mouse. To perform a command by using the keystroke combinations, you press a single keystroke or keystroke combination. Each command in the following table is discussed later in the book.

Table 4.1 DOS Shell Keystroke Commands

Key	Function
F1	Displays context-sensitive help
F3	Exits the DOS Shell, returns to the command line, and removes the DOS Shell from memory (same as Alt-F4)
Alt-F4	Exits the DOS Shell, returns to the command line, and removes the DOS Shell from memory (same as F3)
F5	Refreshes the file list(s)
Shift-F5	Repaints the screen
F7	Moves selected file(s)
F8	Copies selected file(s)
Shift-F8	Extends selection in Add mode
F9	Views file contents
Shift-F9	Accesses the command line without removing the DOS Shell from memory
F10	Activates the menu bar (same as Alt)
Alt	Activates the menu bar (same as F10)
Del	Deletes selected file(s)
+	Expands one level of the current branch in the directory tree
*	Expands all levels of the current branch in the directory tree
Ctrl-*	Expands all branches in the directory tree
- (hyphen)	Collapses the current branch in the directory tree
Alt-Tab	Switches between active task and the DOS Shell, if Task Switching is enabled
Alt-Esc	Cycles through active tasks, if Task Switching is enabled
Shift-↑	Extends selection up
Shift-↓	Extends selection down
Shift-←	Extends selection left
Shift-→	Extends selection right

Key	Function
Esc	Cancels current function
Tab	Cycles forward through areas (left to right, top to bottom)
Shift-Tab	Cycles backward through areas (right to left, bottom to top)
Ctrl-/	Selects all files in the selected directory
Ctrl-F5	Refreshes the selected directory

Using Dialog Boxes

As you work with the DOS Shell, the program routinely displays messages and prompts in pop-up boxes, called *dialog boxes*, on-screen. Any menu item that ends with an ellipsis (...) displays a dialog box when you select the item. When you select Copy from the File menu, for example, the Copy File dialog box, shown in figure 4.6, appears.

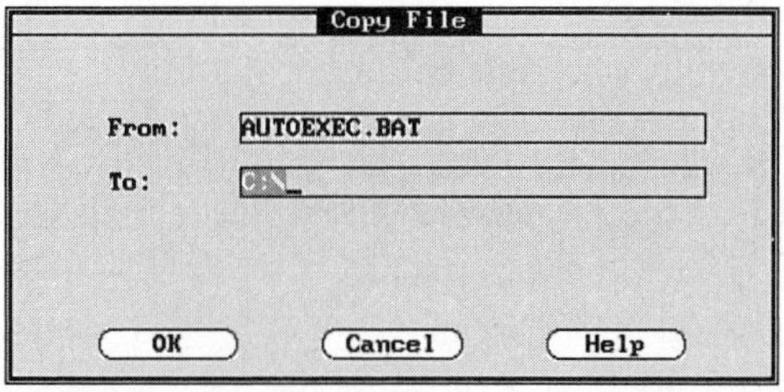

Fig. 4.6

The Copy File dialog box.

Dialog boxes fall into two general categories: those that request information and those that provide information. The Copy File dialog box in figure 4.6 is an example of a dialog box that requests information. Pressing F1, by contrast, displays a dialog box that provides information and is entitled MS-DOS Shell Help. This help screen, shown in figure 4.7, assists you in learning the Shell.

All dialog boxes are built from a standard set of elements: text boxes, list boxes, option buttons, option check boxes, and command buttons. The following sections explain how to use each element.

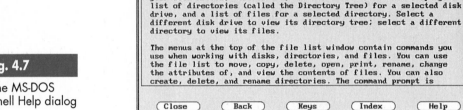

Fig. 4.7

The MS-DOS
Shell Help dialog
box.

Using a Text Box

When you need to type information in a dialog box, the Shell includes
one or more rectangular boxes known as *text boxes*. The Copy File dialog box shown in figure 4.6 contains two text boxes, one labeled From
and one labeled To.

To make an entry in a text box, you first highlight the box. Using the
mouse, move the mouse pointer to the box and click the left button.
Alternatively, you can press Tab or Shift-Tab repeatedly until the text
box is highlighted.

Often the Shell provides a default value in each text box. The text boxes
in figure 4.6, for example, include the default values AUTOEXEC.BAT
and C:\. When you select a text box, the Shell highlights any default
contained in that text box. Typing new text in the text box replaces the
default value.

Sometimes you don't want to replace the entire default value in a text
box. When you want to edit the value, press the right- or left-arrow key
to cause the Shell to remove the highlighting. You then can edit the
existing entry. The same block editing techniques that are explained in
Chapter 14, "Using the DOS Editor," can also be used in text boxes in
the Shell's dialog boxes.

After you make the desired entry or change the value in the text box,
press Enter to accept the value that is displayed in the text box. When
you press Enter, the Shell also closes the dialog box and executes the
command, if any, with which the dialog box is associated.

Using a List Box

Some dialog boxes contain information or a list of choices displayed
in a rectangular area, referred to in this book as a *list box*. A title bar

appears at the top of each list box, as well as a scroll bar on the right side of the list box. Refer to figure 4.7, which shows a help dialog box containing a list box entitled File List Overview.

Often the text or list is too long to fit in the list box, so the Shell enables you to scroll vertically through the contents of the box. To scroll through a list box, use your mouse and the scroll bar, or use the cursor-movement keys.

Using Option Buttons

Some dialog boxes require that you use *option buttons* to select command settings. Each option button is a circle (a pair of parentheses if your screen is in text mode) followed by a command setting. Option buttons always occur in groups—never alone. The buttons in each group are mutually exclusive.

The File Display Options dialog box shown in figure 4.8, for example, contains option buttons listed on the right side of the dialog box, beneath the label Sort By. Displayed file names can be sorted by name, extension, date, size, or disk order, but the Shell does not sort files by more than one of these parameters at a time.

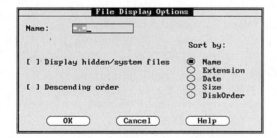

Fig. 4.8

The File Display Options dialog box.

Option buttons operate in a way similar to the buttons on a car radio. When you select a button from the group, any button that was already selected "pops out," or is canceled. Only one button is active at any particular time. The active button is indicated by a dot in the circle (or between the parentheses). The Name option button in figure 4.8 is selected, indicated by the dot in the circle.

To select a different option button, use the mouse to click the desired option button. Alternatively, use the Tab or Shift-Tab key to move the underscore (cursor) to the group of option buttons. Then use the up- or down-arrow key to move the dot to the desired button. Press Enter to select the new option, close the dialog box, and execute the command, if any, with which the dialog box is associated.

Using Option Check Boxes

Some Shell dialog boxes enable you to select the desired command settings by "checking" the appropriate *option check boxes*. An option check box is a pair of brackets followed by a command setting. The File Display Options dialog box in figure 4.8, for example, contains the following check boxes:

■ Display hidden/system files

■ Descending order

An option check box turns a command setting on or off. The setting is checked (or on) when an X appears between the brackets. The setting is off when the space between the brackets is blank. To toggle the setting on or off, use the mouse to click between the brackets. Alternatively, use the Tab or Shift-Tab key to move the cursor to the option check box, and press the space bar. Each time you click the box or press the space bar, the option toggles on or off.

Using Command Buttons

After making any desired entries in text boxes, selecting appropriate option buttons, and checking the correct check boxes, you are ready to execute the DOS Shell command. To do so, select one of the *command buttons*—the rounded-rectangular buttons near the bottom edge of the dialog box.

Most dialog boxes in the DOS Shell contain three command buttons: OK, Cancel, and Help (refer to fig. 4.8). The OK command button activates the choices you made in the dialog box and executes the command, if any, with which the dialog box is associated. The Cancel command button aborts any changes you made in the dialog box and returns to the DOS Shell window. The Help command button accesses the Shell's on-line help facility.

To execute a command button, use one of the following methods:

■ Move the mouse pointer to the desired command button and click the left mouse button.

■ Press Tab or Shift-Tab to move the cursor to the desired command button and press Enter.

> You can execute the command associated with a dialog box by pressing Enter, even though the cursor is not in the OK command button (as long as the cursor is not on one of the other command buttons).

T I P

For Related Information

▶▶ "Mastering Fundamental Editing Techniques," p. 519.

▶▶ "Block Editing," p. 524.

FROM HERE...

Modifying the View

The DOS Shell is quite flexible. In the directory tree area and file list area, you can display directories and file names from any of your computer's disk drives, including directories and file names from two disks at one time. You also can display just the program list, change the entire screen to a graphics mode, and show as many as 60 lines of information on a single screen (depending on the capability of your computer's monitor).

The following sections describe how to modify the display to list directories and files from other disks, to display files from two disks at one time, and to change the amount of information displayed about each file. In addition, the following sections show you how to display the program list full-screen and how to change the number of lines that appear on-screen.

Logging On to a Different Disk and Refreshing the Directory Tree

As you learned in Chapter 3, "Starting DOS," each time you turn on your computer, the operating system (DOS) is loaded from one of your computer's disks. This disk is the boot disk. If your system is configured to start the DOS Shell immediately after your computer boots up, the Shell window lists directories and file names found on the boot disk.

Often, you may need to display the directories and file names on a disk other than the boot disk. Figure 4.8, for example, shows three drive letters: A, B, and C. Drive C is the boot disk; therefore, the directories found in drive C are shown in the directory tree. Drive C's icon is highlighted, indicating that C is the currently selected disk drive.

To display in the directory tree the directories found on another disk, move the mouse pointer to the drive icon of the desired disk and click the left mouse button. Alternatively, press the left- or right-arrow key until the Shell highlights the drive letter you want, and then press Enter. The Shell displays a message that the Shell is reading the disk information and then displays in the directory tree and file list areas of the DOS Shell window the directories and file names from the target disk. Figure 4.9, for example, shows file names from a disk in drive B.

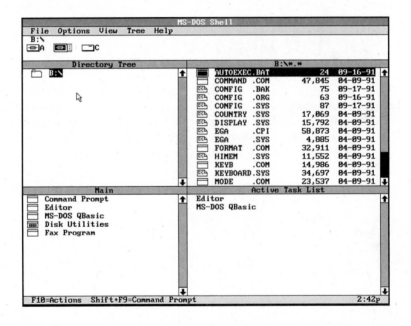

Fig. 4.9

Displaying the directories and file names from the disk in drive B.

Because the DOS Shell enables you to start other programs that may create, modify, or delete files on your disk, the list of files in the DOS Shell window may at times be inaccurate. If you suspect that the directory tree area or file list area does not reflect the actual contents of the disk, use the Shell's Refresh command. To refresh the file list, press F5 or perform the following steps:

1. Select <u>V</u>iew from the menu bar to display the View menu, shown in figure 4.10.

2. Choose <u>R</u>efresh.

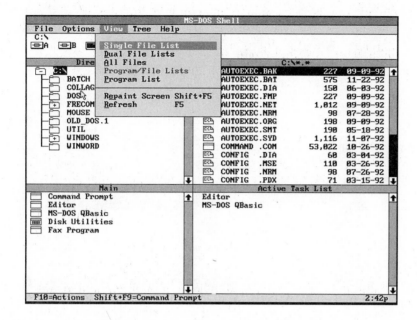

Fig. 4.10

The View menu.

The Shell displays the message Reading Disk Information and then returns to the DOS Shell window and displays the updated list of directories and files in the directory tree and file list areas.

Switching between Dual and Single File Lists

From time to time, you may want the convenience of seeing lists of directories and files from two disks simultaneously. Perhaps you want to copy a file from one disk to another, or maybe you want to compare the list of files on one disk to the list of files on another disk.

The DOS Shell enables you to display two file lists on the same screen by following these steps:

1. Select View from the menu bar to display the View menu (refer to fig. 4.10).

2. Choose Dual File Lists from the View menu.

   The Shell replaces the program list area, at the bottom of the window, with a second disk drive area, directory tree area, and file list area showing the directory tree and file list from the current disk drive (see fig. 4.11). This view is called a *dual file list*.

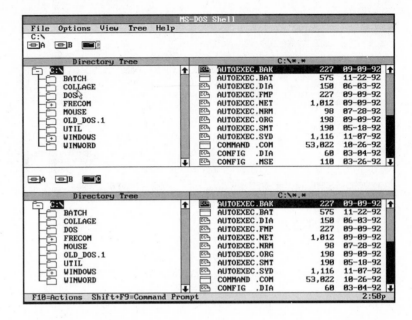

Fig. 4.11

A dual file list.

3. To select a second disk drive in the bottom portion of the window, use the mouse to click the icon in the bottom disk drive area for the drive for which you want to list directories and files.

   Alternatively, use Tab or Alt-Tab to cycle the selection cursor until it highlights the drive icon of the currently selected drive in the bottom disk drive area. Then use the left- or right-arrow key to highlight the desired drive icon, and press Enter.

The Shell lists directories and file names from the second disk in the lower set of directory tree and file list areas (see fig. 4.12). You can switch between the two lists by using the mouse or the Tab key.

Sometimes you want to display a single set of disk drive, directory tree, and file list areas. In addition, you do not want to display the program list area at the bottom of the screen. Use the following procedure to turn on a single list:

1. Select View from the menu bar to display the View menu.

2. Choose Single File List from the View menu.

The window displays a screen similar to the screen shown in figure 4.13, referred to as a *single file list*.

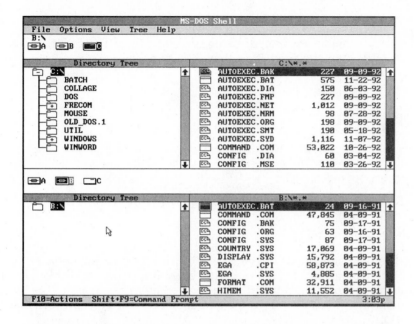

Fig. 4.12

Viewing directories and file names from two disks at one time.

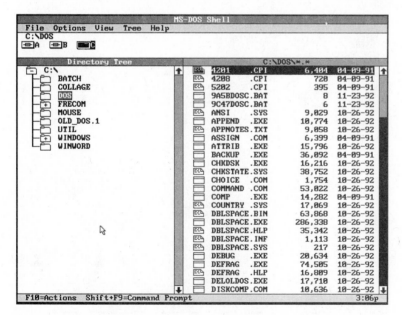

Fig. 4.13

Viewing a single file list.

NOTE When you exit from the DOS Shell, it remembers the changes you made using the View menu. The next time you start the Shell, it will have the same appearance.

Displaying All Files

Occasionally, you may want the Shell window to display all files on a disk, regardless of the directory. To display all files in a single list, complete the following steps:

1. Select <u>V</u>iew from the menu bar to display the View menu (refer to fig. 4.10).

2. Choose <u>A</u>ll Files.

On the right side of the screen, the DOS Shell displays an alphabetical list of the file names of all files on the current disk (see fig. 4.14). The Shell also lists on the left side of the screen information about the file at which the selection cursor is located and about the currently selected file(s).

```
                          MS-DOS Shell
  File  Options  View  Tree  Help
  C:\DOS
  ⌹A  ⌹B  ▃C
                                      *.*
                          GENI    .PAL        410   08-01-91    6:21p
  File                    GLOSSARY.DOC       1,965  10-07-91    9:01p
    Name  : HELP.COM      GLOSSARY.HLP      46,570  03-10-92    3:10a
    Attr  : ...a          GORILLA .BAS      29,434  04-09-91    5:00a
  Selected     B    C     GOTH    .CHR       8,560  08-29-88    2:00a
    Number:    1    1     GOTHIC  .FOT       1,324  04-22-92   10:57a
    Size  :        437    GOTHIC  .TTF      54,200  03-09-92   12:00a
  Directory               GOTHICB .FOT       1,326  04-22-92   10:57a
    Name  : DOS           GOTHICB .TTF      47,912  03-09-92   12:00a
    Size  : 6,057,622     GOTHICBI.FOT       1,340  04-22-92   10:57a
    Files :        126    GOTHICBI.TTF      50,244  03-09-92   12:00a
  Disk                    GOTHICI .FOT       1,330  04-22-92   10:57a
    Name  : EAGLE_AT      GOTHICI .TTF      54,964  03-09-92   12:00a
    Size  : 42,366,976    GRAFTABL.COM      11,205  04-09-91    5:00a
    Avail : 4,222,976     GRAMMAR .DLL     311,808  10-17-91   12:00p
    Files :        872    GRAPH   .EXE     546,304  09-24-91    3:45p
    Dirs  :         19    GRAPH   .HLP     296,643  09-24-91    3:45p
                          GRAPHICS.COM      19,694  10-26-92    6:00a
                          GRAPHICS.COM      19,694  04-09-91    5:00a
                          GRAPHICS.DOC      29,846  10-21-91   12:00p
                 ⌖        GRAPHICS.PRO      21,232  10-26-92    6:00a
                          GRAPHICS.PRO      21,232  04-09-91    5:00a
                          GREP    .COM       7,029  10-23-90    6:00a
                          GR_AM   .LEX     780,688  10-17-91   12:00p
                          HANDOUT .DOT       2,974  03-22-92    1:54p
                          HELP    .COM         413  10-26-92    6:00a
                          HELP    .EXE      11,473  04-09-91    5:00a
  F10=Actions  Shift+F9=Command Prompt                        3:11p
```

Fig. 4.14

The All Files list.

Switching between the Program List and the Program/File Lists

The first time you start the DOS Shell, the DOS Shell window displays the directory tree area, the file list area, and the program list area. Some users prefer to use the Shell primarily as a menu for starting applications programs and thus don't want to view the directory tree and file list every time. The Shell, therefore, provides a view that displays only the program list.

To turn off the directory tree and file list areas and display the program list full-screen, execute the following steps:

1. Select <u>V</u>iew from the menu bar to display the View menu.

2. Choose <u>P</u>rogram List.

The Shell uses nearly the entire screen to display the program list area, as shown in figure 4.15.

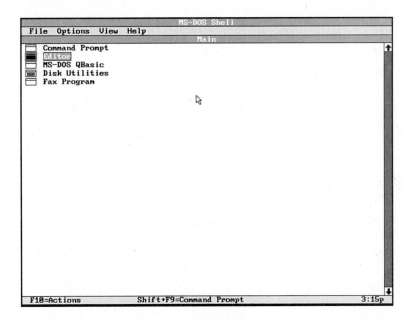

Fig. 4.15

The full-screen program list area.

If you decide later that you want to display the directory tree and file list areas on-screen along with the program list area, complete the following steps:

1. Select <u>V</u>iew from the menu bar to display the View menu.

2. Choose Program/<u>F</u>ile Lists.

The Shell returns to the original view, with the disk drive area, directory tree area, and file list area in the top half of the screen and program list area in the bottom half of the screen.

Understanding the Shell Screen Modes

The Shell window can be displayed in one of several *screen modes*; the number of available screen modes depends on the type of display adapter and monitor you have. Figure 4.1 shows the DOS Shell window in 25-line low-resolution text mode. This setting is the default start-up screen mode when DOS 6.0 is first installed. This mode is one of three screen mode options available to DOS 6.0 users who have a Color Graphics Adapter (CGA).

If you have an Enhanced Graphics Adapter (EGA) or Video Graphics Array adapter (VGA), you can take advantage of additional screen modes that squeeze more lines of text on the screen—up to 43 lines with an EGA adapter and monitor and up to 60 lines with a VGA adapter and monitor. Figures 4.2 through 4.15 show the Shell window in 34-line medium-resolution graphics mode.

To change the screen mode, follow these steps:

1. Choose Options from the menu bar to display the Options menu, shown in figure 4.16.

2. Select Display from the Options menu to display the Screen Display Mode dialog box, shown in figure 4.17.

3. Choose the desired screen mode from the list box.

   Use the mouse and scroll bar or the cursor-movement keys to scroll the list. Click the desired screen mode, or use the arrow keys to highlight the screen mode with the selection cursor.

4. To see what the new screen mode looks like without actually selecting it, choose the Preview command button. The DOS Shell repaints its screen with the new mode, and the Screen Display Mode dialog box remains open.

5. Repeat steps 3 and 4 until you are satisfied with the appearance of the screen.

6. To confirm your choice of a new screen mode, press Enter, or choose the OK command button. If you decide not to change the screen mode, choose the Cancel button or press Esc.

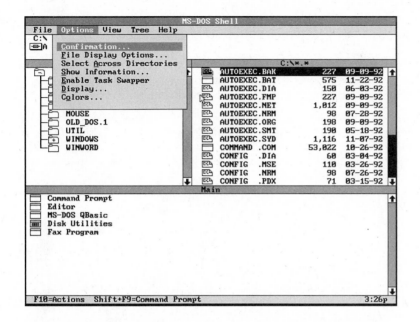

Fig. 4.16

The Options menu.

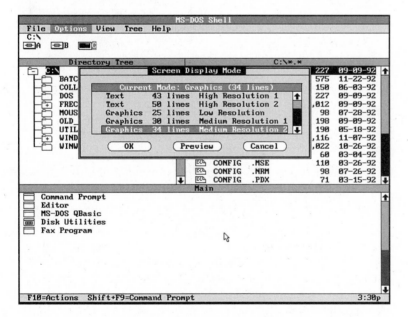

Fig. 4.17

The Screen Display Mode dialog box.

The Shell closes the Screen Display Mode dialog box, returns to the DOS Shell window, and repaints the screen in the new screen mode. If you choose Cancel, the Shell closes the Screen Display Mode dialog box and returns to the DOS Shell window without changing the screen mode.

Using the Help System

At any time during a DOS Shell session, pressing F1 causes a help window to appear. On-line help assists you with the current selection or action so that you can make an informed selection.

The Shell's help system is *contextual*, meaning that DOS looks at the menu item currently highlighted and provides information about that selection. You can go from that help screen to other help screens to get help on additional topics. Figure 4.18 shows a typical help screen.

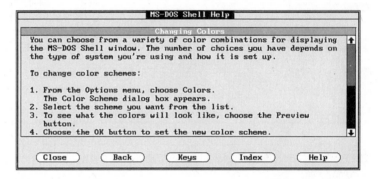

Fig. 4.18

The Changing Colors help screen.

Five command buttons appear at the bottom of a help screen:

■ *Close* returns you to the screen from which you pressed F1.

■ *Back* returns to the preceding help screen.

■ *Keys* displays an index of help information on keystroke commands.

■ *Index* displays the DOS Shell help index, a list of topics on which you can receive help.

■ *Help* displays information on how to use the help system.

Use the mouse and scroll bar or the cursor-movement keys to display the information in which you are interested. Additional related topics are listed in a different color on the help screen. Use the Tab key to highlight the related topic and press Enter, or use the mouse to click the topic. The Shell displays another help screen.

Choose the Close command button or press Esc to return to the screen from which you pressed F1.

Using the Program List

In addition to providing an alternative DOS interface to the command line, the DOS Shell also provides a convenient method for running all the other programs stored in your computer. A program that performs this function is sometimes called a *menuing program*. The Shell's program list area provides menuing capability.

Items listed in the program area of the DOS Shell window fall into two categories: program items and program groups. A *program item* starts a specific software application on your hard disk; a *program group* is a collection of program items or other program groups.

Program groups enable you to group your applications programs by category. For example, you may create a Word Processing group, a Database group, and a Spreadsheet group. By default, the initial list of program items, which you see when you first start the DOS Shell, are in the Main program group. The Main group includes another program group named Disk Utilities, which includes program items that perform disk-related DOS commands.

You can easily tell whether an option listed in the program list area is a program item or a program group. When the DOS Shell window is in text screen mode, program group names are enclosed in brackets. For example, the Disk Utilities program group appears as [Disk Utilities] when the screen is in text mode.

If you have chosen a graphics screen mode, the Shell uses special icons to distinguish between program items and program groups. The following icon appears to the left of program item names:

The following icon appears to the left of program group names:

When you first install DOS 6.0, the program list area lists the program group Main. This group includes the program items Command Prompt, Editor, and MS-DOS QBasic. Selecting a program item starts the selected program. Also included in the main program group is the program group Disk Utilities. Selecting Disk Utilities causes the Shell to display another group of program items, the Disk Utilities group, which consists of DOS utility programs that enable you to copy, back up, restore, format, and undelete disks (see fig. 4.19). You can press Esc to return to the preceding program group or select the Main program group, which appears at the top of the program list.

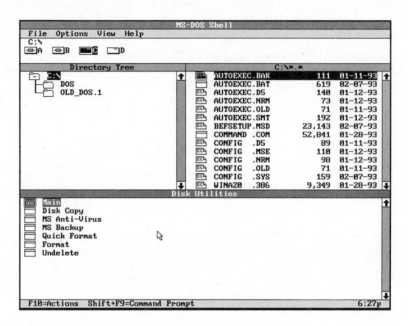

Fig. 4.19

Disk Utilities program items.

The title bar of the program list area displays the name of the current program group. When you first start the DOS Shell, the program list title bar displays the label Main.

Accessing the DOS Command Line

You can move temporarily from the Shell to the DOS prompt, keeping the Shell in memory. Use one of the following methods:

- Position the mouse pointer on the Command Prompt item in the program list area and *double-click*—press twice in rapid succession—the left mouse button.

- Press Tab or Shift-Tab until the program list area is the selected area. If the Command Prompt item is not already highlighted, use the arrow keys to move the selection cursor to this item. Press Enter.

- Press Shift-F9.

The DOS prompt appears. You now can enter DOS commands. To return to the Shell, type **EXIT**, and press Enter.

NOTE   Both the Command Prompt item in the program list and the Shift-F9 keystroke command start a secondary command processor. The same action occurs when you issue the DOS COMMAND command. When you start a secondary command processor, typing the EXIT command is the signal to DOS that you want to return to the primary command processor. When you are in the DOS Shell, COMMAND.COM has loaded and executed DOSSHELL.EXE; typing EXIT after accessing the DOS prompt returns control to DOSSHELL.EXE.

The other way to get to the DOS command prompt is to exit from the DOS Shell. When you use this method, however, DOS removes the Shell from the computer's memory. To exit the Shell, press F3, press Alt-F4, or follow these steps:

1. Select Eile from the menu bar to display the File menu.

2. Choose Exit from the File menu.

The Shell returns you to the DOS prompt. Remember, you have exited the Shell, so to restart the Shell, type **DOSSHELL**, and press Enter.

Starting a Program

When you want to start or run an application listed in the program list, use one of the following methods:

■ Position the mouse pointer on the program item in the program list area and double-click the left mouse button.

■ Press Tab or Shift-Tab repeatedly until the program list area is the selected area. Use the up- and down-arrow keys to move the selection cursor to the desired program item. Press Enter.

■ Move the selection cursor to the program item. Select Eile from the menu bar to display the File menu. Choose Open.

To start the DOS Editor, for example, use one of the preceding methods to select the Editor program item in the Main program group. Similarly, you can start the programming environment MS-DOS QBasic by selecting the MS-DOS QBasic program item in the program list area of the Shell window.

Other methods of starting programs are described in Chapter 10, "Understanding and Using Workgroups."

Accessing the Disk Utilities Program Group

The Disk Utilities program group in the program list area enables you to access several standard DOS commands (refer to fig. 4.19). When you select a command, a dialog box appears in which you can type the standard parameters DOS requires for the command. In all respects, these commands behave exactly as if you had typed them at the DOS prompt. See the following chapters for descriptions of these commands and ways to use them from both the DOS Shell and the command line.

Disk Utilities Item	DOS Command	Chapter Reference
Disk Copy	DISKCOPY	6
MS Anti-Virus	MSAV	18
MS Backup	MSBACKUP	13
Quick Format	FORMAT /Q	7
Format	FORMAT	7
Undelete	UNDELETE	9

Chapter Summary

As you can see, the DOS Shell adds a new dimension to using DOS. Even if you are comfortable using DOS at the DOS prompt, you will want to explore the DOS Shell. Important points covered in this chapter include the following:

■ The DOS Shell is a program that acts as a user interface to the features and capabilities of the MS-DOS operating system.

■ You can scroll quickly through a DOS Shell area in either direction by clicking the scroll box, holding down the left mouse button, and dragging the box in the direction you want the selection cursor to move.

■ When you select a menu name from the menu bar, the Shell displays a pull-down menu.

■ You can modify the view of the DOS Shell window to display more or less information.

- The DOS Shell provides many keystroke command shortcuts. Many of these commands are listed in pull-down menus.

- The Shell window can be displayed in one of several screen modes, depending on the type of display you have.

- At any time during a DOS Shell session, pressing F1 causes a help window to appear.

- You can view the directories of more than one disk at a time by using the dual file lists feature.

- In addition to providing an alternative DOS interface to the command line, the DOS Shell provides a convenient method for running all the other programs stored on your computer.

- Several DOS commands, such as DISKCOPY and FORMAT, are available in the Disk Utilities program item.

Now that you are acquainted with the DOS Shell, the next chapter introduces you to the DOS command line. At the DOS command line, you interact directly with DOS and the DOS command interpreter. The next chapter acquaints you with the syntax requirements of DOS commands and shows you how to list the files on a disk. You will also learn how to obtain help about the various DOS commands from the DOS on-line help system.

Using DOS Commands

Now that you have learned your way around the DOS Shell, you need to become familiar with the DOS command line. This chapter introduces you to the elements that make up DOS commands and teaches you how to issue commands correctly at the DOS prompt.

Key Terms Used in This Chapter

Command	A group of characters that tell the computer what action to take.
Syntax	A specific set of rules you follow when issuing commands.
Parameter	An additional instruction that defines specifically what you want the DOS command to do.
Switch	A part of the command syntax that turns on an optional function of a command.
Delimiter	A character that separates the "words" in a command. Common delimiters are the space and the slash.
Wild card	A character in a command that represents one or more characters. In DOS, the ? wild card represents any single character. The * wild card represents any remaining characters in a "word" in the command.

Understanding DOS Commands

To communicate your need for service to DOS, you enter DOS commands at the DOS command line. Commands are made up of groups of characters that are separated, or *delimited*, by certain other characters. A command you give to DOS is similar to a written instruction you may give to a work associate. Both the DOS command and the written instruction must communicate your intentions using proper form, or *syntax*. Both must communicate what action you want carried out and what the objects of that action are.

If you need to duplicate a sign on a bulletin board so that you can post it on another bulletin board, for example, you may tell a work associate "Copy sign A to sign B. Be sure to verify that you have made no mistakes." Similarly, if you want DOS to copy the contents of disk A to disk B, you give DOS the following instruction:

DISKCOPY A: B:

To verify that the copy is the same as the original, you instruct DOS to compare the two disks:

DISKCOMP A: B:

DISKCOPY and DISKCOMP are the DOS commands that determine what action is to be carried out. The drive letters A: and B: indicate where the action is to be carried out. Although the instructions to duplicate a sign look more natural than the DOS DISKCOPY command, the two are quite similar.

DOS recognizes and responds to over 80 commands. The most useful commands are built into the command processor and are immediately available at the command line. Because of the built-in availability of these commands, they are called *internal commands*.

Other commands are stored as utility programs in a directory on your hard disk or on your DOS disk(s). Because these commands are not built into the command processor, they are called *external commands*. You execute external commands the same way you execute internal commands: by typing the command at the command line.

Learning the "ins and outs" of issuing DOS commands takes some practice. Fortunately, DOS commands have a familiar structure, and you soon will branch out from the examples in this book to your own forms of the DOS commands.

Understanding the Elements of a DOS Command

You issue commands to tell DOS that you need its operating-system services. Although each DOS command provides an individual service, all DOS commands conform to standard rules. Using DOS is easier when you understand the concepts behind the commands. With that understanding, you can generalize many of these rules to different commands.

To begin to understand DOS commands, you need to know two fundamental facts:

- DOS requires that you use a specific set of rules, or *syntax*, when you issue commands.

- Parameters, which are a part of a command's syntax, can change the way a command is executed.

Syntax is the order in which you type the elements of the DOS command. Using proper syntax when you enter a DOS command is like using proper English when you speak. DOS must understand clearly what you are typing in order to carry out the command.

You can think of the command name as the action part of a DOS command. In addition to the name, many commands require or allow further directions. Any such additions are called *parameters*. Parameters tell DOS what action to take or how to apply the action. Using DOS commands is really easy as long as you follow the rules of order and use the correct parameters.

 NOTE Most applications software incorporates the issuing of commands as part of the software's operation. The commands discussed in this book are DOS commands. Be sure that you know the difference between DOS commands, which are issued at the DOS command line, and the commands you learn to use with your applications software.

The Command Syntax

Command syntax can be compared to the phrasing of a spoken or written sentence. The order of the words, the punctuation, and the vocabulary are important ingredients for good communication. When you communicate with DOS, you need to use the proper ingredients so that DOS can interpret your intentions correctly. Like most PC programs, DOS cannot decide to ignore what you "say" but do what you mean. Unfortunately, PCs don't have the capacity for intelligence that people have. If you use improper syntax in a DOS command, DOS objects with an error message—even if the mistake is minor.

This book uses a symbolic form to describe a command's syntax. With this symbolic form, the parts of the command are given names you can relate to. When you actually enter the command, however, you substitute real values for the symbolic names. In this book, symbolic or *variable* text appears in lowercase. In other cases, the examples are commands you can enter exactly as shown. These *literal* commands appear in uppercase letters. Don't worry that you won't be able to tell the symbolic form of a command from a literal example. They are clearly marked in both cases. If you make a mistake and enter a symbolic word in the command line, DOS simply objects with an error message. You won't damage anything.

Some parts of a DOS command are mandatory. These parts represent information that must be included for the command to work correctly. Mandatory parts of a command are the minimum that DOS can understand. When you read that an element of syntax is required, or mandatory, be sure to include a proper value for that element when you enter the command. In this book, mandatory elements are signaled by **bold-face type.**

NOTE When you enter only the mandatory command elements, DOS in many cases uses default parameters for other elements. Because of the defaults, many commands are simple to issue. DOS recognizes the default values because the values are programmed into DOS or because you established the value in an earlier command. Recall the discussion of the logged drive in Chapter 3, "Starting DOS." When you log onto another drive, that drive becomes the *current* drive. If you omit from a command the drive's command-line specifier, DOS uses the current drive.

Syntax elements for which DOS maintains default values are considered *optional.* You do not have to enter optional elements. If you intend for DOS to use a default value, you can save keystrokes by omitting the optional syntax element. DOS accepts commands with all syntax elements present, even though some elements are optional. By including all syntax elements, however, you assert full control over what DOS does. In this book, optional elements are signaled by *italic type.*

Because many DOS commands have several parameters, switches, and defaults, different forms of these commands may be correct. Even though the simple versions of DOS syntax work effectively, most DOS manuals show the complete syntax for a command, which makes the command look complex. For example, the complete symbolic syntax for the DIR command can look like the following:

DIR *d:path\filename.ext /P /W /S /B /L /C /CH /O:sortorder /A:attributes*

You use the DIR command to display a directory of one or more files stored on a disk. This command may look formidable, but don't worry. Command syntax is much easier to understand if you look at the elements on the command line one at a time.

When you enter all syntax elements, DOS uses the exact instructions in place of default values. In the DIR command example, the **DIR** is mandatory. The rest of the command, *d:path\filename.ext /P/W/S/B/L/C/CH/ O:sortorder/A:attributes*, is optional.

The Command-Line Parameters

In addition to the command's name, a DOS command contains syntax elements known as *parameters*. Parameters (sometimes called *arguments*) are the parts of a command line that provide DOS with the objects of the command's action. The objects may be files, system settings, or hardware devices.

In the DIR example, *d:* identifies which disk drive the command will use for its action. *d:* represents the drive parameter in the command. When you give the command, you substitute for *d:* the drive letter of your choice (A:, B:, or C:).

path, a parameter that is introduced in Chapter 8, "Understanding and Managing Directories," refers to the directory path leading to the command. For now, don't worry about *path*.

filename.ext stands for the name of a file, including its extension. In DOS, file names can include up to eight letters. The name also can contain an extension, which consists of a period and up to three more letters. For instance, you may type the file name **MYFILE.123**.

If you pay close attention to the sample syntax and commands, you may note that spaces separate, or *delimit*, the command name and some parameters. In other commands, the slash (/) character separates parameters. Delimiters are important to DOS because they help DOS break apart (or *parse*) the command. For example, the command DIR A: is correct; DIRA: is not.

The Optional Switches

A *switch* is a parameter that turns on an optional function of a command. Switches are special parameters because they usually are not the objects of a command's action; rather, switches modify the command's action. For example, you can use the /W switch with the DIR command to display a wide directory of files, instead of the usual single-column list.

Switches can make a basic command more versatile. In the DIR syntax example, /P, /W, /S, /B, /L, /O, /C, /CH, and /A are switches. Note that each switch is a character preceded by a forward slash (/)—not a backslash (\). Usually, you can use a command's switches in any order or any combination. Not all DOS commands have switches. In addition, switches consisting of the same letter may have different meanings for different commands.

Getting Help from DOS

One of the most convenient features in DOS 6.0 is an on-line help facility. In versions of DOS prior to Version 5.0, you had to memorize command syntax. Version 5.0 added an on-screen syntax summary for each DOS command. In DOS 6.0, complete on-screen help for each DOS command—and many other features of DOS—is now available, as well as the simpler command and syntax summary previously available in DOS Version 5.0

To access on-line help for the use of a particular command, use one of the following procedures:

- Type the DOS command, followed by the switch /?.
- Type **HELP**, followed by the DOS command.

The rest of this section describes each method in detail.

Using the Command-Line Help Switch

The first method for obtaining help—using the /? switch—produces a simple command summary. The command summary displays a brief description of the command's function, the command's correct syntax, a list of the command's switches, and a brief explanation of the effect of each switch.

To get a command summary of the DIR command, for example, type the following command, and then press Enter:

DIR /?

DOS displays the command summary help screen shown in figure 5.1.

```
C:\>dir /?
Displays a list of files and subdirectories in a directory.

DIR [drive:][path][filename] [/P] [/W] [/A[[:]attribs]] [/O[[:]sortord]]
    [/S] [/B] [/L] [/C]

  [drive:][path][filename]  Specifies drive, directory, and/or files to list.
  /P       Pauses after each screenful of information.
  /W       Uses wide list format.
  /A       Displays files with specified attributes.
  attribs    D  Directories    R  Read-only files       H  Hidden files
             S  System files   A  Files ready to archive -  Prefix meaning "not"
  /O       List by files in sorted order.
  sortord    N  By name (alphabetic)      S  By size (smallest first)
             E  By extension (alphabetic) D  By date & time (earliest first)
             G  Group directories first   -  Prefix to reverse order
             C  By compression ratio (smallest first)
  /S       Displays files in specified directory and all subdirectories.
  /B       Uses bare format (no heading information or summary).
  /L       Uses lowercase.
  /C       Displays file compression ratio if on a compressed drive.

Switches may be preset in the DIRCMD environment variable.  Override
preset switches by prefixing any switch with - (hyphen)--for example, /-W.

C:\>
```

Fig. 5.1

Using the DOS command summary help.

Using the On-Line Help System

The second method for obtaining help—typing **help** followed by the DOS command—activates the DOS 6.0 on-line help system, which displays complete information about the command, including examples. The on-line help system displays a detailed description of the command's function, the command's correct syntax, a list of the command's switches, and a detailed explanation of the effect of each switch.

The on-line help system also contains special notes and examples related to each command and lets you view information on related commands or topics with only a few keystrokes. To get the complete on-line help for the DIR command, for example, type the following, and then press Enter:

HELP DIR

DOS displays the on-line help screen shown in figure 5.2.

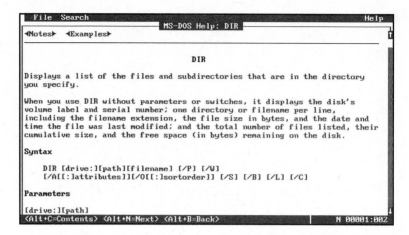

Fig. 5.2

Using the DOS
on-line help
facility.

You can also use the on-line help system by typing **HELP** by itself, and then pressing enter.

DOS starts the on-line help system and displays a table of contents from which you may choose a topic. The next few sections of this chapter describe how to choose topics and move around in the on-line help system.

Navigating the Help System

The on-line help system contains a great deal of information and provides several ways for you to locate, view, and print topics of interest to you. You can use either a mouse or the keyboard to issue commands in the on-line help system; this section describes both methods. For more detailed information about moving around a window, refer to Chapter 4, "Using the DOS Shell."

Because the HELP command provides such complete information, information about a topic or command usually requires more than one screen. In order to view all of the information about a topic, you need to scroll the display forwards and backwards.

To scroll through the text one line at a time, use one of the following methods:

■ Click the downward pointing scroll arrow in the scroll bar at the right edge of the screen to move forward one line. To move backward, click the upward pointing scroll arrow.

■ Press the Ctrl-↓ key combination to move forward; press the Ctrl-↑ key combination to move backward.

To scroll through the text one screen at a time, use one of these methods:

- Click the scroll bar below the scroll box to move forward one screen; click above the scroll box to move backward.

- Press the PgDn key to move forward one whole screen; press the PgUp key to move backward.

In figure 5.2, notice the words *Notes* and *Examples* near the top left corner of the screen. Each word is enclosed with solid, triangular characters. Each of these specially marked words is a jump. A *jump* provides a link to additional information on the currently selected topic or to related topics. Jumps in the body of the help system's text are marked with angle brackets (<>). The word <TREE> at the end of the DIR help text is another example of a jump.

When you select a jump, the on-line help system displays the text related to the topic named by the jump word. To select a jump, use one of the following methods:

- Click the jump with the mouse

- Move the cursor over the jump, and then press Enter

If you select the Examples jump shown in figure 5.2, the help system displays a screen containing examples of the DIR command and explanations of each example. Selecting a jump like <TREE> causes the help system to display the help for the TREE command.

In figure 5.2, notice the solid bar across the top of the screen with the words *File* and *Search*. This area is the help system's *menu bar*. You use the help system's pull-down menus in the same way you use the pull-down menus in the DOS Shell. Refer to Chapter 4, "Using the DOS Shell," for a discussion of pull-down menus.

The choices on the File menu enable you to print a topic or exit the on-line help system. The choices on the Search menu enable you to search for a topic, word, or phrase, and to repeat the last search. Each of these menu choices is discussed in following sections.

Refer again to figure 5.2. Another solid bar appears at the bottom of the screen. The bottom right corner of this area of the help screen displays numbers indicating the current line and column number of the cursor. In figure 5.2, the cursor is at line 1, column 2 of the help text for the DIR command.

At the left edge of this area, three keystroke combinations and their functions are displayed: <Alt+C=Contents> <Alt+N=Next> <Alt+B=Back>.

Each of the labels enclosed in brackets also doubles as a command button (refer to Chapter 4, "Using the DOS Shell," for more information about command buttons). You can click the command button or press the key combination to select the action.

The Next command, Alt-N, causes the on-line help system to display the next topic. The Back command, Alt-B, causes the on-line help system to display the last topic you looked at. The Contents command, Alt-C, causes the on-line help system to display its table of contents. Each item in the table of contents is a jump. To select a topic from the table of contents, position the cursor over the jump and press Enter, or just click the jump.

Table 5.1 summarizes the command keys available in the on-line help system, and their actions.

Table 5.1 On-Line Help Command Keys

Key	Action
Alt	Activates the help system menu
Alt-B	Returns to the last topic you viewed
Alt-C	Displays list of topics covered in the Help system
Alt-F	Opens the File menu
Alt-S	Opens the Search menu
Alt-N	Moves to next topic
Ctrl-↓	Scrolls the screen down one line
Ctrl-↑	Scrolls the screen up one line
Ctrl-Home	Moves to the beginning of the current topic
Ctrl-End	Moves to the end of the current topic
Enter	Selects a menu command or selects the jump under the cursor; the DOS help system displays the text for the jump topic
Esc	Cancels a command; closes a menu or dialog box without making a selection or carrying out the action
F1	Displays context-sensitive help on using the on-line help system
F3	Repeats last search
letter	Moves to next jump beginning with the letter pressed

Key	Action
Shift-*letter*	Moves to previous jump beginning with the letter pressed
PgUp	Scrolls the text up one screen
PgDn	Scrolls the text down one screen
Shift-Ctrl-F1	Moves to the preceding topic
Tab	Moves clockwise to the next jump
Shift-Tab	Moves counterclockwise to next jump

Printing a Topic

The on-line help system enables you to print the text for the currently displayed topic. You may optionally send the output to a file on your disk instead of to the printer. The Print command is located on the File menu. To select the Print command, use one of the following methods:

■ Using your mouse, click the word File on the menu bar. The help system displays the File menu. Click the Print command. The help system opens the Print dialog box shown in figure 5.3. (For information on using dialog boxes, option buttons, text boxes, and command buttons, refer to Chapter 4, "Using the DOS Shell.")

■ Press Alt-F to open the File menu; then press P to select the Print command or press Enter. The Print dialog box appears (refer to fig. 5.3).

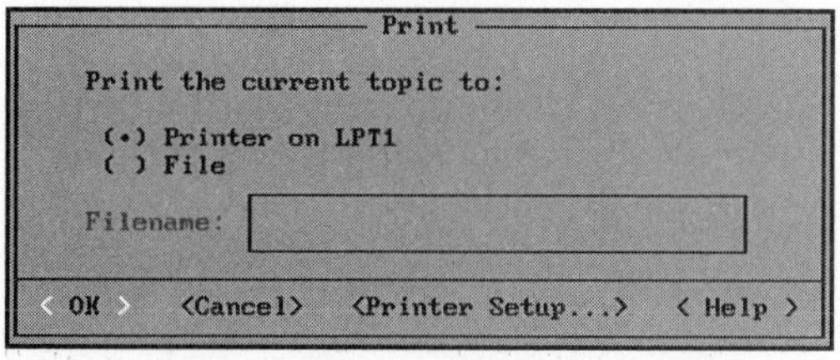

```
┌──────────────────── Print ────────────────────┐
│                                                │
│   Print the current topic to:                  │
│                                                │
│      (•) Printer on LPT1                        │
│      ( ) File                                   │
│                                                │
│   Filename: ┌──────────────────────────────┐   │
│             └──────────────────────────────┘   │
│                                                │
│ < OK >   <Cancel>   <Printer Setup...>  < Help > │
└────────────────────────────────────────────────┘
```

Fig. 5.3

The on-line help system's Print dialog box.

To print the current topic on your printer, simply press Enter or click the OK command button. To send the text for the current topic to a disk file, select the File option button; then, in the text box, enter the name of the file to which you want to send the output. Finally, press Enter or click the OK command button. See Chapter 6, "Understanding Disks and Files," for more information about DOS file names.

Searching for a Topic

You use the Find command to search for a specific topic, word, or phrase. The Find command is located on the Search menu. To select the Find command, use one of the following methods:

■ Using your mouse, click Search on the menu bar. The help system displays the Search menu. Click the Find command. The help system opens the Find dialog box shown in figure 5.4.

■ Press Alt-S to open the Search menu. Press F to select the Find command or press Enter. The help system opens the Find dialog box shown in figure 5.4.

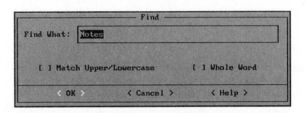

Fig. 5.4

The on-line help system's Find dialog box.

When the Find dialog box first opens, the Find What text box contains the word that the cursor was on when you selected the Find command. In figure 5.4, the cursor was on the word *Notes* when the Find command was selected, so the Find What text box contains the word *Notes*.

Enter the topic, word, or phrase that you want search for in the Find What text box. If the word already in the Find What text box is the word you want to search for, you do not need to type it again. After you specify what word you want to search for, select which of the two Find options you want to use. You may use one, both, or neither of these options.

If you check the Match Upper/Lowercase option check box, you tell the Find command that you only want to find words that exactly match the capitalization used in the Find What box. If you type TREE, for example, and select the Match Upper/Lowercase option check box, the Find command does not consider *tree* or *Tree* to be a match.

If you check the Whole Word option check box, you tell the Find command that you only want whole words that match the text in the Find What box. If you type "dir" in the Find What box, for example, and check the Whole Word option check box, the Find command locates only whole words that match *dir*; *directory* is not considered a match. In this example, if you leave the Whole Word option check box empty, however, Find also considers *directory* to match with *dir*.

You can repeat any search by selecting the Repeat Last Find command on the Search menu, or by pressing F3.

Exiting the Help System

To exit the on-line help system, pull down the File menu and choose the Exit command by doing one of the following:

- Click File to display the File menu; then click Exit. DOS returns to the command line.

- Press Alt-F to pull down the File menu. Use the arrow keys to position the highlight over the Exit command, and then press Enter, or just press X. DOS returns to the command line.

For Related Information

◀◀ "Moving around an Area," p. 88.

◀◀ "Using Pull-Down Menus," p. 90.

◀◀ "Using Command Buttons," p. 96.

▶▶ "Selecting File Names," p. 142.

FROM HERE...

Issuing DOS Commands

Take a moment to become familiar with the instructions used in this book for entering commands. The notation helps you distinguish between what you type and what the computer displays. If you feel that issuing commands is going to be difficult, relax. You don't have to memorize commands instantly; instead, you learn by doing. If you get lost, just back up a few sections and reread the text. Millions of people use DOS commands—we all had to start from scratch and learn how.

Figure 5.5 breaks down the different elements that make up a typical DOS command—the DIR command. As you can see, only two of the switches (/P and / W) are illustrated.

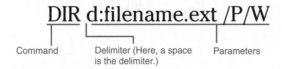

DIR d:filename.ext /P/W

Command   Delimiter (Here, a space   Parameters
           is the delimiter.)

Fig. 5.5

The syntax of the DIR command.

Figure 5.6 is a diagram of the DIR command explained in the preceding sections. This diagram illustrates the steps needed to issue a DOS command, covered in detail in the following sections.

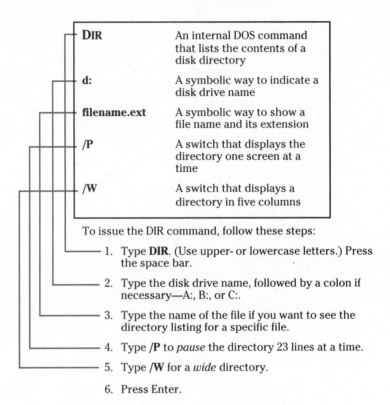

DIR	An internal DOS command that lists the contents of a disk directory
d:	A symbolic way to indicate a disk drive name
filename.ext	A symbolic way to show a file name and its extension
/P	A switch that displays the directory one screen at a time
/W	A switch that displays a directory in five columns

To issue the DIR command, follow these steps:

1. Type **DIR**. (Use upper- or lowercase letters.) Press the space bar.
2. Type the disk drive name, followed by a colon if necessary—A:, B:, or C:.
3. Type the name of the file if you want to see the directory listing for a specific file.
4. Type **/P** to *pause* the directory 23 lines at a time.
5. Type **/W** for a *wide* directory.
6. Press Enter.

Fig. 5.6

Issuing the DIR command.

Typing the Command Name

You enter a command when the command line displays the DOS prompt. This prompt usually consists of the drive letter followed by the greater-than character (>). Notice that immediately following the > is the blinking cursor. As you may recall, the cursor marks the point where the keystrokes you enter appear.

The command name is like a key to the DOS operating system. A command's name identifies the action the command is programmed to perform. COMMAND.COM is the DOS command processor that reads the command you type. COMMAND.COM can carry out several internal commands. The command processor also knows how to load and run the external utility command programs whose names you enter at the DOS prompt.

Enter all DOS command names immediately following the prompt. If the command has no parameters or switches, press the Enter key after you type the last letter of the command name.

You can take advantage of default parameters when you enter a command line. For example, if you type **DIR**, the directory command, at the prompt and then press Enter, DOS supplies the drive parameter (even though you didn't type it). DOS uses the *logged* (current) drive, which—in this case—is drive C.

Adding Parameters

When you are instructed to enter parameters other than switches, this book shows them in one of two ways—lowercase or uppercase. If a parameter is shown as lowercase text, you must supply the value for that text (substitute the appropriate information for the symbolic notation in the book). The lowercase letters are shorthand for the full names of the parts of a command. As in the command name, uppercase letters indicate that you enter letter-for-letter what you see—the literal meaning of the command.

To add a file-name parameter to the DIR command, you can type the following:

DIR C:MYFILE.TXT

In symbolic notation, MYFILE.TXT appears as *filename.ext*.

Remember to separate parameters from the rest of the command. Most of the time the delimiter is a space, but other delimiters, such as the period (.), the backslash (\ ), the slash (/), and the colon (:), are available. Look at the examples in this book to see which delimiter to use.

You can recognize any switches in the sample text by the leading slash character (/). Always enter the switch letter as shown. Do not forget to type the slash. Suppose that you enter the DIR command with a switch character, as follows:

DIR/W

The / serves as the delimiter and tells DOS that a switch is about to follow.

Ignoring a Command Line (Esc)

You occasionally may make a mistake when you are entering a command. Remember that DOS does not act on the command until you press Enter. You can correct a mistake by using the arrow keys or the Backspace key to reposition the cursor. Press the Esc key, however, if you want to type an entirely new command. The Esc key cancels the entry and gives you a new line. Remember that these line-editing and canceling tips work only *before* you press the Enter key. Some commands can be successfully stopped with the Ctrl-C or Ctrl-Break sequence. To restore the system prompt, press Esc.

Executing a Command

The Enter key is the action key for DOS commands. Make a habit of stopping and reading what you type before you press the Enter key. After you press Enter, the computer carries out your command. During the processing of the command, DOS does not display your keystrokes. DOS does remember your keystrokes, however, so be aware that the characters you type could end up in your next command.

DOS stores keystrokes that have not yet been displayed in a *type ahead buffer*. DOS's type ahead buffer, a temporary storage area in RAM, can fill with keystrokes, especially when your PC is hung. When the type ahead buffer fills, your PC beeps when you press an additional key. DOS's use of buffer storage areas also gives DOS some special editing capabilities.

Using the DOS Editing Keys

When you type a command and press the Enter key, DOS copies the line into an input *buffer*—a storage area for command-line keystrokes. You can pull the preceding command line from the buffer and use it again. This feature is helpful when you want to issue a command that is similar to the last command you used. Table 5.2 lists the keys you use to edit the input buffer.

T I P   DOS 6.0 (and Version 5.0) include a utility program called DOSKey. Among other things, DOSKey enables you to reuse DOS commands more easily at the command line. See Chapter 15, "Understanding Batch Files, DOSKey, and Macros," for a discussion of this valuable program.

For Related Information

▶▶ "Using Batch-File Commands," p. 565.

▶▶ "Using DOSKey," p. 590.

FROM HERE...

Using DIR To Look at Files

The DIR command is one of the first commands most DOS users learn. The command quickly provides a list of files, the date and time each file was created or last changed, and the file sizes.

Knowing which files are on your disks and when you created or last changed the files can be important. You can keep a list of files manually—quite a task—or use the DOS DIR command to maintain a list of the files on each of your floppy disks or your hard disk.

Table 5.2 DOS Command-Line Editing Keys

Key	Action
Tab-← →-Tab	Moves the cursor to the next tab stop
Esc	Cancels the current line and does not change the buffer
Ins	Enables you to insert characters into the line
Del	Deletes a character from the line
F1 or →	Copies one character from the preceding command line
F2	Copies all characters from the preceding command line up to, but not including, the next character you type
F3	Copies all remaining characters from the preceding command line
F4	Deletes all characters from the preceding command line up to, but not including, the next character typed (opposite of F2)
F5	Moves the current line into the buffer but does not allow DOS to execute the line
F6	Produces an end-of-file marker (^Z) when you copy from the console to a disk file

Issuing the DIR Command

DIR stands for DIRectory, which is a list of files. The DIR command displays a volume label, five columns of information about the files, the total number of files shown, total amount of disk space used by the files shown, and the amount of unused space on the disk. If the disk you are looking at was formatted with DOS Version 4.0 or later, the directory listing also shows a disk serial number after the volume label.

To try the DIR command, type the following, and then press Enter:

    DIR

DOS executes the command. You have just told DOS to display a list of files from the logged drive. You can also type DIR A: to specify drive A or DIR C: to list the files on drive C. The A: or C: is the optional drive parameter. If you don't specify a drive, DOS uses the logged drive by default.

You can change the logged drive by typing the drive letter followed by a colon, and then pressing Enter. For example, typing A: at the DOS prompt changes the logged drive to drive A. A disk must be in a drive before DOS can make it the logged drive. Remember that you can log only to a drive your system contains. By changing the logged drive, you can switch between a hard disk and a floppy disk, for example.

Using Scroll Control

The term *scrolling* describes what happens as a DOS screen fills with information. When DOS displays text in response to your typing or as a result of a DOS command, the text fills the screen from left to right and top to bottom. As the screen fills, information scrolls off the top of the display. To stop a scrolling screen, press the key combination Ctrl-S (hold down the Ctrl key, and then press S). Press any key to restart the scrolling. On enhanced keyboards, press the Pause key to stop scrolling.

With the DIR command, you can use the /P switch and the /W switch for scroll control. To see more file names on a single screen, you can use the /W switch. The command DIR /W displays only the file names in a wide multicolumn format, in which many files fit on a single screen (see fig. 5.7). This wide format does not include the additional information about each file that a directory listing usually provides.

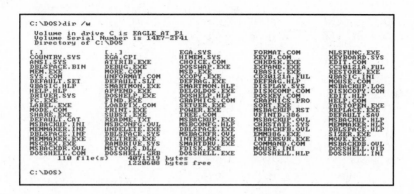

Fig. 5.7

The display
produced by
the command
DIR /W.

For a complete and convenient listing of the directory, use the /P
switch. The command DIR /P pauses the display so that the listing is
presented page by page. Press any key to display the next page of
information.

NOTE When you see the message Press any key to continue,
DOS really means that you should press *almost* any key. If
you press the Shift, Alt, Ctrl, Caps Lock, Num Lock, or Scroll
Lock key, DOS doesn't respond. The easiest keys to press
are the space bar and the Enter key.

For the next example, a diskette with DOS boot files and some of the
DOS external command programs was placed in drive A, and the command DIR /P was used to obtain the following directory listing:

```
Volume in drive A is STARTUP
Volume Serial Number is 1A35-9E2E
Directory of A:\

COMMAND   COM     53460  12-23-92    6:00a
ATTRIB    EXE     11165  12-23-92    6:00a
DEBUG     EXE     15715  12-23-92    6:00a
EXPAND    EXE     16129  12-23-92    6:00a
FDISK     EXE     29333  12-23-92    6:00a
FORMAT    COM     22591  12-23-92    6:00a
RESTORE   EXE     38294  12-23-92    6:00a
SYS       COM      9370  12-23-92    6:00a
CHKDSK    EXE     12267  12-23-92    6:00a
EDIT      COM       413  12-23-92    6:00a
QBASIC    EXE    194313  12-23-92    6:00a
XCOPY     EXE     15820  12-23-92    6:00a
```

```
MSD       EXE     158459 12-23-92    6:00a
DBLSPACE  EXE     269550 12-23-92    6:00a
UNDELETE  EXE      26346 12-23-92    6:00a
QBASIC    HLP     130810 12-23-92    6:00a
QBASIC    INI        132 01-23-93    2:05p
AUTOEXEC  BAT        309 01-22-93    5:36p
CONFIG    SYS        403 01-22-93    5:35p
Press any key to continue . . .

(continuing A:\)
UNFORMAT COM      12738 12-23-92    6:00a
        20 file(s) 1017617 bytes
                    305664  bytes free
```

Examining the Directory Listing

Look at the directory listing in the preceding section. The first line in the listing is the *volume label*, an identification you specify when you prepare the disk. The volume label is optional, but including this label can simplify the job of organizing your disks.

Below the volume label is the *volume serial number*. This number is assigned automatically by DOS (Versions 4.0 and later) when the disk is formatted. DOS uses this number to identify the disk you inserted into a particular drive.

The next lines in the directory listing contain file information. Each line in the directory describes one file, including the file name, extension, size (in bytes), and the date and time you created or last changed the file (assuming that your computer's clock is set correctly or that you entered the time and date when you booted your computer). The next sections look more closely at this information.

The last line of the directory tells you the total number of files listed and the amount of space they take up on the disk. The last line of the directory listing tells you the amount of free space available on the disk. Free space is measured in bytes. This information is useful when you want to determine how many more files a disk can hold.

File Names and Extensions

A file name has two parts—the name and the extension—separated by a period. In the directory listing, however, spaces separate the file name from the extension.

In any single directory, each file must have a unique full name. DOS treats the file name and the extension together as the entire name. The file names MYFILE.123 and MYFILE.ABC are unique because each file has a different extension. The file names MYFILE.123 and YOURFILE.123 are also unique. Many DOS commands make use of the two parts of the file name separately. For this reason, giving each file both a file name and an extension is a good idea.

File names can help you identify the contents of a file. A file name can contain only eight alphanumeric characters; the extension, only three. You may need some ingenuity to come up with unique names that are meaningful.

DOS is particular about which characters you use in a file name or an extension. To be on the safe side, use only letters of the alphabet and numbers—not spaces or a period. DOS truncates excess characters in a file name.

File Size and the Date/Time Stamp

The directory listing's third column shows the size of the file in bytes. This measurement is only an approximation of the size of your file. Your file may use more bytes than indicated. Because computers reserve blocks of data storage for files, files with slightly different data amounts may have identical file-size listings. This factor explains why a word processing memo with only five words can occupy 2K of file space.

The last two columns in the directory listing display a date and a time. These entries show when you created the file or, in the case of an established file, when you last altered the file. Your computer's internal date and time are the basis for the date and time *stamp* in the directory. As you create more files, the date and time stamp become invaluable tools in determining which version of a file is the most recent.

Using Wild-Card Characters with DIR

Perhaps you have seen a Western movie in which a poker-playing cowboy says, "Deuces are wild!" You know that this sentence means that the number two cards can take on a value other than their own. Computerists have borrowed this wild-card concept and applied it to file-name operations on computers. You can use wild-card characters in file names to copy, rename, delete, show directories, or otherwise manipulate file names.

DOS recognizes two wild-card characters: the question mark (?) and the asterisk (*). You can place the ? character in any full file name. The ? matches any one character in that position. The * in a file name or in an extension matches all characters in that part of the full file name.

If you type DIR followed by the file name, the selected list of files is displayed. The long form of the DIR command resembles the following:

    DIR d:filename.ext

Remember to type your actual drive letter instead of the *d:*. In place of *filename.ext*, you can type MYFILE.123, for example. The DIR command you just typed tells DOS to list a directory of all files that match MYFILE.123. The directory listing would list only one file, MYFILE.123. When you use DIR alone, DOS lists all files in the directory. When you use DIR with a file name and extension parameter, DOS lists only files that match that parameter.

Used with wild cards, the DIR command becomes more powerful. If you want to see a listing of all files that have an extension of 123, you can use the * wild-card character. The * replaces every character from the asterisk to the end of the part of the command in which it is located. Suppose, for example, that you type the following:

    DIR *.123

DOS lists any file with the 123 extension, including both MYFILE.123 and YOURFILE.123. If you issue the command DIR MYFILE.*, you may get a listing of MYFILE.123 and MYFILE.XYZ.

T I P   You can give your letter files a LET extension and your memo files an extension of MEM. With this technique, you can use the DIR command with a wild card to get separate listings of the two types of files.

The ? wild card differs from the * wild card. Only the character in the same position as the ? is a match. If you issue the command DIR MYFILE?.123, files like MYFILE1.123, MYFILE2.123 are displayed, but MYFILE10.123 is not. The same rules apply to any other command that accepts wild cards.

The wild-card designation *.* replaces every character in the root file name and every character in the extension. The *.* designation selects *all* the files in a directory.

> **CAUTION:** The *.* specification is a powerful tool; be sure to use it with caution. When used with commands such as DEL, the specification can be dangerous. The command **DEL *.***, for example, deletes *all* files in the directory.

Other examples of wild-card uses with the DIR command are shown in the following list:

Command	Result
DIR MYFILE.123	Presents directory information for the file MYFILE.123
DIR *.123	Lists every file with the extension 123 in the directory
DIR M*.*	Lists each file whose name begins with the letter M
DIR *.*	Lists all files in the directory; the same as typing DIR
DIR *.	Lists all files that have no extension
DIR ???.BAT	Lists all three-letter files that have a BAT extension
DIR MYFILE.???	Lists all the files named MYFILE that have three-letter extensions

Reviewing the DIR Command

The DIR command displays more than a list of file names. As your computing expertise grows, you will find many uses for the information provided by the standard directory listing (see fig. 5.8).

136

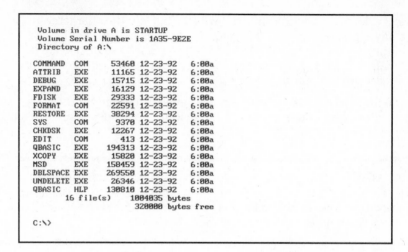

```
Volume in drive A is STARTUP
Volume Serial Number is 1A35-9E2E
Directory of A:\

COMMAND  COM     53460 12-23-92    6:00a
ATTRIB   EXE     11165 12-23-92    6:00a
DEBUG    EXE     15715 12-23-92    6:00a
EXPAND   EXE     16129 12-23-92    6:00a
FDISK    EXE     29333 12-23-92    6:00a
FORMAT   COM     22591 12-23-92    6:00a
RESTORE  EXE     38294 12-23-92    6:00a
SYS      COM      9370 12-23-92    6:00a
CHKDSK   EXE     12267 12-23-92    6:00a
EDIT     COM       413 12-23-92    6:00a
QBASIC   EXE    194313 12-23-92    6:00a
XCOPY    EXE     15820 12-23-92    6:00a
MSD      EXE    158459 12-23-92    6:00a
DBLSPACE EXE    269550 12-23-92    6:00a
UNDELETE EXE     26346 12-23-92    6:00a
QBASIC   HLP    130810 12-23-92    6:00a
       16 file(s)      1004035 bytes
                        320000 bytes free

C:\>
```

Fig. 5.8

The elements
of a standard
directory listing.

The following diagram explains the parts of a directory listing:

APPEND   EXE   10774   10-26-92   6:00a

APPEND is
the file
name, which
can be up
to eight
characters
long.

EXE is
the
exten-
sion.

10774 is
the file
size in
bytes.

The file was
created or
last modified
on October
26, 1992.

Time of
creation
or modifi-
cation was
6:00 a.m.

Chapter Summary

As you can tell, an underlying logic exists for issuing DOS commands. Even though each DOS command has its own characteristics, it also has a defined syntax that may or may not include parameters and switches. The basic knowledge of how to issue DOS commands is an important ingredient in your mastery of DOS. Following are the key points covered in this chapter:

■ You issue commands to DOS for operating system services.

■ The proper phrasing of each DOS command is called the command's syntax.

■ In addition to the name of the command, a syntax line can contain parameters and switches.

■ The DIR command, like many other DOS commands, uses optional parameters. When the optional parameters are omitted, the values are supplied as DOS defaults.

■ You can use the /? command-line switch or the HELP command to get help on any DOS command.

■ You can edit a DOS command line by using special DOS editing keys.

■ Some commands accept wild-card characters (? and *) as substitutes for position-matching in file-name parameters.

The next chapter completes your introduction to DOS by covering the important subject of disks and files. When you begin to use DOS commands, you may find reviewing the ideas presented here helpful.

Understanding Disks and Files

Two of the primary roles of a disk operating system are storing and retrieving data. This chapter introduces you to the fundamental ways in which DOS handles these roles.

To provide data storage and retrieval, the operating system not only must oversee the many technical aspects of the disk hardware but also must provide a bookkeeping method for file storage and retrieval. The disk operating system should provide these services without your needing to know the internal details of the operations.

DOS generally insulates you from the technical details involved in storing and retrieving data on your computer. At times, however, you must handle and prepare for use the magnetic media—typically disks—that actually store the data. This chapter provides a brief overview of the types of disks that may be used in your system and demonstrates several frequently used disk-related commands.

Key Terms Used in This Chapter	
File system	The predefined organization method that a disk operating system uses to get data, in the form of files, to and from a disk
File	A variable-length collection of related information that is referenced by a name

continues

Key Terms Used in This Chapter continued	
Name	The first portion of a file name, consisting of up to eight characters; usually describes the contents of a file
Extension	A file-name suffix, which can include a period and up to three characters; usually describes the type of file
Disk	A magnetic storage medium and the predominant means of file storage for DOS
Disk drive	The electromechanical components that record and play back data to and from the magnetic surfaces of a disk
Hard disk	A built-in fixed disk drive
Floppy disk	Any lower-capacity disk that you can remove from your PC's drive
Minifloppy	5 1/4-inch disk
Microfloppy	3 1/2-inch disk
Diskette	Another term for a 5 1/4- or 3 1/2-inch disk
Platter	A disk contained in a hard disk drive. Most hard disk drives contain two or more platters
Track	A circular section of a disk's surface that holds data
Cylinder	The conceptual alignment of heads on the same track on different sides (and platters) of the same disk
Sectors	Fixed-size components of a track
Format	The specification for a disk's use of its physical space

Introducing the DOS File System

A *file system* is an organized collection of files. As a user, you see the DOS file system at work in the files you organize into directories and subdirectories on your disks. Each file is a named group of data that DOS seems to manipulate as a continuous unit. Behind the scenes, however, DOS uses a complex management strategy, which the DOS file system reflects. A file system includes not only the files but also the internal tables that record the file organization, as well as built-in rules that ensure the consistency of file organization.

Understanding Files

A *file* is a variable-length collection of related information that is referenced by a name. Picture a file cabinet full of file folders, each with a name on the tab. The cabinet itself is not a file; neither are the individual pieces of paper in the folders. Only the named collection of papers in one folder is considered to be a file. Electronic files can be compared with a traditional file cabinet. The drawers are like floppy disks or hard disks, and the file folders are like files (see fig. 6.1).

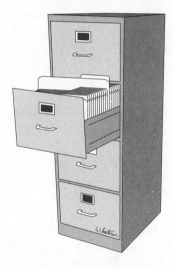

Fig. 6.1

Electronic files compared with a file cabinet.

File names are helpful for locating information in the correct file. Yet the file name itself is not the memo, spreadsheet, or other information you use. Think again of a file cabinet. The information stored on individual papers in the folders is the source of records for the subject named on the file folder. Without properly named folders to group the related papers, access to the information is greatly hindered. Likewise, DOS enables you to group related information in the form of files. DOS and DOS-based applications software enable you to open named files whenever you want to store information on a disk.

In a computer setting, a file can contain data (information), programs (instructions that guide computer tasks), or both. A file can exist on a disk, on magnetic tape, on punch cards, or even in a computer's memory. Files are made up of elements of data or programs. The individual elements can be stored as patterns of holes in a paper tape, as patterns of magnetic fields on the surface of a disk, and in many other ways.

Physical storage techniques for files vary greatly. In all likelihood, however, your computer stores files on disks, which are the predominant means of file storage for DOS. When you see the term *file* in this book, you can count on it to mean *disk file*.

DOS uses file names to identify files. A full *file name* consists of up to eight characters followed by a period (.) and up to three characters called the *extension*. The period and extension are optional.

The first, or *name*, portion of a file name (before the period) often describes the *contents* of the file. Extensions, on the other hand, traditionally are used to describe the *type* of file.

Someone using a word processing application to write a memo might use as the name portion of a file name the name (or a close approximation) of the person who will receive the memo. The extension MEM then can be used. A memo to Mr. Duncan, for example, can be called DUNCAN.MEM. Similarly, the extension .DOC could be used for office-policy document files. A monthly policy statement can be named JAN.DOC.

DOS enables you to use a wide variety of file names. You are free to develop your own file-naming conventions, provided that you stay within the character limits imposed by DOS.

NOTE Differentiating among people is much easier if they have both first and last names. The same is true of files. DOS provides for a name (first name) and an extension (last name). When you name your files, use both parts of the file name so that you can better identify the file later. Many applications add their own file extensions, however; when you use these programs, you simply supply the first portion of a file's name.

Selecting File Names

DOS ensures that every one of your files has a name. In fact, DOS does not provide a way to put file data on a disk without a file name. When a file is created, either by your software or a DOS file-service routine, DOS places the name of that file in a DOS *directory*, which is the DOS equivalent of a library card file. You will learn more about directories later. For now, think of a directory as a table that contains file names and locations.

DOS provides room in each directory entry for an eight-character name and a three-character extension. When you include a file name in a command, you type a period (.) between the file name and the extension.

DOS uses the file-naming convention of the once-dominant CP/M operating system. DOS designers felt that using the CP/M file-naming convention would make the transition from CP/M-based computers to DOS-based computers easier for users. For example, the DIR command, which shows a list of the file names in a directory, also is used in the CP/M operating system. Many file-related concepts were adapted for DOS from the CP/M operating system. As DOS has matured, however, the DOS file system has been enhanced well beyond the capabilities of the original CP/M file system.

The characters you see on your computer screen are the ASCII-code representations of bytes of data. One character is stored in one byte. The name of a directory entry, for example, is 11 bytes long (8 for the first part of the file name plus 3 for the extension). DOS accepts for file names most characters that you would use for "everyday" names. You can use in file names the uppercase and lowercase letters *a* through *z*; DOS automatically stores letters in uppercase in a directory entry. You also can use the numeric characters *0* through *9* and many punctuation characters.

The following list shows the rules for file names.

■ A file name consists of the following items:

a. A name of one to eight characters

b. An optional extension of one to three characters

c. A period between the name and the extension (if an extension is used)

■ The following characters are allowed in a file name:

a. The letters *A* through *Z* (lowercase letters are transformed into uppercase automatically)

b. The numbers *0* through *9*

c. The following special characters and punctuation marks:

$ # & @ ! ( ) – { } ' _ ~ ^ `

- The following characters are *not* allowed in a file name:

    a. Any control character, including Escape (27d or 1Bh) and De-
    lete (127d or 7Fh)

    b. The space character

    c. The following special characters and punctuation symbols:

      + = / [ ] " : ; , ? * \ < > |

- If DOS finds an illegal character in a file name, DOS usually stops
  at the character preceding the illegal one and uses the legal part
  of the name. (A few exceptions to this rule exist.)

- A device name can be part of a name but cannot be the entire
  name. For example, CONT.DAT and AUXI.TXT are acceptable, but
  CON.DAT and AUX.TXT are not.

- Each file name in a directory must be unique.

- A drive name and a path name usually precede a file name. (Path
  names are discussed in Chapter 8, "Understanding and Managing
  Directories.")

To understand why DOS disallows the use of some characters in file
names, you must look below the surface of DOS. Certain characters are
not allowed because DOS does not pass those characters from the keyboard to the command or external command program that controls a
file's name. You cannot, for example, use the Ctrl-G (^G) character in a
file name because Ctrl-G tells an input device to sound the computer's
bell or beep signal. The Escape character produced by the Esc key is
another character that DOS does not accept as part of a file name, because DOS interprets the Esc key as your request to cancel the command line and start again.

Another example of an unacceptable character is Ctrl-S (^S), which DOS
and other operating systems use to stop the flow of characters from
the input device to the output device. Ctrl-S stops screen scrolling, for
example. If you press Ctrl-S while entering a file name, DOS assumes
that you are entering an input-stopping character, not part of a file
name.

You cannot use in a file name any characters that COMMAND.COM
and external-command programs use to divide the parameters and
switches from the command in a command line. Because DOS must
break out or *parse* (distinguish the various components of) the command line, DOS sees certain characters as delimiters of parameters or
as parts of a parameter. The backslash character (\), for example, separates directory names in a path specifier. DOS always reads a backslash
in a command line as part of a path.

Avoiding Reserved Names

DOS reserves names for its built-in input and output devices. You may recall that DOS can treat some PC devices in a high-level way by accepting their names as input or output parameters in a command line. Before using the file name parameters in a command line to look for a file, DOS checks to see whether the file name is a device name. Table 6.1 lists the built-in DOS input and output device names and their purposes.

Table 6.1 DOS Device Names

Device name	Purpose
COMx or AUX	Identifies a serial communication port (x may be the number 1, 2, 3, or 4)
LPTx or PRN	Identifies a parallel printer port (x may be the number 1, 2, 3, or 4)
CON	Identifies the screen and keyboard
NUL	Identifies the "throwaway" or "do nothing" device. The "null" device is used to suppress the output of a program or command; output sent to NUL is neither displayed, stored, or acted on in any way.

Never attempt to write a disk file with a name that is the same as one of the device names listed in Table 6.1. DOS intercepts the device name, even if you add an extension, and tries to use the device—not the file you intend—to complete the command. Use a device name only as a device parameter in a command.

Observing File-Naming Conventions

A *convention* is an informal rule that is not explicitly enforced. DOS file names often follow certain conventions. Although you can use any file name that follows DOS' character and device-name rules, observe DOS file-naming conventions whenever possible. You can, for example, name a memo file and give it a BAT extension, but this extension has a special meaning to DOS because all batch files have the extension BAT. (Batch files are covered in Chapter 15, "Understanding Batch Files, DOSKey, and Macros.") As long as you do not try to execute the memo as a batch file, DOS is happy. If you try to execute the memo file, however, DOS sees the BAT extension and tries to execute it. Of course, the memo cannot be executed.

You can name an EXE file with a COM extension. Although both files are executable, they have internal differences. DOS does not take the extension's name to mean that the file is indeed an EXE or COM file; DOS inspects a key part of the file before deciding how to load and execute the program file. If you name a spreadsheet file as an EXE or COM file, for example, DOS is not fooled into executing the nonprogram file. In all likelihood, your system simply will lock up, and you will have to perform a warm boot to begin again.

Many software manufacturers use certain extensions for special files in their applications. To avert confusion about the contents of a file, avoid using those extensions.

Table 6.2 lists some conventional file name extensions and their meanings. Multiple programs can use the same extensions in their file-naming conventions.

T I P   You don't have to memorize all the file-naming conventions. The documentation supplied with your program describes the file-naming conventions used by that program.

Table 6.2 Common File Name Extensions

Extension	Common use
ARC	Archive (compressed file)
ASC	ASCII text file
ASM	Assembler source file
BAK	Backup file
BAS	BASIC program file
BAT	DOS batch file
BGI	Borland Graphics Interface file (Quattro, Paradox)
BIN	Binary program file
BMP	Windows bitmap file
C	C source file
C++	C++ source file
CBL	COBOL source file
CFG	Program configuration information

Extension	Common use
CHP	Chapter file (Ventura Publisher)
CHR	Character file (Quattro, Paradox)
CNF	Program configuration information
COM	Program file
CPI	Code page information file (DOS)
DAT	Data file
DB	Database file (Paradox)
DBF	Database file (dBASE)
DCT	Dictionary file
DEV	Program device driver file
DIF	Data Interchange Format file
DLL	Windows Dynamic Link Library
DOC	Document file (used by many word processors)
DRV	Program device driver file
DTA	Data file
EPS	Encapsulated PostScript file
EXE	Executable program file
FNT	Font file
GRP	Windows Program Group
HLP	Help file
IDX	Index file (Q&A)
IMG	GEM image (graphics) file
INF	Information file
INI	Initialization files (Windows and other programs)
KEY	Keyboard macro file (ProKey)
LET	Letter
LIB	Program library file
LOG	File logging actions
LST	Listing of a program (in a file)
MAC	Keyboard macro file (Superkey)

continues

Table 6.2 Continued

Extension	Common use
MAP	Linker map file
MSG	Program message file
NDX	Index file (dBASE)
OBJ	Intermediate object code (program) file
OLD	Backup file
OVL	Program overlay file
OVR	Program overlay file
PAK	Packed (archive) file
PAS	Pascal source file
PCX	Picture file for PC Paintbrush
PIF	Program Information File (TopView/Windows)
PRN	Program listing for printing
PRO	Profile (configuration file)
PS	PostScript program file
RFT	Revisable Form Text (Document Content Architecture)
SAM	Ami-Pro document
SAV	Backup file
STY	Style sheet (Ventura Publisher, Microsoft Word)
SYS	System or device driver file
TIF	Picture file in Tagged Image File Format (TIFF)
TMP	Temporary file
TST	Test file
TXT	Text file
WK1	Worksheet file (Lotus 1-2-3 Release 2)
WK3	Worksheet file (Lotus 1-2-3 Release 3)
WKQ	Quattro spreadsheet file
WKS	Worksheet file (Lotus 1-2-3, Releases 1 and 1A)
WQ1	Quattro Pro spreadsheet file
ZIP	Compressed file (PKZIP)

Avoiding Bad File Names

When you enter a file name in a command, DOS may not simply reject
a bad file name; in certain cases, DOS takes some unusual actions. The
following example uses the COPY command to show what can happen.
(Don't worry about learning all about COPY from this example; the
command is covered in detail in Chapter 9, "Managing Your Files.")

The general form of COPY takes a source-file parameter and copies the file
to the destination-file parameter. If the destination file doesn't exist, DOS
creates that file. The example assumes that the source file, TEST.TXT,
already exists on the default drive. To create a new file from the file
TEST.TXT, you can, for example, enter the COPY command as follows:

    COPY TEST.TXT 123456789.1234

Notice that both the file name and the extension given for the destination file name contain an extra character: the file name has the extra
character *9*, and the extension has the extra character *4*. You might
predict that DOS will issue a message warning that the file name and
extension are too long. No such luck! Without issuing a warning, DOS
chops off (*truncates*) the file name to eight characters and the extension
to three characters, and then completes the COPY operation by creating a new file. The resulting file, named by DOS, is 12345678.123. DOS
always discards excess characters in the file name and extension, using
the remaining characters as the file parameter.

Illegal characters in a file name can prevent DOS from carrying out a
command. The following interaction with DOS is an example (again, the
example assumes that the source file already exists):

```
COPY 12345678.123 1[3.123

    File creation error
        0 File(s) copied
```

As you might expect, the illegal character *[* in the target file's extension
stopped DOS from completing the copy operation. If you use the same
[character in a reporting command, such as DIR, DOS issues another
error message. The following sequence shows the error message issued:

```
DIR [

    Parameter format not correct -   [
```

Not every illegal file name character prevents DOS from carrying out a
command, however. In the following example, the semicolon character
is at the end of the destination file's extension:

```
COPY 12345678.123 12345678.12;


   1 file(s) copied
```

DOS carries out the COPY command and creates a new file from the destination parameter. To see the new file's name, issue the DIR command and view the listing, which will resemble the following example:

```
Volume in drive C is MY-486
Volume Serial Number is 196B-8C54
Directory of C:\TEST

.              <DIR>      11-23-92  10:57p
..             <DIR>      11-23-92  10:57p
TEST     TXT       298 11-23-92  10:57p
12345678 123       298 11-23-92  10:57p
12345678 12        298 11-23-92  10:57p
         5 file(s)        894 bytes
                     4839424 bytes free
```

DOS adds the 12345678.12 file because DOS reads the semicolon in the command as a closing delimiter. The remaining part of the target-file parameter becomes the new file's name.

Few experienced DOS users would purposely use illegal characters in a file name, but typos easily can creep into your DOS commands and introduce illegal characters into file name parameters. Type commands carefully, remembering that DOS's reaction to an illegal file name isn't always predictable.

FROM HERE...

For Related Information

▶▶ "Understanding Path Names," p. 238.

▶▶ "Copying and Moving Files," p. 312.

▶▶ "Introducing Batch Files," p. 546.

▶▶ "Understanding the Contents of Batch Files," p. 548.

▶▶ "Creating a Simple Batch File," p. 549.

Examining Disks and Drives

The capability to store named collections of data in files is of little value unless you have a convenient medium on which to store those files. PC designers chose disks as this medium. Disks, both removable and fixed, have a virtual monopoly on file storage in PCs. Tape and CD ROM (Compact Disk Read-Only Memory) finish a distant second and third. Disk drives, DOS's warehouse for file storage, offer convenience, reliability, reusability, and rapid access to files.

Because disks are the primary storage medium for files, understand how disks store files. The following sections explain some basic file-storage concepts.

Understanding the Disk's Magnetic Storage Technique

Disk drives are electromechanical components that record and play back data that is stored on the magnetic surfaces of a disk. Normally, the data is in the form of a file. During the recording, or *writing*, of a file, an electronic circuit translates the PC's electrical data into a series of magnetic fields. These magnetic fields are mirrored (weakly) by the oxide coating of the disk in the drive. In effect, the original data is imprinted magnetically on a disk. The information has changed its state; electrical information is changed to magnetic information.

During the playback, or *reading*, of data from the disk's surface, an electronic circuit translates the magnetic fields back into electrical signals, converting the data back to electrical form. The disk's original magnetic imprint—the file—is not destroyed by the reading operation; the file remains on the disk after it is read. In normal use, only recording over the old imprint, called *overwriting* the disk, changes a disk's imprint. Because many file-related commands overwrite the previous contents of files, use overwrite commands with respect.

Unless you overwrite a file, file storage on a disk is permanent. The disk's recorded magnetic imprint is resistant to weakening and, with proper care, will last for years. Certain magnetic fields, however—such as those produced by motors, magnetic paper-clip holders, ringing telephones, television sets, and speakers—can weaken the magnetic imprint on a disk, making the disk's files unreadable. If the data being translated magnetically from a disk has some loss of integrity, your computer will not be able to fill in missing information or correct invalid information. The result is a *read error*. Read errors can end a work session unpleasantly, because DOS stops your computing when it detects a critical error.

Disk-drive designers strive for perfect data reproduction from computer disks. One bad spot on a disk can result in a message similar to the following:

```
General failure error reading drive A:
```

This message sometimes signals the unrecoverable loss of all data on a disk.

 NOTE   Probably the most frequent cause of this general-failure message is accidental use of an unformatted disk.

Understanding Disk Drives

The mechanical parts and electrical circuits of disk drives are complex. Although disk drives are parts of PC systems, the drives are machines in their own right. DOS relies on the driver programs of the BIOS to signal a drive's electronic circuits to control the drive's mechanical components. You don't have to be concerned about the drive's complexity.

All disk drives have certain common components: read/write heads, head-positioner mechanisms, and disk-spinning motors. All disk drives record on disks. Some disks are removable; some are built into the drive. Both fixed disks and removable disks spin on a center spindle within the disk drive.

Today, many PCs incorporate both fixed disks and removable disks. The BIOS extensions of DOS make provisions for both types of drives.

Even with their common features, fixed and floppy disk drives have some important differences, which the following sections describe. Knowing these distinctions will help you understand how each type of drive operates in your system.

Hard Disk Drives

Drives with built-in disks are called *fixed disk drives* or, because their disks are made of rigid metal, *hard disk drives*. These terms can be shortened to *fixed disk* and *hard disk*. Some seasoned PC users refer to hard disks as *Winchester disks*. Winchester is a name derived from an IBM code name for the sealed disk-drive technology developed by IBM. In this book, the term *hard disk* is used to describe a built-in fixed disk drive.

A hard disk drive can contain more than one hard disk, or *platter*. Multiple platters are arranged in a stack, with space between the individual platters. Hard disk drives have great storage capacity; these drives can hold tens or hundreds of millions of bytes of data.

Figure 6.2 shows a cutaway view of a typical hard disk. The platters are the drive's magnetic disks. A head-positioner arm holds the read/write heads above and below each surface of each platter. When the drive leaves the factory, the components are not exposed, as they are in this figure; the drive is sealed to keep dust, hair, dirt, smoke, and other contaminants out of the delicate mechanical parts.

Hard disks have the advantages of quick operation, high reliability, and large storage capacity. Hard disks have the disadvantage of tying the data stored on the disk to the PC in which the drive is installed. Because the hard disk's platters cannot be removed, the data is tied to the drive.

Hard disks are installed in a PC with mounting hardware and with interconnecting power and data cables. Moving an entire hard disk to another computer simply to use the hard disk's data is, therefore, impractical. When you need to move data between the hard disks of two computers, you can use the XCOPY command or the DOS 6.0 MSBACKUP command. These commands are covered in Part II of this book.

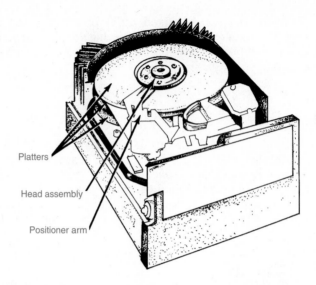

Platters

Head assembly

Positioner arm

Fig. 6.2

An inside view
of the main
components of
a hard disk.

Floppy Disk Drives

In a PC system, the disadvantage of tying data to the hard disk is coun-
terbalanced by the PC's *floppy disk drive*. Floppy disks are protected by
a permanent jacket, which encloses the flexible disk. The flexible disk
inside the jacket is made of Mylar and is coated with sensitive magnetic
film.

The first floppy disks were 8 inches in diameter. By today's standards,
the early 8-inch floppy disks didn't store much data; some 8-inch floppies could store only 320K of data. Today, an 8-inch floppy disk can
store nearly 3 million bytes.

Some early microcomputers used 8-inch floppies as their standard. For
several years, the pioneering microcomputer makers offered the 8-inch
floppy drive as the alternative to such primitive off-line file storage
methods as paper tape and cassette recording.

A smaller version of the 8-inch floppy—the 5 1/4-inch *minifloppy*—
quickly became the floppy of choice for PC designers because of its
size. The 3 1/2-inch *microfloppy* is yet another departure from its larger,
older cousins because it incorporates a rigid plastic case (its jacket) as
a protective cover. The 3 1/2-inch-diameter Mylar disk inside the microfloppy disk is flexible, like the media in 8-inch and 5 1/4-inch floppies.

When you have inserted a disk properly, the label usually faces the top
on horizontal drives and the left on vertical drives (see fig. 6.3). To
complete the insertion of a 5 1/4-inch disk, close the drive door or turn
the latch clockwise.

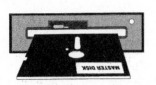

Fig. 6.3

Inserting 5 1/4-inch disks into horizontal and vertical drives.

If the disk does not go in, make sure that the drive doesn't contain another disk. Never jam or buckle a disk during insertion; you could cause permanent damage to the disk.

Insert 3 1/2-inch disks gently, pushing until you hear a click. The drive closes by itself (see fig. 6.4).

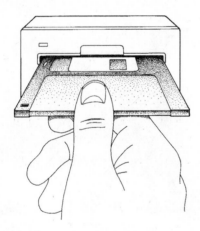

Fig. 6.4

Inserting a microfloppy (3 1/2-inch) disk into a drive.

NOTE You cannot interchange disks of different sizes (diameters) in floppy drives of different sizes. For example, you cannot use a 3 1/2-inch disk in a 5 1/4-inch drive, even though the 3 1/2-inch disk is smaller.

Officially, the smaller two sizes of floppy disks are called *diskettes*; the 8-inch version is called a *disk*. The term *floppy disk* (or *floppy*) refers to any jacket-enclosed disk that you can remove from a PC's drive.

If identifying the type of floppy is important, the size (as in 3 1/2-inch floppy) often is used to make a distinction. *Minifloppy* always refers to 5 1/4-inch floppy disks; *microfloppy* always refers to 3 1/2-inch floppy disks.

The term *disk* can be used to mean any floppy or hard disk when the disk type is clear in context. In other contexts, the term *diskette* is used to refer to both 3 1/2-inch and 5 1/4-inch disks.

You will often store on floppy disks data that should not be erased. To ensure that a floppy disk does not get erased accidentally, write-protect the disk.

To write-protect a 3 1/2-inch microfloppy disk, locate the plastic write-protect shutter and slide it so that the window is open (see fig. 6.5). To write-protect a 5 1/4-inch floppy disk, locate the write-protect notch and cover the notch with a write-protect tab so that the notch is covered (see fig. 6.6).

Fig. 6.5

Microfloppy (3 1/2-inch) disk showing built-in write-protect shutter.

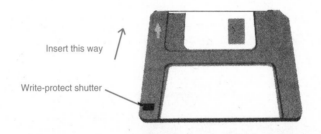

Insert this way

Write-protect shutter

Fig. 6.6

Minifloppy (5 1/4-inch) disk showing write-protect notch.

Insert this way

Write-protect notch

T I P

Most 5 1/4-inch disks are supplied with a sheet of write-protect tabs; if these write-protect tabs are misplaced, you can improvise a write-protect tab with a piece of masking tape or by cutting out a piece of a file-folder or mailing label. Use a piece just large enough to fold over the edge of the 5 1/4-inch disk, covering up the write-protect notch (refer to fig. 6.6). When improvising a write-protect tab for a 5 1/4-inch disk, use only an opaque material that has a strong enough adhesive so that the improvised write-protect tab will not peel off inside the disk drive.

When a disk is write-protected, the drive cannot write new information on the disk even if you inadvertently issue a command that attempts to write data to the disk.

Understanding the Dynamics of the Disk Drive

The dynamics of the disk drive are a function of the drive's electronics. The drive's many components interact with one another, as described in the following sections.

Disk Drive Heads

Disk drives use one or more record/pickup or read/write *heads*. The heads of a disk drive are analogous to the pickup cartridges of phonograph turntables. A cartridge picks up vibrations from the stylus riding in the track and converts those vibrations to electrical energy. Similarly, disk heads convert magnetic energy to electrical data. Although several heads can be used in a disk drive, the electronics of the disk drive accept data from only one head at a time.

Disk drive heads come in different shapes. Figure 6.7 illustrates two common head configurations. The heads are held in position by flexible metal assemblies. A set of wires carrying electrical signals connects to a head and passes through its head-holder assembly, where the wires connect to a flexible ribbon cable. The ribbon cable absorbs wire movements when the head assembly moves. The hard-disk head assembly is small to allow for start-stop control during high-speed head positioning.

On most floppy disks, data is recorded by a head on each side. Floppy drives that use a head on each side of the floppy disk are called *double-sided drives*. Hard disk drives can accommodate more data than one double-sided drive can, however, because hard drives incorporate heads on both sides of each platter.

Using both sides of a disk or platter doubles a drive's storage capacity. Incorporating multiple platters in a hard disk further multiplies the drive's capacity by the number of heads employed.

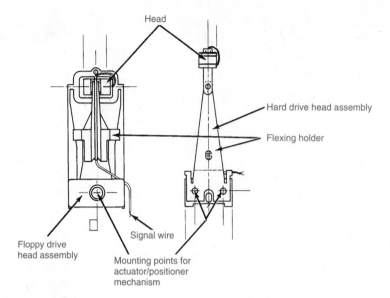

Fig. 6.7

Typical disk drive head assemblies.

Disk Tracks

Regardless of the type of disk drive, all disks spin on a center axis like records spinning on a turntable. A floppy disk spins at 360 revolutions per minute; the rotational speed of a hard disk is 10 times greater (approximately 3,600 rpm). The heads, which are positioned above the spinning surface of the disk, are held and moved in distinct steps by an actuator arm and head positioner. The heads of a floppy disk drive touch the medium; the heads of a hard disk drive ride above the medium on a cushion of air. At each step position, the alignment of the head and the spinning disk produces a circular track.

The track is not a physical track like the groove in a record, but a ring of magnetically recorded data. Unlike a phonograph, which plays a record's contents by following a single spiraling track, a disk drive steps from track to track to retrieve data. Figure 6.8 illustrates the positions of tracks on a disk.

Notice that the tracks are not depicted as a spiral but as concentric circles. The number of concentric tracks available on a disk's surface is determined by the head positioner's mechanical movements, by the density of the magnetic medium, and by the gap between the head and the disk.

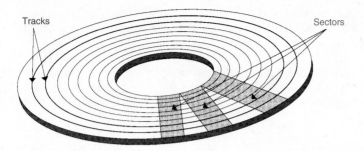

Tracks

Sectors

Fig. 6.8

Concentric tracks
on a disk's
surface.

Disk Cylinders

A disk drive's multiple heads are affixed to a single positioner mechanism. When one head moves one track on its side of a platter (or
floppy), the other heads all move one track on their respective sides of
their respective platters.

Picture a top head riding over Track 10 of Side 1 of a platter, while the
bottom head is riding under Track 10 of Side 2. If the disk has more
than one platter, all the heads assigned to that disk are positioned on
Track 10 of the corresponding platters. This conceptual alignment of
heads on the same track position on different sides of the same platter
is called a *cylinder* (see fig. 6.9), a term derived from the imaginary
shape of the stacked circular tracks at any one stopping point of the
positioner mechanism.

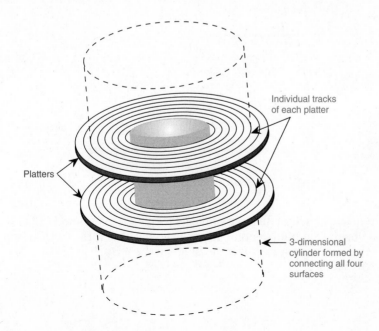

Individual tracks
of each platter

Platters

3-dimensional
cylinder formed by
connecting all four
surfaces

Fig. 6.9

Tracks, platters,
and cylinder.

Because only one head can be active at one time, the drive must activate all its heads in sequence to write (or read) all tracks at the cylinder position. Head activation starts at the top head. To fill a cylinder, a four-head drive writes a track with Head 1, then Head 2, then Head 3, and finally Head 4. The head positioner moves one cylinder, and the sequence repeats. Processing all tracks of a cylinder before moving to the next cylinder is efficient because all heads already are in new track positions.

Disk Sectors

When a disk is blank, as it is when it comes from the factory, the disk contains no tracks and, therefore, no information. DOS has to prepare the disk to accept data. The preparation process is known as *formatting*.

Formatting, as the name implies, places a uniform pattern of format information in all tracks of the disk. The format information in each track enables DOS to slice each track into smaller, more manageable, components of fixed size. These components are called *sectors*.

Figure 6.10 shows the sectors of a floppy disk represented as slices of a disk's surface. The figure shows the boundaries for every other sector. The concentric arcs between the indicated sectors are the disk's tracks. Notice that each track has the same number of sector boundaries (and, therefore, sectors).

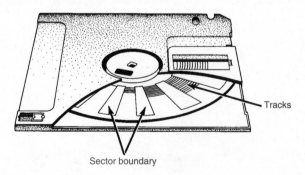

Fig. 6.10

A visual representation of sectors.

DOS reads and writes disk data one sector at a time. Some of DOS' internal file-system bookkeeping is performed by sectors. To DOS, a sector is the disk's most manageable block of data. By default, DOS uses 512-byte sectors.

The number of sectors formatted into each track is tied to the data density the drive uses when reading or writing data. The more dense the recording in a track, and the more tracks on a disk, the more sectors DOS can format.

Designers select the number of tracks and the number of sectors per track with reliability in mind. Floppy disk drives are designed with more margin for error than are hard disk drives. You easily can see why some margin for error is desirable for a drive that must ensure the mechanical alignment of disks that users simply shove into the drive door. Floppy disk drives also must read disks that may have been stored in a place where magnetic fields weakened the disk's magnetic imprint. And despite the protective disk jacket, the magnetic-coated surfaces of many floppy disks can be contaminated by smoke, dust, or fingerprints. A drive must be able to tolerate some disk contamination and still perform without numerous errors. Clearly, no disk drive can avoid errors if the disks it uses are abused. Drive heads cannot read through liquid spills, for example, or through dents made by a ballpoint pen.

Hard disk drives have greater data-storage capacity than their floppy cousins do. A typical PC's hard disk can store at least 10 million bytes of information. This capacity is due in large part to the precision with which the drive's critical components work with the special oxides that magnetically coat the platters. In addition, the working parts of the drive are sealed at the factory in a way that protects the platters, positioners, and heads from contamination. With outside influence on these critical components sealed out, a hard disk drive can offer more tracks and sectors in the same space that a floppy drive occupies. When you consider the fact that most hard disks have more than one platter, each of which is capable of two-sided operation and each of which provides more tracks than a floppy disk can, you begin to see how hard disks get their large storage capacities.

Understanding Disk Formats

Disk drives have a universal way to divide a disk's available physical space. The number of platters, the number of sides, the number of tracks, the number of bytes per sector, and the number of sectors per track are the specific details that factor into this logical division of disk space. The specification for a disk's use of its physical space is called the disk's *format*.

PCs use a variety of disk-drive sizes and formats. Some PCs, for example, can handle both 5 1/4-inch and 3 1/2-inch floppies. Most PC users and software manuals differentiate one format from other formats by using the byte-capacity figure for the desired format. Each new version of DOS has maintained support for the disk formats supported by its predecessors. This support ensures that disks made with older drive formats can be used with current versions of DOS.

Floppy Disk Formats

The first DOS-supported disk drives allowed for twice as many tracks on a 5 1/4-inch floppy disk as the standard 5 1/4-inch disk formats of the time could accommodate. These DOS formats were called *double-density* formats. The original PC disk size and format was 5 1/4-inch, single-sided, 40 tracks, with 8 sectors per track and 512 bytes per sector. These disks are called *single-sided, double-density* (*SSDD*) disks. The capacity of this 8-sector, single-sided format is 160K (K equals 1,024 bytes).

NOTE Computers generally store data in groups of 8 bits. An 8-bit group of data is called a *byte*. By design, digital computers are most efficient when working with numbers as some power of 2. Numbers that are powers of 2 can be represented directly in binary notation.

Computer programmers and designers apply this power-of-2 convention to the expression of a quantity of bytes. A kilobyte, for example, is 2^{10}, or 1,024 bytes, and 2 kilobytes is 2,048 bytes, or 2K. A megabyte, or 1M, equals 1,024K. You need not know about the use of numbers in the power of 2 except to note that capacity expressed in kilobytes (K) or megabytes (M) uses 1,024 as the multiplier rather than 1,000. For scaling purposes, you can think of 1K as representing approximately 1,000 bytes.

The capacity of disk drives is stated in either kilobytes or megabytes. The storage capacity of a hard disk drive is on the order of millions of bytes and usually is expressed in megabytes. The typical capacity of floppies ranges from hundreds of thousands of bytes to slightly more than a million bytes, so a floppy drive's capacity can be described in either kilobytes or megabytes.

The early single-sided format was extended in DOS 1.1 by making the disk format double-sided. All floppies are double-sided, in the sense that they have two sides. But in the formatting sense, the term *double-sided* means that data is recorded on both sides of the disk. Only drives equipped with a second head can accommodate double-sided recording. To differentiate two-sided disks from disks that used only one side for storage, disk makers used the term *double-sided, double-density (DSDD) disks*. When both sides were used for storing data, the format capacity doubled, to 320K. Today, a PC with a single-sided disk drive is rare; most 5 1/4-inch floppy drives are equipped with two heads.

As the design of disk drives became more sophisticated and magnetic materials were improved, the number of sectors per track was increased from 8 to 9 in DOS 2, with no reliability problems. Both DSDD and SSDD formats were given the extra sector per track. This new format, which could store more data than the earlier DSDD and SSDD formats, quickly became popular with users. The single-sided, 9-sector version has a capacity of 180K; the double-sided version has a capacity of 360K. To differentiate between the DSDD and SSDD 8-sector formats and these DSDD and SSDD 9-sector formats, think of the former as DSDD-8 and SSDD-8 and the latter as DSDD-9 and SSDD-9.

The evolution of DOS to Version 3.0 provided for disks with four times (quadruple) the number of tracks of those early standard disks. These 80-track quad-density formats were applied to 5 1/4-inch disks as well as to the new 3 1/2-inch disks. DOS provided one quad-density format of 9 sectors per track, used primarily on 3 1/2-inch disks. This quad-density, 9-sector format is called *QD-9*. The capacity of a QD-9 disk is 720K. Another quad-density, high-capacity quad format of 15 sectors per track is used primarily for 5 1/4-inch disks. The quad-density, 15-sector format is called *HC* (for high capacity) or *QD-15*. The QD-15 format, with a capacity of 1.2M, was popularized by the IBM PC/AT.

For 3 1/2-inch disks, DOS 3.3 added a high-capacity format that supports the 80-track quad density but provides 18 sectors per track. This high-capacity format offers 1.44M of storage space from a microfloppy. This QD-18 format sometimes is called *3 1/2-inch HC*. Boxes of disks intended for formatting to 18 sectors per track usually are labeled *HD*, for high density.

In DOS 5.0, a still-higher-capacity format for 3 1/2-inch disks was added, offering 2.88M of storage. The 2.88M disk format provides 36 sectors per track on 80-track quad-density microfloppies. To use this new format, however, you must have a floppy disk drive and diskettes manufactured specifically to achieve 2.88M storage capacity.

Table 6.3 summarizes the common floppy disk formats.

Table 6.3 DOS Floppy Disk Formats

Format	Tracks	Sectors/Track	Total Sectors	Usable Capacity
SSDD	40	8	320	160K
DSDD	40	8	640	320K
SSDD-9	40	9	360	180K
DSDD-9	40	9	720	360K
QD-9	80	9	1420	720K
QD-15	80	15	2400	1.2M
QD-18	80	18	2880	1.44M
QD-36	80	36	5760	2.88M

Chapter 7, "Preparing and Maintaining Disks," explains the details of the FORMAT command.

Raw Capacity and Usable Capacity

The process of formatting a blank disk places on the disk some data that is not part of the disk's total capacity. A 1.44M disk, for example, holds more than 1.44M bytes of information. You cannot use this extra space, however; the space is reserved for sector-identification and error-checking information. If you buy disks for a 1.44M drive, the identification label may say that the disks have 2M capacity; disks for a 720K drive may indicate 1M capacity.

To understand this apparent discrepancy, you need to understand the difference between total (or raw) capacity and usable (or formatted) capacity. The larger of the two numbers for the same disk is considered to be the *raw capacity* of the disk. Raw capacity includes the space that the formatting information will occupy. The smaller of the two numbers for the same disk is the *usable capacity* of the disk. This number of bytes is available for storing files after the formatting information has been put on the disk.

Fortunately, most manufacturers of hard disks state the capacity of their drives as formatted capacity. Hard disks also lose some overhead space. If you have any doubt as to the meaning of a hard disk's stated capacity, ask the dealer whether the capacity is determined before or after formatting. In this book, *disk capacity* refers to usable capacity after formatting.

Hard Disk Drive Formats

Formats for hard disks nearly always employ 512-byte sectors, usually with 17 sectors per track. *Run-length limited* (RLL) drives use 26 sectors per track, and *enhanced small-device interface* (ESDI) drives ordinarily use 34, 35, or 36 sectors per track.

You can understand the concept of hard disk capacity by remembering the concept of cylinders. Hard disks, you may recall, have two or more heads. Remember that a cylinder is the alignment of all the heads on the same track on both sides of each platter. A disk with 306 tracks on one side of one platter has 306 cylinders. The total number of tracks on the disk is the number of cylinders times the number of heads. The disk's capacity in bytes is the number of tracks times the number of sectors per track times the number of bytes per sector. To obtain the capacity in kilobytes, divide the result by 1,024. To obtain the capacity in megabytes, divide the kilobyte total by 1,024. For approximations of capacity in megabytes, you can divide by a rounded 1,000.

DOS does not provide low-level format data for a hard disk, as it does for a floppy disk. Hard disks normally are given a low-level format at the factory, so users seldom need to initiate a low-level format on a hard disk. DOS uses the low-level format as a base upon which to perform its high-level format.

In a discussion of hard disk formatting, the term *format* refers to the high-level format initiated by the DOS FORMAT command. During the formatting of a hard disk, DOS initializes its bookkeeping tables and then writes "dummy" data into the disk's tracks. From your point of view, formatting a hard disk is the same basic operation as formatting a floppy. DOS keeps the details of the low-level format hidden and out of your way.

T I P

Sometimes the alignment of a hard drive's read/write heads drifts slightly after continual use of the drive. This drifting does not affect the information that has been written to the disk, but the heads may have difficulty locating the information because the low-level format identification information, which is needed to find the data, no longer is aligned beneath the heads. You can eliminate this problem by performing a low-level format of the disk to align the low-level disk tracks with the current location of the heads.

Normally, a low-level format of your hard disk erases all existing data. Certain types of third-party software, however, can perform a low-level format without data loss. The best-known product of this type is SpinRite II (Gibson Research Corporation, Laguna Hills, California).

> **CAUTION:** Several different types of hard disk drives are available. RLL and ESDI drives already have been mentioned. Another type of drive—the Integrated Drive Electronics (IDE) type—never should be given a low-level format, because IDE drives receive special low-level formatting at the factory. If you are unsure what type of hard disk drive you have, check with your dealer or the drive manufacturer before running any programs that perform low-level hard disk formatting.

FROM HERE...

For Related Information

▶▶ "Using the FORMAT Command," p. 180.

▶▶ "Understanding FORMAT's Reports," p. 187.

Trying Some Disk Commands

To get some hands-on practice with disks, try the exercises in the following sections. The exercises build on your knowledge of commands from the last chapter and help reinforce the information about disks and files presented in this chapter.

Determining Your DOS Version with VER

Not all PCs run the same version of DOS. DOS has evolved through six major versions, with minor version changes along the way. Not all commands are available in all versions, and not all commands work exactly the same in all versions. Being able to determine exactly which version you have, therefore, is useful. DOS includes the VER command to help you to do just that.

VER, one of the DOS commands with no parameters or switches, is easy to learn and use. VER is an internal command built into COMMAND.COM. Because VER is internal, COMMAND.COM does not have to find the VER program on the DOS disk (or in the DOS subdirectory).

Clearly, you need to boot DOS on your PC before you can issue any commands. If you haven't started your PC, do so now. If you are uncertain about how to boot, refer to Chapter 3, "Starting DOS." If you want to perform a warm boot (reboot) in a floppy disk system, remember to insert the working DOS disk into drive A, and then press Ctrl-Alt-Del.

Issuing VER is easy. When you see the DOS prompt, simply enter the command as follows:

VER

Don't forget to press Enter to send the command line to DOS.

After you issue the VER command, DOS reports which version of DOS you used to boot the PC. What you see on the screen will look something like this:

```
MS-DOS Version 6.00
```

If you have a PC manufactured by a company that has a special version of DOS, you will see a slightly different message. If you have a Toshiba PC, for example, you may see something like the following:

```
Toshiba MS-DOS Version 6.00
```

In both of these VER reports, you see a manufacturer's name and the DOS version number. The VER report, like the output of many DOS commands, may vary slightly. For information about SETVER, see Chapter 11, "Working with System Information," and Chapter 17, "Configuring Your Computer."

 NOTE When you boot with one version of DOS and then, later in the session, use the external commands from another version, DOS may display an error message. Implementations and versions of DOS often don't mix because of slight differences. If you see an `Incorrect DOS Version` message, chances are good that you booted one version and then used an external command from another version.

Clearing the Screen with CLS

When you issue a series of DOS commands, your screen soon can become cluttered with output text. You occasionally may want to clear the screen before issuing the next command. The internal CLS command can do the job.

Like VER, the CLS command has no parameters or switches. Simply type the following command:

CLS

When you press Enter, DOS clears the screen and places the command prompt and cursor in the upper left corner of the screen.

Copying an Entire Disk with DISKCOPY

Copying one disk (a source disk) to another disk (the target or destination disk) is a practical and useful exercise. DISKCOPY, the external DOS command that performs this task, makes an exact copy of a source disk. DISKCOPY is an ideal command to use when you need to make a copy of a disk, such as a master applications disk.

DOS provides other commands that copy the contents of one disk to another (you learn more about these commands in Part II), but DISKCOPY is the only disk-level copy command offered by DOS.

When you use DISKCOPY, you copy the format and content of the source disk. DISKCOPY uses the formatted capacity of a source disk to determine whether the destination disk has the same format. If you have a 360K-source disk, for example, you must copy it to a 360K-destination disk. Similarly, a 1.2M floppy can DISKCOPY only to a 1.2M floppy.

DISKCOPY is a floppy-disk-only command; you cannot use it to copy a hard disk. Don't worry about harming your hard disk if you accidentally include DISKCOPY in a command line, however; DISKCOPY issues an error message if the disks involved in the operation aren't compatible.

Because DISKCOPY is an external command, you load it from a disk. If the disk that contains DISKCOPY isn't in your current drive, you must use the PATH command to set the correct path before you use DISKCOPY (see Chapter 15, "Understanding Batch Files, DOSKey, and Macros," for information about PATH).The complete correct syntax for DISKCOPY is as follows:

DISKCOPY *sd: dd: /1 /V*

sd: represents the optional name for the drive that holds the disk you want to copy; this drive is called the *source drive*. *dd:* is the optional name of the drive that holds the disk to receive the copy. This *destination drive* sometimes is called the *target drive*. (If you don't specify a drive name, DOS assumes that you want to use the current drive, and prompts you to insert and remove source and destination disks as necessary.) The /1 switch causes DOS to copy only the first side of a double-sided disk. The /V switch instructs DOS to verify that the copy and the original are identical.

As always, type a colon (:) after the drive name. COMMAND.COM needs the colon as an indicator that you are naming a drive as a specifier. Insert a space between the names of the source and destination drives. The space delimits the source and destination drive parameters. If you use a blank, unformatted disk as the destination disk, DOS first formats it.

> If you leave out the drive names in the DISKCOPY command line, DOS uses the current drive as the specifier. To avert confusion, always provide both the source and destination drive names in the command line.

T I P

An example of the DISKCOPY command follows:

    DISKCOPY A: B:

After you issue the DISKCOPY command, DOS prompts you to insert the disk(s) into the proper drives. Make sure that you insert the disks into the correct drives. Write-protect the source disk (by placing a tab over the write-protect notch on a 5 1/4-inch disk or by opening the write-protect slide on a 3 1/2-inch disk) to safeguard its contents in case of a disk mixup.

When the disks are in place, you are ready to continue. Press any key to start the DISKCOPY process. When the process is complete, DOS asks whether you want to make another copy. Press Y to copy another disk or N to exit the command (see fig. 6.11). If the drives or disks are not compatible, an error message appears, and nothing is copied (see fig. 6.12).

If you issue the DISKCOPY command with no drive parameters, DOS uses the current drive to do the copying. DOS prompts you to insert the source and destination disks alternately. Depending on your system's memory, you may swap disks once or several times. Make sure that you don't get the disks confused as you swap them. Be sure to write-protect the source disk to ensure that you don't accidentally overwrite the original data.

```
C:\>DISKCOPY A: B:

Insert SOURCE diskette in drive A:

Insert TARGET diskette in drive B:

Press any key to continue . . .

Copying 80 tracks
9 sectors per track, 2 side(s)

Volume Serial Number is 1EEA-0431

Copy another diskette (Y/N)? N

C:\>
```

Fig. 6.11

A typical DISKCOPY command sequence and messages from DOS.

```
C:\>diskcopy a: b:
Insert SOURCE diskette in drive A:
Insert TARGET diskette in drive B:
Press any key to continue . . .
Drive types or diskette types
not compatible
Copy process ended
Copy another diskette (Y/N)?
```

Fig. 6.12

An error message produced by the DISKCOPY command.

NOTE The designers of DOS provided a way for PCs with only one floppy drive to work with source and destination disks. Many DOS commands (such as DISKCOPY, COPY, and DISKCOMP) treat the single drive as though it were two drives; these commands divide their operations into two phases. If you have one floppy drive (even if you have a hard disk) and issue the command DISKCOPY A: B:, DOS reads the source disk from the floppy drive as drive A and then asks you to insert the destination disk for drive B. On a single floppy drive system, drive B really is drive A. Even though you have one physical drive, DOS treats it logically as two.

DOS can use the drive name B: for some commands by viewing the single drive logically. Your part in the one-drive-as-two operation is to ensure that you insert the correct disk into the drive when DOS prompts you. DOS keeps the identity of the drive straight internally.

Comparing Disks with DISKCOMP

You can confirm that two disks are identical by using the external command DISKCOMP, which compares each track of one disk to each track of another disk sector by sector. Like DISKCOPY, DISKCOMP is a floppy-only command; you cannot use DISKCOMP to compare two hard disks. Further, the disk types and capacities must be the same for both disks in the comparison; any difference in disks made with DISKCOPY is a sign of a problem disk.

One practical use of DISKCOMP is comparing a master disk included with a software package to a working copy of that disk; DISKCOMP will confirm whether the working copy is good.

Normally, you use DISKCOMP to test disks that were made from originals with the DISKCOPY command. Because DISKCOMP doesn't write any information to either disk, both disks can be write-protected. If the disks are identical, DOS displays the message Compare OK.

The syntax for DISKCOMP is similar to that for DISKCOPY. (Also, as is true of DISKCOPY, one drive can act logically as two drives.) Issue the command in the following form:

DISKCOMP *d1: d2: /1 /8*

Because the disks are being compared, not copied, they are referred to as *d1:* and *d2:* rather than as source and destination. The drive specifiers—*d1:* and *d2:*—are optional. (Again, if you don't specify a drive, DOS uses the current drive.) Load the two disks at the DOS prompt; DOS confirms the comparison or points out the differences. The */1* switch causes DOS to compare only the first sides of the disks. The */8* switch compares only the first 8 sectors of each track on the disks.

An example of the DISKCOMP command is as follows:

DISKCOMP A: B:

When the first DISKCOMP operation is complete, DOS asks whether you want to compare another disk.

In the sequence shown in figure 6.13, a working copy of a master disk is being compared to the original master. Notice the comparison errors. The working copy no longer is reliable, or other files have been added to the disk since DISKCOPY was used to make a working copy from the master. The best way to solve the problem is to make a new working copy.

```
C:\>DISKCOMP A: B:

Insert FIRST diskette in drive A:

Insert SECOND diskette in drive B:

Press any key to continue . . .

Comparing 80 tracks
9 sectors per track, 2 side(s)

Compare error on
side 0, track 0

Compare error on
side 0, track 22

Compare another diskette (Y/N) ?N

C:\>
```

Fig. 6.13

Comparing a working copy of a master disk to the original disk.

If you issue the DISKCOMP command with no drive parameters, DOS uses only one drive to carry out the comparison and prompts you to insert the first and second disks alternately. Depending on your system's memory, you will swap disks once or several times. By entering DISKCOMP alone, without parameters, you tell DOS to use the current floppy drive even if your system has two. Make sure that you don't mix up the disks when you're swapping them. If you don't keep track of which disk DOS wants in the drive, you may end up comparing part of a disk to itself.

FROM HERE...

For Related Information

◀◀ "Performing a Cold Boot," p. 67.

◀◀ "Performing a Warm Boot," p. 79.

▶▶ "Setting the Version with SETVER," p. 393.

▶▶ "Using the PATH Command," p. 554.

Chapter Summary

In this chapter, you learned about drives, disks, and files. You also learned about the internal DOS commands VER and CLS, and about the external disk-level commands DISKCOPY and DISKCOMP. Following are the key points covered in this chapter:

- DOS organizes files into a file system that DOS manages.

- Disks are the main storage medium for DOS-based PCs.

- Files are the storage units of disks.

- File names consist of name portions (up to eight characters to the left of the period) and extensions (up to three characters to the right of the period). File name characters must be "legal" to DOS.

- DOS tracks file names in a disk directory. Each file name in a directory must be unique.

- By convention, certain file names refer to specific types of files. You can override file-naming conventions, but observing these conventions makes file names more meaningful.

- DOS uses one of its standard devices when you use a file name that contains the device name. Avoid using the names PRN, CON, NUL, LPT, and COM in file names.

- During formatting, DOS divides disks into tracks, cylinders, and sectors. A disk's storage capacity is governed by the number of sectors on the disk.

- Typical floppy-disk storage capacities are 360K, 720K, 1.2M, 1.44M, and 2.88M. Each floppy drive is designed to work optimally at one of these capacities.

- The VER command reports which DOS version you are using.

- The CLS command clears the screen.

- The DISKCOPY command is an external command that makes a mirror-image copy of a source disk.

- The DISKCOMP command is an external command that compares two disks and reports any comparison errors.

The next chapter begins Part II of this book, which introduces many DOS commands and some additional file-system concepts. You may want to review some of the concepts and rules presented in Part I as you work through Part II.

Putting DOS to Work

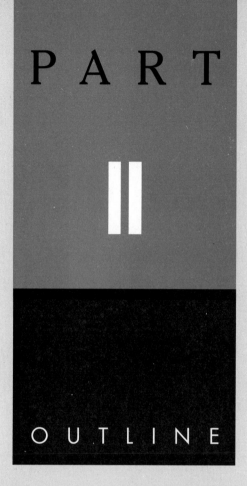

PART

II

OUTLINE

Preparing and Maintaining Disks

I n Chapter 6, "Understanding Disks and Files," you learned the basics of using disks and files in DOS. This chapter builds on that knowledge and introduces useful disk-related DOS commands that you can use from both the DOS Shell and the command line. You learn how to prepare blank floppy disks and hard disks, assign volume labels, transfer the system files, and analyze disks for problems.

This chapter covers the following commands:

FORMAT

UNFORMAT

FDISK

VOL

SYS

CHKDSK

Key Terms Used in This Chapter

Format	Initial preparation of a disk for data storage
Volume label	A name that identifies a particular disk
Track	A circular section of a disk's surface that holds data
Sector	A section of a track that serves as the disk's smallest possible storage unit
Cluster	A unit of one, four, or eight sectors, the smallest amount of disk space that DOS allocates to a file
Disk partition	A division of a hard disk that DOS views as a separate disk
Logical drive	A partitioned section of a hard disk that DOS views as an additional hard disk
Boot sector	A special area in track 0 of each DOS disk; used by DOS to record important information about a disk's format to reference later when working with the disk
Internal command	A DOS command built into COMMAND.COM
External command	A DOS command whose instructions are stored in a file other than COMMAND.COM

Understanding Disk Preparation

Both floppy disks and audiocassette tapes use magnetic media to store information, but in some ways, disks and tapes are different. You cannot just drop a disk into a drive and use the disk; you must prepare your disks before you can store information on them. This preparation process is called *formatting*. DOS's FORMAT command performs this process for disks; you do nothing more than enter the command. FORMAT analyzes a disk for defects, generates a root directory, sets up a storage table, and makes other technical modifications.

Think of unformatted and formatted disks as being comparable to un-lined and lined sheets of paper (see fig. 7.1). The lines on a sheet of paper give you an orderly way to record written information. The lines also act as a guide for whoever reads the information. New unformatted disks are like unlined sheets of paper to DOS.

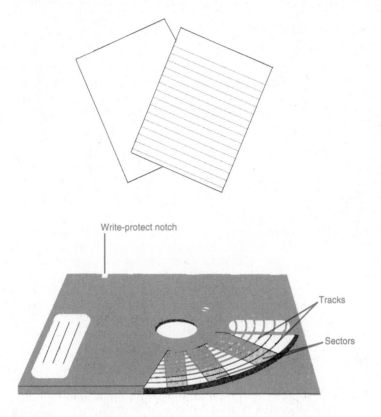

Formatted disks are comparable to lined paper.

Write-protect notch

Tracks

Sectors

Anatomy of a microfloppy disk.

When you format a disk, DOS creates data-storage divisions on the disk's surface. As you learned in Chapter 6, "Understanding Disks and Files," these divisions are concentric circles called *tracks* (see fig. 7.2). DOS decides what type of drive you have and then positions the tracks accordingly. DOS also writes on the disk's first track—track 0—vital information about the disk's format. Later, DOS can read this information quickly to determine how to work with the disk.

As you can see in figure 7.2, each track is divided into segments called *sectors*, which are the smallest divisions of a disk. When you issue the FORMAT command, DOS creates a special disk table called the *file allocation table* (FAT). The FAT, which is always located on track 0, logs every sector on a disk in units of one or more sectors called *clusters*. DOS stores data in the clusters and uses the track number and cluster number to retrieve the data.

A cluster is the smallest unit of storage that DOS allocates for file storage at one time. All DOS commands use tracks and clusters as road maps that enable them to carry out their operations. A standard 5 1/4-inch double-density floppy disk (one that holds 360K of data) has 40 tracks per side. High-density 5 1/4-inch disks (1.2M) and both double-density and high-density 3 1/2-inch floppy disks (720K and 1.44M) have 80 tracks per side. DOS provides FATs and directories suited to the capacities of these disks.

Although formatting disks may become a routine job for you, always be careful during the process because formatting erases all information from a disk. If you format a disk that you used previously, everything stored on that disk disappears. Be careful not to format a disk that contains files you want to keep.

In most cases, a disk formatted with DOS 5.0 or 6.0 can be unformatted with the UNFORMAT command, but only if you unformat before you create or copy files onto the inadvertently formatted disk. (For more information, see the section "Unformatting a Disk" later in this chapter.)

One way to avoid formatting a disk by accident is to label your disks, using the paper labels supplied with the disks. Other precautions are to write-protect 5 1/4-inch disks with a tab and to open the write-protect slide window on 3 1/2-inch disks. In any case, before you try to format a previously used disk, use the DIR command to see which files are on the disk. Then determine whether you can afford to lose those files when you format the disk.

Using the FORMAT Command

The FORMAT command prepares disks for use as external data-storage media. You must format a floppy disk or hard disk before you can use it. You also can reformat disks that have already been formatted.

NOTE When you issue certain external commands like FORMAT, DOS prompts you to insert the proper disk into the drive before DOS carries out the command. If you have a floppy-disk system, remove the disk that contains the FORMAT command, insert the disk to be formatted, and then press any key. Hard-disk systems normally are set up to search for and load an external command from a directory on the hard disk. For more information on this process, see Chapter 8, "Understanding and Managing Directories."

In DOS versions before 5.0, reformatting a disk in effect erased the data stored on the disk. Starting in DOS 5.0, however, the FORMAT command first determines whether the disk contains data. If the disk contains data, FORMAT saves a copy of the boot sector, the FAT, and the root directory in a safe place on the disk where UNFORMAT can find the information when you later need to unformat the disk. You can unformat a disk formatted with DOS 5.0 or 6.0 only if you have not created or copied other files onto the disk.

In DOS 5.0 and 6.0, the FORMAT command clears the disk's FAT and the first character of each file name in the root directory but does not erase any data. (The program also scans the entire disk for bad sectors.) FORMAT then saves the first letter of each file name in a safe place on the disk.

> **CAUTION:** FORMAT is a DOS command that can quickly wipe out the contents of a disk. Even though DOS 5.0 and 6.0 FORMAT command is safer than earlier versions, before you use this command, make sure that you are familiar with its syntax. FORMAT issues warning messages on-screen and prompts you for verification before formatting a hard disk. Take care when you use FORMAT, especially if you use a version of DOS earlier than DOS 5.0. Read the screen prompts, and keep backups of your data.

Formatting Floppy Disks

Formatting floppy disks from the DOS Shell is different from formatting floppies from the command line. Both methods are described in the sections that follow. DOS also provides several formatting options through command-line switches. See the section "Using FORMAT's Switches" later in this chapter for a discussion of how to use the switches when you format disks.

> Mixing formatted disks with unformatted disks is an easy mistake to make when you are working with a fresh box of disks. To avoid a mix-up, place a mark on the label of each disk that you format. The mark may be as simple as a dot, a check, or the letter *F* (for "Formatted").

T I P

Before you begin formatting your first floppy disk, mark the disk's label to indicate that the disk will be formatted. If your computer isn't running, boot from the hard disk or insert the DOS Startup disk into drive A, and then boot your computer.

Formatting a Floppy Disk in the DOS Shell

Perhaps the easiest way to use the FORMAT command is to use it in the DOS Shell. Follow these steps:

1. If the Shell is not loaded, type **DOSSHELL** at the command prompt, and then press Enter. The DOS Shell window appears.

2. Select Disk Utilities in the program-list area. The Shell displays the Disk Utilities program-group list (see fig. 7.3).

3. Select Format in the program-group list. The Format dialog box appears (see fig. 7.4). Notice that the Parameters text box contains the default entry a:.

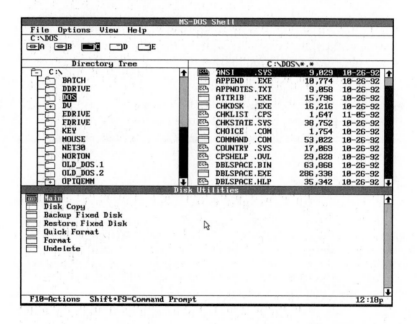

Fig. 7.3

The Disk Utilities program-group list.

4. To format a disk in your A drive, click OK or press Enter.

   To format a disk in a drive other than drive A or to use any of the FORMAT command switches, type the appropriate FORMAT command parameters in the Parameters text box. See "Using FORMAT's Switches" later in this chapter for details on this procedure.

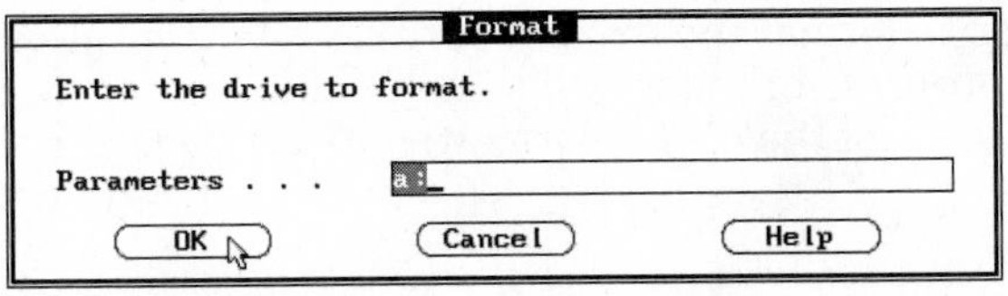

```
┌──────────────────────────────────────────┐
│                  Format                    │
│ Enter the drive to format.                 │
│                                            │
│ Parameters . . .   [a:_                  ] │
│   (   OK  ⤺ )    ( Cancel )    (  Help  )  │
└──────────────────────────────────────────┘
```

Fig. 7.4

The Format
dialog box.

To display a help screen that lists all available parameters for the
FORMAT command, type **/?** in the Parameters text box, and then
press Enter.

T I P

After you click OK or press Enter, the Shell clears the screen and
displays the following prompt at the top of the screen:

```
Insert new diskette for drive A:
and press ENTER when ready...
```

---

5. Remove any disk that may be in drive A and insert the disk that
   you want to format.

6. Press Enter to format the disk.

The messages displayed during the formatting process vary, depending
on whether you are formatting a new disk or a previously formatted
one. When you press Enter at the prompt, the program displays the
message Checking existing disk format, followed by a message
similar to Formatting 1.44M if the disk has not yet been formatted.

If you are formatting a previously formatted disk, DOS displays messages similar to the following as the formatting process begins:

```
Checking existing disk format
Saving UNFORMAT information
Verifying 1.44M
```

DOS is performing a safe format so that you can unformat the disk later,
if necessary, by using the UNFORMAT command. The disk capacity
displayed in the screen message depends on the capacity of your drive
and on the density of the disk you are using (refer to Chapter 6, "Understanding Disks and Files").

As DOS begins to format the disk, the drive's indicator glows, and DOS displays the progress of the formatting operation as a percentage. When 100 percent of the disk is formatted, DOS displays the following message:

```
Format complete

Volume label (11 characters, ENTER for none)?
```

You can give the disk a volume name of up to 11 characters, or you can press Enter to omit the volume name.

Finally, DOS tells you about the disk's formatted capacity in a message similar to the following:

```
1457664    bytes total disk space
1457664    bytes available on disk
    512    bytes in each allocation unit
   2847    allocation units available on disk

Volume Serial Number is 2628-13FD

Format another (Y/N)?
```

To format another disk, insert a different disk, type **Y**, and then press Enter. To quit, type **N** and press Enter. After you type **N** and press Enter, DOS displays the message Press any key to return to MS-DOS Shell.... Press a key on the keyboard to display the DOS Shell window. To return to the Main program list, press Esc or click the Main program-list icon.

 NOTE   During the formatting operation, if the disk has not yet been formatted, FORMAT overwrites every data byte with the hexadecimal value F6. If you want FORMAT to overwrite all data on a previously formatted disk, use the /U switch, which is discussed in the section "Performing an Unconditional Format" later in this chapter.

Performing a Quick Format from the DOS Shell

Sometimes, you want to clear all data from a disk without waiting for the standard formatting procedure to run. DOS 5.0 and 6.0 provide a formatting option—Quick Format—that enables you to reformat a disk quickly. This option is available from both the DOS Shell and the command line.

To quick-format a disk from the DOS Shell, follow these steps:

1. If the Shell is not loaded, type **DOSSHELL** at the command prompt, and then press Enter. The DOS Shell window appears.

2. Select Disk Utilities in the program-list area. The Shell displays the Disk Utilities program-group list.

3. Select Quick Format in the program-group list. The Quick Format dialog box appears (see fig. 7.5). Like the Format dialog box, the Quick Format dialog box includes a Parameters text box that contains the default entry a:.

```
┌─────────────────────────────────────────────────┐
│              ▛▀▀Quick Format▀▀▜                  │
│    Enter the drive to quick format.              │
│                                                  │
│    Parameters . . .  ▐a:▌_____  │
│       ╭────────╮    ╭────────╮    ╭────────╮      │
│       │  OK ▷  │    │ Cancel │    │  Help  │      │
│       ╰────────╯    ╰────────╯    ╰────────╯      │
└─────────────────────────────────────────────────┘
```

Fig. 7.5

The Quick Format dialog box.

4. To quick-format a disk in the A drive, click OK or press Enter. To quick-format a disk in another drive, type the drive letter, followed by a colon (:), and then press Enter.

   The Shell clears the screen and then displays the following prompt at the top of the screen:

   ```
   Insert new diskette for drive A:
   and press ENTER when ready…
   ```

   ---

5. Remove any disk that may be in drive A and insert the disk that you want DOS to quick-format.

6. Press Enter. DOS performs a safe quick format (like the one discussed in the preceding section) and then displays the following message:

   ```
   Checking existing disk format
   Saving UNFORMAT information
   QuickFormatting 1.44M
   ```

The disk capacity stated in the message depends on the capacity of your drive and the density of the disk you are using (refer to Chapter 6, "Understanding Disks and Files").

After the disk has been formatted, DOS displays the message shown in the preceding section and asks whether you want to QuickFormat another (Y/N)?

To format another disk, insert a different disk, type **Y**, and then press Enter. To quit, type **N** and then press Enter. After you type **N** and press Enter, DOS displays the message Press any key to return to MS-DOS Shell.... Press a key on the keyboard to return to the DOS Shell window. To return to the Main program list, press Esc or click the Main icon.

 NOTE The DOS Shell's Quick Format and Format options, listed in the Disk Utilities program group, perform safe formats. Quick Format is faster than Format because Quick Format does not scan the entire disk for bad sectors.

Formatting a Floppy Disk from the Command Line

FORMAT is an *external command*—a program that is not loaded automatically each time you start your computer. COMMAND.COM must load FORMAT from one of your system's drives. Before you can use FORMAT from the command line, therefore, the current disk and directory must contain the program FORMAT.COM, or the directory that contains your DOS program files (including FORMAT.COM) must be in your system's path. (For a discussion of PATH, see Chapter 8, "Understanding and Managing Directories.")

 NOTE The DOS 5.0 and 6.0 Setup programs insert into your system's AUTOEXEC.BAT file a command that ensures that all DOS external commands are in the system's path.

The complete syntax for the FORMAT command is shown in the following:

    FORMAT d: */Q/V:label/F:size/S/B/U/1/4/8/N:sectors/T:tracks*

This syntax shows all the switches that are available with the FORMAT command, but you usually use only a few of them at a time. (All the FORMAT switches are discussed in the section "Using FORMAT's Switches" later in this chapter.)

To format a floppy disk from the command line without using any switches, go to the DOS command prompt, and then follow these steps:

1. To format a disk in drive A, type **FORMAT A:** and press Enter. To format a disk in another drive, type the appropriate drive letter in place of *A*. A message similar to the following appears:

```
Insert new diskette for drive A:
and press ENTER when ready
```

---

2. Remove any disk that may be in drive A, insert the disk that you want to format, and press Enter to begin the formatting process.

The messages displayed during the formatting process are the same as those described in the preceding section.

> **CAUTION:** Versions of DOS earlier than 3.0 do not require you to specify the drive that holds the disk you want to format. In these early versions, if you issue the FORMAT command with no drive parameter, DOS formats the current disk (which may be your working copy of DOS). If you have a floppy-disk system, be sure to write-protect your working copy of DOS so that FORMAT cannot format the DOS disk. As a general rule, remember to specify the drive that you want to format.

Understanding FORMAT's Reports

The primary task of the FORMAT command is to divide the disk into logical storage sectors, but this task is not the command's only purpose. During and after the formatting process, FORMAT issues several reports. Versions of DOS earlier than 4.0 show the track and sector numbers as formatting takes place. In DOS 4.0 and later versions, the FORMAT command provides a continual update of what percentage of the disk has been formatted.

When 100 percent of the disk is formatted, DOS displays the following message:

```
Format complete

Volume label (11 characters, ENTER for none)?
```

You can give the disk a volume name of as many as 11 characters or press Enter to omit the volume name.

Then FORMAT reports the disk's capacity. The report shows the total disk space available (in bytes). If FORMAT finds *bad sectors*—spots on the disk that may not hold data reliably—the command marks these sectors as unusable and displays how many bytes are unavailable because of the bad sectors.

DOS also displays the number of bytes that each *allocation unit* or *cluster* (the smallest group of sectors DOS allocates to a file) can contain and tells you how many allocation units are available on the disk for storage.

The report additionally shows the unique serial number—a random hexadecimal (base 16) number—that DOS has assigned to the disk. DOS uses this number at different times to determine whether you removed a disk from the drive and replaced it with another disk.

The report for a 1.44M formatted disk may resemble the following:

```
1457664   bytes total disk space
1457664   bytes available on disk
    512   bytes in each allocation unit
   2847   allocation units available on disk
Volume Serial Number is 2628-13FD

Format another (Y/N)?
```

To format another disk, insert a different disk, type **Y**, and then press Enter. To return to the DOS prompt, type **N** and press Enter.

Using FORMAT's Switches

To modify and add versatility to FORMAT (and many other DOS commands), you can use parameters called *switches*. You enter these switches in the command line immediately after typing the command. Be sure to type a slash (/) before the switch letter, as in **/S**. The Command Reference provides more details on valid switch combinations.

DOS 5.0 and 6.0 provide an on-line help facility to help you learn the proper syntax for commands you enter in the command line. If you type **FORMAT /?** and press Enter, for example, DOS displays the help screen shown in figure 7.6. If you type **HELP FORMAT** and press enter, you access a great deal more information about disk formatting.

```
C:\>FORMAT /?
Formats a disk for use with MS-DOS.

FORMAT drive: [/V[:label]] [/Q] [/U] [/F:size] [/B ¦ /S]
FORMAT drive: [/V[:label]] [/Q] [/U] [/T:tracks /N:sectors] [/B ¦ /S]
FORMAT drive: [/V[:label]] [/Q] [/U] [/1] [/4] [/B ¦ /S]
FORMAT drive: [/Q] [/U] [/1] [/4] [/8] [/B ¦ /S]

  /V[:label]  Specifies the volume label.
  /Q          Performs a quick format.
  /U          Performs an unconditional format.
  /F:size     Specifies the size of the floppy disk to format (such
              as 160, 180, 320, 360, 720, 1.2, 1.44, 2.88).
  /B          Allocates space on the formatted disk for system files.
  /S          Copies system files to the formatted disk.
  /T:tracks   Specifies the number of tracks per disk side.
  /N:sectors  Specifies the number of sectors per track.
  /1          Formats a single side of a floppy disk.
  /4          Formats a 5.25-inch 360K floppy disk in a high-density drive.
  /8          Formats eight sectors per track.

C:\>_
```

Fig. 7.6

The FORMAT
help screen.

Most of the FORMAT commands that you need to issue are simple. The average DOS user needs only a few of the command's switches; the remaining switches provide advanced features or compatibility with older versions of DOS. Table 7.1 lists the most commonly used switches available with the FORMAT command.

Table 7.1 Commonly Used FORMAT Switches

Switch	Action
/B	Allocates space on the formatted disk for system files by creating hidden files of the same name and size on track 0. Used to create disks that can be made bootable with DOS 4.01 and earlier versions.
/F:size	Specifies the size of the floppy disk to be formatted (such as 160, 180, 320, 360, 720, 1.2, 1.44, and 2.88). You can specify kilobytes or megabytes if you prefer, but doing so is not necessary because DOS understands all the parameters shown here.
/Q	Performs a quick format on a previously formatted disk (DOS 5.0 and 6.0 only).
/S	Copies the system files and COMMAND.COM to the formatted disk.
/U	Performs an unconditional format so that the disk cannot be unformatted with UNFORMAT (DOS 5.0 and 6.0 only).

Table 7.2 lists less commonly used switches that are included for compatibility. The switches listed in this table are preserved from earlier versions of DOS (and still are present in DOS 5.0 and 6.0). Some of the functions listed now are included in the /F:*size* switch; others are used only to format floppy disks for early IBM PCs and compatibles.

Table 7.2 Additional FORMAT Switches

Switch	Action
/N:*sectors*	Enables you to specify the number of sectors per track (between 1 and 99). The functions of this switch have been replaced by the /F:*size* switch.
/T:*tracks*	Specifies the number of tracks per disk side (between 1 and 999). The functions of this switch have been replaced by the /F:*size* switch.
/V:*label*	Enables you to specify the volume label.
/1	Formats a single side of a floppy disk. Usually used with the /8 switch to make disks compatible with DOS 1.0 and 1.1.
/4	Formats a 5 1/4-inch 360K floppy disk in a high-density drive. (A standard 360K drive may not be able to read the resulting disk.) The functions of this switch have been replaced by the /F:*size* switch.
/8	Formats 8 sectors per track rather than 9 or 15. Used for disks that work with older versions of DOS or with early-model disk drives (see the /1 switch).

The following sections describe some of the ways you can use FORMAT's switches.

Performing a Quick Format

One way to clear all data from a disk is to format the disk. Because the formatting procedure can be relatively slow, DOS 5.0 introduced (and DOS 6.0 includes) a *quick-format* capability that you can use only when you reformat a disk that already has been formatted.

To clear data from a disk, type the command **FORMAT /Q** and then press Enter. (For more information about the FORMAT command's Quick Format option, refer to "Performing a Quick Format from the DOS Shell" earlier in this chapter.)

Performing an Unconditional Format

Unless you use the /U switch, the DOS 5.0 and 6.0 FORMAT commands perform a safe format of previously formatted disks. FORMAT first determines whether the disk has been formatted. If the disk has been formatted, FORMAT clears the FAT, boot record, and root directory but does not erase any data. FORMAT then scans the entire disk for bad sectors and saves a copy of the FAT, boot record, and root directory in a safe place on the disk (in the MIRROR image file) where the UNFORMAT command can find them. If the disk has not been formatted previously, FORMAT overwrites every data byte with the hexadecimal value F6.

If you want DOS to overwrite all data on a previously formatted floppy disk (a procedure called *unconditional formatting*), use the /U switch. The following command, for example, unconditionally formats a disk in the A drive:

> FORMAT A: /U

DOS writes the hexadecimal value F6 in every sector in the disk, erasing all existing data.

> **NOTE** All versions of DOS earlier than 5.0 *always* perform unconditional formatting on floppy disks. Most earlier versions of DOS do not overwrite all data when formatting a hard disk but do erase the FAT, root directory, and boot record. COMPAQ DOS 3.2 and earlier versions, AT&T DOS 3.1 and earlier versions, and some Burroughs DOS versions do overwrite all data, even when formatting a hard disk. All DOS versions earlier than 5.0 provide no way to unformat a disk—hard or floppy. The DOS 5.0 and 6.0 FORMAT commands never overwrite all data on a hard disk.

Adding a Volume Label

DOS reserves a few bytes of space on each disk so that you can place a form of electronic identification—a *volume label*—on the disk. A volume label is not unlike a book title—it is simply a name that helps you identify the disk.

In DOS 4.01 and earlier versions, the FORMAT command's /V:*label* switch enables you to place a volume label on a formatted disk. You substitute an 11-character name for the new disk for *label*. (In DOS 5.0 and 6.0, you are prompted for a volume label automatically.) As you learn later in this chapter, the DOS LABEL command can do the same disk-naming job.

NOTE DOS 4.0, 5.0, and 6.0 also assign a volume serial number to each formatted disk. DOS uses this number to determine whether you changed floppy disks.

Each time you use DOS 5.0 or 6.0 to format a disk, DOS displays the message Volume label (11 characters, ENTER for none)?. If you don't want to label the disk, press Enter.

If you have DOS 4.01 or an earlier version, you must use the /V:*label* switch to assign a volume label to a floppy disk during formatting. If you decide to use a name, the following rules apply:

- You can use any of the following characters, in any order, in a volume label:

  The letters *A* through *Z* and *a* through *z*

  The numbers 0 through 9

  The following special characters and punctuation symbols: $ # & @ ! ( ) - { } ' _ ~ ^ `

  A space character (DOS 3.3 and later versions)

- You cannot use any of the following characters in a volume label:

  Any control character (ASCII 31 and lower) and the Del character (ASCII 127)

  The following special characters and punctuation symbols: + = / [ ] ' : ; , ? * \ < > |

When you enter an illegal character in the volume label, DOS 6.0 displays the message Invalid characters in volume label and asks you to enter the volume label again. If you try to type more than 11 characters, your computer beeps. After you type the volume name, press Enter.

Adding System Files

If you want to be able to use a disk to start your computer, the disk must contain hidden DOS system files as well as the command processor (COMMAND.COM). One way to install these system files on a disk is to use the /S switch during the formatting procedure. The /S switch reduces the disk's available storage capacity by as much as 114K.

> **CAUTION:** Don't use the /S switch with FORMAT unless you plan to create a disk from which you can boot.

 NOTE Having at least one bootable system disk as a backup is important in case the disk that contains your working copy of DOS fails or your hard drive develops errors.

When formatting with /S is complete, DOS displays a report similar to the following for a 1.44M disk:

```
System transferred.
Volume label (11 characters, ENTER for none)?
```

After you press Enter, DOS displays the following message:

```
1457664    bytes total disk space
 117760    bytes used by system
1339904    bytes available on disk
    512    bytes in each allocation unit
   2617    allocation units available on disk
 Volume Serial Number is 2A50-1CD2

 Format another (Y/N)?
```

If you need more than one disk that you can use to boot your computer, insert a different disk, type **Y**, and press Enter. To return to the DOS prompt, type **N** and press Enter. You can use any of the formatted disks to start your computer.

If you want a disk that can be made bootable with DOS 4.01 and earlier, use the /B switch. (This switch reserves space for the hidden system files but does not copy COMMAND.COM to the disk.) In these versions of DOS, the system files were placed on track 0. This switch is unnecessary in DOS 5.0 and 6.0 because in these versions, the system files can appear anywhere on the disk.

Formatting Disks of Different Capacities

DOS provides several FORMAT switches that enable you to format floppy disks to any storage capacity supported by the operating system and your hardware.

Each floppy-disk drive in your system has a maximum storage capacity. By default, DOS expects all disks formatted in a particular drive to be formatted to the drive's maximum capacity. On occasion, however, you may want to format a lower-capacity disk. You may, for example, need to format a box of double-density 3 1/2-inch disks (720K) in a high-density (1.44M) 3 1/2-inch drive.

DOS 5.0 introduced the most useful switch for formatting disks of a different capacity: the /F:*size* switch. To format a 720K disk in a 1.44M drive (the A drive), for example, you can use the following command:

FORMAT A: /F:720

Other parameters that you can substitute for the *size* parameter are listed in table 7.1. Table 7.2 lists five other switches that you can use to specify the capacity of a disk. These other switches were designed to format floppy disks for use with earlier DOS versions. The Command Reference includes the syntax for using these switches with the FORMAT command. If you need to use the less-common switches, consult the Command Reference for more information.

Using FORMAT in Another Drive

In Chapter 5, "Using DOS Commands," you learned that COMMAND.COM contains built-in DOS commands called *internal commands* and that commands that reside in separate files on disk are called *external commands*. COMMAND.COM must find and load external commands before executing them. If the external commands are not in the current drive and directory, you must enter a drive parameter—and possibly a path-name parameter—before the command name. The drive parameter is the name of the drive that contains the command's file. In Chapter 8, "Understanding and Managing Directories," you learn how to give DOS the correct path to the external commands.

Suppose that your computer has a hard disk and two floppy drives. You want to format a disk in drive B. You have FORMAT.COM on a disk in drive A and a blank disk in drive B. Follow these steps:

1. To make the drive holding the DOS working disk the default drive, type **A:** and press Enter.

2. To format the unformatted disk in drive B, type **FORMAT B:** and press Enter.

If you had changed to drive B (by typing B: instead of A: in the first step of this example), the command FORMAT B: would produce an error message. Because drive B is not the drive that contains the FORMAT.COM file, DOS cannot find it. One solution to this dilemma is to issue the command as shown in the following:

A:FORMAT B:

DOS finds the FORMAT command on the DOS disk in drive A, as specified in the command, and then formats the unformatted disk in drive B.

For Related Information

◀◀ "Understanding the Disk's Magnetic Storage Technique," p. 151.

◀◀ "Understanding Disk Drives," p. 152.

▶▶ "Helping DOS Find External Commands," p. 240.

FROM HERE...

Preparing the Hard Disk

The following sections explain how DOS divides and formats a hard disk. Be sure to heed all warnings and read all explanations carefully.

> **WARNING:** Many computer dealers install the operating system on a computer's hard disk before you receive the computer. If your dealer has installed an application, such as a word processing program, *do not format the hard disk* unless you also have a copy of the program on floppy disks. If you reformat your hard disk, all programs and data are erased.

Dividing a Hard Disk with FDISK

Before you can format a hard disk, you must *partition* it—that is, divide the hard disk logically into several drives called partitions. A partition is simply a section of the storage area of a hard disk. Many operating systems, including DOS, can use disk partitions, and most systems have some utility program that creates and manages partitions. In DOS, that utility program is the external command FDISK.

NOTE Many computer dealers use FDISK on a system's hard disk before delivering the system to the user. In addition, FDISK is executed automatically by the DOS 5.0 and 6.0 Setup commands during installation. If your hard disk contains files, it already has been partitioned with FDISK and formatted. If you have any questions about the state of your hard disk's preparation, consult your dealer.

Most hard-disk users choose a DOS partition size encompassing the entire hard disk. In other words, the one physical hard disk appears to DOS to be one logical hard disk. FDISK enters into a hard-disk partition table information indicating that the entire disk is available to DOS and that the disk is bootable.

Some PC users want to have on their hard disk DOS and another operating system, and different operating systems use file systems that are not compatible with DOS. FDISK enables you to divide the hard disk into separate, isolated sections so that DOS can use one partitioned section while the other operating system, such as UNIX, uses the other partitioned section. Through separation, each operating system sees its partition as being its own hard disk.

Only one operating system can be active at a time, and the drive in which that operating system is located is called the *active partition*. FDISK controls which partition is active if you have more than one hard-disk partition.

Hard-disk capacities have increased over the last few years. FDISK enables you to divide these larger hard disks into a *boot drive*—called the *primary DOS partition*—and additional hard drives. Each of these additional drives is a *logical drive*. The additional drives are carved out of an area called the *extended DOS partition*. A logical drive is not a separate physical disk, but DOS treats each logical drive as if it were a separate disk. You can use FDISK to partition your hard drive into several logical drives—for example, C, D, and E.

Until DOS 4.0, the largest drive DOS could manage as one partition was 32M. Drives with capacities of more than 32M, however, have been available for some time. FDISK and DOS's extended-partition capability give you a means to use drives larger than 32M. DOS 4.0 and later versions enable you to use your entire hard disk as a single partition.

NOTE Although making a large hard disk into a single logical drive is tempting, doing so may create some disadvantages. If your hard drive is especially large, any command that scans the entire drive—such as DIR or CHKDSK—may take an inordinately long time to complete execution. Unless you have single files that are larger, you may prefer to limit your logical drives to 120M.

CAUTION: You can use the FDISK command to delete an existing partition from the disk partition table. If you delete an existing partition, you lose all data in the files contained in that partition. Be sure that you have backed up or copied any data from a partition that you want to delete. FDISK is not a command to experiment with unless your hard disk contains no data.

The syntax for FDISK, which uses no parameters, is shown in the following:

FDISK

In DOS 3.3 and later versions, you can use FDISK to create more than one DOS partition. After you create a primary DOS partition (or boot disk) with FDISK, you can create an extended DOS partition, which you divide into one or more logical drives.

You must use the FORMAT command to format all primary DOS partitions and logical drives before you can use them. (See the following section "Formatting a Hard Disk" for instructions.) When DOS is the active operating system, as reflected in the partition table (an A appears next to the drive name), it boots from the active DOS partition. You then can switch into one of the logical drives. The primary DOS partition normally is assigned the drive name C.

After you partition the hard disk, DOS treats the logical drives as separate drives and creates a file system for each one when the drive is formatted.

Formatting a Hard Disk

Like floppy disks, you must format a hard disk before you use it. If your hard disk is not formatted using the partitioning features introduced in DOS 5.0, the DOS 6.0 Setup program gives you the option of formatting the hard disk while you install DOS.

Assume that the hard disk (or logical disk) you are going to format is drive C. (If you are formatting another drive, use its drive letter in place of *C* in the example.) If your drive is not the primary DOS partition, you don't need to use the /S switch; DOS boots only from the primary DOS partition. To format drive C, follow these steps:

1. Insert your working copy of the DOS Startup disk into drive A.

2. Switch to that drive by typing **A:** and pressing Enter.

3. Type the following command and press Enter:

   FORMAT C:/S

   FORMAT issues the following warning message and confirmation prompt:

   ```
   WARNING, ALL DATA ON NON-REMOVABLE DISK
   DRIVE C: WILL BE LOST!
   Proceed with Format (Y/N)?
   ```

   This prompt is extremely important. When the prompt appears on-screen, examine it carefully to confirm the disk-drive name (letter) before you type **Y**. If you make a habit of typing **Y** in response to the confirmation prompts of less dangerous commands, you may make a serious mistake with this final FORMAT confirmation prompt.

4. If the specified drive is the one you want to format, type **Y**; if not, type **N** to terminate FORMAT.

   If you type **Y**, FORMAT updates the display with progress reports on the formatting operation. DOS 4.0 and later versions report the percentage of formatting completed; other versions report the head and cylinder count. Depending on the size of the disk being formatted, the process can take from a few minutes to more than half an hour. The greater a disk's capacity, the longer the process takes. When the disk has been formatted, FORMAT issues the message Format complete. FORMAT may not be finished, however. If you used the /S switch, the message System Transferred appears.

   FORMAT next prompts you for the volume label with the message Volume label (11 characters, ENTER for none)?.

5. Type the volume label, and then press Enter. (The discussion of the /V switch in the previous discussion of FORMAT's switches includes a list of acceptable volume-label characters.) If you decide later to change this label, you can use the LABEL command, which is available in MS-DOS 3.1 or PC DOS 3.0 and later versions.

(For more information on LABEL, see "Naming Disks with LABEL" later in this chapter.)

FORMAT displays a report showing the disk space formatted, the bytes used by the system files, defective sectors marked (if any), and the number of bytes available on the disk. Don't be surprised if the report shows some bad sectors in your hard disk. Hard disks, especially those with formatted capacity of more than 21M, frequently have a few bad sectors. These bad sectors are marked as unusable in the FAT and are not allocated to a file.

Checking Partition Status

You can check the status of your partition table by using the FDISK command's /STATUS switch. To do so, type **FDISK /STATUS** at the DOS prompt, and then press Enter. The command shows you a table of your hard disk's partition information (see fig. 7.7) without starting the FDISK program.

```
                                Fixed Disk Drive Status
    Disk    Drv    Mbytes    Free    Usage
     1                639       0     100%
             C:       40
             D:      120
             E:       42
             F:      120
             G:       75
             H:       59
```

Fig. 7.7

Displaying disk partition information.

NOTE If you boot your PC with a version of DOS earlier than 4.0 and you are using a disk larger than 32M, do not expect to find everything that you stored on the disk. Versions of DOS earlier than 4.0 are not designed for extensions that accommodate disks larger than 32M. Furthermore, some third-party disk-utility programs cannot handle the DOS 4.0, 5.0, and 6.0 extensions of the boot sector. If you have DOS 4.0 or a later version and want to use a disk optimizer (such as Norton Utilities) or a rapid-backup program (such as FAST-BACK), make sure that the version you have can handle DOS partitions larger than 32M. (If you use DOS 6.0's DEFRAG or MSBACKUP utility, however, you need not worry.)

Unformatting a Disk

Sooner or later, virtually all PC users format a disk accidentally. The UNFORMAT command (available only in DOS 5.0 and 6.0) is your best chance to undo the damage. UNFORMAT is designed to unformat hard and floppy disks. UNFORMAT also can help you recover from accidental change or damage to a hard disk's partition table. (**Note:** You can only unformat floppy disks that were formatted with the DOS 5.0 or 6.0 FORMAT command. UNFORMAT does not work on floppy disks formatted with earlier versions of DOS.) UNFORMAT has two primary uses:

■ To recover files after an accidental format

■ To rebuild a damaged partition table on your hard disk

Because UNFORMAT completely rebuilds a disk's FAT, root directory, and boot record, use this command only as a last resort. If you accidentally delete a file, for example, use the DOS 6.0 UNDELETE command rather than the UNFORMAT to recover the file. If you accidentally format an entire disk, however, you must use UNFORMAT to recover the disk's data. The degree of success you have in recovering all files depends on which version of DOS you used to format the disk, what switches you used, and what you have done to the disk since you reformatted it.

> **WARNING:** If the disk that you accidentally formatted is a hard disk, *do not* install DOS on it because the DOS files overwrite files you want to recover. *Do not* copy or save files of any kind to the reformatted hard disk. If you have to reboot the computer, use a bootable floppy disk.

NOTE   The DOS 5.0 and 6.0 FORMAT commands create a *MIRROR image file* during the safe format procedure. The MIRROR image file contains a copy of your hard disk's FAT, root directory, and boot record, and saves this information in a safe place on the disk. At the same time, FORMAT creates a hidden file named MIRORSAV.FIL, which contains information required by DOS to locate the MIRROR image file. (This file is "visible" only to the UNFORMAT command and cannot be listed by the DIR command unless you use the /AH switch.) If you use the /U switch with FORMAT, however, no MIRROR image file is created.

When you want to use UNFORMAT after an accidental format, use the following syntax:

UNFORMAT d: */J /L /P /TEST /U*

d: is the drive that contains the disk to be unformatted.

/J causes UNFORMAT to verify that the MIRROR image file accurately reflects the current disk information.

/L searches a formatted disk and lists the file and directory names found.

/P sends all output to a printer.

/TEST provides a test run to indicate whether UNFORMAT can unformat a disk successfully.

/U attempts to unformat a disk without the benefit of a MIRROR image file.

When you want to use UNFORMAT to rebuild a hard-disk partition table, use the following syntax:

UNFORMAT /PARTN */L /P*

/PARTN causes the command to try to rebuild the hard-disk partition.

/L displays the current partition table.

/P sends all output to a printer.

To access help for the UNFORMAT command, use the UNFORMAT /? and HELP UNFORMAT commands. These commands display short help screens summarizing the parameters available in UNFORMAT (see fig. 7.8). Each parameter listed is explained in the following sections.

```
C:\>unformat /?

Restores a disk erased by the FORMAT command or restructured by the RECOVER
command.

UNFORMAT drive: [/J]
UNFORMAT drive: [/U] [/L] [/TEST] [/P]
UNFORMAT /PARTN [/L]

  drive:   Specifies the drive to unformat.
  /J       Verifies that the mirror files agree with the system information
           on the disk.
  /U       Unformats without using MIRROR files.
  /L       Lists all file and directory names found, or, when used with the
           /PARTN switch, displays current partition tables.
  /TEST    Displays information but does not write changes to disk.
  /P       Sends output messages to printer connected to LPT1.
  /PARTN   Restores disk partition tables.

MIRROR, UNDELETE, and UNFORMAT Copyright (C) 1987-1991 Central Point
Software,Inc.

C:\>_
```

Fig. 7.8

The UNFORMAT help screen.

Using the MIRROR Image File To Recover from an Accidental Format

Suppose that you just accidentally formatted a hard disk (or used the DOS RECOVER command incorrectly—see the Command Reference for a discussion of RECOVER). You need to use UNFORMAT, which uses the information stored in the MIRROR image file to restore the FAT, root directory, and boot record to their pre-formatting condition.

To unformat a disk that was safe-formatted, type the following command at the DOS prompt:

UNFORMAT *d*:

(Remember to replace the *d* with the letter of the drive that contains the disk you want to unformat.)

UNFORMAT first tells you to insert a disk into the specified drive and to press Enter. When you follow these instructions, the computer beeps and displays the following warning message:

```
Restores the system area of your disk with
the image file created by MIRROR

WARNING!                WARNING!

This should be used ONLY to recover from the inadvertent use
of the DOS FORMAT command or the DOS RECOVER command.
Any other use of UNFORMAT may cause you to lose data!
Files modified since the MIRROR file was created may be lost.
```

Next, UNFORMAT displays the following message

```
The LAST time MIRROR was used was at hh:mm on mm-dd-yy.
```

For the *hh:mm* and *mm-dd-yy* parameters in these messages, UNFORMAT substitutes the time and date at which MIRROR.FIL was created. UNFORMAT again causes your computer to beep and then displays the following message, substituting the correct drive letter for d:

```
The MIRROR image file has been validated.
Are you SURE you want to update the SYSTEM area
of your drive d (Y/N)?
```

Type **Y** and press Enter to indicate that you want to continue updating the system area of the formatted disk; type **N** and press Enter to quit UNFORMAT and return to the command prompt.

If you choose to update the system area, UNFORMAT writes to the disk's system area the FAT, root directory, and boot record that have been stored in MIRROR.FIL.

NOTE If you have used DOS 5.0 or if you use PC Tools, you have (or had) a separate program called MIRROR. This program creates the same MIRROR image file that the FORMAT command creates. If you used this program on a disk that you are unformatting, the messages you see are slightly different because UNFORMAT finds previous copies of the MIRROR image file. The command displays a message similar to the following:

```
The LAST time MIRROR was used was at hh:mm on mm-dd-yy.
The PRIOR time MIRROR was used was at hh:mm on mm-dd-yy.
If you wish to use the LAST file as indicated
above, press 'L.' If you wish to use the PRIOR
file as indicated above, press 'P.' Press ESC
to cancel UNFORMAT.
```

Suppose that someone in your office accidentally formats drive C, a hard disk that has been protected by MIRROR. You can use UNFORMAT to restore the disk to the way it was before the format—if you have not written any files to the disk. Type the following command at the DOS prompt, and then press Enter:

UNFORMAT C:

UNFORMAT displays the following message:

> The LAST time MIRROR was used was at *hh:mm* on *mm-dd-yy*.
> The MIRROR image file has been validated.
>
> Are you SURE you want to update the SYSTEM area
> of your drive C (Y/N)?

Type **Y** and then press Enter. UNFORMAT uses the MIRROR image file to rewrite the FAT and root directory, restoring the hard disk to the way it was before the accidental formatting (or the last time you issued the MIRROR command).

Recovering from an Accidental Format without a MIRROR Image File

Even if a MIRROR image file is not available for a formatted disk, the UNFORMAT command may be able to recover most of the data. This process takes more time than if a MIRROR image file were available, however, and it does not recover files that were in the disk's root directory.

To use UNFORMAT to unformat a hard disk on which no current MIRROR image file exists, use the following syntax:

UNFORMAT d: /U */L /TEST /P*

Replace **d:** with the letter of the drive that contains the accidentally formatted disk.

The **/U** switch stands for "unformat" and tells UNFORMAT that you are not using a MIRROR image file created by FORMAT.

The optional */L* parameter causes UNFORMAT to list all files and directories found during the UNFORMAT operation. Similarly, */P* causes UNFORMAT to send the entire UNFORMAT process to your printer.

Use the */TEST* option to run a simulation of the process so that you can see which files UNFORMAT can recover before any changes are written to the hard disk.

After you execute the command, UNFORMAT displays the following message:

```
CAUTION !!

This attempts to recover all files lost after a
FORMAT, assuming you've NOT been using MIRROR. This
method cannot guarantee complete recovery of your files.

The search-phase is safe: nothing is altered on the disk.
You will be prompted again before changes are written to
the disk.
Using drive d:
Are you SURE you want to do this?
If so, type Y; to cancel the operation, press any other
key.
```

To continue with the unformat operation, type **Y** and then press Enter. Press any other key to cancel the process.

While searching the disk, UNFORMAT displays the following message:

```
Searching disk…
pp% searched, mm subdirectories found.
Files found in the root: 0
Subdirectories found in the root: mm
```

UNFORMAT does not find any root-level files, but it substitutes for *mm* the number of root-level subdirectories that it finds. (Refer to Chapter 6, "Understanding Disks and Files," for a discussion of files, and see Chapter 8, "Understanding and Managing Directories," for a discussion of the root directory.) As UNFORMAT searches the disk, the command continually updates the last message, substituting the percentage of the disk read for *pp* and the number of subdirectories found for *mm*.

After UNFORMAT completes its search of the disk's data, the command lists the subdirectories found. Depending on which version of the FOR-MAT command was used, UNFORMAT may or may not be able to re-cover the names of subdirectories. If it cannot, UNFORMAT gives each subdirectory a name in the format SUBDIR.*nnn,* with *nnn* representing a number ranging from 1 to 512. If UNFORMAT can find the subdirectory names, it displays them and then displays a message similar to the following:

```
Walking the directory tree to locate all files…

Path=D:\
Path=D:\DIRNAME\
Path=D:\
```

In this message, *D* is the drive name, and *DIRNAME* is the subdirectory. This message is repeated for each subdirectory found. UNFORMAT then lists the number of files found, including subdirectories, and displays the following warning:

```
Files found: nn
Warning!  The next step writes changes to disk.
Are you sure you want to do this?

If so, type Y; to cancel the operation, press any other
key.
```

To proceed with the unformat operation, type **Y** and press Enter. UNFORMAT checks for file fragmentation.

If you have not used a program such as PC Tools Compress to unfragment the files on your hard disk, individual files may be broken into fragments on the hard disk. When UNFORMAT locates a fragmented file, the command has no way to find the next segment of the file; therefore, UNFORMAT asks whether you want to truncate or delete the file. UNFORMAT tells you the total size of the file as well as the number of bytes in the first fragment. To recover this fragment of the file, type **T** and press Enter. To direct UNFORMAT to omit this file from the new directory, type **D** and press Enter.

After UNFORMAT deletes or truncates all fragmented files, it rebuilds the FAT, root directory, and boot record by using the information found during the search. Finally, UNFORMAT indicates how many files were recovered and displays the message Operation completed.

At the end of the process, most files that were neither truncated nor deleted are intact, but UNFORMAT may include in a file data that doesn't belong to that file. This error can occur if a file is fragmented into two blocks of data that at some point are separated on the disk. If the other file is later deleted, leaving an unallocated space, this space may seem to UNFORMAT to be part of the file. The only way to discover this type of error is to use the file. If the file is a program, run it; if the file is not a program, display the file's contents.

Rebuilding a Partition Table

UNFORMAT also enables you to recover from a corrupted hard-disk partition table. Such an error normally generates the DOS message Invalid drive specification. To recover from this problem, you first must issue the UNFORMAT command with the /PARTN switch and then use UNFORMAT without this parameter to restore the FAT, root directory, and boot sector.

To recover from a corrupted hard-disk partition table, follow these steps:

1. Boot your computer (with a floppy disk, if necessary) and display the DOS prompt.

2. Change to a drive that contains the UNFORMAT file, UNFORMAT.COM. If your only hard disk is inaccessible because of partition-table corruption, use a copy of DOS on a floppy disk. (UNFORMAT.COM is contained on the Startup disk, one of the disks used during DOS installation.)

3. Type the following command at the DOS prompt:

   UNFORMAT /PARTN

   UNFORMAT prompts you to insert the disk containing the file PARTNSAV.FIL and to type the name of that disk drive.

4. Insert the disk that contains the copy of the partition table created by MIRROR (see Chapter 18, "Getting the Most from Your Hard Drive," for more information).

5. Type the letter of this drive and press Enter.

   MIRROR rebuilds the partition table from the file PARTNSAV.FIL found on the floppy disk. After UNFORMAT has rebuilt the partition table, the program prompts you to insert a master DOS disk into drive A and press Enter. To complete this process, you need a bootable backup disk that contains your system files and the UNFORMAT command. (If you have not yet made a bootable backup disk, refer to the explanation of the /S switch in "Using FORMAT's Switches" earlier in this chapter.)

6. Insert a bootable DOS disk into the A drive, and then press Enter. UNFORMAT causes your computer to reboot.

7. Use the copy of UNFORMAT on the floppy to restore the FAT, root directory, and boot record, following the steps described in "Using the MIRROR Image File To Recover from an Accidental Format" earlier in this chapter.

Naming Disks with LABEL

The external command LABEL adds, modifies, or changes a disk's volume label. In DOS, a *volume label* is a name given to a physical or logical disk. The LABEL command is available in PC DOS 3.0 and later versions and in MS-DOS 3.1 and later versions.

If a disk's volume label is blank (if you or another user pressed Enter when FORMAT or LABEL prompted for the label), you can use the LABEL command to add a volume label.

DOS displays the volume label when you issue commands such as VOL, CHKDSK, DIR, and TREE. In DOS 3.2 through DOS 4.0, FORMAT asks for a hard disk's volume label before reformatting the disk. Giving each disk (physical and logical) a volume label is a good idea. A disk with a unique volume label is easier to identify than one that doesn't have a label.

The syntax for the LABEL command is shown in the following:

LABEL *d:label*

d: is the name of the drive that holds the disk you want to label.

label, the optional label text that you supply as the new volume label, can include up to 11 characters. (The acceptable characters for a volume label are listed in the section "Adding a Volume Label" earlier in this chapter.) DOS immediately updates the specified or default drive's label with no warning prompt. If you do not supply the *label* parameter, LABEL automatically prompts you for a new label.

To change the current volume label on a disk, enter the following command:

LABEL

DOS responds with a message similar to the following:

```
Volume label in C is BOOT DISK
Volume serial number is AB02-07E8
Volume label (11 characters, ENTER for none)?
```

You enter the text for the volume label; DOS assigns the new label. If you simply press Enter in response to the prompt, you are telling DOS to delete the current label without replacing it. DOS confirms your decision by displaying the message Delete current volume label (Y/N)?

If you type **Y**, and then press Enter, DOS deletes the current label. If you press Enter only or type any character other than **Y** or **N**, DOS repeats the prompt.

Keep in mind the following special restrictions when you use LABEL:

- You cannot use the LABEL command in a networked drive.

- In DOS 3.2 and later versions, you cannot use LABEL on a disk in a drive that is affected by the SUBST or ASSIGN command.

NOTE   Some third-party programs can edit the volume label of a hard disk formatted with a version of DOS earlier than 3.1. Ask your computer dealer to recommend one of these third-party programs or to upgrade your DOS version to 6.0.

Examining Volume Labels with VOL

The internal command VOL is convenient when you want to view a disk's volume label or to verify that a label exists. VOL accesses the disk's volume label from the root directory and then displays the label created during the disk's formatting or modified by a subsequent LABEL command.

You can use VOL freely because it is a display-only command; it does not change any files or the label name.

The syntax of the VOL command, shown in the following, is simple:

VOL *d:*

d: is the optional name of the drive whose volume label you want to see. If you omit a value for *d:*, DOS displays the label for the default drive.

To see the volume label of the disk in drive A, for example, type the following command, and then press Enter:

VOL A:

DOS responds with a message similar to the following:

```
Volume in drive A: is WORK DISK 1.Z
Volume serial number is AB2F-1A7E
```

CHKDSK, TREE, and DIR include the volume-label display in their output.

Using SYS To Transfer the DOS System

All DOS disks have a DOS file system, but only disks with the DOS system files and COMMAND.COM can be used to start the computer. The external command SYS transfers (copies) the hidden system files from a bootable system disk. Some versions of SYS (in DOS versions before 3.3) do not transfer COMMAND.COM and, thus, require you to use COPY to transfer COMMAND.COM to the target disk. DOS 3.3 and later versions transfer COMMAND.COM as a part of the operation of SYS.

As explained earlier in this chapter, you can make a disk bootable by using the /S switch with the FORMAT command. You can use the SYS command when you need to make an already formatted disk bootable. The disk must have room for the system files that SYS intends to transfer, and those system files must be compatible with your version of DOS.

To use SYS successfully, observe the following rules:

■ The destination disk must be formatted.

■ The destination disk must contain sufficient free space for the two hidden system files and COMMAND.COM (183,808 bytes for DOS 6.0 system files), must already contain earlier versions of the system files, or must have been formatted with the /B switch.

■ In DOS 3.3 or earlier versions, system files have to be contiguous. If a disk contains user files and does not contain the two system files, DOS issues the error message No room for system on destination disk.

■ You cannot use SYS in a networked drive. If you want to use SYS in a networked drive, you must log off the network or pause your drive. (For the exact restrictions, consult your system's network documentation).

■ You must include the destination-drive parameter in the SYS command. SYS will not transfer a copy of the system to the current drive; the destination must be a different drive. The source drive for the system files always is the current drive. In DOS 4.0 and later versions, you also can specify a source-drive parameter (meaning that you can have a source other than the current drive).

 NOTE If you are unsure which DOS version is on the boot disk, you can issue the VER command to have DOS display the version. Remember that one of the hidden files is the input-output (I/O) system, which contains device drivers for the implementation of DOS on a particular computer. Although many implementations of the I/O system file are compatible with one another, some may not be. For this reason, do not mix different DOS versions or implementations when you use the SYS command. In fact, never mix different versions of DOS on one computer.

The syntax for the SYS command is shown in the following:

SYS d:

If you are using DOS 4.0 or a later version, you also can provide the source drive for the system files, using the following syntax:

SYS *ds:* **dd:**

dd: is the target, or *destination*, drive for the system files. You must specify a drive name (letter) for drive **dd:**. The drive specified by *ds:* is the drive used for the *source* of the system files.

Suppose that you are using DOS 6.0 with a hard disk and have an empty disk that you want to make bootable for use with another computer. Follow these steps:

1. Insert the formatted disk into drive A and make sure that your current PATH setting includes the directory that contains SYS. (For information on the DOS path, see Chapter 8, "Understanding and Managing Directories.")

2. Type the following command:

   SYS C: A:

SYS replies with the message System transferred. The system files now are on the disk in drive A. You now can use this disk to boot your computer.

NOTE The C: in step 2 is optional depending on whether drive C is current. If you are logged onto drive C, C: already is the default source for the system files, and therefore, you don't need to add it to the command line.

Analyzing a Disk with CHKDSK

The external command CHKDSK analyzes a floppy or hard disk. CHKDSK checks a disk's FAT, directories, and, if you want, the fragmentation of the files on the disk. (*Fragmentation* is the scattering of parts of a file across a disk.)

CHKDSK is DOS's self-test command. CHKDSK makes sure that the internal tables that keep files in control are in order. Although the technical details of how CHKDSK performs its analysis are beyond the scope of most casual DOS users, the better you understand CHKDSK, the more comfortable you will be when the command uncovers problems. Just because you don't understand exactly how CHKDSK works doesn't mean that you must avoid using it.

CHKDSK checks for the following problems in the FAT:

- Unlinked cluster chains (lost clusters)
- Multiply-linked clusters (cross-linked files)
- Invalid next-cluster-in-chain values (invalid cluster numbers)
- Defective sectors where the FAT is stored

CHKDSK checks for the following problems in the directory system:

- Invalid cluster numbers (out of range)
- Invalid file attributes in entries (attribute values that DOS does not recognize)
- Damage to subdirectory entries (CHKDSK cannot process them)
- Damage to a directory's integrity (its files cannot be accessed)

Optionally, CHKDSK repairs problems in the FAT caused by lost clusters and writes the contents of the lost clusters to files. CHKDSK also can display all files and their paths (paths are discussed in Chapter 8, "Understanding and Managing Directories").

NOTE Running CHKDSK periodically on your hard disk and important floppies is good practice. Because the FAT and the hierarchical directory system work together to track file names and locations, a problem in the FAT or one of the directories is always a serious problem. In all likelihood, CHKDSK can find and correct most problems in a disk's internal bookkeeping tables.

The CHKDSK command uses the following syntax:

CHKDSK *d:path\filename.ext /F/V*

d: is the optional drive name to be checked. If the drive name is omitted, DOS uses the current drive.

path is the optional path to the directory that contains the files you want to analyze for fragmentation. If you omit a path name but specify a file name in the command line, DOS uses the current directory.

filename.ext represents the optional file name and extension for the file to be analyzed for fragmentation. If you don't include a file name, CHKDSK does not check for fragmentation.

/F is the optional *fix* switch, which instructs CHKDSK to repair any problems that it encounters.

/V is the *verbose* switch, which instructs CHKDSK to provide file names on-screen as it analyzes the files.

When the process is complete, CHKDSK displays a screen report of its findings. This report summarizes disk and system memory usage. Figures 7.9 and 7.10 show typical CHKDSK reports.

> Take advantage of the CHKDSK command's capability to make a "dry run" of its checking routines. You can use this feature to assess reported problems. Before issuing CHKDSK with the /F switch, for example, issue the command without the switch. CHKDSK without /F prompts you if the command finds a problem (as though you had used the /F switch). After you have assessed the findings of CHKDSK and have taken remedial actions (such as those that follow), you can issue CHKDSK with the /F switch so that the command can fix the problems that it finds.

T I P

DOS stores every file as a chain of clusters. (Each cluster is a group of sectors; clusters are referred to as *allocation units* in DOS 4.0 and later versions.) Each entry in the disk's directory points to the entry in the FAT that contains the list of clusters allocated to a file.

CHKDSK processes each directory, starting at the root and following each subdirectory. CHKDSK checks the cluster chain by using the directory entry's FAT pointer and then compares the size of the file (in bytes) with the size of the FAT's allocation (in clusters). CHKDSK expects to find enough chained clusters in the FAT to accommodate the file, but not more than are necessary. If CHKDSK finds too many clusters, it displays the following message:

```
Allocation error,

size adjusted
```

The file is truncated (excess clusters are deallocated) if you use the /F switch.

CHKDSK makes sure that each of the FAT's clusters is allocated only once. In rare circumstances—for example, if power problems or hardware failures occur—DOS can give two different files the same cluster. By checking each cluster chain for cross-linked files, CHKDSK can report mixed-up files. Each time you see the message `filename is cross-linked on cluster nnnnn`, copy the file reported in *filename* to another disk. CHKDSK reports another file with the same message. Copy the second file to another disk also. Chances are good that the contents of the two files are mixed up, but you have a better chance of recovering the files if you save them to another disk before CHKDSK "fixes" the problem.

CHKDSK expects every cluster in the FAT to be available for allocation, part of a legitimate directory-based cluster chain, or a marked bad cluster. If CHKDSK encounters any clusters or cluster chains that are not pointed to by a directory entry, CHKDSK issues the message `x lost clusters in Y chains`. CHKDSK then asks `Convert lost chains to files (Y/N)`? This message appears even if you didn't use the /F switch.

If you used the /F switch and you press Y, CHKDSK turns each cluster chain into a file in the root directory. Each file created has the name *FILEnnnn.CHK*. (*nnnn* is a number, starting with 0000, that increments by 1 for each file created by CHKDSK.) If you did not use the /F switch and you press Y, nothing happens. CHKDSK, however, does tell you what it would have done had you used the /F switch.

> **NOTE** You can use the DOS TYPE command to examine the contents of a text file, and you may be able to use a word processing program to put the text back into its original file. The TYPE command doesn't do you any good, however, for a binary (program or data) file. If the problem is with a program file, you may need to use the DOS COMP or FC command to compare your disk's binary files with their counterparts from your master disks.

```
C:/>chkdsk

Volume EL MONSTRO! created 11-11-1992 4:33p
Volume Serial Number is 195D-7B68
Errors found, F parameter not specified
Corrections will not be written to disk


       84 lost allocation units found in 4 chains.
   172032 bytes disk space would be freed

 32974848 bytes total disk space
    83968 bytes in 4 hidden files
    83968 bytes in 27 directories
 31514624 bytes in 1341 user files
  1120256 bytes available on disk

     2048 bytes in each allocation unit
    16101 total allocation units on disk
      547 available allocation units on disk

   655360 total bytes memory
   592112 bytes free
```

Fig. 7.9

A typical report produced by CHKDSK with **no** parameters.

```
E:\>chkdsk \que\msdos6\*.*

Volume Data Files  created 01-31-1992 6:00p
Volume Serial Number is 195D-7B68

 32974848 bytes total disk space
  1693696 bytes in 5 hidden files
   122880 bytes in 50 directories
 31006720 bytes in 1217 user files
   151552 bytes available on disk

     2048 bytes in each allocation unit
    16101 total allocation units on disk
       74 available allocation units on disk

   655360 total bytes memory
   562416 bytes free

E:\QUE\MSDOS6\D6-CH07.SAM Contains 2 non-contiguous
blocks

E:\>_
```

Fig. 7.10

The report produced when CHKDSK is issued with a path.

The disk does not lose any sectors physically. A lost-cluster report does not indicate that the clusters are bad; lost clusters indicate only that DOS made a bookkeeping error in the FAT, which makes some clusters appear to DOS to be lost. The clusters are not tied to a directory entry, yet they are marked as being in use.

The lost-cluster problem is most likely to occur when you are running a disk-intensive program such as dBASE IV or WordPerfect. Although these programs are not to blame for lost clusters, programs such as these increase DOS's exposure to bookkeeping errors. Programs that use disk files to swap sections of program and data too large for memory may ask DOS to read and write work files hundreds of times in an afternoon of computing. Power glitches or interruptions, heated hardware components, and electrical interference can turn a cluster-chain number into a different number at the critical moment when DOS is writing the number into the FAT. Still, when you consider the millions of bytes for which DOS is responsible in a typical PC, DOS's reliability record is superb. CHKDSK recovers most clusters that DOS bookkeeping errors lose.

When you use CHKDSK, the following rules apply:

- CHKDSK begins execution immediately after you enter the command. If you use a one-disk system, use the drive B: parameter to allow time for DOS to change from the disk containing CHKDSK to the disk you want to analyze.

- CHKDSK reports problems found during operation but does not repair the problems unless you include the /F switch in the command line.

- Run CHKDSK at least once a week. Run CHKDSK daily during periods of extreme file activity.

- CHKDSK converts lost clusters to files if you type **Y** in response to the Convert lost chains to files (Y/N)? prompt. CHKDSK places the files in the disk's root directory under the name *FILEnnnn.CHK*.

- If CHKDSK terminates because the root directory has no more entries available for converted chain files, clear the current *FILEnnnn.CHK* files by erasing them or by copying them to another disk or directory. After the files are cleared from the root, reissue CHKDSK.

For a sample CHKDSK exercise, suppose that you are copying a group of files from your hard disk to a floppy. During the copy operation, the lights flicker and then go out completely. In a few seconds, power is restored to normal. Your computer reboots DOS and awaits your input.

Power problems during file operations such as COPY can cause DOS's bookkeeping job to be interrupted. The directory and the FAT may contain errors. To ensure that no errors go undetected, issue the CHKDSK command on the floppy disk, as follows:

CHKDSK A:

CHKDSK begins to analyze the floppy disk in drive A and then displays the following report:

```
Volume SCRATCH DISK created 09-12-1989  11:23a
Errors found, F parameter not specified
Corrections will not be written to disk
A:\DBASE1.OVL
Allocation error, size adjusted
   730112 bytes in total disk space
   415744 bytes in 4 user files
   314368 bytes available on disk
     1024 bytes in each allocation unit
      713 total allocation units on disk
      307 available allocation units on disk
   655360 total bytes memory
   409856 bytes free
```

Because you did not use the /F switch, CHKDSK did not repair the problem. You can examine the problem further before reissuing CHKDSK with the /F switch. Look at a directory listing of the files on drive A to see whether you can determine the nature of the allocation problem. Consider the following directory listing:

```
Volume in drive A is SCRATCH DISK
Volume Serial Number is 1982-BA9A
Directory of  A:\
DBSETUP  OVL    147968 10-21-88  12:22a
DBASE3   OVL     85024 12-28-88   9:04p
DBASE6   OVL    114832 10-20-88  11:22p
DBASE1   OVL         0 09-12-89   1:46a
       4 File(s)     314368 bytes free
```

The last directory entry, DBASE1.OVL, shows a file size of 0 bytes. A 0-byte file size never results from a successful COPY operation, so the file's directory-size entry is suspicious. To clarify the nature of the allocation error, compare the CHKDSK report with the directory listing generated by the DIR command.

The CHKDSK report shows 415,744 bytes in the four files. When you total the bytes in the directory listing, you can account for only 347,824 bytes in the four files. Both CHKDSK and the directory listing show 314,368 bytes available on the disk. CHKDSK and DIR both report available disk bytes as the number of bytes in unallocated disk clusters—not the difference between the capacity of the disk and the number of bytes in the disk's files. Both commands get the disk's remaining capacity indirectly from the FAT.

Because both commands agree on the FAT's calculation, you must assume that the directory entry for DBASE1.OVL is incorrect in its reflection of the file's size. CHKDSK can repair the directory entry. Issue the CHKDSK command again, this time using the /F switch, as shown in the following:

CHKDSK A: /F

CHKDSK displays the following message:

```
Volume SCRATCH DISK created 09-12-1989   11:23a
A:\DBASE1.OVL
Allocation error, size adjusted
 730112 bytes in total disk space
 415744 bytes in 4 user files
 314368 bytes available on disk
    1024 bytes in each allocation unit
     713 total allocation units on disk
     307 available allocation units on disk
 655360 total bytes memory
 409856 bytes free
```

To confirm that the suspected directory problem is repaired, list the directory of the disk again. The following report appears:

```
Volume in drive A is SCRATCH DISK
Volume Serial Number is 1982-BA9A
Directory of  A:\
DBSETUP  OVL     147968 10-21-88   12:22a
DBASE3   OVL      85024 12-28-88    9:04p
DBASE6   OVL     114832 10-20-88   11:22p
DBASE1   OVL      65536 09-12-89    1:46a
        4 File(s)        314368 bytes free
```

Notice that DBASE1.OVL shows 65,536 bytes rather than 0. The available capacity of the disk remains unchanged. Now the total bytes shown in the directory listing are within a few thousand of the difference between the disk's capacity and the total bytes free. You can account for this small difference by considering the fact that some of the files do not fill their last allocated cluster. The error in the directory is corrected, and the disk is ready for use again.

Chapter Summary

This chapter presented the important FORMAT command and other disk-level DOS commands. The chapter covered the following key points:

- You must format both hard and floppy disks before you use them to store files.

- Formatting sets up a directory for file name and status information, and also creates a file-allocation table (FAT) that tracks the availability of storage space on the disk.

- FORMAT accepts several switches, including the /S switch, which makes the disk bootable; the /F switch, which enables you to specify disk capacity; the /U switch, which performs an unconditional format; and the /Q switch, which performs a quick format.

- Before you can format a hard disk, you must partition it by using FDISK.

- Disk partitions can be DOS partitions or partitions of another operating system.

- DOS partitions are either *primary* (bootable) partitions or *extended* partitions divided into one or more logical drives.

- DOS views logical drives as being the same as physical disks and assigns each logical drive its own drive letter.

- The UNFORMAT command restores a disk that has been formatted inadvertently.

- The LABEL command adds or changes a disk's volume label.

- The VOL command displays a disk's volume label.

- The SYS command transfers the DOS system files from a bootable disk to another disk. You can use SYS to upgrade a disk's DOS version.

■ CHKDSK is a disk-level command that finds and fixes problems. CHKDSK analyzes a disk's FAT and directory system.

■ When you include the /F switch in the command, CHKDSK can repair most problems that it encounters.

The next chapter, "Understanding and Managing Directories," introduces DOS's hierarchical directory system, explaining how to use DOS commands in a multilevel-directory system.

Understanding and Managing Directories

This chapter covers the DOS file-management strategy, teaching you the role of directories and explaining their hierarchical structure. The chapter explains in detail how to understand and navigate the path to each file and program on your disks. You also learn how to change special file attributes that determine such characteristics as whether a file can be erased, listed in the directory, or accessed as a read-only file.

Key Terms Used in This Chapter

Directory	A disk-based table of file names and other file-related information that DOS uses with the file allocation table (FAT) to access a file's data content.
Root directory	A master directory created on each disk by FORMAT.
Subdirectory	An additional named directory created by a user.

continues

Key Terms Used in This Chapter continued

Attribute	A directory-based indicator of a file's status. Attributes include read-only, archive, system, hidden, and volume label.
Relative path	The path from the current directory where the root and intervening directories are taken from DOS defaults.
Absolute path	The path named from the root directory, including all intervening subdirectories.

Reviewing Your Knowledge of Disks

To help you learn about directories, a quick review follows on some of the concepts concerning DOS disks. As you recall, DOS uses a drive name or parameter to reference each disk drive on your system; DOS uses letters, such as A, B, and C, as names for the drives.

Before DOS can use a disk in a drive, the disk must be formatted. The FORMAT operation establishes key tables on each disk along with vital information about the disk's format. DOS uses the tables and disk information as a template for managing the disk's storage capabilities. When you format a disk, DOS creates a root directory and file allocation table on the disk.

Because each disk has the necessary tables to act as an independent storage medium, DOS enables you to use multiple disks. DOS keeps track of the logged drive and uses that drive as the current drive. DOS stores the current drive's name internally. When you issue a command without an optional drive parameter, DOS uses the stored drive letter. If you type the command DIR without specifying a drive letter, for example, DOS produces a directory listing from the current drive. In this case, DOS appears to approach its file system as a single set of files.

If you use a drive parameter with a command, DOS accesses the file-system tables from the specified disk drive. When you type the command DIR B:, DOS produces a listing of the contents of the disk in drive B even if drive A is the current logged drive. DOS commands can access files on all types of disks. If DOS can format a disk on your system, DOS can use that disk. With a drive parameter, you have immediate access to any disk on your system, and you access the files on any disk by using commands that work with any other disk.

Understanding the Role of Directories

The directory is an important table created by the FORMAT command on each disk. Each DOS-formatted disk has one directory, called the *root directory* because it is the root of the disk's file system. DOS uses the directory as a kind of index system for finding files. Individual entries in this index system are called *directory entries*. DOS allows for a fixed number of directory entries in the root directory. This number is the same for disks with the same format but varies with different formats. Disks with larger capacities have more root directory entries.

By using DOS commands, you can see much of the makeup of a directory. The DIR command accesses and displays selected parts of directory entries, as in this example:

```
Volume in drive A is QUE BRUCE
Volume  Serial Number is 0773-09E8

Directory of  A:\

DBSETUP     OVL          147968 10-21-88      12:22a
DBASE3      OVL           85024 12-28-88       9:04p
DBASE6      OVL          114832 10-20-88      11:22p
DBASE1      OVL           65536 09-12-89       1:46a

        4 file(s)         413360 bytes
                          314368 bytes free
```

The DIR command, however, does not display *all* the elements of a directory entry. Table 8.1 lists the components of a directory entry.

Table 8.1 The Main Features of DOS Directories

Feature	Example	What Is Stored
File name	THANKYOU	Eight-character file prefix
File name extension	DOC	Three-character file suffix
File attributes	R (read-only)	Special status information about this file used by DOS
Time	10:22	The time of creation or last modification
Date	11-14-91	The date of creation or last modification
Starting cluster	576	The number of the first cluster allocated to this file by DOS in the FAT
File size	1024 bytes	The number of bytes in this file

You undoubtedly recognize the file name, extension, time, and date components of a directory entry as the ones displayed by the DIR command. DIR also displays the file size. These components, or *fields*, of a directory entry contain information useful to you as well as to DOS (see fig. 8.1). DIR displays this information to assist your file-management activities.

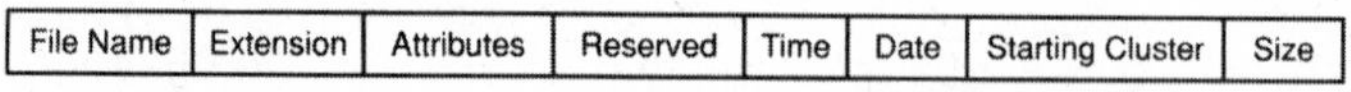

Fig. 8.1

The fields of a directory entry.

File Name	Extension	Attributes	Reserved	Time	Date	Starting Cluster	Size

NOTE   DOS also stores volume labels in directory entries, using the combined file name and extension fields to form an 11-byte (11-character) field (see Chapter 7, "Preparing and Maintaining Disks"). The FORMAT and LABEL commands write your choice of a volume name into the root directory entry for a disk. DOS knows that the directory entry is a volume label because the volume label attribute for the entry is set.

The starting cluster and file attribute fields, shown in table 8.1 and in figure 8.1, are not included in the DIR command's displayed output. The starting cluster field contains the cluster number of the first cluster

DOS has allocated for a particular file's storage. The file attribute field contains special status information that DOS uses to determine how the file is to be managed internally. Because these two fields are not as visible or as self-explanatory as the fields displayed in the DIR listing, the next two sections describe them in detail.

For Related Information

◀◀ "Preparing the Hard Disk," p. 195.

◀◀ "Dividing a Hard Disk with FDISK," p. 195.

◀◀ "Formatting a Hard Disk," p. 197.

FROM HERE...

Chaining through a File

The starting cluster field of a file's directory entry is the key to the file's storage allocation as tracked in the FAT (file allocation table). You recall that DOS creates a FAT for each disk during formatting. For each cluster (allocation unit) on the disk, the FAT indicates whether the cluster is allocated to a file. Much as a restaurant hostess looks at a table chart for a place to seat you, DOS looks at the FAT for available clusters when a file is created or enlarged. When you arrive early at a restaurant, it is nearly empty, and the hostess seats you in the general vicinity of other guests, leaving other sections of the restaurant unused. When DOS allocates files on a freshly formatted disk, DOS uses the first cluster and sequences through a connected series of clusters, leaving many clusters unused at the end of the FAT. When you leave the restaurant, the hostess marks your table as being available. Likewise, when you erase or shorten a file, DOS marks the released clusters in the FAT as being available and uses them to store another file.

You may have had a dining experience in which the hostess did not have enough adjacent tables to seat your entire party. Your group is fragmented across two or more tables with other parties seated at tables between the parts of your group. You can remain connected as a group by telling the waiter, "We're with those people over there," as you point to the other table.

When a DOS command or applications program asks DOS to store a file on the disk, DOS checks the FAT, finds the next available cluster, and stores a portion of the file there. If that cluster cannot accommodate the entire file, DOS finds the next available cluster and stores part of the file there. DOS does not look for the largest available block of clusters, so the entire file may not fit the first group of available clusters. If the disk has a great deal of file activity, a file may be split into many pieces, scattered around the disk. This disconnected cluster condition is known as *file fragmentation*. Although file fragmentation can slow DOS's access to the file, this method of storing files makes efficient use of all available space.

DOS connects all clusters of a file by recording in the current cluster's entry in the FAT where the next cluster is located. When a file is allocated to more than one cluster, each cluster entry in the FAT "points" to the next cluster that contains more of the file, using the next cluster number as a pointer. The result is a chain of clusters that comprises the map of a file's disk storage. The FAT, as a storage map, tells DOS exactly where to go on the disk to get all the parts of a file.

When you ask for a file by name, using a DOS command, DOS looks for the "who" identity of the file in the directory, which stores file names and starting clusters. To access the file from the disk, DOS needs to know the "where" identity of the file. Using the starting cluster, found in the directory, DOS then consults the FAT to identify the chain of clusters that holds the contents of the file.

> **CAUTION:** Do not use disk-unfragmenting utilities on a DoubleSpace drive.

NOTE   DOS uses the directory and the FAT to allocate and access files. If the values in these DOS tables become corrupted due to power surges, physical damage, or media failure, DOS cannot access the files and storage areas on the disk effectively. If you have important files on a damaged disk, you may be able to reduce the damage by using certain DOS commands.

The FORMAT command, by default, or when used with the quick option, makes a copy of the FAT, root directory, and boot sector and places the file in a safe place (see Chapter 7, "Preparing and Maintaining Disks"). If some calamity befalls any of these crucial tables, you can use the UNFORMAT command to recover them.

The CHKDSK command uses the directory and the FAT to check the proper tracking of each cluster and directory entry on a disk (see Chapter 7, "Preparing and Maintaining Disks"). CHKDSK detects improper relationships in the cluster chains of files and the sizes of directory entries. CHKDSK fixes a disk by adjusting improper file allocation sizes, eliminating circular references in cluster pointers, and making other technical adjustments in the FAT and directories.

The RECOVER command, included in DOS 5.0 and earlier versions, was designed to reestablish a file in a new location on disk with a new directory entry if the existing FAT or directory entries were damaged. Some of the recovered file's content, however, probably will be lost. RECOVER does include a provision to recover an entire damaged disk. This full version of the command is meant for *informed* users only, however, and even then should be used only as a last resort, because the command sometimes can cause more harm than good.

RECOVER is not included as a utility in DOS 6.0. If you upgraded from an earlier version to DOS 6.0, however, RECOVER still may reside on your hard disk. Do not use RECOVER to recover a DoubleSpace drive.

Understanding File Attributes

The file attribute field in the directory entry is a one-byte entry that stores a number of characteristics about each file but is not displayed in a normal directory listing. Each characteristic stored in the file attribute field is referred to as a file attribute. Each file can have more than one file attribute. Each file attribute is represented in the attribute byte by a single bit, often called an attribute bit. Table 8.2 lists the attributes and their purposes in DOS. You can view and modify most attribute bits by using the DOS Shell or the ATTRIB command; DOS manages some attribute bits directly.

Table 8.2 File Attributes and Their Meanings	
Attribute Bit	**Meaning**
Archive	This file has been created or modified since you issued the last DOS command that resets this attribute (such as BACKUP or XCOPY).
Hidden	This file is bypassed by most DOS file-management commands and does not appear in a directory listing. Hidden files, however, are listed by the DOS Shell in the file list area.
Read-only	This file can be accessed for information but cannot be erased or modified. (Note that you can erase a read-only file by using the DOS Shell.)

continues

Table 8.2 Continued

Attribute Bit ·	Meaning
Subdirectory	This attribute identifies the entry as a directory rather than data or a program.
System	This file is a DOS system file.
Volume label	This entry is the volume label for a disk. The entry does not identify an actual file.

The *archive attribute* works with certain DOS file-management commands to determine which files the commands process. XCOPY, for example, includes an optional switch that causes XCOPY to examine a file's archive attribute before copying the file to its destination. If the archive attribute is not turned on (set), XCOPY bypasses the file.

The underlying reason for having archive attributes is similar to the reason for having a small metal flag on a mailbox. The flag acts as a synchronizer of activity so that the carrier makes only necessary stops. The mail carrier passes by the mailbox each delivery day as part of the mail delivery and pickup operation. If the mail carrier has no mail to deliver to the box on a particular day, and no letters are being mailed, stopping at the box is a waste of the mail carrier's time. The owner of the mailbox can raise the red metal flag as an indicator that the box contains letters to mail, and the carrier, seeing the flag, stops to pick up the letters. After emptying the box, the carrier lowers the flag.

Likewise, the archive attribute of a file is a "flag" for the command that processes the file. When DOS adds or modifies the contents of a file, DOS sets the archive attribute, analogous to raising the mailbox flag. Commands that have the capability to use the archive attribute can "look" to see whether the flag (archive attribute) is raised (set) and then process the file only if the archive attribute is set. When commands like XCOPY and BACKUP see that the archive attribute is turned on in a file's directory listing, the commands assume that the file is new or has changed since the last XCOPY or BACKUP command. You can use the archive attribute in these ways to make copies or backups of files that have changed since your last backup or copy using XCOPY. If only a few files have been added to or changed on a disk, only a few files are included in the backup copy operation. DOS bypasses the files whose "flags" are not raised, saving time and disk space.

Some DOS commands automatically change the archive attribute when a file is added or modified. You can use such commands as XCOPY to reset the attributes. DOS also supplies the ATTRIB command, which directly changes a file's archive attribute. ATTRIB in DOS 3.2 and later versions turns on an archive attribute (sets it) and turns it off (resets, or clears, it). With ATTRIB, you can control the files that commands like XCOPY process. (Using XCOPY's /A switch or /M switch causes XCOPY to copy only files whose archive file attribute is set. See the Command Reference for a listing of all switches available for use with XCOPY.)

A file entry with the *hidden attribute* turned on is "invisible" to most DOS file-management commands. Hidden files have file names and extensions like normal user files but are not processed by the DIR and COPY commands. The two DOS system files on the boot disk are examples, as are the files that manage a DoubleSpace drive.

You can detect the presence of hidden files with the ATTRIB or CHKDSK command. Using ATTRIB (starting with DOS 5), you can also list hidden files. CHKDSK merely indicates the number of hidden files on the disk.

The *subdirectory attribute* indicates to DOS that the entry is not intended for a user file but for an additional directory called a subdirectory. (Subdirectories are explained in later sections of this chapter.) When carrying out file-management commands, DOS knows to bypass a file with the subdirectory attribute turned on.

The *system attribute* indicates that a file is an operating system file. The two DOS system files have this attribute in addition to the hidden attribute. You need not worry about the system attribute; it does not affect your DOS work.

The *volume label attribute* indicates that the directory entry involved is not for a file. This attribute tells DOS that the file name and extension fields should be combined to provide an 11-character volume label for the disk. Only a volume label entry can have this attribute set (turned on).

The archive, hidden, read-only, and system attributes are the only attributes you can change directly through DOS. DOS controls the other attributes without your intervention.

Changing File Attributes with the DOS Shell

You can change file attributes from within the DOS Shell, which enables you to change file attributes on one or more files at a time.

NOTE The following discussion focuses on how to change the file attributes of a selected file or files in the current directory on the logged disk. A discussion of how to use the DOS Shell to change directories and to log onto another disk is found in the second half of this chapter. See also Chapter 9, "Managing Your Files," for details on how to use the mouse and keyboard to select the files whose attributes you want to change.

To change the file attributes on a single file, start the DOS Shell and follow these steps:

1. Select the file list area of the DOS Shell window by pressing Tab until the title of the right-hand window is highlighted, or by clicking when the mouse pointer is in it.

2. In the file list area, select the file whose attributes you want to change. Use the mouse pointer to click the file name, or use the up- or down-arrow key to move the selection cursor to the file name.

3. Select File from the menu bar to display the File menu.

4. Choose Change Attributes to display the Change Attributes dialog box, shown in figure 8.2.

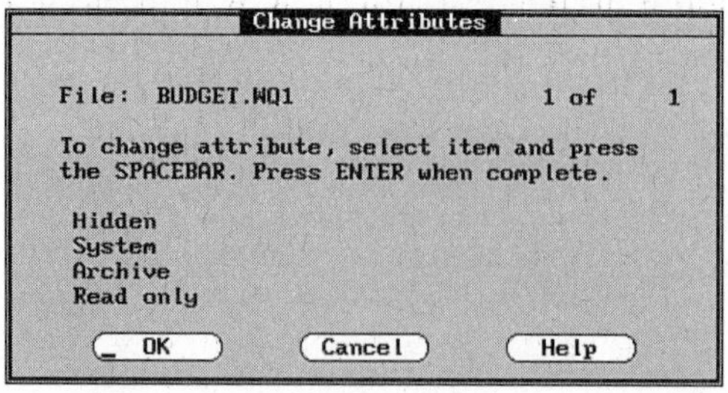

```
┌──────────────────[ Change Attributes ]──────────────────┐
│                                                          │
│   File:  BUDGET.WQ1                    1 of      1       │
│                                                          │
│   To change attribute, select item and press            │
│   the SPACEBAR. Press ENTER when complete.               │
│                                                          │
│        Hidden                                            │
│        System                                            │
│        Archive                                           │
│        Read only                                         │
│        ( _  OK  )      ( Cancel )      ( Help )          │
└──────────────────────────────────────────────────────────┘
```

Fig. 8.2

The Change Attributes dialog box.

The Shell lists four attributes in the Change Attributes dialog box: Hidden, System, Archive, and Read Only. A triangular pointer appears to the left of each attribute that is set (turned on).

5. To change an attribute setting, use the mouse pointer to click the attribute name, or use the up- or down-arrow key to move the selection cursor to the attribute name and press the space bar. (**Note:** The selection cursor appears as soon as you press the up- or down-arrow key.)

Each attribute acts as a toggle switch. Select the attribute once to turn it on. Select the attribute again to turn it off.

6. After you have made all desired changes to attribute settings, choose the OK button to execute the command and set the new attributes.

The Shell also enables you to change file attributes on multiple files by following these steps:

1. Use the mouse pointer or keyboard to select the names of the files whose attributes you want to modify.

2. Select File on the menu bar to pull down the File menu.

3. Choose Change Attributes. The Shell displays the Change Attributes dialog box, this time listing options to change files one at a time or to change all selected files (see fig. 8.3).

Fig. 8.3

Changing the file attributes of multiple files.

If you want to give different selected files different file attributes, choose the first option. When you want all selected files to have the same attribute settings, choose the second option. The Shell then displays a Change Attributes dialog box similar to the one shown in figure 8.2.

4. To change an attribute setting, use the mouse pointer to click the attribute name, or use the up- or down-arrow key to move the selection cursor to the attribute name and press Enter. (*Note:* The selection cursor appears as soon as you press the up- or down-arrow key.)

5. After you have made all desired changes to attribute settings, choose the OK button to execute the command and set the new attributes.

If you choose the Change Selected Files One at a Time option from the dialog box shown in figure 8.3, you must repeat steps 4 and 5 for each selected file.

Changing File Attributes with the ATTRIB Command

In addition to the DOS Shell Change Attributes command, the external DOS command ATTRIB enables you to manipulate several file attribute bits in a file's directory entry. You can issue the ATTRIB command in three ways:

- The following syntax displays on-screen a file's current attribute values:

   ATTRIB *d:path***filename.ext**/*S*

- The following syntax sets (turns on) file attributes:

   ATTRIB +A +H +R +S *d:path***filename.ext**/*S*

- The following syntax resets (turns off) file attributes:

   ATTRIB -A -H -R -S *d:path***filename.ext**/*S*

d: is an optional parameter that specifies the disk containing the files whose attributes you want to list or change.

path\ is an optional parameter that indicates the directory path containing the selected files. You learn about paths in the section "Understanding Path Names" later in this chapter.

filename.ext is a mandatory parameter that specifies the file or files whose attributes you want to list or change. By using wild cards (* and ?), you can specify multiple files in this parameter.

The optional */S* switch (DOS 3.3 and later versions only) instructs ATTRIB to process files that match the file parameter in all subdirectories of the path directory. You learn about subdirectories in the section "Expanding the File System through Subdirectories" later in this chapter.

The plus (+) operator in front of each attribute letter (A, H, R, or S) instructs ATTRIB to set the respective attribute bit. Conversely, the minus (-) operator turns off the attribute.

You can specify the various attributes one at a time or all together in the command line. You can manipulate the H and S attributes with the ATTRIB command only in DOS Version 5.0 or later.

Establishing Read-Only Files

The DOS Shell and the ATTRIB command give you control over file attributes. In particular, the read-only attribute makes DOS unable to overwrite (change) or erase (remove) a file. Commands like COPY, ERASE, and XCOPY normally can remove or overwrite an existing file.

When you add a file to a directory (through an applications program or through DOS), the read-only attribute is off, and the file can be overwritten or erased. DOS commands and applications programs are free to perform destructive operations on the file.

If you set the read-only attribute of a file, DOS commands that normally overwrite or erase files do not affect the file. Marking a file as read-only protects the file much like write-protecting a disk protects the contents of the disk. You can use the DOS Shell or the ATTRIB command to write-protect important files, ensuring that careless use of the COPY or ERASE command does not destroy the files.

Suppose, for example, that you have created a spreadsheet file named BUDGET.WQ1, which contains the yearly budget figures for your company. You want others in your department to view this spreadsheet, but you don't want them to make any changes. Use the following command to make the BUDGET.WQ1 file read-only:

ATTRIB +R BUDGET.WQ1

Alternatively, select the file list area of the DOS Shell and select the BUDGET.WQ1 file name. Follow the steps described in the section "Changing File Attributes with the DOS Shell" earlier in this chapter to display the Change Attributes dialog box. Initially, only the archive attribute is turned on. Use the mouse or the arrow keys to select the Read Only option in the dialog box to turn on the read-only attribute. Finally, select OK to execute the command. The Shell returns to the DOS Shell window.

Now your colleagues can view the BUDGET.WQ1 file, but they cannot change or erase it. If someone tries to issue the command ERASE BUDGET.WQ1, for example, DOS responds with the message Access Denied and does not erase the file.

 NOTE The DOS Shell Delete command, discussed in Chapter 9, "Managing Your Files," warns you if you attempt to delete a file whose read-only attribute is turned on, but the Shell enables you to delete the file if you confirm your choice.

The FDISK and FORMAT commands do not observe the read-only status of a file. FDISK and FORMAT are disk-level commands; therefore, they don't look at disk directories when doing their jobs. Don't rely on the read-only attribute of a file to protect the file from a disk-level command.

After you use the ATTRIB +R command to mark a file as read-only, you can use the ATTRIB -R command to reset (turn off) the read-only attribute. To reset the read-only attribute of BUDGET.WQ1, for example, type the following command at the command prompt, and press Enter:

    ATTRIB -R BUDGET.WQ1

The file is again subject to DOS commands that can overwrite or erase the file.

To turn off the read-only attribute by using the DOS Shell, follow the same procedure you used to turn on each attribute. Each attribute acts as a toggle switch, so the Shell turns the read-only attribute back off.

Making COMMAND.COM Read-Only with ATTRIB

COMMAND.COM is an important program file. To protect the file against accidental erasure or overwriting, you can make it read-only by using the ATTRIB command. Assume that COMMAND.COM is in the root directory of your C disk. To determine the current attribute settings, type the following command at the command prompt, and press Enter:

    ATTRIB C:\COMMAND.COM

DOS displays the following information:

```
A        C:\COMMAND.COM.
```

By default, the A (archive) attribute is set, as denoted by the letter A, which is displayed to the left of the file name. The R (read-only) attribute is not set. To turn on the read-only attribute, issue the following command:

    ATTRIB +R C:\COMMAND.COM

COMMAND.COM is now a read-only file. To verify the change, issue the following command:

ATTRIB \COMMAND.COM

DOS responds as follows:

```
A    R      C:\COMMAND.COM
```

The letter R now appears, as well as the letter A. The R indicates that the file's read-only attribute is set.

For Related Information

▶▶ "Using DOS To Manage Files," p. 282.

▶▶ "Finding Files," p. 288.

▶▶ "Using the Shell To Display File Information," p. 292.

FROM HERE...

Expanding the File System through Subdirectories

The DOS creators designed one master directory with a predetermined number of file entries to limit the space occupied by the directory. Recall that FORMAT establishes one fixed-length directory for each disk. Keeping this directory small is important because the larger the directory, the less space is left on the disk for your files. The creators first established a cap on the number of entries in this directory to fix its size. This cap number was proportional to the capacity of the disk. Thus, floppies had fewer file entries in the master directory (fewer bytes) than hard disks had. For most DOS users, however, one directory is not sufficient for effective file management.

The FORMAT-provided directory, called the root directory, is not intended to accommodate every possible file a disk can hold. DOS does not limit directory entries to those of the root directory; you can also enter files into expansion directories, or *subdirectories*. DOS provides a disk with a root directory, but you can add to the file system as many subdirectories as you require.

In the root directory or in a subdirectory, DOS still enters the name and the first cluster number of a file's FAT entry. The DOS subdirectory is a special file that DOS uses much like the root directory. Because DOS appears to work with the root directory and subdirectories in the same way, DOS users often call subdirectories "directories." Although internally DOS manages the root directory and subdirectory differently, subdirectories safely can be called directories.

DOS provides a few commands to manage the subdirectory system, including commands to create, remove, and change the current directory. You learn about these commands in detail later in this chapter, but the following paragraphs introduce them briefly.

A freshly formatted disk contains only one directory, the root directory. With the MKDIR (MAKE DIRECTORY) command, you can create a subdirectory. You can create a subdirectory called LETTERS (you can use any file name DOS accepts), for example, and keep in this new subdirectory all the letter files you create. Subdirectories have the advantage of holding files of some common type or purpose.

To change the current directory and focus DOS's attention on the LETTERS subdirectory, you can use the CHDIR (CHANGE DIRECTORY) command. DOS keeps track of the current directory in the same way it tracks the current drive. After you change to a directory, the new directory becomes the current directory for that disk. When you boot DOS, the current directory is the root directory of the boot disk.

If you want to remove the LETTERS subdirectory, you can use the RMDIR (REMOVE DIRECTORY) command, but the directory must contain no files. DOS does not enable you to delete a directory and make orphans of the files in that directory.

Subdirectories in DOS 2.0 and later versions, as well as the commands that support the subdirectories, are a great advancement over the single fixed directories of DOS 1. The feature that gives the most efficiency to the DOS file system is the hierarchical relationship among the subdirectories—each subdirectory can, in turn, contain other subdirectories, which also can contain subdirectories, and so on.

Understanding the Hierarchical Directory System

You can arrange your DOS directories and subdirectories in a hierarchy. The term *hierarchy* means an organization or arrangement of entities. Entities can refer to people, objects, ideas, files, and so on. To a genealogist, entities in a hierarchy may be people in a family tree. To

DOS, entities in a hierarchy are directories in a directory system. In either case, the hierarchy begins with the root entity. In a family tree, the root entity may be great-great-grandfather Isaac Watson. In DOS, this core entity is the root directory. In genealogy, people can trace their roots through their parents and then through their parents' ancestors. People know who their forefathers are, based on the relationships of the family tree. In DOS, subdirectories can trace their paths back to the root directory. DOS subdirectories and their files are identifiable by their relationships to other subdirectories.

You can create many subdirectories from the root. (This chapter later covers the commands for creating and deleting subdirectories.) The root is the parent of each subdirectory. You also can create subdirectories stemming from other subdirectories so that the new subdirectories have another subdirectory as their parent directory. Figure 8.4 illustrates how subdirectories are arranged hierarchically from the root. You can see that the arrangement does resemble that of a family tree. Indeed, the DOS directory system is often called a *tree-structured* directory system.

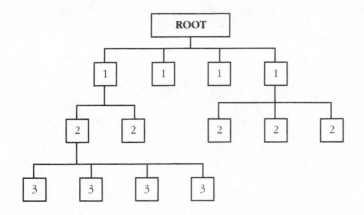

Fig. 8.4

Hierarchical levels of a DOS directory tree.

Figure 8.4 represents a directory with three levels of subdirectories. Because you create the subdirectories on your disks, your directory may have more or fewer levels. Regardless of the number of levels, the relationship among the subdirectories is important.

The base of this tree structure is the root directory. In a family tree, David may be the son of Wayne, who is the son of Alex, the son of John. John is the head, or root, of the family tree for David. Another way to represent David's identity in this family tree is as follows:

John\Alex\Wayne\David

In this example, each level of the family tree is separated by a backslash character. This David is different from the preceding David:

Isaac\Virgil\Robert\David

Both share the name David, but their relationships to their parents are unique.

DOS directories share the same kind of identity relationships as families. With DOS 2.0 and later versions, every DOS disk can have a family of directories (subdirectories) that stems from the root directory. DOS enables you to add directories in levels like generations. The directory LETTERS is a first-level subdirectory, for example, LETTERS is created as an offspring of the root directory. The root has no name as such and is simply referenced on the command line as the backslash (\) character.

To refer to the file MEMO.DOC located in the LETTERS subdirectory, you can use the name \LETTERS\MEMO.DOC. If the MEMO.DOC file is located on a drive other than the current drive, you must specify disk, directory, and file name parameters, such as C:\LETTERS\MEMO.DOC. C: is drive parameter, \LETTERS is the directory parameter, and MEMO.DOC is the file name parameter. The root directory of drive C is the parent directory of LETTERS, and LETTERS is the parent directory of the file MEMO.DOC.

Understanding Path Names

Each directory, including the root directory, can contain user files. Two files can have the same file name and extension as long as the files reside in different directories. When you specify a file name in a DOS command, DOS needs to know the names of the directories, starting from the root, that lead to the file. This sequence of directory names leading to a file is called the file's *directory path*, or just the file's *path*.

When specifying a file's path, use a backslash (\) to separate one directory name from another. This backslash is DOS's directory delimiter. In symbolic notation, the path for a file appears as follows:

d:\dir1\dir2\dir3+\filename.ext

d: is the drive letter. The first \ is the DOS name for the root. *dir1\dir2\dir3+* indicates a chain of directories in which the directory to the left of another directory is the parent. The plus sign (+) indicates that more (or fewer) directory names are allowed. All characters between the first \ and the final \ comprise the file's directory path. The *filename.ext* parameter is the name of the file.

To see how the path parameter works with DOS, look again at the DIR command. Recall that issuing DIR alone on the command line causes DOS to display a list of files found in the current directory of the logged drive. DOS supplies the drive and directory parameter for the command by using the current drive and current directory. You can, however, instruct DOS to display a list of files found in a different drive and directory by explicitly specifying the path to that drive and directory.

When you boot DOS, the current directory is the root directory of the boot disk. If you want to see the files in another directory, the \DOS subdirectory, for example, you must include the path parameter in the directory command. To see the COM extension files in \DOS from the root of the logged drive, issue the following command:

>   DIR \DOS*.COM

If your current drive is A and you want to see the COM files on drive C in the \DOS directory, issue the following command:

>   DIR C:\DOS*.COM

You can log onto the \DOS directory by using the command CHDIR \DOS; \DOS becomes the current directory on the current disk (later in this chapter is a discussion of CHDIR). If you don't specify a directory parameter in a DOS command, DOS assumes that you mean to use the current directory, \DOS. Thus, to see the COM files in the \DOS directory, issue the following command:

>   DIR *.COM

This command produces the same list of files as the command DIR \DOS*.COM issued from the root directory. DOS supplies the \DOS path by default. Many DOS commands work with optional path parameters. When you don't supply a path, DOS uses the current drive and current directory as the default path. Check the syntax for each command to see whether you can take advantage of the default path.

Using PROMPT To Display a Full Path

While you are reading about the hierarchical directory system, you may want to confirm that your DOS prompt is displaying the current drive and current directory, referred to collectively as the *full path*. The internal command PROMPT enables you to display the full path as part of the DOS prompt. DOS 5.0 and later versions supply the appropriate prompt command automatically in AUTOEXEC.BAT, a special program file that runs each time you boot your computer. If your command prompt does not already show the path, issue the following command:

PROMPT pg

After you issue the PROMPT command, DOS shows the full path in the prompt. When you are logged onto the \DOS directory on drive C, for example, the command prompt is C: \DOS>.

The $p parameter in the PROMPT command tells DOS to display the full path as part of the prompt. $g tells DOS to display the greater-than symbol (>) at the end of the prompt. This prompt reminds you of where you are working in the hierarchical directory system.

Unless this PROMPT command is included in your system's AUTOEXEC.BAT file, the prompt returns to its former look as soon as you reboot. (For a full discussion of the PROMPT command, see Chapter 11, "Working with System Information.")

Helping DOS Find External Commands

When you issue an external DOS command, DOS cannot execute the command unless the program can locate the DOS external program file. You can tell DOS where the program file is located in three ways:

- Log on to the disk and directory that contains the command.

- Supply the path in the command line.

- Establish a DOS search path to the command's directory.

So far, you have learned how to log on to the drive and directory that contain the external command file. In this case, DOS finds the command by using the default drive and path.

If you want to use an external command located on another drive or directory, you can supply the drive and path information as a part of the DOS command. If drive B is the current drive and the CHKDSK external program is on the working DOS disk in drive A, for example, you can issue the following command:

A:CHKDSK

DOS looks on drive A for the CHKDSK program and analyzes the disk in drive B, the current drive.

In another example, if the CHKDSK command is in a directory named \DOS on drive C, and you are logged onto drive B, you can analyze the disk in B with the following command:

C:\DOS\CHKDSK

Drive B is the current drive, so you must specify C as the drive parameter. You must also specify the directory where CHKDSK resides, \DOS. A \ character separates the path from the file name parameter. With the drive parameter and path to the command given in the command line, DOS finds and executes the CHKDSK command and analyzes the disk in drive B.

The most convenient method to help DOS find external commands is to use the PATH command to establish a search path for DOS to use. DOS designers anticipated that you would not want to log on to the drive containing an external command or give the directory path every time you use a command. The PATH command enables you to give DOS a list of directories through which to search each time you issue an external command or type the name of a batch file or executable program file.

NOTE

The PATH command enables DOS to locate and execute program files with COM and EXE extensions. Batch files with BAT extensions also are located and executed through the search path. If you supply a path to a program on the command line, however, DOS does not search the path alternatives if the program is not in the directory you specify.

You can include up to 127 characters in the PATH command. If you are unsure of your current PATH setting, you can issue the PATH command without parameters. DOS then shows the current PATH setting.

The PATH command does not help DOS find data files. A similar command, APPEND, provides a list of directories through which DOS searches for data files. The APPEND command is discussed in the Command Reference section.

The syntax of the PATH command is as follows:

PATH=d1:path1\ ;d2:path2\ ;+

The equal sign (=) is optional; you can just use a space. **d1:** is the first drive and contains **path1**. If DOS doesn't find a specified program file in the current directory, DOS looks for the program next in path1 on disk d1. The semicolon (;) character following **path1** marks the end of the first path. **d2:path2** is a second drive and path combination for

DOS to search if the specified program is not in the first path. ;+ indicates that you can add other alternative paths to the command. DOS searches for a program from left to right through the path alternatives. You normally should give the drive parameters with the path parameters because you don't want DOS to search for a directory on the default drive when the directory is on another drive.

Nearly all hard disk users take advantage of the PATH command. DOS 6.0's installation program, as well as the installation programs for many applications programs, add to or modify the PATH statement in the AUTOEXEC.BAT file. Program instructions usually recommend which path alternative you should add. Read the documentation that comes with your applications programs to determine the appropriate PATH command. For DOS use on a hard disk, you certainly want to include the directory that holds the DOS external commands. You then can issue DOS external commands from any drive or directory without specifying the drive or directory where the DOS program files reside. Thanks to the PATH command, internal and external commands are equally convenient.

Suppose, for example, that the DOS external program files are located in a directory named \DOS on your computer's C drive. To include the external commands in your search path, issue the following command:

    PATH C:\DOS

DOS looks in C:\DOS for any program not located in the current directory. If you have other applications programs, you can add their directories to the path. To add dBASE's directory to the path, for example, issue the following command:

    PATH C:\DOS;C:\DBASE

Notice that the semicolon separates the two directory names. When you issue the command to start dBASE at a command prompt, DOS first tries to find the program in the current directory. DOS then searches C:\DOS for the dBASE program, and failing to find it there, searches C:\DBASE, where the file is located.

T   I   P   Use PATH in your AUTOEXEC.BAT file so that the paths are automatically established when you boot. See Chapter 11, "Working with System Information," for more information.

For Related Information

▶▶ "Changing the Command Prompt with PROMPT," p. 414.

FROM HERE...

Working with Directories through the DOS Shell

DOS 6.0 provides both DOS Shell commands and internal DOS commands (for use at the command line) that manage directories. The Shell commands generally involve the directory tree area of the DOS Shell window. The following sections describe how to use the DOS Shell's directory tree area.

Understanding the Directory Tree

When you first start the DOS Shell, the DOS Shell window is divided into the drive area, at the top of the screen, and three larger areas: the directory tree area, the file list area, and the program list area (see fig. 8.5, but refer to Chapter 4, "Using the DOS Shell," for a full discussion of the DOS Shell window).

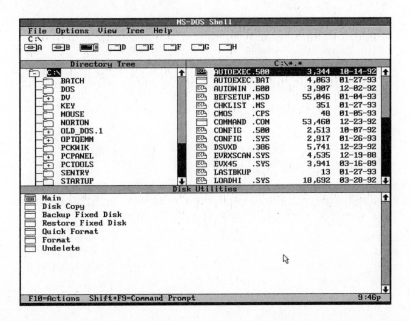

Fig. 8.5

The DOS Shell window.

The drive area at the top of the DOS Shell window indicates the selected disk by highlighting one of the drive icons. Figure 8.5, for example, shows that C is the selected drive.

As explained earlier in this chapter, DOS manages files on your disks by maintaining file information in a hierarchical directory structure. The directory tree area, in the upper left quadrant of the window, graphically depicts this directory structure. At the top of this area, the root directory of the logged disk is shown as a folder-shaped icon, or as a pair of brackets ([ ]) if the DOS Shell is in text mode. All other directories are shown as folder-shaped icons (or pairs of brackets). These other directories are listed below the root icon and connected to the root icon by a vertical line. The name of each directory is listed to the right of its icon.

At any time during a session with the DOS Shell, one directory name is highlighted. This highlighted directory is referred to as the *selected directory*. When you first start the Shell, the directory that is current when you start the program is the selected directory (usually the root directory of the boot disk). The file list area of the DOS Shell window, in the upper right quadrant of the screen, lists the file names in the selected directory.

Selecting a Different Disk and Refreshing the Tree

To display the directory structure of a different disk, you must select the icon for that disk in the drive area of the DOS Shell window. Use one of the following methods to select a different disk:

- Move the mouse pointer to the icon for the target disk drive, and click the left mouse button.

- Press Ctrl-*d*, substituting the disk drive letter for *d*.

- Press Tab or Shift-Tab to select the drive area of the DOS Shell window. Use the left- or right-arrow key to highlight the drive letter of the target drive. Then press Enter to confirm your choice.

After you select a new drive, the Shell displays the selected drive's directory structure in the directory tree area. The list of files from the selected directory also displays in the file list area.

Occasionally, the Shell does not recognize that you have altered the directory or file structure on the disk and consequently displays an inaccurate list of directories, files, or both. To force the Shell to re-read the directory tree and file list from the disk, press F5, or do the following:

1. Select <u>V</u>iew from the menu bar to display the View menu.

2. Choose <u>R</u>efresh.

The DOS Shell displays the message `Reading Disk Information` and then returns to the DOS Shell window. The directory tree and file list areas now accurately reflect the contents of the disk.

To refresh just the selected directory, press Ctrl-F5.

Occasionally, you may need to display the directory trees of two disks at the same time on one screen. At other times, you may want to see more of the directory tree than can be displayed within the standard half-screen format of the directory tree area. In either case, refer to Chapter 4, "Using the DOS Shell," for a description of how to display a dual file list and a single file list.

Navigating the Directory Tree

Often you need to display the file names in a directory other than the currently selected directory. Use one of the following methods to select a different directory in the directory tree:

■ Use the mouse to click the target directory name. If the directory tree is too long to view in its entirety in the directory tree area, use the scroll bar on the right side of the directory tree area to scroll the target directory name into sight. Then click the directory name.

■ Press Tab or Shift-Tab repeatedly until you select the directory tree area of the DOS Shell window. Use the up- and down-arrow keys to scroll through the directories. As you scroll up or down, the Shell displays in the file list area the names of files found in each directory in the directory tree.

Expanding and Collapsing Branches

As you recall, the DOS directory structure is tree-like. The root directory is like the trunk of a tree, with all other directories growing out like branches of a tree. The DOS Shell graphically represents this tree-like nature in the directory tree area of the DOS Shell window as an upside-down tree.

The DOS directory structure can have multiple levels, but initially the Shell shows only the first level of the tree. Each first-level directory—a directory attached directly to the root—is depicted as a branch of the tree. Just as branches of a real tree can have offshoot branches, each DOS directory can contain offshoot directories. The Shell indicates that a directory contains other directories by placing a plus sign (+) in the directory icon. Figure 8.5 shows plus signs in the directory icon for the following directories:

DV
OLD_DOS.1
OPTQEMM
PCPANEL
PCTOOLS

To *expand* (show the directories subordinate to) by one level a directory tree branch that shows a + in its directory icon, use the mouse to click the + in the directory icon, or do the following:

1. Select the directory tree area that contains the target directory icon.

2. Move the selection cursor to the directory name.

3. Press the + key, or select Expand One Level from the Tree menu.

The Shell then shows the next level of directories beneath the selected directory. Figure 8.6, for example, shows the expanded DATABASE directory containing three second-level directories: ACCESS, DBASE, and PARADOX.

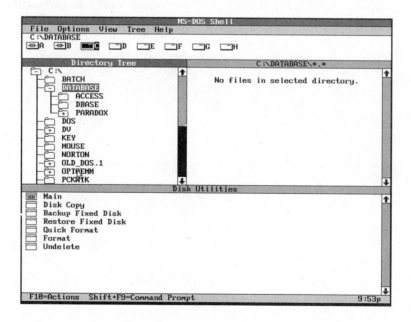

Fig. 8.6

Expanding a directory tree branch.

> **NOTE** Notice that the file list area in figure 8.6 indicates `No files`
> `in selected directory`. The DATABASE directory is a
> major division of the overall hard disk directory, used
> merely to hold the four subordinate directories. This ap-
> proach provides an easily understandable structure for
> the hard disk directory. Refer to "Keeping a Clean Root
> Directory" later in this chapter for more information on
> this subject.

Offshoot directories can contain more offshoots. Earlier in this chapter,
the relationship among directory levels is described as analogous to a
family tree—child, parent, grandparent, and so on. When a second-level
directory contains one or more third-level directories, the Shell shows
a plus sign (+) in the second-level directory icon. The directory icon of
the FOXPRO directory shown in figure 8.6, for example, indicates that
this branch of the DATABASE directory also contains at least one directory. To expand one level of the FOXPRO branch, follow the procedure
you used to expand one level of the DATABASE branch.

If you do not remember precisely where a directory is located in the
directory tree, expanding branches one level at a time may become
tedious. When you want to expand all levels beneath a particular directory branch, use the following procedure:

1. Use the mouse to click the directory name, or use the arrow keys
   to move the selection cursor to the directory name.

2. Press the * key, or select Expand All from the Tree menu.

The Shell expands all levels of the tree below the currently selected
directory. Figure 8.7, for example, shows the fully expanded DATABASE
branch of drive C's directory tree.

The opposite of expanding a directory branch in the directory tree area
is *collapsing* a branch. When you first start the DOS Shell, you may notice that a root directory's icon contains a minus sign (–). After you
expand a directory branch, the icon for the expanded branch also contains a minus sign. These minus signs are a reminder that you can collapse the branch. To collapse a branch whose icon contains a –, click
the directory icon with your mouse, or use the following procedure:

1. Select the directory name.

2. Press the – key, or choose Collapse Branch from the Tree menu.

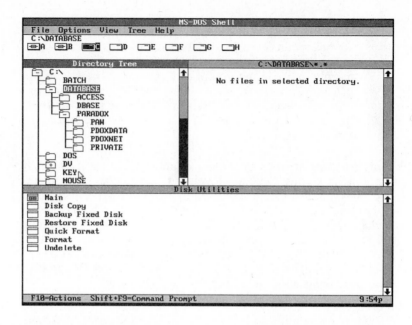

Fig. 8.7

The fully expanded DATA-BASE branch.

To collapse the entire tree, click the root directory icon or do the following:

1. Select the root directory name at the top of the directory tree.

2. Press the – key, or choose <u>C</u>ollapse Branch from the Tree menu.

The Shell collapses the entire tree down to the root level and places a + in the root directory icon.

FROM HERE...

For Related Information

◄◄ "Modifying the View," p. 97.

Creating Directories

Because the only automatically available directory on a DOS disk is the root, you must add any additional directories. Even after you establish a workable directory structure for your computer, you occasionally need to create new directories on your disks. DOS enables you to add directories to a disk through the DOS Shell or through the internal MKDIR (or MD) command. The following sections discuss both methods of adding directories.

Understanding the Addition of a Directory

When you instruct DOS to create a new directory, whether through the DOS Shell or through the MKDIR command, DOS does some work behind the scenes before complying.

First, DOS verifies that the given (or implied by default) parent directory exists. You cannot create two directory levels with one command. Next, DOS confirms that the new directory has a unique name. To confirm uniqueness, DOS ensures that the parent directory does not contain an entry for a file with the same name as the proposed directory's name. Because subdirectories are files, DOS has no convenient means of separating a directory from a normal file with the same name.

After confirming that the new directory name is unique in the parent directory, DOS allocates a file for the new directory and marks the new file entry in the parent directory as a subdirectory.

DOS completes two entries in the new directory. The name of the first entry is always . (called "dot"). The dot entry in a directory refers, or points, to the directory that contains it. You can think of the dot entry as an alias for the current directory's name, analogous to the pronoun *me*. The second entry is always named .. (called "dot-dot"). DOS uses this dot-dot entry to point to the parent of the current directory. This entry is an alias for the parent directory's name and is analogous to the name Mom or Dad.

 NOTE Every subdirectory you create automatically contains the . and .. alias entries. If you use the DIR command to view a subdirectory's file entries, you always see the . and .. entries.

On the command line, COMMAND.COM accepts the alias entries . and .. as legitimate parts of path specifiers. When specifying a directory path in a DOS command, you can use the .. alias any time as shorthand to indicate the path of the current directory's parent. Some examples of .. in commands are included in this chapter.

When you create a directory, whether through the DOS Shell or at the command line, follow these naming guidelines:

■ All characters allowed in a normal file name can be used in a directory name.

■ A directory name cannot be the name of a standard DOS device, such as AUX, PRN, and CON.

■ A directory name cannot duplicate a file name in the intended
parent directory, although you could create a directory called
DAD in a directory containing the file DAD.TXT.

Creating a Directory in the Shell

To create a new directory by using the DOS Shell, do the following:

1. Select the directory tree area of the DOS Shell window.

2. Select the directory to be the parent of the new directory.

3. Select File from the menu bar to display the File menu.

4. Choose Create Directory from the File menu.

   The Shell displays the Create Directory dialog box shown in
   figure 8.8. This dialog box indicates the name of the parent
   directory, C:\SPREADSH in figure 8.8.

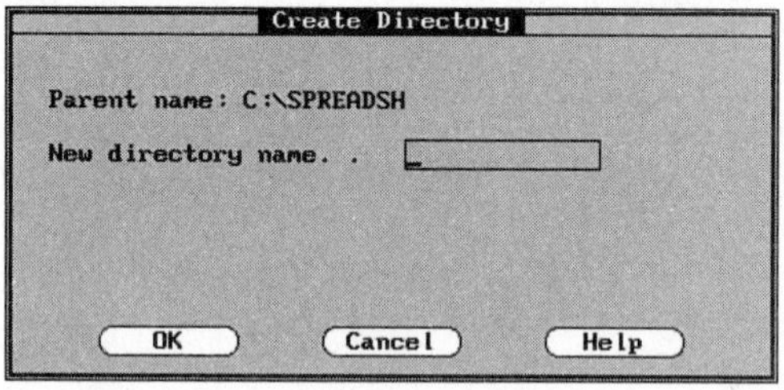

Fig. 8.8

The Create
Directory dialog
box.

```
┌──────────────────[ Create Directory ]──────────────────┐
│                                                          │
│   Parent name: C:\SPREADSH                               │
│                                                          │
│   New directory name. .  [                    ]          │
│                                                          │
│                                                          │
│       (  OK  )      ( Cancel )      ( Help )             │
└──────────────────────────────────────────────────────────┘
```

5. Type the name of the new directory, and press Enter or click OK.

The Shell creates the new directory and returns to the directory tree
area of the DOS Shell window. The Shell also adds to the tree an icon
for the new directory.

T   I   P   Assigning directory names that in some way describe the files they
contain is often helpful, even though the name you give a directory
has no effect on the data in these files. Directory names such as DA-
TABASE, UTILITY, and WINDOWS, for example, are more descriptive
than DIR-ONE, FILES, or PROGRAMS.

Creating Directories with MKDIR (MD)

DOS provides the internal MKDIR, or MD, command, which you use to tell DOS to make a new directory. The MKDIR and MD names for this command are identical in operation. Anywhere you see MKDIR in the following discussions, you can substitute MD if you prefer.

When you use the MKDIR command, follow these guidelines:

■ The specified or implied parent directory of the intended directory must exist. MKDIR (MD) cannot make more than one directory at a time. On a disk with only a root directory, for example, the command MKDIR \PROG\DATA does not work.

■ MKDIR (MD) does not change the current directory to the new directory. To change to the new directory, you need to use CHDIR (CD).

When you issue the MKDIR command, you are instructing DOS to add a new directory to some part of the file-system tree. The following syntax and examples use the MKDIR version of the command. The syntax for the MKDIR command is as follows:

MKDIR *d:path***name**

The *d:* parameter is optional. It indicates the disk where the new directory is to be added. If you omit d:, DOS uses the default drive.

The *path*\ parameter is also optional. It indicates the directory path to which the new directory is to be added. If you omit *path*\, DOS uses the current directory.

The **name** parameter is not optional. You must specify the name for the new directory.

The length of the full path (drive, path, and new directory name) must not exceed 63 characters, including delimiters. The full path name is the measure for length. If you are creating a directory relative to your current directory, you must count your current directory's full path length including the implied root \ character as being part of the 63-character limit.

> **NOTE**
>
> When you begin a path parameter with the \ character, you are telling DOS how to locate the directory or file from the root directory—the file's *absolute* path. If you specify a path that does not begin with \, DOS assumes that you are specifying a path *relative* to your current directory. If, for example, your current directory is \DOS, and you want to add the directory \DOS\DRIVERS, you can issue the command

MKDIR DRIVERS. Notice that no leading \ appears in front of the new directory name DRIVERS. When you omit the leading \, DOS adds the current directory path to the path parameter you specified in the command in order to form the complete path parameter.

Relative path parameters also work with other DOS commands. You can see instances of relative paths as path parameters in other examples.

For this example, assume that you currently are logged on to drive C and have a formatted floppy disk in drive A with no subdirectories on it. If you are using DOS on a hard disk, the examples that follow assume that you have used PATH to establish a path to the directory that contains the external DOS commands (see "Helping DOS Find External Commands" earlier in this chapter). To create the directory \DATA on the disk in drive A, enter the following command:

    MKDIR A:\DATA

DOS makes the new directory, DATA, on the disk in drive A. You can achieve the same result by issuing the MKDIR command while logged on to the root directory of drive A. You use the relative path form of a path parameter as in the following:

    MKDIR DATA

The directory is created directly from the root even though no disk name or beginning backslash is given in the command line. DOS uses the current (default) drive, A, and makes the directory relative to the current directory, the root. If you do not specify a path, DOS makes the current directory the parent directory of your new directory.

Changing the Current Directory with CHDIR (CD)

When you are working at the DOS command line, DOS remembers the current directory and the current drive name. You issue the CHDIR, or CD, command to change the current directory to a new current directory. If you omit a path parameter, in most commands, DOS searches only the current directory when looking for files or programs.

NOTE   CHDIR and CD initiate the same command; their usage is identical.

The CHDIR command is the hierarchical directory system's navigation command. Its primary use is to change the current directory.

CHDIR alone (with no parameters) is the "Where am I?" command. If you use the CHDIR command this way, DOS reports the current directory's path name without changing your current directory. Issuing only CHDIR tells DOS to report where commands using no drive and path parameters do their work.

The syntax for CD, or CHDIR, is as follows:

CHDIR *d:path*

The *d:* parameter is optional; it indicates the disk drive where the directory is located. Using this parameter does not change the current logged drive, but this parameter enables you to change the current directory on a drive without first logging onto that drive. If you omit the drive parameter, DOS uses the current drive.

The *path* parameter is the name of the new current directory. The *path* parameter can begin with the **..** alias, which instructs the command to begin at the parent of the current directory.

When using the CHDIR command, follow these guidelines:

■ The drive and path parameters in the command line must be valid.

■ If the path parameter begins with \ , CHDIR assumes that the directory specified in the path is absolute—from the root.

■ If the path parameter does not begin with \ , CHDIR assumes that the directory given in the path is relative—from the current directory.

■ When you specify a drive parameter but no path parameter, CHDIR reports the current working directory for the specified disk.

■ When you omit the path parameter and the drive parameter from the command line, CHDIR reports the current working directory of the currently logged drive.

You can always change to the root directory of the logged disk by using the command CHDIR \.

T I P

Suppose, for example, that the current directory on drive A is \DIR1. To receive a report of the logged (default) directory of a disk, you issue the CHDIR command in the following form:

CHDIR A:

CHDIR reports drive A's logged directory as the following:

```
A:\DIR1
```

Suppose that the logged disk is drive C and that the current directory of C is \KEEP. To see the default directory, issue the command in the following form:

CHDIR

CHDIR reports as follows:

```
C:\KEEP
```

To change the default directory of the disk in drive A to \FILES when the logged drive is C, issue the following command:

CHDIR A:\FILES

DOS changes the default directory in A to \FILES. To confirm the change, issue the following command:

CHDIR A:

CHDIR replies as follows:

```
A:\FILES
```

The subdirectories \WORDS\MEMOS and \WORDS\DOCS have \WORDS as their parent directory. To change the directory in the current drive C from \WORDS\MEMOS to \WORDS\DOCS, issue the following command:

CHDIR ..\DOCS

Notice that the alias for the parent directory of the current directory (.. with no leading \) acts as a shorthand substitute for the same full command:

CHDIR \WORDS\DOCS

To change from the \WORDS\DOCS directory on the current drive to \WORDS (the parent directory of \WORDS\DOCS), you issue the following command:

CHDIR ..

DOS changes to \WORDS as the current directory of the logged disk. The use of the .. alias as the only parameter of the command always changes to the parent of the current directory unless the current directory is the root. The root has no parent.

For Related Information

▶▶ "Listing Files with DIR," p. 405.

▶▶ "Using DOSSHELL," p. 413.

▶▶ "Changing the Command Prompt with PROMPT," p. 414.

▶▶ "Altering the Look of the Screen with MODE," p. 416.

FROM HERE...

Deleting Directories

Just as you occasionally need to add a directory to a disk, you may need to delete a directory. DOS enables you to remove empty directories at the end of a directory branch in the directory tree. In other words, you can remove an empty directory at the lowest level of a directory branch.

You can delete a directory in the DOS Shell or at the command line. The sections that follow describe both methods.

Deleting a Directory in the Shell

To remove a directory in the DOS Shell, use the following procedure:

1. Delete all files and other directories contained in the directory you want to delete (see Chapter 11, "Working with System Information").

2. Select the directory name in the Shell directory tree area.

3. Press the Del key, or choose File from the menu bar and then Delete from the File menu.

If you attempt to delete a directory that contains one or more files or directories, the Shell does not delete the directory. Instead, the Shell displays an error message.

Removing an Unneeded Directory with RMDIR (RD)

When you need to remove a directory from your directory tree structure, you can use the RMDIR, or RD, command from the DOS command line.

 The two command names RMDIR and RD are different names for the same command; the actions of both names are identical.

RMDIR removes directories at the lowest level of a directory path. Just as you can create a directory structure with MKDIR, you can remove a directory structure with RMDIR. RMDIR enables you to rearrange your directory system if you change your mind about your current choices for directories or their names.

 DOS 6.0's DELTREE command enables you to rename directories from the command line. Using the DOS Shell to rename a directory (beginning with DOS 5.0), however, is easier. Alternatively, you can remove a directory and then create a new directory with the name you want.

The syntax for RMDIR is as follows:

RMDIR *d:***path**

The *d:* parameter is optional; it specifies the disk that contains the directory to be removed. If you omit *d:* from the command line, DOS assumes that the current (logged) disk holds the directory you want to remove.

The **path** parameter is required. It specifies the directory path of the directory you want to remove. If **path** begins with a backslash (\), DOS assumes that the path to the directory name is absolute from the root. If the **path** parameter does not begin with a backslash, DOS assumes that the path to the directory name is relative from the current directory of *d:*.

Deleting a subdirectory is similar to deleting a user file. Subdirectory entries are special files to DOS. Unlike user files, however, subdirectories may contain user files and subdirectory entries. DOS does not "orphan" a subdirectory's files and lower subdirectories by deleting the subdirectory. When you issue the RMDIR (RD) command to delete a subdirectory, DOS first checks to ensure that the subdirectory is empty.

> **NOTE** An empty subdirectory contains the . and .. file entries, but DOS knows that these two entries are part of the subdirectory bookkeeping function. The presence of only the . and .. files in the directory indicates to DOS that the directory is empty.

DOS also checks to ensure that the current directory is not the directory you are deleting. You cannot delete a current directory.

> Hidden files that don't appear in a DIR command listing of the directory are considered user files; you cannot remove the directory if it contains hidden files. Use the ATTRIB command or the DOS Shell to uncover the presence of hidden files on a disk (DOS 5.0 or later).
>
> **T I P**

After determining that the subdirectory you want to delete is empty and is not the current directory, DOS removes the directory from the file system.

When using the RMDIR command, follow these guidelines:

- The directory you remove must be empty.

- The root directory is not a subdirectory. You cannot remove a root directory.

- The number of characters in the full path name (drive, path, and directory) to be removed cannot exceed 63.

- A directory affected by a SUBST command cannot be removed.

- Do not remove directories from a drive that is affected by a JOIN or an ASSIGN command.

The SUBST, JOIN, and ASSIGN commands are covered in Chapter 12, "Controlling Devices."

When you are maintaining files, you may create a directory to contain files for a special purpose of limited duration. Perhaps you keep a few files that need to be checked in a special directory. After you check the files, you no longer need to keep the files separate, or you may not need the files at all. The directory itself may be of no further use to you, and you may want to remove the directory from your disk.

As an example, assume that drive E of your system includes the directory \BC\DSWORK\DONE, which contains program files that have been checked by their author. The files and the directory are no longer needed, so you can remove them. First, log on to drive E. Then, to change to the \BC\DSWORK directory, use the following command:

CHDIR \BC\DSWORK

You are now logged on to the parent directory of \BC\DSWORK\DONE. To see the name of the directory to be deleted, type the following command:

DIR *.

DOS reports the directory on-screen as follows:

```
Volume in drive E is LOGICAL E
Volume Serial Number is 45E1-AH0B

Directory of  E:\BC\DSWORK

.    <DIR>         7-05-92       11:54a
..   <DIR>         7-05-92       11:54a
DONE <DIR>         7-11-92        9:42a

   3 File(s)            0 bytes
              200704 bytes free
```

DONE, the name of the directory you want to delete, is displayed in this DIR listing. The file name parameter included in the DIR command (*.) causes DOS to display all file names contained in the current directory that have no file name extensions.

Now, because you are logged on to the parent directory of the directory you want to delete, you can issue the RMDIR command with no drive and path parameters as follows:

RMDIR DONE

Sometimes when you try to delete a directory, DOS responds with the following message:

```
Invalid path, not directory,
or directory not empty
```

This DOS message tells you that one of the following situations has occurred:

- The full path you specified does not exist on the disk.
- The path you specified names a file, not a directory.
- The directory you are asking DOS to delete still contains files or subdirectories.

You must determine which message applies to your situation by using a process of elimination.

First, check the current directory with the CHDIR (no path parameter) command. Use DIR to look at the parent. Finally, determine whether the DONE directory contains user files or subdirectories. Change to that directory by using the following command:

CHDIR DONE

Notice that you do not have to give an absolute path to change to DONE. DOS changes to DONE relative to the current directory. You can accomplish the same directory change by issuing the following command:

CHDIR \BC\DSWORK\DONE

This second form is the absolute path form of CHDIR.

When you are logged on to DONE, issue the DIR command. For this example, you see the following directory listing:

```
Volume in drive E is LOGICAL E
Volume  Serial Number is 45E1-AH0B

Directory of  E:\BC\DSWORK\DONE

.     <DIR>         8-11-92   10:23a
..    <DIR>         8-11-92   10:23a
DWIMDOS   C   3439    6-03-92    5:23p
DWIM1     C   5414    6-04-92   11:07a
DWIM2     C  11625    6-06-92    5:39p

       5 file(s)      20478 bytes
                     200704 bytes free
```

The directory listing of the DONE directory shows that the directory is not empty. You can erase all files that contain the PRO extension to empty the directory (erasing files is covered in the next chapter); then verify that the directory is empty by issuing another DIR command. The DIR command reports the following:

```
Volume in drive Eis LOGICAL E
Volume Serial Number is 45E1-AH0B

Directory of     E:\BC\DSWORK\DONE

.     <DIR>                  8-11-92    10:23a
..    <DIR>                  8-11-92    10:23a

        2 file(s)                    0 bytes
                           255280 bytes free
```

Now only the . and .. alias directory entries remain. You can change to the parent directory by using the following shorthand command:

    CHDIR ..

From this parent directory, you can remove the now empty DONE directory with the following command:

    RMDIR DONE

The E:\DIR\DSWORK\DONE directory is removed.

Using DELTREE To Delete Directories That Contain Files

DOS 6.0's new DELTREE command enables you to delete directories that contain files—even complete branches of a directory tree. This command removes the directory you specify and everything in it—subdirectories, files, and files in subdirectories.

The syntax for DELTREE is as follows:

    DELTREE /Y d:**path**

The optional d: parameter specifies the disk that contains the directory branch to be removed. If you omit d: from the command line, DOS assumes that the current (logged) disk holds the directory to be removed.

The required **path** parameter specifies the topmost level of the directory branch to be removed. If **path** begins with a backslash (\), DOS assumes that the path to the directory name is absolute from the root. If the path parameter does not begin with a backslash, DOS assumes that the path to the directory name is relative from the current directory of *d:*.

The */Y* parameter is optional. Because DELTREE is a potentially dangerous command, capable of wiping out hundreds of files at a time, DOS normally displays the message Delete *d:path* and all its subdirectories? [Y/N]. (If you type **Y** and press Enter, the command proceeds; if you type **N** and press Enter, the operation stops.) If you use the */Y* parameter, however, the message does not appear, and DELTREE proceeds as though you had typed **Y**.

NOTE DELTREE deletes everything, including hidden files. Be sure that you no longer need anything in any of the directories subordinate to the one you name before proceeding. To make sure, first issue the DIR command (with the /S parameter) or the TREE command, which is discussed later in this chapter.

In the previous example, if you had not already deleted E:\BC\DSWORK\DONE, you could use the following command:

    DELTREE E:\BC\DSWORK\DONE

This command deletes the DONE directory and everything in it. Similarly, the following command deletes the DSWORK directory and everything in it, including the DONE directory:

    DELTREE E:\BC\DSWORK

Renaming Directories

Even if you are careful in the way you name directories, you will invariably want to change a directory name sooner or later. Suppose that you just upgraded from Quattro Pro 3.0 to Quattro Pro 4.0, for instance, and you want to rename a directory from QPR3DAT (for Quattro Pro 3.0 data) to QPRO4DAT (for Quattro Pro 4.0 data).

To rename a directory using the DOS Shell, follow these steps:

1. Select the directory name in the directory tree.

2. Choose File from the menu bar to display the File menu.

3. Select Rename from the File menu.

The Shell displays the Rename Directory dialog box. This dialog box lists the current directory name followed by a text box labeled New Name.

4. Type the new name in the text box; then press Enter or click OK.

The Shell renames the directory and immediately registers the change in the directory tree area of the DOS Shell window.

 DOS 6.0's MOVE command enables you to rename directories from the command line and also moves files from one directory to another. The syntax of the MOVE command for renaming directories is as follows:

MOVE *d:***path newname**

The optional *d:* parameter specifies the disk that contains the directory branch to be removed. If you omit *d:* from the command line, DOS assumes that the current (logged) disk holds the directory to be removed.

The required **path** parameter specifies the directory that you want to rename. If **path** begins with a backslash (\), DOS assumes that the path to the directory name is absolute from the root. If the path parameter does not begin with a backslash, DOS assumes that the path to the directory name is relative from the current directory of *d:*.

The required **newname** parameter is the new name that you want to give the directory.

Continuing the previous example, you can use the following command to rename the directory C:\SPREADSH\QPRO3DAT:

MOVE C:\SPREADSH\QPRO3DAT QPRO4DAT

The preceding command uses the absolute path syntax. If the C:\SPREADSH directory were current, you could use the following command, expressing relative path syntax:

MOVE QPRO3DAT QPRO4DAT

> **CAUTION:** You can specify a complete path, including a drive name, in the **newname** parameter, but doing so is risky. If you make a mistake, the error message Unable to open source appears.

NOTE You can use the MOVE command to move files from one directory to another, even if the directories are not on the same drive. The command cannot move directories themselves, however, from one location to another.

Listing Directories with TREE

The files in your hierarchical directories probably are organized much the same way you physically organize floppy disks. Perhaps you keep directories for letters, applications programs, memos, and many other categories, just as you keep disks with categories of files. As the number of directories and files grows, however, your ability to remember which directory holds which file decreases. Instead of asking yourself which disk holds your file, your question becomes, "Which directory holds my file?"

DOS provides an external command—TREE—that lists all the directories of a disk as a tree structure similar to the DOS Shell directory tree. The TREE command also can list the files in the directories. If you have a hard disk, you may find the TREE command especially useful.

The TREE command syntax is as follows:

TREE *d:path* */F/A*

d: is an optional parameter that indicates the drive whose directories you want to list. If you omit *d:*, TREE lists the directories on the current disk drive.

TREE with DOS 3.3 and later versions accepts the optional *path* parameter. This parameter names the directory where TREE is to start processing the listing. If you omit the *path* parameter, TREE begins processing from the root directory.

TREE in DOS 3.3 and earlier versions accepts only the single switch */F*, which directs TREE to list the files in the directories. Use this switch if you are trying to locate a file. If you do not give the switch, TREE displays only a list of the disk's directories, not the disk's files.

In DOS 4.0 and later versions, TREE displays the directory tree with line graphics characters. The */A* switch uses nongraphics characters to draw the tree.

Trying Hands-On Examples

The hypothetical examples given with the explanations of the directory-management commands illustrate how the commands work, but hands-on examples can be helpful also. The exercise in this section uses a practice disk in drive A. You can try the MKDIR, CHDIR, TREE, and RMDIR commands on the practice disk. The exercise assumes that DOS is in drive C and that a PATH command tells DOS where the external FORMAT, LABEL, and TREE commands are located on drive C.

If you have two floppy disks rather than a hard disk, use DOS in drive A and perform the exercise on a disk in drive B, which should be your logged drive. You need to give the location of the drive that contains your external commands when using the FORMAT, LABEL, and TREE commands, as in A:TREE. Be sure that your working DOS disk is write-protected.

If you have only one floppy drive, you can use drive parameters that make DOS use the one drive as two. With DOS on a disk designated as A, start by formatting a disk with the command FORMAT B:. Log onto drive B. DOS asks you to insert the disk for drive B. You leave the new formatted disk in the drive. When you issue the TREE and LABEL commands, issue them as A:TREE and A:LABEL. DOS asks you to insert the disk for drive A. At that time, remove the practice disk and insert the DOS disk. Be sure that your working DOS disk is write-protected.

 NOTE Your version of DOS may produce slightly different messages and displays from those shown. As usual, these differences are minor and don't affect the exercise.

Preparing the Exercise Disk

For this exercise, to avoid disturbing a useful disk, use a blank or surplus floppy disk. If you have a formatted blank disk, you can skip this part of the exercise. If you are using a previously formatted disk, use the DIR command on the disk to ensure that it is empty.

Insert the blank disk into drive A and issue the following command:

    FORMAT A:

DOS responds with the following message:

```
Insert new diskette for drive A:
press ENTER when ready...
```

Press Enter, and the formatting process begins. When FORMAT is finished, you see the following message:

```
Volume label  (11 characters, ENTER for none)?
```

Respond to this prompt by pressing Enter. (You add a volume label for the disk in a later step.) DOS reports the results of the formatting of the floppy and displays the following prompt:

```
Format another (Y/N)?
```

Press N and press Enter. FORMAT terminates, and DOS returns to the DOS prompt.

Performing the Exercise

First, log on to the A drive by typing **A:** and pressing Enter. Now, for the practice, issue the LABEL command as follows:

    LABEL

DOS responds with the following prompt:

```
Volume in drive A has no label
Volume  Serial Number is 394A-17EE
Volume  label (11 characters, ENTER for none)?
```

Enter the volume label **PRACTICE**, and press Enter. You can use this disk for later practice sessions if you want, but for now, you use it to work with the directory commands.

Issue the DIR command on the formatted disk. You see the following:

```
Volume in drive A is PRACTICE
Volume  Serial Number is 394A-17EE

Directory of A:\

File not found
```

Notice that the directory report is for A:\. You may be used to reading this report as a report for the entire disk, but it is actually a report for the contents of drive A's root directory. The line File not found is a good indicator that the disk has no files or subdirectories, but remember that a hidden file is not listed by DIR. Because this disk is freshly formatted, it contains no files or subdirectories—just the root directory provided by FORMAT.

Issue the following command:

    MKDIR \LEVEL1

DOS creates a directory named \LEVEL1, which stems from the root directory. Your disk light comes on momentarily as DOS writes the directory entry for \LEVEL1 into the root. Now issue the DIR command again. The DIR report looks like the following:

```
Volume in drive A is PRACTICE
Volume  Serial Number is 394A-17EE

Directory of A:\

LEVEL1      <DIR>     10-31-92  4:54p

        1 file(s)      0 bytes
                   1457152 bytes free
```

Notice that the directory listing is still of the root of drive A. Making the new directory did not change the current directory. The new directory is listed in its parent (the root) directory. To make \LEVEL1 the current directory, issue the following command:

    CHDIR LEVEL1

The DOS prompt appears as follows (assuming that the command PROMPT pg is in your system's AUTOEXEC.BAT file):

```
A:\LEVEL1>
```

Now issue the DIR command again. You see the following directory listing:

```
Volume in drive A is PRACTICE
Volume  Serial Number is 394A-17EE

Directory of A:\LEVEL1

 .       <DIR>   10-31-92     4:54p
 ..      <DIR>   10-31-92     5:54p

         2 file(s)          0 bytes
                      1457152 bytes free
```

The listing verifies that the directory being shown is of A:\LEVEL1. The two dot files are the only files in the directory. Notice that the two dot files are listed as directories. Remember that the dot directory is representative of \LEVEL1 itself. To test this representation, issue the DIR command as follows:

DIR .

You see the A:\LEVEL1 directory again.

The .. entry is representative of a directory's parent directory. Try the following command:

DIR ..

You see the A:\ (root) directory listing again. **Remember:** Using .. as a path parameter is a quick way to reference a path from a parent directory while a subdirectory is the current directory.

Now you can add a subdirectory to \LEVEL1 by issuing the following command:

MKDIR LEVEL2

Again, the path specified in the command is a relative path because no leading \ is used. DOS creates a new directory named \LEVEL1\LEVEL2 by adding the current directory, \LEVEL1, and the parameter of the MKDIR command, LEVEL2. Issue the DIR command now. You see the following:

```
Volume in drive A is PRACTICE
Volume  Serial Number is 394A-17EE

Directory of A:\LEVEL1

.          <DIR>  10-31-92    4:54p
..         <DIR>  10-31-92    5:54p
LEVEL2     <DIR>  10-31-92    4:56p

       3 file(s)         0 bytes
          1456640 bytes free
```

The new directory is listed in the \LEVEL1 parent directory. Now change to the new directory with the following command:

CHDIR LEVEL2

Again, the CHDIR parameter is a relative path to the new directory from its parent. The following DOS prompt appears:

```
A:\LEVEL1\LEVEL2>
```

The disk now has two subdirectories as a single branch of the root directory. Note that you can reach LEVEL2 only by passing through LEVEL1 because LEVEL1 is part of LEVEL2's path.

Now issue the CHDIR \ command to make the root the current directory. The prompt should be A:\> again. To see the directory structure you have created on drive A, issue the TREE command. A message similar to the following appears:

```
Directory PATH listing for Volume PRACTICE

Volume Serial Number is 394EA-17EE

A:.
    LEVEL1

        LEVEL2
```

You can see that the structure is a main branch from the root to \LEVEL1 and an additional branch from \LEVEL1 to \LEVEL1\LEVEL2. DOS enables you to create directories in a branch, one level at a time. The next command tries to create two levels of a new branch. Issue the following command:

MKDIR \SUB1\SUB2

Because \SUB1 has not been created, DOS refuses to create \SUB1\SUB2. You get the following error message:

```
Unable to create directory
```

If you create SUB1 and then SUB2, you have no problem. Do so now with the following two commands:

MKDIR \SUB1
MKDIR \SUB1\SUB2

Notice that the parameters for the MKDIR commands use paths as absolute paths from the root. You can create these two directories with these two commands from any current directory on the disk. All the necessary path information is in the parameters. None of the path information comes from DOS's current directory default. To see the new structure of the disk's directory system, issue the TREE command again. The following output appears:

```
Directory PATH listing for Volume PRACTICE

Volume Serial Number is 394EA-17EE

A:.

    LEVEL1

            LEVEL2

    SUB1

            SUB2
```

You can show the new branch in the directory tree containing \SUB1 and \SUB1\SUB2 by using the following command:

CHDIR \SUB1\SUB2

Your prompt reflects the new current directory. To illustrate that you can manage other directories from the current directory, issue the following command:

DIR \LEVEL1\LEVEL2

DOS displays a listing of \LEVEL1\LEVEL2 even though the current directory for drive A is \SUB1\SUB2. Note that the only two files in the listing are the dot files. In other words, the \LEVEL1\LEVEL2 directory is empty. To delete \LEVEL1\LEVEL2, issue the following command:

RMDIR \LEVEL1\LEVEL2

You can delete the directory because it is empty. Notice that the path specified in the RMDIR command is absolute. You must reference another branch in the directory tree from the root when your current directory is in another branch. For now, return to the root and look at the directory tree by issuing the following commands:

CHDIR \
TREE

The directory tree now appears as follows:

```
Directory PATH listing for Volume PRACTICE
Volume Serial Number is 394EA-17EE
A:.
LEVEL1
SUB1
    SUB2
```

Notice that \LEVEL1\LEVEL2 is now gone. You have created and then removed part of the directory structure.

You can continue to build on the \SUB1 directory branch by adding another subdirectory to \SUB1. Issue the following command:

MKDIR \SUB1\SUB_TOO

\SUB1\SUB_TOO is at the same level as \SUB1\SUB2 and stems from the same branch. Both directories have \SUB1 as their parent directory. The output of TREE shows the new relationship as follows:

```
Directory PATH listing for Volume PRACTICE

Volume Serial Number is 394EA-17EE

A:.
    LEVEL1

    SUB1

      SUB2

      SUB_TOO
```

Make \SUB1\SUB_TOO your current directory with the following
command:

CHDIR \SUB1\SUB_TOO

The DOS prompt indicates the new current directory. You can make
your current directory \SUB1\SUB2 by using the parent dot-dot alias in
the current directory. Issue the following command:

CHDIR ..\SUB2

The prompt now reads A:\SUB1\SUB2>. How does the .. parameter in
the CHDIR parameter work? Remember that in any subdirectory, DOS
takes the .. entry to represent the parent directory. In this case, the
parent directory is \SUB1. When DOS sees the .. in the path parameter,
DOS assumes that \SUB1 is substituted. The resulting parameter indicates \SUB1\SUB2 to DOS. DOS is able to change to the other second-
level directory in the \SUB1 branch without seeing \SUB1 as a literal
part of the CHDIR command's parameter.

Reviewing the Exercise

If you have completed the exercise, you have successfully created,
navigated, and modified a disk's directory structure. When you work
with directories in your daily computer activities, the directory management you use is not much different from that demonstrated in the
exercise. If you observe the rules and syntax of the directory-level
commands, you can create a directory structure that fits your file organization categories perfectly. If you use the DOS Shell to manage your
directories, you may find the process even easier.

If you're still a bit uncomfortable with the concept of hierarchical directories and their management, keep the practice disk for more exercises. You may find that practice results in proficiency in just a short time. Don't be afraid to talk with other DOS users about their personal preferences for ways to arrange directories. No single best way exists.

Giving full, absolute path parameters in directory commands is the surest way to work with directories. An absolute path parameter tells DOS exactly which directory you intend the command to affect. You may want to develop the habit of using full path parameters to avoid copying or deleting files in relatively specified directories. Don't worry about DOS getting a relative path parameter mixed up. DOS does what you tell it to do. Telling DOS what to do through full path parameters helps to ensure that *you* aren't getting mixed up.

If you use .. and relative path parameters, always have a good sense of where you are in the directory system. Using .. and relative paths saves command keystrokes, but always use these convenient "shortcuts" with care.

Putting Hierarchical Directories To Work for You

DOS supplies each disk with a root directory. Beyond the root, you can use the directory-management commands to create a directory tree in any architecture you want. DOS enables you to control the external look of your directory tree while the operating system manages the internal bookkeeping tasks of the hierarchical directory system. Still, some planning on your part can help make your directory system design easy to use.

The following sections suggest some directory structures and tips. Each DOS user has individual tastes in creating a directory structure. You may want to consider the following suggestions for your use or as food for thought. If you already have your directories arranged, keep these suggestions in mind for the next time you reorganize your hard disk.

Keeping a Clean Root Directory

The root directory for a 360K floppy can hold 112 file entries. Both 1.2M and 1.44M floppies hold 224 entries. If you have the DOS program files on your boot floppy, you can quickly exhaust these numbers as you add small files to the boot disk. You are not limited, however, by the number of files you can create in a subdirectory (as long as space remains on the disk for the files' contents).

If you have a hard disk, consider keeping the root directory as clean as possible. Keep in the root only the few necessary files that DOS needs to get started. With an uncluttered root directory on your hard disk, you can be a more efficient file manager.

Some files, however, need to be in the root of your boot disk. If you are using an AUTOEXEC.BAT file, it must reside in the root directory of the boot disk. The same rule applies to the CONFIG.SYS file, if you include one. If the disk is bootable, the hidden DOS system files also are located in the root directory, but the FORMAT or SYS command put them there. The system files remain in the root unless you use special disk-editing software to change the hidden and system attributes so that you can erase or move these files. Be aware that if you erase or move the system files by using a third-party program, DOS does not boot.

COMMAND.COM is normally in the root by virtue of the /S switch of the FORMAT command. The root of a bootable disk is a good place for COMMAND.COM. You do not have to leave COMMAND.COM in the root, however, if you make some entries in the CONFIG.SYS (see Chapter 17, "Configuring Your Computer") and AUTOEXEC.BAT files (see Chapter 15, "Understanding Batch Files, DOSKey, and Macros"). A good directory for COMMAND.COM is \DOS. In your CONFIG.SYS file, add the following line:

SHELL=C:\DOS\COMMAND.COM C:\DOS /P

NOTE If you are using DOS 5.0 or later versions, you don't need to perform this fine-tuning because it is performed when you install DOS. In these versions, the DOS installation program, Setup, automatically adds the SHELL command to your CONFIG.SYS file. Setup also installs a copy of COMMAND.COM in the \DOS directory on your hard disk.

When DOS boots, it takes the assignment of the SHELL command and uses the path and file name to find the command processor. Be sure not to misspell any parts of the full path name. DOS locks up at boot time if the assignment to SHELL is an incorrect file. Of course, a working copy of DOS on a floppy disk makes any SHELL error (or any other hard disk boot failure) easier to recover from. Be sure that \DOS is present on the disk. After you put this line in CONFIG.SYS, do not reboot until you have copied COMMAND.COM to \DOS from the root with the following command:

COPY \COMMAND.COM \DOS /V

(Chapter 9, "Managing Your Files," discusses the COPY command.)

With COMMAND.COM copied to \DOS, you can erase COMMAND.COM in the root. The command is as follows:

ERASE \COMMAND.COM

 NOTE If you get the error message Access denied when you attempt to erase COMMAND.COM, you may have previously used the DOS Shell or the ATTRIB command to make COMMAND.COM read-only. Refer to the discussions of setting and resetting attributes earlier in this chapter for help in turning off the read-only attribute. After the read-only attribute is reset, you can erase COMMAND.COM.

When you reboot, DOS finds COMMAND.COM in the \DOS directory of your boot disk, and your boot disk's root directory is free of the file.

Some users keep device drivers, the programs specific to the operation of input/output devices, in the root directory. If you have these types of files in your root directory, you can move them. The next section discusses driver files.

Some batch files are often located in a root directory. Batch files are ideal for relocation from the root because you can put them in another directory and use the PATH command to lead DOS to them. The next section also gives some considerations for finding a home for batch files.

When you are copying a floppy disk full of files to your hard disk, you can easily forget to use CHDIR to change the intended destination directory. If you rely on the convenience of DOS defaults instead of using the full destination path name in the COPY command, you can end up with your root full of files from the floppy because of wrong parameters in COPY.

If your root directory is fairly clean (containing only a few files), you can recover from this kind of mistake by copying everything in the root to an empty temporary subdirectory. When the subdirectory contains the root's normal files and the errant files, you can erase all files in the root. The hidden DOS files remain because you cannot erase them. Then you can copy the root's necessary files back to the root from the temporary directory. The root should contain only the files it contained before the mistake. If you make a regular printout of the command TREE /F, you can double-check the root's content. When the root is back to normal, erase the temporary directory's contents. Now you're back where you started. Try your original COPY command again, but this time with the correct destination parameters.

Including a Directory To Store DOS Programs

The DOS external commands and other DOS programs, such as QBasic, EDIT, DEBUG, and Setup, have one important element in common: these programs are all files that relate directly to the functions of DOS. Including a directory to hold these programs and their associated files is a good idea. The name for this DOS directory can be \DOS, and as the name implies, the \DOS directory is a subdirectory of the root. Some users follow the UNIX operating system's convention of keeping the utility commands in a directory called \BIN. Either name works from an organizational point of view.

 NOTE When you use the DOS 6.0 installation program, Setup, to install DOS on a hard disk, the program automatically places all DOS external command files in the \DOS directory on your system's boot disk.

When you issue a PATH command on the command line or in an AUTOEXEC.BAT file, position the \DOS entry right after the root entry. Don't forget to include the drive parameter with each alternative search path in the PATH command line. Because all your external DOS commands are located in the second search path, you should get a good response when you are working in DOS.

Many users prefer to make a subdirectory of \DOS called \DOS\DRIVERS to hold their DOS device drivers (those files with the SYS extensions) as well as device drivers included with applications programs or hardware. Because device drivers are loaded during the processing of CONFIG.SYS at boot time, you must include the full path name to the drivers you need in each command that loads a driver in the CONFIG.SYS file. Chapter 17, "Configuring Your Computer," covers the DEVICE configuration command and CONFIG.SYS. An example of a CONFIG.SYS line is as follows:

DEVICE=\DOS\DRIVERS\MOUSE.SYS

Separating the drivers from the DOS commands can make your tree listings from the TREE command or in the DOS Shell directory tree more indicative of the function of the file group in each subdirectory in the \DOS tree branch.

Creating a \BAT directory (or similar name) for all batch files is another good idea. Include this directory in the PATH command so that DOS can locate the batch files.

Ensuring Uniform Directories for Applications Programs

Many applications programs create directories to store sample files, tutorials, and auxiliary utilities, as well as data for the applications. Although many of these programs suggest default directory names when you install the software, often you are prompted to choose your own directory names. In most cases, you can let the package install with the default names for directories. You may not want to use the default names, however, if you have an older version of the package and want to keep the older version. dBASE III Plus and dBASE IV and Lotus 1-2-3 Releases 2.1, 2.2, and 3 are examples of programs that have several versions. When you install new software, be careful not to overwrite program or data files you want to keep. Often, the best policy is to install new software in a directory different from a previous version's.

If you have an applications package that does not create directories during installation, consider how you want to structure directories for the package and its data. You can copy WordStar Release 7, for example, to a directory named \WS. The directory or directories for your WordStar document files should be subordinate to the \WS directory so that all WordStar's associated files form a branch of the directory tree and are not spread across branches. You can create a \WS\MEMOS directory for your memo documents and a \WS\FORMS for office-form master documents.

Keeping associated files in the same branch of the directory tree also makes the job of backing up files easier. The command XCOPY /S copies all files from the named directory and its subdirectories. You can use this command to make convenient partial working backups of one branch of the directory tree if all associated files you want to back up are in that branch. (See Chapter 13, "Understanding Backups and the Care of Data," for a full discussion of backing up files.)

Using a Temporary Directory

DOS requires a directory for the temporary files that it creates during various operations. On many occasions, a temporary directory comes in handy for holding files you are preparing for another use. An example is the use of the temporary directory for recovering from an incorrect COPY command that deposited files in the wrong directory. You can create a directory called \TEMP to act as a temporary storage location for these files. A hard disk system with a single floppy disk drive is not a convenient system on which to copy floppy disks. The drive gets the job done, but the COPY command, using the same drive for the source and the target, asks for multiple disk swaps. You can use the DISKCOPY command, which may require fewer swaps, but any fragmentation of the original disk is mirrored on the copy.

If you are making multiple copies of an original, a simple and speedy way to make the copy is to copy the floppy's source files to the hard disk's \TEMP directory. You then can copy the files from the \TEMP directory to the destination floppy in the single floppy drive. This process reduces disk swapping, and the copies can be finished faster thanks to the hard disk's extra speed. When the copies are finished, you can erase the contents of \TEMP so that it is ready for your next use.

NOTE   DOS 5.0 and later versions *require* a directory for temporary files. The Setup program automatically sets up the \DOS directory as the repository for temporary files by adding this line to your AUTOEXEC.BAT file:

SET TEMP=C:\DOS

If you create a \TEMP directory, you may want to edit this command so that DOS uses the \TEMP directory for temporary files. To do so, change it to the following:

SET TEMP=C:\TEMP

(See Chapter 11, "Working with System Information," for information about the SET command.)

Keeping Files in \KEEP

Sometimes a file is like a favorite old shirt. You just don't know whether you want to get rid of the file. You leave it in a subdirectory like you leave an old shirt in the corner of your closet. You may need the file again, but then again, you may not. In either case, you may be too distracted by other issues to make a decision about the file's disposition when you stumble across it yet another time. Soon, you change directories and forget about the file—that is, until your disk space gets short. Then you begin digging through the dark corners of your subdirectory closets trying to find a file or two to discard. And at "disk space running out" time, you feel less equipped to make a decision about a file's importance than ever before. In confusion, you decide to erase the old file.

If this series of events strikes a familiar chord, consider creating a \KEEP directory. When you find a file that has questionable future use, but you don't want to be bothered with making a decision about its disposition at the moment, move the file to \KEEP. As always, make sure that the file does not overwrite a different file with the same name. (Always give your files descriptive names, avoiding generic names such as TEMP or SAVE.) You see in the next chapter that you can always rename files as a function of COPY.

Erase the copy of the file from its original subdirectory to keep that subdirectory uncluttered. When a week is up, \KEEP may have several files in it.

At this point, you may not have saved any disk space, but you have done some housecleaning in a few directories. Now comes the hard part. Before \KEEP contains more bytes of files than your floppy can hold on one disk, sit down and decide which files stay and which ones go. You may copy some back to their original directories. Some you may erase, and some you may copy to a "just in case" floppy disk for an archive copy. Before you store the floppy, issue the following command:

    DIR *d:*/W >PRN

d: is the name of your floppy disk. This command with the /W switch sends a wide directory report to your printer. Put the printed copy in the disk's envelope for reference. With the floppy disk holding the \KEEP "keepers," you are free to erase the contents of \KEEP. If you use this method regularly, you develop a better sense of the files that are important; those that aren't as important, you can erase.

FROM HERE...

For Related Information

▶▶ "Fine-Tuning Your Computer with CONFIG.SYS and AUTOEXEC.BAT," p. 663.

▶▶ "Understanding DOS 6.0 Boot Options," p. 681.

Chapter Summary

In this chapter, you learned about hierarchical directories and related concepts. You saw how the FAT and directories contain the what-and-where values for a file, which DOS uses to locate data about a file. This chapter also covered the commands you use to manage the hierarchical directory structure. Understanding how DOS directories relate to one another is an important step toward mastering the DOS directory-level commands and using file-level commands effectively.

In this chapter, you learned the following key points:

- Directories store the entries for each file. Each file has a name, time, and date of creation or modification, file attributes, and file size.

- The starting cluster stored in a file's directory entry points to a chain of clusters in the FAT that log the file's location on the disk.

- File attributes indicate special status for a file. Attributes are read-only (read/write), hidden, system, volume label, subdirectory, and archive.

- The ATTRIB command enables you to control the read-only, archive, system, and hidden attributes.

- DOS creates the root directory when formatting a disk, and you add subdirectories through the MKDIR command. You name a subdirectory by using any legal DOS file name and optional extension.

- The root directory and subdirectories form a hierarchical tree structure.

- You can change to a directory with the CHDIR command. That directory then becomes the current directory.

- The command PROMPT pg causes the DOS prompt to display the current drive and directory as a part of the DOS prompt.

- The PATH command helps DOS find and execute a program file, such as an external command, when the program file is not in the current directory.

- All DOS disks have a root directory.

- You can use the DOS Shell to view the hierarchical directory structure in the directory tree.

- You can use the DOS Shell to create, rename, and delete directories.

- The MKDIR (MD) command creates (makes) new directories.

- The CHDIR (CD) command changes default (current) directories.

- The TREE command reports your directory tree structure.

- The RMDIR (RD) command removes empty directories.

- A DOS-specific directory gives better control of external DOS command path searches.

- Directories for applications software packages should be uniform in structure. Many applications create their own directories when you install the package.

- Using a \TEMP directory can make file copying on a single floppy drive system easier.

- Using a \KEEP directory can keep directories less cluttered.

The directory-level commands lend themselves to practice and experimentation. You can use your existing directory layout to try variations of these commands. You may want to refer to this chapter from time to time as you work with the commands that take directory parameters.

Understanding the concept of the path is important to understanding the file-management commands presented in the next chapter. In Chapter 9, you learn all the commands you need to manage files from the command prompt and how to manage files from the DOS Shell.

Managing Your Files

After you have installed DOS on your computer, created your directories, and installed programs, you are ready to start your favorite program and get down to the business of computing. In a sense, you have set up housekeeping on your PC.

Most programs generate files as you work with them. You begin to accumulate files on your computer's disks in much the same way that you accumulate possessions in your home or office. Fortunately, DOS provides useful file-management commands in the DOS Shell and at the command line. This chapter covers these file-management commands.

You learn about using the Shell and the DOS command line to find, view, rename, delete, undelete, copy, move, and verify the contents of files. You also learn how to run program files and how to use the DOS Shell to associate specific file names with programs so that selecting a file causes the Shell to run the associated program. You even see how to run multiple programs simultaneously by using DOS's task swapper.

Key Terms Used in This Chapter

Binary file	A file containing instructions or data that has meaning to the PC but cannot be displayed or printed as ASCII characters
Character string	A series of ASCII characters
End-of-file marker	In a text file, a Ctrl-Z (^Z) ASCII character, which tells DOS that the end of the usable portion of a file has been reached
Sorting	The ordering of a list of items
Task	A program that DOS has loaded into memory
Text file	A file containing only standard ASCII characters

Using DOS To Manage Files

DOS always has provided commands for basic management of files on your computer. Beginning with DOS 4.0, however, you also can perform file-management chores through the DOS Shell. Although managing files from the DOS Shell is easy—you select options from a menu instead of typing commands at the DOS command line—you need to understand how to perform the same tasks from the command line. Sometimes, issuing a simple command from the command line is more efficient than waiting for the DOS Shell to load. At other times, you may need to use a computer on which the Shell is not loaded. The following sections describe how to use both the DOS Shell and the command line to manage files.

To get the most out of this chapter, you must be familiar with concepts discussed in preceding chapters. In particular, the discussions in this chapter depend heavily on concepts and techniques introduced in Chapters 4, 5, 6, and 8. If you haven't yet read those chapters, read them before continuing.

Selecting Files in the DOS Shell

In the DOS Shell, file-management operations are performed primarily through the File menu. The active menu options displayed in the File

menu, however, vary according to which area of the window is active.
Although the menu options displayed when the directory tree is active
are the same as the options displayed when the file list is active, many
of these menu options are dimmed (not valid) when the directory tree
is active. Most of the Shell file-management operations described in
this chapter are performed with the file-list area active. (Refer to Chapter 4, "Using the DOS Shell," for a full discussion of how to select areas
in the DOS Shell window.)

The DOS Shell's file-management commands operate on all selected
files. At any time, you can select any number of files. The Shell displays
both the name and the file-list icon of each selected file in reverse
video. Selected files need not be from the same directory.

Selecting a Single File

To select a single file, follow these steps:

1. Activate the directory-tree area.

2. Use the mouse and scroll bar or the cursor-movement keys—up
   arrow (↑), down arrow (↓), PgUp, PgDn, Home, and End—to scroll
   through the directory tree until the name of the directory containing the files you want to select appears.

3. Use the mouse or the up- and down-arrow keys to move the selection cursor to the target directory.

4. Activate the file-list area.

5. Use the mouse and scroll bar or the cursor-movement keys to
   scroll the file list until the name of the file you want to select
   appears.

6. Click the name of the file to be selected (the target file). Alternatively, use the cursor-movement keys to move the selection cursor to the target file, and then press the space bar.

To indicate that a file is selected, DOS displays the file name and file-list
icon in reverse video.

 NOTE   A file is not selected until the icon is displayed in reverse
video. Simply highlighting the file name with the selection
cursor is not sufficient to select the file.

Selecting Multiple Files

If you want to apply a DOS Shell command to several files, applying the command simultaneously to all the files is more efficient than applying it to one file at a time. After you select the first file, you can select the other files in either of the following ways. This procedure is referred to in the DOS Shell as *extending the selection*:

■ Hold down the Ctrl key and click the name of the file that you want to select.

■ Press Shift-F8. When the message ADD appears in the status bar, move the selection cursor to the name of the file you want to select, and then press the space bar. Press Shift-F8 again to turn off the ADD message.

The icon and file name of each selected file appear in reverse video (see fig. 9.1).

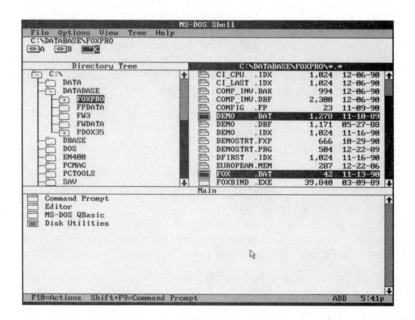

Fig. 9.1

Selecting several files in the DOS Shell.

T I P You can use either of the preceding selection methods to deselect a selected file.

Frequently, you may want the Shell to work on several files that are listed one after the other in the list area. To select contiguous files, you can select each file individually, using the previously discussed method. But the Shell provides an easier way to select files as a group.

To select files in the DOS Shell, follow these steps:

1. Select the first file.

2. Use one of the following procedures to select the remaining files:

   ■ Use the mouse to position the pointer on the last file you want to select, press the Shift key, and click the left mouse button.

   ■ While holding the Shift key, use the cursor-movement keys to move the selection bar to the last file.

   The Shell selects all the files. To indicate that these files are selected, the Shell displays the file names and their icons in reverse video.

In the file-list area shown in figure 9.2, all files between and including DEMO.BAT and FOX.BAT are selected.

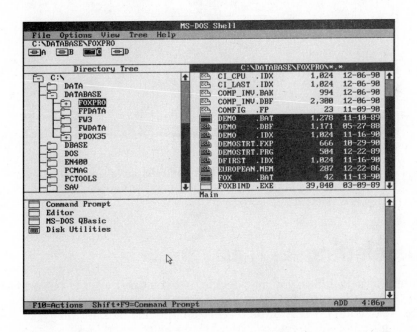

Fig. 9.2

Selecting several contiguous files in the DOS Shell.

Selecting All Files

To select all the files in a directory, follow these steps:

1. Select the directory in the directory-tree area.

2. Activate the file-list area.

3. Press Ctrl-/, or choose File from the menu bar to display the File menu (see fig. 9.3).

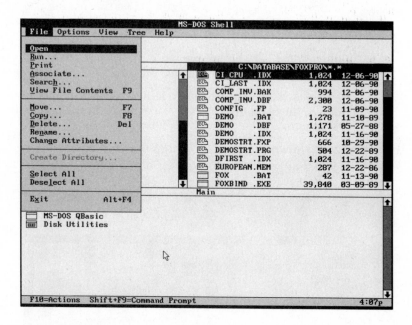

Fig. 9.3

The File menu.

4. Choose the Select All option. The Shell displays the file names and icons of all files in the directory in reverse video, indicating that they are selected.

Deselecting All Files

After you select files, you may decide that you don't want to perform a DOS Shell operation on that group of files. Perhaps you want to start a fresh selection process by *deselecting* all selected files. Normally, selecting a different directory also deselects all selected files.

You also can deselect all selected files in one procedure. Use the mouse to click anywhere in the file area, or press the space bar. Alternatively, choose Deselect All from the File menu. The Shell removes the reverse video from all file-list icons and all file names except the one on which the selection cursor is located.

Selecting Files across Directories

By default, the DOS Shell enables you to select files in only one directory at a time. By selecting a different directory, you deselect all selected files. Occasionally, however, you may want to perform a file-management operation on files from several directories. For example, you may want to copy to a floppy disk one file from each of three directories on your hard disk. You can perform this copy by using the Shell to select files across directories.

Before you can select files in several directories, you must do the following:

1. Choose Options from the menu bar to display the Options menu (see fig. 9.4).

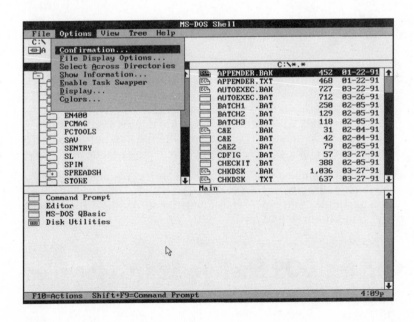

Fig. 9.4

The Options menu.

2. Choose Select <u>A</u>cross Directories. The Shell removes the <u>O</u>ptions menu from the screen.

The next time you display the <u>O</u>ptions menu, the Shell displays a small diamond (♦) to the left of the Select <u>A</u>cross Directories option. This symbol indicates that the capability to select files in several directories is enabled. Now you can select a different directory without deselecting all selected files.

To copy files from three directories to a floppy disk in one procedure, first select the directories and then the files, one at a time. Then you use the <u>F</u>ile menu's <u>C</u>opy command to copy all the selected files to the floppy disk.

FROM HERE...

For Related Information

◄◄ "Understanding the DOS Shell Window," p. 84.

◄◄ "Using the DOS Shell Menus," p. 89.

Finding Files

Personal computers commonly have storage media that can hold millions of bytes of information in hundreds or even thousands of files. Ideally, you keep the files on your computer's hard disk organized and cataloged by program and by subject matter. In reality, however, you may have many files with similar-looking file names scattered throughout your hard disk, making finding a specific file a daunting task. The DOS Shell's file-finding capability can come to the rescue.

DOS 6.0's DIR command and the Shell's Searc<u>h</u> command enable you to scan a specific directory or an entire hard disk for all files with names that fit a particular pattern. The following sections describe how to use these DOS methods to find files.

Using the DOS Shell To Search for Files

You often have a good idea of what a file's name is but are not exactly sure how it is spelled. The DOS Shell enables you to search the entire selected disk or a specific directory for every file whose file name matches given criteria.

When you want to search for a file or group of files from within the DOS Shell, use the following procedure:

1. Activate the drive area, the directory-tree area, or the file-list area.

2. Select Search from the File menu. The Shell displays the Search File dialog box (see fig. 9.5).

Fig. 9.5

The Search File dialog box.

A message in the Search File dialog box indicates which directory currently is selected in the directory-tree area. Below this message is the Search For text box, which contains the default search criterion *.* (pronounced *star dot star*). The search criterion defines the file-name pattern for which you want the Shell to search.

The DOS wild-card character (*) in the search criterion tells the Shell to search for every file with any file name and any file-name extension. Clearly, the default criterion is too broad for your usual needs, and you will have to specify new criteria.

3. Type the search criteria in the Search For text box. When you specify the criteria, you can use any valid file name, as well as the DOS wild-card characters * and ?.

Suppose that you want to search for your budget spreadsheet but cannot remember which directory contains that file. Because you are not sure whether the file name is BUDGT.WQ1, BUDGET.WQ1, or BUDGET.WK1, you would type the following search criterion in the text box:

BUDG*.W?1

The Search File dialog box also contains an option check box labeled Search Entire Disk (by default, the check box contains an X) and three command buttons: OK, Cancel, and Help.

4. Click OK or press Enter. The Shell searches the entire selected disk, clears the screen, and displays a list of the file names that meet the criterion.

Figure 9.6 shows the results of the BUDG*.W?1 search.

```
                              MS-DOS Shell
    File  Options  View  Tree  Help
                         Search Results for: BUDG*.W?1
     📄 C:\WORD_PRO\ENDATA\BUDGT.WK1                                        ↑
     📄 C:\SPREADSH\QPRO2DAT\BUDGET.WQ1




















    F10=Actions  Esc=Cancel                                          4:11p  ↓
```

Fig. 9.6

Search results for
BUDG*.W?1.

If the Shell cannot find a file name that matches the criteria, the following message appears:

```
No files match file specifier
```

Sometimes, you want to narrow your search to a single directory. In such a case, follow this procedure:

1. Select the target directory in the directory-tree area.

2. Choose Search from the File menu. The Search File dialog box appears.

3. Type the search criteria in the text box.

4. Toggle off the Search Entire Disk check box (click this check box to remove the X).

5. Click OK or press Enter. The Shell searches only the selected directory and displays a list of file names that meet the search criteria.

You can apply all of the Shell's file-management commands to the file list that the Search command generates.

Searching for Files with the DIR Command

To find a file on your disk from the command line, you can use the /S switch with the DIR command. The /S switch +instructs DOS to search the current directory and all directories below the current directory.

If you want to search a specific directory, first use the CHDIR command to change to that directory. To search the entire disk, change to the root directory. At the DOS prompt, type **DIR**, followed by the search criterion. The search criterion can be a specific file name or can contain wild-card characters (* and ?). To complete the command, add the /S switch, and then press Enter.

To search the current disk for your budget spreadsheet (as in the example in the preceding section), change to the root directory, and then type the following command:

DIR BUDG*.W?1 /S

When you press Enter, DOS displays a listing similar to the following:

```
         Volume in drive C is QUE BRUCE
          Volume Serial Number is 1628-BA9A

      Directory of C:\SPREADSH\QPRO4DAT

      BUDGET     WQ1      4037     10-05-92     2:00A
                 1 files(s)          4037 bytes


      Directory of C:\WORD_PRO\ENDATA

      BUDGET     WK1       5120    04-07-92     8:51p
                s 1 files(s)          5120 bytes

   Total files listed:
                 2 files(s)          9157 bytes
                            9400320 bytes free
```

Using the Shell To Display File Information

By default, the DOS Shell lists the name, size, and directory date of each file in the selected directory. But the operating system stores additional information about each file. The Show Information command in the DOS Shell enables you to display that additional information.

To display additional information about a file within the DOS Shell, follow these steps:

1. Move the selection cursor to the target file name in the DOS Shell window's file-list area.

2. Choose <u>S</u>how Information from the <u>O</u>ptions menu. The Show Information dialog box appears (see fig. 9.7).

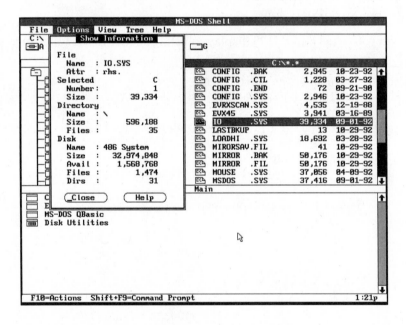

The Show Information dialog box is one of the few dialog boxes that provide information without asking you for any input. Under the headings File, Selected, Directory, and Disk, the dialog box lists information about the highlighted file (refer to fig. 9.7).

The File section of the Show Information dialog box displays the file name (including the extension) as well as file attributes. Each currently set attribute is indicated in the Attr line by a character: *r* for read-only, *h* for hidden, *s* for system, and *a* for archive. (Refer to Chapter 8, "Understanding and Managing Directories," for a discussion of file attributes.) In figure 9.7, the Show Information dialog box lists information for the file IO.SYS. Because IO.SYS is one of two read-only, hidden DOS system files, the Attr line shows the characters *r* (for read-only), *h* (for hidden) and *s* (for system).

The names of the drives currently stored in the Shell's buffer appear to the right of the Selected heading in the dialog box. If you have logged on to more than one drive during the current Shell session, this section of the dialog box contains two columns. The Selected row lists the two most recently selected drives; the first column shows the current drive, and the second column shows the drive you selected immediately before the current one. The Number line shows the number of files currently selected on the disk. The Size row shows the total bytes of disk storage occupied by all the selected files (on both disks, if two disks are listed).

The Directory section of the Show Information dialog box displays the name of the currently selected directory, the total size of all files in that directory, and the total number of files in that directory. In figure 9.7, the directory name is a backslash (\), which indicates that the current directory is the root.

The dialog box's Disk section displays information about the disk drive. The Name row is the current drive's volume label (applied during formatting or with the LABEL command); the Size row represents total storage space on the current disk; and the Avail entry shows how much free space is available for new files. The Files row displays the number of files stored on the disk; and the last entry, Dirs, shows the number of subdirectories on the disk.

For Related Information

◀◀ "Understanding File Attributes," p. 227.

FROM HERE...

Controlling the File-List Display

When you use the Shell to display file names, the names appear in alphabetical order. When you use the DIR command at the DOS command line, DOS normally lists files in the order in which the names are
stored on the disk. At times, however, listing files in some other order
is convenient. The following sections describe how to change the order
in which files are displayed in the DOS Shell and how to use the DIR
command to display files in a different order.

Using the Shell To Control the File-List Display

Normally, the Shell displays in the file list all files in the current directory, listing them in ascending alphabetical order (*A* through *Z*). Sometimes, however, you want the program to display a more-limited group
of file names in the Shell window. You may want to find a particular file
name or to list a certain category of files (all spreadsheets, for example). At other times, you may want the files to be listed in a different
order, perhaps by date or by size. You can limit the files listed in the
file-list area of the DOS Shell window, and you can change the order in
which the Shell lists file names. To perform either task, you use the File
Display Options command.

To limit the files listed in the file-list area, follow these steps:

1. Choose File Display Options from the Options menu. The Shell
    displays the File Display Options dialog box (see fig. 9.8).

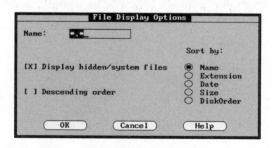

2. The entry in the Name text box determines which files the Shell
    lists in the file-list area. This text box contains the default value
    ., which causes the Shell to list all files from the selected
    directory.

3. To cause the Shell to limit the file listing, type a file-name criterion in the Name text box. You can use either or both of the DOS wild-card characters. The asterisk (*) takes the place of any string of characters, and the question mark (?) takes the place of any single character.

Suppose that the currently selected directory is C:\DOS and that you want to display all files in the directory with the EXE extension. You would type the following criterion in the Name text box:

*.EXE

4. After you type a new file-name criterion, click OK or press Enter. The Shell returns to the DOS Shell window and repaints the screen. The file-list area now contains only file names that meet the new criterion you specified.

The file-list area of the DOS Shell window shown in figure 9.9, for example, lists only file names with the extension EXE.

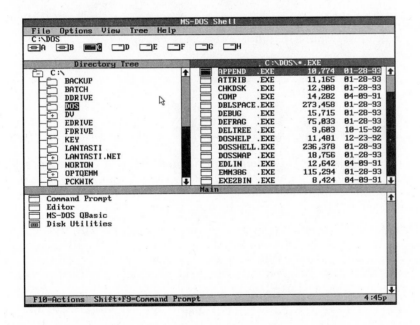

Fig. 9.9

The File-list area showing only files with the extension EXE.

If no files meet the criterion, the Shell displays the message No files match file specifier.

To change the order in which the Shell lists file information, follow these steps:

1. Choose File Display Options from the Options menu. The File Display Options dialog box appears.

2. Click one of the five option buttons under the Sort By heading:

Option	Result
Name	Sorts by file name
Extension	Sorts by file extension
Date	Sorts by creation or modification date
Size	Sorts by file size
DiskOrder	Displays the tile names in the order in which they appear in the directory

3. Click OK or press Enter. The DOS Shell lists files in the new sort order. The Shell continues to use the new file-name criterion and the new sort order until you change either setting or exit the Shell.

T I P Don't forget to change the file-name criterion to *.* after you finish looking at a limited list of files. Otherwise, you may get confused and think that some of your files are missing.

Using DIR To Control the File-List Display

Chapter 5, "Using DOS Commands," introduces the DIR command and two of its switches, /P and /W. In DOS 5.0 and 6.0, the DIR command has five additional switches, which enable you to control the list of files displayed at the command line by the DIR command.

By default, DIR lists the names of all files except those with the hidden or system attribute. Files are listed in no particular order. By adding certain switches to the DIR command, you can make DOS list only file names that have specified attributes. You also can make DOS list file names in a specific sorted order.

The complete syntax of the DIR command is shown in the following:

DIR *d:path\filename /P/W/Aattributes/Osortorder/S/B/L/C*

Refer to Chapter 5, "Using DOS Commands," for discussions of the *d:*, *path*, and *filename* parameters and of the */P* and */W* switches.

The /Aattributes switch enables you to list only files that have one or more specific file attributes. Substitute one or more of the following codes for the *attributes* parameter:

Attribute Code	Meaning
A	Archive attribute
D	Directory attribute
H	Hidden attribute
R	Read-only attribute
S	System attribute

The /C switch has no affect on normal drives but displays the degree of compression for each file in an additional column on DoubleSpace drives.

To see a listing of all hidden files in the current directory, for example, type the following command, and then press Enter:

DIR /AH

DOS lists all files that have the hidden attribute.

You can include attribute codes in any combination and in any order. For example, you can list all file names with the read-only attribute and the archive attribute by issuing the following command:

DIR /ARA

When you press Enter, DOS lists file names that have both attributes.

To list only file names that do not have a certain attribute, insert a minus sign (–) before the attribute code. To see all files that are not directories and that don't have the archive bit, for example, type the following command at the command line, and then press Enter:

DIR /A-A-D

If, in a DIR command, you include the /A switch with no attributes parameter, DOS lists all file names, regardless of file attribute—even the names of hidden and system files.

The /Osortorder switch enables you to determine the order in which DOS lists file names. To cause DOS to sort the file list in a particular order, substitute for the *sortorder* parameter one of the following sort codes:

Parameter Code	Meaning
E	Sorts alphabetically by file extension
D	Sorts chronologically by date and time
G	Groups directories first
N	Sorts alphabetically by name
S	Sorts numerically by file size
C	Sorts in order of degree of compression

You can include sort codes in any combination. The order of the sort codes in the DIR command denotes the priority of each sort criterion. The command DIR /ONE, for example, sorts the file names first by name and then by extension. The command DIR /OEN sorts files by extension (for example, grouping all COM files together and all EXE files together) and then sorts the files by name. If you include the /O switch in a DIR command without specifying a sort code, DOS sorts the file names alphabetically.

By default, all sorting is in ascending order: *A* through *Z*, smallest to largest, earliest to latest. Precede a sort code with a minus sign (–) to reverse the sort order: *Z* through *A*, largest to smallest, latest to earliest.

For a discussion of the */S* switch, refer to "Searching for Files with the DIR Command" earlier in this chapter.

Use the */B* switch to display a "bare" file list: a list of file names only. The default file list generated by the DIR command shows the name of each file in the directory, the file name extension, the file size, and the date and time when the file was last changed. Occasionally, you may want to see only the name of each file. Perhaps you want to print a list of the files on a floppy disk. In such a case, insert the disk into drive A, and then issue the following command:

    DIR A: /B

DOS lists on-screen the names of all files in the current directory of the disk in drive A. DOS does not list file size or file date and time. To send this list to the printer, issue the following command:

    DIR A: /B >PRN

The */L* switch, used with the DIR command, instructs DOS to display file names in lowercase letters.

Establishing a Default Directory Display

If you find that you continually use one or more of the seven switches available for use with the DIR command, record the switch(es) as an environment variable named DIRCMD. Add the following command to your AUTOEXEC.BAT command:

SET DIRCMD=*switches*

Substitute for *switches* the switch or switches you want DOS to use by default. If you want DOS to sort file names alphabetically and to pause scrolling after each screenful of information, for example, include the following command in AUTOEXEC.BAT:

SET DIRCMD=/ON/P

Reboot the computer. DOS creates the environment variable DIRCMD and gives it the value /ON/P. Each time you issue the DIR command, DOS automatically adds these two switches.

You can override a switch that is recorded in the DIRCMD by preceding the switch with a minus sign (–). To override the /P switch that currently is recorded in DIRCMD, for example, issue the DIR command as follows:

DIR /-P

DOS lists all file names without pausing at the end of each screenful of information.

For Related Information

◀◀ "The Command-Line Parameters," p. 117.

◀◀ "The Optional Switches," p. 118.

FROM HERE...

Viewing Files

As you work with files in the Shell, you occasionally need to view the contents of a file. In many programs, a file on one of the distribution disks includes information that supplements the program's manuals. Typically, you are instructed to read this file (often named READ.ME, README.TXT, or a similar name) before you install the software in your system. Such files normally contain only ASCII characters; a file that contains only ASCII characters often is called an *ASCII file*.

Understanding Bytes

To DOS, a file simply is a stream of bytes. A byte contains 8 bits (binary digits) and can represent more than one kind of value in your PC. A byte can be encoded to represent a number, a computer instruction, a table, or even an ASCII character. Usually, computer professionals represent bytes as one of two general types: ASCII and binary.

An ASCII byte contains a code that represents one of 256 possible ASCII characters. Files composed entirely of ASCII codes are called ASCII files. The DOS TYPE command and the DOS Shell's View File Contents command (File menu) both work with ASCII files. Not all ASCII codes, however, represent readable text characters such as letters, numbers, and punctuation symbols.

Some ASCII codes are device-control codes; a device detects and uses a code that controls the device's operation. Ctrl-S is one control code; a device that detects Ctrl-S in a character stream stops sending its stream of characters. You can use Ctrl-S to stop a display from scrolling off the screen, for example. When the control characters are not being used to control a device, they can represent special characters—such as a smiling face or musical notes—on-screen. Other ASCII codes produce special characters on-screen but have no device-control meaning. These ASCII codes produce lines and corners of boxes and other graphical characters or foreign-language characters.

Binary files are composed of bytes that represent instructions and data. The contents of these files have no character equivalents. Only software programs can read binary files and make sense of their contents. You can use the DOS TYPE command to force display of the contents of a binary file as ASCII code, but the display is gibberish, filled with random characters and symbols. To view the contents of binary files expressed as hexadecimal (hex) codes, use the DOS Shell.

When you need to view the contents of an ASCII file, you can use either the TYPE command or the DOS Shell's View File Contents command. You also can use this Shell command to display the contents of any file, even a *binary file* (one that contains non-ASCII codes). The following sections describe both file-viewing methods.

Using the Shell To View a File

When you want to view the contents of a file from within the DOS Shell, follow these steps:

1. Select the target file in the file-list area.

2. Choose View File Contents from the File menu.

When the file you want to view contains only ASCII characters, the Shell displays the ASCII-file viewer. One of the files distributed with DOS 6.0, for example, is named APPNOTES.TXT and contains only ASCII text. To view the contents of APPNOTES.TXT, select its name in the file-list area, and then choose View File Contents from the File menu. The Shell displays the file in the ASCII viewer (see fig. 9.10).

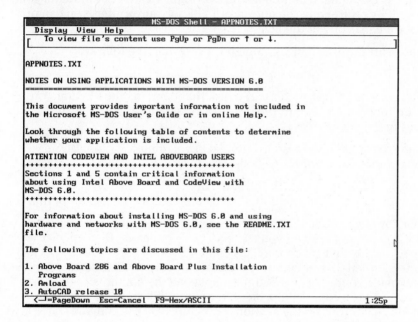

To scroll through the file, use the cursor-movement keys (PgUp, PgDn, ↑, and ↓). Alternatively, you can use the mouse to click the labels PgUp, PgDn, ↑, or ↓, which are displayed near the top of the window (refer to fig. 9.10). Press Esc to return to the DOS Shell window.

When the file you want to view contains data other than ASCII characters, the Shell uses the hexadecimal (base 16, often referred to as *hex*) viewer. If you select the DOS command-processor file, COMMAND.COM, and press F9, for example, the Shell displays the contents of the file as four columns of hexadecimal codes and one column of ASCII characters. (This information normally has meaning only to programmers and to the computer.) As in the ASCII viewer, you can scroll through the file by using the cursor-movement keys or the mouse.

Non-ASCII files, such as COMMAND.COM, frequently contain at least some ASCII text. You can switch between the ASCII and hex viewers by pressing F9.

Using the TYPE Command To View Files

When you need to see the contents of an ASCII text file, you can use the TYPE command as well as the DOS Shell's View File Contents command. By redirecting the output of TYPE to your printer, you can produce a hard copy of the file.

The syntax for the TYPE command is shown in the following:

TYPE *d:path***filename.ext**

The optional *d:* parameter is the disk that contains the file that you want to view. If you omit the drive, DOS assumes that you want to view files in the default drive.

The *path*\\ parameter also is optional. If you omit the path, DOS assumes that you want the default directory.

Replace **filename.ext** with the name of the file you want DOS to display. This parameter is not optional. Wild-card characters are not permitted.

TYPE is designed to display the contents of a text file that contains ASCII characters. When you issue a TYPE command, DOS opens the specified file and sends the file's contents to the screen as ASCII characters. When DOS encounters a Ctrl-Z character (ASCII decimal 26; the end-of-file character), DOS stops displaying the contents of the file and returns to the command prompt. (For more information about the end-of-file character, see the section "Using the COPY Command" later in this chapter.)

When you use TYPE to view a text file, the file's contents can fill and begin to scroll off the screen faster than you can read the text. You can press Ctrl-S or the Pause key (available only on the Enhanced Keyboard) to stop scrolling, but the text you want to see may already have scrolled off the screen. MORE displays a screenful of a command's output and then pauses until you press a key. You can use the MORE filter with the TYPE command as shown in the following example:

TYPE AUTOEXEC.BAT | MORE

The | character in this command is the DOS *pipe* character, which instructs DOS to send a command's output to the filter that follows the pipe character. Piping to MORE causes DOS to pause the scrolling of the screen when the screen fills. Press any key to display the next screenful.

T I P

An even easier way to display an ASCII file one screen at a time is to *redirect* a file into the MORE command without using the TYPE command at all. Use the following syntax:

MORE < *d:path***filename.ext**

The < symbol causes DOS to use the specified file parameter as input to the MORE filter. DOS displays the file, one page at a time, displaying the message - - More - - at the end of each page. To display a file in the C:\DOS directory, for example, type the following command (replacing **filename.ext** with the file name and extension of the file you want to view), and press Enter:

MORE < C:\DOS\filename.ext

If you want a simple printed copy of the contents of a text file, you can redirect the output of the TYPE command to the printer by using the special redirection character: the greater-than sign (>). To print the contents of the README.TXT file, for example, make sure that your printer is on-line, and then issue the following command:

TYPE README.TXT >PRN

Your printer prints the file. (Because TYPE does not format the text into pages, the printed output may not break at page boundaries.)

When you use the TYPE command, remember the following guidelines:

■ The output of TYPE stops when the command encounters the first Ctrl-Z in the file.

■ Because TYPE does not accept wild cards in the file-name parameter, use of the command is limited to a one file at a time.

■ TYPE tries to interpret any file as an ASCII text file, even if the file contains non-ASCII data. If you use a binary file (such as a COM or EXE file) as the file parameter, TYPE's output may produce graphical characters, control-character sequences, and beeps. TYPE's output may even lock up your computer, forcing you to reboot.

■ You can pause TYPE's output by pressing Ctrl-S or Pause. Press any key to resume scrolling.

■ You can terminate TYPE's output by pressing Ctrl-C or Ctrl-Break.

Printing Files from the DOS Shell

The DOS Shell has an option that uses the DOS PRINT command. You first must load PRINT.COM from the DOS prompt. At the command prompt, type the following command, and then press Enter:

    PRINT

DOS displays the following message:

    Name of list device [PRN]:

If your printer is attached to the computer's first parallel printer port (LPT1), simply press Enter. Otherwise, type the appropriate printer-port device name, and then press Enter. DOS displays a message similar to the following:

    Resident part of PRINT installed
    PRINT queue is empty

This message indicates that the PRINT program is loaded in memory as a memory-resident program. Now you can use the PRINT command (as described in the Command Reference) or the DOS Shell's Print command to print files.

Restart the DOS Shell, and then follow these steps to print a file:

1. In the DOS Shell window's file-list area, select the file or files that you want to print.

2. Choose Print from the File menu. The Shell sends all selected files to the PRINT command's *print queue*: a holding area on the disk.

   The print queue, which is controlled by the PRINT command, contains files that are waiting to be printed. Files are printed in the order in which they are sent to the print queue. The memory-resident portion of the PRINT command controls the flow of data to the printer. You can continue with other operations in the Shell as the selected files print.

Starting Programs

The DOS Shell provides several ways to start a program. A sophisticated capability for starting programs in the Shell's program-list area is
explained fully in Chapter 16, "Configuring the DOS Shell." The following sections describe some of the other Shell methods and the procedure for starting a program from the command line.

Running a Program in the Shell

When you want to run a program and you know the exact start-up command, you can use the DOS Shell's Run command to start the program
by following these steps:

1. Activate the drive area, the directory-tree area, or the file-list area
   in the DOS Shell window.

2. Choose Run from the File menu. The Shell displays the Run dialog
   box, which contains the Command Line text box (see fig. 9.11).

Fig. 9.11

The Run dialog
box.

3. Type the appropriate start-up command for the program in the
   Command Line text box.

4. Press Enter. DOS blanks the screen and executes the command,
   which in turn starts the program.

After you quit the program, DOS returns to the DOS Shell window.

A second way to run a program from within the Shell requires that you
first locate the program file and display its name in the file-list area.
(The file must have the extension EXE, COM, or BAT.) Then you can
start the program by performing one of the following steps:

■ Double-click the program file's name.

■ Select the file name, and then press Enter.

■ Select the file name, and then choose Open from the File menu.

T I P   The Run command works only when the program you are trying to run is located in a directory specified in the current path (see the discussion of PATH in Chapter 11, "Working with System Information") or when you include a complete path name before the name of the program. The PATH command is most useful when you have created a DOS batch file for each program that you routinely use. (Batch files are explained in Chapter 15, "Understanding Batch Files, DOSKey, and Macros.")

See Chapter 16, "Configuring the DOS Shell," if you are interested in an even more powerful and convenient method of starting programs: customizing the DOS Shell's program-list area.

T I P   The Shell denotes program files—files that have the extensions EXE, COM or BAT—with the following icon:

The Shell denotes all other types of files with the following icon:

Starting Associated Programs in the Shell

Probably the most convenient way to start programs from the file list area is a procedure called *launching*—starting a program by selecting one of the program's data files. Before you can use this procedure to start a particular program, however, you must *associate*—assign or identify—at least one of that program's file extensions. Then you can start the program by selecting a file name that has the associated extension.

Associating Files with Programs

Many programs create and work with files that have distinctive file name extensions. Lotus 1-2-3 files have the extensions WKS, WK1, or WK3; Microsoft Word document files have the extension DOC; and dBASE database files have the extension DBF. The DOS Shell enables you to associate particular extensions with a specific program so that you can start the program and load a file with an associated extension in one step.

The DOS 6.0 Shell provides two procedures for associating one or more file extensions with a program.

To specify that all extensions be associated with a particular program, follow these steps:

1. In the file-list area, select the program or batch file with which you want to associate specific extensions. (The program must use COM, EXE, or BAT extensions.)

2. Choose Associate from the File menu. The Shell displays the Associate File dialog box.

   This dialog box contains a message that indicates the name of the program. The dialog box also contains a text box labeled Extensions.

3. In the Extensions text box, type the extension(s) that you want to associate with the application or batch file (see fig. 9.12).

Fig. 9.12

The Associate File dialog box with file extension specified.

   Do not type a period at the beginning of each extension. If you type more than one extension, press the space bar between entries.

4. Click OK or press Enter.

Suppose that you want to associate the extensions TXT and INI with the DOS Editor (discussed in Chapter 14, "Using the DOS Editor"). Type the following command in the Associate File dialog box, and then press Enter:

TXT INI

The second method of associating a file extension with a program starts with the data file rather than the program file. As an alternative to the preceding procedure, follow these steps for each file extension that you want to associate with a program:

1. In the file-list area, select a file whose extension you want the Shell to associate with a specific program. Again using the DOS Editor as an example, you can select a file with the extension TXT, such README.TXT, which is distributed with DOS 6.0.

2. Choose Associate from the File menu. The Shell displays another Associate File dialog box, this one containing a text box in which you can type the program's directory path and file name. If the current file extension already is associated with a program, the Shell displays the program's path and file name in the text box.

3. In the text box, type the program's complete file name, including the extension. If the file is in a directory that's not included in the PATH statement, type the directory path as well as the file name.

4. Click OK or press Enter.

 NOTE Program-to-file extension associations are stored in an ASCII file called DOSSHELL.INI. You can use any text editor, including the DOS Editor, to edit this file.

Launching Files in the Shell

After you associate a file extension with a program in the Shell, starting the program and loading an associated file in one procedure—often called *launching the file*—is easy. To launch a file, follow these steps:

1. Select the data file whose associated program you want to run.

2. Choose Open from the File menu or press Enter. The Shell starts the associated program and tries to load the selected data file.

As an alternative to steps 1 and 2, double-click the data file name.   **T I P**

If you associated the TXT extension with the DOS Editor (EDIT.COM), for example, you can start the Editor and load README.TXT by double-clicking the README.TXT entry in the DOS Shell window's file-list area.

NOTE When you use the method discussed in this section to launch a file, the Shell executes a command that has the same effect as typing at the command prompt the program name followed by a space and the data file name. When you select README.TXT, for example, the Shell executes the following command:

EDIT README.TXT

Although this procedure is successful in many cases, not all programs can load data files that are typed as a part of the start-up command. If the Shell starts the associated program but fails to load the data file, you must issue the appropriate commands in the program to load the data file.

After you finish running a program that you launched by using the Shell, DOS displays the following message:

```
Press any key to return to MS-DOS Shell...
```

If you press any key on the keyboard, DOS again displays the DOS Shell window.

Using the Task Swapper

The DOS 5.0 Shell introduced a significant new feature that has been retained in DOS 6.0: the capability to load more than one program at a time. DOS accomplishes this feat through a technique called *task swapping*. To activate this feature, choose Enable Task Swapper from the Options menu. The Shell adds an active task-list area to the window (see fig. 9.13). Initially, nothing is listed in this area because no program (other than the Shell) is active.

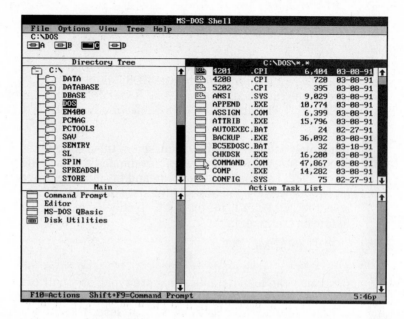

The DOS Shell window with an active task-list area.

With the task swapper enabled, you still start programs by using any of the methods described earlier in this chapter. But after you start a program, you can jump back to the DOS Shell instantly without exiting the program. Simply press Alt-Esc or Alt-Tab, and the screen returns to the DOS Shell window, where the program (or associated data file) is listed in the active task-list area. DOS has swapped the contents of memory (RAM) to disk, freeing space in memory so that you can run another program.

Suppose that you start the DOS Editor by selecting Editor from the program-list area. After you work in the DOS Editor, you decide that you want to return to the DOS Shell to format a disk. Press Alt-Tab or Alt-Esc. DOS clears the screen, displays the label MS-DOS Shell at the top of the screen, and then displays the DOS Shell window. The DOS Editor now is listed as an active task in the active task-list area (see fig. 9.14).

After you return to the DOS Shell window, you can use any DOS Shell command or load another program.

After using the task swapper to load more than one program, you can press Alt-Tab or Alt-Esc to return to the Shell window. The Shell adds each open program to the list in the active task-list area. To jump to one of the active tasks, select the appropriate file name in the active task list, and then press Enter. Alternatively, double-click the file name.

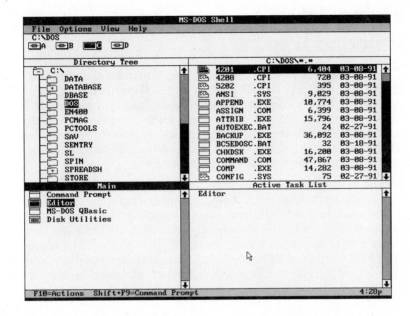

Fig. 9.14

Using the task
swapper.

CAUTION: Do not load a 3270 terminal-emulation or telecommunications program under the task swapper. If you load a terminal
emulator, your session with the mainframe computer may be disconnected unexpectedly, resulting in potential data loss. If you
load a telecommunications program, data transmission will fail if
you switch to another program.

T I P

The fastest way to switch between active tasks is to hold down the
Alt key and tap the Tab key. *Do not release the Alt key.* The Shell
displays the name of the task at the top of the screen. Still holding
down the Alt key, press the Tab key again to see the name of the
next task. Repeat this keystroke until the target task name appears.
Finally, release the Alt key. The Shell switches to the target task.

When you quit a program, the Shell removes the program's name from
the active task list. When the active task-list area is empty, you can
disable the task swapper by choosing Enable Task Swapper from the
Options menu again.

Starting Programs from the Command Line

To start a program from the command line, you must change to the directory that contains the program and then type the correct start-up command. Typically, you type the program name and press Enter. With many programs, you can select certain features or options by adding special parameters to the start-up command. (Consult the documentation that comes with your software to determine the most appropriate start-up command for each of your programs.)

Often, the most convenient practice is to include in your computer's PATH command the directory that contains a program. This practice normally enables you to start the program without first changing to the directory that contains the target program. When in doubt, check your software's documentation to determine whether adding the program to the PATH command will benefit you. (For more information on the PATH command, refer to Chapter 8, "Understanding and Managing Directories.")

FROM HERE...

For Related Information

▶▶ "Issuing the SET Command," p. 424.

▶▶ "Using Batch-File Commands," p. 565.

▶▶ "Using Multiple Start-Up Commands," p. 616.

▶▶ "Providing Information through Replaceable Parameters," p. 617.

Copying and Moving Files

Probably the most common file-related function is copying files from one disk or directory to another. Another common task for many PC users is copying one or more files from one storage location to another location and then deleting the original files. The result is that the files are moved from the first location to the second. The following sections describe how to use DOS (from the Shell and from the command line) to copy and move files.

Copying files is a fundamental job for disk operating systems. MS-DOS provides the COPY command (for use at the command line) as well as several ways to copy files in the Shell.

The DOS copy operation enables you to copy files as well as to copy data to and from logical devices. Figure 9.15 diagrams the copy operation used with several possible inputs and two possible outputs. Three of the possible inputs consist of more than one file or logical device. DOS can join two or more inputs into one output in a process called *combining*. You may never need to use all these inputs and outputs, but they are available with the command.

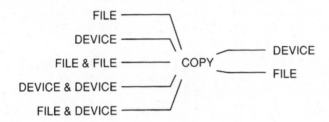

Fig. 9.15

Possible inputs and outputs in a copy operation.

When you perform a copy operation, remember the following guidelines:

- The source parameter must contain at least one of the following parameters: path, file, or device.

- If the source-file parameter is omitted, all files in the specified directory and drive are copied. This situation is equivalent to supplying *.* as the source-file parameter.

- You can specify additional source-file parameters by using the + operator to combine the files.

- If the source-file parameter contains a wild card and the destination parameter is a file name, the destination file will be the combination of source files that matches the source-file parameter.

- If COPY detects an attempt to copy a single source file to itself (same drive, directory, file name, and extension), the copy operation is aborted.

- The optional destination parameter consists of a combination of drive, path, and file-name parameters. If you don't provide a drive or path, DOS uses the current drive or path for the destination. If you don't specify a destination file name, DOS uses the source file's name as the destination parameter.

COPY definitely is a versatile file-management workhorse. A incorrect COPY operation, however, can do nearly as much damage as an incorrect ERASE command. Be sure to treat COPY with respect. Many programs include warning messages as part of their internal file-copying commands. The DOS COPY command gives no warning when it is about to overwrite existing files, but the Shell's Copy command does.

Copying Files in the Shell

With the DOS Shell, you can copy one or more files in a directory, between directories, or between disks, using any of several approaches. The approach described in this section—the dual-file-list method—is the quickest and easiest to learn and use.

To perform the copy operation using the dual-file-list method, you first must select the source and target drive and directory and create a dual file list. Complete the following steps:

1. Select the source drive and directory (those that contain the files you want to copy).

2. Choose Dual File Lists from the View menu to switch to the dual file list.

   NOTE Under certain specific circumstances, you can skip this step. For example, you can drag selected files to another directory on the same disk without opening a dual file list. Completing this step, however, always produces the result that you want.

3. Use the mouse or the cursor-movement keys to select the target drive and directory in the second directory tree.

4. Use the mouse or keyboard to select, in the first (upper) file list, the files that you want to copy.

   Figure 9.16 shows an example of a dual-file-list display. C:\SPREADSH\QPRO2DAT is displayed in the top file list area; A:\SPREADSH\BUDGET appears in the bottom file list.

The remaining steps for completing the copy operation differ, depending on whether you want to use the mouse or the keyboard. If you use a mouse, complete the following steps:

1. Position the mouse pointer on a selected file in the upper file list. Hold down the Ctrl key while you press and hold the left mouse button. While holding down both the Ctrl key and the mouse button, drag the mouse pointer to the target drive letter in the lower drive area or, alternatively, to the target directory's name in the lower directory tree.

   When you begin to drag the mouse, the pointer changes from an arrow (or a block, in text mode) to a circle (or two exclamation-point symbols, in text mode). When the pointer enters the second directory tree, the circle becomes a file icon (or a diamond, in text mode). If you are copying several files, the file icon resembles a stack of three papers.

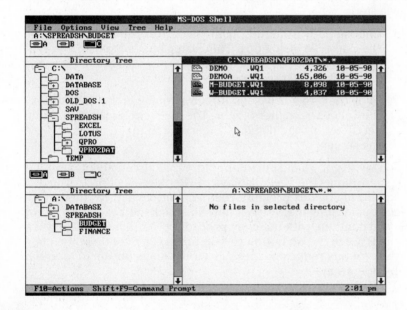

Fig. 9.16

Using the dual-file-list display to copy files.

NOTE

When you are copying files to a different disk, you don't have to hold down the Ctrl key; holding down the mouse button is enough. If you drag files to another directory on the same disk without holding down the Ctrl key, however, the Shell assumes that you want to *move* the files rather than *copy* them.

After you release the mouse button and Ctrl key, the Shell displays the Confirm Mouse Operation dialog box, which contains the following query:

```
Are you sure you want to copy
the selected files to
d:\path\filename
```

2. To confirm that you want the Shell to copy the selected file(s) to the target directory, click Yes.

If you don't have a mouse, complete the copy procedure by following these steps:

1. Choose Copy from the File menu or press F8. The Shell displays the Copy File dialog box. This dialog box contains the From and To text boxes. The Shell lists the source files in the From text box and the source directory in the To text box.

2. Type the target drive and directory name in the To text box, and then click OK or press Enter. The Shell copies the files to the target directory and displays a message to that effect in the center of the screen.

If you try to copy a file into a directory that already contains a file with the same name, the Shell displays the Replace File Confirmation dialog box. This dialog box prompts you to confirm whether you want to replace the existing file with the new file. Click the Yes button to copy the file and continue with the copy procedure (if other files have yet to be copied). Click the No button to skip the file and continue the copy procedure for any remaining files. Click the Cancel button to terminate the copy operation.

Moving a File in the Shell

When the Shell moves a file, the program copies the file from one storage location to another and then deletes the file from its original location. Therefore, the steps for moving one or more files with the DOS Shell are nearly the same as those for copying files. When you want to move one or more files, follow steps 1 through 4 of the copy procedure (refer to the preceding section). Then perform the steps listed in this section for mouse users or for keyboard users.

If you are using a mouse, perform the following steps to complete the move operation:

1. Position the mouse pointer on one of the selected files in the upper file list. Hold down the Alt key while you press and hold down
   the left mouse button. While holding both the Alt key and the
   mouse button, drag the mouse pointer to the target drive letter in
   the lower drive area or to the target directory's name in the lower
   directory tree.

   When you start dragging the mouse, the pointer changes from an
   arrow (or a block, in text mode) to a circle (or two exclamation-
   point symbols, in text mode). When the pointer enters the second
   directory tree, the circle becomes a file icon (or a diamond, in text
   mode). If you are copying several files, the file icon resembles a
   stack of three files.

   After you release the mouse button and Alt key, the Shell displays
   the Confirm Mouse Operation dialog box, which contains the following query:

   ```
   Are you sure you want to move
   the selected files to
   d:\path\filename
   ```

2. To confirm that you want the Shell to move the selected file, click
   Yes.

If you don't have a mouse, complete the move procedure by following
these steps:

1. Choose Move from the File menu or press F7. The Shell displays
   the Move File dialog box. This dialog box contains two text boxes,
   one labeled From and another labeled To. The Shell lists the
   source files in the From text box and the source directory in the
   To text box.

2. Type the target drive and directory name in the To text box, and
   then click OK or press Enter. The Shell moves the files to the target directory and displays a message to that effect in the center of
   the screen.

If you attempt to move a file into a directory that already contains a file
with the same name, the Shell displays the Replace File Confirmation
dialog box. This dialog box prompts you to confirm whether you want
to replace the existing file with the new file. Click the Yes button to
move the file and continue with the move procedure (if other files have
yet to be moved). Click the No button to skip the file and continue the
move procedure for any remaining files. Click the Cancel button to terminate the move operation.

Setting Confirmation Preferences

By default, the Shell displays a dialog box each time you use a mouse to delete a file, replace a file, or perform a copy or move operation. In each case, you must click OK or press Enter to confirm that you want to complete the operation.

For new DOS Shell users, having to confirm actions that may cause loss of data is beneficial. For seasoned users, however, each confirmation dialog box may be more of a nuisance than a safeguard. The Shell, therefore, enables you to change your confirmation preferences so that the confirmation dialog boxes don't appear.

To change one or more confirmation preferences, choose Confirmation from the Options menu. The Shell displays the File Options dialog box, which contains the following check boxes:

■ *Confirm on Delete.* When checked, this option requires the Shell to ask you before the Shell deletes a file.

■ *Confirm on Replace.* When checked, this option instructs the Shell to prompt you for confirmation before the Shell copies a file over another file with the same name.

■ *Confirm on Mouse Operation.* When checked, this option requires that you confirm each mouse operation.

Click the check box that corresponds to the confirmation requirement that you want to disable, and then click OK or press Enter to confirm this change and return to the DOS Shell window.

Using the COPY Command

You can copy files not only by using the DOS Shell's copy procedure but also by using the COPY command at the command line. Symbolically, the COPY command says the following:

COPY from *this source* to *this destination*

In a COPY command, the order of the parameter requirements always moves from the source to the destination, or target. The correct syntax for the COPY command is shown in the following:

COPY *d1:path1***filename1.ext1** *d2:path2\filename2.ext2/V/A/B*

For combining files, the syntax is shown in the following:

COPY *d1:path1***filename1.ext1** */A/B* +
d2:path2\filename2.ext2 /A/B
d0:path0\filename0.ext0

d1:, *d2:*, *d0:* are valid drive names. If you omit a drive parameter, DOS uses the current drive.

path1, *path2*, and *path0* are path parameters. If you omit a path parameter, DOS assumes that you mean the current directory.

The + character delimits source files that are to be combined.

filename1.ext1, *filename2.ext2*, and *filename0.ext0* are file-name and extension parameters. You must provide a source path or file parameter.

The ellipsis (...) signifies that other drive, path, and source file-name parameters may be included in a combine operation.

The */V* switch verifies that the copy has been recorded correctly.

The */A* and */B* switches have different effects on the source and destination files. For the source file, */A* treats the file as an ASCII file. The command copies all the information in the file up to, but not including, the first end-of-file marker (ASCII decimal 26). DOS ignores anything after the end-of-file marker. The */B* switch copies the entire file (based on its size, as listed in the directory) as if the copied file were a program file (binary). Any end-of-file markers are copied.

For the destination file, */A* adds an end-of file marker to the end of the ASCII file after it is copied. */B* does not add the end-of-file marker to this binary file.

Sometimes, you want to change a file's date and time attribute to today's date and time. Use the following command:

COPY /B *filename.ext+,,*

T I P

Copying All Files in a Directory

As you add and delete disk files, the free space for new file information becomes spread around the surface of the disk. This phenomenon is called *fragmentation*. DOS allocates data-storage space by finding the next available disk space. If the next available space is too small to hold an entire file, DOS uses all that space and puts the rest of the file in the next available space. Fragmented files diminish disk performance.

If you use DISKCOPY on a fragmented floppy disk, you get an exact image of the fragmented disk. To avoid copying the fragmentation, or to make an efficient copy of a fragmented floppy disk, use the copy operation (from the Shell or the command line).

Suppose that all source files are in the source floppy's root directory. Format the destination disk, if necessary, and make sure that the disk has enough room to hold all the source files. Then copy the source files to the destination disk. Insert the source disk into drive A and the destination disk into drive B, and then type the following command:

    COPY A:*.* B:

This command copies all files on the disk in drive A to the disk in drive B, keeping the same file names.

Alternatively, you can copy all the files on a floppy disk to a directory of your hard disk. To copy all files on drive A to the \TEMP directory on drive C, for example, you type the following command:

    COPY A:*.* C:\TEMP

Combining Text Files

Although you can use COPY to combine any files, the combine operation is most effective when the files are ASCII text files. In most cases, combining binary files results in an unusable destination file.

For the following examples, assume that the current directory contains three text files, all with TXT extensions. The files and their contents are listed in the following:

File	Contents
INTRO.TXT	Combining is
BODY.TXT	the joining of files
ENDING.TXT	into a new file.

To join the three files into a fourth file, type the following command:

    COPY INTRO.TXT+BODY.TXT+ENDING.TXT ALL.TXT

The resulting file, ALL.TXT, contains the text from the three source files. To verify ALL.TXT, issue the following command:

    TYPE ALL.TXT

TYPE sends the contents of ALL.TXT to the screen. DOS displays the following:

```
Combining is the joining of files into a new file.
```

Copying from a Device to a File

A common and handy use of the COPY command is copying to a file keystrokes entered from the keyboard or console device. (*CON* is the device name for *console*; for all practical purposes, CON is the keyboard.) You can use the resulting text file as a batch file, a configuration file, a memo, and so on.

To practice copying from the keyboard to a file, you can create a simple batch file that changes the current directory to \123R3 and starts Lotus 1-2-3 Release 3. The command that creates the batch file is shown in the following:

        COPY CON C:\DOS\RUN123.BAT

When you press Enter, DOS displays the cursor on the next line; the DOS prompt does not appear. Now you can start typing the file by following these steps:

1. Type **C:** and then press Enter. The cursor drops to the next line.

2. Type **CD\123R3** and press Enter. The cursor drops to the next line.

3. Type **LOTUS** and press Enter. The cursor drops to the next line.

4. Press the F6 function key or the Ctrl-Z key combination to indicate the end of the file. DOS displays the end-of-file marker (^Z).

5. Press Enter. The ^Z code indicates to DOS that you are finished entering data into the file. DOS responds with the message
    `1 file(s) copied.`

To confirm that the new file is the way you want it, you can use the TYPE command to review the contents of the file.

 If you try this example on your system, be sure to use the appropriate directory names for DOS and Lotus 1-2-3.

Using the MOVE Command

In DOS 6.0, you can move files not only by using the DOS Shell's move procedure but also by using the MOVE command at the command line. Symbolically, the MOVE command says the following:

        MOVE from *this source* to *this destination*

In a MOVE command the order of the parameter requirements always moves from the source to the destination, or target.

The correct syntax for the MOVE command is shown in the following:

> **MOVE** *ds:paths***filenames.exts** *dt:patht***filename.extt**

You must specify at least one source parameter and only one target parameter.

ds: is a valid drive name of the drive containing the file to be moved. If you omit a drive parameter, DOS uses the current drive.

paths is a path parameter for files to be moved. If you omit a path parameter, DOS assumes you mean the current directory.

filenames.exts is a file name and extension parameter for the source file(s). You may use wild-card characters. You must provide a source path or file parameter.

dt is a valid drive name for the target of the MOVE command. If you omit a drive parameter, DOS uses the current drive as the target.

patht is a path parameter for the target directory of the MOVE command. If you omit a path parameter, DOS assumes you mean the current directory.

filenamet.extt are the file-name and extension parameters for the target file. You must provide a target drive, path, or file parameter, and it must be different from the source. If you omit a target parameter, the message Required parameter missing appears.

> **CAUTION:** If you omit a path parameter from *both* the source and the target, you either copy or rename the source file, depending on whether the specified target file name exists. If the name exists, you copy the source file over the target file, eliminating the target file. If the name does not exist, you rename the source file.

If your source parameter includes only one file, you can rename the file as you move it by specifying a new file name and/or extension as part or all of the target parameter. If your source parameter includes more than one file, you may not use a file-name and extension parameter as part of the target parameter; however, if you do, DOS assumes you mean the target file to be the target for all the files to be moved, and the message Cannot move multiple files to a single file appears. You must, however, specify either a drive or a directory as the target.

For example, to move a file called BUDGET.WQ1 from a directory called C:\SPREADSH\QPRO4DAT to a directory called D:\OLDFILES (assuming neither directory is current), you enter this command:

MOVE C:\SPREADSH\QPRO4DAT\BUDGET92.WQ1 D:\OLDFILES

If the move is successful, DOS displays the following message:

```
c:\spreadsh\qpro4dat\budget92.wq1 =>
   c:\oldfiles\budget92.wq1 [ok]
```

> **WARNING:** If the source and target parameters represent the same file, DOS erases the file without warning you.

 NOTE You can use the MOVE command to rename directories. See Chapter 8, "Understanding and Managing Directories," for the instructions and syntax.

Renaming Files

If copying files is the most common file-related function of DOS, renaming files probably follows close on its heels. The reasons for renaming a file are many. You may want to use the current file name for another file, or perhaps you want to create a name that better describes the contents of the current file. Whatever the reason, DOS enables you to rename a file through the Shell or from the command line.

The DOS rename operation changes the name in a file's directory entry, but the file and its physical location on the disk remain unchanged. Because two files in the same directory cannot have the same name, DOS will not change a file name if the new file name already exists.

Whether you carry out the DOS rename operation from the Shell or at the command line, remember the following guidelines:

- You can use the commands REN and RENAME interchangeably at the command line. Both commands produce identical results.

- You must supply both an old file name and a new file name. The file names can contain wild cards for DOS to use in pattern matching.

■ You cannot use the rename operation to move a file from one directory or disk to another directory or disk. (You use the MOVE command for this purpose.)

Renaming a File from the Shell

To rename a file in the Shell, follow these steps:

1. In the file-list area, select the file whose name you want to change.

2. Choose Rename from the File menu. The Shell displays the Rename File dialog box. This dialog box displays the current file name as well as a text box labeled New Name.

3. Type the new file name in the New Name text box, and then click OK or press Enter. The Shell changes the name and returns the screen to the DOS Shell.

Renaming Files from the Command Line

The internal RENAME (or REN) DOS command is your command-line tool for altering the name of an existing file. RENAME modifies a file's name without changing the file's content.

The syntax for the RENAME command is shown in the following:

RENAME *d:path***filename1.ext1 filename2.ext2**

The *d:* parameter is the drive that contains the file to be renamed. The *path*\ indicates the directory that contains the file.

The file currently is named **filename1.ext1**. Wild cards are allowed in the file name, the extension, or both.

filename2.ext2 is the new name for the file. The new file name can be a new literal name, or the new file name can contain wild cards. You cannot specify a drive or path for **filename.ext2**; both the drive and the path must be the same as for the original file name. You must provide both **filename1.ext1** and **filename2.ext2**.

Suppose that you used your word processing program to prepare a sales report and you want to give the backup file (SALES.BAK) a more descriptive name. After you log on to the appropriate disk and directory, issue the following command:

RENAME SALES.BAK SALES_08.REP

Perhaps you want to rename the EXPENSE.YTD file, keeping the same root name but making the extension more descriptive. You can specify the entire old name and an entire new name in the command line, as in the preceding example. An easier way, however, is to use the * wild card for the root file name and change only the extension. First, make sure that only one file with the root file name of EXPENSE is available for RENAME to process with a *.YTD specifier, and then issue the following command:

> RENAME *.YTD *._92

The new name for the EXPENSE.YTD file is EXPENSE._92. The *.YTD parameter tells DOS to find all files with YTD extensions. The new file-name parameter *._92 tells DOS to rename the found files' extensions as _92 extensions but to keep the root file names the same.

If you are not sure which files a wild-card parameter will match, issue the DIR command, using the wild-card pattern that you plan to use in the file-name parameter. DIR lists the matching file names. Study these names carefully to see whether using the wild-card pattern with the RENAME command produces the result that you expect.

T I P

Deleting Files

Because no disk has unlimited storage space and because nearly every file eventually becomes obsolete, DOS provides a way to erase or delete files from your disks. You can use DOS from the Shell or from the command line to delete files from the disk.

When you execute a delete operation, DOS locates the file in the directory and marks the directory entry with a special internal indicator. DOS considers this space to be available for reassignment when a new file is being added to the directory. By reclaiming a deleted file's directory entry, DOS can control the expansion of a subdirectory or reclaim one of the limited root-directory entries.

Understanding the Delete Operation

The delete operation does not affect the contents of a file's allocated clusters. Deleting a file does not record over the file's data in the way erasing a cassette tape records over existing audio; rather, DOS alters its bookkeeping records in the directory and in the file allocation table (FAT). The directory entry for the file receives a special indicator, and the FAT cluster chain for the file is deallocated. DOS marks the file's clusters as being "free."

The DOS bookkeeping records for the deleted file remain relatively intact until another file is added to the directory or until another file is expanded or added in any directory. Beginning with DOS 5.0, you can use the UNDELETE command to reverse the effect of deleting a file. The UNDELETE utility (discussed in the later section "Recovering Deleted Files with UNDELETE") takes advantage of the fact that DOS does not erase a file's content when you delete the file. UNDELETE "fixes" the deleted file's directory entry and reconstructs the deleted file's cluster chain. If another file has been added, however, the UNDELETE command may not be able to recover the deleted file because DOS may have reallocated some of or all the storage space assigned to the deleted file.

When you are executing a delete operation, remember the following guidelines:

■ At the command line, the DEL (or ERASE) command does not erase files marked with the read-only attribute, the hidden attribute, or the system attribute. The Shell's Delete command deletes a file, regardless of the file's current attributes; but if the file is marked with the read-only attribute, the hidden attribute, or the system attribute, you first must confirm the operation.

■ The delete operation does not remove a directory, erase a volume label, or erase a hidden or system file.

■ If you type **DEL subdirectory_name**, DOS tries to delete all the files in the specified subdirectory.

Using the DOS Shell To Delete a File

To use the DOS Shell to delete one or more files, follow these steps:

1. In the file-list area, select the file(s) you want to delete.

2. Choose <u>D</u>elete from the <u>F</u>ile menu or press Del. DOS displays the Delete File confirmation dialog box.

The Shell displays different dialog boxes, depending on whether you are deleting one or multiple files. When you are deleting several files, the Shell lists the selected files in the Delete text box.

3. To continue the delete operation, click OK or press Enter; to terminate the operation, click Cancel.

   If you are deleting a single file, the Shell displays only the name of the file that you are about to delete and asks you to confirm the operation. Click Yes or press Enter to delete the file.

   If several files are selected, the Shell asks you to reconfirm the deletion of each file. Click the Yes button once for each file. The Shell erases each file and then returns the screen to the Shell window.

CAUTION: If you turned off the Confirm on Delete check box in the File Options dialog box, the Shell does not ask you to confirm that you want to delete each file. Rather, the Shell deletes the file(s) as soon as you issue the command.

If you attempt to delete a file whose read-only attribute is set, the Shell displays the following message:

T I P

```
Warning! File is Read Only!
```

To continue with the deletion, click Yes or press Enter.

Deleting Files from the Command Line

The internal DEL and ERASE commands remove files from the disk, returning to the disk the space occupied by the deleted files. When you use DEL or ERASE to erase a file, DOS no longer can access the file. The erased file's directory entry and storage space become available to DOS for storage of another file.

NOTE   You can use ERASE and DEL interchangeably; the commands produce identical results.

DEL is a necessary file-management command. Unless you erase unwanted or unnecessary files from a disk, the disk eventually reaches full storage capacity. You need to erase files from a hard disk so you can use the disk for primary data storage. DEL is DOS's "throw it away" command.

> **CAUTION:** Because DEL (or ERASE) deletes files from your disk, use the command with caution. DEL accepts wild cards in the file parameter. A momentary lapse of your attention while you use DEL can eradicate important data in the blink of an eye.

The syntax for the DEL and ERASE commands is shown in the following:

DEL *d:path***filename.ext** */P*

ERASE *d:path***filename.ext** */P*

d: is the optional drive containing the disk that holds the file(s) to be erased. If you omit the drive parameter, DOS uses the logged drive.

path is the optional directory path to the file(s) to be erased. If you omit the path parameter, DOS assumes that you mean the current directory.

filename.ext is the file-name parameter for the file(s) to be erased. You can use wild cards in the file name and extension. Normally, a file-name parameter is required. If you don't specify a file name, you must specify a path. DOS then assumes that you want to delete all files in the path.

The */P* switch is available with DOS 4.0 and later versions. Using the optional /P switch causes DEL (or ERASE) to prompt you for confirmation before DOS deletes each file. Type **Y** to instruct DOS to delete a file, or type **N** to skip the file without erasing it.

Deleting Unwanted Files

Suppose that you have completed and delivered a series of memos composed in your word processing program. That program automatically creates in the C:\WP directory a backup file, with a BAK extension, for each memo. You want to keep the memo files on disk so that you can refer to them, but after the memos are safely delivered, you do not need the BAK files. You can erase the files with BAK extensions one at a time, or you can issue the DEL command as follows:

DEL C:\WP*.BAK

In this command line, the *.BAK file-name parameter instructs DOS to delete only the files with the BAK extension. When the DEL command completes its work, all files with BAK extensions are removed from the directory. Because this command line includes drive and path parameters, you can issue the command from any logged disk and current directory and still erase the BAK files in C:\WP.

Recovering Deleted Files with UNDELETE

Because of the way DOS deletes files, reversing the process is relatively easy—but only if you act promptly. When DOS deletes a file, DOS changes one character in the file name recorded in the directory area of the disk so that the target file no longer is listed. As far as DOS is concerned, the file is gone. DOS does not erase the modified file name from the directory, however; likewise, DOS doesn't erase any data from the disk.

Eventually, as you add new files to the disk, DOS reallocates the disk space assigned to the deleted file, causing new data to overwrite the old data. Soon, the file and its data are gone permanently. But if you use the DOS 6.0 UNDELETE command before DOS has a chance to overwrite a deleted file's data, you can reverse the DELETE operation.

> If you discover that you accidentally deleted a file, immediately try to recover it. The longer you wait, the less likely you are to recover the file completely by using the UNDELETE command.

T I P

Using UNDELETE from the DOS Shell

DOS 6.0 enables you to use UNDELETE from the DOS Shell or from the command line.

> **CAUTION:** Using UNDELETE from the DOS Shell may not be good practice. DOS first saves the contents of the computer's memory to a disk file and then executes the UNDELETE command. The disk file DOS creates may overwrite some of or all the data that you want to recover. A safer method is to exit the Shell (by pressing F3) and then run UNDELETE from the command line.

When you are using the Shell and want to recover an accidentally deleted file, complete the following steps:

1. Activate the program-list area of the DOS Shell window.

2. Select the Disk Utilities program-group item to display the Disk Utilities program group in the program-list area.

3. Choose the Undelete program item. The Shell displays the Undelete dialog box, which contains a text box labeled Parameters. The Parameters text box contains a default value of /LIST.

4. To see a list of deleted files, click OK or press Enter.

The following section describes other parameters that you can type in the Parameters text box. When you learn how to use these parameters, you can use them to undelete files from the DOS Shell.

Using UNDELETE from the Command Line

The syntax of the UNDELETE command is shown in the following:

UNDELETE *d:path\filename.ext /LIST/DT/DOS/ALL*

d: is the optional parameter that specifies the drive containing the disk that holds the deleted file(s).

path is the optional parameter that specifies the path to the directory that contains the deleted file(s).

filename.ext specifies the file(s) that you want to undelete. You can use wild cards to indicate multiple files. By default, if you do not specify a file name, DOS attempts to undelete all deleted files in the current directory or in the directory specified by the *path* parameter.

The */LIST* parameter causes UNDELETE to list the deleted files that can be recovered.

The */DT* switch instructs DOS to use the delete-tracking method of recovering the specified file(s). (This method is described in the following section.) If no delete-tracking file exists, DOS does not proceed. By default, UNDELETE uses the delete-tracking method when no switch is specified; when no delete-tracking file exists, the program uses information in the DOS directory to recover files.

/DOS causes DOS, in its attempt to undelete files, to rely on the information still stored in the DOS directory instead of using the delete-tracking method.

The */ALL* switch attempts to recover all deleted files without further input from you. When used with this switch, UNDELETE first looks in the delete-tracking file for information about the deleted files and then uses information from the DOS directory.

The UNDELETE command has two approaches to recovering a deleted file: the *delete-tracking* method and the *DOS* method. The following sections discuss both methods.

Recovering Files with UNDELETE Installed

Ideally, your AUTOEXEC.BAT file contains a command that causes the DOS UNDELETE command to load its deletion-tracking option or its delete-sentry option. These options load a memory-resident portion of the regular UNDELETE command. You specify which option you want to use by including in the command line switches that load UNDELETE as a resident program.

UNDELETE's delete-sentry option actually saves a specified number of deleted files in a hidden directory for a specified number of days. This option ensures that deleted files can be undeleted completely provided that UNDELETE was resident with this option when the files were deleted.

UNDELETE's deletion-tracking option constantly tracks and maintains a list of all files deleted from your computer. UNDELETE saves the deletion-tracking information in the *deletion-tracking file*. This file— PCTRACKR.DEL—has the system attribute; DOS does not list the file when you use the DIR command. Using the memory-resident version of the small but powerful UNDELETE option is crucial if you want maximum protection against accidental file deletions.

By default, UNDELETE tries to read the hidden directory and decipher the encrypted file names. If the file you want to recover isn't in that directory, or if you didn't use the delete-sentry option, UNDELETE tries to read the deletion-tracking information in the deletion-tracking file, PCTRACKR.DEL. If PCTRACKR.DEL doesn't exist, UNDELETE attempts to recover files through the DOS directory. You also can use the /DS switch to force UNDELETE to use the delete-sentry directory or the /DT switch to force UNDELETE to use the deletion-tracking file. In theory, when you use the /DS switch, the UNDELETE command terminates if no delete-sentry files match the file specification you enter; actually, you get an `Invalid parameter specifications` message.

The /DT switch causes the command to ignore files in the delete-sentry directory to use only the deletion-tracking information in PCTRACKR.DEL. If this file does not exist, or if no files are reported in it, UNDELETE terminates.

Suppose that you want to recover a file and have installed UNDELETE with the delete-sentry option. Change to the directory that contains the deleted file, and then type the following command:

UNDELETE *filename.ext*

Be sure to substitute the name of the file that you want to recover for *filename.ext*. When you press Enter, DOS displays a message similar to the following:

```
UNDELETE - A delete protection facility

Copyright  1987-1993 Central Point Software, Inc.
All rights reserved.

Directory: C:\SPREADSH\QPRODAT
File Specifications: BUDGET.WQ1
   Searching Delete Sentry control file...
    Delete Sentry control file contains    1 deleted files.
   Searching deletion-tracking file....
    Deletion-tracking file contains   0 deleted files.

   Of those,    0 files have all clusters available,
                0 files have some clusters available,
                0 files have no clusters available.

   MS-DOS directory contains    0 deleted files.
   Of those,    0 files may be recovered.

Using the Delete Sentry method.
   Searching Delete Sentry control file....
    BUDGET   WQ1    4037    11-29-92    4:58p       ...A Deleted 12-5-92 1:32a

This file can be 100% undeleted. Undelete (Y/N)?n
```

This message indicates, in place of *filename.ext*, the name of the file you specified. The message then indicates the total number of deleted files by this name listed in the Delete Sentry directory; the total number of files by this name in the deletion-tracking file; the number of files by this name that have all clusters available and, therefore, are recoverable; the number of partially recoverable files; and the number of files that are not recoverable.

Next, the DELETE command's message may indicate that the deleted file still is listed in the MS-DOS directory. Such a file may have been deleted when UNDELETE was not resident in memory as well as when delete tracking was active.

Finally, the UNDELETE message lists the first file matching *filename.ext* that DOS found in the Delete Sentry directory. If this file is recoverable (that is, if the file's clusters have not yet been reallocated to another file), DOS asks whether you want to undelete the file. To recover the file, type **Y**. DOS recovers the file and displays the following message:

```
File successfully undeleted.
```

The UNDELETE message also lists any other files with the same name in the Delete Sentry directory. The files are listed one by one, starting with the most recently deleted files. For each file, UNDELETE asks whether you want to recover the file. If additional files with the same name are listed in the deletion-tracking file, UNDELETE repeats the procedure for each of these files.

If recovering a file creates a duplicate file name in the directory, UNDELETE displays the following message:

```
The filename already exists. Enter a different filename.

Press "F5" to bypass this file.

If you want to recover this file, type a unique file name
(one that does not already exist in the current direc-
tory). Otherwise, press F5 to skip this file.
```

NOTE You may have created and deleted same-named files in a particular directory more than once. (In fact, every time you save a file on which you are working, you delete the preceding version and create a new one.) So don't be alarmed or confused if UNDELETE asks more than once whether you want to recover a particular file. Normally, you recover the most recently deleted version of the file and discard the others.

Occasionally, by the time you realize that you need to recover an accidentally deleted file, other files may have reused some of the file's clusters. In such a case, UNDELETE displays the following message:

```
Only some of the clusters for this file are
available. Do you want to recover this file
with only the available clusters? (Y/N)
```

Press Y to recover the available bytes or N to skip the file. If you wait too long before attempting to recover a file, you may not be able to recover the file because other files are using all its clusters. In this case, UNDELETE tells you so and displays the message `Press any key to continue.`

Sometimes, even though most of a file still is on disk, the clusters in the first part of the file may have been reused by another file. In such a case, UNDELETE loses its "map" to the rest of the file and displays the following message:

```
Starting cluster is unavailable. This file cannot be
recovered with the UNDELETE command. Press any key to
continue.
```

If you want to know which deleted files you still can recover, type the following command:

UNDELETE /LIST

UNDELETE displays, from the Delete Sentry directory, the deletion-tracking file, and/or the DOS directory, a list of deleted files from the current directory.

T I P   If a deletion-tracking list is too long to fit in one screen, you can use Ctrl-S to pause the display. Press any key on the keyboard to resume scrolling. Do *not* use redirection or the MORE filter; these actions create disk files that may overwrite some or all of the data that you want to recover.

CAUTION: If you delete all the files in a directory and then delete the directory, you cannot recover any of the deleted files from that directory. UNDELETE cannot recover a a`deleted directory.

The UNDELETE command is a product of Central Point Software, licensed by Microsoft Corporation for distribution as part of DOS 6.0. Another Central Point Software product, PC Shell, can recover a deleted directory. (PC Shell is part of the PC Tools utility package.)

Using the DOS Directory To Recover a File

If you were not using UNDELETE's resident portion when you accidentally deleted the file that you want to recover, you can try to recover the file by using the information stored in the DOS directory. Type the following command:

> UNDELETE *filename.ext* /DOS

Substitute for *filename.ext* the name of the file that you want to recover.

UNDELETE displays a message similar to the following:

```
Directory: C:\SPREADSH\QPRODAT
File Specifications: BUDGET.WQ1

     Delete Sentry Control file not found.
     Deletion-tracking file not found.
     MS-DOS Directory contains 1 deleted files.
     Of those,  1 files may be recovered.

Using the MS-DOS Directory.

  ?UDGET    WQ1    4037   11-29-92    4:58p   ...A
Undelete (Y/N)?
```

Type **Y** to recover the file or **N** to skip the file. After you type Y, UNDELETE displays the following prompt:

```
Enter the first character of the filename.
```

Because the DOS directory no longer has any record of this first character, you must supply the letter. Type the letter that you want UNDELETE to use as the beginning letter of the file name. UNDELETE recovers the file and displays the following message:

```
File successfully undeleted.
```

Using the Microsoft Undelete Program for Windows

If you use Microsoft Windows, the DOS 6.0 Setup program probably installed the Windows utilities in their own program group in the Windows Program Manager. The Windows Tools group includes an Undelete program. When you open this program, Windows displays a screen similar to the one shown in figure 9.17, listing the deleted files in whatever directory was current when you started Windows. The following sections explain how to set up and use Microsoft Undelete for Windows.

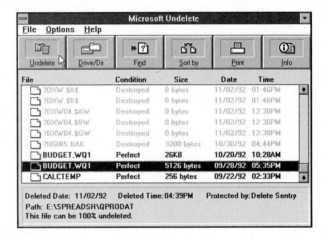

Fig. 9.17

Using the Windows Undelete program.

Configuring Microsoft Undelete

If you have installed the DOS version of UNDELETE in your AUTOEXEC.BAT file, you need not configure Microsoft Undelete. If you have not installed UNDELETE, however, choose Configure Delete Protection from the Options menu. This command displays a dialog box in which you can choose one of the following options:

- Delete Sentry

- Delete Tracking

- No Delete Protection

You already have seen what each of these options do. If you install Delete Protection through Windows, UNDELETE will be installed in your AUTOEXEC.BAT file automatically.

Selecting Files To Recover

If the default directory does not contain the file that you want to recover, click the Drive/Dir button or choose Change Drive/Directory
from the File menu. A dialog box appears in which you can type the
correct directory path in a text box or choose the directory from a list
box. When you click OK, the main window shows the deleted file in
your chosen directory (refer to fig. 9.17). When you select a file, Windows displays the following information below the directory window:

- The date and time when the file was deleted, if known (this information is available only if Delete Sentry is used)

- The protection method in use when the file was deleted, if any
  (if none, Windows displays the message Protected by: DOS)

- The current drive and directory

- The probability that the file can be recovered

If the directory where the deleted file was stored is not current, click
the Find button or choose Find Deleted File from the File menu. The
Find Deleted Files dialog box appears (see fig. 9.18).

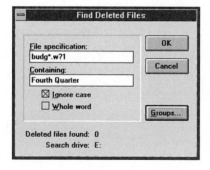

Fig. 9.18

The Find Deleted
Files dialog box.

In this dialog box, you can type the name of the file that you want to
find and also some text from the file; this information helps Undelete
locate the correct version of the file. If you want to narrow the search
further, click the Groups button to display a list of all the file types
whose extensions are associated with a program in Windows. You can
narrow the search more by clicking one or more of the listed groups.
After you finish specifying what to search for, click OK.

If Undelete finds any matching files, it displays the files in the directory
window.

Recovering Files

When you see the file that you want to recover, select it, and then perform one of the following actions:

- Click the Undelete button.
- Choose Undelete from the File menu.
- Choose Undelete To from the File menu.

If you use either of the first two methods, Undelete simply recovers the file in its current location. If the prognosis for recovery is not good, however, you may want to use the Undelete To command so that you can recover the file to another drive.

You may have to search the disk to find the data that was in the file. If you're not successful the first time, Undelete To enables you to try again without disturbing the data on the original disk.

If you use the Undelete command and recover the file, the information in the Condition column changes to read Recovered, as shown in figure 9.19.

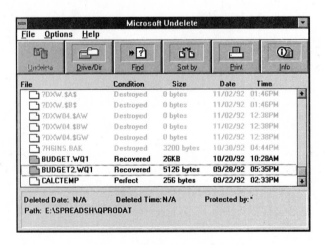

Fig. 9.19

Successfully undeleting files.

If you want to recover a file whose name is being used by another file, the message File already exists appears. Choose OK, and you see a dialog box in which you can enter a new name for the file. As you can see in figure 9.19, both files named BUDGET.WQ1 have been recovered, but one has been renamed.

Using Other Options

Microsoft Undelete includes several other options that are not available when you try to recover a deleted file from the DOS prompt:

- *Sorting.* The Sort By button and the Sort By command (Options menu) enable you to sort the file names displayed in the Undelete window by name, date, size, directory date and time, deletion date and time, or condition.

- *Printing.* You can group the files in the display by directory and then print them by clicking the Print button or choosing Print List from the File menu.

- *Displaying information.* Click the Info button or choose File Info from the File menu to display a box in which all the information about a deleted file is conveniently grouped in one place.

- *Selecting files.* The Options menu contains two commands that you can use to select groups of files for recovery. Choose Select by Name to display a dialog box in which you enter a file name. If you include a wild-card pattern in the file name, all matching files will be selected. You then can choose the Unselect by Name command to narrow the selection.

- *Deleting files.* If you installed the Delete Sentry option, you can choose Purge Delete Sentry File from the File menu to get rid of all the files—or selected files—in the Sentry directory. You may want to use this command if you are running low on disk space and need to install a new program.

Searching for Text with FIND

The FIND command, used from the command line, searches one or more files for a string of ASCII text and then displays the lines of text that contain the search string. FIND is useful on occasions when you know some of the text that a file contains but cannot recall which file contains the text. FIND uses the known text to help you locate the file.

The syntax for the FIND command is shown in the following:

FIND /C/N/V/I "string" d:path\filename...

"string" (the quotation marks are mandatory) specifies the ASCII characters that you want DOS to find.

d:path\filename... represents the drive, path, and file name of the file. The ellipsis indicates that you can specify more than one file.

The /C switch instructs DOS to count the number of lines that contain "string".

The /N switch instructs DOS to indicate a line number for each occurrence of "string" in a file.

The /V switch instructs DOS to display all lines that do not contain "string".

The /I switch instructs DOS to ignore the case of the characters in "string".

 NOTE When you use /C and /V together, the command counts the number of lines that do not contain "string". When you use /V and /N together, the command displays and numbers the lines that do not contain "string".

When you use the FIND command, consider the following guidelines:

- Use FIND only for ASCII text files.

- The string parameter is case-sensitive. The string LOOK is not the same as the string look, unless you use the /I switch.

- The string parameter must be enclosed in quotation marks. If the string contains a quotation mark, type two quotation marks together (""). FIND searches for occurrences of ".

- Find looks for input from the standard input device (keyboard) if filename is not specified.

- You cannot use wild cards in filename.

When you don't specify switch options, the FIND command reads each specified file and displays each line that contains a particular ASCII string.

You can use the FIND command to modify or filter output from other DOS commands. FIND often is used with redirection and piping. If you need to search a text file for lines that include certain information, redirecting the output to a file or to your printer probably is more useful that displaying the information. Then you can use the list as a reference while you use a text editor or word processing program to look at the entire original file.

The FIND command often is useful as a word-search utility. Suppose that you forgot the name of the memo that you sent to your boss. You know that the memo's name is MEMO1, MEMO2, or MEMO3 and that you always use the title *Supervisor* in memos to your boss. You can use *Supervisor* as a search string. Type the following command:

> FIND "Supervisor" MEMO1 MEMO2 MEMO3

DOS lists each line that contains the string *Supervisor*. The form of the listing is shown in the following:

```
- - - - - MEMO1
- - - - - MEMO2
Supervisor of Communications
- - - - - MEMO3
```

As you can see, the line that contains the word *Supervisor* is listed below the file name MEMO2, indicating that the file for which you are looking for is MEMO2. (No lines are listed below MEMO1 or MEMO3.)

Turning on Verification with VERIFY

The VERIFY command controls whether the DOS VERIFY setting is on or off. When VERIFY is on, data written to a disk by a DOS command or a program is *verified*—read by DOS and compared with the original. This verification is the same as that performed by DOS when you use the COPY command with the /V switch. When VERIFY is on, you do not need to use /V with COPY. When VERIFY is off, data written to disk is not verified.

When VERIFY is on and you use commands such as COPY, BACKUP, RESTORE, XCOPY, DISKCOPY, and REPLACE, you are assured that data hasn't been written to a bad sector on the disk. The verification operation can slow the execution of these commands, however. In most disk-intensive activities, a program is 20 percent to 40 percent slower during disk input/output than when VERIFY is off. You have to weigh the added assurance of data integrity against the inconvenience of slower execution. Many users turn on VERIFY while they work with critical files and turn VERIFY off for normal DOS work.

You can issue the VERIFY command in any of the following three forms:

VERIFY ON

VERIFY OFF

VERIFY

When you boot the computer, VERIFY is off (the default setting). Use VERIFY ON to turn on VERIFY. Later, you can use VERIFY OFF to turn off VERIFY.

Use the VERIFY command alone, with no parameters, to see the current setting of VERIFY.

When you use VERIFY, consider the following guidelines:

■ If you issue VERIFY with no parameter, DOS responds with the message VERIFY is ON or VERIFY is OFF.

■ If VERIFY is on, specifying a /V switch in a COPY command has no additional verification effect.

■ You cannot use VERIFY to verify a network drive.

If you plan to perform a critical backup operation on your hard disk, for example, you can add an extra level of confidence by turning on VERIFY. During the backup procedure (see Chapter 13, "Understanding Backups and the Care of Data"), DOS verifies that each sector is written without error to the backup disk(s). To turn on VERIFY, issue the command **VERIFY ON**.

To see whether VERIFY is on or off, type **VERIFY** at the DOS prompt. DOS responds as follows:

    VERIFY is ON

When you no longer want verification, you can turn off the feature by typing **VERIFY OFF**.

 Unlike PROMPT and PATH, the VERIFY setting is not stored in the DOS environment. VERIFY is an internal indicator, or *flag*.

Selectively Updating a Disk with REPLACE

The external command REPLACE, introduced in DOS 3.2, is a special COPY command. REPLACE enables you to update existing files in the target directory with new versions of files with the same name in the source directory. Conversely, you can use the REPLACE command to copy from the source directory only the files that don't already exist in the target directory.

When you issue the command with no switches, REPLACE reads the source disk and directory for files that match the command line's source-file parameter. DOS transfers all matching files to the destination disk and path. Unlike COPY, REPLACE cannot rename the files as they are copied to the destination; therefore, no target file name is allowed (or needed).

The REPLACE command has many practical applications. For example, you can use REPLACE to collect on a floppy disk the most recent versions of common files from a group of PCs. You also can use REPLACE to upgrade software on your hard disk.

The syntax of the REPLACE command is shown in the following:

> **REPLACE** *d1:path1***filename.ext** *d2:path2 /A/P/R/S/W/U*

d1: is the optional source-drive parameter. If you omit this parameter, DOS assumes that you mean the current drive.

The optional *path1* parameter is the path of the source files. If you omit the source-path parameter, DOS assumes that you want the current directory.

The **filename.ext** parameter, which represents the name of the source file(s), is required. Wild cards are allowed in the file name and extension.

d2: represents the target drive, where the files will be replaced. If you omit this parameter, DOS uses the current drive.

path2 represents the target path, where the files will be replaced. If the target-path parameter is omitted, DOS assumes that you want the current directory of the target disk.

The /A switch instructs DOS to add new files to the target disk. RE-PLACE copies only the source files that do not already exist in the target directory. You cannot use the /A switch with /S or /U.

The /P switch prompts you for confirmation before DOS replaces each file. To confirm the replacement, type **Y**. To reject replacement, type **N**.

The /R switch instructs DOS to replace read-only files as well as other files.

The /S switch instructs DOS to search all subdirectories of the target directory for a file that matches each source file. You cannot use /S with /A.

The /W switch instructs DOS to wait for you to press a key before executing the copying operation.

The /U switch instructs DOS to copy source files with a more recent date and time than target files with the same names. You cannot use /U with /A.

When using the REPLACE command, consider the following guidelines:

- REPLACE is available in DOS 3.2 and later versions.

- You must include a source file-name parameter with REPLACE. The file-name parameter may contain wild cards.

- The destination parameters may include a drive and a path name but may not include a file name. You can omit the destination drive or path, or both; REPLACE assumes default values for omitted destination parameters.

- You cannot use the /A switch with the /U or /S switch. All other switch combinations are allowed.

Suppose that you want to update the \PROGRAMS directory on your computer's hard disk in drive C. The new files are on a floppy disk in drive A. The current directory listing for C:\PROGRAMS is shown in the following:

```
Volume in drive C is HARD DISK
Volume Serial Number is 2F7F-16CD
Directory of  C:\PROGRAMS
.               <DIR>         11-03-89     12:31p
..              <DIR>         11-03-89     12:31p
RESULT    DAT         810  08-24-90      1:32p
JUDE      DAT          56  12-12-90     10:15p
PROFILE   DAT         850  08-11-90      4:46p
RESULTS   DAT         911  08-24-90      2:46p
```

```
TESTS     DAT       488  08-26-90      3:47p
CONVERT   SYS        40  09-01-90      5:54p
GEN4SYS   BAS      6556  09-01-90      5:37p
MONITOR   BAS       993  06-22-90     12:10p
       10 file(s)   10934272 bytes free
```

A directory listing of drive A also shows several files:

```
Volume in drive A is COLLECTION
Volume Serial Number is 1B22-1ED1
Directory of  A:
PROCED    DOC     19712  10-29-91      7:34p
RESULT    DAT       810  08-25-91     11:06a
FRM_SR1   DAT       372  08-18-91     11:18a
JUDE      DAT        56  12-14-91     11:15p
FRM_PRL   DAT      9280  08-19-91      2:32p
PROFILE   DAT       850  08-11-91     10:46p
CROSS     DAT      1463  08-26-91      3:48p
RESULTS   DAT       911  08-24-91     10:55p
TESTS     DAT       488  08-28-91      2:17p
CONVERT   SYS        40  09-01-91      5:54p
GEN4SYS   BAK      6556  09-01-91      5:37p
MONITOR   BAK       993  06-22-91     12:10p
IO        BAK     22736  08-23-91     12:42p
       13 file(s)    6582 bytes free
```

Notice that some of the file names appear in both directories. If you want REPLACE to copy these files from the floppy disk to the C:\PROGRAMS directory, for example, issue the following command:

> REPLACE A:*.* C:\ PROGRAMS

As REPLACE processes the files, you see the following message:

```
Replacing C:\PROGRAMS\RESULT.DAT
Replacing C:\PROGRAMS\JUDE.DAT
Replacing C:\PROGRAMS\PROFILE.DAT
Replacing C:\PROGRAMS\RESULTS.DAT
Replacing C:\PROGRAMS\TESTS.DAT
Replacing C:\PROGRAMS\CONVERT.SYS
6 file(s) replaced
```

This replacement list includes all the files that the two directories have in common. The files in drive A that were not in \PROGRAMS were not copied. The files in \PROGRAMS that were not in drive A remain intact. REPLACE makes the updating operation much easier than issuing a series of COPY commands.

Using Interlnk To Communicate with a Laptop Computer

A new DOS 6.0 feature, Interlnk, enables you to access drives and printers on a remote computer as though they were part of your computer. You can use this feature to transfer files from a laptop or notebook computer to your desktop computer, to print files located on your portable computer on a printer attached to your desktop computer, and even to run programs directly from the remote computer.

When you use Interlnk, one computer—the *server*—becomes the completely passive "slave" of the other. Before you start, decide which computer you want to work on. The server should be the computer with the resources—files or printers—that you want to use remotely.

Setting Up Interlnk

To use Interlnk, you first must connect either the serial or parallel ports of both computers. If you want to use a serial port, you must use a serial cable with pins 2 and 3 crossed (a "null-modem" cable). If you want to use the parallel (printer) ports, you must have a serial cable with 25 pins at each end, all of which are connected (a "straight-through" cable).

> **NOTE** After you install Interlnk as a device driver on the server, DOS thereafter regards that computer as having one or more additional disk drives, even when the two computers are not connected. SMARTdrive, for example, attempts to cache the nonexistent drives, and DOSSHELL shows the drives in the drive bar. To get rid of the drive messages, you must remove the command that loads Interlnk from your CONFIG.SYS file or precede it with a REM statement such as the following:
>
>   REM DEVICE=C:\DOS\INTERLNK.EXE

Next, decide which computer you will be using. On that computer, add the following line to your CONFIG.SYS file, and then reboot your computer:

DEVICE=C:\DOS\INTERLNK.EXE

Normally, Interlnk scans all your drives and all your ports when this device driver loads. If you have a serial mouse and plan to run Microsoft Windows, add a parameter that tells Interlnk which port is connected to the remote computer. If you are using a second printer port for your connection, for example, type the following line:

DEVICE=C:\DOS\INTERLNK.EXE /LPT2

This command prevents Interlnk from examining all your serial and parallel ports (and from disrupting your mouse operations in the process).

After you connect your computers and load the device driver on one, you must load Intersvr on the remote computer (the server). Issue the following command on that computer:

INTERSVR

A screen similar to the one shown in figure 9.20 appears.

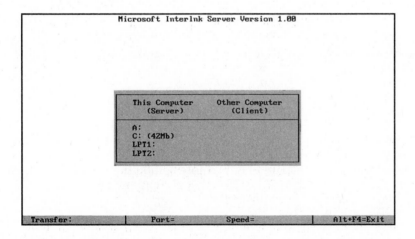

Fig. 9.20

Setting up the server.

Next, return to your other computer and issue the following command:

INTERLNK

A message similar to the following appears:

```
Scanning

Port=LPT2

This Computer          Other Computer
   (Client)               (Server)
. . . . . . . . . . . .   . . . . . . . . . . . . . . . . . . . . . . . .
   D:         equals    A:
   E:         equals    C:(42Mb)
   LPT1:      equals    LPT2:
```

This message tells you that drive A of the remote computer now is available to you as drive D of your local computer and that drive C of the remote computer now is drive E of your local computer.

Using Interlnk To Transfer Files

To see a directory on drive C of the remote computer, type the command **DIR F:**. To copy files from one computer to the other, you simply issue a COPY (or XCOPY) command, with a drive of one computer as the source and a drive of the other computer as the target. To copy C:\SPREADSH\BUDGET.WQ1 from your local computer to the server, for example, issue a command such as the following:

    COPY C:\SPREADSH\BUDGET.WQ1 D:\SPREADSH

Using a Remote Printer

Suppose that your remote computer is connected to a laser printer and your local computer isn't. The status report indicates that LPT1 of your computer is linked to LPT2 of the remote computer. Assuming that the laser printer is attached to LPT2 on that computer, you simply would tell your program to print its file to LPT2.

Installing Interlnk Remotely

If one of your computers is running DOS 6.0 and the other is running another version of DOS, the non-DOS 6.0 computer will not have Interlnk installed. Interlnk can install itself on the remote computer, however, if Interlnk is running on the local computer and if the computers are connected via serial—not parallel—ports. On the local computer, issue the following command:

INTERLNK /RCOPY

You are prompted to select the serial port to be used. After you indicate that port, go to the remote computer and type the following commands:

MODE COM*n*:2400,N,8,1,P

CTTY COM*n*:

In these commands, *n* represents the number of the serial port you are using on the remote computer. This parameter forces the remote computer to accept input from the specified serial port.

When you finish typing these commands, return to the computer on which Interlnk is installed and press Enter. Messages on both computers tell you that INTERLNK.EXE and INTERSVR.EXE are being copied. On the receiving computer, the message looks like the following example:

```
Loading bootstrap

Receiving INTERSVR.EXE (37266) 100%

Receiving INTERLNK.EXE (17133) 100%
```

The files are placed in the current directory of the receiving computer. Both computers then return to DOS.

You can use either computer as the client or the server, provided that you install the device driver in the server's CONFIG.SYS. If the remote computer is running an early version of DOS, however (3.3 or earlier, for example), you may not be able to access files on the server that were created in DOS 5.0 or 6.0, especially if those files are larger than 32M.

Running Programs Remotely

After you are linked to another computer by Interlnk, you can use that computer's drives as if though they were part of your local computer. Thus, you can run a program on the remote computer from the command line as you would run one on your local computer. (For more information, refer to the section "Starting Programs from the Command Line" earlier in this chapter.)

Because programs on the remote computer do not appear on your local computer's PATH, you must make one of the following choices:

- Make the drive that contains that program the current drive.
- Make the directory in which the program resides the current directory.
- Type the command that runs the program.

    or

    Type a command in the format ***d:\path\program***. *d:* is the drive, *path* is the complete path from the root directory, and *program* is the command.

Which technique is appropriate depends on how the program works. If the program must be run from its home directory when it is not on the path, for example, use the first option. Otherwise, you may use the second technique.

The preceding techniques actually just load the program from the remote computer and run it on your local computer. Consequently, you may encounter problems if the program is set up to use specific aspects of the remote computer's hardware that the local computer lacks. Suppose, for example, that the two computers have different types of screens. The program may be set up to display text and graphics on the remote computer's screen and may be unable to display anything on your local computer.

Another problem occurs if the program expects to find specific files on a particular drive but cannot access the drive because the drive names have been changed. Drive C still is drive C of your local computer, but drive C of the remote computer now is known to DOS as drive E of your local computer. If the program needs to find certain files in drive C, it cannot find those files unless they also exist in the same directory of your local computer. (In such a case, don't run the program from the remote computer; use the version on your local computer instead.)

Chapter Summary

DOS offers many useful file-management commands, both through the DOS Shell and at the command line. Use these commands to arrange your files and to keep your computer's disks well-organized and accessible. As you gain experience with file-management commands, you probably will want to incorporate additional switches or take more advantage of DOS defaults.

In this chapter, you learned the following key points:

■ The names of DOS devices are reserved. If you use a reserved name for a file parameter, DOS uses the device.

■ The end-of-file character ^Z marks the end of many ASCII files.

■ The RENAME operation changes the name of an existing file.

■ The DELETE operation removes files from a directory. Erased files no longer are available to DOS.

■ The UNDELETE command can recover deleted files.

■ The TYPE command displays an ASCII file's contents.

■ The COPY operation copies and combines files.

■ The VERIFY command manages DOS's internal VERIFY setting.

■ The REPLACE command selectively updates files on the target disk with files of the same name on the source disk.

In Chapter 10, "Understanding and Using Workgroups," you learn how to use workgroups.

Understanding and Using Workgroups

NOTE This chapter covers Workgroup Connections—a program available from Microsoft that enables you to use data from a Windows for Workgroups or LAN Manager network. However, you probably will need more information on Windows for Workgroups or LAN Manager. See the program documentation and Que's *Connecting Windows for Workgroups 3.1* and *Using Windows 3.1*, Special Edition.

Available as a separate product that you can use with DOS 6.0 is a series of utilities called Workgroup Connections. Workgroup Connection provides a way for computers that are not running Windows for Workgroups to access network resources.

A *network* is a group of computers that are linked through network adapter cards and cables. The most popular type of network used with PCs is a *local-area network* (LAN). A *workgroup* is a group of computers and people in an office network that have been logically associated—that is, they need access to the same type of information or the same printer. Workgroups usually are set up according to what people in the office do. For example, one network may connect all computers in a business, but people in the accounting office may comprise one workgroup and people in the marketing office may comprise another.

Workgroup Connection is a separate utility you can purchase for DOS 6.0. This group of utilities enables you to perform the following tasks:

- Share files with other computers in the network
- Share printers with other computers in the network
- Send and receive electronic mail

This chapter explains how to install Workgroup Connection on your computer, share files and printers, and use electronic mail.

Using Workgroup Connection

Workgroup Connection gives you access to the Windows for Workgroups network. You can read and write files to *shared directories*—directories on the hard drive of a computer that users in the LAN can access. As a Workgroup Connection user, you can access directories that a Windows for Workgroups or LAN Manager user decides to share with other users. You cannot, however, share your computer's directories with other people in the network.

Besides using shared directories, you can use a shared printer—that is, a printer attached to another computer. You cannot share a printer that is attached to your computer with other network users unless you are running Windows for Workgroups on your computer or you are attached to a LAN Manager network using its remote printing capability.

This section explains how to set up a network adapter card in your computer, install Workgroup Connection, and share network resources such as directories and printers.

Understanding Workgroup Connection

Workgroup Connection is a program which serves to extend DOS running on your computer. Along with a network adapter, Workgroup Connection provides access to mail, hard drives, and printers on other computers that are attached to the network. Suppose, for example, that you have a hard drive C on your computer. Workgroup Connection can let you assign drive D to the hard drive of your coworker's computer across the hall. If your coworker also has a printer attached to her computer, Workgroup Connection enables you to print your documents on that printer. With Workgroup Connection, you can also send and receive electronic mail messages with your coworkers who are on the network.

Computer networks are designed to be modular. This modular approach does not lock you into any one type of network component. You can use a wide range of computers and network adapters and still hook up to the network. Workgroup Connection copies a series of driver programs that enable you to get into the network. If you change your network adapter from an Intel EtherExpress to an SMC Arcnet, for example, you do not have to change everything—only one driver program.

The driver programs stay resident in your computer's memory while your computer is turned on. Another term for this type of program is *memory-resident* or *terminate and stay resident* (TSR). Workgroup Connection's WCSETUP program modifies the CONFIG.SYS file in the root directory of your hard drive (with your permission, of course). WCSETUP adds the lines that call up the driver programs your computer needs to get into the network.

Planning for Workgroup Connection Setup

Most of the information in this section has been determined when Windows for Workgroups or LAN Manager was set up. You may need to talk to the person managing the network before proceeding. Before you install Workgroup Connection, familiarize yourself with the following definitions:

- *Workgroup name.* The workgroup name is the name that your network administrator assigns to the workgroup. If you do not have a workgroup name, you and the people with whom you want to share directories and printers need to choose one.

- *Computer name.* The computer name is the name that appears in the network to identify your computer. Although many people use their own names to identify their computers, this practice might not work from an administrative standpoint. What would happen, for example, if you changed computers?

  You need to come up with a name that identifies your computer— for example, ADMIN1, ADMIN2, EVEREX TEMPO LX, or AUTOCAD COMPUTER.

- *User name.* The user name is the name that appears in the network to identify you. First names are fine unless two or more people in the workgroup have the same first name. Some workgroups use initials; others use the first letters of first names and the first six or seven letters of last names.

  Examples of user names include TOM, WORDPROCESSOR1, DBIERER, and EILEENB.

Setting Up Your Network Adapter Card

Network adapters, which are similar to video adapter cards and internal modem cards, are cards that plug into your computer. As is true of any other type of board that plugs into your computer, the network adapter card's settings must be adjusted so that the network adapter does not interfere with the operation of other adapters in your computer.

You can change your adapter settings by moving jumpers, switching micro switches on the card, or running the setup program that comes with the adapter. If you have an Intel EtherExpress adapter, you have no jumpers or switches to set; you need to plug in the board and run the setup program. This program checks your computer and makes firmware changes in the adapter card so that it does not conflict with the settings of any other card in your computer.

> **WARNING:** Never remove or plug in an adapter card while your computer's power is on. Turn off the power first. Another precaution you can take is to touch the metal case of your computer before adding or removing a card so that any static electricity that may have built up discharges. Static electricity can harm a computer card.

T I P If your computer does not boot up after you add a network adapter, turn off the computer and remove the card. If your computer boots up fine without the network adapter card, the adapter's settings are conflicting with another setting on another card in your computer. Change the adapter's settings and try again until your computer boots properly.

T I P Always keep a written record of the settings you make to each adapter card in your computer; then be sure to update these records each time you add, change, or remove cards.

Understanding Types of Network Adapters

Many different types of network adapters are available. Table 10.1 lists some of these types.

Table 10.1 Types of Network Adapters

Adapter Type	Cable Type	Distance	Transmission Speed	Largest Manufacturers
Ethernet	RG/58 Coax, RG/8 or RG/11 Coax, and Twisted Pair[1]	3035 feet with repeaters or hubs[2] (for twisted pair)	10 mpbs[3]	3Com, Intel, SMC[4], Tiara, Novell/Eagle, Thomas Conrad
Arcnet	RG/62 Coax and Twisted Pair	20,000 feet (with active hubs)	2.5 mpbs	SMC, Thomas Conrad, Tiara
Token Ring	Twisted Pair	5,000 feet (with MSAUs[5] and repeaters)	4 or 16 mbps	IBM, Proteon, Thomas Conrad, Intel

[1] *Twisted Pair wire is like the wire used for telephones, except that the pair of wires has a certain number of twists per foot to break up the magnetic field that otherwise would develop and interfere with the signals traveling over the wire.*

[2] *Repeaters and hubs are black boxes that have many inputs and outputs. The signals from the network cards go into these boxes and come out boosted in strength. These boxes act very much like the signal amplifiers/splitters used with cable TV. RG/58, /8, /11, and /62 is computer-network coaxial cable very much like the cable used for cable TV.*

[3] mbps *stands for million bits per second. Network adapters are rated according to how quickly they transmit information over the LAN. Each character, such as the letter A, for example, in a file that is copied over the network is coded into what is known as a* byte. *A byte is composed of 8* bits. *Information on the LAN is transmitted one bit at a time. An Ethernet adapter can transmit 10 million bits every second, meaning that roughly 1.25 million characters can travel on the LAN every second. Depending on the driver programs running on your computer, the actual number of characters transmitted per second may be 10 percent to 20 percent lower because of the extra computer processing required by the driver programs.*

[4] *SMC stands for Standard Microsystems Corporation.*

[5] *MSAU stands for multistation access unit—a fancy term for a hub in the Token Ring world.*

Other, less-popular types of network adapters include FDDI (Fiber-Distributed Digital Interface), CDDI (Copper-Distributed Digital Interface), wireless, and infrared.

Choosing Network Adapter Settings

You need to be aware of several settings when you set the switches and jumpers on your network adapter or run its setup program. These settings include interrupts, I/O addresses, base memory addresses, DMA channels, and node addresses. Table 10.2 summarizes what you need to know about these settings. The numbers shown in the Typical Settings column for I/O Address, Base Address, and Node Address are computed using the hexadecimal (base 16) numbering system.

Table 10.2 Network Adapter Settings

Setting	Typical Settings	Description
IRQ	2 through 15	The Interrupt Request (IRQ) is the main way that a computer identifies the cards plugged into its slots. Each card literally can *interrupt* the computer by using an interrupt line. If you have your network adapter set to interrupt 3, for example, whenever the adapter receives information from the LAN, the adapter interrupts the computer on line 3.
I/O Address	2E0, 300, 0A20	The Input/Output (I/O) address is the start of a series of addresses that a computer uses to transmit and receive LAN data. This address also is known as a *port*. The port is like the porthole in a ship; a computer uses this window to send and receive information. You can think of the I/O address as being like a mailbox. When you want to mail a letter, you place it in the mailbox and put the flag up; when you are expecting a letter, you check your mailbox.

Setting	Typical Settings	Description
Base Address	C0000, D0000	This address is used for many purposes. Many network adapters use part of the computer's main memory as a *buffer*, where they store information that is coming in from or going out to the LAN. Other adapters include a special memory chip called a *ROM* chip. This chip contains a set of instructions that the network adapter uses in sending and receiving LAN information. Some adapters use the computer's main memory to store the information contained in their ROM chips. Main memory usually is much faster than a ROM chip.
DMA	0 through 7	DMA stands for Direct Memory Access. DMA enables a network adapter to send and receive LAN information quickly. If a network adapter supports DMA, the computer gives that adapter special treatment in transferring information to its main memory. You can think of DMA as being like a commuter lane on a freeway: if you have a certain number of people in your car, you can use a special lane.
Node Address	000000000001, 00804E478F04	The node address—a unique number assigned to each network adapter—enables the computer to identify which network adapter is sending data and where information should be sent. You have to set the node address manually if you have an Arcnet network adapter. Ethernet and Token Ring adapters have this address put into a chip at the factory. (You can override assigned addresses by running a software program.) Two or more network adapters with a duplicate node address can cause problems in a network.

Not all network adapters use all these settings. Some network adapters have additional special settings.

T I P   Before you set up your network adapter, read the manual provided by the manufacturer. Check to see whether the adapter is set to its default setting. Many vendors provide a software setup program that displays the proper switch settings. Try the network adapter at its default setting. If the default does not work, change the settings one at a time until you find a setting that works. Be sure to write the settings down in a logbook for later reference.

Testing Your Network Adapter

Most network adapters come with software to test the status of the adapter. Before testing the adapter, however, be sure that the adapter is set up and does not prevent your computer from booting up properly. Write down the your network adapter settings. Insert the adapter card into your computer and attach the card to the network cabling. Then turn on your computer.

To test the adapter, put the test disk in your floppy drive or copy the software into a subdirectory of your hard drive. Locate and run the test utility. (You may need to consult the manual that comes with the adapter to determine the name of the test utility.)

Network adapter test utilities vary greatly from card to card. Most test utilities test the following:

- *Network adapter settings.* Study the readout presented to you by the test software to determine whether the settings displayed by the test utility agree with the settings you wrote down for the adapter before installing it. If the settings do not agree, turn off your computer and remove the adapter. Use the adapter's manual to set the adapter card to the proper settings.

- *Internal Test.* This test confirms that chips on the adapter are functioning properly. If the adapter fails this test, replace the network adapter. If a new network adapter also fails the test, run a thorough diagnostic test of your computer to be sure it is functioning properly.

- *Network Communications Test.* The communications test checks to see whether the adapter is sending and receiving data through the LAN. Most test utilities enable you to specify a certain number of packets to send and receive. Any number from 1,000 to 5,000 packets is sufficient to test your network adapter. If your adapter fails this test, verify that the settings are correct and that the adapter passes the internal test. You can also check your network cabling and connectors. Most adapters fail this test if they are not properly cabled to the network.

After you successfully complete the text and have your network adapter set up and the settings written down, you are ready to install Workgroup Connection.

Installing Workgroup Connection

Before you begin to install Workgroup Connection on your computer, you need to know the following key pieces of information:

- The name of your network adapter
- The network adapter's interrupt request (IRQ)
- The network adapter's base address
- A name for the computer running Workgroup Connection
- The workgroup name

This information is the key to installing Workgroup Connection successfully. You can obtain the first three items, which deal with the network adapter, as you install the adapter card. You make up the fourth item—the computer name. The fifth item—the workgroup name—was determined when the first copy of Windows for Workgroups was installed.

To install Workgroup Connection, insert the Workgroup Connection disk into your floppy drive, and then follow these steps:

1. At the DOS prompt, start the setup program by typing **A:WCSETUP**. The initial screen appears:

```
Setup for Workgroup Connection ----------------------------
Welcome to Setup for Workgroup Connection.
Setup prepares Workgroup Connection to run on your computer.
 * To get additional information about a Setup screen, press F1.
 * To set up Workgroup Connection now, press ENTER.
 * To quit Setup without installing Workgroup Connection, press F3.
```

2. Press Enter to continue. The directory-path screen appears.

3. Type the directory path to which Workgroup Connection files will be copied (for example, C:\WGC), and then press Enter. SETUP begins examining your system files.

A list of network adapters supported by Workgroup Connection appears.

4. Locate the name of the network adapter installed in your computer and press Enter. WCSETUP copies the necessary drivers to your hard disk and configures the drivers.

   The next screen prompts you for a computer name and displays a list of characters you cannot use—! # $ % & ( ) ^ _ ' { } ~, for example.

5. Type a name for you computer. This name, which is used to identify your computer, can be up to up to 15 characters long.

6. After you type the computer name, press Enter. The workgroup name screen appears.

7. Type the workgroup name, and then press Enter. This name must agree with the name your network administrator has chosen for your workgroup. If the Workgroup name you enter does not agree, you may not be able to access shared directories or printers properly.

   After you enter the Workgroup name, the Workgroup Connection settings screen appears (see fig. 10.1).

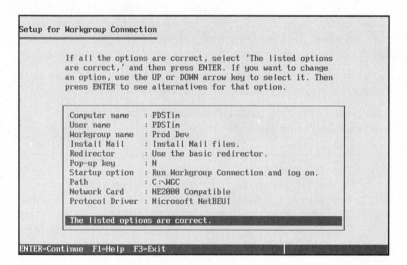

Fig. 10.1

The Workgroup Connection settings screen.

8. Make any changes you want. Table 10.3 summarizes the settings that you can change.

9. After you review the settings, select The Listed Options Are Correct, and then press Enter. SETUP completes copying the Workgroup Connection files to the directory that you specified and sets up the network connections according to your settings by modifying your CONFIG.SYS and AUTOEXEC.BAT files. A final screen shows that you successfully completed the setup.

10. To reboot your computer so that the Workgroup Connection drivers can load, press Enter. To quit WCSETUP without rebooting your computer, press F3. Quitting without rebooting doesn't affect your new setup. You can quit without rebooting if you want to return to the DOS prompt and not use Workgroup Connection at this point.

   After the computer restarts, the network drivers are loaded into memory. If you elected to log on when you start the network, a prompt appears, asking you to enter your user name.

11. The user name that you entered during setup is the default. If this name is correct, press Enter. Otherwise, enter the desired user name and press Enter.

12. At the password prompt, press Enter if you don't want to use a password. If you do want to use a password, type a password and press Enter. A prompt appears, asking you to confirm your password. If you typed a password, type it again then press Enter. You now are logged on to the network.

You can change your setup at any time by typing **WCSETUP** and pressing Enter.

Table 10.3 Workgroup Connection Settings

Option	Description
Computer name	The computer name that you selected
User name	Initially the same as the computer name but can be changed
Workgroup name	The workgroup name you selected
Install Mail	Initially reads Install Mail Files. You have the option of installing or not installing mail files. Choose Install Mail Files if you want to send and receive mail through the network. If you are short on disk space, choose Do Not Install Mail Files. (Mail files take approximately 270K of disk space.)

continues

Table 10.3 Continued

Option	Description
Redirector	You have two options: Basic and Full. The Basic redirector is a memory-resident Workgroup Connection program that provides standard workgroup functions, including connecting network drives for directory sharing and printer sharing. The Full redirector provides more-advanced connections for network-aware programs. Choose this option if you are connecting to a network (such as LAN Manager) that uses an OS/2 program that makes use of features such as *named pipes*, which enable network programs to access resources on many computers. The Full redirector requires more disk space than the Basic redirector does.
Pop-up key	This option enables you to choose which key you use in conjunction with Ctrl-Alt to call up the Workgroup Connection pop-up menu, which enables you to access shared directories and printers without exiting the program that is running. Some programs use certain Ctrl-Alt key combinations. The default is Ctrl-Alt-N. If a program already uses Ctrl-Alt-N, you can choose another letter.
Startup option	You can choose among three options: ■ *Run Workgroup Connection Only.* Activates Workgroup Connection but doesn't log you on to the LAN automatically. When you choose this option, you must log on to the network manually to use shared resources. ■ *Run Workgroup Connection and Log On.* Runs Workgroup Connection and automatically logs you on to the network. When you log on, you can connect automatically to whatever network resources— such as shared directories and printers— you establish. ■ *Run Workgroup Connection, Log On, and Load Pop-Up.* Connects and logs on your computer and loads the memory-resident Workgroup Connection menu. The pop-up menu option (which requires an extra 29K of memory) enables you to connect to network resources without leaving the program that you are running. If you are

Option	Description
	using Word for DOS and want to print, for example, you can open the Workgroup Connection pop-up menu by pressing Ctrl-Alt-N inside Word. The pop-up menu appears, enabling you to connect to a shared printer in the network.
Path	The drive and directory you selected to contain the Workgroup Connection files.
Network Card	The network adapter card that SETUP selected. Examine this setting to ensure that SETUP selected the correct card and the correct settings for the card. (For more information, see the sidebar titled "Checking Your Network Card Settings.")
Protocol Driver	The network communications protocol used in your Windows for Workgroup network (Microsoft's NetBEUI). Support for other protocols is limited. An example of another protocol is TCP/IP, a protocol used in many UNIX and U.S. government computer networks.

Checking Your Network Card Settings

For Workgroup Connection to work properly, the settings of the Workgroup Connection network card driver must match the settings of the network card itself. You make these settings when you run WCSETUP. The settings are as follows:

■ The name of the card

■ The interrupt request (IRQ)

■ The base address

When you install the network card, write down the settings you made. When you view the settings you made during Workgroup Connection setup (refer to fig. 10.1), select the Network Card option and press Enter to call up the network-drivers configuration screen. This screen contains three options:

■ Change driver for network card.

■ Edit settings for network card driver.

■ Driver configuration is correct.

continues

Checking Your Network Card Settings continued

If the name of the network card is incorrect, choose Change Driver for Network Card, and then press Enter. From the list of network cards that appears, select the correct name for your card, and then press Enter. You return to the network-drivers configuration screen. Then follow these steps:

1. Choose the Edit Settings for Network Card Driver option and press Enter. A screen displaying Drivername, IOBASE, and INTERRUPT appears.

   If any of these settings is incorrect, select the option and press Enter. A new screen appears, listing selections for the option. Make the correct selection and press Enter.

2. After you select the correct driver name, IOBASE, and INTER-RUPT, choose The Listed Options Are Correct and press Enter. You return to the network-drivers configuration screen.

3. From the network drivers configuration screen select Driver Configuration Is Correct and press Enter. You return to the screen that lists all the Workgroup Connection settings.

4. Select The Listed Options Are Correct and press Enter. Your connections now are set correctly.

NOTE

If, when selecting the correct network adapter name, you don't see your adapter listed, you must supply the drivers on a disk provided by the manufacturer. Workgroup Connection and Windows for Workgroups use a type of driver known as an NDIS driver. Most vendors put the letters *NDIS* in the file names of their drivers.

From the network adapters list, select Network Card Not Shown on List Below. Insert the manufacturer's driver disk in a floppy drive. At the prompt, type the path to the proper driver and press Enter. WCSETUP loads the driver and moves you to the adapter-settings screen.

Operating Workgroup Connection

Now that you have successfully installed Workgroup Connection, the next step is to put it to use. This section shows you how the utilities that come with Workgroup Connection work.

Understanding NET and the Connections Menus

Workgroup Connection comes with a workgroup utility program called NET.EXE. After you install this utility on your computer, you can use NET.EXE to perform the functions of a workgroup client—that is, connect to and disconnect from shared directories and shared printers.

Workgroup Connection gives you access to shared directories and printers on the network. These elements are known as *connections*. You can use NET.EXE as a Connections menu system or as a command-line utility. The menu for using shared directories (the default) is the Disk Connections menu; the menu for using shared printers is the Printer Connections menu.

You can access the Disk Connections menu in one of two ways. If you chose to load this pop-up menu during setup, you can access the Disk Connections menu by pressing Alt-Ctrl-N (unless you changed the default shortcut key from N to another letter). If you didn't install Workgroup Connection as a TSR, change to the directory containing the Workgroup Connection files and run the Net program by typing **NET** and pressing Enter. The Disk Connection menu appears (see fig. 10.2).

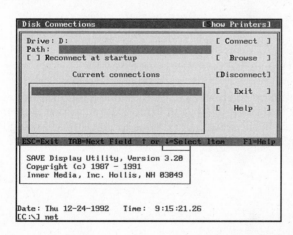

Fig. 10.2

The Disk Connections menu.

Table 10.4 summarizes the options available in this menu. You can move to any Disk Connections option by pressing Tab or by pressing Alt and the underscored letter in the option name.

Table 10.4 Disk Connections Menu Options

Option	Description
Drive	Lists the letter of the drive to which you want to connect. You can connect drive letters from A to the last drive letter specified in your CONFIG.SYS file.
Path	Lists the path, which consists of two backslash characters (\\) followed by a computer name and a directory name. To access a directory called SOUNDS on a computer named WILBUR, for example, you type **\\WILBUR\SOUNDS**.
Reconnect at Startup	Reconnects this drive each time you run Workgroup Connection and log on
Current Connections	Displays a list of currently connected drives and their paths
Show Printers	Switches you to the Printer Connections menu, through which you can view and control network printing
Connect	Connects the drive to the path that you specify
Browse	Checks the network to determine what computers and shared directories for each computer are available
Disconnect	Disconnects the drive from the path
Exit	Exits the Disk Connections menu
Help	Provides information on using the Disk Connections menu

Notice that the option Show Printers displays the Printer Connections menu. Most of the options in the Printer Connections menu are the same as those in the Disk Connections menu. The following list shows the differences between the Disk Connections and Printer Connections menus.

Printer Connections Menu Option	Description	Disk Connections Menu Replacement
Port	The printer port name to assign for your computer	Drive
Show Disks	Switches between the Disk Connections and Printer Connections menus	Show Printers
Show Queue	Displays the activity of a shared printer and enables you to Pause, Resume, or Delete a print job that you sent to the shared printer	None

A quicker way to manage disk connections and printer connections is to issue NET commands at the DOS command line. You can use several command-line parameters with the NET command to manage your connections.

The syntax you use to issue command-line parameters is as follows:

NET *parameter*

Table 10.5 lists and explains the parameters you can type after the NET command.

Table 10.5 Available NET Parameters

Parameter	Description
/?	Displays a list of the command-line parameters
command /?	Reveals additional options available for a *command*. Commands such as NET USE and NET PRINT have a dozen additional options each. To get help from the DOS prompt on the NET LOGON parameter, for example, type **NET LOGON /?**.
CONFIG	Displays the computer name, user log-on name, software version, redirector version, directory where Workgroup Connection was loaded, and workgroup name
HELP	Displays a help screen listing the various NET parameters

continues

Table 10.5 Continued

Parameter	Description
LOGOFF	Logs off of the network
LOGON	Logs on to the network. If you have any connections that have been marked Reconnect at Startup, those connections are established at this time. This parameter indicates that a record of these connections saved from the last network session was used to reestablish the network connections.
PASSWORD	Enables you to change your log-on password
PRINT	Enables you to print and manage jobs you have printed to a shared printer queue. (For more information, see the section "Using a Shared Printer" later in this chapter.)
START	Starts Workgroup Connection. If you specified the memory-resident program when you installed Workgroup Connection, the Connections menus are loaded into memory. The Basic or Full redirector loads into memory. You also can start without being prompted to enter a user log-on name. If you start the program without entering your name, Workgroup Connection assumes that you want to use the default log-on name.

Startup Options include the following:

- *BASIC*. Loads the basic redirector.

- *FULL*. Loads the full redirector.

- */LIST*. Lists the Workgroup Connection components loaded so far.

- *NETBEUI*. Loads the Microsoft NetBIOS interface.

- *NETBIND*. Binds the protocols and network adapter cards.

- *POPUP*. Loads the pop-up menu interface.

- *WORKSTATION*. Starts the default redirector (specified during installation).

- */YES*. Starts Workgroup Connection without waiting for you to enter a log-on name and password. This option assumes that you want to use the default log-on name and password (the ones you used when you installed Workgroup Connection).

Parameter	Description
STOP	Stops Workgroup Connection and the pop-up menu, if it is resident in memory
TIME	Synchronizes the time on your computer with the time on a Microsoft LAN Manager time server (a file server running LAN Manager, if you have one in your network). This command includes option flags that enable you to specify another workgroup.
USE	Connects a drive or port to a shared directory or printer in the network. (Additional options are mentioned throughout this chapter.)
VER	Displays the version of Workgroup Connection that you are using.
VIEW	Displays a list of computers and shared resources. To view the resources of a particular computer, type **NET VIEW \\computer** (*computer* is the computer name).

Take some time to become familiar with the connections menus and with the NET command and its parameters. You use these menus and commands to access shared directories and printers.

Entering the Network

Before you can use any of the features of Workgroup Connection, you must log on to the network. If you selected the Run Workgroup Connection and Log On option when you installed Workgroup Connection, you are prompted to log on to the network every time you boot your computer.

Logging on to the network consists of entering your user name and a password, if you selected a password when you first logged on to the network. Because Workgroup Connection remembers the user name you chose when you installed Workgroup Connection, entering your user name amounts to nothing more than pressing Enter. If you elected to use a password, you then are prompted to type your password and press Enter.

You can log on to and log off of the network by using the NET command from the DOS command line. The syntax for logging on is shown in the following:

NET LOGON *username password /YES*

If you type only **NET LOGON** and then press Enter, you are prompted to type your user name and password. You can, however, type your user name and password in the command line, as you see in the syntax. If you include the optional */YES* switch, DOS uses your default user name and password to log you on to the network.

Exiting the Network

After you log on to the network, you can log off at any time. The syntax for logging off the network is shown in the following:

NET LOGOFF */YES*

The */YES* switch is optional. Simply typing **NET LOGOFF** at the command line logs you off the network.

Be aware that if you log on to the network and then try to log on to the network again, Workgroup Connection assumes that you are another user trying to log on to the network, and the following message appears:

```
You are currently logged on as username.
You must first log off before logging on again.
Do you want to log off? (Y/N) [N]:
```

If you press Enter, you choose the default setting (No) and remain logged on to the network. If you type **Y**, however, and then press Enter, you are logged off the network. Workgroup Connection assumes that you want to log in again and prompts you for a new user name. This practice is useful if you have a computer that several people use because when you type Y, Workgroup Connection leaves you at a logon prompt screen so that the next user can logon.

If you are attached to a shared directory or a shared printer, you also are prompted to disconnect from the directory or printer before you log off.

Stopping Workgroup Connection

Each time you start your computer, you also start the network connection because of the NET START command that WCSETUP placed in your AUTOEXEC.BAT file. When the network is started, you can access any of the Workgroup Connection features.

You can stop Workgroup Connection, however, by using the STOP parameter. The syntax for stopping the utility is shown in the following:

NET STOP *option*

In place of *option*, you may use one of the following parameters:

Option	Description
BASIC	Stops the basic network redirector
FULL	Stops the full network redirector
NETBEUI	Stops the NetBIOS interface
POPUP	Unloads the NET pop-up utility from memory but doesn't stop the network connection
WORKSTATION	Stops the default redirector

By typing **NET STOP**, you stop all access to the network. If you are logged on to the network and connected to a shared directory or shared printer, the program prompts you to end those connections and log off before stopping the network connection.

After you stop Workgroup Connection, you can start it. To start the connection, you use the following syntax:

NET START *option /LIST*

The */LIST* switch displays a list of the options that are loaded into memory. The following table lists the options that you can use in place of *option*.

Option	Description
BASIC	Loads the basic network redirector
FULL	Loads the full network redirector
NETBEUI	Loads the NetBIOS interface
POPUP	Loads the NET pop-up utility into memory as a TSR
WORKSTATION	Loads the default redirector

Why would you want to stop and then restart a connection? Suppose that you have been using the Basic redirector and now need to use the features of the Full redirector. You can type the command NET STOP BASIC, followed by the command NET START FULL. The full redirector is loaded into memory for use.

374

Suppose instead that you want to load NET as a TSR. Issue the command NET START POPUP. NET loads as a TSR that you can activate by pressing the hot key (Alt-Ctrl-N).

Using a Shared Directory

The Workgroup Connection feature that probably is used most often is directory sharing. The following sections explain how to connect and disconnect network drives.

Connecting to a Network Drive

Connecting to a network drive assigns a drive letter to a shared directory. To connect to a network drive, you can run the NET program or use the pop-up Disk Connections menu.

To connect to a network drive by using the pop-up menu, follow these steps:

1. Press Alt-Ctrl-N. The Disk Connections menu appears.

2. Choose the Drive option, and then type the desired drive letter.

3. Choose the Path option, and then type the desired path. To connect to the SOUNDS shared directory on the server PDS, for example, type **PDS\SOUNDS**.

   If you don't know the path, choose the Browse option, which opens the Browse dialog box (see fig. 10.3).

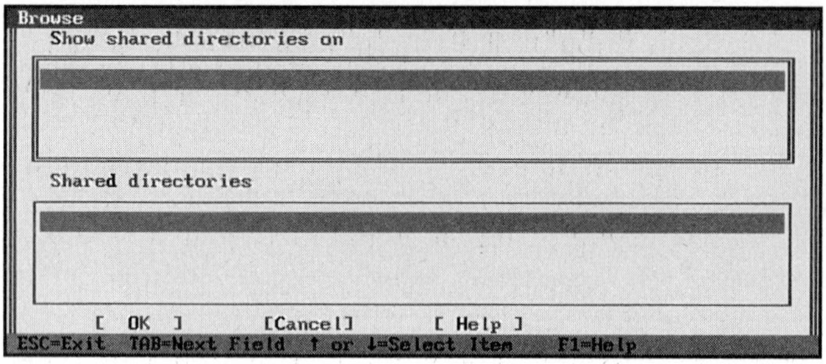

```
Browse
  Show shared directories on



  Shared directories



      [  OK  ]      [Cancel]      [ Help ]
ESC=Exit  TAB=Next Field  ↑ or ↓=Select Item   F1=Help
```

Fig. 10.3

The Disk Connections Browse dialog box.

4. In the <u>S</u>how Shared Directories On list box, select the desired computer, and then press Tab or Alt-D to move to the Share<u>d</u> Directories list box from which you select the desired shared directory. Choose <u>O</u>K to return to the Disk Connections menu.

5. Click the <u>C</u>onnect button.

6. Choose E<u>x</u>it to leave the Disk Connections menu.

You also can connect to a network drive from the DOS command line by issuing the NET command, as follows:

NET USE *d*: *server**shared_dir*

or

NET USE * *server**shared_dir*

The asterisk (*) means that the next available drive letter is used, although you also can use a specific drive letter. The command NET USE F: \\PDS\BOOK, for example, assigns the shared directory BOOK to your F drive.

Disconnecting from a Network Drive

You may need to disconnect from a network drive from time to time for any of the following reasons:

■ The computer containing the shared directory went down.

■ The access type of the shared directory changed while you were connected.

■ You ran out of drive letters and need to use this drive letter to connect to another directory.

To disconnect from a network drive, follow these steps:

1. Press Alt-Ctrl-N. The Disk Connections menu appears.

2. In the Current Connections list box, select the drive from which you want to disconnect.

3. Choose the Disconnect option. The drive disappears from the Current Connections list box.

To disconnect a network drive from the DOS command line, use the following syntax:

NET USE d: /DELETE

To disconnect from network drive F, for example, you type NET USE F: /DELETE and press Enter.

Using a Shared Printer

Workgroup Connection enables you to assign printing from a local port to a shared printer. When you are running a program, any printing that normally would be directed to one of the parallel ports (LPT1, LPT2, and so on) is redirected to the print queue for the shared printer.

The following sections explain how to connect to, disconnect from, and manage connections with shared printers in your network.

Connecting a Port to a Network Printer

In a network connection, a *local parallel port* (that is, a port on your computer) is assigned to a shared printer. To connect to a network printer, you can issue the NET command or use the Printer Connections menu.

To access the Printer Connections menu, start the NET menu by pressing Alt-Ctrl-N or by typing **NET** and pressing Enter. The default is to the Disk Connections menu. To change to the Printer Connections menu, shown in figure 10.4, press Alt-S.

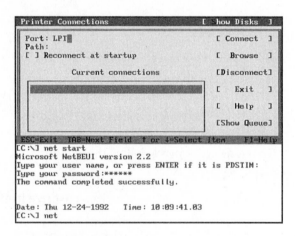

Fig. 10.4

The Printer Connections menu.

To connect to a network printer, follow these steps:

1. Access the Printer Connections menu by pressing Alt-S.

2. Choose Port, and then type the desired port number (1, 2, or 3). You can define up to three printer connections at the same time.

3. For the <u>P</u>ath option, type the desired path. The path consists of two backslash characters (\\), the computer name, another backslash, and a directory path. To access a printer called SPEED_DEVIL on computer TASMANIAN, for example, you type **\\TASMANIAN\SPEED_DEVIL**.

If you don't know the path to the printer, choose the <u>B</u>rowse option, which opens the Browse dialog box (see fig. 10.5).

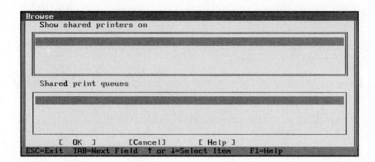

Fig. 10.5

The Printer Connections Browse dialog box.

In the <u>S</u>how Shared Printers On list box, select the desired computer. Press Tab or Alt-D to move to the Share<u>d</u> Print Queues list box, and then select the desired shared printer queue. Choose <u>O</u>K to return to the Printer Connections menu.

4. Choose <u>C</u>onnect. The new printer connection appears in the Current Connections list.

5. Choose E<u>x</u>it to return to the command line.

You can connect to a shared printer from the command line in much the same way that you connect to a shared directory from the command line. Use the following syntax:

NET USE port#: \\server\queue

To attach the printer LASER01 from the server PDS01 to your LPT1 port, for example, you type **NET USE LPT1: \\PDS01\LASER01**. Thereafter, anything that you send to LPT1 is redirected to LASER01, which is connected to PDS01.

Disconnecting from a Network Printer

You may need to disconnect from a network printer from time to time for any of the following reasons:

- The computer containing the shared printer went down.
- The access type of the shared printer changed while you were connected.
- You decide to connect different printers to your three allowed ports.

To disconnect from a network printer, follow these steps:

1. Access the Printer Connections menu by pressing Alt-Ctrl-N and then Alt-S.

2. In the Current Connections list box, select the printer from which you want to disconnect.

3. Choose Disconnect. The printer disappears from the Current Connections list box.

You also can disconnect a printer by typing the NET command at the command line, as follows:

NET USE port#: /DELETE

To disconnect the shared printer from your LPT2 port, for example, you type **NET USE LPT2: /DELETE**.

Managing Print Queues

You have a certain degree of control over jobs that you place in the print queue of a shared printer. You can view the status of the print queues to determine how busy a printer is. If a queue is busy, you may decide to print to another queue. (If you place a job in print queue for a printer that is already being used, you do not affect the other user's print job; you can affect only jobs that you place in the queue.) Only the local user using the host computer (where the shared printer is attached) can manage any jobs in the queue.

To view and manage your jobs in the queue, choose Show Queue from the Printer Connections menu. The Print Queue dialog box appears, listing the available print queues (see fig. 10.6).

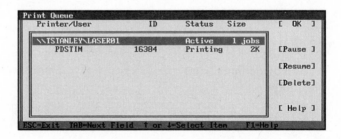

Fig. 10.6

The Print Queue dialog box.

This dialog box has two major sections: the print-queue list and the command buttons. Table 10.6 summarizes the four columns of information in the print-queue list.

Table 10.6 Print-Queue List Information

Column	Description
Printer/User	Displays the *computer name**printer name* of the shared printer. If the printer is printing a job or has jobs in the queue, the name of the user who generated the job is listed.
ID	Displays an identifying number assigned by Windows for Workgroups so that the program can keep track of the job.
Status	Lists the status of the printer. Printer status codes are Active (for printers that are ready to print) and Paused (for printers that are ready but paused by the local user). When jobs are being printed, this column also lists the status of the job. Job-status codes are Printing (when the job is printing successfully) and Paused (for jobs paused by the initiators or the local user).
Size	Indicates how many jobs are stacked up for each printer. If jobs are printing, you also see a list of the sizes of the jobs (in kilobytes).

You also can perform print-queue-management functions by clicking the following command buttons, which are listed on the right side of the dialog box:

- *OK*. Returns to the Printer Connections menu.

- *Pause*. Pauses the currently selected job until you release the pause. This option is useful for stopping printing if you must change paper or service the printer in some way. (You can pause only your own print jobs; the local user can pause any user's print jobs.)

- *Resume*. Restarts a print job that you paused earlier.

- *Delete*. Deletes a job that is waiting in the queue. You may need to delete a job if you decide to print the same job to another queue. Delete your first job so that you don't tie up the first printer needlessly.

- *Help*. Accesses the help screen.

You also can use the command line to manage your print queue by using the following syntax:

NET PRINT port pjob#

The *port* option is the port to which you assigned a shared printer. The *pjob#* option is the number of the print job in the queue.

You also can add the following options after the NET PRINT command:

/DELETE	Deletes a print job
/PAUSE	Pauses a print job
/RESUME	Resumes a paused print job

To examine the queue, type **NET PRINT *port***. To examine the queue for your port LPT1, for example, you type NET PRINT LPT1:. If you now have seven jobs in the queue and want to delete job 4, you type NET PRINT LPT1 4 /DELETE.

Sending and Receiving Mail

Microsoft Mail is an electronic mail utility that enables you to send and receive mail messages within your workgroup. The Mail program is located in the same directory you installed Workgroup Connection. You can set up Mail on a computer that is running Workgroup Connection. Tell the system which post office to use, enter your password, and fill out the post-office account-information screen.

After Mail is set up, the following events need to occur in order for you to access Mail in the future:

■ The computer serving as the mail server must be up and running Windows for Workgroups.

■ You need to connect a drive to the post-office directory.

The concepts for Mail under Workgroup Connection are the same as those for Mail under Windows for Workgroups. For more information on this topic, see Que's *Connecting Windows for Workgroups 3.1* and *Using Windows 3.1*, Special Edition.

Starting Mail

The command to start Mail from Workgroup Connection uses the following syntax:

MAIL -D*drive mailbox_name* -P*password*

Table 10.7 summarizes the command's syntax and additional options.

Table 10.7 Mail Start-Up Options

Option	Explanation
–D*drive*	Specifies the Mail database. *drive* specifies the drive containing the workgroup post-office directories (the Mail database).
mailbox_name	The name of your mailbox. (This option isn't required. If you don't enter your mailbox name here, the program prompts you for the name later.)
–*x*	*x* represents the number of lines on your mail screen (25 to 50).
–C	Tells Mail that you are using a color monitor.
–E*drive*:*path*	Tells Mail where your graphics programs (such as Paintbrush) are located. If you are sending messages that contain graphics and want to be able to access these graphics immediately, use this parameter. Mail searches the *path* indicated for graphics programs. If you are using a program called VPIC.EXE in the GRAPHICS directory, for example, you type **-eC:\GRAPHICS\VPIC.EXE** after the MAIL command.
–H or –?	Shows the help screen for the MAIL command.
–I*drive*:*path*	Tells Mail where to store temporary graphics files it may need to create when processing messages that contain graphics. If you don't have enough room on your C drive, for example, you can specify a directory called EXTRA on drive D by typing **–iD:\EXTRA**.
–M	Tells Mail that the memory-resident programs MONITOR or MICRO are loaded. These programs notify you immediately if you have an incoming mail message.
–N*x*	Mail checks for new mail every *x* seconds. (*x* can range from 1 to 999 seconds.) If you use 1 for *x*, you receive notice of new mail quickly but may find that your system slows. A value of 999 checks for new mail approximately every 15 minutes. If you use a value of 0, your computer doesn't check the post office for mail until you get into the Mail program.

continues

Table 10.7 Continued

Option	Explanation
-P*password*	Enables you to enter a password from the command prompt. Otherwise, the system stops and waits for you to enter the password.
-S*type*	Enables you to specify your monitor type: ■ CGA (Color Graphics Adapter) ■ EGA (Enhanced Graphics Adapter) ■ HERC (Hercules Graphics Adapter) ■ VGA (Video Graphics Array) ■ MONO (monochrome)
-V	Reduces the "snow" on some graphics screens. If you don't have any screen problems when you use Mail, don't use this parameter. If you see flickers and snow on-screen, exit Mail and reenter, using this flag.
-X	Sets the notification method.
-W*x*	Sets the color scheme. *x* represents any number from 1 to 15. These numbers correspond to the set of 16 foreground/background colors that are standard in DOS.

Suppose, for example, that the following conditions are true: the WGPO directory is connected to drive G; the mailbox name is Eileen; and the password is MELLO. To access Eileen's mail screen, using these specifications, you type the following command:

    MAIL -dG: EILEEN -pMELLO

> **CAUTION:** You must know the drive and/or directory that contains your mailbox data. The directory (usually named WGPO) should contain the workgroup post office. If you don't specify the drive and/or directory, Mail does not start.

Sending Messages

Sending a message involves three main actions:

- *Addressing the message.* From your personal address list or the post-office address list, you need to select the names of the people whom you want to receive the message.

- *Composing the message.* Type the text of the message. You also can attach a file to the message. The attached file "rides" along with the message; the recipient can detach the file.

- *Processing the message.* You have several choices: you can save the message to a folder for later use, erase the message, or transmit it. A transmitted message is placed on the LAN and sent to the post office. The message resides in a file in the post-office computer until the recipients of the message pick up their mail. If the recipients don't pick up their mail in the designated period, the mail is considered to be undeliverable.

To compose a message, first choose Compose from the Mail main menu. The Compose window appears (see fig. 10.7).

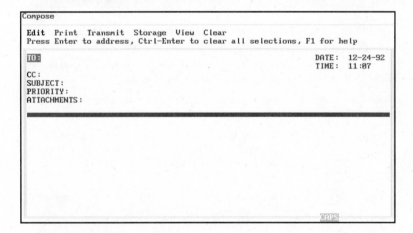

```
Compose
Edit  Print  Transmit  Storage  View  Clear
Press Enter to address, Ctrl-Enter to clear all selections, F1 for help

TO:                                          DATE:  12-24-92
                                             TIME:  11:07
CC:
SUBJECT:
PRIORITY:
ATTACHMENTS:



                                                              CAPS
```

Fig. 10.7

The Compose window.

The Compose window contains the following fields:

- *TO.* The recipient of the message. You can select one or more names from the post-office list or your personal address list.

- *CC.* The recipient of a copy of the message. You can select one or more names from the post-office list or your personal address list.

- *SUBJECT.* The title or subject of the message.

■ *PRIORITY*. The level of the message, as shown in the following:

1	High priority
2-4	Moderate priority
5	Low priority
R	Highest priority; causes a Return Receipt to come back to you when read

You may not be able to use the PRIORITY option, depending on restrictions set by the administrator of your workgroup post office.

■ *ATTACHMENTS*. Enables you to add files to your message.

■ *DATE*. Today's date. (This field cannot be changed.)

■ *TIME*. The current time. (This field cannot be changed.)

You also can use the following function keys while you compose a message:

Key	Description
F1 (Help)	Calls up the help system, which is available at any time. If you are working on a specific field, pressing F1 can give you help on that field.
F2 (Format)	Formats the text of the message as a paragraph, starting with the current line.
F3 (Preferences)	Enables you to change preferences while you compose the message.
F4 (Highlight)	Enables you to change the appearance of the highlight. To change a block of text to a specific type of highlight, first select it by using F6, and then press F4.
F5 (Include)	Enables you to insert (include) a DOS file into your message. This option is useful when you want to create a form to use on a regular basis. Create the form, using a text editor, and then press F5 to bring the form into your message so that you can complete and send it.
F6 (Mark)	Starts selecting text at the cursor location. Use the arrow keys to move the highlight to the end of the block of text that you want to select.
F7 (Copy)	Enables you to copy the selected text to a paste buffer (available only when you have some text selected).

Key	Description
F8 (Paste)	Brings whatever is in the paste buffer to the cursor location (available only when you have text in the paste buffer).
F9 (Cut)	Enables you to cut the selected text to a paste buffer (available only when you have text selected).
F10 (Delete)	Enables you to delete the selected text (available only when you have text selected).
Insert	Toggles between insert and overtype modes. In insert mode, all characters to the right of the cursor move to the right when you type. In overtype mode, all characters to the right of the cursor are overwritten.

After you finish composing your message, press Esc to return to the Compose menu.

From the Compose menu, you have several options: you can edit, print, transmit, store, view, or clear the message. You probably will want to transmit the message. To send the message, choose Transmit in the Compose menu. If you have the Confirmation option set, choose Yes to confirm that you want to Transmit the message). The message is sent to the post office.

Receiving Messages

You can receive messages in the following circumstances:

- When you enter Mail
- When you choose Update from the main menu
- At time intervals determined by what you specified when you entered Mail. The MAIL –Nx option enables you to change this parameter (refer to table 10.7 earlier in this chapter).

After you receive a mail message, you can read it by following these steps:

1. Choose Read from the Main menu. A reverse highlighted bar appears in the Contents Listing screen. The Contents Listing screen appears.

2. Select the message that you want to read. The size of the message appears on the top right side of the screen.

3. Press Enter to display the contents of the message.

Chapter Summary

Workgroup Connection is a product you can purchase separately from DOS 6.0. Workgroup Connection provides access to a network. The most important feature of Workgroup Connection is its ability to connect you with other network computers' hard drives, printers, and electronic mail. This chapter gave you an overview of Workgroup Connection and explained how to install and configure a network adapter card and how to install Workgroup Connection. In this chapter, you also learned how to use the NET utility, enter and exit the network, and stop Workgroup Connection. Finally, you learned how to install the Mail utility and how to send and receive electronic mail.

The next chapter, "Working with System Information," explains how you can control the DOS interface.

Working with System Information

C hapters 1 through 5 of this book introduce the fundamentals of DOS and how these fundamentals relate to you and your hardware. Chapters 6 through 9 show you the commands associated with your disks, directories, and files. This chapter covers commands that enable you to control your DOS interface.

You can use these commands to change or display your system information, such as the date and time assigned to your files. If you use DOS 4.0 or later versions, you may issue a command to invoke the DOS Shell. If you use an earlier version of DOS, you can use several commands to adjust the appearance of the screen.

The commands covered in this chapter are called *system information commands*. This chapter covers the following commands:

DATE

TIME

VER

SETVER

MEM

DIR

DOSSHELL

PROMPT

MODE

COMMAND

EXIT

SET

These commands, as well as their parameters and switches, are also described in the Command Reference.

Changing the Date and Time

When DOS saves a new file to disk, it assigns a date and time stamp to the file; this stamp is placed in the directory entry with the file name, attributes, and starting cluster information for the FAT. The computer reads the date and time assigned to a file as the current date and time.

If your computer is a 286 (AT-class), 386, or 486, a battery-backed clock keeps the date and time in memory after you set them. Even when the computer is turned off, power from the battery goes to the chip containing the clock, and the date and time remain current. In a PC or XT you can use an add-on, battery-backed clock for this purpose. When you have an add-on clock, you must run a special program (packaged with the clock) to transfer date and time information to DOS.

Setting the date and time becomes increasingly important as you create more files on your computer. Because the DOS file-naming rules limit you to only eight characters in the root file name and three characters in the file extension (which is generally used to indicate the file type), the names of your files may not be very descriptive. In this situation, you can use the date and time stamp to tell which file is the most recent. On computers without a clock or with a clock and a dead battery, however, the date and time are set to the same value each time you turn on the computer. This situation makes it difficult for you—or DOS—to tell the difference between an old file and a revised or new file. In addition, some DOS commands work by comparing file dates. If you have no clock or your battery is dead, enter the current date and time each time you start your computer. This precaution helps you avoid the confusion that can result from having many files assigned similar date and time stamps.

Occasionally checking your computer's date and time is worthwhile. All batteries eventually fail and need replacing. All clocks in personal computers lose time. How much time your clock loses depends on the programs you run on your computer.

The clock that keeps the date and time in a PC is controlled by an electronic component in the computer—the *system timer*. This chip is the heartbeat of the computer. Everything the computer does takes a known amount of time. The system timer provides a regular pulse that controls all the functions occurring in the computer.

One of these functions is to update the clock that DOS uses to tell the time (and consequently the date). Commands or other programs that cannot afford to be interrupted while they are working tell DOS not to interrupt them until they finish operating. A typical example is a communications program that waits for a character to be sent from another computer. If DOS is busy performing other tasks, such as updating the clock, the program may miss the character. Consequently, this type of program disables the interrupts—the program tells DOS to do nothing else for the period of time that it needs full control. During these times, the clock is not updated. These periods are only a few seconds, but the effect is cumulative, and eventually the time loss is noticeable.

If you do not have an AUTOEXEC.BAT file, which runs when you start your computer, DOS prompts you for the date and time when you boot the computer. DOS also shows you the current settings and allows you to change them. On a 286 (AT-class), 386, or 486, you can probably accept the current settings because the date and time are loaded from the battery-backed clock.

If you have an AUTOEXEC.BAT file that lacks DATE and TIME commands, DOS uses its current settings. If you see that a file you have just edited has the wrong date and time, change the current settings by using the DATE and TIME commands.

Issuing the DATE Command

The syntax for the internal DATE command is shown in the following:

DATE *today*

or

DATE

If you type DATE at the DOS prompt, DOS shows you the current setting and prompts you for a new date. You can change the date without being prompted by including the new date on the command line.

The *today* parameter specifies the month, day, and year. The exact syntax depends on the COUNTRY code set in your CONFIG.SYS file. (Chapter 20, "Understanding the International Features of DOS," includes a discussion of the country code settings.) The syntax for *today* can be in one of the following forms:

COUNTRY Code	Format
North America	*mm-dd-yy*
	mm-dd-yyyy
Europe	*dd-mm-yy*
	dd-mm-yyyy
East Asia	*yy-mm-dd*
	yyyy-mm-dd

The abbreviations are as follows: *mm* is the month, *dd* is the day, and *yy* and *yyyy* are the year.

To enter the date December 23, 1992, on a machine configured for North America, type the following:

DATE 12-23-92

You also can type the year in its full form (1992, for example). If you use two digits, DOS assumes the 19. Instead of the hyphen, you can use periods or slashes as separators. Leading digits are not required. If the month is January, for example, you can type **1** (instead of **01**) for the month.

If you want to change the date, letting DOS prompt you for the date is the best way to use this command because the current date appears in the correct format, and you can copy the syntax rather than remember it. Following is an example of how the DOS screen might appear if you let DOS prompt you for the current date:

```
C:\>DATE
Current date is Mon 09-18-1992
Enter new date (mm-dd-yy): 12-23-1992
```

Pressing Enter when DOS prompts you for a new date retains the current setting. If you don't enter the date correctly or if you select a date out of the DOS range, DOS displays the error message Invalid date and then again displays the Enter new date prompt.

Notice that DOS displays the day of the week in addition to the other date information. You can use the DATE command to determine the day of the week for a particular date. To do so, issue the DATE command to see the new setting, but do not change the setting.

DOS 3.3 and later versions actually change the battery-backed clock as well as the system clock setting when you use the DATE command. Versions of DOS before 3.3 do not update the date permanently in the battery-backed clock; those versions keep the date you enter only while the computer is on. When you turn off the power, the date value reverts to the one stored in the battery-backed clock. To change the clock permanently for earlier versions of DOS, use the SETUP program supplied with your computer.

Issuing the TIME Command

The syntax for the internal TIME command is as follows:

TIME *now*

or

TIME

As with DATE, if you type only TIME and press Enter at the command prompt, DOS shows you the current setting and prompts you for a new time. You can change the time without being prompted by including the new time on the command line as a parameter.

The *now* parameter specifies hours, minutes, and seconds. The exact syntax for *time* depends on the COUNTRY code setting in your CONFIG.SYS file.

You can use either a 12-hour or a 24-hour clock. The following shows the syntax for the 24-hour clock:

hrs:mins:secs.1/100secs

The abbreviations mean the following: *hrs* is the hour, a number from 0 to 23; *mins* is the minutes, a number from 0 to 59; *secs* is the seconds, a number from 0 to 59; and *1/100secs* is the number of one-hundredth seconds, a number from 0 to 99. The 24-hour clock starts with midnight as 00:00.

DOS 4.0 and later versions use the 12-hour clock; the syntax is the same as for the 24-hour clock except that *hrs* is a number from 1 to 12, and you add an *a* or *p* to signify A.M. or P.M. If you do not add an *a* or *p*, DOS assumes A.M. You can also enter a 24-hour time, and DOS displays it in the 12-hour format.

In either format, do not include spaces between the parameters. Also, in the case of the 12-hour version, do not include spaces between the end of the time elements and the *a* or *p*. You can use a period instead of a colon when separating the hours, minutes, and seconds, or a comma in place of a period when separating the seconds from the hundredths of a second.

You do not have to specify all the parts of the time. DOS sets any missing elements to zero (using the 24-hour clock notation). To set the time to 8:25 P.M., for example, you would type one of the following lines:

TIME 20:25

TIME 8:25p

Either command sets the time to 8:25 P.M. The seconds and hundredths of a second are set to zero. To set the clock to 12:30 A.M., you would type the following:

TIME :30

Letting DOS prompt you for the time is the easiest way to use this command because DOS shows the syntax, just as it does with DATE. Following is an example of how the DOS screen might appear if you let DOS prompt you for the current time:

```
C:\>TIME
Current time is 2:35:07.23p
Enter new time: 2:40p
```

You can use the COUNTRY command to change the format DOS uses to display the time (see Chapter 20, "Understanding the International Features of DOS").

NOTE As with the DATE command, DOS Versions 3.3 through 6.0 actually change the setting in your battery-backed clock when you execute the TIME command. Earlier DOS versions do not update the time in the battery-backed clock; when you turn off the power to your computer, the time setting reverts to the one in the battery-backed clock. You need to use the SETUP program supplied with your computer to change the clock permanently with these earlier versions.

For Related Information

▶▶ "Understanding COUNTRY.SYS," p. 755.

FROM HERE...

Displaying the Version with VER

DOS includes an internalx command that displays the DOS version the computer is using. Knowing how to use the VER command is invaluable if you ever work with an unfamiliar computer. Some commands, such as DISKCOMP, FORMAT, and XCOPY work differently or are not available with different DOS versions. If you do not know which version of DOS a computer is using, the VER command can tell you.

When you issue the VER command, DOS displays a message such as `MS-DOS Version 6.00` that shows the version of DOS that was used to boot the computer. If a computer with a hard disk is booted from a floppy disk, the version of DOS may not be what you expected. Suppose that your hard disk is formatted for DOS 6.0, but you use a Version 3.3 floppy disk to boot your computer. The Version 6.0 commands on your hard disk will not work while your computer is running a different version of DOS; the message `Incorrect DOS Version` appears when you try to use one of the Version 6.0 commands.

Sometimes DOS can be slightly different even within the same version. Some computer manufacturers supply DOS packages specially designed to work with their machines, so you may see a different message if you use a different product. COMPAQ Computer Corporation's version of DOS, for example, includes COMPAQ's name with the version number. Because of the differences between these versions, you may be able to track down problems on an unfamiliar computer more easily if you first determine the exact DOS version number and its manufacturer.

Setting the Version with SETVER

When a new version of DOS is released, some time passes before software manufacturers can upgrade popular applications programs to take full advantage of DOS's new features. Many programs ask the operating system to tell them which version of DOS the computer is running. If a program does not recognize the version of DOS in memory, it may refuse to run. One or more of your applications programs, therefore, may refuse to run because they have not been certified by the manufacturer to run properly with DOS 6.0.

You can get a reluctant program to run in DOS 6.0 in two ways:

- Contact the software manufacturer or your dealer to find out whether you need a program upgrade.

- Use the SETVER command to add the name of the program to DOS 6.0's *version table*. The version table is a list of programs with DOS version numbers listed next to them. When a program listed in the version table loads into memory and asks DOS for its version number, DOS reports the version number listed in the version table rather than the actual version number—6.0. The application is fooled into running in DOS 6.0.

The first option is the better choice. By checking with the manufacturer, you can determine whether the applications program has been tested in DOS 6.0.

> **CAUTION:** If you use SETVER, you run the risk, however slight, that your program may become corrupted if it is incompatible with DOS 6.0.

The SETVER command operates as both a device driver and an executable command. Before DOS can use the version table, you must load SETVER.EXE as a device driver. Include the command in your CONFIG.SYS file so that it executes every time you start your computer. If SETVER.EXE is not in your CONFIG.SYS file, you need to add it. Use the following syntax to add SETVER.EXE to your CONFIG.SYS file:

DEVICE=*d:path***SETVER.EXE**

The parameters *d:* and *path*\ are the disk and directory that contain the SETVER.EXE external program file. If you are using DOS 6.0, the installation program creates a default CONFIG.SYS file for you, which includes the following command:

DEVICE=C:\DOS\SETVER.EXE

After the device driver SETVER.EXE is loaded into memory, DOS can use the version table to report different DOS versions to applications programs listed in the version table.

To see whether your program is already in the version table, use SETVER from the command line. To do this, type **SETVER** at the command line; do not add switches, file names, or parameters. DOS displays a two-column listing with program names in the first column and the DOS version number the programs will work with in the second column. Microsoft has already tested the programs listed in the initial version table and determined that they operate properly in DOS 6.0. The version list that appears on your screen should resemble the following:

```
KERNEL.EXE      5.00
NETX.COM        5.00
NETX.EXE        5.00
NET5.COM        5.00
BNETX.COM       5.00
BNETX.EXE       5.00
EMSNETX.EXE     5.00
EMSNET5.EXE     5.00
XMSNETX.EXE     5.00
XMSNET5.EXE     5.00
DOSOAD.SYS      5.00
REDIR50.EXE     5.00
REDIR5.EXE      5.00
REDIRALL.EXE    5.00
REDIRNP4.EXE    5.00
EDLIN.EXE       5.00
BACKUP.EXE      5.00
ASSIGN.COM      5.00
EXE2BIN.EXE     5.00
JOIN.EXE        5.00
RECOVER.EXE     5.00
GRAFTABL.COM    5.00
LMSETUP.EXE     5.00
STACKER.COM     5.00
NCACHE.EXE      5.00
NCACHE2.EXE     5.00
IBMCACHE.SYS    5.00
XTRADRV.SYS     5.00
WINWORD.EXE     4.10
EXCEL.EXE       4.10
LL3.EXE         4.01
REDIR4.EXE      4.00
REDIR40.EXE     4.00
MSREDIR.EXE     4.00
WIN200.BIN      3.40
METRO.EXE       3.31
WIN100.BIN      3.40
HITACHI.SYS     4.00
```

```
MSCDEX.EXE     4.00
NET.EXE        4.00
NETWKSTA.EXE   4.00
DXMA0MOD.SYS   3.30
BAN.EXE        4.00
BAN.COM        4.00
DD.EXE         4.01
DD.BIN         4.01
REDIR.EXE      4.00
SYQ55.SYS      4.00
SSTDRIVE.SYS   4.00
ZDRV.SYS       4.01
ZFMT.SYS       4.01
TOPSRDR.EXE    4.00
NETBEUI.DOS    5.00
NET.COM        3.30
```

When you run one of the programs listed in the first column of the version table, DOS reports to the program the DOS version number listed in the second column.

If you try to run a program and it displays an error message stating that you are using an incompatible version of DOS, you may want to try adding the program to the version table. Type the SETVER command using the following syntax:

SETVER *c:path***filename.ext n.nn**

The *c:path*\ parameter indicates the disk and drive where the SETVER.EXE file is located on your system.

The **filename.ext** parameter is the name and extension of the command that starts the program in question.

The **n.nn** parameter is a DOS version number that the program will recognize. Consult the program's documentation to determine with which versions of DOS the program can run. You can also use SETVER to delete program names. The syntax for using SETVER to delete programs from the version table is shown in the following:

SETVER *d:path***filename.ext** */DELETE /QUIET*

The two switches—/DELETE and /QUIET—can be abbreviated as /D and /Q.

For an example of how you use SETVER, assume that you want to run a program called GOODPROG.EXE, but the program runs only with DOS

Versions 3.0 to 3.3. To add GOODPROG.EXE to the version table, type the following command at the command prompt and press Enter:

SETVER GOODPROG.EXE 3.30

DOS displays the following series of messages, including an initial warning:

```
WARNING - The application you are adding to the MS-DOS
version table may not have been verified by Microsoft
on this version of MS-DOS. Please contact your software
vendor for information on whether this application will
operate properly under this version of MS-DOS. If you
execute this application by instructing MS-DOS to re-
port a different MS-DOS version number, you may lose or
corrupt data, or cause system instabilities. In that
circumstance, Microsoft is not responsible for any loss
or damage.

Version table successfully updated

The version change will take effect the next time you
restart your system.
```

To verify that the application has been added to the version table, execute SETVER again without switches or parameters. The added application appears at the end of the list. The modified table takes effect, however, only after you restart or reboot your computer.

If you later decide to delete a program from the version list, use the /D switch and the *filename* parameter. To delete GOODPROG.EXE from the version table, for example, type one of the following commands at the command line and press Enter:

SETVER GOODPROG.EXE /DELETE

SETVER GOODPROG.EXE /D

DOS deletes the application name from the version table and displays the message Version table successfully updated. The version change takes effect the next time you restart your system.

If you are using a batch file to delete a program name from the version table, you may want to suppress the preceding message. To prevent this message from appearing on-screen, add the /QUIET switch in addition to the /DELETE switch.

Displaying the Amount of Free and Used Memory

DOS 4.0 and later versions include the external MEM command, which you can use to provide system information. The command shows the free and used memory on the system and can show which programs and devices are loaded in the system. (For a complete discussion of the types of memory, see Chapter 17, "Configuring Your Computer.")

Issuing the MEM Command

The following line shows the syntax for the MEM command:

MEM /*DEBUG* /*CLASSIFY* /*FREE* /*MODULE:programname* /*PAGE*

All switches are optional. You can abbreviate each switch by typing only the first letter (/D, /C, /F, /M:*programname* /P). You can use the /PAGE switch, which tells DOS to pause at the end of each page, with all the other switches. You cannot use any of the other switches together, however. You cannot use /DEBUG with /CLASSIFY, /FREE, or /MODULE, for example.

The /*DEBUG* switch lists all the loaded programs and device drivers. This listing includes the name, size, position, and type of each item.

The /*CLASSIFY* switch lists the programs loaded into conventional memory as well as in *upper memory*, the 384K area of memory between 640K and 1M that is usually reserved for use by certain system devices, such as your monitor.

The /*FREE* switch lists the free areas of conventional and upper memory. The /*MODULE:programname* switch shows the way a program module is currently using memory. You must specify the program name after the /MODULE switch. The *MEM* /*MODULE* switch lists the areas of memory the program module is using and shows the address and size of each area.

Understanding the Operation of MEM

To see a "short" version of the memory report that indicates the amount of free conventional memory, EMS memory, and XMS memory, type **MEM** (do not include a switch). DOS displays a report similar to the following:

```
Memory Type        Total =  Used  +  Free
----------------   ------   ------    ------
Conventional        640K      43K      597K
Upper               155K      87K       68K
Adapter RAM/ROM     229K     229K        0K
Extended (XMS)*    7168K    2304K     4864K
----------------   ------   ------    ------
Total memory       8192K    2663K     5529K

Total under 1 MB    795K     130K      665K

Total Expanded (EMS)                7872K (8060928 bytes)
Free Expanded (EMS)*                5040K (5160960 bytes)

* EMM386 is using XMS memory to simulate EMS memory as needed.
  Free EMS memory may change as free XMS memory changes.

Largest executable program size      597K  (610880 bytes)
Largest free upper memory block       37K   (38064 bytes)
MS-DOS is resident in the high memory area.
```

This report gives you three types of information about every type of memory in your system, in three columns: the total amount, the amount currently being used, and the memory available for you to use for programs.

The first line describes the conventional memory: the total amount (generally 640K, where 1K = 1,024 bytes), the amount of memory currently being used, and the amount of free memory. The next line shows you the amount of upper (reserved) memory and adapter RAM/ROM in the same format. These two amounts total 384K, which, in addition to the conventional memory, is the total amount of memory that DOS addresses—1,024K.

The MEM report then tells you the total amount of extended memory that has been mapped (converted) to XMS memory, the amount currently in use, and the amount available for use. In the example, 7,168K of XMS memory of the original 8192K (or 8M) are available.

The next line shows the total amount of memory under 1M and the amount available to you for running programs. This amount may be misleading because the figure lumps together the amount of free conventional and free reserved memory. Most programs cannot use both of these types of memory as if they were contiguous.

The first two long lines below the totals show the total amount and free amount of *expanded* memory in your system. A footnote explains that the EMM386.EXE memory manager creates expanded memory from the pool of XMS memory as needed. Finally, MEM indicates whether MS-DOS currently is loaded in the high memory area.

Sometimes, MEM's short report doesn't provide enough information to meet your needs. The three available switches produce longer versions of the report. Because these reports don't fit on a single DOS screen, use the /PAGE switch to display one page of the report at a time.

The reports generated by MEM's /CLASSIFY (/C) and /DEBUG (/D) switches are highly technical in content. To execute the MEM command with the /DEBUG switch, type the following:

    MEM /DEBUG

A report similar to the following appears:

Conventional Memory Detail:

Segment	Total		Name	Type
00000	1039	(1K)		Interrupt Vector
00040	271	(0K)		ROM Communication Area
00050	527	(1K)		DOS Communication Area
00070	2656	(3K)	IO	System Data
			CON	System Device Driver
			AUX	System Device Driver
			PRN	System Device Driver
			CLOCK$	System Device Driver
			A: - C:	System Device Driver
			COM1	System Device Driver
			LPT1	System Device Driver
			LPT2	System Device Driver
			LPT3	System Device Driver
			COM2	System Device Driver
			COM3	System Device Driver
			COM4	System Device Driver
00116	5568	(5K)	MSDOS	System Data
00272	10608	(10K)	IO	System Data

```
         1136    (1K)    XMSXXXX0   Installed Device=HIMEM
         3104    (3K)    EMMXXXX0   Installed Device=EMM386
         1488    (1K)               FILES=30
          256    (0K)               FCBS=4
          512    (1K)               BUFFERS=20
          976    (1K)               LASTDRIVE=K
         3008    (3K)               STACKS=9,256
00509      80    (0K)    MSDOS      System Program
0050E    2640    (3K)    COMMAND    Program
005B3      80    (0K)    MSDOS      -- Free --
005B8     272    (0K)    COMMAND    Environment
005C9     128    (0K)    VSAFE      Environment
005D1    6688    (7K)    VSAFE      Program
00773     144    (0K)    MSDOS      -- Free --
0077C   13616   (13K)    UNDELETE   Program
00ACF     176    (0K)    MEM        Environment
00ADA   88368   (86K)    MEM        Program
0206D  522528  (510K)    MSDOS      -- Free --
```

Upper Memory Detail:

Segment	Region	Total		Name	Type
0C13A	1	44304	(43K)	IO	System Data
		44272	(43K)	DBLSSYS$	Installed Device=DBLSPACE
0CC0B	1	48	(0K)	MSDOS	-- Free --
0CC0E	1	28800	(28K)	SMARTDRV	Program
0D316	1	128	(0K)	MOUSE	Environment
0D31E	1	14672	(14K)	MOUSE	Program
0D6B3	1	38064	(37K)	MSDOS	-- Free --
0F001	2	800	(1K)	IO	System Data
		768	(1K)	SETVERXX	Installed Device=SETVER
0F033	2	31952	(31K)	MSDOS	-- Free --

Memory Summary:

Type of Memory	Total		=	Used		+	Free	
Conventional	655360	(640K)		44240	(43K)		611120	(597K)
Upper	158800	(155K)		88736	(87K)		70064	(68K)
Adapter RAM/ROM	234416	(229K)		234416	(229K)		0	(0K)
Extended (XMS)*	7340032	(7168K)		2359296	(2304K)		4980736	(4864K)
Total memory	8388608	(8192K)		2726688	(2663K)		5661920	(5529K)

```
Total under 1 MB     814160   (795K)      132976  (130K)      681184  (665K)

Handle      EMS Name      Size
------      --------      ------
     0                    060000
     1                    010000

Total Expanded (EMS)                     8060928  (7872K)
Free Expanded (EMS)*                     5160960  (5040K)

* EMM386 is using XMS memory to simulate EMS memory as needed.
  Free EMS memory may change as free XMS memory changes.

Memory accessible using Int 15h              0     (0K)
Largest executable program size         610880   (597K)
Largest free upper memory block          38064    (37K)
MS-DOS is resident in the high memory area.

XMS version  3.00; driver version  3.09
EMS version  4.00
```

The first column shows the starting address of each item that MEM found. The address is listed in hexadecimal (base 16) notation. The second column shows the size, in kilobytes, of each program or driver. The third column shows the name of the program or device driver loaded into memory. The final column includes the type of item listed. The types include the system files IO.SYS, MSDOS.SYS, and COMMAND.COM; programs; installed device drivers and system device drivers; environment; and any data areas the programs may need.

To see a listing of programs, drivers, and free space in conventional and upper memory, type the following command and press Enter:

MEM /C

DOS shows you a report similar to the following:

```
Modules using memory below 1 MB:

Name        Total       =   Conventional   +  Upper Memory
--------    ---------------   ----------------   ----------------
MSDOS       16461   (16K)      16461   (16K)         0    (0K)
HIMEM        1152    (1K)       1152    (1K)         0    (0K)
EMM386       3120    (3K)       3120    (3K)         0    (0K)
COMMAND      2912    (3K)       2912    (3K)         0    (0K)
```

```
VSAFE        6816     (7K)        6816     (7K)           0    (0K)
UNDELETE    13616    (13K)       13616    (13K)           0    (0K)
DBLSPACE    44320    (43K)           0     (0K)       44320   (43K)
SMARTDRV    28800    (28K)           0     (0K)       28800   (28K)
MOUSE       14800    (14K)           0     (0K)       14800   (14K)
SETVER        816     (1K)           0     (0K)         816    (1K)
Free       681184   (665K)      611120   (597K)       70064   (68K)
```

Memory Summary:

Type of Memory	Total		=	Used		+	Free	
----------------	-------------			-----------------			----------------	
Conventional	655360	(640K)		44240	(43K)		611120	(597K)
Upper	158800	(155K)		88736	(87K)		70064	(68K)
Adapter RAM/ROM	234416	(229K)		234416	(229K)		0	(0K)
Extended (XMS)*	7340032	(7168K)		2359296	(2304K)		4980736	(4864K)
----------------	-------------			-----------------			----------------	
Total memory	8388608	(8192K)		2726688	(2663K)		5661920	(5529K)
Total under 1 MB	814160	(795K)		132976	(130K)		681184	(665K)
Total Expanded (EMS)				8060928	(7872K)			
Free Expanded (EMS)*				5160960	(5040K)			

```
* EMM386 is using XMS memory to simulate EMS memory as needed.
  Free EMS memory may change as free XMS memory changes.

Largest executable program size       610880    (597K)
Largest free upper memory block        38064     (37K)
MS-DOS is resident in the high memory area.
```

> **NOTE** Because some of the report scrolls off the screen before you can read it, you may want to use the /P switch to tell DOS to pause after each page. To do so, type the following:
>
> MEM /C /P
>
> DOS displays the report one page at a time. Press any key when you are ready to display the next page.

The third and fourth columns of the report, titled Conventional Memory and Upper Memory, show you how much memory is allocated to any particular driver or program. Use the Upper Memory column to determine whether any drivers or programs are loaded in upper memory, and use the memory summary at the end of the report to see how much upper memory is still free.

Before attempting to move a driver or program from conventional to upper memory (using DEVICEHIGH or LOADHIGH), compare the driver or program's size (in the Conventional Memory Size column) to the available upper memory block (UMB) size shown at the bottom of the memory summary. The available UMB must be at least as big as the driver or program before you can load the driver or program into upper memory.

A quick way to see a listing of free memory space without searching through one of the longer reports is to use the /FREE switch, as shown in the following:

    MEM /F

If you use this switch, MEM lists the free areas of conventional and upper memory. This report shows you the segment address and size of each free area of conventional memory and the largest free block in each region of upper memory. The switch also summarizes your overall memory use. A sample of the report follows:

```
Free Conventional Memory:

  Segment        Total
  ------      ----------------
    005B3          80    (0K)
    00773         144    (0K)
    00ACF         176    (0K)
    00ADA       88368   (86K)
    0206D      522528  (510K)

  Total Free: 611296  (597K)

Free Upper Memory:

  Region    Largest Free      Total Free      Total Size
  ------   --------------   --------------   --------------
      1     38064  (37K)     38112  (37K)    126032 (123K)
      2     31952  (31K)     31952  (31K)     32768  (32K)
```

You can also send the MEM report to your printer by using the following command:

    MEM /C > PRN

This command redirects the report to the DOS device PRN, your computer's first printer port.

After you identify a driver or memory-resident program that appears to be the right size to fit in the available UMB, edit your CONFIG.SYS or AUTOEXEC.BAT to add DEVICEHIGH or LOADHIGH to the appropriate command or program file. Reboot your computer and issue the MEM /C command again to see whether the driver or program loaded.

To arrive at the best combination of device drivers and memory-resident programs loaded into upper memory, you may have to experiment a little. DOS loads programs in the largest available UMB first, so try loading the largest drivers and programs first by placing their start-up commands earliest in CONFIG.SYS or AUTOEXEC.BAT.

For Related Information

▶▶ "Upper Memory Blocks," p. 639.

▶▶ "Optimizing Your Computer's Memory," p. 639.

FROM HERE...

Listing Files with DIR

The DIR command is one of the first commands most DOS users learn. The command quickly gives you a list of your files, along with the date and time you created them, and the file sizes. If you type only DIR, you are using only a fraction of the command's full power.

Issuing the DIR Command

The syntax of the DIR internal directory command is shown in the following:

DIR *d:path\ filename /P /W /A:attributes /O:order /S /B /L*

The abbreviations are as follows: *d:* is the drive; *path* is the path name; and *filename* is the name of the file you want to display (optional). You use the switches, listed in table 11.1, to control what the DIR command displays.

Table 11.1 DIR Switches

Switch	Action
/P	DIR displays one screen full of information and then pauses. Pressing any key causes DIR to continue the listing.
/W	DIR displays only the file names, without the size, date, or modification time of the files. Files are listed in columns across the screen, rather than one per line.
/A:*attributes*	DIR displays only files that have, or lack, file attributes you specify, such as read only, hidden, or system files (DOS 5.0 and 6.0 only).
/O:*order*	DIR lists files in a different sorted order, such as alphabetical order by name (DOS 5.0 and 6.0 only).
/S	DIR lists the contents of subdirectories (DOS 5.0 and 6.0 only).
/B	DIR lists file names only, one per line (DOS 5.0 and 6.0 only).
/L	DIR lists all file names in lowercase (DOS 5.0 and 6.0 only).

The /A:*attributes* switch enables you to list only the files that have at least one attribute you specify. Substitute one or more of the following codes for the *attributes* parameter:

Attribute	Description
D	Directory attribute
R	Read-only attribute
H	Hidden attribute
A	Archive attribute
S	System attribute

The /O:*sortorder* switch enables you to choose the order in which DOS lists file names. To cause DOS to sort the file list in a particular order, substitute one of the following sort codes for the *sortorder* parameter:

Attribute	Description
N	Sorts files alphabetically by name
S	Sorts files numerically by file size
E	Sorts files alphabetically by file extension
D	Sorts files chronologically by date and time
G	Groups directories first before showing files

When you issue the DIR command and any of the parameters are missing, DOS assumes the current status. If you omit the path name, DOS assumes the current subdirectory; if you omit the drive, DOS assumes the current drive.

Understanding the Operation of DIR

Almost all computers sold today come with hard disks (also called *hard drives*). A hard disk holds many times the number of files that a floppy disk can hold. Unless you organize your hard disk, you can end up with directory listings that fill the screen many times over. Using a hierarchical system of directories and subdirectories can help you avoid many of these problems, but having many directories also can effectively "hide" files. Learning to use the DIR command, along with organizing your hard disk sensibly, makes all your files easily accessible.

Consider the simplest form of the DIR command. Typing DIR at the DOS prompt when C:\DOS is the current directory gives you the full listing of the directory C:\DOS. The volume label and serial number are displayed first. Then each file in the directory is listed in the following fashion:

```
EGA  SYS    4885   6-10-91      5:00a
```

The information displayed is most of the information stored in the directory table. The file attributes do not appear, but DOS uses them to determine whether to display a file. Hidden files are not included in this list. The location of the first cluster in the file allocation table (FAT) for the file also is not displayed because knowing the file's starting cluster is of no use to you.

At the end of the listing, DOS indicates the total number of files in the directory, the total number of bytes used by the listed files, and the total number of bytes free on the current disk. The DIR report for C:\DOS, for example, may show the following information:

```
87 files    2105291 bytes
         8935424 bytes free
```

If you add up the size of each listed file on the disk and subtract the result from the total disk capacity, that number and the number of free bytes shown in the directory listing probably do not match, but the directory listing is correct. Remember that hidden files are not shown and, more important, the size of the file is not necessarily the same as the amount of disk space it occupies.

When you create a file, no matter how small, DOS allocates a whole number of clusters on the disk for the file. The directory listing shows the file length in bytes and calculates the free space, based on the number of free clusters on the disk. These free clusters are remaining positions on the disk not yet allocated to another file. (See Chapter 2, "Understanding the Role of DOS," for more information about the file storage system.)

The free space reported by DIR is the number of unallocated clusters (also called allocation units) multiplied by the size of a cluster (1,024 bytes on most hard disks). You can also use CHKDSK to obtain a report of the total number of allocation units available on the disk.

Displaying a Screenful of Information with DIR

If you add the /P switch to the DIR command, DOS pauses the scrolling of the screen at the end of each screenful of information. Pressing any key displays the next page of information. This switch works much like the MORE filter, discussed in Chapter 9, "Managing Your Files." The /P switch is convenient because it is built into the DIR command, so you do not need to have the MORE filter in the search path.

To see more file names, use the /W switch. When you use the /W switch, a directory listing like the one shown in figure 11.1 appears.

```
Volume in drive C is El Monstro!
Volume Serial Number is 1A42-7BD0
Directory of C:\DOS

[.]            [..]            EGA.SYS         FORMAT.COM      ASSIGN.COM
NLSFUNC.EXE    COUNTRY.SYS     EGA.CPI         HIMEM.SYS       KEYB.COM
KEYBOARD.SYS   ANSI.SYS        ATTRIB.EXE      CHOICE.COM      CHKDSK.EXE
EDIT.COMDBL    SPACE.BIN       DEBUG.EXE       DOSSWAP.EXE     CHKLIST.MS
EXPAND.EXE     FDISK.EXE       MEM.EXE         MORE.COM        MSD.EXE
QBASIC.EXE     RESTORE.EXE     SYS.COM         UNFORMAT.COM    XCOPY.EXE
DOSSHELL.VID   DOSSHELL.INI    DOSSHELL.COM    DOSSHELL.GRB    DEFRAG.EXE
DEFRAG.HLP     WNGRAFIC.DLL    MSMOUSE.COM     QBASIC.HLP      SMARTMON.EXE
CPAV.EXE       SMARTMON.HLP    DISPLAY.SYS     DOSSHELL.EXE    COMP.EXE
HELP.HLP       DOSHELP.EXE     APPEND.EXE      DELOLDOS.EXE    DISKCOMP.COM
DISKCOPY.COM   DRIVER.SYS      FASTHELP.EXE    DOSHELP.HLP     DOSKEY.COM
EDIT.HLP       FC.EXE          JOIN.EXE        FIND.EXE        GRAPHICS.COM
GRAPHICS.PRO   HELP.COM        LABEL.EXE       LOADFIX.COM     SETVER.EXE
SORT.EXE       FASTOPEN.EXE    MODE.COM        MWBACKUP.EXE    MWBACKUP.HLP
PRINT.EXE      POWER.EXE       NETWORKS.TXT    README.TXT      REPLACE.EXE
REPORT.EXE     SHARE.EXE       SUBST.EXE       TREE.COM        VFINTD.386
MWBACKF.DLL    MWBACKR.DLL     MSBACKUP.EXE    MSBACKUP.OVL    MSBACKFB.OVL
MSBACKFR.OVL   MSBACKDB.OVL    MSBACKUP.HLP    MSBACKDR.OVL    MSBCONFG.OVL
MSBCONFG.HLP   CHKSTATE.SYS    MEMMAKER.HLP    MEMMAKER.INF    MONOUMB.386
UNDELETE.EXE   MWUNDEL.EXE     MWUNDEL.HLP     WNTOOLS.GRP     MWGRAFIC.DLL
DBLWIN.HLP     MSTOOLS.DLL     MWAVDOSL.DLL    MWAVDRVL.DLL    MWAVDLG.DLL
MWAVSCAN.DLL   MOUSE.INI       MSAV.INI        MSBACKUP.INI    MWAV.INI
MYSHELL.INI    QBASIC.INI      UNDELETE.INI    SMARTMON.LOG    MWAV.EXE
BETAINFO.INI   MWAVABSI.DLL    MWAV.HLP        MWAVSOS.DLL     MWAVMGR.DLL
MWAVTSR.EXE    VSAFE.COM M     SAV.EXE         DBLSPACE.EXE    DEFAULT.SET
MSAVIRUS.LST   MSAV.HLP        MSAVHELP.OVL    DBLSPACE.HLP    DBLSPACE.INF
DBLSPACE.SYS   DOSSHELL.HLP    EMM386.EXE      SIZER.EXE       MEMMAKER.EXE
APPNOTES.TXT   DELTREE.EXE     INTERLNK.EXE    EDLIN.EXE       EXE2BIN.EXE
GRAFTABL.COM   RECOVER.EXE     INTERSVR.EXE    MOVE.EXE        MSCDEX.EXE
RAMDRIVE.SYS   SMARTDRV.EXE    COMMAND.COM

     148 file(s)      6281141 bytes
                      1069056 bytes free
```

Fig. 11.1

A directory listing resulting from using the /W switch.

With hierarchical directories, your directory listing includes sub-directory names and files. In the wide listing, directory names are enclosed in brackets ([ ]).

Because the file names are grouped so closely together, a wide listing can be useful when you want to see the types of files in a directory.

Using DIR To Control the File List Display

Chapter 6, "Understanding Disks and Files," introduces you to the DIR command and two of its switches, /P and /W. Beginning with DOS 5.0, the DIR command has five additional switches that enable you to control the list of files displayed at the command line by the DIR command.

By default, DIR lists file names of all files except those with the hidden attribute or system attribute. Files are listed in no particular order. By adding certain switches to the DIR command, you can cause DOS to list only file names that have specified attributes or to list file names in a specific sorted order, as explained in this section.

Using the /A:*attributes* Switch

As mentioned earlier, by using the /A:*attributes* switch, you can list only the files that have at least one attribute you specify. You can substitute one or more of the following codes for the *attributes* parameter:

D	Directory attribute
R	Read-only attribute
H	Hidden attribute
A	Archive attribute
S	System attribute

If you include in a DIR command the /A switch with no attributes parameter, DOS lists all file names—even the file names of hidden and system files—regardless of file attribute. To see only a listing of all hidden files in the current directory, however, you type the following command and press Enter:

    DIR /AH

DOS lists all files that have the hidden attribute.

You can use attribute codes in any combination and in any order. You can list all file names with the read-only attribute and the archive attribute, for example, by issuing the following command:

    DIR /ARA

DOS lists file names that have both attributes.

To list only file names that do *not* have a certain attribute, insert a minus sign (–) before the attribute code. To see all files that are not directories and that don't have the archive bit, for example, type the following command at the command line and press Enter:

    DIR /A–A–D

Using the /O:*sortorder* Switch

As mentioned earlier, the /O:*sortorder* switch enables you to choose the order in which DOS lists file names. When you want DOS to sort the file list in a particular order, substitute one of the following sort codes for the *sortorder* parameter:

N	Sorts files alphabetically by name
S	Sorts files numerically by file size
E	Sorts files alphabetically by file extension
D	Sorts files chronologically by date and time
G	Groups directories first before showing files

You can include sort codes in any combination. The order of the sort codes is the order in which the DIR command chooses the criterion by which to sort your files. The command DIR /O:NE sorts the file names first by name and then by extension. The command DIR /O:EN sorts files by extension (for example, grouping all COM files together and all EXE files together) and then sorts the files by name. If you include the /O switch in a DIR command without specifying a sort code, DOS sorts the files alphabetically by name.

DOS assumes that all sorting should be done in ascending order—A through Z, smallest to largest, earliest to latest. DOS uses these criteria (the default setting) unless you precede your sort codes with a minus sign (–) to reverse the sort order—Z through A, largest to smallest, latest to earliest.

Using the /B and /L Switches

You can use the /B switch to display a "bare" file list—a list of file names only. The default file list generated by the DIR command shows the name of each file in the directory, the file name extension, the file size, and the date and time the file was last changed. Occasionally, you may want to see just the file name of each file. Perhaps you want to print a list of the files on a floppy disk. Place the disk in drive A and issue the following command:

    DIR A: /B

DOS lists all file names of files in the current directory of the floppy disk in drive A. DOS does not list file size or file date and time. If you would rather send this list to the printer, issue the following command:

    DIR A: /B >PRN

The /L switch, when used with the DIR command, causes file names to appear in lowercase letters.

Searching for Files with the DIR Command

To find a file on your disk from the command line, you can use the /S switch with the DIR command. If you want to search a specific directory, first use the CHDIR command to change to that directory. To search the entire disk, change to the root directory.

At the DOS prompt, type **DIR**, followed by the name of the file or files for which you want DIR to search. This name can be a specific file name or can contain wild-card characters (* and ?). To complete the command, add the /S switch and press Enter. The /S switch causes DOS to search the current directory and all subdirectories of the current directory.

Suppose, for example, that you created a number of budget spreadsheets using your spreadsheet software and saved these spreadsheets on your hard disk. You want to make a copy of the budget spreadsheet files, but you cannot remember the directory where they are located. However, you do remember that all the files start with the letters *BUDG*. You can use the DIR command to search the hard disk for the location of the files. Change to the root directory or your hard disk, and type the following command:

DIR BUDG*.* /S

When you press Enter, DOS displays a listing similar to the following:

```
    Volume in drive C is QUE BRUCE
    Volume Serial Number is 1628-BA9A
    Directory of C:\SPREADSH\QPRO4DAT
BUDGET   WQ1   4037 10-05-92  2:00A
        1 files(s)  4037 bytes

Directory of C:\WORD_PRO\ENDATA
BUDGET   WK1   5120 04-07-92  8:51p
        1 files(s)  5120 bytes

Total files listed:
        2 files(s)  9157 bytes
                 9400320 bytes free
```

Customizing the DIR Command

If you find that you continually use one or more of the seven switches with the DIR command, you can avoid typing them repeatedly by recording the commonly used switches as an environment variable named DIR, using the following command:

SET DIRCMD=_switches_

For the _switches_ parameter, substitute the switch or switches you want DOS to use automatically. If, for example, you want DOS to sort file names alphabetically and to pause scrolling after each screenful of information, include the following command in your AUTOEXEC.BAT:

SET DIRCMD=/ON/P

Reboot the computer. DOS creates the environment variable DIRCMD and gives it the value /ON/P. Each time you issue the DIR command, DOS adds these two switches.

You can override a switch that is recorded in the DIRCMD by preceding the switch with a minus sign (–). To override the /P switch that is currently recorded in DIRCMD so that DOS lists all file names without pausing at the end of each screenful of information, for example, issue the DIR command as shown in the following:

DIR /–P

For Related Information

◀◀ "Managing Files," p. 59.

◀◀ "Trying Some Disk Commands," p. 166.

▶▶ "The MORE Filter," p. 456.

FROM HERE...

Using DOSSHELL

With DOS 4.0 and later versions, DOS includes an optional graphical user interface called the DOS Shell. By using the DOS Shell, you can select items from a list of options rather than learn each of the individual commands. If you are a new user, the DOS Shell is helpful because it enables you to perform basic DOS functions without extensive training.

The DOS Shell is actually a program. You can run the program from the DOS prompt, or you can have DOS run the Shell at boot time from the AUTOEXEC.BAT file. Chapter 4, "Using the DOS Shell," describes the various features of the Shell program.

Changing the Command Prompt with PROMPT

The default command prompt shows the current drive and a greater-than sign. The PROMPT command enables you to change from this display to a more informative and friendly prompt.

Typing **PROMPT pg** at the command prompt changes the prompt to give you the full subdirectory path on the disk. This new prompt enables you to see the current directory at all times. If you use a hard disk, this display is the minimum recommended prompt setting because navigating subdirectories can be difficult if you don't know your current position.

The PROMPT command has many more features. In its most extensive form, the command requires the ANSI.SYS device driver (see Chapter 19, "Understanding ANSI.SYS"). Even without using the ANSI.SYS device driver, however, you can choose from many different command prompts.

Issuing the PROMPT Command

The syntax for the PROMPT command is shown in the following:

PROMPT *string*

The *string* consists of text, a series of character pairs, or both. Each character pair, called a *meta-string*, consists of a dollar sign, followed by one of the following characters:

t d p v n g l b q h e _

The string can contain any text or any number of meta-strings in any order. Table 11.2 lists the different meta-strings.

Table 11.2 Meta-Strings for Use with the PROMPT Command

Meta-String	Displayed Information or Result
$_	Carriage return/line feed (moves the cursor to the beginning of the next line)
$b	Vertical bar character (|)
$d	Date
$e	Esc character
$g	Greater-than sign (>)
$h	Backspace (moves the cursor one space to the left)
$l	Less-than sign (<)
$n	Current drive
$p	Current path
$q	Equal sign (=)
$t	Time
$v	DOS version

Understanding the Operation of PROMPT

The PROMPT pg command shows the current path, followed by the greater-than sign. As an alternative, consider the following command:

    PROMPT Date: $d Time: t_pg

This command displays the following prompt:

```
Date: Mon 03-22-1993 Time: 2:35:07.23
C:\WP\MEMOS>
```

Two of the meta-strings require further explanation. You use the Esc character ($e) in association with the ANSI.SYS driver (see Chapter 12, "Controlling Devices," for more information). In the same way that you use the dollar sign to indicate to DOS that the next character is a meta-string, you use the Esc character to signal ANSI.SYS that the next few characters are an ANSI.SYS command.

You can use the Backspace character ($h) to remove characters from the prompt. In the preceding sample PROMPT, for example, the seconds and hundredths of a second in the displayed prompt are more of a distraction than they are helpful. You can alter the command as follows:

PROMPT Date: $d Time: thhhhhh_pg

The result is the following improved prompt:

```
Date: Mon 03-22-1993 Time: 2:35
C:\WP\MEMOS>
```

If you don't like the current prompt, type **PROMPT** at the command line, and DOS resets the prompt to the current drive letter and a greater-than sign (for example, C>). Remember, if you use sub-directories, the best practice is to use PROMPT pg.

FROM HERE...

For Related Information

▶▶ "Installing ANSI.SYS," p. 736.

Altering the Look of the Screen with MODE

You can use the external MODE command to customize the number of characters per line and the number of lines displayed on-screen. You can also use the MODE command to set the configuration of your computer ports (such as your printer port) and for code page switching.

NOTE Certain areas of memory in your system store the character tables for your video screen and your keyboard. By switching tables, you can configure MS-DOS 6.0 to use alternate character tables to suit your national language and customs. These tables are called *code pages*. For more information about code pages, see Chapter 20, "Understanding the International Features of DOS."

You can attach two types of displays to the same computer: a monochrome adapter and display, and a color graphics adapter and display. You switch between the displays by using the MODE command. Switching displays is particularly handy when you use graphics programs, such as a drawing program. MODE enables you to use the color display to show graphics programs and drawings and the monochrome display to show text or word processing programs.

When you type at the keyboard on a two-display system, you see the keystrokes only on one of the displays. This display is the *active display*. The keyboard and active display make up the console. DOS uses CON as the device name for the console.

Selecting the Display Type

To change the display characteristics, you can use two forms of the MODE command with any version of DOS. Additional forms are available with DOS 4.0 and later versions. You can use the following syntax, which works with any version of DOS, for the simplest form of the MODE command:

>   **MODE** *dt*

The abbreviation *dt* is the display type and mode. Available options are 40, 80, BW40, BW80, CO40, CO80, or MONO.

The 40 and 80 refer to the number of columns of text displayed. DOS sees text as columns of letters, but what this setting means for you is that you can choose between 40 and 80 characters per line. BW stands for black and white; CO stands for color; and MONO refers to the monochrome display adapter.

To set the number of columns (characters per line) displayed on the active display to 40 or 80, respectively, type either of the following:

>   MODE 40

>   MODE 80

To select the display attached to the monochrome display adapter as the active display, type the following:

>   MODE MONO

The monochrome display always displays 80 columns.

To select the color graphics display as the active display, use one of the following commands:

>   MODE CO40

>   MODE CO80

MODE BW40

MODE BW80

The first two options select the color mode of the color display with 40 or 80 columns. The last two options select the color display but use the black-and-white display modes with 40 or 80 columns.

Shifting the Screen on a Color Graphics Adapter

The second form of the MODE command, available in all versions of DOS, is for use on a Color Graphics Adapter only. This form, which does not work on an Enhanced Graphics Adapter (EGA) or a Video Graphics Array (VGA), enables you to configure your PC to work with a television instead of a specially designed computer monitor. It moves the horizontal position of the image on your screen. If you cannot see the far-left or far-right character on your screen, the following command corrects the problem:

MODE *dt,s,T*

The *dt* parameter is the display type described in the preceding section. The *s* parameter can have the value *R* to move the image to the right or *L* to move the image to the left. If the display is in 80-column mode, MODE moves the image two characters to the right or left. If in 40-column mode, MODE moves the image one character to the right or left. The optional *T* parameter, when used, causes MODE to display a test pattern, which you can use to align the display.

If you type **MODE CO80,R,T**, a line of 80 characters appears across the screen, along with the following prompt:

```
Do you see the leftmost 0? (y/n)
```

If you respond **Y** to the prompt, this image moves two positions to the right of its preceding position. If you respond **N** to the prompt, the screen moves farther to the right. Using the L option works in the same way but moves the image to the left.

If you operate your system after shifting the screen, you have a little less memory available for your application. (The MODE command uses less than 1K of memory.) To display the image in an adjusted position, DOS places a small program into memory. This program intercepts all output to the screen, adjusts it, and then sends the output or image to the screen. The program in memory is the *memory-resident portion* of the MODE command. Other versions of the MODE command also leave a part of the command resident.

Using MODE To Adjust the Number of Columns or Lines On-Screen

DOS 4.0 introduced two additional MODE command options that you can use to alter your screen modes. In DOS 4.0 and later versions, you can adjust the number of columns or the number of lines displayed on-screen. You must install the ANSI.SYS device driver before either of the forms can adjust your screen, however.

The syntax for the first form of the MODE command is shown in the following:

MODE CON COLS=a **LINES=**b

COLS= sets the number of columns displayed on the screen to a, and **LINES=** sets the number of lines displayed on the screen to b. If you omit a setting for the number of columns or the number of lines, the current setting is preserved.

Valid numbers for a are 40 or 80. Valid numbers for b on a VGA screen are 25, 43, or 50; valid numbers for b on an EGA screen are 25 or 43.

If ANSI.SYS loads via the CONFIG.SYS file, typing the following command gives you a display mode 80 columns wide and 43 lines high on a computer with an EGA or VGA adapter and monitor:

MODE CON COLS=80 LINES=43

After you set the display mode, you can start your application program. The display mode remains, unless the application resets it. If you use the preceding MODE on a computer with an EGA screen, for example, you can use WordPerfect in 43-line mode without adjusting any settings in WordPerfect.

Not all applications can "see" that the extra lines are available. Try some MODE CON commands to determine whether you can use the extra lines. Using MODE CON to set your screen to 43 or 50 lines makes it easier to view long DIR listings, but the type is very small and may be difficult to read.

Another MODE command option, added in DOS 4.0 and still available, enables you to alter the number of lines displayed without specifying that the screen is the console. This form, which is really a variation on the MODE CON theme, is handy when you use an auxiliary console instead of CON. Chapter 12, "Controlling Devices," introduces the CTTY command, which establishes another device as the standard input and output device.

The syntax for this form of the MODE command is shown in the following:

    *d:path***MODE** *dt,b*

In this syntax, *dt* is the display type and *b* is the number of lines to be displayed. The acceptable values for *dt* and *b* are as previously described, but not all combinations of values for *dt* and *b* are possible. For example, you cannot adjust the number of lines on a monochrome or CGA monitor. The following table lists the workable combinations of parameters with the MODE command for setting the display type:

Mode Option	MDA	CGA	EGA	VGA
CO40,25		✔	✔	✔
CO40,43			✔	✔
CO40,50				✔
CO80,25		✔	✔	✔
CO80,43			✔	✔
CO80,50				✔
BW40,25		✔	✔	✔
BW40,43			✔	✔
BW40,50				✔
BW80,25		✔	✔	✔
BW80,43			✔	✔
BW80,50				✔
MONO	✔			

On a VGA system, you can alter the display type to color with 40 columns and 50 lines by typing the following command:

    MODE CO40,50

All forms of the MODE command that adjust the display are similar in syntax and purpose. An incorrect command does not damage anything, and DOS provides reasonably clear error messages. If the ANSI.SYS driver is required and not installed, for example, DOS displays the following error message:

```
ANSI.SYS must be installed to perform requested function
```

For Related Information

▶▶ "The CTTY Command," p. 444.

FROM HERE...

Loading a Secondary Command Processor

The COMMAND command enables you to load a second copy of COMMAND.COM, the system's command processor. Many programs do this automatically when they enable you to go to a DOS command prompt without exiting from the program.

Issuing the COMMAND Command

The syntax for COMMAND is shown in the following:

> **COMMAND** *d:path\ /P /MSG /E:aaaaa /C string*

For this command, *d:path* is the drive and the path position of the COMMAND.COM file you are loading. The other parameters are explained briefly in the list that follows and in more detail in the next section:

Parameter	Description
/P	Makes the second copy of the command processor permanent
/MSG	Causes DOS to load DOS messages into memory instead of reading the messages from disk every time they are needed
/E:*aaaa*	Enables you to adjust the number of bytes of memory that the command processor reserves for its environment
/C *string*	Enables you to pass a string of characters to the command processor being started

Understanding the Operation of COMMAND

COMMAND.COM, your command processor, reserves a small amount of memory called the *environment*; COMMAND.COM uses this memory space to store variables, such as your PATH, PROMPT, and COMSPEC. If you load another copy of COMMAND.COM but omit the *d:path* parameter, the second command processor inherits the contents of the first command processor's environment. If you include the *d:path* parameter, the second command processor does not inherit the old environment and only keeps the COMSPEC path specified by *d:path*.

When you leave the second command processor by using the EXIT command, the first command processor's environment remains unchanged, even if you changed the second command processor's environment while you were working with it. The second copy is actually a shell over the first copy; DOS assumes that you want the same environment because, with the same environment, you don't have to reenter all your variables. When you exit a copy of the command processor, DOS assumes that any changes you made to the environment are no longer needed.

The optional /P switch makes the second copy of the command processor permanent. The first command processor is no longer available, and DOS runs your AUTOEXEC.BAT file if you have one. Remember, if you use the /P switch, you cannot use the EXIT command to exit the second copy of the command processor and return to the first one. You have to turn your computer off and reboot.

The /MSG switch causes DOS to load DOS messages into memory instead of reading the messages from the disk every time they are needed. If you have a floppy disk system, using this switch improves the performance of DOS, but you lose some memory space.

The /E:*aaaaa* switch enables you to adjust the number of bytes of memory that the command processor reserves for its environment. The minimum value for *aaaaa* is 160, and the maximum is 32768. Each variable stored in the environment takes up space, and you may find that you run out of room in the environment. If, for example, the environment needs to store long settings (such as the long prompt used in the earlier PROMPT command example), you may need to adjust the size of the environment. If you see the message Out of environment space, enlarge the environment.

The /C *string* option enables you to pass a string of characters to the command processor you are starting. This option generally was used in batch files (see Chapter 15, "Understanding Batch Files, DOSKey, and Macros") in DOS versions before 3.3 but is no longer needed with DOS 3.3 and later versions, where it has been replaced by the CALL command.

Using EXIT To Leave the Current Copy of the Command Processor

Use the EXIT command to leave the current copy of the command processor and return to the previously loaded copy. The syntax for the EXIT command is shown in the following:

EXIT

No options or switches exist for this command. You cannot use the EXIT command if the second command processor was started by using the /P switch.

Using EXIT and COMMAND Together To Start and Exit Secondary Command Processors

Used together, the COMMAND and EXIT commands provide two interesting uses. If you have specified an alternate location with the file COMMAND.COM, you use the COMMAND command to load the second processor. If, for example, the DOS command processor is in the root directory and another command processor is loaded in the OTHER subdirectory, you can type the following command:

COMMAND C:\OTHER /E:320

This command loads the second COMMAND.COM and assigns it an environment size of 320 bytes. You can use the second command processor to execute commands using the 320-byte environment. When you are finished using the secondary command processor, type **EXIT** to return to the primary command processor.

The other use for this command pair is when you have set up a complex environment and you want to execute a command with a basic environment without changing the existing environment. In this case, you can start the second command processor with the *d:path*\ option. If necessary, you can change the environment by using the SET command (covered in the next section). Execute the desired commands in the altered environment, and then exit the second command processor.

If the command processor is in the root directory of drive C, type the following command:

COMMAND C:\

This command loads a second copy of the command processor. The new environment includes only a setting for COMSPEC, showing that the command processor is loaded in C:\. The prompt does not have a setting and shows up in the form C>. You then execute any desired commands in the new environment. After you have finished issuing the commands, type **EXIT** to exit the the second command processor and return to the first command processor. All the environment settings for the first command processor stay as they were originally.

The principles DOS uses to execute this command are also used by applications programs that enable you to suspend your program temporarily and go to DOS. When you select the DOSSHELL command within your word processor, for example, the program starts a second command processor. All the existing information is kept in memory with the first command processor. You execute DOS commands in the second command processor and type **EXIT** when the commands are complete. The first command processor is then active, and you return to your application program.

Changing the Environment

The SET command enables you to adjust the DOS environment. This command shows the current settings in the environment, or you can use the command to add or change environment variables.

Issuing the SET Command

The syntax for the SET command is shown in the following:

SET *name=string*

You can type **SET** at the command prompt without any variables. The command then lists all the current settings for environment variables.

The variable *name=* is the name of the environment variable. The most frequently used environment variables are COMSPEC, PROMPT, and PATH. You can choose your own variable names in addition to these three, however.

The parameter *string* is the value to which you want to set the variable. In the case of PATH, the *string* can be the list of directories through which you want DOS to search to find program files. If you use the *name=* parameter without a value for *string*, the variable specified is a null value (contains nothing).

Changing the Environment Variables with SET

Suppose that you want to use the SET command to change the environment variables. The following three commands change the COMSPEC, PROMPT, and PATH:

SET COMSPEC=C:\SYS\COMMAND.COM

SET PROMPT=pg

SET PATH=C:\;C:\DOS;C:\SYS;

The first command tells DOS that the command processor, COMMAND.COM, is located in the SYS subdirectory of drive C. The second command sets the prompt to include the current path and a greater-than sign. The third command places the root directory, the DOS directory, and the SYS directory of drive C onto the path.

You can set the prompt and path by using the specific commands. If your command processor is not located in the root directory of the boot drive, you must include an appropriate SHELL directive in CONFIG.SYS. In DOS 5.0 and later versions, a properly constructed SHELL directive automatically sets the COMSPEC variable correctly. In earlier versions, you must add the SET COMSPEC= command to the AUTOEXEC.BAT file with a string that points to the command processor. If you do not add this command, your system can fail when you boot your computer or when you leave an application program that needs to reload the command processor. This failure occurs because the system cannot find the command processor. Refer to Chapter 17, "Configuring Your Computer," for information on how to use the SHELL directive in CONFIG.SYS to tell the system where to find the command processor.

Setting Your Own Environmental Variables with SET

You can also use the SET command to set custom variables in the environment. These variables usually are the names of directories or switches that programs use. The programs know to look for a particular variable in the environment and to take the values and use them in the program.

A word processing program, for example, may look for a dictionary file called DICT in the current directory. If you use the SET command, however, a different directory can contain the dictionary file. During installation, the program probably will insert a SET command into the batch file that invokes the program. This command can use the following form:

    SET DICT=C:\WP\DICT

This command enables the program to look in the WP directory for the dictionary file instead of looking in the current directory. Remember that setting a variable in the environment is useful only to programs that know to look for that variable.

Each variable stored in the environment occupies space. If a program needs a large variables set, you may have to increase the area of memory set aside for the environment when DOS is booted. You make this change through the SHELL command in CONFIG.SYS (see Chapter 17, "Configuring Your Computer").

FROM HERE...

For Related Information

▶▶ "Understanding CONFIG.SYS," p. 630.

▶▶ "Using the SHELL Command," p. 669.

Chapter Summary

This chapter introduced the commands you use to see and change the DOS system information. The following key points were covered in this chapter:

- The DATE and TIME commands alter the date and time used by DOS when you save files to disk.

- The VER command displays the current booted version of DOS.

- The MEM command provides extensive information about the memory, programs, and devices currently running.

- The DIR command, one of the most commonly used DOS commands, provides a list of the files in a directory or on a disk.

- The PROMPT command alters the appearance of the command prompt. On systems that use hierarchical directories, changing the prompt setting to PROMPT pg is advisable. The current path always is displayed.

- The MODE command can alter the appearance of the screen. You can alter the number of lines, number of columns, and current display.

- The COMMAND command enables you to execute DOS commands in a different environment or temporarily suspend programs while you use DOS.

- The EXIT command returns you to your program or to the first copy of the command processor.

- The SET command enables you to change individual environment variables. These variables include PROMPT, PATH, and COMSPEC.

Chapter 12, "Controlling Devices," covers the commands that you use when you work with devices. You learn how to control input and output devices. Chapter 12 also completes the coverage of the DOS core commands.

Controlling Devices

Devices—hard disks, printers, video displays, keyboards, and modems, for example—can supply input to the computer, receive output from the computer, or both. This chapter discusses the commands that control the devices connected to your computer. You use these commands to redirect input and output, select alternate keyboards, print graphics and text files, and alter the names assigned to parts of your hard disk.

DOS supplies additional commands to help you interact with devices. With three elements called *filters*, DOS is responsible for channeling information between devices. You can use these filters—MORE, FIND, and SORT—to modify information as it passes from files to the screen. Table 12.1 lists and explains the functions of the commands and filters discussed in this chapter.

Table 12.1 Control Device Commands and Filters

Command	Function
CLS	Clears screen
GRAPHICS	Prints graphics screens
PRINT	Prints in background

continues

Table 12.1 Continued

Command	Function
ASSIGN	Redirects file input/output
JOIN	Joins two disk drives
SUBST	Substitutes a drive name for a path
CTTY	Selects a different console
	Makes the serial port the console
MODE	Controls device operations
	Redirects a parallel port to a serial port
	Changes the typematic rate

Filter	Function
MORE	Pauses the display of text
FIND	Finds strings of text
SORT	Sorts information

Table 12.2 lists and explains the functions of the operators you use in the redirection commands and filters.

Table 12.2 Operators

Operators	Function
<	Redirects a command's input
>	Redirects a command's output
>>	Redirects a command's output and appends the output to the target, if one exists
|	Passes the output from one command to another as input

Key Terms Used in This Chapter

Queue	A list of files to be printed
Buffer	A portion of memory reserved for storing data
LCD	A liquid-crystal display; a type of screen found on most laptop and notebook computers

Redirection	Sending the output from a command or program to a device other than the one expected (usually the screen); sending input to a command or program from a point other than the one expected (usually the keyboard)
Pipe	Sending information that normally goes to the screen to another program by using the pipe symbol (l)
Filter	A program that modifies information coming from a program before the information reaches the screen or is piped to another program

The CLS Command

The internal command CLS clears the screen, removing all visible text. CLS then displays the prompt so that you can continue to issue DOS commands. CLS clears only the on-screen display. If your system uses two screens, CLS clears only the active display, not both screens.

The CLS command, which has no switches, uses the following syntax:

CLS

Clearing the screen does not change the mode of the display. If, for example, you used the MODE command to change your screen display to 40 columns, the screen clears when you issue the CLS command; CLS then redisplays the DOS prompt in 40-column mode. All other attributes that you set previously—for example, if you define a background color and foreground color by using ANSI.SYS escape sequences—are also retained. (For more information on MODE, see Chapter 11, "Working with System Information.")

You frequently use the CLS command in batch files. By inserting a CLS command at the end of the AUTOEXEC.BAT file, for instance, you can remove all the messages that memory-resident programs may display as they load into memory.

For Related Information

◀◀ "Altering the Look of the Screen with MODE," p. 416.

▶▶ "Understanding the Contents of Batch Files," p. 548.

FROM HERE...

The GRAPHICS Command

You may have tried to use the Print Screen key (PrtSc on some keyboards) to print the contents of your screen to a printer; if so, you may have discovered that this method works only when your screen is in text mode.

If your monitor is a CGA, EGA, or VGA, the external command GRAPHICS enables you to use the Print Screen key to print graphics screens also. When you execute GRAPHICS, a portion of the program remains memory-resident. When you next press Print Screen (or Shift-PrtSc), all ASCII code characters that would otherwise print as text are converted to graphics before the information is sent to the printer.

Issuing the GRAPHICS Command

Use the following syntax for GRAPHICS with DOS Version 3.3 and later:

GRAPHICS *printer d:path\filename /R /B /LCD /PRINTBOX:STD*

printer is the type of printer you are using. Table 12.3 lists the values you can use for the *printer* parameter. If your printer is not listed, it may be compatible with one of the other printers on the list. Refer to your printer's instruction manual for details. If you do not specify a printer, DOS assumes the GRAPHICS printer type.

Table 12.3 List of Printer Types and Settings	
Printer Type	**Model Name**
COLOR1	IBM PC Color Printer with black ribbon, which prints in gray scales
COLOR4	IBM PC Color Printer with RGB (red, green, blue) ribbon, which prints four colors
COLOR8	IBM Personal Computer Color Printer with CMY (cyan, magenta, yellow, and black) ribbon, which prints eight colors
DESKJET	Hewlett-Packard Deskjet printer (DOS 5.0 and 6.0 only)
GRAPHICS	IBM PC Graphics Printer, IBM ProPrinter, or IBM Quietwriter printer
GRAPHICSWIDE	IBM PC Graphics Printer with an 11-inch carriage, or IBM ProPrinters II and III

Printer Type	Model Name
HPDEFAULT	Any Hewlett-Packard PCL printer (DOS 5.0 and 6.0 only)
LASERJET	Hewlett-Packard LaserJet (DOS 5.0 and 6.0 only)
LASERJETII	Hewlett-Packard LaserJet II (DOS 5.0 and 6.0 only)
PAINTJET	Hewlett-Packard PaintJet printer (DOS 5.0 and 6.0 only)
QUIETJET	Hewlett-Packard QuietJet printer (DOS 5.0 and 6.0 only)
QUIETJETPLUS	Hewlett-Packard QuietJet printer (DOS 5.0 and 6.0 only)
RUGGEDWRITER	Hewlett-Packard RuggedWriter printer (DOS 5.0 and 6.0 only)
RUGGEDWRITERWIDE	Hewlett-Packard RuggedWriter wide printer (DOS 5.0 and 6.0 only)
THERMAL	IBM PC-Convertible thermal printer
THINKJET	Hewlett-Packard ThinkJet printer

d:path\filename is the drive, path, and file name of a printer profile file (DOS Version 4.0 and later). This file supports the printers of other manufacturers. If your printer doesn't fit into one of the categories supported by GRAPHICS, you can create a custom printer profile for use with GRAPHICS. The *\filename* parameter refers to the *profile file*, which specifies how graphics are translated for various printers. The profile file is an ASCII text file with two types of information for each printer in the file. A profile can include information about how the printer is controlled—selecting printer colors or adjusting the darkness of the printed piece. The second section of the profile lists the translation from the screen to the printer.

GRAPHICS.PRO is the profile file supplied with DOS. If you want to create a custom profile file for your printer, make a copy of the supplied GRAPHICS.PRO file and modify it. This exercise is also useful if you are interested in the programming aspects of DOS. Modifying the GRAPHICS.PRO file is not necessary for most printers.

T I P

/R forces the printer to print a monochrome text screen as you see it—black background and white text. When you use the /R switch with a color screen, the darkest colors (black or blue) are converted to black; light colors are converted to white or light gray; and other colors are printed as different shades of gray on a *gray scale* for contrast. If you don't use the /R switch, all on-screen information that is white prints as black, and all black on-screen information (usually the background) prints as white. The paper color in the printer is assumed to be white.

T   I   P   If the on-screen colors don't have a sharp enough contrast, the GRAPHICS command may "miss" the difference between colors and produce an all-white or all-black printout. If this problem occurs, try altering your screen colors before you print.

/B prints the background color. Use this switch only if you have a color printer, after you specify COLOR4 or COLOR8 as your printer type. If you try to use the /B switch with a black-and-white printer, DOS displays the following message:

```
The /B switch is invalid with black and white printers.
```

/LCD is a switch designed for use with the IBM PC-Convertible, which comes with a small liquid-crystal display (LCD) screen. /LCD forces the printer to print the screen as it appears, with the size of the screen and characters smaller than on normal monitors. You can also use this switch with any other laptop computer that has an old-style, smaller LCD screen like the IBM PC-Convertible. Most laptops now have a full-sized LCD screen and don't require the use of this switch.

/PRINTBOX:STD sets the printbox size to *standard* or normal size, as it appears on monochrome and VGA monitors of standard size and shape. You use this setting to print the screen when you work with Quattro Pro, Microsoft Word, or other programs in graphics mode. You also use this setting to print the contents of a narrow LCD screen if you want it to appear as if it were on a standard monitor. By typing /PRINTBOX:LCD, you can use this switch to force the printer to print in LCD mode (a longer form of the /LCD switch, shown above). You can abbreviate the /PRINTBOX switch to /PB.

Using GRAPHICS To Print a Screen Image

Suppose that you have an IBM ProPrinter printer. If you use a mono-chrome system and want to print a screen image with the background as black and the text as white, type the following command:

GRAPHICS /R

After GRAPHICS loads into memory, you can create the screen of inter-est and press Print Screen to print to the printer.

To print eight-color images (including the background color) on an IBM Personal Computer Color Printer with a CMY ribbon installed, type the following command:

GRAPHICS COLOR8 /B

On the PC Convertible with an attached full-sized monitor, you can send the screen image to the IBM PC-Convertible thermal printer by typing the following:

GRAPHICS THERMAL /PB:STD

Changing the command to GRAPHICS THERMAL /PB:LCD or GRAPHICS THERMAL /LCD prints the image as it normally appears on the liquid-crystal display.

Rules for Using GRAPHICS

■ After you load GRAPHICS, you can press the Print Screen (Shift-PrtSc) key to print graphics screens on listed graphics printers.

■ If you omit the /PB and /LCD switches, GRAPHICS uses the previous printbox setting.

■ You can print up to 8 colors on a color printer.

■ You can print up to 19 shades of gray on a black-and-white printer.

The PRINT Command

In Chapter 9, "Managing Your Files," you learned that the COPY com-mand can transfer information from one device to another. The com-mand COPY LETTER.TXT PRN, for example, copies the file named LETTER.TXT to the device PRN, the printer. During this copying pro-cess, the computer is not available for other use.

Because the external command PRINT enables you to print in the background, you can do other work while you print a document. Printing occurs during the idle times—when the computer waits for you to type at the keyboard, for example. You also can queue for printing more than one file at a time.

Issuing the PRINT Command

The external PRINT command uses the following syntax:

> **PRINT** */D:device /B:size /U:ticks1 /Q:qsize*
> */M:ticks2 /S:ticks3 d1:path1\filename1 /P /T /C*
> *d2:path2\filename2 /P /T /C...*

d1:path1\filename1 is the drive, path, and file name of the first file you want to print.

d2:path2\filename2 is the drive, path, and file name of the next file you want to print. The ellipsis (...) means that you can list more files. Wild cards are permitted in the file names.

Like GRAPHICS, PRINT leaves a portion of itself in memory after you issue the command, and the switches change how the PRINT command works. You can only specify the */D:device*, */Q:qsize*, */B:size*, */U:ticks1*, */M:ticks2*, and */S:ticks3* optional switches when you first issue the PRINT command. These switches are explained in the following list:

- *■* */D:device* names the serial or parallel port to which your output device is attached. Acceptable values include all DOS output devices and ports, such as LPT1, LPT2, LPT3, PRN, COM1, COM2, COM3, COM4, or AUX.

- *■* */Q:qsize* specifies the maximum number of files—from 4 to 32—that can be queued at a time. If the switch is omitted, 10 files is the default queue size.

- *■* */B:size* determines the size of buffer used in the printing process. The data for printing is taken from the disk in chunks the size of the specified buffer. Increasing the buffer size causes the PRINT command to read data from the disk in bigger chunks. The minimum buffer size is 512 bytes; the maximum is 16K. If you don't specify the buffer size, the default size is 512 bytes. Remember that the larger you make the buffer, the less RAM you have for running applications programs.

- *■* */U:ticks1* determines how long the PRINT command waits for the printer to be available. In most cases, the PRINT command sends data to the printer faster than the printer can actually print. The printer can store some of this information in a built-in memory buffer. When this memory buffer fills, the printer sends a busy signal to the computer. The printer transfers the data in the buffer to the print head and prints the data. When space for more data becomes available in the printer's memory buffer, the printer stops sending a busy signal, and PRINT sends more data.

The */U:ticks1* switch changes the number of clock ticks that PRINT waits before sending data to the printer. The default setting is 1, but you can change the setting to as high as 255. If the printer is busy, PRINT first tries to send the data and then waits the number of clock ticks set by this switch. If the printer is still busy, PRINT immediately transfers control back to DOS for other tasks without using the rest of the clock ticks set aside for it by the */S:ticks3* switch.

■ */M:ticks2* specifies the number of system clock ticks that the PRINT command waits for the printer to print a character. *ticks2* can be set to any value between 1 and 255; the default value is 2.

■ */S:ticks3* determines the number of clock ticks allocated to the background printing. Too high a value for this switch causes the computer to respond sluggishly to other commands that you execute while you print in the background. A low value slows the printing process. The range of values is 1 to 255; the default value is 8.

You can use the following switches at any time to control the action of the PRINT command; to do so, at the prompt, type the command and the name of the file you want to affect and add the desired switch:

■ The */P* switch places a file in PRINT's queue. The preceding file and all subsequent files on the command line are printed.

■ The */C* switch cancels the printing of some files. The file name issued before the /C and all files after the /C on the same command line are removed from the print queue. (The printer alarm sounds if you cancel the currently printing file with the /C switch.) You must issue the /P switch to add files to the queue again.

■ The */T* switch terminates printing. All files are removed from the queue, including the file being printed. The printer alarm sounds, a file cancellation message prints, and the paper advances to the next page.

If you enter file names without a /P, /C, or /T switch, DOS uses the /P switch as a default so that all files are placed in the queue for printing. If, at the prompt, you type PRINT with no switches, a list of all files in the queue appears. This list includes the name of the file that is currently printing and the order of files yet to print. This command also displays any error messages. If, for example, you forget to turn on the printer, the following error message appears:

```
Errors on list device indicate that it may be off-line.
Please check it.
```

Using PRINT To Print Several Files

You do not have to enter the names of all the files to print at one time. You can issue the PRINT command several times to add or remove files from the print queue. You can specify the parameters that affect the way PRINT operates only when you first issue the command. After you first issue the PRINT command, you use the command only to enter file names for printing or to cancel printing.

If you enter the PRINT command for the first time without specifying a device, PRINT prompts you for a device name. The default, PRN, is the first parallel port (LPT1) on your computer. Pressing Enter at the DOS prompt accepts the default.

To start PRINT with the default settings, type **PRINT**.

If you are in no hurry to collect the printed output of files and want to use the computer while the printer prints your files, you can readjust the default installation settings for PRINT. By changing the /M:*ticks2* or /S:*ticks3* settings, you can give your computer better response time. (As mentioned earlier, /M:*ticks2* alters the maximum length of time that can elapse while the printer prints a character before DOS displays an error message, and /S:*ticks3* determines the number of clock ticks that DOS allocates for background printing.) To alter the default settings, you can type the following when you invoke the PRINT command for the first time:

PRINT /D:PRN /M:1 /S:25

If you are unconcerned about the sluggishness of the keyboard, you can improve the speed of the background printing by altering the buffer size, as well as adjusting /M:*ticks2* and /S:*ticks3*. You might type in the following command, for example:

PRINT /D:PRN /B:16384 /M:1 /S:25

Experiment with these variables until you find a setting that is acceptable. A sluggish keyboard is not always tolerable. If the response time is too slow, you can make errors—for example, you may assume that a program didn't accept your keystrokes and try to retype the command, while the program was only waiting to regain control.

By using a combination of the /P, /T, and /C switches, you can adjust the order in which the files print. Suppose, for example, that you want to print five files: LETTER1.TXT, MEMO1.TXT, REPORT1.TXT, REPORT2.TXT, and REPORT10.TXT. Type the following on the command line:

PRINT /D:PRN LETTER1.TXT /P MEMO1.TXT REPORT1.TXT
    REPORT2.TXT REPORT10.TXT

If you then decide that you want to print REPORT10.TXT before REPORT2.TXT, type the following command, which removes REPORT2.TXT from the print queue and adds the file to the end of the queue:

PRINT REPORT2.TXT /C REPORT2.TXT /P

You can cancel all files to be printed by typing the following command:

PRINT /T

General Rules for Using PRINT

- You can only specify the /D:*device*, /Q:*qsize*, /B:*size*, /S:*ticks3*, /U:*ticks1*, and /M:*ticks2* optional switches the first time that you issue the PRINT command.

- If you specify /D:*device*, you must type this switch first, before all other switches.

- If you issue /P, the preceding file and all subsequent files entered on the command line by the PRINT command are printed until a /T or /C switch is issued.

- If you issue /C, the preceding file and all subsequent files are canceled.

- The files print in the order that you enter them at the command line.

- A page-eject sequence is sent to the printer at the end of a file.

- You cannot use the printer for other purposes while PRINT is in operation. You cannot, for example, use Print Screen when PRINT is in effect.

continues

> **General Rules for Using PRINT continued**
>
> ■ The files being printed must be on the same disk drive.
>
> ■ You cannot alter files that are in the print queue or being printed.
>
> ■ Specifying a nonexistent device causes unpredictable behavior by the computer.
>
> ■ Tab characters in the printed file are converted to blanks, up to the next 8-column boundary.

The ASSIGN Command

You use the external command ASSIGN to redirect all DOS read-and-write (input and output) requests from one drive to another. Each drive is a DOS device. By using the ASSIGN command, DOS can interrogate a different disk than the one actually specified on a command line.

 NOTE   This command exists only in DOS Versions 1.0 through 5.0. If you have an earlier version of DOS, you can still use this command because it is included in the SETVER table. For details on the use of ASSIGN, see the command reference in this book. For more information about SETVER, see Chapter 17, "Configuring Your Computer."

The syntax for the ASSIGN command is shown in the following:

ASSIGN d1=d2 .../STATUS

d1 is the drive letter for the original disk drive; **d2** is the drive letter for the reassignment.

The ellipsis (**...**) indicates that more than one drive can be reassigned on a single command line.

/STATUS (available in DOS 5.0 only), issued with no other parameters, displays a listing of current drive assignments.

For Related Information

▶▶ "Setting the Version with SETVER," p. 663.

FROM HERE...

The JOIN Command

You can use the JOIN command to add a disk drive to the directory structure of another disk. For example, the external command JOIN enables you to use a floppy disk in such a way that it appears to DOS to be part of a hard disk. You can also use JOIN if you have two hard disks: drive C and drive D. JOIN can attach drive D to a subdirectory on drive C, for instance.

 NOTE The JOIN command exists only in DOS Versions 3.1 through 5.0. If you have an earlier version of DOS, you can still use this command if you add it to the SETVER table. For details on the use of JOIN, see the command reference in this book. For more information about SETVER, see Chapter 17, "Configuring Your Computer."

The syntax for JOIN is shown in the following:

>   **JOIN d1:** *d2:\path/D*

The directory structure of floppy disk *d1* is added to the directory structure of hard disk *d2*.

d1: is a valid disk drive name that becomes the alias or nickname. **d1:** may be a nonexistent disk drive.

d2:path is the valid disk drive name and directory path that will be nick-named **d1:**.

/D deletes the alias.

The SUBST Command

The external command SUBST is the inverse of the JOIN command. Instead of grafting a second disk onto the tree structure of a disk, the SUBST command splits a disk's directory structure in two. In effect, the SUBST command creates an alias disk drive name for a subdirectory.

Issuing the SUBST Command

You can use the SUBST command to perform different functions.

To establish an alias, use the following syntax:

>   **SUBST d1: d2:pathname**

To delete an alias, use this form:

SUBST d1: /D

To see the current aliases, use the following form:

SUBST

The SUBST command replaces a path name for a subdirectory with a drive letter. After a SUBST command is in effect, DOS translates all I/O requests to a particular drive letter back to the correct path name.

The alias drive created by the SUBST command inherits the directory tree structure of the subdirectory reassigned to a drive letter.

 NOTE As the default, DOS assigns the LASTDRIVE= parameter a value of E. Higher drive designators, however, can be made by inserting a LASTDRIVE= parameter into the CONFIG.SYS file. DOS then establishes each of the drive letters up to and including the specified LASTDRIVE as DOS devices. When you use the SUBST command, DOS understands that you are referring to a device.

Using SUBST To Reference a Path with a Drive Letter

SUBST is commonly used in two different situations. If you want to run a program that does not support path names, you can use the SUBST command to assign a drive letter to a directory. The program then refers to the drive letter, and DOS translates the request into a path. If, for example, the data for a program is stored in C:\WORDPROC, you can type the following to tell the program that the data is stored in drive E:

SUBST E: C:\WORDPROC

After the substitution is made, you can issue the following command:

SUBST

The following message appears:

```
E: => C:\WORDPROC
```

To disconnect the substitution of drive E for the C:\WORDPROC directory, type the following command:

SUBST E: /D

The other use for SUBST is to reduce typing long path names. When a PC is used by more than one person, path names can become quite long because each user may use a separate section of the hard disk to store data files and common areas of the disk to store programs. If the paths \USER1\WORDDATA and \USER1\SPREDATA exist on drive C, the typing needed to reach files in the directories can be reduced by using the following command:

SUBST E: C:\USER1

Issuing a directory command on drive E produces the following listing:

```
Volume in drive E is HARD DISK C
Volume Serial Number is 1573-0241
Directory of  E:\


.               <DIR>      05-02-92   12:07p
..              <DIR>      05-02-92   12:07p
WORDDATA        <DIR>      05-02-92    1:59p
SPREDATA        <DIR>      05-22-92    2:08p
       4 File(s)            0 bytes
                      3477824 bytes free
```

The volume label given is the label from drive C, but the directory itself is the contents of C:\USER1.

As with JOIN and ASSIGN, you can use the SUBST command to fool software that insists on using an otherwise unusable drive. For example, a friend may have written an applications program that makes direct reference in its code to a directory on drive C. You can fool your friend's program by using SUBST to attach drive D to a subdirectory on your drive C.

 NOTE Do not use the following DOS commands in conjunction with drives that you create with the SUBST command: BACKUP, CHKDSK, DISKCOMP, DISKCOPY, FDISK, FORMAT, LABEL, RECOVER, RESTORE, and SYS.

General Rules for Using SUBST

■ d1: and d2: must be different.

■ You cannot specify a networked drive as d1: or d2:.

■ d1: cannot be the current drive.

■ d1: must have a designator less than the value in the LASTDRIVE statement of CONFIG.SYS. (See Chapter 17, "Configuring Your Computer," for more information on CONFIG.SYS.)

■ Do not use SUBST with ASSIGN or JOIN.

■ Remove all SUBST settings before you run DISKCOPY, DISKCOMP, FDISK, PRINT, FORMAT, LABEL, BACKUP, RECOVER, SYS, or RESTORE.

■ Beware of using CHDIR, MKDIR, RMDIR, APPEND, and PATH with any drives reassigned.

The CTTY Command

DOS can take information or data from and send it to different kinds of devices. Any device that you can use to give information to DOS is called an *input device*, and any device DOS can send information to is an *output device*. DOS uses your keyboard and screen as the standard input and output devices. Together, these two devices make up the *console*, known to DOS as the *CON device*. The internal command CTTY enables you to tell DOS that you want to use a different device for input and later enables you to restore the keyboard and screen as the console.

Use the one of the following syntax lines for the internal command CTTY:

CTTY *device*

CTTY CON

device is the name of a DOS device which can be used for input.

CTTY causes DOS to intercept the I/O request calls that normally come from the keyboard and go to the screen; the command redirects these calls to the device you specify.

By typing the command CTTY COM1, for example, you designate COM1 as the device that sends and receives standard input and output. This command is used in association with specialized programs that need input from a different source than the keyboard.

Typing CTTY CON from the auxiliary device restores the console to the keyboard and display.

You can also use CTTY if the computer is attached to an intelligent bar code reader that collects information from packages. This reader, in association with a specialized program, may not need to use the display or keyboard.

You probably will not need to use the CTTY command. DOS usually can gather information through devices without altering the input and output devices. Certain applications programs, however, benefit from your use of CTTY. One example is the DOS external program INTERLNK, which requires the CTTY command in order to transfer itself to another computer (see Chapter 9, "Managing Your Files," for more information on INTERLNK).

General Rules for Using CTTY

■ You can use the character-based devices AUX, COM1, COM2, COM3, or COM4 as the alternate console.

■ The physical device attached to the relevant AUX, COM1, COM2, COM3, or COM4 must be able to accept input and provide output.

■ Programs that do not use DOS function calls will not make use of the alternate console.

For Related Information

◄◄ "Using Interlnk To Communicate with a Laptop Computer," p. 346.

FROM HERE...

The MODE Command

MODE is one of the more versatile external commands supplied with DOS. DOS Versions 4.0, 4.01, 5.0, and 6.0 extended this versatility still further. MODE sets the operational modes of serial and parallel ports and redirects information from parallel ports to serial ports. MODE can also set display modes, and you can use MODE with code pages. For more information about display modes and code pages, see Chapter 11, "Working with System Information," and Chapter 20, "Understanding the International Features of DOS," respectively.

Using MODE To Control Device Operations

This section introduces the MODE functions that relate to devices. You can use MODE to set a variety of devices—the serial ports and parallel ports. To read about all functions of the MODE command, turn to the Command Reference later in this book.

Using MODE To Change Parallel Port Settings

A *parallel port* transmits data by transferring (usually to a printer) an entire byte at one time. The MODE command adjusts the number of lines per inch on your printer, the number of columns per line, and the retry feature.

Issuing the MODE Command

Use the following syntax for the external MODE command, which changes the parallel printer characteristics:

MODE LPT*n*: *cpl,lpi, P*

LPT*n*: is the parallel port name. *cpl* is the number of characters per line. The default cpl setting is 80. *lpi* is the number of lines per inch. The default setting for lpi is 6. *P* specifies continuous retries on time-out or "busy" errors.

An additional version of the command, which is available with DOS Version 4.0 and later, uses the following syntax:

MODE LPT*n*: *COLS=wid, LINES=lpi, RETRY=action*

wid is the number of columns per line: 80 or 132; *lpi* is the number of lines per inch: 6 or 8; and *action* is the message you want DOS to return or the action DOS should take when the printer port is busy.

When you use the MODE command to adjust the parallel port setting, this command alters only two items seen on the printout itself: the characters per line and the lines per inch. In general, printing is performed directly from an applications program, which is able to set many more parameters for a particular printer. The program operates by sending to the printer Escape sequences that can adjust the printed output accordingly.

The retry setting is more significant. In DOS Version 4.01 and earlier, the MODE command either performs no retry when it receives a time-out error or retries continuously when the P option is included. When data is sent to the printer, the port expects to see return signals from the printer indicating that the data was received. If no signals are received within a particular period of time, a time-out error occurs. By default, DOS does not try again to send information to the printer and returns an error message to the screen. If you include the P option, DOS continuously tries to send the data; this prevents the error message from being displayed. Pressing the Ctrl-Break key combination stops the retrying process.

In DOS Versions 4.0 through 6.0, various retry options are available. If you don't specify a retry option, DOS doesn't continue to try to send data when a time-out error occurs. When you use the retry option, you can select from a list of options. Although the B setting is no longer available in DOS 6.0, it is listed here for compatibility with DOS 5.0. The following list explains the various options:

- The *B* setting (DOS Version 5.0 and earlier) returns a busy signal to the device driver when the port is busy.

- The *R* setting causes a ready signal to be returned from the port— even if the port is busy. Then, when the printer does become ready, the data is ready to send, and an error message does not appear on-screen.

- The *E* option is most commonly used when the printing is done in the background (by PRINT or a network print queue). The data is not transferred to the printer until the port is not busy.

- The *N* setting (*NONE* in DOS 4.0 and 4.01) indicates that no retry action is taken.

- The *P* option (in DOS 5.0 and 6.0) causes DOS to try the printer continuously until the busy state ends.

Using MODE To Print a Large File

In some cases, you must use the P option to print a file. Consider a large DOS file that you want to copy to the printer. If the file is larger than the storage capacity of the printer, the printer port will be busy at some point during the data transfer. If the printer remains busy for too long, an error message appears on-screen; DOS thinks the printer is defective, and the printing process aborts.

Specifying P in DOS Version 3.3 and earlier or RETRY=B in DOS Versions 4.0 and 5.0 causes DOS to wait until the printer is ready to receive data. (The B option is no longer available in DOS 6.0, but you can use the P option for this purpose.) Use the following command for LPT1 in DOS Version 3.3:

MODE LPT1:,,P

For DOS Versions 4.0, 4.01, and 5.0, use the following command:

MODE LPT1 RETRY=B

For DOS Version 6.0, use the following command:

MODE LPT1 RETRY=P

If the file is large and you want to be able to fit more lines of text on a page, you can print the file with a higher number of lines per inch (8 instead of 6). Also, you can specify 132 columns per line instead of 80. This setting is not a problem for a wide-carriage printer, which accepts wide paper. If you are using a printer that accepts 8 1/2-inch paper, however, you must set the printer to print in a condensed character mode, which can fit 132 columns on a line of 8 1/2-inch paper.

When the printer is attached to LPT2, use the following command to fit as much information as possible on a page:

MODE LPT2:132,8

General Rules for Using MODE To Change Parallel Port Settings

■ The default values of the port are reset if you reset or initialize the printer.

■ If you omit a parameter from the command line, the setting for that parameter is not changed.

■ Do not use any of the retry options when printers are being shared on an IBM PC network.

Using MODE To Change the Serial Port

You can use another option of the MODE command to alter the functions of the serial ports. This command works in a way similar to the parallel port adjustments. DOS changes the parameters that are sent to and from the device driver.

Issuing MODE To Adjust Serial Ports

The acceptable serial ports are COM1, COM2, COM3, and COM4. The serial port can receive and transmit data only one bit at a time. The signaling rate (the number of times per second that data is transmitted) is the *baud rate*. The amount of data transferred in a second is referred to as the *bps* (bits per second).

You can use the MODE command to adjust the baud settings and change the amount of data sent in a fixed time. Although it is called a baud setting, the numbers used are actually the number of bits transmitted per second. Acceptable baud settings are 110, 150, 300, 600, 1200, 2400, 4800, 9600, and 19200. You need to use only the first two digits of the number to set the baud rate.

The most common devices attached to a serial port that you need to set from DOS are serial printers and plotters. Although modems are serial devices, you usually don't adjust them from DOS. Communications programs, however, use the DOS functions to make adjustments to the serial ports.

Use the following syntax to change the serial port:

MODE COM*y***:** *baud,parity,databits,stopbits,P*

The elements of the commands are explained in the following list:

- **COM***y***:** is the name of the serial port device.

- *baud* is the baud rate. You must specify the baud rate for the serial port.

- *parity* is the parity.

- *databits* is the number of data bits. The default number of data bits is 7.

- *stopbits* is the number of stop bits. The default number of stop bits is 1 for all baud rates except 110, when 2 stop bits are set as the default.

- *P* specifies continuous retries on time-out errors.

With DOS Version 4.0 and later, you can also use the following syntax:

MODE COMy: *BAUD=baud PARITY=parity DATA=databits STOP=stopbits RETRY=action*

action is the message you want DOS to return when the port is busy.

With versions of DOS prior to Version 4.0, the retry feature provided two choices when a time-out error occurred: no retry or continuous retries when you included the P option. When data is sent to the printer, the port expects to see signals from the printer indicating that the data was received. If no signals are received within a particular period of time, a time-out error occurs. By default, DOS does not try again to send information to the printer and returns an error message to the screen. If you include the P option, DOS continuously tries to send the data; this prevents the error message from being displayed. The Ctrl-Break key combination stops the retrying process.

With DOS Version 4.0 and later, more retry options are available. If you do not specify a retry option, DOS doesn't try again to send data when a time-out error occurs. When you use the retry option, you can select from the following four options:

- The *R* setting causes a ready signal to be returned from the port even if the port is busy. Then, when the printer does become ready, the data is ready to send and an error message does not appear on-screen.

- The *E* option is most commonly used when you are printing in the background (using PRINT or a network print queue). The data is not transferred to the printer until the port is not busy.

- The *N* option specifies no action; this setting is the default.

- Available in DOS Versions 5.0 and 6.0, the *P* action specifies continuous retry.

Using MODE To Set the Serial Port

To set the first serial port to communicate at 2400 bps, with 8 data bits, 1 stop bit, and no parity, you can type one of the following commands:

MODE COM1 2400,N,8,1

or

MODE COM1 24,N,8,1

If you are using DOS Version 3.3 or later, you can type the following instead to get the same settings:

MODE COM1 BAUD=24 DATA=8 STOP=1 PARITY=NONE

NOTE The printer or plotter needs to be set to receive data in the same format in which the serial port is sending the data— that is, the same baud rate, parity, and so on.

General Rules for Using MODE with Serial Ports

■ If you set a retry option, a portion of MODE remains resident unless you use the DOS Version 4.0 RETRY=none option.

■ The retry option slows the performance of foreground tasks when computers are being shared on an IBM PC network.

■ DOS Version 4.0 and later can include Mark or Space parity settings. All versions of DOS support *none*, *odd*, and *even* parity settings.

Using MODE To Redirect a Parallel Port to a Serial Port

The final MODE setting you can use with ports is the command to redirect a parallel port to a serial port.

Issuing the MODE Command To Redirect Ports

Use the following syntax for the MODE command that changes the parallel printer to a serial printer:

MODE LPT*n*:=COM*y*:

LPT*n*: is the name of the parallel printer port; **COM*y*:** is the name of the serial port.

After you use MODE, DOS channels to the serial port all I/O requests that a program sends to the parallel port. The conversion of data from byte-wide to bit-wide is handled automatically by the electronics associated with the port.

Using MODE To Redirect Ports

Some early programs don't directly support serial printers. To use a serial printer, you can set a serial port and redirect a parallel port to that serial port. This process enables you to print when you use a serial printer and use a program that doesn't directly support the printer.

You initialize a serial port with DOS Version 3.3 by using a command similar to the following:

> MODE COM2 2400,E,7,2

With DOS Version 4.0 and later, you may type the following command instead:

> MODE COM2 BAUD=24 DATA=7 STOP=2 PARITY=EVEN

You then follow the initialization command by typing the following command:

> MODE LPT1=COM2

All data that normally goes to LPT1 is transmitted to COM2 at 2400 bps, with 7 data bits, 2 stop bits, and even parity.

General Rules for Using MODE To Redirect Ports

- ◼ Any parallel port can be redirected to any serial port.

- ◼ The serial port must be initialized with both speed and data characteristics before the parallel port is redirected.

- ◼ The initialization of the serial port must include the retry option if the attached device is a printer.

Using MODE To Change the Typematic Rate

When you press a key on the PC keyboard, a character appears on-screen. If you continue to hold the key down, the pressed character repeats on-screen. The number of times a second the key is repeated is known as the *typematic rate*.

With versions of DOS prior to Version 4.0, you need an add-on utility program to alter the keyboard typematic rate. You now can make this setting from DOS.

Issuing the MODE Command To Set the Typematic Rate

Following is the syntax for the MODE command that changes the typematic rate:

> **MODE CON RATE=***rate* **DELAY=***delay*

rate is the number of repetitions per second. The rate parameter can have values in the range 1 through 32. These values represent a repeat rate of from 2 to 30 characters per second (the higher the value, the faster the repeat rate). The default value is 20 for an IBM AT and 21 for an IBM PS/2, which is equivalent to approximately 10 characters per second.

delay is the time delay before DOS starts repeating a key. You can adjust both the delay and the rate. The delay is specified in 1/4-second intervals. The range for the delay is 1 through 4, making a total possible delay of 1 second.

Using MODE To Set a Delay

To set the keyboard so that the delay before the key repeats is 0.75 seconds and the rate value is 24, type the following:

> MODE CON RATE=24 DELAY=3

For Related Information

◀◀ "Altering the Look of the Screen with MODE," p. 416.

▶▶ "Understanding Code Page Switching," p. 763.

FROM HERE...

The Redirection Commands

DOS uses three standard devices: one for input, one for output, and one for errors. The main input/output device is the console, which is DOS's name for your keyboard and screen. The keyboard is the standard input device, and the display is the standard output and error device. In short, you type commands on the keyboard, and the commands and any error messages appear on-screen.

DOS enables you to choose the devices that you will use to input and output information; this process is called *redirection*. (Error messages are always sent to the screen.)

Issuing the Redirection Commands

The redirection symbol, which looks like an arrow (> or <), shows the input's source and destination. Use the following syntax for redirecting a program or command's input:

> *command < inputdevice*

The syntax for redirecting a program or command's output is shown in the following:

> *command > outputdevice*

The syntax for redirecting and appending to an existing file is shown in the following:

> **function** *command >> outputdevice*

inputdevice is the source of the input; *outputdevice* is the destination of the output. *command* can specify almost all applications programs or DOS commands. With the redirection command, you can use any DOS output device as an *outputdevice*, and you can use any DOS input device as an *inputdevice*.

Normally, redirected input comes from a file. Some devices, however, such as a mouse or a bar code reader, can also be used as a source of input. For example, you can write a file that consists of the keystrokes used to operate a program, or you can use the output from a mouse as the input for a program.

Most DOS users redirect output more often than they redirect input. The DIR > PRN command, which redirects the output of a directory to the printer, is a common example of redirection. When you issue this command, DOS redirects the output (the directory listing itself) to the PRN device instead of sending the listing to the screen. This command produces a hard copy listing of the directory.

Another common use is redirecting output to a file. To review the statistics of the MEM /C command, for example, type the following command:

> MEM /C > CLASSIFY.MEM

> **CAUTION:** Take care when you use the > operator. If you use >
> and refer to an existing file, DOS overwrites the existing file with
> the new output.

When you use redirection commands with pipes and filters, discussed
later in this chapter, the command becomes even more powerful.

Using Redirection To Print the Output of Commands

If you want to redirect to the printer a copy of your disk's directory
structure and a list of the files on your hard disk, type the following:

TREE C:\ /F >PRN

The TREE command does not supply a directory listing that includes
file sizes. If you want to create a full listing of all the directories on your
hard disk by using redirection to append the output of the command,
you specify that each directory be listed and then specify that the
output be appended to a file. You then can print the full list. To perform this task, you type a command similar to the following for each
directory:

DIR C:\ /S >> FULLIST.DIR

The DIR command lists the files in all the directories on drive C. The /S
switch causes the DIR command to display all subdirectories. You can
then substitute the names of other drives for C.

If you are testing programs that require a large amount of user input,
the following redirection method is useful. For example, you can type
the following:

PROGRAM < C:TESTPAT

This command results in the file TESTPAT supplying the input to PRO-
GRAM. The redirection process enables you to construct a file that
contains the correct keystrokes needed to operate a program. You then
can test the program's basic operation before all the error-trapping
sequences are included. These sequences handle situations when the
incorrect key is typed on the keyboard.

General Rules for Using Redirection

■ Do not use redirection on a DOS command line that includes CALL, FOR, or IF.

■ Using > and referring to an existing file causes DOS to overwrite the existing file with the new output.

■ Using >> adds the output to an existing file or creates a new file if the file does not exist.

The MORE Filter

DOS uses elements called *filters* to channel information between devices. You can use these filters to modify information as it passes from files to the screen. Filters, which work only on ASCII text files, are often used with the redirection symbols so that the input can come from a source other than the keyboard or be sent to a device other than the screen.

Piping is another feature used with these commands. You use the pipe symbol (I) to send output information that normally goes to the screen as input to another program. Piping, a form of redirection, diverts information destined for a device but then makes the information become the input from a device to another program.

The MORE filter buffers information from the input device or file and sends the data to the monitor one screen at a time.

Issuing the MORE Filter

The syntax for the MORE filter, which has no switches, is shown in the following:

MORE

MORE is commonly used in the following ways:

MORE < *filename* (where *filename* is the input file)

or

command I **MORE** (where *command* is any command or program)

MORE collects—and saves in a temporary disk file—information that normally goes to the screen. When a screen of input is obtained, MORE sends that information to the standard output device all at the same time. The text is channeled through the MORE filter until the end-of-file. Press any key when DOS displays the -- More -- prompt; this action displays the next screen. After all the information is displayed on-screen, DOS erases the temporary file created by MORE.

Using MORE To Pause the Screen

When you use MORE to pause directory listings, the filter serves a function similar to the /P switch that is available with the DIR command.

The most common use of MORE, however, is to pause the TYPE command. To read the contents of a README.DOC file one page at a time, for example, type the following:

TYPE README.DOC | MORE

or

MORE <README.DOC

Both syntax forms work identically. To see the contents of a file, you can use the TYPE command. If the output of the file flows off the screen, reissue the command by pressing F3, and add the pipe character (|) and MORE.

General Rules for Using MORE

- Do not use MORE alone. MORE is a filter, which requires input to redirect or pipe.

- To view additional screens full of information, press any key when DOS displays the -- More -- prompt.

- Ctrl-Break terminates the command without displaying any other screens.

The FIND Filter

The FIND filter finds strings of ASCII text in files. This filter is often used in association with redirection and piping.

Issuing the FIND Filter

Use the following syntax for the FIND Filter:

FIND /C /N /V /I "string" d:path\filename ...

"string" specifies the ASCII characters for which you want to search.

d:path\filename is the drive, path, and file name of the file to search. The ellipsis (...) indicates that you can specify more than one file to search.

/C causes FIND to count all the lines that contain the "string". You use the /C switch to count the number of lines with the ASCII string; the text itself isn't passed to the screen.

/N causes FIND to include line numbers of the lines that contain the "string". You use the /N switch to locate the line numbers within the text file. The line numbers listed are the line numbers in the original text file, not just sequential numbers. If the third, fifth, and sixth lines in the text file contain the string, for example, the line numbers displayed are 3, 5, and 6, not 1, 2, and 3.

/V causes FIND to search only for lines that do not contain the "string". Only these lines are passed on to the screen.

/I (DOS Version 5.0 and later only) makes FIND insensitive to case: upper- and lowercase letters are considered the same.

 NOTE You can use /C and /V together. The count displayed is the number of lines that do not contain "string". You can also use /V and /N together. The lines that do not contain "string" are displayed with their appropriate line numbers.

If you use FIND without options, the filter reads each of the files you specify and displays all lines that contain the ASCII string you are looking for. DOS filters the information that normally goes to the output device. All lines that include the ASCII string are displayed on-screen.

Like the other filter commands, FIND is often used with redirection and piping. If you search a text file for lines that include specific information, redirecting the output to a file may be helpful. You then can use the list as a reference while you look at the whole of the original file.

Using FIND To Find Files on Disk

You can use the FIND command to find on disk all files that have a certain extension. To find all files that have the extension LET, for example, type the following command:

DIR /S /B | FIND ".LET"

Because the /S switch is used with this DIR command, all files whose names contain LET—either in the root or extension—are listed under the name of the directory containing them. Because the /B switch is used, the file names are listed in the form FILENAME.EXT, with a period instead of spaces separating the file name and its extension. Therefore, you can search for .LET instead of LET. In this form, each file name is preceded by its directory path.

The DIR command with the /S option lists all the files on a disk. The output for DIR that normally goes to the screen is filtered through the FIND command. The output from FIND is then displayed on-screen.

You can also use the FIND filter with text files as a word-search utility. Suppose, for example, that you forget the name of the memo you sent to your boss, but you know that the file is either MEMO1, MEMO2, or MEMO3. You also know that you always use your boss's title, *Supervisor*, in memos. You can find the memo you need by typing the following:

FIND "Supervisor" MEMO1 MEMO2 MEMO3

When you issue this command, each line that contains *Supervisor* is listed. The listing appears in the following form:

```
---------- MEMO1


---------- MEMO2


Supervisor of Communications


---------- MEMO3
```

General Rules for Using FIND

- Use FIND only on ASCII text files.

- The *"string"* parameter is normally case-sensitive, that is, FIND regards the uppercase string *LOOK* as different from the lowercase string *look*. In DOS Version 5.0 and later, you can use the /I switch to make the search case-insensitive.

- To cause FIND to search for a quote in a string, type two quote marks together (""). FIND then searches for occurrences of ".

- If you do not specify a *filename*, FIND uses the standard input device.

- You cannot use wild cards in *filename*.

The SORT Filter

The third DOS filter is SORT, which sorts the information from an ASCII file before displaying the result on-screen. Like FIND and MORE, SORT often is used with redirection and piping.

Issuing the SORT Filter

Use the following syntax for the SORT filter:

SORT */R* */+n*

/R reverses the sort order; *n* is the offset column for the sorting process.

The SORT filter processes information that normally goes to your screen or other output device. The text from the input is analyzed on a line-by-line basis and sorted according to the ASCII binary values of the characters. This order is alphabetical, but SORT doesn't discriminate between upper- and lowercase letters.

When you use SORT with redirection or piping, more sophisticated sorting occurs. The most common use of SORT is to sort a directory listing into a text file, which you can then can print.

The offset—the */+n* option—in the command shows the leftmost column to be sorted. With a directory listing, you can sort by date or file size rather than by root name. Table 12.4 lists the offset values for a directory listing.

Table 12.4 Offset Values for SORT	
Offset Value	**Sorting By**
1	Root name
10	File extension
14	File size
24	File date
34	File time

The sorted output appears on-screen; the original directory listing itself remains unchanged.

NOTE In DOS Versions 5.0 and 6.0, you can sort a directory listing by using the /O switch. This use of SORT is not as vital as it once was. To sort a directory by name, you can use the following command:

>   DIR \ /ON

Similarly, you can use /OE to sort by extension, /OS to sort by size, and /OD to sort by date and time combined. You still need to use SORT if you want to sort the directory by time alone.

Using SORT To Sort Subdirectories

You can use redirection and piping, as well as the FIND and SORT filters, in many ways. In DOS 4.0, 4.01, or 5.0, for example, you can create a sorted list of the subdirectories in the root directory by using the process outlined in the next paragraphs.

To create a sorted list of subdirectories in the root directory, follow these steps:

1. Type the following command:

>   TREE C:\ /A | FIND "-" | SORT /+2 >TEMP.LST

   When issued with the /A switch, the TREE command produces a listing that utilizes the nongraphics character set. The FIND filter then removes all lines that are not subdirectory names. The output from FIND is sorted by SORT on column 2, and the output is redirected to a temporary file.

2. Use the temporary file as the input to the FIND filter, which removes all directories that are not in the root by typing the following command:

FIND /V "|" <TEMP.LST

The result is an alphabetical list of all subdirectories in the root directory.

> **NOTE** Although the preceding commands work in DOS Versions 5.0 and 6.0, the DIR command can perform essentially the same work in a simpler manner by combining switches /AD (directories only), /S (include subdirectories), and /O (sort alphabetically by name), as shown in the following:
>
> DIR /AD /S /O

General Rules for Using SORT

- If *n* is not specified, column 1 is assumed.

- Lines are sorted according to their ASCII binary values with two exceptions: SORT is not case-sensitive. For example, *A* and *a* are sorted as they occur in the source file. Characters with values over 127 are sorted in the order determined by the current COUNTRY code setting. (See Chapter 20, "Understanding the International Features of DOS," for more information.)

- The output file name must be different from the input file name when you use redirection.

Chapter Summary

This chapter discussed the commands associated with changing how DOS interacts with devices. These commands range from basic commands that clear a screen to advanced filtering and redirection commands. The following important points were covered:

- Use the CLS command to clear the active display.

- Use the GRAPHICS command to print graphics screens on supported printers.

■ The PRINT command is a background printing program.

■ Use the ASSIGN, JOIN, and SUBST commands to change the device names assigned to disk drives and directories.

■ Use the CTTY command to change standard input and output devices.

■ Use the options available with the MODE command to adjust settings for serial and parallel ports.

■ You can use MODE with DOS Versions 4.0, 5.0, and 6.0 to alter the keyboard typematic rate.

■ You use the MORE, FIND, and SORT filters with text files. The filters are frequently used with redirection and piping.

The next chapter, "Understanding Backups and the Care of Data," which concludes Part II of this book, discusses the steps you can take to care for your data.

Understanding Backups and the Care of Data

Desktop computers commonly contain hard disk drives that can store thousands of pages of information. If your computer contains a hard disk, it almost certainly contains millions of bytes of software—the programs that run your computer. The hard disk probably also contains thousands or even millions of bytes of data—the information you or someone else has typed into the system. The software and data represent a significant investment in money and effort that would be lost if your hard disk were damaged or erased.

This chapter explains how to protect your computer files from a variety of menaces such as static electricity, excessive heat, and erratic electrical power. Most important, in this chapter you learn how to use several DOS commands, including XCOPY, and the two hard-disk backup programs, MSBACKUP and Microsoft Backup for Windows, to back up the files on your system and then to restore these files in the event of damage to or erasure of your disk.

NOTE If you have never learned how to back up your disk files or produce duplicates, now is time to learn. If you use the ideas covered in this chapter, you can avoid the sinking feeling that comes from losing a significant amount of hard work to a hard disk crash, accidental disk format, or accidental file erasure.

Key Terms Used in This Chapter

Surge protector	A protective device inserted between a power outlet and a computer's power plug. By acting as a circuit breaker, a surge protector helps block power surges that can damage the computer's circuits.
Static electricity	A high-voltage charge that builds on objects (including people) and that can be discharged when another object is touched. Static electricity discharges can damage electronic circuits.
Ground	An electrical path directly to earth. Grounds can dissipate static discharges safely. A PC chassis normally is grounded, but this grounding is not always adequate to stop a static discharge.
Voltage regulator	An electrical device that keeps voltage fluctuations from reaching an electrical device. Regulators usually don't stop all power surges.
Full backup	A special series of disks containing all the data stored on a hard disk, along with information about the previous location of the data files.
Intermediate backup	A series of disks containing copies of all files modified since the most recent full backup.

Avoiding Data Loss

Today's personal computers are reliable and economical data processing machines. Like all machines, however, computers are subject to failures and operator errors. Table 13.1 lists some hardware and software problems discussed in this chapter and suggests ways to prevent these problems.

Table 13.1 Hardware and Software Problems and Prevention Techniques

Problem	Prevention
Static electricity	Use antistatic liquid or floor mat; place a "touch pad" on desk.
Overheating	Clean clogged air vents; remove objects that block vents; use air-conditioned room during the summer.
Damaged disks	Don't leave disks to be warped by the sun; use protective covers; avoid spilling liquids on disks; store disks in a safe place; avoid magnetic fields from appliances (televisions, microwave ovens, and so on); do not use a ball-point pen to write on flexible disks.
Data loss	Keep current backups of your hard disk and any diskettes that contain important data; scan for viruses; use delete-tracking.
Viruses	Always scan a questionable disk for viruses before copying any files to your hard disk.

Always be cautious about your computer's environment. If your power fluctuates and lights flicker, you may need to purchase a *line voltage regulator* from your computer dealer.

Your computer may perform erratically when it is too hot. Because circuits are not reliable when they overheat, you may get jumbled data. Make sure that your computer has room to breathe by cleaning the air vents.

You generate static electricity on your body when humidity is low, when you wear synthetic fabrics, or when you walk on carpet. Just by touching your keyboard while carrying a static charge, you can send an electrical shudder through your computer, causing a data jumble or circuit failure. Fortunately, you can avoid static problems by touching your grounded system cabinet before touching the keyboard. If static electricity is a serious problem for you, ask your dealer about antistatic products, which are inexpensive and easy to use.

Preventing Software Failures

A minority of software packages have flawed instructions called *bugs*. Software bugs are usually minor and rarely cause greater problems than keyboard lockups or jumbled displays. The potential does exist for a software bug to cause your disk drive to operate in an erratic way, however. Fortunately, most companies test and debug their software before marketing the packages. Performing a backup of your disks is your best insurance against damage caused by bugs.

Software *viruses* are purposely created software bugs with the potential to cause a great deal of damage to your files. Most viruses are additional program codes hidden in a COM file like COMMAND.COM. A virus most often does its damage by altering the disk's file allocation table (FAT) and marking clusters as bad or unavailable. A virus also has the capability of initiating a FORMAT or destroying a disk partition table.

Viruses "multiply" through the exchange of software between users. If you load an infected COM file onto your PC, the virus can quickly infect your COMMAND.COM file. Unfortunately, you can back up an infected file, and when the file is restored, the virus continues to do its dirty work. Your best defense against a virus is to install only reputable software from a source who can attest to the program's operation. If you are hit by a virus, you may have to fall back to your write-protected master DOS disks and rebuild your system from the ground up. DOS 6.0, however, includes a pair of programs—Microsoft Anti-Virus (MSAV.EXE) and Windows Anti-Virus (MWAV.EXE)—that can monitor your system constantly to detect viruses. If necessary, these programs can also remove any viruses they find. For details on these programs, see Chapter 18, "Getting the Most from Your Hard Drive."

Preventing Mistakes

As you gain skill, you may use DOS commands that can result in the accidental loss of files. When you use commands such as COPY, ERASE, and FORMAT, you may inadvertently remove important data. For this reason, study what you typed before you press Enter. It is easy to develop a typing rhythm that carries you straight through confirmation prompts into the clutches of disaster.

Although you can use Ctrl-C, Ctrl-Break and, if necessary, Ctrl-Alt-Del to abandon commands, you are stopping what is already underway, and these "panic buttons" may not contain the damage. Because you are likely to make mistakes at one time or another, always have a backup copy of all important data.

DOS versions since 5.0 are more forgiving than previous versions of DOS. These DOS versions include a safe, reversible FORMAT command, as well as an UNDELETE command that you can use to recover from an accidental DEL or ERASE command.

For Related Information

▶▶ "Understanding How Viruses Spread," p. 725.

▶▶ "Guarding against Infection," p. 732.

FROM HERE...

Combining Copying and Directory Management with XCOPY

The external command XCOPY is an enhanced version of COPY that, among other capabilities, can create directories on the destination disk. XCOPY is therefore handy for copying a portion of your directory tree to another disk. XCOPY is a sophisticated copy command with many uses.

The XCOPY command addresses the needs of three types of computer users: those who use more than one computer, those who have hard disks, and those who want more control over which files are copied than is provided by the standard COPY command. Almost all PC users fit into at least one of these categories, so XCOPY is an important command to know and use.

XCOPY syntax is similar to COPY syntax, but the switches are more complex. XCOPY syntax is as follows:

> **XCOPY** *ds:paths\filenames.exts dd:pathd\filenamed.extd*
> */V/P/W/S/E/A/M/D:date*

In this command, *s* means source. The *source files* are the files to be copied. If you omit the source disk drive name (*ds:*), the current disk drive is used. If you omit the source path name (*paths*), the current directory on the drive is used. You can use wild cards in the source file name (*filenames.exts*). If you omit the file name, XCOPY assumes that you want to specify the wild card *.* and copies all files in the given path. You must include at least one source parameter.

With XCOPY, *d* means destination. If you do not specify a destination disk (*dd:*) or path name (*pathd*), XCOPY uses the current disk directory. If you omit the destination file name (*filenamed.extd*), files on the source disk retain their names on the destination disk.

In an XCOPY operation, DOS may not always recognize whether a particular parameter refers to a file or to a directory. When ambiguity arises, XCOPY asks whether the destination is a file name or path name.

Consider the following command, for example:

        XCOPY C:\WORDS*.* A:\WORDS

If no directory named WORDS exists on the destination disk, DOS cannot determine whether you intend to create a file or a directory named WORDS on the A disk.

XCOPY displays the following message:

```
Does WORDS specify a file name
or directory name on the target
(F = file, D = directory)?
```

Press F when the destination (target) is a file name, or D when the destination is a directory. Unlike COPY, XCOPY creates directories on the destination disk as needed.

NOTE If you append a backslash to the name of the target directory, XCOPY automatically assumes that the target is a directory, not a file. In the previous example, if you use the command XCOPY C:\WORDS*.* A:\WORDS\, you will not have to specify that the target is a directory. XCOPY creates the \WORDS directory if it does not exist.

Understanding the Operation of XCOPY

XCOPY is best described as a hybrid between COPY and BACKUP/RE-STORE. XCOPY and COPY duplicate files between directories and disks. Unlike COPY, however, XCOPY does not copy files to a nondisk device, such as the printer (PRN) or the console (CON). Like BACKUP and RE-STORE, XCOPY can copy files selectively and traverse the directory tree to copy files from more than one directory. XCOPY also can make a destination directory when one does not exist. This directory capability makes XCOPY useful for duplicating a directory branch onto another disk.

Like COPY but unlike BACKUP, XCOPY copies files that are directly usable. (You cannot use files processed by BACKUP until you have processed them with RESTORE.)

When using the XCOPY command, consider the following guidelines:

- XCOPY cannot copy hidden source files.

- XCOPY does not overwrite read-only destination files.

- If a file parameter is omitted in the XCOPY syntax, XCOPY assumes the *.* full wild-card pattern as the file parameter.

- If you include the /D switch, the date parameter must be entered in the format of the system's DATE command or in the format indicated by the latest COUNTRY command.

- The /V switch performs the same read-after-write checking as the SET VERIFY ON global verify flag.

- To use XCOPY to copy empty source subdirectories, you must specify both the /S and /E switches.

Understanding XCOPY's Switches

XCOPY has eight switches, which are described in this section. The Command Reference section gives a complete table of XCOPY's switches.

/V is the familiar verify switch. XCOPY verifies that it has copied the files correctly.

/W causes XCOPY to display the message Press any key to begin copying file(s) and waits for you to insert the source disk. This switch is particularly useful in batch files.

/P is the prompt switch. XCOPY displays the name of the file to be copied and asks whether the file should be copied. Press Y to copy the file or N to skip it. When you answer Y, XCOPY immediately copies the file.

The */S* and */E* switches affect the way XCOPY handles additional subdirectories. These two switches tap the full power of XCOPY. COPY limits itself to handling the files from one directory; XCOPY starts with the named or current directory (source) and can process the files in all additional subdirectories of the source directory, all lower subdirectories of these subdirectories, and so on. XCOPY traverses the subdirectory tree and can copy complete directory branches from one disk to another.

The /S switch copies subdirectories and the directory specified in the command. The /S switch instructs XCOPY to copy all designated files from the current and subsequent subdirectories to a parallel set of subdirectories on the destination disk drive. Assume, for example, that you want to copy to the disk in drive A all the files in the C:\WORDS directory and all files in the two subdirectories of C:\WORDS: \WORDS\LETTERS and \WORDS\CONTRACTS. You want XCOPY to create on the destination disk any directories necessary to hold the files from the source disks. To perform this operation, you issue the following command:

    XCOPY C:\WORDS*.* A: /S

The command executes in the following sequence:

1. XCOPY copies all files in \WORDS to the current directory on drive A.

2. If the subdirectory \LETTERS doesn't already exist on drive A, XCOPY creates \LETTERS. XCOPY then copies all files from WORDS\LETTERS to the subdirectory \LETTERS on drive A.

3. Similarly, XCOPY creates \CONTRACTS, if necessary, on the destination disk and copies all files from the subdirectory WORDS\CONTRACTS to the corresponding subdirectory on drive A.

In essence, XCOPY lifts a copy of the directory tree starting at the source directory and transplants the copy to drive A.

 NOTE   XCOPY does not place the copied files from the subdirectories into a single directory. XCOPY places files from one subdirectory into a parallel subdirectory. If the subdirectory does not exist on the destination, XCOPY creates the subdirectory.

The /E switch affects the operation of the /S switch. If XCOPY encounters an empty subdirectory on the source drive, XCOPY /S skips the empty subdirectory. If you give the /S and /E switches together, XCOPY also creates empty subdirectories on the destination drive. The /E switch has no effect without the /S switch.

The switches */M*, */A*, and */D:date* add extra filters to the *filenames.exts* parameter. The /M and /A switches tell XCOPY to copy only files that have been modified since the last archival procedure that turned off the archive attribute. In Chapter 8, "Understanding and Managing Directories," you learned about the archive attribute stored in the directory with each file name. When you create or change a file, this attribute is turned on. XCOPY, when used with the /A switch, copies only files that have their archive attribute set. The command does not affect the archive bit. When you use the /M switch, XCOPY copies only files with the archive bit set and then turns off the archive attribute for each archived file.

NOTE The BACKUP command can select files based on the archive attribute. If XCOPY has cleared this flag, however, BACKUP does not process the file. If you use the commands XCOPY /M and BACKUP /M (the switches have identical meaning for the two commands), the backup you make using BACKUP may not be complete.

The */D:date* switch selects files based on their *directory date*, the date of the file's creation or modification. XCOPY copies files created or modified on or after the date specified.

Using XCOPY Effectively

Using XCOPY, you can control by date or archive attribute the files copied; you can copy complete subdirectory trees; and you can confirm which files to copy. The command has several ideal uses: copying files selectively between disks or directories, performing a quick hard disk backup (backing up only a few critical files in several subdirectories), and keeping the directories of two or more computers synchronized.

With COPY, your control is limited. COPY duplicates all files that match the given name—an all-or-nothing approach. If you use the /P switch with XCOPY, however, DOS asks whether you want to copy each file.

XCOPY is practical to use if you want to make backup copies of less than a disk full of files from several directories. Instead of BACKUP, you may prefer to use the command XCOPY /A to select files that have changed since the last backup.

Keep the following points in mind when you use XCOPY to back up a disk:

■ If you suspect that the files cannot fit on one disk, be sure to use the /M switch. As XCOPY copies each file, the command resets the file's archive attribute bit. When the destination disk fills, XCOPY stops. Change disks and restart the XCOPY command, again using the /M switch. XCOPY copies the files whose archive bit has not yet been reset.

■ XCOPY cannot break a large source file between destination disks. If you need to back up a file that doesn't fit on a single floppy disk, you must use BACKUP.

A favorite use of XCOPY is to synchronize the contents of the hard disks of two computers. Many people have one computer at work and another at home. If both computers have hard disks, keeping the copies of programs and data files current is a major task. Which files did you change today? Which machine has the more current version?

When you want to keep separate hard disks synchronized, you may find XCOPY's /A, /D:*date*, and /S switches especially useful. The /S switch forces XCOPY to traverse your disk's directory structure, playing a hunting game for source files. Whether you use /A or /D depends on how often you copy files between the machines. If you copy files between the machines frequently, you may prefer the /A switch. If you let many days pass between synchronizing your computers' contents, you may find that the /D switch works better. Use the /D switch if you have run BACKUP on the source machine since you last used XCOPY. BACKUP resets the archive attribute so that XCOPY's /A switch does not catch all files changed between XCOPY backups.

Duplicating a Directory Branch

For this example, assume that your hard disk has a subdirectory named \WPFILES that contains a few word processing files. \WPFILES also has two subdirectories. The first, \WPFILES\MEMOS, contains your current memos. The second, \WPFILES\DOCS, contains your document files. You want to keep a current set of the files in these three directories stored on a floppy disk. To copy all the files in this directory branch to the floppy, issue the following command:

XCOPY C:\WPFILES A:\WPFILES\ /S

XCOPY immediately begins to read the source directories. DOS displays the following messages:

```
Reading source file(s)...
C:\WPFILES\LET9_1.WP
C:\WPFILES\LET9_2.WP
C:\WPFILES\LET9_3.WP
C:\WPFILES\LET9_4.WP
C:\WPFILES\LET9_5.WP
C:\WPFILES\DOCS\SCHEDULE.DOC
C:\WPFILES\MEMOS\SALES.MEM
    7 File(s) copied
```

Because you included the /S switch, XCOPY copied the files in C:\WPFILES, C:\WPFILES\MEMOS, and C:\WPFILES\DOCS. The A:\WPFILES path parameter causes XCOPY to ask whether the name specifies a directory or a file. \WPFILES conceivably could be a user file in the root directory. The full path name of each file is echoed to the screen as the file is copied to drive A. When the command finishes, the \WPFILES directory branch has been copied to drive A.

As another example, assume that your PC experiences a hardware failure and needs to go to the shop for repairs. You want to use your floppy disk that contains the \WPFILES directory branch to place the \WPFILES directory branch on a second computer's hard disk. Enter the following command:

XCOPY A: C: /S

XCOPY reverses the copy process described in the preceding paragraphs by copying all the files on drive A to corresponding subdirectory locations on drive C.

Comparing Files with FC

The external command FC (for *file comparison*) compares two files or two sets of files to find differences in the files. Any differences are reported on-screen. When a copied file is extremely important, you can use FC to compare the file with the original. If differences are found, you know that a problem may exist with the copy. (Normally, DOS detects data integrity errors while reading and writing files. But if you want to be sure that two files are the same, you can ease your mind by using FC.)

PC DOS Versions 1.0 through 5.0 and MS-DOS Versions 3.3 through 5.0 include a simpler file-comparison command, COMP. This command, however, is less versatile than FC, provides less information, has fewer options, and cannot compare files of different lengths.

The FC command has two general syntax forms. One form uses the /B switch for a forced binary comparison; the other form uses the remaining switches in an ASCII comparison. The two forms of syntax are as follows:

FC */B d1:path1***filename1.ext1** *d2:path2***filename2.ext2**

or

FC */A/C/L/LBn/N/nnnn/T/W d1:path1***filename1.ext1**
*d2:\path2***filename2.ext2**

 Although placing all switches before other parameters in an FC command is conventional (and required in some earlier versions of DOS), this practice is not necessary in DOS 6.0.

d1: is an optional parameter that specifies the drive containing the first file to be compared. If the first drive parameter is omitted, FC assumes the default drive.

path1 is the path of the directory containing the first file. If the first file's path is omitted, FC assumes the default directory.

filename1.ext1 is the file name of the first file. This parameter is mandatory. If you use wild-card characters in this parameter, all files matching this parameter are compared with the second file.

d2: is the drive containing the second file to be compared. If the second drive parameter is omitted, FC assumes the default drive.

path2 is the path of the directory containing the second file. If the second file path is omitted, the command assumes the default directory.

filename2.ext2 is the file name of the second file. This parameter is mandatory. If you use wild-card characters in this parameter, the first file is compared with all files matching it.

> **NOTE** If you use wild-card characters in both the first and second file names, FC compares the files as sets. That is, only those files whose names match in other respects are compared.
>
> If you use the command FC *.WK1 *.BAK, for example, FC compares each worksheet file having the extension WK1 with the worksheet file having the same base name and the extension BAK. FC does not compare every worksheet file with every backup file.

/A instructs FC to abbreviate its output (DOS 3.2 and later versions), displaying only the first and last lines of each set of differences separated by an ellipsis (...).

/B performs a binary (byte-by-byte) comparison, showing the hexadecimal address and value of every differing byte.

/C causes FC to ignore the case of alphabetic characters when making comparisons.

/L instructs FC to compare the files in ASCII mode, even when the files have EXE, COM, SYS, OBJ, LIB, or BIN extensions (DOS 3.2 and later versions).

/LBn sets the number of lines in FC's buffer to n. The default number is 100 (DOS 3.2 and later versions). If the number of consecutive non-matching lines exceeds the buffer size, FC aborts the compare operation.

/N instructs FC to include the line numbers of lines reported in the output (DOS 3.2 and later versions).

/nnnn establishes the number of lines that must match after a difference in order to resynchronize FC.

/T instructs FC to view tab characters as literal characters rather than tab-expanded spaces (DOS 3.2 and later versions).

/W instructs FC to compress *white space*—tabs, empty lines, and spaces—into a single space for purposes of file comparison.

Understanding the Operation of FC

FC works in two modes: ASCII and binary. FC defaults to ASCII mode comparison when the files to be compared do not have EXE, COM, SYS, OBJ, LIB, or BIN extensions.

In ASCII mode, FC compares two files on a line-by-line basis. Lines from both files are held in a line buffer. FC uses the lines in the buffer to compare the first file to the second.

If FC detects a difference, FC displays the first file name followed by the last matching line and the mismatching line(s) from the first file. FC then displays the next line to match in both files.

After displaying mismatch information about file 1, FC repeats the same sequence for file 2. The file 2 name is displayed first, followed by the last matching line and the mismatching lines from file 2, ending on the next line that matches in both files, thus synchronizing the two files.

FC can help you determine whether the contents of two files are different by showing you the extent and location of any mismatch FC finds. You can use this output as an alternative to a side-by-side comparison of the file contents.

In binary mode, FC compares two files byte for byte. At the first difference, the byte offset position in the first file is reported along with the value of the two files' bytes at the position. The offset and byte values are reported in hexadecimal (base 16) form. This form of FC is essentially equivalent to the older COMP command.

T I P   If you are comparing two files that are not the same, you can quickly stop the reporting of differences by pressing Ctrl-C or Ctrl-Break.

In binary mode, FC does not attempt to resynchronize the two files by finding an adjusted point of byte agreement. If one file has an additional byte at one place in the file, FC reports the additional byte and all subsequent bytes of the file as mismatches.

If one file is longer than its comparison file, the binary mode compares as many bytes as are present and then reports that one file is longer. When a binary file comparison results in a long listing of differences, you may want to stop the FC operation by pressing Ctrl-C.

Only one switch is available in the binary mode. The /B switch causes the comparison to be binary even if file extensions indicate that the files are not binary. You use the /B switch to compare two text files in binary mode. You may find situations in which you would rather have the binary-mode output format of FC than the ASCII mode format. Binary mode format reports differences as pairs of hexadecimal values. You then can see the values of characters, such as Ctrl-G (bell), that do not produce printed output.

When you use FC, keep in mind that the default number of lines that must match in an ASCII comparison after a difference has ended is two. The files then are considered resynchronized. The number of "must match" lines can be changed using the /nnnn switch by setting nnnn to the desired value.

Using FC To Compare a Copied File to Its Original

Suppose that you are copying the ANSI.SYS file from your hard disk to a floppy disk to use for an important demonstration on another PC. When the copy completes, you set the disk on the edge of your desk and go to the break room to get coffee. When you return, you notice that the disk has fallen off your desk and landed against the small transformer that runs your cassette recorder. You are worried that the magnetic field from the transformer has damaged ANSI.SYS. To verify that the copied ANSI.SYS is good, you compare it to the original by using the following command:

    FC A:ANSI.SYS C:\DOS\DRIVERS\ANSI.SYS

After a few seconds, FC reports FC: No differences encountered. The copy of ANSI.SYS seems to be good.

Comparing Two Text Files

The following example demonstrates the operation of FC. Suppose that two similar text files, ORIGINAL.TXT and ANOTHER.TXT, are located in the default directory of the current drive. ORIGINAL.TXT contains the following:

```
This is the first line.
This is the second line.
1
2
3
4
5
This is the last line.
```

ANOTHER.TXT contains the following:

```
This is the first line.
This is not the third line.
1
2
3
4
5
6
7
8
9
This is the last line.
```

Note that ANOTHER.TXT has four more lines than ORIGINAL.TXT, and that the second lines of the files contain differing text. These simple files illustrate how FC reports differences. You can use the principles illustrated here to understand the result of comparisons of more complex files.

If, for example, you want to compare the two files that are in the same directory, you issue the following command:

FC ORIGINAL.TXT ANOTHER.TXT

FC reports the following:

```
Comparing files ORIGINAL.TXT and ANOTHER.TXT
***** ORIGINAL.TXT
This is the first line.
This is the second line.
1
***** ANOTHER.TXT
This is the first line.
This is not the third line.
1
*****


***** ORIGINAL.TXT
5
This is the last line.
***** ANOTHER.TXT
5
```

```
6
7
8
9
This is the last line.
*****
```

FC displays the lines before and after the mismatched line, if any exist.
FC also finds mismatches that are not on equivalent lines so that it can
match text even when one file contains material not found in the other.
The second report concerning ANOTHER.TXT shows all the lines between the one containing the numeral 5 and the one containing the text
This is the last line. Only these two matching lines appear in the
report concerning ORIGINAL.TXT.

Understanding Microsoft Backup

Compared to floppy disks, hard disks have many advantages. Hard
disks are faster, have larger storage capacities and root directories,
support multiple partitions, and never require a disk swap. A file on a
hard disk can be many times the size of a file on a floppy disk. Commands like COPY and XCOPY enable you to keep a few duplicate files
on a floppy for backup purposes, but DOS provides a pair of special
programs specifically designed for the big jobs: Microsoft Backup
(MSBACKUP.EXE) and Microsoft Backup for Windows
(MWBACKUP.EXE).

By default, the Setup program installed one of these programs when
you installed DOS 6.0 on your computer. If your system has Microsoft
Windows, however, you have the option of installing both programs.
As you might expect, Microsoft Backup for Windows can be used
only within Microsoft Windows. The DOS version, however, can be
used either at a command prompt or in a DOS window within Microsoft
Windows.

Both backup programs are full-featured programs that enable you to
perform the following tasks:

- Copy files from a hard disk to another disk, usually a floppy disk.

- Restore the copied files to their original location or to another
  disk of your choice.

■ Compare files on your backup copies with the originals to ensure their validity.

Both programs have several types of menus and many options to enable you to copy only those files you want to copy and to ease the process of making backup copies on a regular basis. Because the programs are rather similar, this chapter focuses on MSBACKUP. Relevant differences in the Windows version are noted.

> **NOTE** If you do not now use Microsoft Windows but plan to add that operating environment to your system at a later time, you must reinstall DOS 6.0 to install the Windows version of the backup program.

> **NOTE** The files copied to the backup disk do not have the same format as files on your hard disk or files copied with the COPY or XCOPY commands. The directories of disks written by the backup programs show only one file per disk, taking all the available space, as in the following example:
>
> ```
> Volume in drive A is DEFAULT FUL
> Directory of A:\
> EE21123A 001    1457664 11-23-92    4:11p
>         1 file(s)     1457664 bytes
>                           0 bytes free
> ```
>
> These files may actually contain the data that originally appeared in many files on your hard disk, along with information about their original location. Before you can use these files, they must be restored, using the Restore portion of one of the Backup programs.

Both versions of the Backup program can read backup disks created by the other version. You need not worry, therefore, about losing access to backup data if you switch from one version of the program to the other.

Backup disks contain not only special copies of files but also directory information about each file. This information enables the programs to copy the backup files to their original locations in the directory tree.

The Backup programs can spread a single file across more than one floppy disk. This capability enables you to copy to multiple disks files that are too big to fit on a single disk. If a backup operation uses more than one disk, each disk is linked internally to the next disk to form a backup set.

During the backup operation, each disk in a set is filled to capacity before the next disk is requested. If a file is only partially written to a backup disk when the disk reaches full capacity, the remainder of the file is written to the next disk in the set.

Like XCOPY, the Backup programs can copy files selectively. You can specify a directory or branch of directories, a file name, a file name patterned after a wild card, and additional selection switches. By taking advantage of the programs' selectivity, you can maintain more than one set of backup disks, each set having its own logical purpose.

You can, for example, keep one backup set that contains every file on your hard disk. This set is insurance against data loss resulting from a hard disk failure or crash. You may have another backup set that contains only the files that have their archive attributes turned on. With an archive set for each day of the week, you can recover a week's worth of data between complete backups. When your hard disk fails, you replace it, restore using the full set, and then update with the daily sets.

You can lose the data on your hard disk in many ways. If you have not replicated the data, you may be forced to re-create the data and suffer the consequences of permanent data loss if you cannot re-create data. If you have never experienced a disk-related failure, don't be overconfident. With 10 million hard disk users working on their computers for an average of 8 hours per day, over 250,000 people will experience a hard-disk-related failure this year. You could be next.

Configuring the Backup Programs

Before you can create backups of your data with either backup program, you must first test the program for compatibility. If you have not previously run the program, the test is performed automatically the first time you do so. A special program runs through some of the backup program's menus, making selections as though you were running the program yourself. This program tests your floppy disk drives and the speed of your processor chip and hard disk. Periodically, dialog boxes appear and ask you for permission to continue. You respond by selecting "buttons" similar to those you have seen in dialog boxes in the DOS Shell and the DOS Editor. You select options in the same way: by pressing the highlighted letter, by moving the highlight to the desired button with the Tab or Shift-Tab key, or by clicking the desired button with the mouse. In the DOS version, a highlighted button has pointers at its left and right ends and is a different color from the other buttons. In the Windows version, the highlighted button is simply a different color.

The program then displays a dialog box that gives you the option of choosing the drive and medium you want to use for the compatibility test (see fig. 13.1). To select a different capacity disk, move the high-light to the appropriate entry with the cursor keys; then press the space bar. Choose OK when the setting conforms to your choice. (If you have only one low-density drive, this option is not available.) If you have two drives of the same type, the program uses both, alternating backup disks between the drives.

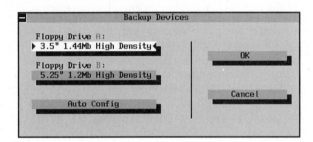

Fig. 13.1

Choosing a disk drive and capacity for backups.

The program then selects a group of files to back up and completes a backup. This procedure requires two floppy disks of the type you selected. Make sure these do not contain any data you want to save because the disks will be erased completely. The program instructs you when to insert the disks. When the backup is complete, the program compares the data on the backup disks with the source files to verify that the backup is accurate.

NOTE Even after you configure one of the backup programs, you still have to configure the second program. However, the backup files that either program creates can be read by the other program.

Your computer will probably pass the compatibility test. If it does, you can proceed to make backups with the program. However, the program may display the following warning message:

```
DMA Buffer size too small. You will not be able to per-
form a backup, compare, or restore until the DMA buffer
size is increased. See 'Troubleshooting' in your MS-DOS
manual.
```

If this message appears, and you have an 80386 or 80486 microprocessor, use the DEVICE command to load the memory manager EMM386.EXE in your CONFIG.SYS file. Add the parameter D=64 to the command, as shown in the following:

> DEVICE:C:\DOS\EMM386.EXE D=64

If you have an 8088 or 80286 microprocessor and do not use an expanded memory manager, you will not encounter this problem, but the program may still fail the compatibility test. (See Chapter 17, "Configuring Your Computer," for details on EMM386.EXE and the CONFIG.SYS file.)

> Most commercial expanded memory managers include a parameter that you can use to enlarge the DMA buffer. If you use an expanded memory manager other than EMM386.EXE, consult the documentation for details.

T I P

When you finish running the tests—and assuming that you selected the default buttons—the programs save all the settings on every menu to a file called DEFAULT.SET. Continue to select the default buttons until you return to a DOS prompt or the Windows Program Manager.

Understanding Microsoft Backup Functions

Both the DOS and Windows backup programs have five basic functions: Backup, Compare, Restore, Configure, and Quit. In the DOS version, the dialog box shown in figure 13.2 contains buttons representing each function. In theWindows version, the functions are represented by a series of icons near the top of the screen (see fig. 13.3).

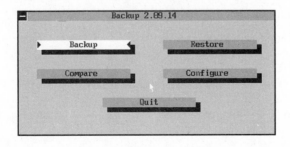

Fig. 13.2

The opening DOS Backup dialog box.

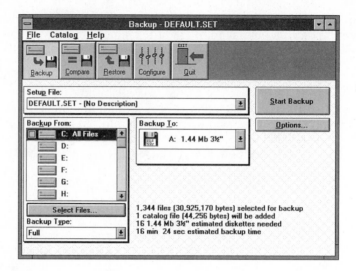

Fig. 13.3

The opening
Backup for
Windows screen.

The functions are listed in the following:

■ _B_ackup duplicates all or selected files from your hard disk on
floppy disks.

■ _C_ompare compares the files in a set of backup floppy disks to
their source on the hard disk to verify that the copies are
accurate.

■ _R_estore copies the files on your backup floppy disks to the hard
disk, in either their original location or a new location, or to another floppy disk in usable form.

■ _Configure_ enables you to select default settings for the program. In
the DOS version, the following choices are available:

Change the number of rows of text shown on the screen.

Switch to a display using normal text characters instead of the
graphics characters shown in the illustrations here.

Adjust the way your mouse behaves.

Change the screen colors.

■ _Quit_ enables you to exit the program.

The Configure options, which appear in figure 13.4, are similar to the
options found on DOSSHELL's _O_ptions menu. You can also select a
different drive or disk capacity for your backups or send your backups
to a _DOS path_—that is, a directory on your hard disk.

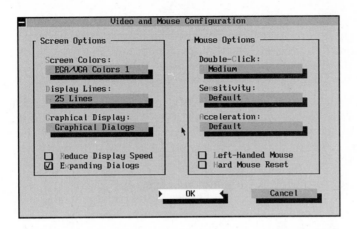

Fig. 13.4

Changing DOS
Backup's display
options.

Both programs have pull-down menus at the top of the screen. The File
menu enables you to load and save *setup files*—files that contain all the
settings you will use for a particular type of backup or restore. The File
menu also enables you to print the contents of *catalog files* containing a
list of the files that have been backed up. Both backup programs have a
Help menu as well, which explains techniques and procedures. The
Windows Backup program has a third menu, a Catalog menu, which
enables you to select catalog files for restore or comparison. This menu
does not appear in the DOS version; however, you can select catalog
files after you have chosen to perform a restore or compare.

Setting Up a Backup Policy

Every PC user should develop a *backup policy,* a defined method of
backing up data on a regular basis. Your policy may include making and
keeping more than one backup set. The backup programs allow for
three basic types of backups:

■ A *full* backup copies every file on your hard disk. Keep at least two
full backup sets so that you can re-create your system if your hard
disk is destroyed; you need not make both copies at the same
time.

■ An *incremental* backup copies only new files or files that have
been changed since the last full backup was performed. You use
an additional set of disks for the incremental backup set. You may
complete several backups between full backups, depending on
how many files you work with and how large the files are. Each
time you perform an incremental backup, you add any files that
are new or modified since the previous new or incremental
backup.

■ A *differential* backup, like a partial backup, copies only files that are new or have been changed since the last full backup and requires a separate set of disks from the full backups. With a differential backup, however, you reuse the same floppy disks for each backup until you perform your next full backup.

The distinction between incremental and differential backups lies with the archive bit. When you perform a full backup, the backup programs turn off the archive attribute for any file that is backed up. When you modify or create a file, DOS turns on the new or modified file's archive attribute.

When you perform an incremental backup, the backup programs turn off the archive bit so that each incremental backup includes only files created or modified since the previous incremental backup. When you perform a differential backup, however, the backup programs *do not* turn off the archive bit. Therefore, every file modified or created since the previous full backup is copied. The differential backup is appropriate if you work with the same few files daily and do not need several generations of each file.

T I P   You can use the ATTRIB command to determine the current archive attribute setting for each file on your system. If you want to make sure that a particular file is backed up by an incremental backup procedure, use ATTRIB to turn on the archive attribute.

You can perform a full backup weekly, monthly, or at some other interval. The intervening (incremental or differential) backup intervals reduce your risk of data loss between full backups. The time between performing intermediate backups depends on the amount of risk to your data you are willing to take. In a business setting, you may reduce your risk to an acceptable level by performing an intermediate backup every other day. If your PC activity level is high, you may need to perform an incremental backup daily. If your PC activity is minimal, a differential backup once every two weeks may be frequent enough to reduce your risk to a manageable level.

In addition to these three types of backups, you can create backup sets for special purposes. You can select files to include in, or exclude from, the backup. You can select these files individually, by directory, according to a wild-card pattern, by date, or by attribute, and save the selections in a setup file. You learn how to select files for backups later in this chapter.

Issuing the MSBACKUP Command

The syntax for the MSBACKUP command is shown in the following:

MSBACKUP *filename* */Ttype* */video*

All of the switches are optional.

filename is the name of a setup file. If you created setup files for different types of backups, you can load one automatically by specifying the file on the command line. If you do not specify a setup file, MSBACKUP loads DEFAULT.SET and applies the settings to the drive specified in that file. If no drive is specified, MSBACKUP applies the settings to the default drive.

/Ttype specifies the type of backup. Specify the type with a single letter: */TF* for full, */TD* for differential, */TI* for incremental. The */Ttype* switch overrides the backup type specified in the setup file.

/video specifies the type of video display to be used. Use */LCD* for laptops or other LCD screens, */BW* for black and white, or */MDA* for monochrome displays, including those attached to Hercules-type adapters. Do not specify a video type for a color display.

For Related Information

▶▶ "Understanding CONFIG.SYS," p. 630.

FROM HERE...

Using Microsoft Backup

DOS provides a pair of special programs specifically designed for the big jobs: Microsoft Backup (MSBACKUP.EXE) and Microsoft Backup for Windows (MWBACKUP.EXE). Using Microsoft Backup, you can perform a full, incremental, or differential backup; compare backups files to the original files; select which files to backup; and restore backup files. The following sections explain how to perform these tasks.

Performing a Full Backup

In this section, you learn how to complete a full backup. First you learn how to use MSBACKUP and Microsoft Backup for Windows.

Performing a Full Backup with MSBACKUP

To perform a full backup in DOS, follow these steps:

1. Enter the following command:

   MSBACKUP

   The program scans drive C (unless you specified a different drive and saved the information in the default setup file, DEFAULT.SET), reads its directories, and then presents its opening screen.

2. Choose the Backup button. As shown in figure 13.5, the default setup file is loaded, and the selected backup type is Full. To perform a full backup, select the drive to back up from the Backup From list by double-clicking the appropriate drive, or by using the cursor-movement keys to move the highlight to the drive and pressing the space bar. You may choose more than one drive. Each time you choose a drive, Backup scans the drive and adds the selected files to the totals.

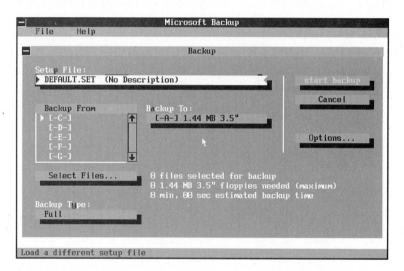

Fig. 13.5

The Backup screen.

As you select files to back up, the Backup screen shows you exactly what is required. A message similar to the following appears:

```
1,316 files (with catalog) selected for backup
24 1.44 MB 3.5" floppies needed (maximum)
15 min, 50 sec estimated backup time
```

Backup formats any target disks that are not formatted and compresses the data on the backup disks so that the capacity of the disks required may be less than the amount of data you need to back up.

NOTE The Windows Backup program indicates how many bytes of data are selected for backup and compresses the files so that fewer backup disks and less time are required to complete a backup.

3. Choose §tart Backup. The program begins by creating a backup catalog, listing the files to be backed up and the options chosen. The following message appears:

```
Insert diskette #1 in drive A:
```

As the backup progresses, a display similar to figure 13.6 appears.

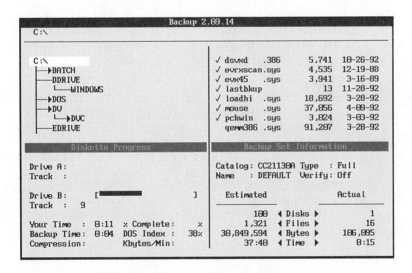

Fig. 13.6

Viewing the progress of a backup.

4. When the disk is full, the program prompts you to insert the next disk, and so on until the backup is complete.

As you remove each disk, label the disk "Full Backup #*nn*," where *nn* is the number of the disk in the series. Date the label also. When the backup is complete, the opening screen reappears.

Comparing the Backup to the Original Files

The first time you use a series of disks for a backup, compare the backups to the originals to verify that the disks are readable and accurate. You don't want to discover that your backup is unusable when you want to use it to recover a hard disk!

To perform a compare, follow these steps:

1. Choose Compare. A screen similar to the main Backup screen appears.

2. Choose Backup Set Catalog, and select the setup file you used for the backup. (If you haven't saved any setup files, this will be DEFAULT.SET.)

3. Select the drive or drives from the Backup From list; the number of files to compare changes from 0 to the number of files you backed up.

4. The program prompts you to insert each disk in turn, and a progress screen keeps you apprised of events.

At the end of the process, the dialog box indicating that no errors were found or the errors were corrected will probably appear. If this is not the case, you may want to discard the disks that contain the errors, replace them with new ones, and repeat the backup.

NOTE When you quit the program, you may be told that you have not saved your changes in the DEFAULT.SET setup file. In this case, you are asked if you want to save your changes or discard them. You may find it more helpful to save your settings explicitly to other files, which you can load either from within the program or from the command line. To save a backup setup, choose Save As from the File menu, and specify a file name and, optionally, a drive and directory where the setup file should be stored. The program automatically supplies the extension SET.

Performing a Full Backup in Windows

The procedure for performing a full backup in Windows is essentially the same as for DOS. The primary difference is the appearance of the screen. When the program loads, you see a message warning you not to use your disk drives while a backup, restore, or compare operation is in progress. You can prevent this message from reappearing each time you load the program by checking the Disable This Message box.

Otherwise, you proceed the same way you would in DOS. You can work in other programs while the backup is proceeding. A beep informs you when you must change disks.

Performing Intermediate Backups

Two types of intermediate backups are possible: incremental and differential. The difference depends on the status of the archive bit for selecting files. The incremental backup resets the archive bit after completion, and the differential backup does not.

Performing an Incremental Backup

To perform an incremental backup, choose Backup Type, and then choose Incremental from the dialog box. The backup proceeds as the full backup proceeds. Mark each disk in the set with the number and the date belonging to the increment for this backup. Store the completed set in a safe place, and avoid mixing the disks with disks from another backup set.

For example, you may perform an incremental backup every Tuesday and Friday and run a full backup every two weeks. Under this plan, you accumulate four incremental backup sets before you need to repeat the backup cycle and reuse the disks.

 No matter what type of backup you perform, the backup programs erase the target disks; therefore, each incremental backup must start on a new target disk. You cannot add backup files to disks that have been used as part of a set. By default, the backup programs warn you when the disk you are using is part of an existing backup set and give you the options of overwriting the disk, placing a different disk in the drive, or canceling the backup.

Performing a Differential Backup

If you use the differential backup method, you have just one intermediate backup set. The first time you do an intermediate backup in a backup cycle after a full backup, start with disk number 01 in your intermediate backup set. You may need more than one disk to complete the backup. Because the differential method does not reset the archive bit, the next intermediate backup set includes all the files included in the first intermediate backup set. Consequently, you can reuse the same backup disks for each intermediate backup set. To perform a differential backup, select Differential from the Backup Type dialog box, and proceed as you would with a full backup.

The differential method has the advantage of using fewer backup disks than the incremental method. On the other hand, you retain only one intermediate copy of your files that have been modified or created since the previous full backup. If you think you may need to examine successive iterations of a file, use the incremental method.

Special-Purpose Backups

You are not limited to full and intermediate backups of entire disks. You can specify any file or group of files to be included in a backup. When you complete a project, for example, you may want to back up all the files associated with that project in a special series for archival purposes. Or you may want to back up such files daily in a series of incremental or differential backups. Both backup programs provide the means to make any number of special-purpose backups.

To select a group of files for a special backup, first make sure that your backup type is Full. Otherwise, you cannot include files that do not have their archive bit set. Next, choose Select Files. The backup program scans the default (or selected) drive to see how many files and directories are on it and displays a screen similar to the DOS Shell, with drives at the top, directories at the left, and files at the right (see fig. 13.7). The status line displays the following message:

```
Select entire directories with right mouse button or Spacebar
```

You also see a series of buttons at the bottom of the screen. The Shell-like window and the buttons provide two different (although complementary) ways to select files for backing up. These procedures differ somewhat in the two backup programs.

Selecting Files Manually

When you choose Select Files and go to the selection screen, you see that the root directory of the current drive is highlighted. To select an entire directory, move the highlight to it; then double-click, press the space bar, or click once with the right mouse button. A pointer appears next to the root directory, and check marks appear next to the file names. To select only some of the files in a directory, select the files individually in the file window, or select the directory containing them and then deselect the files you want to exclude. To select or deselect a file, follow the same procedure you use to select a directory.

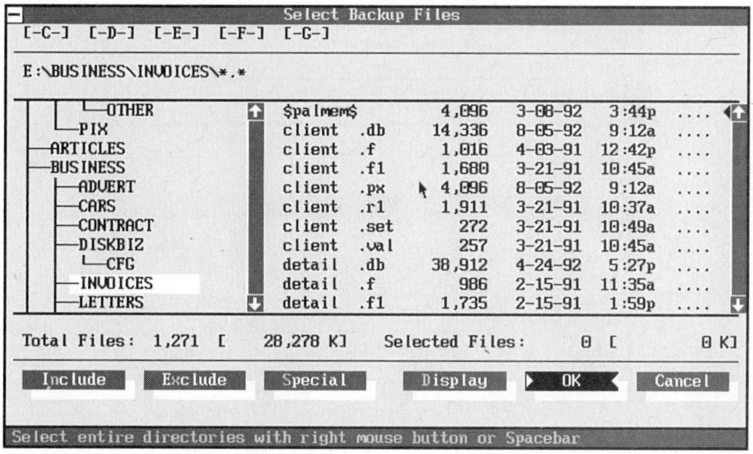

```
┌─┐                  Select Backup Files
│─│
 [-C-]  [-D-]  [-E-]  [-F-]  [-G-]

E:\BUSINESS\INVOICES\*.*
          └─OTHER        ↑  $palmem$      4,096    3-08-92    3:44p  ....  ⬆
           └─PIX            client  .db   14,336    8-05-92    9:12a  ....
    ─ARTICLES               client  .f     1,016    4-03-91   12:42p  ....
    ─BUSINESS               client  .f1    1,600    3-21-91   10:45a  ....
        ─ADVERT             client  .px ▶  4,096    8-05-92    9:12a  ....
        ─CARS               client  .r1    1,911    3-21-91   10:37a  ....
        ─CONTRACT           client  .set     272    3-21-91   10:49a  ....
        ─DISKBIZ            client  .val     257    3-21-91   10:45a  ....
          └─CFG             detail  .db   38,912    4-24-92    5:27p  ....
        ─INVOICES           detail  .f       986    2-15-91   11:35a  ....
        ─LETTERS        ↓   detail  .f1    1,735    2-15-91    1:59p  ....  ⬇

Total Files:  1,271  [     28,278 K]   Selected Files:      0 [        0 K]

  ┌ Include ┐   ┌ Exclude ┐   ┌ Special ┐   ┌ Display ┐  ▶  OK  ◀   ┌ Cancel ┐

Select entire directories with right mouse button or Spacebar
```

Fig. 13.7

Selecting files to back up.

When only some of the files in a directory are selected, the pointer next to the directory name changes to this symbol: >.

Press Alt-N to select the Include button, and then choose OK. This action selects all the files in all the subdirectories of the root directory— that is, the entire drive. Choose OK; the Backup screen reappears.

You select files and directories for backup in Microsoft Backup for Windows the same way as in MSBACKUP. The main difference is the manner in which selection information is displayed. A series of symbols lets you know in detail which directories have some or all files selected and whether some or all the selected files will be backed up. (Files may be selected and not backed up if you have chosen an intermediate type of backup, or if you have given the program explicit instructions not to back up some of the selected files, as described in the next section.) Choosing the Legend button displays the description of the symbols shown in figure 13.8.

If you want to reuse the selections you have made, be sure to save the selections in a setup file; if you don't do this, your selections are saved in the DEFAULT.SET file. To save your selections in a setup file, choose Save Setup As from the File menu. The Save Setup File dialog box appears, enabling you to give the backup set a name and a description (see fig. 13.9). You can optionally choose a different drive and directory for the setup file. (The default is C:\DOS.) Figure 13.9 shows the Windows version of the dialog box, but the DOS version is very similar.

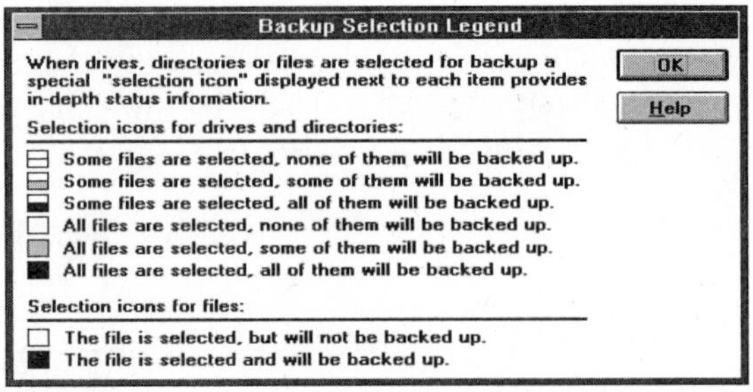

Fig. 13.8

Fig. 13.8

File selection
legend in
Microsoft Backup
for Windows.

Backup Selection Legend

When drives, directories or files are selected for backup a
special "selection icon" displayed next to each item provides
in-depth status information.

Selection icons for drives and directories:

- Some files are selected, none of them will be backed up.
- Some files are selected, some of them will be backed up.
- Some files are selected, all of them will be backed up.
- All files are selected, none of them will be backed up.
- All files are selected, some of them will be backed up.
- All files are selected, all of them will be backed up.

Selection icons for files:

- The file is selected, but will not be backed up.
- The file is selected and will be backed up.

OK   Help

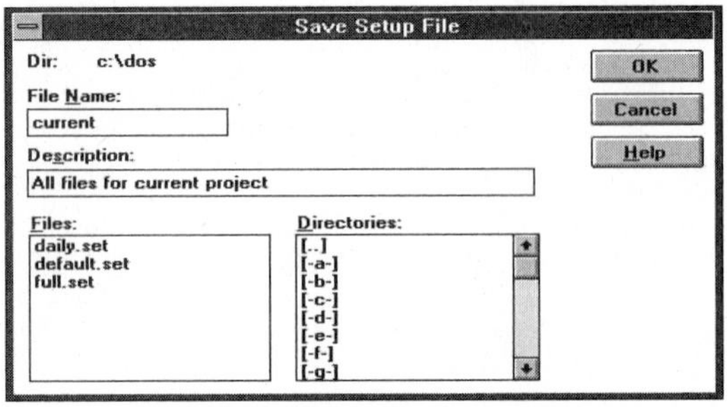

Fig. 13.9

The Save Setup
File dialog box.

Save Setup File

Dir: c:\dos

File Name:
current

Description:
All files for current project

Files:
daily.set
default.set
full.set

Directories:
[..]
[-a-]
[-b-]
[-c-]
[-d-]
[-e-]
[-f-]
[-g-]

OK   Cancel   Help

The next time you want to perform a backup of this type, load the setup
file. In the DOS version, you can load the setup file from the command
line or by choosing Open Setup from the File menu. In the Windows
version, you can load the setup file from within the program using the
same command. (The Open Setup File dialog box is similar to the Save
Setup File dialog box.) Under some mysterious circumstances, you
sometimes have to choose the appropriate drive from the Backup From
list to activate your selections; usually, however, you do not.

Choosing Files Using Selection Criteria

The buttons at the bottom of the file selection screen give you many
ways to select files to include in or exclude from a backup. These buttons also control other aspects of the program:

- *Include* (*Include* in Microsoft Backup for Windows) and *Exclude*
  enable you specify a path to include or exclude, and a file name.
  The file name may include a wild-card pattern. You can optionally
  check a box to include all subdirectories of the specified path.

  In addition to selecting files to include, you may want to *exclude*
  the following types of files, even from a full backup:

Configuration files that are regenerated and updated every time you use an applications program

Backup files created by applications programs (usually having the extension BAK, or some other extension including the characters B and K)

Temporary files (usually having the extension TMP or an extension including the $ sign)

■ *Special* enables you to exclude read-only, hidden, system, or copy-protected files, or select files by date.

■ *Display* enables you to determine whether the files appear in the file window sorted by name, extension, size, date, or attribute, and whether selected files appear before unselected files when the screen is refreshed.

The *Display* button in Microsoft Backup for Windows, in addition to the functions available in MSBACKUP, enables you determine which of the directory data appears in the file window. You can selectively exclude the file date, file time, file size, and file attributes. You can also rearrange the display so that the directory window appears above the file window instead of to its left.

Microsoft Backup for Windows includes two other buttons:

■ *Legend* displays the Backup Selection Legend window (refer to fig. 13.9).

■ *Print* enables you to print a list of the files selected for backup, either to the printer or to a file. (You can print the contents of the setup file from either program by choosing Print from the File menu.)

Editing the Include/Exclude List in MSBACKUP

When you choose Include or Exclude, the dialog box contains a button labeled Edit Include/Exclude List. Choosing this button produces the dialog box shown in figure 13.10. You can select an entry to copy, delete, or edit.

To edit a selection, choose Edit. This command displays the Edit dialog box shown in figure 13.11. In this dialog box you can specify a drive, path, and file name, including wild-card patterns. You can choose whether to include or exclude the specified files and whether to apply the selection to subdirectories of the current directory.

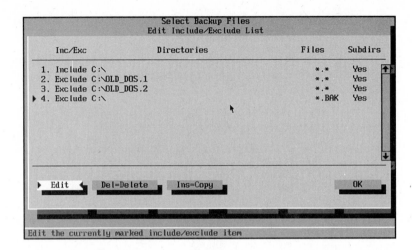

Fig. 13.10

The MSBACKUP
Edit Include/
Exclude List.

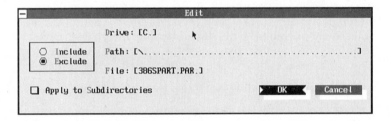

Fig. 13.11

Editing file
specifications.

To use the Edit dialog box effectively, you first must copy an existing specification in the Edit Include/Exclude List dialog box (refer to fig. 13.10). Then select one of the copies, and choose Edit. After you enter the Edit dialog box, you can enter any specifications you want.

NOTE In MSBACKUP, you need not include a drive name in a specification for inclusion or exclusion. By not specifying a drive name, you can apply the same specifications to any or all drives and select the drives from the Backup From list. In Microsoft Backup for Windows, you must include a drive name. However, you can load a setup file created by MSBACKUP in Microsoft Backup for Windows.

Editing the Include/Exclude List in Microsoft Backup for Windows

In Microsoft Backup for Windows, a single dialog box contains the list of included and excluded file specifications and the fields for editing specifications (see fig. 13.12). You do not need to edit existing specifications. You can just enter your criteria (which must include a drive name), and choose Add.

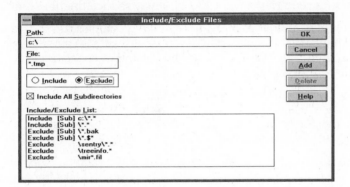

Fig. 13.12

Including and excluding files in Microsoft Backup for Windows.

Using Other Backup Options

Both backup programs give you additional options concerning their behavior. To view or change these options, use the Options button on the Backup screen. Figure 13.13 shows the resulting dialog box in Microsoft Backup for Windows, with the default options selected. The options—and the defaults—are the same in MSBACKUP.

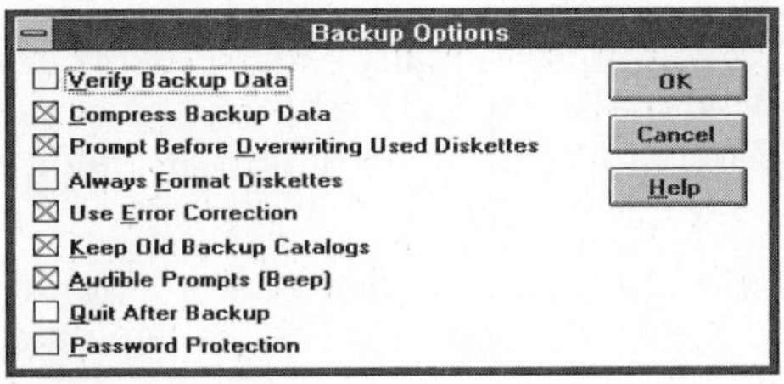

Fig. 13.13

The Backup Options dialog box.

The Backup Options dialog box contains the following options:

- *Verify Backup Data* forces the backup program to read the file from the backup disk after it is written and compare it to the original file. This process ensures that the backup is safe and accurate; when you use this option, however, the backup takes nearly twice as long.

- *Compress Backup Data* causes the program to compress the data before writing it to the backup disk. Compression results in the backup requiring fewer disks and may reduce the time required.

- *Prompt Before Overwriting Used Diskettes* causes the program to display a warning before writing backup data on a used disk. You can then choose to overwrite the files on the backup disk or use a different disk.

- *Always Format Diskettes* forces the program to format every backup disk before writing to it so that the backup programs always format an unformatted disk or a badly formatted disk. Choosing this option increases the time required for a backup.

- *Use Error Correction* adds special coding to each backup disk to make recovering the data easier if the backup disks become damaged or worn out. This option decreases the amount of data you can fit on each backup disk, but the extra margin of safety is worth the loss.

- *Keep Old Backup Catalogs* prevents the programs from erasing the previous catalog when you perform a full backup. If, as suggested, you have two separate full backup series, leave this option selected so that you can use the catalogs to locate files to be restored.

- *Audible Prompts (Beep)* causes the computer to beep every time a prompt appears.

- *Quit After Backup* automatically closes the program when your backup procedure is complete. This option is useful when you are running MSBACKUP from a batch file or running Microsoft Backup for Windows in the background.

- *Password Protection* enables you to enter a password, which will thereafter be required to access the backup data or the catalog.

Restoring Backup Files

Performing a backup operation is akin to buying an insurance policy. You hope you never have to use it, but if disaster strikes, you have a way to replace the loss. To reinstate lost data onto your hard disk, choose the Restore button in either program.

> **NOTE** The DOS 6.0 backup programs can restore only data backed up with one of these programs or with one of the Norton backup programs, published by Symantec Corporation. DOS 6.0 includes an external RESTORE command, which is the only command that can read files copied to a backup set by the BACKUP command from earlier versions of DOS. Consult the Command Reference later in this book for details on the use of this command.

The Restore option enables you to restore an individual file, selected files, or an entire hard disk.

Both Backup programs provide the same facilities when restoring files, but they are arranged somewhat differently. When you choose Restore, the program loads the most recent backup set catalog and displays the Restore screen shown in figure 13.14. The catalog's name appears in the Backup Set Catalog field. The drive and capacity used for the backup appear in the Restore From field, and Original Locations appears in the Restore To (or Restore To) field.

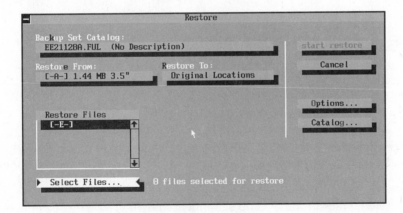

Fig. 13.14

The Restore screen.

To choose another backup set for restore, select Backup Set Catalog, and choose one of the other files listed. If the file is not in the default catalog directory (C:\DOS), choose Catalog and then choose Load; then select the drive and directory from the appropriate list before choosing the catalog file.

If your hard disk contains no catalog file for the backup series from which you wish to restore, choose Catalog and then Retrieve. The program asks you to place the last disk of the backup series in your drive, and the backup program reads the catalog from the disk. If the program cannot read the catalog, if the catalog is missing, or if the disk is damaged, choose Catalog and then Rebuild. The program asks you to insert each backup disk from the series beginning with disk 1. The backup program reconstructs the catalog from the data on the backup disks.

> **NOTE**   The Catalog command appears on a button in MSBACKUP and on the menu bar in Microsoft Backup for Windows.

By default, the programs restore files to their original locations. If the file's original directory is no longer on the destination disk, the program creates the directory before restoring the file. The programs make directory entries for files that are no longer on the destination disk and allocate the next available space in the FAT for the restored file's allocation.

You can restore to other drives or other directories. To do so, choose Restore To (or Restore To in the Windows version), and select Other Drives or Other Directories. You may want to use this option to restore an older version of a file without destroying your current version. By default, the programs automatically overwrite existing files of the same name in the same location. If you choose either of the alternative locations, you will have a chance to enter both a drive name and a directory path after you begin the restore.

You may restore all or only some of the files in a backup set. To restore all the files, select the drive(s) in the Restore Files list. This action selects all the files in the backup set that were originally on the selected drive.

To select individual files to restore, choose Select Files. You again see a screen similar to the DOS Shell screen. However, only those drives included in the backup appear on the drive bar, and no file names appear in the file window if the current directory did not include any files that were backed up. In Microsoft Backup for Windows, directories that contain no files in the backup set appear in light gray. You select files and directories to restore the same way you selected files and directories for backup.

When the correct entries appear in all fields of the Restore screen, choose Start Restore. Like the Backup module, the Restore module prompts you for the disks of the backup set.

NOTE Restoring a full backup set to a freshly formatted disk eliminates any file fragmentation that may have existed on the disk when you backed up the files. Restoring an incremental backup set, however, may result in fragmented destination files. As you may recall, fragmentation doesn't affect the file's integrity, but it may slow disk performance slightly.

When you restore files, keep the following guidelines in mind:

- The destination disk must already be formatted. The restore operation, unlike the back up operation, has no provision to format the destination disk.

- Files restored to a freshly formatted disk are not fragmented.

WARNING: If you have copy-protected files on your hard disk when you do a backup, they may not restore properly to a destination disk. Ideally, you uninstall copy-protected software using the manufacturer's suggested procedure prior to performing the backup; then reinstall the copy-protected programs after the restore operation. This practice may not be practical, however. Keep in mind that you may have to reinstall copy-protected software after restoring a complete disk.

Restoring Files after a Disk Failure

This section presents an example of restoring files. Assume that you are using a backup policy that includes a weekly full backup on Friday and an incremental backup each Wednesday. You have two backup sets. The first set from Friday contains all files. The second set contains only files modified or created after Friday, but before Thursday.

Now suppose that you are saving a worksheet file on Thursday morning when a workman begins to use a large drill next door. DOS reports the following message:

```
General Failure on drive C:
```

You abort the spreadsheet session and run CHKDSK to ensure that your FAT and directory system are in order. (Chapter 7, "Preparing and Maintaining Disks," covers the operation of CHKDSK.) DOS reports hundreds of lost clusters.

You have had an electrical noise-induced hard disk failure. You have no choice but to reformat your hard disk and then fall back to your backup disks. This process requires the steps discussed in the following paragraphs.

You first need to reboot your computer with a DOS Startup disk in drive A because the DOS utilities on your hard disk may be corrupt. After you format your hard disk, copy the external DOS commands back to the hard disk from the DOS master disks. You will use MSBACKUP for the restore because you have not yet restored Windows. Use the PATH command to set a search path to the DOS directory so that DOS can locate the MSBACKUP command.

In case of total disk failure, restore your backup sets in chronological order. Restore your latest full backup set first. Locate the disks from your full backup set and put them in their proper order. Then issue the MSBACKUP command. You probably will have to configure the program all over again. When you have completed this process, choose Restore.

Put the last disk into drive A and choose Catalog and then Retrieve. Select the appropriate drive(s) in the Restore Files list. Choose Start Restore.

DOS lists the full path and file names of the files being restored on the progress screen. When all the files from the first disk are restored to the hard disk, DOS prompts you for the next disk in the backup set. This cycle repeats until you have completed the restore operation.

After restoring the full backup set, you must restore the incremental backup set. Because you want to restore all the files in the incremental backup set, you use the same procedures you used to restore the full backup set. The operation proceeds in the same fashion.

After both backup sets are restored, run CHKDSK to ensure that the hard disk is in order. Keep both backup sets intact until you have determined that your hard disk is performing correctly. Run CHKDSK several times during the day. If all is in order, perform a full backup at the end of the day.

Performing a Selective Restore

This section discusses how to perform a selective restore operation. Assume that last week you accidentally deleted the database file CLIENT.DB from your INVOICES directory. You discovered the error today and have already tried, unsuccessfully, to use the UNDELETE command. Luckily, an up-to-date version of the CLIENT.DB file is on your most recent backup set.

To restore only the \BUSINESS\INVOICES\CLIENT.DB file from the backup set, load the backup program you use, choose Restore, select the appropriate backup set, and choose Select Files.

You again see a tree and file window, as shown in figure 13.15. Select the file from the file window.

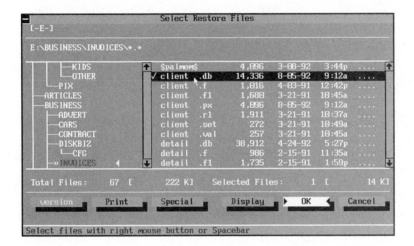

Fig. 13.15

Selecting a file to restore.

As in the complete restore example, RESTORE prompts you to insert the first disk. You can insert the first disk, or if you know the disk number that holds the CLIENT.DB file, you can insert that disk. RESTORE bypasses any files on the source disk that are not included in the destination parameter you gave in the command. When RESTORE encounters the file \BUSINESS\INVOICES\CLIENT.DB, the program lists the file name on the progress screen and copies the file to the destination disk.

For Related Information

◄◄ "Analyzing a Disk with CHKDSK," p. 212.

FROM HERE...

Chapter Summary

This chapter covered the important DOS commands and procedures that enable you to ensure the integrity of your data and, even more important, protect yourself from data loss. Following are the key points covered in this chapter:

■ You can protect your computer hardware equipment by following common-sense safety precautions.

■ You can protect yourself from computer viruses by purchasing only tested software and using MSAV or Microsoft Anti-Virus for Windows to check any new software.

■ The COMP and FC commands compare a file for differences.

■ XCOPY is a versatile copy command that can create subdirectories while copying.

■ The MSBACKUP command produces special copies of your program and data files backup sets. Backup sets usually are used for recovering lost data.

■ The RESTORE command reads files from backup sets and restores the files to their original directories on another disk.

■ You can protect yourself from data loss by faithfully following a backup policy.

Chapter 14, "Using the DOS Editor," introduces the DOS Editor. This text processor is a simple yet reasonably powerful tool for creating configuration files and short documents.

Getting the Most from DOS

PART

III

OUTLINE

Using the DOS Editor

T he DOS Editor, which was introduced in DOS 5.0, is a *text proces-sor*, a kind of mini-word processor. The Editor is the perfect tool for creating short text documents and editing text files.

When you try the DOS Editor, you are in for a pleasant surprise. The Editor is so easy and intuitive to use that you will likely become a regular user.

This chapter explains how to use the basic features of the DOS Editor, including how to use its menus and shortcut commands and how to create, edit, save, and print text.

Key Terms Used in This Chapter

Text file	A file that contains only ASCII text charac-ters (without special formatting characters). The DOS Editor works only with text files.
Editing command	One of the commands available from a pull-down menu.
Shortcut key	A keystroke combination that immediately activates an editing command, bypassing the menu system.
Dialog box	A window that pops open when the DOS Editor needs more information before exe-cuting a command.

continues

Key Terms Used in This Chapter continued

Highlighted option	A command or option that appears in inverse video. The highlighted option executes when you press Enter.
Location counter	The two numbers at the right end of the status bar that indicate the cursor's current row and column.
Scroll bars	The two matte strips (a vertical strip along the right edge and a horizontal strip near the bottom edge) used with a mouse to move through the file.
Clipboard	An area of memory where text can be stored temporarily.
Selected text	A block of text you highlight with various Shift-key combinations. Selected text can be deleted, moved, and edited as a single block.
Insert mode	The editing mode in which a typed character is inserted into the existing text at the current cursor position.
Overtype mode	The editing mode in which a typed character replaces the character at the current cursor position.
Place marker	A document location designated with a special keystroke combination and to which the cursor can be moved immediately by a particular keystroke combination.

Understanding the DOS Editor

The DOS Editor falls into a class of programs known as text editors. As the name implies, a *text editor* works with files that contain pure text (as opposed to *binary* files, which contain programming instructions).

Listed are some of the typical tasks for which the DOS Editor is ideally suited:

■ Creating, editing, and printing memos (and other text documents).

■ Viewing text files whose contents are unknown.

■ Creating or modifying various system configuration files, such as AUTOEXEC.BAT and CONFIG.SYS.

- Writing and modifying batch files. (Batch files are discussed in Chapter 15, "Understanding Batch Files, DOSKey, and Macros.")

- Writing and saving README files. Many computer users place a README file in a hard disk subdirectory (or on a floppy disk) to explain the contents of other files in the subdirectory (or on the disk).

- Creating and viewing files that are uploaded to or downloaded from electronic bulletin boards, such as CompuServe.

- Writing programs for programming-language environments that don't include a resident editor.

Be aware that document files produced by some word processors aren't pure text files. The files may contain special formatting or printer-control characters. Most word processors can import the pure text files created with the DOS Editor. The Editor, however, may not successfully import word processor document files that contain certain formatting characters.

For Related Information

▶▶ "Introducing Batch Files," p. 546.

▶▶ "Creating a Simple Batch File," p. 549.

FROM HERE...

Files Required To Run the DOS Editor

The DOS Editor is part of the DOS 6.0 package. The Editor is invoked by the external command EDIT, which runs the program EDIT.COM. When you run the Editor, EDIT.COM calls on two other files: QBASIC.EXE and EDIT.HLP. Only QBASIC.EXE is required. EDIT.HLP contains the text of the help messages, but the Editor works without this file.

Starting the DOS Editor

You can start the DOS Editor from the DOS Shell or from the command line.

If you're running the DOS Shell, select Editor from the Main program group in the program list area (refer to Chapter 4, "Using the DOS

Shell," for more about starting a program from the DOS Shell). After you select Editor from the DOS Shell menu, a box labeled File to Edit pops open. A message inside the box prompts you to supply a file name. To start the Editor without loading a specific file, just press Enter. If you want to load a text file into the Editor, however, type the file's name, including the path if the file is not located in the default directory. Then press Enter to start the DOS Editor with your designated file loaded and ready for editing.

If you're running the Editor from the command line, type **EDIT** at the DOS prompt, and press Enter.

Regardless of which method you choose for starting the Editor, it now initializes. A preliminary screen appears (see fig. 14.1).

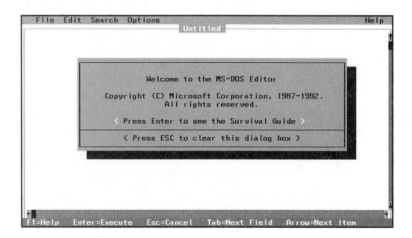

Fig. 14.1

The preliminary DOS Editor screen.

You now must press either Enter or Esc:

- Enter activates the Survival Guide. (The Survival Guide provides help about using the DOS Editor.)

- Esc clears the box in the center of the screen and prepares the Editor for working on a text file.

Press Esc. Now the DOS Editor screen is blank, and you can begin writing a text file. Your screen should look like the screen shown in figure 14.2.

FROM HERE...

For Related Information

◀◀ "Understanding the DOS Shell Window," p. 84.

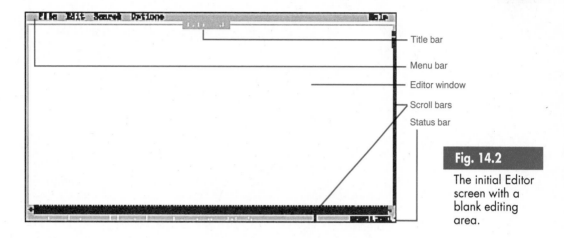

Title bar

Menu bar

Editor window

Scroll bars

Status bar

Fig. 14.2

The initial Editor screen with a blank editing area.

Getting Acquainted with the Initial Editor Screen

Take a moment to look at your screen (or refer to fig. 14.2). The screen is composed of several elements.

The *menu bar* lists the available menus: File, Edit, Search, Options, and Help. The *title bar* contains the name of the text file being edited (it is now Untitled). The *status bar* describes the current process and shows certain shortcut key options.

Scroll bars are a vertical strip along the right edge and a horizontal strip just above the status bar. The scroll bars are used with a mouse to move through the file. (Mouse techniques are described in the section "Using a Mouse" later in this chapter.)

The *Editor window* is the large area in which the text of your file appears. The *cursor* is the flashing underscore character that indicates where typed text will appear.

Navigating the DOS Editor

The DOS Editor provides several ways to perform most commands. The Editor has a user-friendly set of menus from which you can select options. Many of these options require you to enter further information in an on-screen box known as a *dialog box*.

The Editor enables you to execute many commands by pressing special shortcut keys. You also can use a mouse to execute commands.

The sections that follow describe how to use menus, dialog boxes, shortcut keys, and a mouse in the DOS Editor.

Understanding the Menu System

The DOS Editor menu system provides many editing commands. The menu bar contains the following options: File, Edit, Search, Options, and Help. Selecting any of these options displays a pull-down menu. The File option displays a menu that enables you to load files, save files, and print files. The Edit menu is used to cut and paste text. The Search menu is used for finding and replacing specified text. The Options menu can be used to reconfigure environment options, and the Help menu provides access to on-line help.

To activate the menu bar, press Alt. The first letter of each menu name is highlighted. Press the first letter of the menu name. Press Alt and then F, for example, to activate the File menu (Alt-F). Similarly, press Alt-E to display the Edit menu, Alt-S to display the Search menu, Alt-O to display the Options menu, or Alt-H to display the Help menu.

Every time you open a main menu, the first command on the submenu is highlighted. You can move this highlight to the other commands by pressing the up- or down-arrow key. As you move the highlight, notice that the status bar displays a brief description of the highlighted command.

On a menu, one letter of each command is highlighted. On most systems, the highlighted letter appears in high-intensity white. To execute a command, move the highlight to that command and press Enter, or press the key that corresponds to the highlighted letter.

Depending on which editing commands you have executed previously, some commands in a menu may not be available. In such a case, the menu shows the command name in a dull color (usually gray), and no highlighted letter appears in the name. If you try to execute an unavailable command, the DOS Editor sounds a beep and refuses to execute the command.

The Esc key (Escape) is the "oops" key. Pressing Esc closes the menu system and returns you to the Editor.

In the pull-down menus, an ellipsis (...) following the name of a command indicates that a dialog box opens when you issue that command. (Sometimes, depending on the circumstances, a command without the ellipsis also opens a dialog box.)

Understanding Dialog Boxes

When you execute a menu command, it may execute immediately or, depending on the command and the current context, a dialog box may pop up. A dialog box means that the DOS Editor needs more information before the command can be completed. If, for example, you execute the command to save a new file, the Editor first needs to know what name to give the file. A dialog box prompts you for the necessary information.

For example, if you activate the Search menu and then select Change, the DOS Editor displays the Change dialog box (see fig. 14.3).

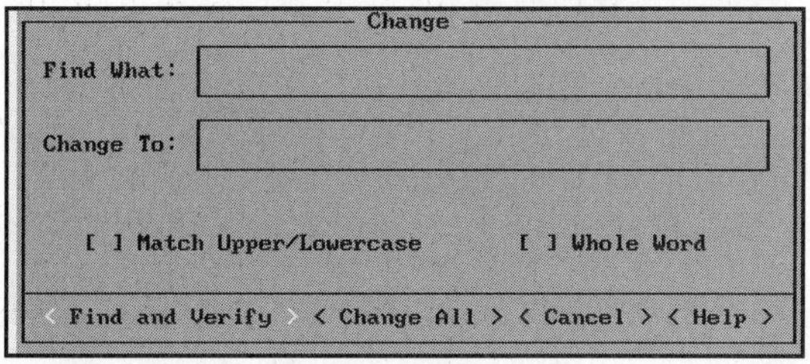

```
┌─────────────────────────── Change ───────────────────────────┐
│                                                               │
│  Find What: [                                               ] │
│                                                               │
│  Change To: [                                               ] │
│                                                               │
│                                                               │
│     [ ] Match Upper/Lowercase        [ ] Whole Word           │
│                                                               │
│  < Find and Verify >  < Change All >  < Cancel >  < Help >    │
└───────────────────────────────────────────────────────────────┘
```

Fig. 14.3

The Change dialog box.

The DOS Editor uses dialog boxes to get a variety of information. Sometimes you must type something, such as a file name or a search string in a text box. Sometimes you must choose from a list of options. At other times, you select from a series of command buttons (refer to Chapter 4, "Using the DOS Shell," for a discussion of dialog boxes, text boxes, option buttons, and command buttons).

When a DOS Editor dialog box opens, the following three keys have special significance:

- Tab moves the cursor from one area of the dialog box to the next area. After you specify information in one area, use Tab to move to the next area.

- Esc aborts the menu option and returns you to the Editor. Use Esc when you change your mind and decide against issuing a particular command.

- Enter is the "go ahead" key. Press it when all options in the dialog box are as you want them and you are ready to execute the command. You press Enter only once while you are working inside a dialog box. Use Tab, not Enter, to move the cursor from one area of the dialog box to the next area. (Be careful. Most people tend to press Enter after they type information, such as a file name. Remember, when you need to specify additional information inside the dialog box, press Tab, not Enter.)

In every dialog box, one command button is enclosed in highlighted angle brackets. The highlighted brackets identify the action that takes place when you press Enter.

To highlight the angle brackets of the command you want, press Tab repeatedly. Be sure not to press Enter until you have specified everything satisfactorily.

When you are working with a dialog box, Alt is an "express" key. By pressing Alt and a highlighted letter, you activate an option even if the cursor is in another area.

Using Shortcut Keys

For convenience, many commonly used DOS Editor menu commands have an associated *shortcut key*. Pressing this shortcut key while you are working with the Editor executes the command directly, bypassing the menu system. Table 14.1 provides a complete list of shortcut keys.

Table 14.1 DOS Editor Keyboard and Mouse Shortcuts

Shortcut Key	Effect	Mouse
F1	View help on menu or command	Click right button on desired item
Shift-F1	View help on getting started	Click Getting Started (Help menu)
Ctrl-F1	View next help topic	Click Next (status bar)
Alt-F1	Review preceding help screen	Click Back (status bar)
Shift-Ctrl-F1	View preceding help topic	None
F3	Repeat the last Find	Click Repeat Last Find (Search menu)
F6	Move between help and desired window	Click inside editing
Shift-F6	Make preceding window active	Click inside window
Shift-Del	Cut selected text	Click Cut (Edit menu)
Ctrl-Ins	Copy selected text	Click Copy (Edit menu)
Shift-Ins	Paste text from clipboard	Click Paste (Edit menu)

Shortcut Key	Effect	Mouse
Del	Erase selected text	Click Clear (Edit menu)
Ctrl-Q-A	Change text	Click Change (Search menu)
Ctrl-Q-F	Search for text string	Click Find (Search menu)
Esc	Terminate Help System	Click Cancel (status bar)
Alt	Enter Menu-selection mode	None
Alt-Plus	Enlarge active window	Drag title bar up
Alt-Minus	Shrink active window	Drag title bar down

Using a Mouse

A mouse is an excellent pointing device for computer applications. The DOS Editor supports a mouse. You can execute menu commands and many editing tasks with a mouse. If your system is mouseless, you can get along fine; if you have a mouse, try it and see what you think.

NOTE The DOS Editor works with any Microsoft-compatible mouse and driver. If you have a mouse, you presumably know how to install and activate your mouse driver. Microsoft supplies a mouse driver as part of the DOS 6.0 package, but you should use it only if you have a Microsoft mouse.

When the mouse is active, you see a special mouse cursor on-screen. The mouse cursor is a small rectangle, about the size of one text character, that moves as you move the mouse. Notice that the regular blinking cursor remains active. You can continue to use all the keyboard commands and features. Refer to table 14.1 for a comprehensive list of mouse techniques.

Following are some additional mouse pointers:

- To open a menu, click the menu name in the menu bar.
- To execute a menu command, click the command name in the menu.

- To set an option in a dialog box, click that option.

- To abort a menu, click a location outside the menu.

- To move the cursor in the file, click at the location you want.

- To select text, *drag* the mouse over the text. That is, move the mouse pointer to one end of the text to be selected; then press and hold down the mouse button while you move the mouse across the text to be selected.

- To activate the Editor window while a help screen is visible, click anywhere inside the Editor window.

- To expand or shrink the Editor window while a help screen is visible, drag the title bar of the Editor window up or down.

- To scroll the screen horizontally one character, click the left or right arrow at either end of the horizontal scroll bar.

- To scroll the screen vertically one character, click the up or down arrow at either end of the vertical scroll bar.

- To scroll text vertically to a specific position, move the mouse cursor to the *scroll box* (the inverse-video rectangle inside the vertical scroll bar). Then drag the scroll box along the scroll bar to the desired position.

- To scroll text one page at a time, click the vertical scroll bar somewhere between the scroll box and the top or bottom of the scroll bar.

- To scroll horizontally several positions at once, click the horizontal scroll bar somewhere between the scroll box and the left or right end of the scroll bar.

- To execute a dialog-box action enclosed in angle brackets, click the name between the brackets.

- To execute any keystroke action enclosed in angle brackets in the status bar, click the name inside the angle brackets.

For Related Information

FROM HERE...   ◄◄ "Using Dialog Boxes," p. 93.

Mastering Fundamental Editing Techniques

Editing is a skill—almost an art. Some editing techniques are simple, others more complex. Many editing tasks can be performed in more than one way.

This section discusses the fundamental editing skills, which include moving the cursor, scrolling, and inserting and deleting text.

Moving the Cursor

With text in the DOS Editor, you can move the cursor around the text in several ways. The Editor provides two alternative cursor-movement interfaces:

- *Keypad interface*. The specialized IBM PC keys—the arrow keys, Ins, Del, and so on—govern most editing activities. To move the cursor up, for example, you use the up-arrow key.

- *Control-key interface*. Ctrl-key combinations govern most editing activities. To move the cursor up, for example, you press Ctrl-E. This interface is used in the word processing program WordStar.

Generally, the DOS Editor accommodates both camps. Most editing techniques are available with both the keypad and Control-key (WordStar-style) sequences. A few techniques, however, can be performed with only one method. This chapter focuses on the keypad style. The Control-key combinations are mentioned only when required by a particular editing technique.

Table 14.2 summarizes the cursor-movement commands.

Table 14.2 Cursor-Movement Commands

Effect	Keypad	Control-key style
Character left	Left arrow	Ctrl-S
Character right	Right arrow	Ctrl-D
Word left	Ctrl-left arrow	Ctrl-A
Word right	Ctrl-right arrow	Ctrl-F
Line up	Up arrow	Ctrl-E

continues

Table 14.2 Continued

Effect	Keypad	Control-key style
Line down	Down arrow	Ctrl-X
First indentation level	Home	None
Beginning of line	None	Ctrl-Q-S
End of line	End	Ctrl-Q-D
Beginning of next line	Ctrl-Enter	Ctrl-J
Top of window	None	Ctrl-Q-E
Bottom of window	None	Ctrl-Q-X
Beginning of text	Ctrl-Home	Ctrl-Q-R
End of text	Ctrl-End	Ctrl-Q-C
Set marker	None	Ctrl-K *n*
Move to marker	None	Ctrl-Q *n*

Look at the far right end of the status bar, in the lower right corner of the DOS Editor screen. You see two numbers, separated by a colon. The two numbers indicate the cursor's current location in your file. The first number is the current row; the second, the current column.

Use the arrow keys to move the cursor, and watch the numbers change. Press Num Lock; an uppercase N appears next to the location numbers to indicate that Num Lock is on. Press Num Lock a few more times to toggle the indicator on and off. Press Caps Lock; an uppercase C appears next to the location numbers, left of the N, to indicate that the Caps Lock key is on.

Scrolling

Scrolling is the movement of text inside the Editor window. When you scroll, you bring into view a portion of the file currently not visible in the Editor window. Scrolling, which can be horizontal as well as vertical, keeps the cursor at the same row and column number but moves the text in the window.

Table 14.3 summarizes the scrolling commands. For large-scale scrolling, you use the PgUp and PgDn keys. Try using these keys by themselves and with the Ctrl key.

Table 14.3 Scrolling Text

Effect	Keypad	Control-key style
One line up	Ctrl-up arrow	Ctrl-W
One line down	Ctrl-down arrow	Ctrl-Z
Page up	PgUp	Ctrl-R
Page down	PgDn	Ctrl-C
One window left	Ctrl-PgUp	
One window right	Ctrl-PgDn	

Inserting Text into a Line

You can insert text into an existing line. Move the cursor to the position at which you want to insert text. Type the text you want to insert. As you type, text to the right of the cursor moves right to accommodate the inserted text. You can move off the line by using any of the cursor-movement keys. Do *not* press Enter to move off the line. Pressing Enter splits the line in two.

Deleting Text from a Line

You can use one of the following two methods to delete a few characters from a line:

- Move the cursor to the character you want to delete. Press the Del key. To delete consecutive characters, continue pressing Del.

- Move the cursor to the character immediately to the right of the character you want to delete. Press the Backspace key.

Most people find the first method more natural. Try both methods and make your own choice.

Splitting and Joining Lines

Sometimes you need to split a line of text into two lines. Move the cursor to a position beneath the character that you want to begin the second line of text. Press Enter. The line splits in two, and the second half moves down to form a new line. Succeeding lines are pushed down to accommodate the new line.

Conversely, you can join two lines to form one line. Position the cursor in the second line, and press Home to move the cursor to the left end of the line. Press Backspace. The second line moves up to the right end of the first line. Lines beneath the split line move up one line.

Inserting and Deleting an Entire Line

To insert a blank line between two lines, move the cursor to column 1 in the lower of the two lines, and then press Ctrl-N; or press Home (to move the cursor to the left end of the current line), and press Enter. Then move the cursor up to the new blank line.

To delete an entire line, place the cursor anywhere on the line, and then press Ctrl-Y.

Overtyping

By default, the DOS Editor operates in *Insert* mode. If you type new text while the cursor is in the middle of a line, that new text is inserted at the cursor location. Instead, you can *overtype*. In Overtype mode, the new text replaces the former text.

To activate Overtype mode, press Ins. The cursor changes from a blinking line to a blinking box. The larger cursor signifies Overtype mode, in which any new character you type replaces the character at the cursor location.

To return to standard Insert mode, press Ins again. The Ins key acts as a toggle switch that alternates between Insert and Overtype modes.

Learning Special Editing Techniques

In addition to the basic editing techniques, the DOS Editor provides several special editing features. The sections that follow describe how to use the automatic indenting, tab, and place marker features.

Using Automatic Indent

When you type a line and press Enter, the cursor drops down one line but returns to the column where you began the preceding line. This feature is convenient when you want to type a series of indented lines.

For example, assume that you type the following line and press Enter:

This line is not indented

The cursor moves to the beginning of the next line. Then press the space bar three times to move the cursor to column 4 and type the following:

But this line is

Press Enter again. Note that the second time you press Enter, the cursor moves to the next row, but remains indented at column 4. Type **So is this one** and press Enter. The cursor remains indented.

Now, press the left-arrow key until the cursor returns to column 1. Type **Back to no indentation** and press Enter.

The short text block looks like the following:

```
This line is not indented
    But this line is
    So is this one
Back to no indentation
```

Using Tab

By default, tab stops are set every eight spaces. When you press the Tab key, the cursor moves to the right to the next tab stop. All text to the right of the cursor moves right when you press Tab. Additional tabbing techniques follow.

To indent an existing line a full tab position, move the cursor to column 1 of the line, and press Tab.

To remove leading spaces and move a line to the left, move the cursor anywhere on the line, and then press Shift-Tab.

To indent or "unindent" an entire block of lines, select the lines by using one of the Shift keystrokes shown in table 14.4. Then press Tab to indent the entire block, or Shift-Tab to "unindent" the entire block.

To change the number of default tab stops, first select Display from the Options menu. Press Tab several times to move the cursor to Tab Stops; type a new value for the number of characters per tab stop, and then press Enter to close the dialog box.

Using Place Markers

A *place marker* designates a specific location—a row and column—in your text. You can set as many as four place markers. After setting a place marker, you can move the cursor instantly from anywhere in the file to that marker's location. The markers are invisible; no character displays in the text to indicate a set marker.

To set a place marker, press and release Ctrl-K, then press a number key from 0 through 3. This action associates the cursor's current position with the marker having the number whose key you pressed. To move the cursor to a previously set place marker, press and release Ctrl-Q, then press the number of the marker (0 through 3).

Block Editing

You can edit blocks of text as a single unit. Block editing requires that you understand two relevant concepts: *selecting text* (which identifies the block of text to be edited) and the *clipboard* (which temporarily stores a block of text in a reserved area of memory).

This section describes the following techniques:

- Selecting text for block operations
- Using the clipboard
- Cutting and pasting blocks of text

Selecting Text

A block of selected text is always one continuous piece. The block may be one character, a few characters, a line, several lines, a paragraph, or even an entire file. Selected text appears in reverse video.

Follow these steps to select a block of text:

1. Move the cursor to one end of the block.

2. While you hold down the Shift key, use the cursor-movement keys to highlight the block.

Table 14.4 lists the keys used for selecting text. In general, the keys you use to select text are the same as those you use to move the cursor, but you also press Shift when using them to select text.

Table 14.4 Selecting Text

To select	Use this key combination
Character left	Shift-←
Character right	Shift-→
To beginning of line	Shift-Home
To end of line	Shift-End
Current line	Shift-↓
Line above	Shift-↑
Word left	Shift-Ctrl-←
Word right	Shift-Ctrl-→
Screen up	Shift-PgUp
Screen down	Shift-PgDn
To beginning of text	Shift-Ctrl-Home
To end of text	Shift-Ctrl-End

After you have selected (highlighted) a block, you can deselect it by pressing any arrow key. (Do not use Shift, however; Shift expands or shrinks the selection.) The highlighting disappears, indicating that the entire block has been deselected.

Understanding the Clipboard

The clipboard is a text storage area in memory; the clipboard acts as a kind of halfway house for blocks of text. You can place a block of text into the clipboard and later retrieve the block. The clipboard has many uses. Its most common use is to *cut and paste*—to move or copy a block of text from one place in the file to another.

The clipboard stores only one block of text at a time. When you place text in the clipboard, the incoming text completely replaces the previous contents of the clipboard. Changing the block of text in the clipboard is always an all-or-nothing affair. You cannot add or subtract incrementally. Similarly, retrieval is all-or-nothing. You cannot move only part of the clipboard's contents into your file.

Working with Text Blocks

The DOS Editor supports four block-oriented editing techniques (see table 14.5). Each technique is available by using the Edit menu or by pressing the appropriate shortcut key. (Press Alt-E to activate the Edit menu.)

Table 14.5 Block-Editing Techniques

Menu Command	Shortcut Key	Description
Cut	Shift-Del	Deletes selected text from a file and places that text in clipboard.
Copy	Ctrl-Ins	Places in clipboard a copy of selected text from file; text in file remains selected.
Paste	Shift-Ins	Inserts contents of clipboard into the file at cursor; clipboard contents remain intact. If file currently has selected text, clipboard text replaces the selected text.
Clear	Del	Deletes selected text from file; contents of clipboard are not affected.

For example, to select the first three lines of text in a file, press Ctrl-Home to return the cursor to the beginning of the file. While holding down the Shift key, press the down-arrow key three times. You have selected the first three lines of the file; they now are displayed in reverse video (highlighted).

After the three lines are selected, you can use one of the block-editing commands. To activate the Edit menu, press Alt-E. The DOS Editor displays the Edit menu shown in figure 14.4. You can now use one of the menu commands. Alternatively, you can use one of the shortcut keys to operate on the selected block, even without displaying the Edit menu.

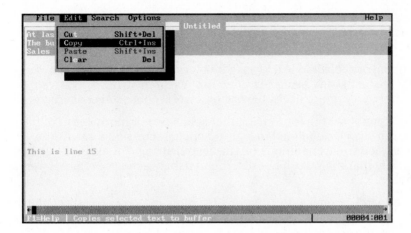

Fig. 14.4

The Edit menu.

When you perform copy operations, a copy of the selected text moves to the clipboard but isn't deleted from the original location. If you perform a cut command, however, the DOS Editor places the highlighted text into the clipboard and removes the selected text from its original location.

After text has been copied or cut into the clipboard, you can use the paste operation to copy the clipboard's contents to a new location in the file. Move the cursor to the desired target location and select Paste from the Edit menu, or press Shift-Ins (the shortcut key for Paste). A copy of the clipboard text is inserted at the cursor's location. (The clipboard still holds a copy of the pasted text. You can insert additional copies of the clipboard text at other locations in the file.)

Pressing Del or selecting the Clear command from the Edit menu permanently deletes the selected text from the file without placing a copy of the text in the clipboard.

Searching and Replacing— the Search Menu

The Search menu offers several options for searching for and replacing text. These capabilities are most useful in long files.

From the Search menu, you can perform the following actions:

- Find one or more occurrences of a designated text string

- Replace one or more occurrences of a designated text string with a second text string

A *text string* is a sequence of one or more consecutive text characters. These characters can be letters, digits, punctuation, or special symbols—any characters you can type from the keyboard.

Finding or replacing text always involves a *search string*, which is simply the text string being searched for. A search string can be a single character or, more likely, a word or several consecutive characters.

You cannot search for a string that spans two or more lines. The search string is confined to a group of characters on a single line. You can place some conditions on the search string. For example, you can specify that the search not discriminate between upper- and lowercase letters.

The search begins at the cursor's location and proceeds through the file. If the end of the file is reached before the search string is found, the search continues at the top of the file until the entire file has been traversed. Table 14.6 summarizes the three commands available from the Search menu.

Table 14.6 Search Menu Commands

Command	Shortcut Key	Description
Find...	None	Opens a dialog box in which you specify the search string; finds the search string in your file
Repeat Last Find	F3	Searches for the text specified in the last Find command
Change...	None	Replaces one text string with another

Using the Find Command

To use the Find command, first activate the Search menu by pressing Alt-S. Your screen looks similar to figure 14.5.

Select Find. The Find dialog box opens, with the cursor on the Find What text box (see fig. 14.6). The word that is at the cursor's current location in the file (or the currently selected text) appears in the text box. If you want to search for this word, press Enter. Otherwise, type the correct search string, and press Enter. The DOS Editor locates the first occurrence of the search string in your file and selects (highlights) the text found.

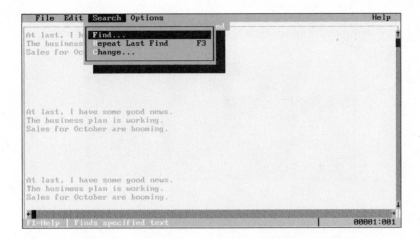

Fig. 14.5

The Search menu.

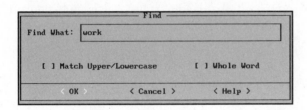

Fig. 14.6

The Find dialog box.

You can press F3, or select Repeat Last Find on the Search menu. The Editor moves to the next occurrence of the search string (if any).

As shown in figure 14.6, you can use the following check boxes in the dialog box to place conditions on the search:

- *Match Upper/Lowercase.* If you select this check box, a successful search occurs only when the upper- and lowercase letters in the text exactly match those in the search string. If this option is not selected, upper- and lowercase letters are considered the same.

- *Whole Word.* If this option is selected, the search string must exist as an independent word that cannot be embedded inside a larger word. The character that immediately precedes and immediately follows the search string must be a space, a punctuation character, or one of the special characters (such as <, *, or [ ]).

Using the Change Command

In addition to just searching for text, you can use the DOS Editor to search for specific text and then replace the text with other text.

Activate the Search menu by pressing Alt-S. Select the Change command. The Editor displays the Change dialog box (see fig. 14.7).

The first text box in the Change dialog box is labeled Find What. Type the text you want the Editor to find in this text box (the target text). The second text box is labeled Change To. Type the text you want entered. A completed Change dialog box is shown in figure 14.8.

This dialog box contains two check boxes: Match Upper/Lowercase, and Whole Word. Refer to the preceding section for a discussion of these check boxes.

After making the appropriate entries in the text boxes and selecting any desired check boxes, choose from among the following three command buttons:

■ *Find and Verify* finds each occurrence of the target string, one after another. (You specify the target string in the Find What dialog box.) As each occurrence of the target string is found, a second dialog box opens. This second box gives you the choice of making the substitution, skipping to the next occurrence, or canceling the remaining searches. Find and Verify is the default option, which you automatically select by pressing Enter.

■ *Change All* changes all occurrences of the target string to the string specified in the Change To box. The changes occur all at once. A dialog box informs you when the substitutions are complete.

■ *Cancel* aborts the Change command, closing the dialog box without making any substitutions. This option is equivalent to pressing Esc.

After the DOS Editor finishes the find-and-replace operation, it displays a second dialog box. This second box contains the message Change complete. If no matching text can be found, the box displays the message Match not found. Select the OK command button to return to the Editor window.

Managing Files

The DOS Editor closely oversees your disk files. You can manage your directories with a complete save-and-load capability.

Overview of the File Menu

The File menu is your command center for loading and saving files. Six commands are available on the File menu (see fig. 14.9).

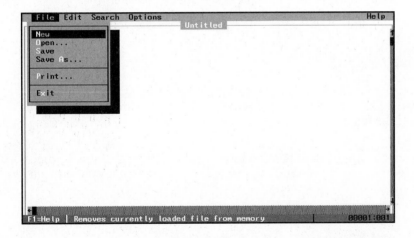

Fig. 14.9

The File menu.

The New command clears the file currently in the DOS Editor. The result is a clean slate, as though you had just initialized the Editor. This command does not affect other copies of the file. If the file previously was saved on disk, for example, the disk copy is not erased; only the working copy in the Editor is erased.

Open loads a file from disk into the DOS Editor environment. You can use this command also to see a list of file names in any directory.

Save saves the current file to disk.

Save As saves the current file to disk after prompting you for the file name.

Print prints all or part of the text in the DOS Editor environment.

Exit ends the editing session and returns to the DOS Shell or the command-line prompt.

> **NOTE** When you are working with files, keep in mind these maxims:
>
> 1. Until you name a file, the Editor displays the temporary name *Untitled* in the title bar.
>
> 2. When you save a file, the Editor adds the extension TXT to the file name if you don't specify another extension.
>
> 3. If you try to exit the Editor or open a new file without first saving a working file in the Editor, a dialog box opens to warn you.

Saving a File

When you save a file for the first time, you must specify two file attributes: the file path (the directory or disk on which to save the file) and the file name.

The DOS Editor stores files on disk in ASCII format. Such files are text files that can be manipulated by most text editors and word processors. You can view ASCII files directly from the DOS command line by using the TYPE command.

Using the Save As Command

Follow these steps to save the current Untitled file with a new file name:

1. Select Save As from the File menu. In the dialog box that opens, the current path is shown below the words *File Name* (see fig. 14.10). A list box, below the label *Dirs/Drives*, lists the directories and disk drives available on your system.

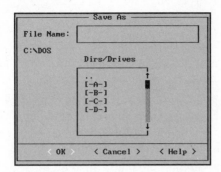

Fig. 14.10

The Save As
dialog box.

2. Type the new file name in the File Name box. You may specify any file extension as part of the file name. Typical file extensions for ASCII text files are TXT and DOC.

3. Press Enter to save the file.

The DOS Editor saves the file to disk in the directory specified by the current path.

Save As is commonly used for storing a file the first time you create it and for saving a second version of a file in a different directory or with a different name from the first version. For example, assume that you are editing a file named MYWORK.TXT. After making a few changes, you decide to save the new version of the file under the name MEAGAIN.TXT. Display the File menu, and select Save As. The DOS Editor displays the Save As dialog box.

The File Name text box contains the current file name, MYWORK.TXT. Type **MEAGAIN.TXT** and press Enter. The DOS Editor stores the file on disk as MEAGAIN.TXT, changing the name in the title bar accordingly. The file MYWORK.TXT remains stored on disk. Remember that if you continue editing the file on-screen, you are editing MEAGAIN.TXT (as indicated in the title bar), not MYWORK.TXT.

To store a file in a directory other than that specified by the current path, type the new directory path as part of the file name. For example, if you type the file name **\MEMOS\PLAN.BID**, the DOS Editor stores the file with the name PLAN.BID in the directory \MEMOS. After you save the file, the name PLAN.BID appears in the title bar. The next time you issue the Save As command, the default directory path is specified in the dialog box as C:\MEMOS. If you save a new file without including an explicit path, the file is saved in the C:\MEMOS directory.

You can use this technique to save files on different disk drives. To save a file named MYFILE.TXT in the root directory of the disk in drive A, for example, type the file name as **A:\MYFILE.TXT**.

Using the Save Command

Use Save to store a file you have already named. No dialog box appears. The current version of the file in the DOS Editor is saved to disk under the existing file name.

Using Save on an unnamed (untitled) file has nearly the same effect as using Save As; the Editor opens a dialog box similar to that shown in figure 14.10 so that you can enter a file name.

When you use the Save command while editing an existing file, the Editor doesn't prompt you for a file name. Instead, the Editor simply saves the new edited version of the file in place of the old version on disk. As you edit a file, use Save periodically to update the file on disk.

Using the Open Command To Load a File

After text files are stored on disk, you can load a file into the DOS Editor with the Open command. Because this command lists files in any directory, you also can use Open to search your directories for specific file names. When you select Open, a dialog box pops open (see fig. 14.11).

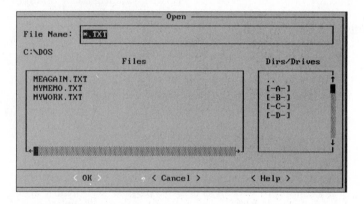

The Open dialog box.

The Open dialog box contains the File Name text box. By default, this box contains *.TXT, the wild-card file name for all files with the extension .TXT. The current directory path (C:\DOS in figure 14.11) is below the File Name text box. In the File Name text box, type a file name, a directory path, or a name using the * and ? wild-card characters.

To change the default path, specify a path in the File Name text box, and press Enter. Otherwise, the DOS Editor looks in the current directory for files with the extension TXT.

The Files list box contains the names of all files that satisfy the current directory-path and file-name specification. In figure 14.10, the Files box shows all files that satisfy the path and file-name specification C:\DOS*.TXT.

The Dirs/Drives list box lists available directories and disks. You can move the cursor to the Dirs/Drives list box by pressing Tab repeatedly. Then press the up- and down-arrow keys to move the highlight to one of the directories or drives listed in the box. Press Enter to change the default path.

To load a specific file into the DOS Editor, you can use the File Name box or the Files box. To use the File Name box, type in the box the name of the specific file, including a path (or rely on the default path shown below the box). If you don't specify an extension, the Editor assumes the TXT extension. For example, to load the file MYFILE.TXT, which is found in the current directory, type **MYFILE**, and press Enter.

You also can select a file name from the Files list box if it contains the file name you want. First, press Tab to move the cursor to the Files list box. Then use the arrow keys to highlight the target file name. Alternatively, you can press the first letter of the file name to move the highlight. When the name you want is highlighted, press Enter.

The DOS Editor loads the file so that you can edit or view it.

Loading a File When You First Start the DOS Editor

You can load a file when you first start the DOS Editor. The technique you use depends on whether you start the Editor from the DOS Shell or from the command line:

- *If you are starting the Editor from the DOS Shell,* after you select Editor from the DOS Shell menu, a box labeled File to Edit pops open. A message inside the box prompts you to supply a file name. When you type the file name, include the path if the file isn't located in the default directory. Then press Enter to start the Editor with your designated file loaded and ready for editing.

- *If you are starting the DOS Editor from the command line,* at the DOS prompt, type **EDIT**, followed by a space and the file name. Include the path if the file isn't in the current directory. For example, to start the Editor with the file \SALES\MYFILE.TXT loaded, type the following line:

    EDIT \SALES\MYFILE.TXT

The following notes apply when you load a file when starting the DOS Editor (whether you start it from the DOS Shell or from the command line):

- The Editor does not assume the extension TXT or any other extension if you don't specify an extension as part of the file name.

- The Editor initializes directly without taking the intermediate step of asking whether you want to see the help material in the on-screen Survival Guide.

- If the Editor cannot locate the specified file, the Editor assumes that you want to create a new file with that name. Accordingly, the Editor initializes with a fresh slate that includes your designated file name in the title bar. After you enter data into the file, you can save it directly with the Save command. (You don't need to use Save As and specify the file name a second time.)

Using the New Command

Use New when you want to stop work on one file and create a new file. If you haven't saved the old file, the DOS Editor opens a dialog box for confirmation. Otherwise, the old file clears, and the screen looks as though you had just initiated the Editor. You see a blank editing area with Untitled in the title bar.

Printing a File

Your computer system probably includes a printer. Whether you have a dot-matrix, daisywheel, or laser printer, follow these steps to print a copy of the file currently loaded in the Editor. You can print selected text or the complete file.

1. Activate the File option on the main menu.

2. Select Print. This command opens the Print dialog box (see fig. 14.12).

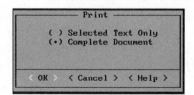

Fig. 14.12

The Print dialog box.

3. Choose from among the following option buttons:

■ *Selected Text Only* prints only selected text, which appears in reverse video in the Editor. (Selecting text is explained earlier in this chapter.) This option is the default when a block of text is selected.

■ *Complete Document* prints the entire file. This option is the default when no text is selected.

4. Press Enter to begin printing. Make sure that your printer is turned on and is on-line.

Exiting from the DOS Editor

When you have finished editing files, you may want to leave the DOS Editor. Display the File menu and choose the Exit command. If the file already has been saved, the Editor returns to the DOS Shell or to the command line, depending on how you started the program.

If you try to quit without first saving the document you have been editing, the Editor opens a dialog box to ask whether you want to save the file. Select the Yes command button to save the file and exit Editor. Select the No command button to exit from the Editor without saving any changes to the current file. Select the Cancel button to close the dialog box and return to the Editor. To get help information about the dialog box, select the Help button.

Starting the DOS Editor with Optional Switches

When you start the DOS Editor from the command line, four special parameter switches are available. These switches are listed in table 14.7.

To display the maximum number of lines when starting the DOS Editor, for example, use the following command:

EDIT / H

A file name can be specified with one of the command options, as in the following example:

EDIT \ SALES\ MYFILE /H

Use the /B switch if you run the DOS Editor on a computer system with a color video adapter but a black-and-white monitor. (Many laptop computers have this configuration.) At the DOS prompt, activate the Editor as follows:

    EDIT /B

Table 14.7 Optional Switches for the EDIT command	
Switch	**Description**
/B	Displays the DOS Editor in black and white, even when a color graphics adapter is present.
/G	Updates Editor screens as quickly as possible on systems with CGA (Color Graphics Adapter) video. (**Note**: Some computer systems cannot support this option. If screen flicker occurs when you choose /G, your hardware is not compatible with this option.)
/H	Displays the maximum number of lines possible with your video hardware. EGA (Enhanced Graphics Adapter) and VGA (Video Graphics Array) systems can produce more than the standard number of lines on-screen.
/NOHI	Effectively displays the Editor on monitors that do not support high intensity.

Customizing the DOS Editor Screen

Colors on the DOS Editor screen are preset. You can customize most of these colors and other attributes from the Options menu by using the Display command. If you have a color system, you may want different colors for the foreground and background text. If you don't use a mouse with the Editor, you may want to remove the scroll bars.

Changing Colors and Removing Scroll Bars

To change screen colors in the DOS Editor, display the Options menu and select Display. A dialog box similar to figure 14.13 opens.

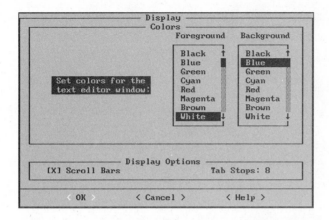

Fig. 14.13

The Display
dialog box.

With the cursor on the Foreground box, you can select a new foreground text color by pressing the up- and down-arrow keys. The
Foreground box cycles through the colors available with your video
hardware. Note that as you press the arrow keys, the text to the left
of the dialog box (Set colors for the text editor window) displays with the current foreground and background colors. Select a
new foreground color by moving the highlight to the color you want.
Don't press Enter yet. You have more selections to make before closing
this dialog box.

Press Tab to move the cursor to the Background box. Select a new
background color; the process is similar to the one you followed to
select a new foreground color.

Now press Enter to return to the Editor screen. The new colors should
be in use.

If you don't use a mouse, you may want to consider removing the scroll
bars from your screen. Many users think that the screen looks less
cluttered without the scroll bars. To see what you prefer, try the following exercise.

Reopen the dialog box by displaying the Options menu and selecting
Display. Press Tab several times to move the cursor to the Scroll Bars
check box. The X inside the brackets indicates that scroll bars are
displayed.

Press the space bar or S to unselect the check box. Removing the X
indicates that you want to deselect the display of scroll bars. Press
Enter, and the scroll bars are gone (see fig. 14.14).

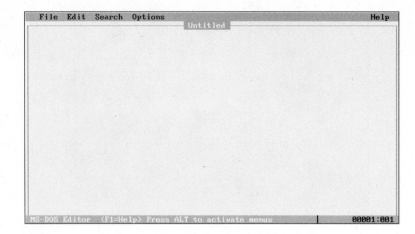

```
 File   Edit   Search   Options                                    Help
                            Untitled
```
```
 MS-DOS Editor   <F1=Help> Press ALT to activate menus        00001:001
```

Fig. 14.14

The Editor screen
with scroll bars
removed.

Saving Customized Settings

If you change one or more display options, the DOS Editor creates a
file named QBASIC.INI and stores it in the directory containing the
EDIT.COM and QBASIC.EXE files. (For most systems, this directory is
\DOS.) The QBASIC.INI file contains a record of the new screen configuration. When you later restart, the Editor uses QBASIC.INI to restore the
screen with your customized settings.

Every time you start the Editor, it looks for QBASIC.INI in the default
directory or in the directory chain established by the PATH statement
in your AUTOEXEC.BAT file. If you restart from a different directory, be
sure that the Editor has access to the QBASIC.INI file.

If you want to start the Editor with the original screen configuration,
simply erase the QBASIC.INI file.

NOTE   The DOS Editor "borrows" the programming editor from the
QBASIC.EXE file. Thus, the DOS Editor shares the editing
environment found in the QBasic programming language.
Similarly, the DOS Editor and QBasic share the initial con-
figuration file (QBASIC.INI). Whether you run the DOS
Editor or QBasic, the initial configuration is saved in the
QBASIC.INI file.

Using the Help System

The DOS Editor provides on-line help through the Help menu (see fig. 14.15). Help screens include information about menus and commands, shortcut keys, dialog boxes, keyboard actions, and even about the help system itself.

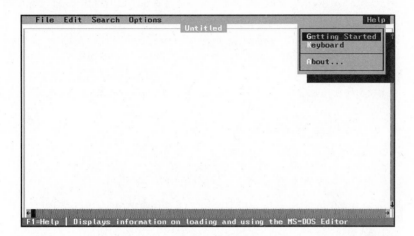

Fig. 14.15

The Help menu.

Three categories of information are available from the Help menu:

- *Getting Started* provides information about starting the Editor, using the menu and command system, and requesting help.

- *Keyboard* explains the different editing keystrokes and shortcuts for moving the cursor around your text file.

- *About* shows the Editor version number and copyright information.

The following are general notes on using the Help system:

- To activate the Help system at any time, press Alt-H.

- To move the cursor to the next help topic, press Tab. When the cursor is on the topic you want, press Enter to view the help screen.

- To activate the Getting Started help menu at any time, press Shift-F1.

- To close a help window and exit the help system, press Esc.

- A help screen opens in a separate window. The title bar of this window shows the help topic on display. For example, if you request help on the Save command from the File menu, the title bar of the help window reads HELP: Save command.

- The F1 key provides express help. To get help on any menu, command, or dialog box, press F1 when the cursor or highlight is on the desired item.

- For help when an error message occurs, move the cursor to the Help option in the error-message box, and press Enter.

- Sometime, at your leisure, consider browsing through all the help screens. To browse, press Shift-F1, and then press Ctrl-F1 repeatedly.

- To scroll any particular help screen, press PgUp or PgDn.

- When help is active, a separate help window opens in addition to the Editor window. You can move the cursor between the help and the Editor windows by pressing F6 (or Shift-F6).

- When a help window and the Editor window are open simultaneously, you can enlarge or reduce the size of the active window by pressing Alt-plus or Alt-minus. (Here, *plus* and *minus* refer to the + and – keys on the numeric keypad.)

- To cut and paste text from a help screen into your file, first use the normal editing keys to select the text on the help screen. Copy the selected lines to the clipboard. Press F6 to activate the Editor window and then, using the normal editing keys, paste the help text into your file. Now reactivate the help screen by pressing F6 again.

- When the help system is active, as in all editing contexts, the status bar at the bottom of the screen displays useful keystrokes. If you want to execute a command shown enclosed in angle brackets, press the indicated keystroke or click the mouse when the mouse cursor is on the command name in the status bar.

- The Editor keeps track of the last 20 help screens you have viewed. To cycle back through previously viewed screens, press Alt-F1.

- When you start the Editor, the initial dialog box gives you the option of seeing the Survival Guide. If you press Enter to see the Guide, the help system is activated. A help screen displays information about getting started with the Editor and using the help system.

■ The Editor stores the text of the help screens in a file named EDIT.HLP. To display any help screen, the Editor must have access to this file. The Editor searches for EDIT.HLP in the current directory or in directories specified by the PATH statement of your AUTOEXEC.BAT file. Normal DOS installation automatically places this file in the default \DOS directory. If for some reason, EDIT.HLP is located outside your PATH specifications, however, you can supply the Editor with the path to EDIT.HLP by selecting the Help Path command on the Options menu.

Chapter Summary

The DOS Editor is a text processor with which you can create, edit, and save text files. Among the Editor's features are full-screen editing, pull-down menus, shortcut keys, mouse support, and on-line help.

Although not in the same class as sophisticated word processors, the Editor is a considerable improvement from Edlin, the line-oriented editor (and the only text editor) supplied with earlier versions of DOS. The new editor is easier to use and more powerful than Edlin.

The DOS Editor is perfectly suited for creating short text documents such as memos, README files, and batch files.

In this chapter, you have mastered the following concepts and skills:

■ Navigating the menus and dialog boxes of the DOS Editor

■ Basic editing techniques in the Editor

■ Editing blocks of text

■ Searching for and replacing selected text

■ Managing files through the Editor

■ Customizing your screen in the Editor

In Chapter 15, you learn how to work with batch files, use DOSKey, and create macros.

Understanding Batch Files, DOSKey, and Macros

When you discover that you're performing a certain task on your computer repeatedly, you should look for a way to get the computer to do more of the work. Your computer can perform most tasks faster than you can, and it doesn't make mistakes.

DOS has always enabled you to automate your use of DOS commands by creating batch files. A *batch file* is a text (ASCII) file containing a series of commands that you want DOS to execute. When you type the batch file name, DOS executes these commands in the order you specified when you created the batch file. This chapter explains how to create and use DOS batch files.

In Chapter 14, "Using the DOS Editor," you learned how to create text files with the Editor. In this chapter, you use the Editor to create batch files. You learn about batch file commands and the AUTOEXEC.BAT file, and you see some examples of batch files you can modify to suit your needs.

In addition to batch files, you can use the DOSKey program to make the command line more efficient. DOSKey stores in the computer's memory the commands you type at the DOS command line, enabling you to use these commands again without retyping them. DOSKey also enables you to store a series of commands in memory and assign them to a new command name called a *macro*. You can execute the stored commands simply by typing the name of the macro. This chapter teaches you how to use these DOSKey features.

Key Terms Used in This Chapter

AUTOEXEC.BAT	A special batch file that DOS automatically executes during the booting process. This file, usually placed in the root directory, is an ideal place to include commands that initialize the operation of a PC.
Batch file	A text file containing commands that DOS executes as though the commands were entered at the DOS prompt. Batch files always have the BAT extension.
Flow control	The capability to control the order in which DOS processes lines of a batch file.
Macro	A series of DOS commands stored in memory under a single name. You execute a macro by typing its name.
Meta-string	A series of characters that in DOS takes on a meaning different from the string's literal meaning. DOS displays substitute text when the program finds meta-strings in the PROMPT command.

Introducing Batch Files

The idea of getting a computer to do work in convenient, manageable batches predates the personal computer by several years. The earliest computers were large and expensive, and they could do only one job at a time. But even these early machines were fast. Making them wait for keyboard input between jobs was inefficient.

Batch processing was developed to make computers more productive. Collections of tasks to be carried out consecutively were put together *off-line*—that is, without using the computer's resources. The chunks, or batches, of tasks then were fed to the computer at a rate that kept the computer busy and productive.

Today, computers are less expensive than human resources are. Batch processing enables computers to carry out a series of tasks automatically so that people don't have to waste time typing frequently used or complex commands.

A batch file is a text file that contains a series of DOS commands. Most commands used in batch files are familiar to you, having been explained in previous chapters of this book. Other commands, which control the flow of action in batch files, are available only in batch files. DOS executes the commands in a batch file one line at a time, treating each command as though you issued it individually.

You can use batch files to automate a DOS process. Using a set of commands in a batch file, you actually create a new, more powerful command. After a few experiments, you will find this DOS feature quite handy.

Recognizing a batch file in a directory listing is easy; batch files always have the file name extension BAT. You can execute a batch file by typing the file name at the DOS prompt and then pressing Enter. To execute the batch file SAFE.BAT, for example, you would type **SAFE** at the command line and press Enter. COMMAND.COM looks in the current directory for a file named SAFE that has the BAT extension; if it finds such a file, it reads the file and executes the DOS commands that the file contains.

> You can use the PATH command to give DOS alternative directories to search for the batch file you enter. PATH tells COMMAND.COM where to find BAT files as well as where to find EXE and COM files.
>
> **T I P**

Batch files are useful for issuing frequently used commands whose parameters you have trouble remembering. For example, you can run the Backup program by typing MSBACKUP and then selecting options from the program. But what if you have saved several sets of options in setup files for different circumstances? You could create batch files to run MSBACKUP with the proper setup file when you issue a simple command such as DAILYBAK.

Batch files can *echo* (display) messages that you designate. This text-display capability is useful for presenting instructions or reminders on-screen. You can compose messages that describe how to execute a command or that contain syntax examples and reminders. Batch files also can use the TYPE command to display text from another file.

In some ways, batch files resemble computer programs. DOS has a host of special commands that are used primarily in batch files. Although you can type some of these commands at the DOS prompt, their main use is in batch files. These commands introduce flow-control and decision-making capabilities into a batch file.

Understanding the Contents of Batch Files

Batch files consist entirely of ASCII text characters. You can create batch files in the DOS Editor, in Edlin, and in nearly any other text-editing or word processing program. (If you use a word processing program, you must use a setting that omits the special formatting and control characters that many such programs use for internal purposes.)

The easiest way to create a short batch file, however, is to use the COPY command to redirect input from the keyboard (the CON device) to a file (see Chapter 9, "Managing Your Files," for more information).

When you create batch files, observe the following rules:

- Batch files must be ASCII files. If you use a word processing program, be sure that the program saves the file without formatting characters.

- The name of the batch file, which can be one to eight characters long, must conform to DOS's file-name rules. Make batch-file names meaningful so that they are easier to remember.

- The file name must end with the BAT extension.

- The file name cannot be the same as a program file name (a file with an EXE or COM extension).

- The file name cannot be the same as an internal DOS command (such as COPY or DATE).

- The batch file can contain any valid DOS commands that you can enter at the DOS command line. (Typos cause errors.)

- You can include in the batch file any program name that you usually type at the DOS command line. DOS executes the program as though you had entered its name at the command line.

- Use only one command or program name per line in the batch file. DOS executes batch files one line at a time.

You start a batch file by typing its file name (excluding the extension) at the DOS prompt and then pressing Enter. The following list summarizes the rules DOS follows when it loads and executes a batch file:

■ DOS looks first to the drive and directory specified in the command.

■ Unless you specify the drive name before the batch-file name, DOS uses the current drive.

■ Unless you specify a path, DOS searches the current directory for the batch file.

■ If the batch file is not in the current directory or in the path you specified in the command, DOS searches the directories specified in the last PATH command you issued.

■ When DOS encounters a syntax error in a batch file's command line, DOS displays an error message, skips the incorrect command, and executes the remaining commands in the batch file.

■ You can stop a batch file by pressing Ctrl-C or Ctrl-Break. DOS displays the following prompt:

```
Terminate batch job (Y/N)?
```

Type **N** to skip the current command (the one being carried out) and proceed to the next command in the batch file. Type **Y** to abort execution of the batch file and return to the DOS prompt.

For Related Information

◄◄ "Copying from a Device to a File," p. 321.

FROM HERE...

Creating a Simple Batch File

One task that you may perform repetitively is copying and comparing files. Tasks consisting of the same series of commands are ideal candidates for batch files.

In this section, you create a simple batch file, using the COPY command to redirect input from the keyboard (the CON device) in order to create an ASCII text file. (Remember that you also can use the DOS Editor,

Edlin, or another text-editing or word processing program to create ASCII text files.)

Suppose that you often work with two spreadsheet files called SALES.WK1 and CUSTOMER.WK1. You frequently update these files and store them in the directory \STORE on drive C. After you update the files, you normally copy them to a disk in drive A and compare the copies on the floppy disk with the originals on the hard disk.

To begin creating a batch file that automates this process, type the following line at the DOS prompt and then press Enter:

    COPY CON COPYCOMP.BAT

This COPY command redirects console (keyboard) input to the file COPYCOMP.BAT. After you press Enter, DOS drops the cursor to the first blank line below the DOS prompt at the left of the screen and then waits for further instructions. Type the following three lines, pressing Enter after each line:

    ECHO OFF
    COPY C:\STORE A:
    FC C:\STORE A:/L

After you enter the last line in the file, press F6 or Ctrl-Z (both keys produce the characters ^Z) to signal DOS that it has reached the end of the file; then press Enter. DOS displays the following message:

```
1 file(s) copied
```

DOS copies the three lines into a file named COPYCOMP.BAT.

> **CAUTION:** When you use COPY CON to create a text file, check each line before pressing Enter. You can use Backspace and the DOS command-line editing keys (listed in Chapter 5, "Using DOS Commands") to edit the current line. After you press Enter, DOS moves the cursor down to the next line, and you cannot correct any errors in previous lines. You can abort the process without saving the file, however, by pressing Ctrl-C.

The first line of the COPYCOMP batch file, ECHO OFF, instructs DOS not to display the batch file's commands as the batch file executes. In other words, when you run the batch file, you do not see the command lines themselves on-screen; you see only the results of their actions.

> **T I P**
>
> The ECHO OFF command, which appears on-screen, prevents subsequent commands from appearing on-screen. If you are using DOS 3.3 or a later version, however, you can prevent the ECHO command from displaying by preceding the ECHO command with the @ character, as in the following command:
>
> @ECHO OFF

The second line of COPYCOMP.BAT copies the desired files from their source location in C:\STORE to the destination root directory of drive A.

The final line of the batch file uses COMP.COM, an external DOS command that compares the copied files with the originals. Although you can use the /V (verify) switch with COPY, using FC is more thorough.

Now that the COPYCOMP.BAT batch file is complete, you can run the file by typing the following command at the DOS prompt and then pressing Enter:

COPYCOMP

DOS first copies the two files from the C:\STORE directory to drive A and then compares both copies with both original files.

Understanding the AUTOEXEC.BAT File

The batch file named AUTOEXEC.BAT has special significance to DOS. When you boot your computer, DOS searches for this file in the root directory. When an AUTOEXEC.BAT file is present, DOS executes the commands contained in the file; otherwise, DOS prompts you for the date and time (refer to Chapter 3, "Starting DOS," for a full discussion of the boot process).

The AUTOEXEC.BAT file is optional; not every PC has this file. Most users, however, include an AUTOEXEC.BAT file of their own design on their boot disk because the file enables them to establish automatic operating parameters.

AUTOEXEC.BAT is intended to be a convenience to you. You can omit this file, enter a few preliminary commands, and then start your PC work session, accomplishing the same result as an AUTOEXEC.BAT file. Unless you have a good reason not to, however, take advantage of this

DOS feature by placing repetitive initialization commands in AUTOEXEC.BAT.

Some software packages come with installation programs that create or modify AUTOEXEC.BAT. These programs typically create AUTOEXEC.BAT if it doesn't exist or add commands to AUTOEXEC.BAT if it does exist. The installation program for DOS 6.0, for example, creates an AUTOEXEC.BAT file on your hard disk.

If you have doubts about which commands to include in your AUTOEXEC.BAT file, the following sections give you some ideas. Refer also to Chapter 17, "Configuring Your Computer," to learn more about using AUTOEXEC.BAT.

 NOTE   The AUTOEXEC.BAT file is a special batch file only in the sense that DOS executes AUTOEXEC.BAT each time you boot your computer. In every other sense, AUTOEXEC.BAT works the same way as any other batch file.

You can include any valid DOS command in the AUTOEXEC.BAT file, subject to the following guidelines:

■ The full file name must be AUTOEXEC.BAT, and the file must reside in the root directory of the boot disk.

■ The contents of the AUTOEXEC.BAT file must conform to the rules for batch files.

■ When DOS executes AUTOEXEC.BAT after a boot, DOS does not prompt for date and time automatically. You must include the DATE and TIME commands in your AUTOEXEC.BAT file if you want to review the date and time every time you reboot. Most users do not use DATE and TIME in AUTOEXEC.BAT, however, because most PCs have a battery-operated clock that correctly maintains the system's date and time.

FROM HERE...

For Related Information

◄◄ "Performing a Cold Boot," p. 67.

▶▶ "Reviewing AUTOEXEC.BAT," p. 630.

▶▶ "Fine-Tuning Your Computer with CONFIG.SYS and AUTOEXEC.BAT," p. 663.

Understanding the Contents of AUTOEXEC.BAT

Using AUTOEXEC.BAT is an excellent way for you to set up system defaults. That is, AUTOEXEC.BAT is the place to put commands you want DOS to execute every time you start your system. For example, you can use AUTOEXEC.BAT to tell your computer to change to the directory that holds your most commonly used program and start the program. This way, AUTOEXEC.BAT starts your program as soon as you boot your computer. You can use this technique, for example, to instruct DOS to start the DOS Shell each time you turn on your computer.

> Floppy-disk users often make each program disk bootable and place a different AUTOEXEC.BAT file on each disk. To start any particular program, they insert the program disk and reboot the computer. DOS does the rest.

T I P

Table 15.1 lists the commands that most frequently are included in simple AUTOEXEC.BAT files.

Table 15.1 AUTOEXEC.BAT File Commands

Command	Function
CD	Changes to the directory in which you normally work
DATE	Enables you to enter the correct time so that DOS can acccurately "stamp" new and modified files, providing the correct date to programs that request that information.
DIR	Displays a listing of the root directory as soon as the computer boots
ECHO	Enables you to include a message as part of your start-up
PATH	Establishes the directory path that DOS searches for executable files (EXE, COM, and BAT extensions)
PROMPT	Customizes the system prompt

continues

Table 15.1 Continued	
Command	**Function**
TIME	Enables you to enter the correct time so that DOS can accurately "stamp" new and modified files, providing the correct time to programs that request that information*

* This command is unnecessary if your computer has a battery-operated system clock.

Most of these commands are self-explanatory. The more complex commands are covered in the following sections.

Using the PATH Command

The PATH command tells DOS where to search for COM, EXE, and BAT files (see Chapter 8, "Understanding and Managing Directories," for more information on external commands). In this section, you learn how to use the PATH command in the AUTOEXEC.BAT file.

Suppose that you installed the operating-system files in the \DOS directory on your hard disk, C. You want to be able to issue DOS external commands from any directory on the disk without specifying the directory that contains the operating-system files. To accomplish this task, type the following command in the AUTOEXEC.BAT file:

PATH C:\DOS

If you want DOS to search the root directory first and the \DOS directory next, type the following PATH command in AUTOEXEC.BAT:

PATH C:\;C:\DOS

To cause DOS to search a third directory, add that directory's name to the PATH command, and so on. Notice that semicolons (;) separate the directory names.

After AUTOEXEC.BAT executes the PATH command, when you issue a command at the command line, DOS searches the directories listed in the PATH command. If DOS cannot find the program in the current directory, the program searches the first directory listed in the PATH command (in this example, the root directory), and then the second directory in the PATH command, and so on. DOS continues to search directories in turn until the executable file is found or until all alternatives are exhausted. If DOS cannot find an executable file by the specified name in any directory in the PATH, DOS displays the following message:

```
Bad command or file name
```

The path specified in AUTOEXEC.BAT becomes DOS's default search path. You can change this default path by issuing the PATH command manually at the DOS prompt or through another batch file.

Using the PROMPT Command

The default DOS prompt (A> or C>) is rather spartan. This DOS prompt tells you the identity of the current logged drive but nothing else (A> for the floppy-disk drive A and C> for the hard-disk drive C). By using the PROMPT command, however, you can change the prompt to any of a wide variety of forms and even to include useful system information.

The syntax for the PROMPT command is as follows:

PROMPT text

The *text* parameter can be any string of characters. DOS creates the prompt from this character string, interpreting the characters literally. If you include the word *HELLO* in the PROMPT command, for example, DOS displays HELLO as part of the DOS prompt.

Certain character strings have special meaning to DOS, however, when you use them in the PROMPT command. These special character strings are two-letter codes, sometimes referred to as *meta-strings*. DOS substitutes current system information or a special character for each meta-string.

The following section explains meta-strings.

Understanding Meta-Strings

A PROMPT command meta-string consists of two characters, the first of which always is the dollar sign ($). DOS interprets meta-strings to mean something other than the literal meaning of the characters.

Several PROMPT command meta-strings convey current system information. If you include the meta-string $t in the PROMPT command, for example, DOS displays the current system time in HH:MM:SS format.

Other meta-strings used in the PROMPT command cause DOS to display literally characters that DOS otherwise would interpret as part of a command syntax. For example, DOS normally recognizes the symbols > and < as redirection characters and the vertical bar (|) as the pipe character. You may, however, want to include one or more of these symbols in a prompt without causing DOS to perform redirection or piping. To use one of these characters in the DOS prompt for a purpose other than redirection or piping, you must use the appropriate meta-string.

Table 15.2 lists the PROMPT command meta-strings and their meanings.

Table 15.2 Meta-Strings for Use with the PROMPT Command	
Meta-string	**Meaning**
$_	Carriage return/line feed (moves the cursor to the beginning of the following line)
$b	Vertical bar or pipe character (	)
$d	Current system date
$e	Escape character
$g	Greater-than symbol (>)
$h	Backspace character (moves the cursor one space to the left)
$l	Less-than symbol (<)
$n	Current drive name
$p	Current drive and path
$q	Equals sign (=)
$t	System time
$v	DOS version

Customizing Your Prompt

You can use the meta-string characters with the PROMPT command to produce your own DOS prompt. Because you can use other characters in addition to meta-strings, you can experiment with different combinations of meta-strings and phrases.

 Issuing the PROMPT command alone, with no parameters, restores the prompt to the original default (A> or C>).

If you want your prompt to tell you the current DOS path, for example, type the following command:

    PROMPT THE CURRENT PATH IS $P

If the current drive is C and the current directory is \DOS, the preceding PROMPT command produces the following DOS prompt:

```
THE CURRENT PATH IS C:\DOS
```

By adding the meta-string $g, you can add the greater-than symbol (>) to the prompt. The new version of the command is as follows:

PROMPT THE CURRENT PATH IS PG

Your DOS prompt appears as follows:

```
THE CURRENT PATH IS C:\DOS>
```

Using meta-strings and characters, you also can display other system information in the prompt, including the system date and time and the DOS version. The following PROMPT command displays the date and time above the path and encloses the path in brackets:

PROMPT $D :$T$_[$P]

After you issue this command, the prompt resembles the following example:

```
Mon 01-04-1993: 9:26:00.48
[C:\]
```

The $_ meta-string causes the prompt to move down one line before displaying the path.

You can use the $h meta-string to erase part of the prompt. The $t meta-string, for example, causes DOS to display seconds and hundredths of seconds. Using the $h meta-string several times, you can erase the seconds and hundredths of seconds, making the prompt less cluttered. The PROMPT command is as follows:

PROMPT D:THHHHH_[$P]

After you issue this command, DOS displays a prompt similar to the following example:

```
Mon 01-04-1993: 9:26
[C:\]
```

> **NOTE** The $e meta-string represents the Escape character (ASCII decimal 27). This meta-string is used with a special file named ANSI.SYS, a device driver file. (Refer to Chapter 19, "Understanding ANSI.SYS," for a discussion of device drivers.) Using the PROMPT command and ANSI.SYS codes, you can customize your system prompt further, even adding color if you want.

FROM HERE...

For Related Information

◄◄ "Helping DOS Find External Commands," p. 240.

►► "Understanding Device Drivers," p. 632.

Examining AUTOEXEC.BAT Files

The contents of users' AUTOEXEC.BAT files may vary, but most AUTOEXEC.BAT files contain a few of the same commands. The following sample AUTOEXEC.BAT file executes useful start-up commands:

```
DATE
TIME
PATH=C:\;C:\DOS;C:\KEEP;C:\;
PROMPT $P$G
CD\BATCH
DIR
ECHO Good Day, Mate!
```

Following are explanations of the lines in this file:

- *DATE* prompts you to enter the correct date so that DOS can accurately date-stamp new and modified files.

- *TIME* prompts you to enter the correct time so that DOS can accurately time-stamp new and modified files.

- *PATH=C:\;C:\DOS;C:\KEEP;C:\;* instructs DOS to search the named directories to find files that have EXE, COM, or BAT extensions.

- *PROMPT PG* customizes the system prompt to show the current drive and path and the greater-than (>) symbol.

- *CD\BATCH* makes \BATCH the current directory. This directory may contain batch files that start programs on your hard disk.

- *DIR* displays a listing of the current directory.

- *ECHO Good Day, Mate!* displays Good Day, Mate! as part of your start-up procedure.

You easily can see whether AUTOEXEC.BAT exists in your root directory or on your logged floppy disk. First, log onto your hard disk and change to the root directory. To look at the directory listing of all files with BAT extensions, type the following command, and then press Enter:

DIR *.BAT

To view the contents of AUTOEXEC.BAT on-screen, type the following command:

TYPE AUTOEXEC.BAT

To get a printed copy of the AUTOEXEC.BAT file, redirect output to the printer by using the following command:

TYPE AUTOEXEC.BAT >PRN

Alternatively, you can use the COPY command to copy the file to the printer, as follows:

COPY AUTOEXEC.BAT PRN

If you choose not to print a copy of your AUTOEXEC.BAT file, make sure that you write down the contents before you make any changes. Be sure that you copy the syntax correctly. This copy serves as your worksheet.

You can use your copy of AUTOEXEC.BAT to see whether a PROMPT or PATH command is contained in the batch file. If you want to add or alter PROMPT or PATH commands, mark the additions or changes on your worksheet. Use your paper copy of the AUTOEXEC.BAT file to check for proper syntax in the lines you change or add before you commit the changes to disk.

Always make a backup copy of your existing AUTOEXEC.BAT file before you make any changes in the file. To save the current version, you can copy it with a different extension. To create a copy named AUTOEXEC.OLD, for example, type the following command, and then press Enter:

COPY AUTOEXEC.BAT AUTOEXEC.OLD

DOS copies the contents of AUTOEXEC.BAT to the file AUTOEXEC.OLD. You now can modify your AUTOEXEC.BAT file by using the DOS Editor, Edlin, or another text-editing or word processing program. If you use the COPY CON method, you have to start from scratch and type the entire new version of the batch file.

If you find that the new AUTOEXEC.BAT file does not work or does not perform appropriately, you can erase the new file. Then, using the RENAME command, you can rename the AUTOEXEC.OLD file AUTOEXEC.BAT, and you are back where you started.

Understanding Replaceable Parameters

The batch files discussed so far in this chapter carry out exactly the same functions every time you use them. You may want a particular batch file to operate on different files each time you use it, however, even though the commands in the batch file are fixed. When you use *replaceable parameters* in a batch file, you can cause the same parameter to do different things.

A parameter is an additional instruction that defines the task that you want the DOS command to do. When you type the name of the batch file at the DOS prompt, you can include up to nine parameters. DOS assigns a variable name to each parameter, starting with 1 and going up to 9. (DOS always assigns the variable name 0 to the name of the batch file itself.)

You can use each variable in your batch file by preceding the variable name with the percent sign (%). This combination of the percent sign and the variable name is the replaceable parameter.

When used in a batch file, each replaceable parameter, numbered %0 through %9, holds the place for a parameter in one or more commands of a batch file so that you can provide the actual value of the parameter at the time you execute the batch file.

Consider the COPYCOMP.BAT batch file discussed earlier in this chapter:

```
ECHO OFF
COPY C:\STORE A:
COMP C:\STORE A:
```

Each time you execute this batch file, it copies all files from the C:\STORE directory to the A disk and then compares the files. Suppose that you want to make this batch file more versatile so that you can use it to copy and compare the files in any directory. Revise COPYCOMP.BAT as follows:

```
ECHO OFF
COPY %1 %2
COMP %1 %2
```

Notice that %1 and %2 replace C:\STORE and A:, respectively. These parameters are the replaceable parameters.

After making these changes in COPYCOMP.BAT, you can use the batch file to copy and compare the files from any directory to any disk or directory. To copy and compare the files in the \SPREADSH\QPRO2DAT directory on the C drive with the files on a disk in the B drive, for example, type the following command, and then press Enter:

COPYCOMP C:\SPREADSH\QPRO4DAT B:

DOS copies all files from C:\SPREADSH\QPRO4DAT to the disk in drive B and then compares the original files with the copies to ensure that the copy procedure was effective.

To see how DOS replaces the parameters, create a batch file called TEST1.BAT and type the following line into this file:

@ECHO %0 %1 %2 %3 %4 %5 %6 %7 %8 %9

After you create this file, type **TEST1**, followed by one space. Then type your first name, your last name, street address, city, state, ZIP code, and age, with each entry separated by spaces. Your screen should look similar to the following example:

```
C\:>TEST1 DAVID SMITH 1234 PINE STREET ANYTOWN IN 46032 39
TEST1 DAVID SMITH 1234 PINE STREET ANYTOWN IN 46032 39
C\:>
```

The batch-file command instructs DOS to display the parameters 0 through 9. In the preceding example, these parameters are the following:

Parameter	Word
%0	TEST1
%1	DAVID
%2	SMITH
%3	1234
%4	PINE
%5	STREET
%6	ANYTOWN

continues

Parameter	Word
%7	IN
%8	46032
%9	39

Now try to "shortchange" DOS by not specifying a sufficient number of parameters to fill every variable marker. Run TEST1 again, but this time, type only your first name. Your screen should resemble the following example:

```
C>TEST1 DAVID
TEST1 DAVID
C>
```

DOS displays the batch-file name and your first name. No other information is echoed to the screen. You specified fewer parameters, and DOS replaced the unfilled markers with nothing. In this case, the empty markers did no harm.

Some commands you use in a batch file, however, may require that a replaceable parameter not be empty. If you include DEL in a batch file with a replaceable parameter and the parameter is empty, you see the following error message:

```
Invalid number of parameters
```

You can use the IF command (discussed later in this chapter) to avert such errors.

In the remainder of this section, you learn how to construct a batch file that takes advantage of replaceable parameters. Suppose that you use several computers daily, but one of the hard-disk systems is your "workhorse," where you store all the files that you want to keep. You use floppy disks to move information from computer to computer. After copying a file back to a hard disk, you usually delete the file from the floppy disk. Deleting the file removes it from the process so that the file is not accidentally copied to the hard disk again later. You use the following steps to transfer data from a floppy disk to a hard disk:

1. Copy file from the floppy disk to the hard disk with the verify switch on.

2. Erase the file from the floppy disk.

To simplify this process, you can create a batch file called C&E.BAT (copy and erase). Type the following commands in the file:

```
COPY A:%1 C:%2 /V
ERASE A:%1
```

To use the C&E.BAT file, type the following command at the DOS prompt:

```
C&E oldfilename newfilename
```

The first parameter, *oldfilename*, represents the name of the file you want to copy from the floppy disk to the hard disk; *newfilename* is the new name for the copied file (if you want to change the file name as the file is being copied).

Suppose that you put a disk containing the file NOTES.TXT into drive A and want to copy the file to the hard disk. Type the following command at the DOS prompt:

```
C&E NOTES.TXT
```

The screen appears as follows:

```
C>COPY A:NOTES.TXT C: /V
1 file(s) copied
C>ERASE A:NOTES.TXT
C>
C>
```

Notice that even though you didn't type the parameter *newfilename*, DOS carried out the batch file, keeping the same file name during the copy. DOS copied NOTES.TXT from drive A to drive C and then deleted the file on the disk in drive A. The %2 parameter was dropped, and the file did not get a new name during the copy operation.

One benefit of creating a batch file that copies a file using parameters is that you can use a path name as the second parameter. By specifying a path name, you can copy the file from the floppy disk to a different directory on the hard disk. To copy NOTES.TXT to the WORDS directory, for example, type the following command:

```
C&E NOTES.TXT \WORDS
```

The screen display is as follows:

```
C>COPY A:NOTES.TXT C:\WORDS /V
1 file(s) copied
C>ERASE A:NOTES.TXT
C>
```

Because \WORDS is a directory name, DOS copies the file NOTES.TXT into the directory \WORDS, following the rules of syntax for the COPY command. The batch file takes advantage of these syntax rules.

> **NOTE** Patience and persistence are important in understanding batch files. Many PC users who tried to avoid using batch files finally experimented with one or two examples; these users picked up the concept rapidly and now produce batch files that anyone would be proud to have created. Give yourself a chance to learn batch files by completing the exercises in this chapter. You can use the sample batch files as templates and apply them to specific situations. When you learn how to compose batch files, you will have harnessed one of DOS's most powerful features.

Your use of batch files is not limited by your own imagination. If you pick up almost any personal-computer magazine, you can find a few useful batch files introduced in a feature or an article. You can use these featured batch files verbatim or modify them for your own special situation.

Even if you don't regularly create your own batch files, you can use your knowledge of batch-file principles. Many programs are started by batch files rather than by the name of the actual program file. With your knowledge of batch files, you can use the TYPE command to display the contents of any batch file so you can see what the batch operation is doing.

Many software programs use the commands in an installation batch file to install the main files. You can understand how an installation proceeds if you read the installation batch file. Knowing what the batch file does can help you avert installation conflicts. Suppose that you use drive B to install a program supplied on a 5 1/4-inch disk, because your drive A is a 3 1/2-inch drive. Many installation batch files, however, assume that the files are to be installed in drive A. To prevent this conflict, you can modify a version of the installation batch file by changing all instances of A: to B:. When you run your modified installation batch file, you can install the new software without a hitch.

Working with batch files also can serve as a meaningful introduction to programming. The batch-file commands covered in this chapter give batch files the kind of internal flow and decision-making capabilities that programming languages offer. Of course, don't expect batch files to equal the versatility of a full-featured programming environment. But batch files certainly can assume a programming flavor. By using batch files, you can increase DOS's usefulness significantly.

Using Batch-File Commands

DOS includes special commands that often are used in batch files. Table 15.3 lists batch-file commands for DOS 3.3 through 6.0.

Table 15.3 Batch-File Commands

Command	Action
@	Suppresses the display of the command line on-screen (DOS 3.3 and later)
CALL	Runs another batch file and returns to the original batch file (DOS 3.3 and later)
CHOICE	Halts processing until a specified key is pressed (use the IF ERRORLEVEL command to determine which key was pressed)
CLS	Clears the screen and returns the cursor to the top corner of the screen
COMMAND /C	Invokes a second copy of the command processor, COMMAND.COM, to call another batch file (necessary in versions before 3.3)
ECHO	Turns on or off the display of batch commands as they execute; also can display a message on-screen
FOR..IN..DO	Permits the use of the same batch command for several files; the execution "loops"
GOTO	Jumps to the line following the specified label in a batch file
IF	Permits conditional execution of a command
PAUSE	Halts processing until a key is pressed; displays the message `Press any key to continue…`
REM	Enables you to insert into a batch file comments that describe the purpose of an operation
SHIFT	Shifts the command-line parameters one parameter to the left

You can use any of the commands listed in table 15.3 in a batch file; you can use some of them at the DOS system level as well. For example, you can type **ECHO** with or without an argument at the DOS prompt. DOS displays the string you type after ECHO or, if you provide no argument, tells you whether ECHO is ON or OFF. If you type **PAUSE** at the DOS prompt, DOS displays the message `Press any key to continue…` and waits for a keystroke.

Although these two commands are not very useful at the DOS prompt, the FOR..IN..DO command structure can be quite useful at the operating-system level to carry out repetitive commands.

The following sections explain the batch commands and their uses.

Displaying Messages and Inserting Comments

The ECHO command does two things. ECHO ON and ECHO OFF turn on and off the display of lines from batch files as the commands are executed, and ECHO also displays messages.

ECHO can display a message up to 122 characters long (the 127-character DOS command-line limit, minus the length of the ECHO command, minus a space).

You can use REM (which stands for *remark*) in a batch file to remind you what the batch file does. When you review a batch file some time after you create it, you may no longer remember why you used certain commands or why you constructed the batch file in a particular way. Leave reminders in your batch file by using REM statements, which don't appear on-screen when ECHO is off. The REM comments make the batch file self-documenting, a feature that you and other users will appreciate later.

If you want the batch file to display particular messages, use ECHO. Messages set with ECHO appear on-screen whether or not you set ECHO OFF.

To insert a blank line between messages, type a semicolon (but no space) after the ECHO command, as follows:

        ECHO;

Clearing the Screen and Suppressing Screen Display

You can use the DOS CLS command at the DOS prompt to clear the screen at any time. In batch files, CLS commonly is used after the ECHO OFF command to clear the screen, providing a clear space for your batch file's messages. The syntax of that command is as follows:

        ECHO OFF
        CLS

Branching with GOTO

When you run a batch file, DOS normally processes commands one line at a time, from the beginning of the batch file to the end. When you use the DOS GOTO command, however, you can change the order in which DOS executes batch commands by instructing DOS to branch to a specific line in the file.

The syntax of GOTO is as follows:

GOTO label

The DOS GOTO command uses *label* to specify the line in the file to which DOS should send the execution of the file. A batch-file label is a separate line that is not a command per se. A label consists of a colon followed by one to eight characters. The label name can be longer than eight characters, but DOS reads only the first eight characters.

When DOS encounters a GOTO command in the batch file, DOS starts at the beginning of the batch file and searches for a label matching the one specified by GOTO. DOS then jumps execution to the batch-file line following the line with the label.

Consider the following batch file, LOOP.BAT. This file is similar to the TEST.BAT batch file you created previously, with the addition of the GOTO and PAUSE commands.

```
:LOOP
@ECHO OFF
ECHO Hello, %1
PAUSE
GOTO LOOP
```

To test the batch file, type **LOOP DAVID**. The screen shows the following message:

```
Hello, DAVID
Press any key to continue…
```

The batch file begins by echoing Hello, DAVID and then waits for you to press a key. After you press a key, DOS again displays the following message:

```
Hello, DAVID
Press any key to continue…
```

When you press a key again, DOS executes the GOTO LOOP command, causing execution of the batch file to return to the line labeled :LOOP at beginning of the file. DOS again displays the messages and pauses.

This batch file is an example of what programmers call an *infinite loop*. The program never stops on its own. To abort the batch file, you must press Ctrl-C or Ctrl-Break. DOS asks Terminate batch job (Y/N)? If you type **Y**, DOS returns to the DOS system prompt.

This simple example illustrates the operation of GOTO. You seldom will create infinite loops on purpose, but you should be able to use the GOTO command to control the order in which DOS executes batch-file commands.

Using the IF Command

The IF command is a "test and do" command. When a given condition is true, the IF command executes a stated action. When the given condition is false, IF skips the action. If you are familiar with programming languages, such as BASIC, you should find the DOS IF command familiar.

The IF command tests the following three conditions:

- What the ERRORLEVEL of a program is
- Whether a string is equal to another string
- Whether a file exists

The following sections explain these tests.

Using IF To Test ERRORLEVEL

The first condition that IF can test is ERRORLEVEL. The proper syntax for testing the ERRORLEVEL is as follows:

IF *NOT* ERRORLEVEL number command

ERRORLEVEL is a code left by a program when it finishes executing. A better name for this condition might be "exit level." This form of the IF command determines whether the value of ERRORLEVEL is greater than or equal to a number specified in the *number* parameter. Conversely, by adding the optional word *NOT*, you can determine whether the value of ERRORLEVEL is *not* greater than or equal to the value of the *number* parameter. If the specified condition is true, DOS executes the command specified in the *command* parameter. Otherwise, DOS skips to the next line in the batch file without executing *command*.

In DOS 3.3 and later versions, the only DOS commands that leave an ERRORLEVEL (exit) code are BACKUP, DISKCOMP, DISKCOPY, FORMAT, GRAFTABL, KEYB (DOS 4.0 and later), REPLACE, RESTORE, and XCOPY. Many other programs generate exit codes, however.

An exit code of zero (0) usually indicates that the command was successful. Any number greater than 0 usually indicates that something went wrong when the program executed. The following exit codes, for example, are generated by the DISKCOPY command:

Code	Meaning
0	Successful operation
1	A read/write error occurred that did not terminate the disk-copy operation
2	The user pressed Ctrl-C
3	A "fatal" read/write error occurred and terminated the copy procedure before it was completed
4	An initialization error occurred

An IF command in a batch file enables you to test for the exit code generated by a DOS command or program to determine whether the command or program worked properly.

When you use ERRORLEVEL to test exit codes, DOS tests whether the exit code is equal to or greater than the specified *number* parameter. If the exit code is equal to or greater than the number, DOS executes the *command* parameter. If the exit code does not meet the condition, DOS skips the *command* parameter and executes the next command in the batch file. You can think of this condition as a BASIC-like statement, as follows:

IF exit code >= number THEN do command

The IF ERRORLEVEL command is most useful with the new DOS 6.0 command CHOICE. When your batch file uses this utility, the file can pause for keyboard input. The utility puts a value in ERRORLEVEL related to the key pressed. You then can make your batch file branch or perform some other task based on the key pressed. A batch file otherwise does not accept keyboard input except when the input is provided on a batch-file command line. (For more information, see the section "Pausing for Input in a Batch File" later in this chapter.)

Suppose that you want to create a batch file named DCOPY.BAT that makes disk copies in your A drive, using the DISKCOPY command and the verification switch (see Chapter 6, "Understanding Disks and Files"). If the disk-copy procedure terminates before completion, you want the batch file to inform you of the cause.

Create a batch file named DCOPY.BAT that contains the following lines:

```
@ECHO OFF
DISKCOPY A: A: /V
IF ERRORLEVEL 4 GOTO INIT_ERR
IF ERRORLEVEL 3 GOTO FATL_ERR
IF ERRORLEVEL 2 GOTO CTRL-C
IF ERRORLEVEL 1 GOTO NON_FATL
ECHO DISKCOPY successful and verified!
GOTO END
:INIT_ERR
ECHO Initialization error!
GOTO END
:FATL_ERR
ECHO Fatal error! DISKCOPY stopped!
GOTO END
:CTRL-C
ECHO Someone pressed Ctrl-C!
GOTO END
:NON-FATL
ECHO A non-fatal error occurred. Check data!
:END
```

To run this batch file, type **DCOPY** at the command line, and then press Enter. DOS displays the following message:

```
Insert SOURCE diskette in drive A:
Press any key to continue…
```

When you press a key, DOS begins the disk-copy procedure. After the DISKCOPY command in the batch file executes, the batch file runs through a series of IF ERRORLEVEL tests.

First, the batch file tests for an initialization error (exit code = 4). If the exit code equals or is greater than 4, DOS skips to the line labeled :INIT_ERR and displays the message `Initialization error!`

Next, the batch file checks for exit code 3. If the exit code is 3, execution of the batch file skips to the :FATL_ERR label and displays the message `Fatal error! DISKCOPY stopped!`

The batch file again tests the exit code and branches to the :CTRL_C label if an exit code of 2 is detected. The batch file also branches to the :NON_FATL label when the exit code is 1.

Finally, if no errors are detected by the series of IF ERRORLEVEL commands, the batch file displays the following message:

DISKCOPY successful and verified!

Using IF To Compare Strings

The second use for the IF command is to test whether string 1 equals string 2. The syntax of the batch command is as follows:

IF *NOT* **string1==string2 command**

This form of the IF command determines whether the first character string, *string1*, is the same group of characters as *string2*. Usually, one string is a replaceable parameter. If the two strings are identical, this condition is true, so DOS executes the command specified in the *command* parameter. Otherwise, DOS skips to the next line in the batch file without executing *command*. By adding NOT to the IF command, you can test for the condition when the two strings are not the same.

Assume that you want to create a batch file named DAYBACK.BAT that backs up your hard disk each day of the week. On Fridays, you want the batch file to perform a complete backup. On Mondays through Thursdays, you want the batch file to perform an additive incremental backup. Use the DOS Editor or another text editor to create the following batch file:

```
@ECHO OFF
CLS
IF "%1"="" GOTO TRY_AGAIN
IF %1==FRI GOTO FULL
IF %1==MON GOTO ADD
IF %1==TUE GOTO ADD
IF %1==WED GOTO ADD
IF %1==THU GOTO ADD
:TRY_AGAIN
ECHO Try again! Type DAYBACK and day of week (MON-FRI).
GOTO END
:FULL
ECHO Insert first disk of backup set.
PAUSE
C:
CD \
BACKUP C: A: /S
GOTO END
:ADD
ECHO Insert last disk of backup set.
```

```
PAUSE
C:
CD \
BACKUP C: A: /S/M/A
:END
```

To run this batch file, type **DAYBACK**, followed by the three-letter abbreviation for the day of the week (MON, TUE, WED, THU, or FRI), and then press Enter.

The first IF command in DAYBACK.BAT checks to make sure that you have typed the day of the week. If you don't provide enough parameters with the IF command, DOS replaces the replaceable parameter with a null value. (In batch files, null values must be enclosed in quotation marks to prevent a syntax error.)

The remaining IF commands determine whether you typed *FRI* or another day of the week. If you type *FRI*, the batch file branches to the :FULL label and performs a full backup. If you typed MON through THU, the file jumps to the :ADD label and performs an additive incremental backup. If you typed anything else, the batch file instructs you to try again.

NOTE The :END label often is used to mark the end of the batch file. In the preceding batch file, execution branches to the :END label after a full backup, after an incremental backup, or after you are instructed to try again. When you use this technique, DOS executes only a portion of the batch file each time you run it, skipping the portions of the batch file that don't apply. Because the :END label is the last line in the batch file, the batch file ends at that point.

In the DAYBACK.BAT example, the replaceable parameter in the first IF command is enclosed in quotation marks because programmers commonly use quotation marks to delimit character strings. Actually, a comparison with any letter, number, or symbol can do the job. One common procedure is to use a single period instead of quotation marks, as shown in the following example:

    IF %1 . == . GOTO TRY_AGAIN

If you don't enter a parameter for %1, DOS interprets the line as follows:

    IF . == . GOTO TRY_AGAIN

Use the syntax that is easiest for you to remember and understand.

If %1 equals nothing, DOS branches to the line following the label TRY_AGAIN and displays the message Try again! Type DAYBACK and day of week (MON-FRI).

If %1 equals something other than nothing, DOS does not branch to NOTHING; instead, DOS executes the second IF command in the batch file, which tests whether you typed *DAYBACK FRI*, and so on. Notice that GOTO statements are used to jump around the parts of the batch file that should not be executed.

> When you use the IF command, DOS compares strings literally. Uppercase characters are different from lowercase characters. If you run DAYBACK by typing **DAYBACK Fri**, DOS compares Fri with the uppercase FRI and decides that the two strings are not the same. The IF test fails, and no backup operation is performed.
>
> **T I P**

Using IF To Look for Files

The third type of IF command tests whether a given file is on disk. The syntax for this form of the IF command is as follows:

IF *NOT* EXIST filename command

This form of the IF command determines whether the file specified in the *filename* parameter exists on your computer's disk (or doesn't exist, if you add NOT). If the file does exist, the IF command executes the command specified in the *command* parameter.

If you want to test for a file in a drive other than the current drive, type the drive name before *filename* (for example, IF EXIST B:CHKDSK.COM).

You can use IF EXIST when you start a word processing program. Perhaps you use a file called TEMP.TXT to store temporary files or to write blocks that are to be read into other documents. You can use IF EXIST to test for the existence of the file and to erase the file, if it does exist.

Your batch file, called WORD.BAT, would look like the following example:

```
@ECHO OFF
CLS
CD \DOCUMENT
IF EXIST TEMP.TXT DEL TEMP.TXT
\WORDS\WP
CD \
```

In this batch file, ECHO is turned off, and the screen is cleared. The current directory is changed to \DOCUMENT—the directory where you store your word processing documents.

Next, the IF command tests for the existence of TEMP.TXT. If the file does exist, DOS deletes the file. Finally, DOS starts your word processing program from the \WORDS subdirectory.

Notice the last line of the batch file: CD \. When your word processing program starts, the batch file is suspended temporarily. After you quit your word processing program, control is given back to the batch file. The batch file then executes its last line, CD \ , which changes back to the root directory. The batch file ends.

FROM HERE...

For Related Information

◄◄ "Copying an Entire Disk with DISKCOPY," p. 168.

Pausing for Input in a Batch File

Before DOS 6.0, the only way to affect the execution of a batch file after the file started was to press Ctrl-C or Ctrl-Break. These key combinations enabled you to cancel a single command or to end the entire operation. DOS 6.0 gives you a means of temporarily halting the execution of a batch file and accepting limited user input. You can use this feature to decide whether or not to process certain commands, to branch to a different part of a batch file, or even to present a menu and accept any of a series of choices.

To employ this capability, you use the CHOICE command. The command's syntax is as follows:

    CHOICE */C:choices /N /S /T:c,nn message*

Following are explanations of the components of this command:

- */C:choices* lists the keys that can be pressed. If you don't specify *choices*, the default is YN.

- */N* prevents the display of acceptable keys at the end of the prompt.

- */S* instructs CHOICE to pay attention to the case of the key pressed; this feature enables you to use *Y* and *y* for different choices.

■ *T:c,nn* causes CHOICE to act as though you pressed the key represented by *c* if you don't make a choice within *nn* seconds.

■ *message* is the optional prompt to be displayed.

You respond to the key pressed by using a series of IF ERRORLEVEL commands. By default, the choices are Y and N. Y has the ERRORLEVEL code 2, and N has the ERRORLEVEL code 1.

Making a Two-Way Choice

If you don't specify which keys should be pressed, CHOICE assumes Y and N, and adds [Y,N]? to the end of whatever message you choose to include. This feature is extremely useful if you want to decide whether to load a certain program when your computer starts. For example, you might type the following commands near the end of your AUTOEXEC.BAT file:

    CHOICE Back up hard disk
    IF ERRORLEVEL 2 MSBACKUP

When the AUTOEXEC.BAT file reaches the first line, DOS displays the following message:

```
Back up hard disk[Y,N]?
```

If you have not yet backed up your hard disk today, you would type **Y**, which generates the ERRORLEVEL code 2. DOS then executes the MSBACKUP program. If you have backed up your hard disk, you would type **N**. You need not test for this code, however, because it's the only other alternative. DOS then executes any commands following these lines in AUTOEXEC.BAT, but MSBACKUP doesn't run.

Creating a Simple Menu

Because you can specify any keys as choices, you could use CHOICE to create a simple menu, using the */C:choices* parameter to specify the keys to be pressed. You might use a command such as the following:

    CHOICE/c:swd Load Spreadsheet, Word Processor, or Database
    Manager

DOS displays the following message:

```
Load Spreadsheet, Word Processor, or Database
Manager[S,W,D]?
```

The ERRORLEVEL codes for the specified keys read from left to right. Thus, pressing D generates a code of 3; pressing W, a code of 2; and pressing S, a code of 1. You might think of the following lines as reading like the following example:

```
IF ERRORLEVEL 3 DB
IF ERRORLEVEL 2 WP
IF ERRORLEVEL 1 SS
```

IF ERRORLEVEL, however, automatically assumes that all numbers lower than the one specified also are true. If you type D, for example, DOS loads your word processing program as soon as you exit from your database manager and your spreadsheet program as soon as you exit from your word processing program.

You can deal with this situation in either of two ways. One way is to add a second command that changes the flow of execution. Your file would have to resemble the following example:

```
CHOICE/C:swd Load Spreadsheet, Word Processor, or Database
Manager
IF ERRORLEVEL 3 DB
IF ERRORLEVEL 3 GOTO END
IF ERRORLEVEL 2 WP
IF ERRORLEVEL 2 GOTO END
IF ERRORLEVEL 1 SS
:END
```

The second way to deal with the limitation of the ERRORLEVEL directive is to have each test execute a batch file instead of a program. (After you pass control to a second batch file, DOS does not return to the original file unless you use CALL or COMMAND /C.) For this command to work properly, the batch files must appear either in the current directory or in a directory in the path that precedes the directories containing the programs.

T I P

Always give a user a way to get out of a command without choosing any of the proffered alternatives. You can break out of the CHOICE command, for example, by pressing Ctrl-C or Ctrl-Break. These key combinations tell DOS to skip to the following line. But you could include a third alternative, such as Quit, as shown in the following example:

```
CHOICE /C:YNQ Back up hard disk
IF ERRORLEVEL 3 MSBACKUP
IF ERRORLEVEL 3 GOTO END
IF ERRORLEVEL 1 IF NOT ERRORLEVEL 2 GOTO END
other commands
:END
```

Creating a Display Menu

You can use the other switches provided with CHOICE to create a display menu. You create text to explain the choices and suppress the display of characters at the end of the optional message. You might create a batch file called MENU.BAT and type the following commands:

```
@ECHO OFF
CLS
ECHO;
ECHO;
ECHO Press S to load Spreadsheet
ECHO Press W to load Word Processor
ECHO Press D to load Database Manager
ECHO Press Q to quit
ECHO;
CHOICE /C:SWDQ /N /T:Q,10 Your choice?
IF ERRORLEVEL 4 GOTO END
IF ERRORLEVEL 3 GOTO DB
IF ERRORLEVEL 2 GOTO WP
ECHO Loading spreadsheet program...
SS
GOTO END
:WP
ECHO Loading word processing program...
WP
GOTO END
:DB
ECHO Loading database management program...
DB
:END
```

When you type the command **MENU**, DOS clears the screen and displays the following message:

```
Press S to load Spreadsheet
Press W to load Word Processor
Press D to load Database Manager
Press Q to quit
Your choice?
```

If no key is pressed within 10 seconds, the CHOICE command issues a Q, and the DOS prompt returns.

T I P   You can construct very elaborate menus by using the ASCII box-drawing characters, ANSI Escape sequences (to establish colors), and the CHOICE command. See Chapter 19, "Understanding ANSI.SYS," for a discussion of the uses of ANSI.SYS.

Using FOR..IN..DO

FOR..IN..DO is an unusual and extremely powerful batch command. The command's syntax is as follows:

FOR %%variable IN (set) DO command

variable is a one-letter name that takes on the value of each item in *set*. You can use this command in the DOS command line as well as from within a batch file. When you use the command in the command line, however, use only one percent sign (%) instead of two (%%) in front of the variable. You must use two percent signs in a batch file so that DOS does not confuse *variable* with a replaceable parameter.

The *set* parameter is the list of items, commands, or disk files whose value you want *variable* to take. You can use wild-card file names with this parameter. You also can use drive names and paths with any file names you specify. If you have more than one item in the set, use a space or a comma between the names.

The *command* parameter is any valid DOS command that you want to perform for each item in *set*.

Using a FOR..IN..DO Batch File

An interesting example of the use of FOR..IN..DO is a batch file that compares file names found on a disk in drive A with the file names found on another disk and then produces a list of the files on both disks. Create the batch file CHECKIT.BAT, entering the following lines:

```
@ECHO OFF
CLS
IF "%1"=="" GOTO END
FOR %%a IN (B: C: D: E: b: c: d: e:) DO IF "%%a"=="%1" GOTO
    COMPARE
ECHO Syntax error: You must specify a disk to compare.
ECHO     Be sure to leave a space before directory.
GOTO END
:COMPARE
%1
IF "%2"=="" GOTO SKIP
CD %2
:SKIP
ECHO The following files are on both disks:
FOR %%a IN (*.*) DO IF EXIST A:%%a ECHO %%a
:END
```

Insert into drive A the disk that you want to compare, and then use the following syntax:

CHECKIT drive *directory*

drive is the drive that contains the other disk that you want to compare, and *directory* is the directory that you want to compare. This batch file substitutes the drive you specify for %1 in the batch-file commands and substitutes any directory you specify for %2. The directory is optional; if you specify a drive and directory, separate their names with a space. Otherwise, the batch file treats the drive and directory as one replaceable parameter (%1). If you don't specify a directory name, DOS compares the current directory of the drive with the current directory of the disk in drive A.

Suppose that you want to compare the list of files in drive A with the list of files in the \GAMES directory in drive B. Type the following command at the command line:

CHECKIT B: \GAMES

The batch file determines which files in the \GAMES directory of the disk in drive B also are on the current directory of the disk in drive A.

When the CHECKIT batch file is called, DOS first determines whether %1 is empty (%1 is empty if you typed no drive letter or directory after

CHECKIT in the command line). If %1 is empty, the batch file displays an error message, branches to the end of the file, and quits without performing a comparison.

If you specify a disk drive, DOS goes to the third line of the batch file and determines whether the drive letter is a valid drive letter. Valid drive letters are B, C, D, E, b, c, d, and e. (If your system has more or fewer drives, the list changes to reflect your configuration.) If no valid drive letter is found, or if you don't include a colon (:) and space after the drive letter, the batch file displays a message and branches to the end of the batch file.

If you specified a valid drive, CHECKIT branches to the :COMPARE section of the program. When executing the first line in this section, DOS logs onto the drive you specified in the command line (the drive designation replaces %1 in the batch file). The batch file determines whether you included a directory parameter; if you did include this parameter, DOS changes to that directory.

Finally, the batch file displays a message and then looks at all the file names in the current directory to see whether a file with the same name exists in drive A. For every match found, the batch file lists the file name.

Using FOR..IN..DO at the DOS Prompt

You may find that you want to issue commands such as the ones in CHECKIT at the DOS prompt. Instead of using the batch file for the preceding example, you can change subdirectories manually and then type the FOR..IN..DO line (the line that does all the work in the batch file) at the DOS prompt. If you do use FOR..IN..DO outside a batch file, DOS requires that you enter only one percent sign.

You can also use FOR..IN..DO if you copy files from a disk to the wrong subdirectory on a hard disk. Use this command to delete the files from the hard disk.

Using FOR..IN..DO with Other Commands

FOR..IN..DO works equally well with commands and file names. Instead of naming a set of files, you can name a series of commands that you want DOS to carry out. Consider the following example:

FOR %%a IN (COPY DEL) DO %%a C:*.*

In a batch file, this line first copies all the files on drive C to the current directory and then erases the files from drive C. Instead of specifying the drive and file, you can use a replaceable parameter in the line, as follows:

FOR %%a IN (COPY DEL) DO %%a %1

To use this batch file, you first must change to the destination directory (for example, D:\BAK). When you invoke this version of the batch file, you type the names of the files that you want to copy and remove. If you name the batch file MOVER.BAT, you can type the following command to invoke the file:

MOVER C:\WP

MOVER.BAT copies all the files in the subdirectory C:\WP to D:\BAK and then erases the files in C:\WP. This file works much like the C&E.BAT file you created earlier in this chapter.

Moving Parameters with SHIFT

The SHIFT command moves the parameters in the command line that invoked the batch file; each parameter moves one parameter to the left. SHIFT tricks DOS into accepting more than 9 replaceable parameters (10 if you include the batch file name, which is %0). The diagram of SHIFT is as follows:

%0 ←%1 ←%2 ←%3 ←%4 ←%5...
↓
bit bucket

In this diagram, parameter 0 is dropped. The old parameter 1 becomes parameter 0. The old parameter 2 becomes parameter 1; parameter 3 becomes 2; parameter 4 becomes 3; and so on. A command-line parameter that previously was 11th in line and not assigned a parameter number now becomes parameter 9.

The following batch file, SHIFTIT.BAT, is a simple example of the use of the SHIFT command:

```
@ECHO OFF
CLS
:START
ECHO %0 %1 %2 %3 %4 %5 %6 %7 %8 %9
SHIFT
PAUSE
GOTO START
```

Suppose that you type the following text:

SHIFTIT A B C D E F G H I J K L M N O P Q R S T U V W X Y Z

The screen shows the following message:

```
SHIFTIT A B C D E F G H I
Press any key to continue…
```

Notice that the batch file name is displayed because %0 holds the name of the batch file. Press a key to continue; DOS now displays the following message:

```
A B C D E F G H I J
Press any key to continue…
```

In this case, the file name has been dropped into the bit bucket. %0 now equals A. All the parameters have shifted one to the left. Each time you press a key to continue, SHIFT continues moving down the list of parameters you typed. Press Ctrl-C when you want to stop.

SHIFT has many uses. You can use it to build a new version of the C&E.BAT file you created earlier in this chapter. The following modified version of the copy-and-erase batch file, called MOVE.BAT, shows a use for SHIFT:

```
@ECHO OFF
CLS
:LOOP
COPY %1 /V
ERASE %1
SHIFT
IF NOT %1. == . GOTO LOOP
```

This batch file copies and erases the specified file or files. The batch file assumes nothing about the files to be copied; you can specify a disk drive, a path, and a file name. The batch file copies the files to the current directory and then erases the files from the original disk or directory.

The last two lines shift the parameters to the left, determine whether any parameters remain, and then repeat the operation if necessary.

Running Batch Files from Other Batch Files

On some occasions, you may want to run a batch file from another batch file. Running batch files from within batch files is particularly useful when you want to create a menu batch file that can start several different programs.

This section discusses three ways to run batch files from other batch files. One method is a one-way transfer of control. The other two methods involve running a second batch file and returning control to the first batch file. These techniques are useful if you want to build menus with batch files or to use one batch file to set up and start another batch file.

Shifting Control Permanently to Another Batch File

The first method of calling a second batch file is simple: include the root name of the second batch file as a line in the first batch file. The first batch file runs the second batch file as though you had typed the second batch file's root name at the DOS prompt.

To run BATCH2.BAT, for example, include in BATCH1.BAT the following line:

    BATCH2

DOS loads and executes BATCH2.BAT. Control passes in only one direction: from the first batch file to the second. When BATCH2.BAT finishes executing, DOS displays the system prompt. You can consider this technique to be an interbatch-file GOTO. Control goes to the second file but doesn't come back to the first file.

Calling a Batch File and Returning Using CALL

In all versions of DOS, you can call a second batch file from the first, execute the second batch file, and return to the first batch file. In DOS 3.0 through 3.2, you use COMMAND /C (discussed in the following section). In DOS 3.3 and later versions, you use the CALL command.

The syntax of the CALL command is as follows:

CALL *d:path***filename** *parameters*

d:path\ represents the optional disk drive and path name of the batch file that you want to execute. *filename* is the root name of the batch file. When you type the CALL command, you can specify any parameters that you want to pass to the batch file you are calling. You can place the CALL command anywhere in the first batch file.

When DOS executes a CALL command, DOS temporarily shifts execution to the called batch file. As soon as the called batch file stops, DOS returns to the first batch file and continues execution with the line immediately following the CALL command.

The following three batch files demonstrate how CALL works:

BATCH1.BAT

```
@ECHO OFF
CLS
REM This file does the setup work for demonstrating
REM the CALL command or COMMAND /C.
ECHO This is the STARTUP batch file
ECHO The command parameters are %%0-%0 %%1-%1
CALL batch2 second
ECHO MEM from %0
MEM
ECHO Done!
```

BATCH2.BAT

```
ECHO This is the SECOND batch file
ECHO The command parameters are %%0-%0 %%1-%1
CALL batch3 third
ECHO MEM from %0
MEM
```

BATCH3.BAT

```
ECHO This is the THIRD batch file
ECHO The command parameters are %%0-%0 %%1-%1
ECHO MEM from %0
MEM
```

The first line of BATCH1.BAT sets ECHO OFF. The second line clears the screen. The next two lines in BATCH1 are remarks intended only to document the purpose of the batch file.

The two ECHO lines are similar for all three batch files. The first of the two lines identifies the batch file being used. The second ECHO line shows the 0 parameter (the name by which the batch file was invoked) and the first parameter (the first argument) for the batch file. Notice that to display the strings %0 and %1, you must use two percent signs (%%0 and %%1). If you use a single percent sign, DOS interprets the string as a replaceable parameter and does not display the actual percent symbol.

Each CALL statement in the first and second batch files invokes another batch file. BATCH1.BAT calls BATCH2.BAT, and BATCH2.BAT in turn calls BATCH3.BAT. In each case, a single argument passes to the batch file being called: *second* to BATCH2.BAT and *third* to BATCH3.BAT. Each batch file then displays its name (by using the %0 variable) and runs MEM. When DOS reaches the end of each called batch file, DOS returns to the calling batch file.

NOTE   MEM was introduced in DOS 5.0. Use CHKDSK instead of MEM if you are using an earlier version of DOS.

After you type the batch files explained in the preceding paragraphs, make sure that your printer is ready (the power is on, paper and ribbon are loaded, and so on). Press Ctrl-PrtSc to activate the printer, and then type **BATCH1 FIRST**.

When the printer finishes running, turn off the printer's capability to print echoed lines by pressing Ctrl-PrtSc again (you don't need to turn off the printer's power). If you don't have a printer to record the information displayed on-screen, press Ctrl-S to pause the screen as needed. After you view the screen, press any key to resume the screen display.

Check the printout or the screen display for the largest executable program size provided by the MEM command (in other words, the largest block of memory available for use by an executable program). This number grows larger after each batch file is executed and removed from memory. Figure 15.1 shows the output from a 486 computer when BATCH1 FIRST is typed.

```
This is the STARTUP batch file.
The command parameters are %0-BATCH1 %1-FIRST.
This is the SECOND batch file.
The command parameters are %0-batch2 %1-second
This is the THIRD batch file.
The command parameters are %0-batch3 %1-third.

MEM from batch3.

Memory Type              Total      =    Used     +    Free

Conventional             640K            51K           589K
Upper                    0K              0K            0K
Adapter RAM/ROM          384K            384K          0K
Extended (XMS)           7168K           1488K         5680K

Total memory             8192K           1923K         6269K
Total under 1 MB         640K            51K           589K

     EMS is active.
     Largest executable program size   589K (603056
     bytes)
     Largest free upper memory block   0K (0 bytes)
     MS-DOS is resident in the high memory area.
     MEM from batch2.


Memory Type              Total      =    Used     +    Free


Conventional             640K            51K           589K
Upper                    0K              0K            0K
Adapter RAM/ROM          384K            384K          0K
Extended (XMS)           7168K           1488K         5680K

Total memory             8192K           1923K         6269K
Total under 1 MB         640K            51K           589K

     EMS is active.
     Largest executable program size   589K (603152
     bytes)
     Largest free upper memory block   0K (0 bytes)
     MS-DOS is resident in the high memory area.
     MEM from batch1.


Memory Type              Total      =    Used     +    Free

Conventional             640K            51K           589K
Upper                    0K              0K            0K
Adapter RAM/ROM          384K            384K          0K
Extended (XMS)           7168K           1488          5680K
Total memory             8192K           1923K         6269K
Total under 1 MB         640K            51K           589K

     EMS is active.
     Largest executable program size   589K (603152 bytes)
     Largest free upper memory block   0K (0 bytes)
     MS-DOS is resident in the high memory area.
     Done!
```

Fig. 15.1

The output produced by issuing the BATCH1 FIRST on a 486 computer.

Each time you use the CALL command, DOS temporarily uses 80 bytes of RAM until the called batch file finishes running. Because DOS uses that much memory for each nested CALL command, you can run out of memory. (A *nested* CALL command is a CALL command from a called batch file.) Not many people nest CALL commands deeply in batch files. The accumulated memory-usage problem does not occur when a single batch file calls multiple other batch files. In that case, you can use the CALL command as many times as you want and use only the same 80 bytes of RAM for each call.

You can use batch files like the ones described in this section with all versions of DOS by making three changes. First, delete the @ character in the first line of BATCH1.BAT. The @ feature is not available with versions of DOS earlier than 3.3. Second, change the CALL commands to COMMAND /C. The CALL command also was introduced in DOS 3.3. Finally, for versions before to DOS 5, substitute CHKDSK for MEM.

Calling a Batch File with COMMAND /C

If you use a version of DOS earlier than 3.3, you cannot use the CALL command, but you can use COMMAND.COM—the command interpreter—to call other batch files. The syntax of COMMAND, when used in a batch file to call another batch file, is as follows:

COMMAND /C *d:path***filename** *parameters*

The main difference between the syntaxes of CALL and COMMAND is that you must use the /C switch. As is true in the CALL command, *d:path* represents the optional disk drive and path name of the batch file that you want to execute, and *filename* is the name of the batch file. Similarly, you can specify any parameters that you want to pass to the batch file you are calling. You can place the COMMAND /C command anywhere in the first batch file.

When COMMAND.COM executes the called batch file, two copies of COMMAND.COM are in memory. When the called batch file finishes executing, the second copy of COMMAND.COM is removed from memory, and the original copy regains control.

If you use COMMAND /C in the example batch files, the results are almost identical to the results when CALL is used. Each copy of COMMAND.COM, however, uses more memory than the CALL command does. The amount of memory used by COMMAND.COM varies among versions of DOS—particularly in DOS 5.0 and 6.0, which use approximately 1K less memory for COMMAND.COM than earlier versions do.

Another difference between CALL and COMMAND /C is worth noting. Because COMMAND loads a new version of COMMAND.COM, any changes you make to the environment while the second batch file is being processed are lost when you return to the calling batch file. If you use CALL, however, environment changes made during execution of the called batch file are "permanent" during the current DOS session or until they are changed again by some other command. These changes are available to the calling batch file as well as to subsequent programs run by the same command processor.

To better understand this process, consider the following examples (because these batch files use both the CALL command and COMMAND /C, you must use DOS 3.3 or a later version to test them):

TEST1.BAT

```
@ECHO OFF
SET VAR1=ONE
SET VAR2=
SET VAR3=
ECHO The environment before calling TEST2.BAT:
SET
PAUSE
COMMAND /C TEST2
ECHO The environment after returning from TEST2.BAT:
SET
PAUSE
CALL TEST3
ECHO The environment after returning from TEST3.BAT:
SET
```

TEST2.BAT

```
@ECHO OFF
SET VAR2=TWO
ECHO The environment while TEST2.BAT is executing:
SET
PAUSE
```

TEST3.BAT

```
SET VAR3=THREE
ECHO The environment while TEST3.BAT is executing:
SET
PAUSE
```

To run these batch files, type **TEST1**, and then press Enter. A message similar to the following appears on-screen:

```
The environment before calling TEST2.BAT:
COMSPEC=C:\DOS\COMMAND.COM
PROMPT=$P$G
PATH=C:\;C:\DOS
TEMP=C:\DOS
VAR1=ONE
Press any key to continue…
```

This message indicates the DOS environment before calling TEST2.BAT.
Notice that the environment variable *VAR1* is set to the value ONE.
Press any key, and the preceding message reappears with the following
line added:

```
VAR2=TWO
```

TEST1.BAT calls TEST2.BAT by using the COMMAND /C method. While
TEST2.BAT is executing, a second copy of COMMAND.COM is loaded
into memory. TEST2.BAT creates the environment variable *VAR2* and
gives it the value TWO. Press any key to display a third message, as
follows:

```
The environment after returning from TEST2.BAT:
COMSPEC=C:\DOS\COMMAND.COM
PROMPT=$P$G
PATH=C:\;C:\DOS
TEMP=C:\DOS
VAR1=ONE
Press any key to continue…
```

After DOS returns from TEST2.BAT, the second copy of
COMMAND.COM no longer is in memory, and the environment variable
VAR2 has disappeared. Press any key to display a fourth message, as
follows:

```
The environment while TEST3.BAT is executing:
COMSPEC=C:\DOS\COMMAND.COM
PROMPT=$P$G
PATH=C:\;C:\DOS
TEMP=C:\DOS
VAR1=ONE
VAR3=THREE
Press any key to continue…
```

Notice that the new environment variable *VAR3* has a value of THREE. Again, press any key. The final message appears:

```
The environment after returning from TEST3.BAT
COMSPEC=C:\DOS\COMMAND.COM
PROMPT=$P$G
PATH=C:\;C:\DOS
TEMP=C:\DOS
VAR1=ONE
VAR3=THREE
Press any key to continue…
```

Because TEST3.BAT was called with the CALL command, the environment remains intact when DOS returns to TEST1.BAT, and the environment variable *VAR3* still exists.

Using DOSKey

A welcome feature introduced in DOS 5.0 is the keyboard-utility program DOSKey. DOSKey is a memory-resident program that enables you to edit and reuse DOS commands without retyping them. The program also enables you to create new commands, referred to as *macros*, that can take the place of several DOS commands. Yet DOSKey occupies only about 4K of memory. The following sections explain how to load DOSKey into your computer's memory and how to use the program's capabilities.

Loading DOSKey

DOSKey is a memory-resident (terminate-and-stay resident, or *TSR*) program, first available in DOS 5. This program enables you to edit commands in the DOS command line easily. DOSKey also stores in a buffer in memory a running history of the commands you issue at the command. DOSKey then enables you to reuse those commands without retyping them.

Before you can use DOSKey's features, you must load the program into memory. To load DOSKey from the command line, type the following command, and then press Enter:

DOSKEY

The message DOSKey installed. appears on-screen. After this message appears, all DOSKey features are available.

The most convenient way to load DOSKey is to include the program in AUTOEXEC.BAT. Simply include the command DOSKEY somewhere in your AUTOEXEC.BAT file, and DOSKey loads each time you turn on your computer.

See Chapter 17, "Configuring Your Computer," for instructions on loading DOSKey into upper-memory blocks (UMBs). This technique, which makes DOSKey available without the use of any conventional (below 640K) memory, is available only on 80386 (DX or SX) or 80486 systems.   **T I P**

As is true of most DOS commands, DOSKey has several available switches. The full syntax of the command to install DOSKey is as follows:

DOSKEY */REINSTALL/BUFSIZE=size/MACROS/HISTORY /INSERT /OVERSTRIKE*

Following are explanations of the components of this command:

■ */REINSTALL* installs another copy of DOSKey and clears the command-history buffer. This command does not, however, remove existing copies of DOSKey that already are in memory.

■ */BUFSIZE* sets the size of the command buffer. The *size* parameter represents the number of bytes that the buffer occupies in memory. The default size is 512 bytes; the minimum size is 256 bytes.

■ */MACROS* displays a list of the currently defined DOSKey macros.

■ */HISTORY* displays the contents of the command-history buffer.

■ */INSERT* instructs DOS to insert new text into the existing text at the cursor position. (You cannot use this switch with */OVERSTRIKE.*)

■ */OVERSTRIKE*, the default condition, instructs DOS to insert new text in place of existing text at the cursor position. (You cannot use this switch with */INSERT.*)

As is true of all DOS 6.0 commands, you can display a list of available switches by typing either of the following commands and then pressing Enter:

DOSKEY / ?

or

HELP DOSKEY

Editing the Command Line

A primary purpose of DOSKey is to facilitate editing of DOS commands. If you are a typical PC user, you issue the same or similar commands frequently, and you don't always type each command correctly the first time. DOSKey can save you typing by enabling you to edit commands without typing them from scratch every time you notice an error.

Suppose that you want to see a directory listing of all files with the WQ1 extension in the \SPREADSH\QPRO2DAT directory in the C drive. In haste, however, you type the DIR command as follows:

DOR C:\SPREADSH\QPRO2DAT*.WQ1

Before you press Enter, you realize that you mistyped the DIR command, but you don't want to retype it. When DOSKey is loaded, you can use the following procedure to correct the mistake:

1. Press the Home key to move the cursor to the left end of the command line.

2. Use the right-arrow key to move the cursor to the O in the word DOR.

3. Type I to correct the error.

4. Press Enter.

DOS displays the directory listing as you requested.

Even before you load DOSKey, DOS provides some command-line editing capability. Table 15.4 lists the normal DOS command-line editing keys, which are available whether or not you make DOSKey memory-resident.

Table 15.4 DOS Command-Line Editing Keys	
Key	**Action**
⊢← →⊣	Moves the cursor to the following tab stop
Esc	Cancels the current line and does not change the buffer

Key	Action
Ins	Enables you to insert characters into the line
Del	Deletes a character from the line
F1 or →	Copies one character from the preceding command line
F2	Copies all characters from the preceding command line up to, but not including, the next character you type
F3	Copies all remaining characters from the preceding command line
F4	Deletes all characters from the preceding command line up to, but not including, the next character typed (opposite of F2)
F5	Moves the current line into the buffer but prevents DOS from executing the line
F6	Produces an end-of-file marker (^Z) when you copy from the console to a disk file

The keys listed in table 15.5 supplement the normal DOSKey command-line editing keys.

Table 15.5 Additional DOSKey Command-Line Editing Keys

Key	Action
←	Moves the cursor one character to the left
→	Moves the cursor one character to the right
Backspace	Moves the cursor one character to the left; in Insert mode, also erases character to the left
Ctrl-←	Moves the cursor one word to the left
Ctrl-→	Moves the cursor one word to the right
Ins	Toggles between Replace mode (the default) and Insert mode
Home	Moves the cursor to the left end of the command line
End	Moves the cursor to the space after the last character in the command line
Esc	Erases the command line

Reusing Commands

In addition to enhancing DOS's command-line editing capabilities, DOSKey adds a capability that was not previously available in DOS: you can redisplay a command that you issued earlier during the current DOS session. You then can execute the command without changing it, or you can use the DOS and DOSKey editing keys to make modifications before executing the command.

After you load DOSKey into memory, the program maintains in memory a buffer that contains a history of DOS commands issued at the command prompt during the current DOS session. DOSKey enables you to reuse the commands in this command-history buffer.

Suppose that earlier during the current DOS session, you issued the following COPY command:

COPY C:\DATABASE\FOXPRO\MAIL.DBF C:\WORD_PRO\WP

Now you want to issue the following similar command without retyping the entire command:

COPY C:\DATABASE\DBASE\MAIL.DBF C:\WORD_PRO\WP

To edit the earlier command, follow these steps:

1. Press the up-arrow key repeatedly until the original COPY command appears in the command line.

2. Use the DOS and DOSKey editing keys to change the command.

3. Press Enter.

In addition to the up-arrow key, DOSKey provides the keys listed in table 15.6 for use in retrieving commands from the command-history buffer.

Table 15.6 DOSKey Command-Buffer-History Keys

Key	Action
↑	Displays the preceding DOS command
↓	Displays the DOS command issued after the one currently displayed, or displays a blank line when you are at the end of the list
Alt-F7	Clears the command-history buffer
Alt-F10	Clears all macro definitions
F7	Displays the contents of the command-history buffer in a numbered list

Key	Action
F8	Searches for the command that most closely matches the characters typed at the command line
F9	Prompts for a line number (where line number refers to the number displayed next to a command in the command-history listing generated by pressing F7); type the number to display the corresponding command
PgDn	Displays the last command stored in the DOSKey command buffer
PgUp	Displays the earliest command issued that still is stored in the DOSKey command buffer

To view the entire list of commands currently stored in the command-history buffer, press F7. DOSKey lists all commands contained in the buffer, one on each line, with a number at the left end of each line. The oldest command—the command issued earliest in the current DOS session—is number 1. Subsequent commands are listed in the order in which you issued them.

DOSKey provides another way for you to see the entire list of commands in the command-history buffer. Type the following command, and then press Enter:

DOSKEY /HISTORY

DOSKey generates the same list of commands as the F7 command, but without line numbers.

T I P

To create a batch file that contains all the commands in the current command-history buffer, use the following command syntax:

DOSKEY /HISTORY > filename.BAT

Substitute for *filename* the name that you want to give the batch file. After you issue this command, the new batch file contains all the commands from the command-history buffer, including the command that created the batch file itself. Use the DOS Editor, Edlin, or some other text editor to delete the last command and any other commands you don't want to include in the batch file.

You can use the up-arrow key to display previously issued commands. Each time you press the up-arrow key, DOSKey displays the preceding command. After you display one or more previous commands by pressing the up-arrow key, you can use the down-arrow key to move back down through the commands to the most recent command. Sometimes, however, selecting a command from the list generated by pressing F7 is easier. To use this method, press F9. DOSKey displays the following message:

    Line number:

Type the number that corresponds to the desired command in the list of commands generated by pressing F7. DOSKey displays the selected command in the command line for you to edit or execute.

When you want to move quickly to the first command in the buffer, press PgUp. To go to the last command in the buffer, press PgDn.

If you want to clear the command-history buffer, press Alt-F7. DOSKey abandons the contents of the command-history buffer.

DOSKey also can help you locate a command quickly. Type the first several characters of the command you need to find, and then press F8. Suppose that you want to locate the following command:

    COPY C:\DATABASE\FOXPRO\MAIL.DBF C:\WORD_PRO\WP

Type **COPY** and press F8. Each time you press F8, DOSKey shows you the next command that contains the COPY command. When the desired command is displayed, you easily can edit and reuse the command with minimal typing.

FROM HERE...

For Related Information

▶▶ "Upper Memory Blocks," p. 639.

Creating and Using Macros

In addition to providing command-line editing capabilities and the command-history buffer, DOSKey enables you to create your own DOS commands, referred to as *macros*. A DOSKey macro is similar to a batch file but is contained in memory rather than on disk. Each macro can contain one or more DOS commands, up to a maximum of 127 characters.

DOSKey macros are similar to batch files in the following ways:

- Macros can contain multiple DOS commands.

- Macros are invoked by typing a name at the DOS prompt.

- Macros can use replaceable parameters.

Macros differ from batch files in the following ways:

- Macros are stored in memory (RAM); batch files are stored on disk.

- Macros are limited to 127 characters; batch files have unlimited maximum length.

- Ctrl-C or Ctrl-Break stops a single command in a DOSKey macro; Ctrl-C or Ctrl-Break stops an entire batch file.

- The GOTO command is not available in macros.

- One macro cannot call another macro, and you cannot call a macro from within a batch file.

- Macros can define environment variables but cannot use them.

The following sections explain how to create and run DOSKey macros.

Creating Macros

DOSKey enables you to create macros at the command line or through a batch file. The syntax for creating a macro is as follows:

DOSKEY macroname=command(s)

The *macroname* parameter is the name that you want to give the macro. Use any keyboard characters in the name except <, >, |, or =. Do not include a space in the macro name; use an underscore or hyphen instead if you want the macro name to have the appearance of two words.

The *command* parameter can include any number of DOS commands, subject to the following rules:

- The entire command cannot exceed 127 characters (the DOS command-line limit).

- Each pair of commands must be separated by the characters *$t*.

■ Instead of using the redirection and piping operators (<, >, and |), use *$l*, *$g*, and *$b*, respectively.

■ The ECHO OFF command is not effective in macros. Commands always appear on-screen.

When you want to use replaceable parameters in a macro, use the codes $1 through $9 rather than %1 through %9. Suppose, for example, that you often use the REPLACE command to keep current copies of particular subdirectory files on floppy disks so that you can take the files with you. To do this, however, you must issue the REPLACE command twice for each subdirecotry you want to keep current. An easier method is to create the following macro called UPD:

```
DOSKEY UPD=REPLACE \C:$1\$2 A:\$1 /U $T REPLACE C:\$1\$2
    A:\$1 /A
```

DOSKey has a special type of replaceable parameter that is not available in batch files. The characters *$** represent not just one parameter, but all the characters that you type in the command line to the right of the macro name. This type of replaceable parameter is useful when you don't know ahead of time how many parameters or switches you might type when you execute the macro.

Suppose that you want to create a macro to help you format floppy disks in drive A, a 3 1/2-inch high-density drive. You want to be able to type **FA 720** to format a 720K disk and **FA 1.44** to format a 1.44M disk. Occasionally, however, you may want to use one or more of FORMAT's switches, such as the /S switch to create a system disk, the /Q Quick Format switch, or the /U unconditional format switch. To create the FA macro, type the following command:

```
DOSKEY FA=FORMAT A: /F:$*
```

To confirm that DOSKey has stored the macros you defined, type the following command, and then press Enter:

```
DOSKEY /MACROS
```

DOSKey lists all macros currently stored in the DOSKey macro buffer. Assuming that you defined the UPD and FA macros, the preceding command displays the following lines:

```
UPD=REPLACE \C:$1\$2 A:\$1 /U $T REPLACE C:\$1\$2 A:\$1
   /A
```

> **T I P**
>
> You easily can save a copy of the entire contents of the macro buffer by using redirection. To create a file named MACROS.BAT that contains all the current macros, type the following command and press Enter:
>
> DOSKEY /MACROS > MACROS.BAT
>
> If you want to use this batch file later to re-create the macros during a future session, edit the file, adding DOSKEY to the beginning of each line.

Because DOSKey macros reside in memory rather than on disk, all macros are erased when you turn off or reboot the computer. One disadvantage of using DOSKey macros is that you need to reenter commonly used macros each time you turn on your computer. You can overcome this drawback, however, by using AUTOEXEC.BAT to define the macros that you use most often. To make the UPD and FA macros routinely available, for example, include the following commands in AUTOEXEC.BAT:

```
DOSKEY UPD=REPLACE \C:$1\$2 A:\$1 /U $T REPLACE C:\$1\$2
    A:\$1 /A
DOSKEY FA=FORMAT A: /F:$*
```

Every time you turn on or reboot your computer, the preceding commands create the MOVE and FA macros in the DOSKey macro buffer.

The first DOSKEY command in AUTOEXEC.BAT loads the program as memory-resident, even if the command also is defining a macro.

Running Macros

Using a DOSKey macro is as easy as using any other DOS command. Simply type the macro name at the command line, and then press Enter. If the macro has any replaceable parameters, include appropriate values in the command line.

Suppose that you want to use the UPD macro to maintain current copies of files. Simply type the following:

UPD *dirname filespec*

As with a batch file, *dirname* is the first replaceable parameter, $1, and *filespec* is the second, $2. To keep current all files in C:\PROJECT1, type **UPD PROJECT1 *.*** and press Enter.

Perhaps you want to use the FA macro created in the preceding section to format a 1.44M disk. You want to use Quick Format, make this disk bootable, and assign the volume label BOOT_DISK. Type the following command at the DOS prompt, and then press Enter:

FA 1.44 /Q /S /V:BOOT_DISK

DOS first displays the command in the following format:

```
FORMAT A: /F:1.44 /Q /S /V:BOOT_DISK
```

Then DOS prompts you as follows:

```
Insert new diskette for drive A:
and press ENTER when ready…
```

Press Enter to proceed with the formatting operation. DOS displays messages indicating the progress and successful completion of the procedure. Finally, DOS displays the following message:

```
QuickFormat another (Y/N)?
```

Type **Y** if you want to use the same switch settings to format another disk, or type **N** to return to the DOS prompt.

Chapter Summary

Batch files and macros can make your computer do the hard work for you, replacing repetitive typing with commands that execute automatically. As you work with batch files and macros, remember the following key points:

■ You must give batch files the BAT extension.

■ You invoke batch files by typing the name of the batch file (without the extension) and pressing Enter. You can specify an optional drive name and path name before the batch file name.

- You can include in a batch file any command that you can type at the DOS prompt.

- AUTOEXEC.BAT is a special batch file that DOS calls when you boot your computer.

- Each word (or set of characters) in a command separated by a delimiter is a parameter. When you use a batch file, DOS substitutes the appropriate parameters for the variable markers (%0 through %9) in the file.

- You can use the ECHO command to turn on or off the display of DOS commands being executed by the batch file.

- The PAUSE command causes the batch file to suspend execution and then displays a message on-screen.

- Use the REM command to leave comments and reminders in your batch file; the comments do not appear on-screen when ECHO is off.

- Use the CLS command to clear the screen completely.

- You can use the GOTO command to create a loop in the batch file.

- IF tests for a given condition.

- CHOICE enables you to prompt for input and create menus.

- FOR..IN..DO can repeat a batch-file command for one or more files or commands.

- SHIFT moves command parameters to the left.

- The @ character suppresses the display of a single line from a batch file.

- COMMAND /C and CALL invoke a second batch file and then return control of the computer to the first batch file.

- DOSKey enables you to redisplay a command that you issued earlier during the current DOS session.

- DOSKey macros are stored in memory (RAM).

- Macros can contain multiple DOS commands but are limited to 127 characters.

- The GOTO command is not available in macros.

In the next two chapters, you learn about configuring your computer system. Chapter 16, "Configuring the DOS Shell," describes how to configure the DOS Shell, and Chapter 17, "Configuring Your Computer," explains how to take full advantage of your computer's memory and peripheral devices.

Configuring the DOS Shell

This chapter shows you how to fine-tune DOS 6.0's DOS Shell to meet your requirements. The discussions here follow up on topics introduced in Chapter 4, "Using the DOS Shell."

In Chapter 4, you learned how to switch among dual file lists, a single file list, and the program list, and how to change the Shell screen mode. This chapter teaches you how to change screen colors in the Shell.

Chapter 4 also taught you how to use the program-list area to start an application. Now that you are more familiar with the Shell and with DOS in general, you are ready to learn how to customize the program list. This chapter explains how to build a menu system by adding program groups and program items to the program-list area of the DOS Shell window, as well as how to tailor these elements to your specifications.

Key Terms Used in This Chapter

Color scheme	A collection of color settings that are applied as a group to the DOS Shell
Program group	A collection of program items and other program groups, displayed as a group in the program-list area of the DOS Shell window
Program item	An option listed in the DOS Shell program-list area that enables you to start a particular software program or DOS utility

Setting Screen Colors

When you start the DOS Shell for the first time, the program sets screen colors according to its default settings. If you are happy with the default color scheme, you can skip this section of the chapter.

In an effort to make color selection quick and easy, the designers of the DOS Shell provided eight predefined color schemes. Each color scheme sets the colors that the Shell uses to display the various components of the DOS Shell window: background color, text color, menu color, and so on. Instead of having to set the color for each component separately, you simply choose one of the ready-made color schemes.

To choose a different color scheme for the Shell, follow these steps:

1. Display the DOS Shell window by typing **DOSSHELL** at the DOS prompt.

2. Choose Colors from the Options menu. The Color Scheme dialog box appears (see fig. 16.1).

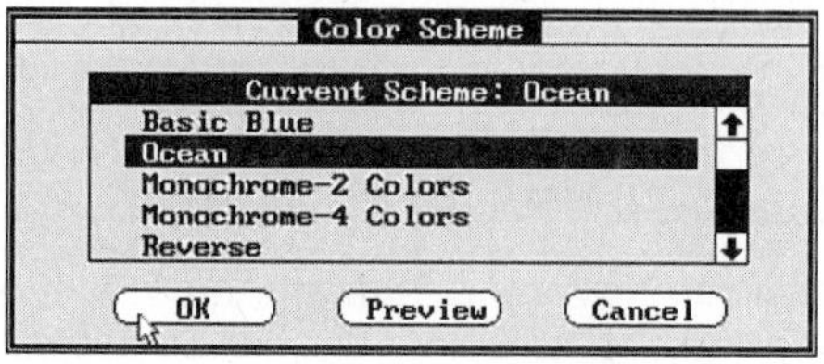

Fig. 16.1

The Color Scheme dialog box.

This dialog box contains a list box and three command buttons. The title bar of the list box indicates the name of the current color scheme. For example, the list box in figure 16.1 indicates that the Ocean is the current color scheme.

3. To choose a different color scheme, use the mouse and scroll bar to display and select your choice, or use the cursor-movement keys to move the selection bar to the new color-scheme name. Then click the OK command button or press Enter. The DOS Shell window reappears, painted with the new colors.

You may want to experiment with the color schemes without permanently changing the settings. The Shell provides a way for you to preview a color scheme before actually adding it to the DOS Shell configuration. To preview a color scheme, follow these steps:

1. Move the selection bar to a different color setting in the Color Scheme dialog box, and then click the Preview command button. The Shell changes the screen colors to the new scheme but does not remove the Color Scheme dialog box from the screen.

2. If you like the new colors, choose the OK button to accept the change and return to the Shell window. Otherwise, move the selection bar to another color scheme and click Preview, or click Cancel to revert to the original color scheme.

Creating Custom Colors

In addition to the predefined color schemes, you can create custom color schemes by editing the DOS Shell configuration file, DOSSHELL.INI.

Locate the file DOSSHELL.INI in the directory that contains your operating-system files (usually C:\DOS). Load DOSSHELL.INI into the DOS Editor (discussed in Chapter 14, "Using the DOS Editor") or into another text editor that can handle lines more than 256 characters long without truncating or splitting the lines.

Without making any changes in the file, scroll through DOSSHELL.INI until you see the following lines:

```
color =
{
   selection =
   {
   title = Basic Blue
   foreground =
      {
         base = black
         highlight = brightwhite
         selection = brightwhite
         alert = brightred
         menubar = black
         menu = black
         disabled = white
         accelerator = cyan
         dialog = black
         button = black
         elevator = white
         titlebar = black
         scrollbar = brightwhite
         borders = black
```

continues

Creating Custom Colors continued

```
        drivebox = black
        driveicon = black
        cursor = black
    }
    background =
    {
            base = brightwhite
            highlight = blue
            selection = black
            alert = brightwhite
            menubar = white
            menu = brightwhite
            disabled = brightwhite
            accelerator = brightwhite
            dialog = brightwhite
            button = white
            elevator = white
            titlebar = white
            scrollbar = black
            borders = brightwhite
            drivebox = brightwhite
            driveicon = brightwhite
            cursor = brightblack
    }
    }
    selection=
```

These lines mark the beginning of the color-scheme section of DOSSHELL.INI. Use your text editor's block-copy feature to copy the lines, beginning with *selection* = and ending with the right brace (}) that appears in the line above the second occurrence of *selection* =. With your cursor on the first occurrence of selection=, paste the text you copied. Now, you can make changes to the new color selection.

Use the editor to change the name in the *color* = line to the name you want to give the new color scheme. Finally, use the editor to change the color settings within the copied lines. If you want the menu bar to have a cyan background color, for example, edit the *menubar* line in the *background* = section so that the line reads as follows:

```
menubar = cyan
```

For Related Information

◄◄ "Files Required To Run the DOS Editor," p. 511.

◄◄ "Changing Colors and Removing Scroll Bars," p. 538.

FROM HERE...

Working with Program Groups

The program-list area of the DOS Shell window provides a convenient method of running the programs stored on your computer. The Shell enables you to create menus, referred to as *program groups*, in which you can list all the programs stored on your computer.

When you start the Shell for the first time, the program-list area of the Shell window displays the Main program group. This program group consists of three program items and one program group, as shown in figure 16.2.

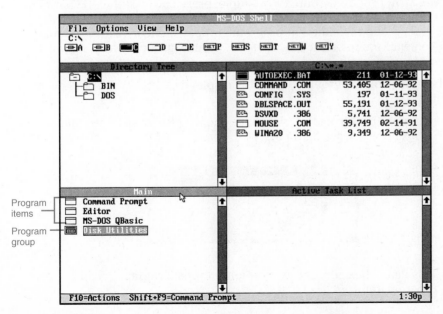

Fig. 16.2

The Main program group.

By default, the Main program group includes the following program items:

- Command Prompt
- Editor
- MS-DOS QBasic

The Main group also includes the Disk Utilities program group, which in turn consists of six external DOS commands that are used primarily for disk management: Disk Copy, Microsoft Anti-Virus, Microsoft MS-Backup, Quick Format, Format, and Undelete.

By creating your own program groups within the Main group, you easily can organize your software programs according to your work habits. You might, for example, divide your programs according to software type, creating a word processing group, a database group, a spreadsheet group, and a graphics group. Alternatively, you might decide to split programs into groups according to subject matter, establishing a Business Productivity group, a Personal Management group, and a Rest and Relaxation group.

Adding a Program Group

To add a new program group, make the program-list area the active area of the DOS Shell window, and display the program group to which the new group is to be added. If you want to add a new program group to the Main program group, for example, press Esc until the title bar of the program-list area displays the title Main. When you want to add a program group to a different program group, use the mouse or cursor-movement keys to select the intended "parent" group in the program-list area.

When the program group you want is displayed, complete the following steps:

1. Choose New from the File menu. The New Program Object dialog box appears (see fig. 16.3).

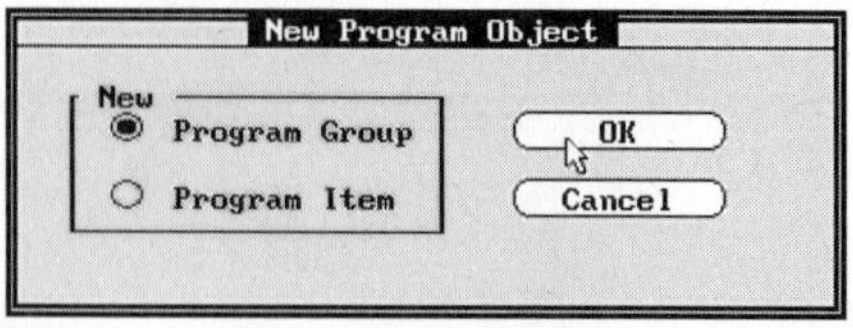

Fig. 16.3

The New Program Object dialog box.

This dialog box contains two option buttons: Program Group and Program Item.

2. Click the Program Group option button, and then click the OK command button or press Enter. The Add Group dialog box appears (see fig. 16.4).

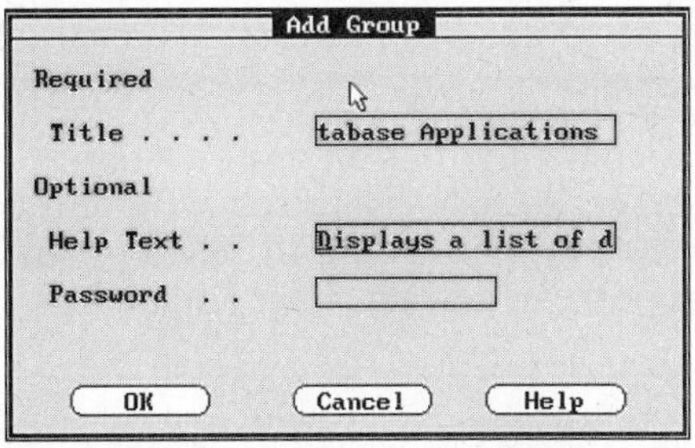

```
┌────────────────────────────────────────────┐
│               ▓Add Group▓                    │
│                                              │
│  Required                                    │
│                          ⌖                   │
│    Title . . . .    │tabase Applications│    │
│                                              │
│  Optional                                    │
│                                              │
│    Help Text . .    │Displays a list of d│   │
│                                              │
│    Password  . .    │                    │   │
│                                              │
│                                              │
│      ( OK )       ( Cancel )     ( Help )    │
│                                              │
└────────────────────────────────────────────┘
```

Fig. 16.4

The Add Group dialog box.

This dialog box contains three text boxes: Title, Help Text, and Password. You must type an entry in the Title text box, but entries in the Help Text and Password text boxes are optional.

3. Type a program-group title in the Title text box. (You can use up to 23 characters, including spaces.) This title will be the name, or menu option, that appears in the program-list area when the parent program group is displayed.

   If you are creating a program group for your database applications, for example, you might type **Database Applications** in the Title text box. This title will appear not only in the program-list area, but also in that area's title bar when a program group is activated.

4. Type a help message, if you choose, in the Help Text text box. (The message can be up to 255 characters long, even though the Shell can display only 20 characters at a time in the text box; the text in the text box scrolls to the left as you type past the 20th character.)

   For a Database Applications group, for example, you might type the help message **Displays list of database applications**.

   Afterward, whenever you press F1 while the Database Applications item is highlighted, the help message appears.

   The Shell displays help messages in the Shell Help dialog box (see fig. 16.5 later in this section) and formats the help message to fit in the dialog box. If you want a line to break at a particular point, type the characters ^**m** (or ^**M**) at that point. Any following text starts on the next line when the help message is displayed in the Help dialog box.

5. Type a password, if you choose, in the Password text box. (The password can be up to 20 characters long, including spaces.)

> **WARNING:** Using a password to limit access to a DOS Shell program group provides only minimal security. Any user with access to your computer easily can bypass the Shell and start programs from the DOS command line instead.

6. Click the OK command button or press Enter. The Shell adds the new program group to the selected program group. Now, if you select the new program group, the Shell opens an empty file-list area so that you can add program items.

Adding Custom Help Features

The Shell enables you to build links to the built-in DOS Shell help messages from your custom help messages. These links provide more ways for users to get help when they are confused or want to do something new.

When you type a help message in the Add Group dialog box, enclose in double quotation marks the word or words you want to display as a link to another help message. Type the help-message reference number, enclosed in tildes (~), just to the right of the link word(s). You can determine the help-message reference number by displaying or printing the DOS Shell help file, DOSSHELL.HLP.

To create a link that displays a help screen discussing the program list, for example, type the following text in the Help Text text box of the Add Group dialog box:

^m^mRelated Topic^m " Program List Procedures"~R102~

Thereafter, when the user presses F1 while the program-list selection bar is resting on Database Applications, the Shell displays a help message similar to the one shown in figure 16.5.

Fig. 16.5

The Sample help message.

Modifying Program-Group Properties

After you create a program group, you can change the parameters that define it—its *properties*—through the Shell File menu. To change a program group's properties, follow these steps:

1. Activate the program-list area. If the group that contains the properties you want to change is not included in the Main group, select the program group that includes the target group.

2. Use the mouse or cursor-movement keys to move the selection bar to the name of the program group that contains the properties you want to modify.

3. Choose Properties from the File menu. The Program Group Properties dialog box appears (see fig. 16.6).

```
┌─────────────────────────────────────────────────┐
│            Program Item Properties               │
│                                                  │
│  Program Title . . . .  [Paradox              ]  │
│                                                  │
│  Commands  . . . . . .  [PARADOX_             ]  │
│                                                  │
│  Startup Directory . .  [C:\DATABASE\PDOX35\P35DATA] │
│                                                  │
│  Application Shortcut Key  [                  ]  │
│                                                  │
│  [ ] Pause after exit      Password . .  [    ]  │
│     ( OK )   ( Cancel )   ( Help )   ( Advanced...) │
└─────────────────────────────────────────────────┘
```

Fig. 16.6

The Program Group Properties dialog box.

This dialog box essentially is a copy of the Add Group dialog box (refer to fig. 16.4), except that the title, help message, and password for the selected group already appear in the text boxes.

4. Make any desired changes in the title, help message, and password, and then click OK or press Enter. Alternatively, click Cancel to return to the Shell window without changing any of the program group's properties.

Deleting a Program Group

Through the File menu, you also can remove a program group. Before deleting a program group, make sure that all items in the group are deleted (see the section "Deleting a Program Item" later in this chapter).

To delete a program group, follow these steps:

1. Move the selection bar to the name of the group that you want to delete.

2. Choose <u>D</u>elete from the <u>F</u>ile menu or press Del. The Delete Item dialog box appears (see fig. 16.7).

The Delete Item
dialog box.

3. Select 1. Delete This Item. Then click OK or press Enter. The Shell deletes the program group from the selected program-group list.

NOTE If you attempt to delete a program group before it is empty, the Shell displays an error message box.

Changing the Order of a Group's Listings

Placing the groups that you use most frequently near the top of the group listing is convenient, enabling you to find these groups quickly. You can place groups in any order you want. To move a group from one place to another in the menu list, follow these steps:

1. Move the selection bar to the group that you want to move.

2. Choose Reorder from the <u>F</u>ile menu. The Shell displays the following message in the status line:

```
Select location to move to, then press ENTER. ESC to cancel.
```

3. Use the cursor-movement keys to move the selection bar to the desired new location for the selected group, and then press Enter. The Shell moves the group to the new position.

You can repeat these steps as often as necessary to produce the order you want for your groups.

Working with Program Items

After you create program groups, the next step in building your menu system is adding program items. The following sections describe how to add program items, as well as how to modify, copy, and delete existing program items in the program group. (To reorder program items, follow the procedure described in the preceding section.)

Adding a Program Item

Adding a program item is similar to adding a program group. When you want to add a program item to a particular group, make the program-list area the active area of the DOS Shell window, and then display the program group to which you want to add the program item. If you want to add a program item to the Database Applications program group, for example, press Esc until *Main* appears in the title bar of the program-list area, and then use the mouse or cursor-movement keys to highlight Database Applications.

After the program group is selected, follow these steps:

1. Choose New from the File menu. The New Program Object dialog box appears (refer to fig. 16.3).

2. Click the Program Item option button, and then click the OK command button or press Enter. The Add Program dialog box appears (see fig. 16.8).

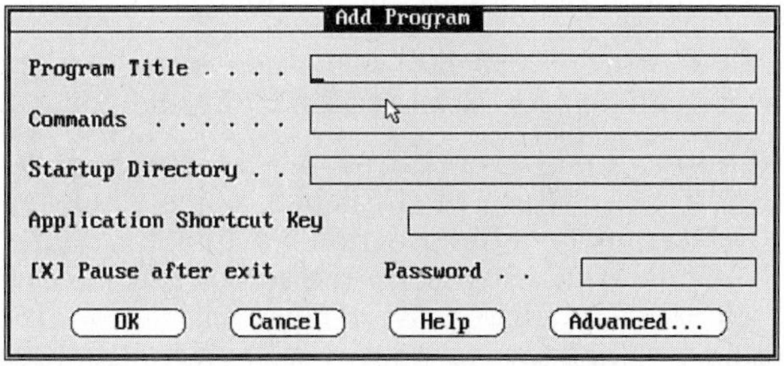

```
┌─────────────────────██ Add Program ██───────────────────┐
│                                                          │
│  Program Title . . . . [                              ]  │
│                                                          │
│  Commands  . . . . . . [                              ]  │
│                                                          │
│  Startup Directory . . [                              ]  │
│                                                          │
│  Application Shortcut Key  [                          ]  │
│                                                          │
│  [X] Pause after exit     Password . .  [            ]  │
│    ( OK )    ( Cancel )    ( Help )    ( Advanced... )   │
└──────────────────────────────────────────────────────────┘
```

Fig. 16.8

The Add Program
dialog box.

This dialog box contains five text boxes: Program Title, Commands, Startup Directory, Application Shortcut Key, and Password. You must type entries in the Program Title and Commands text boxes, but entries in the Startup Directory, Application Shortcut Key, and Password text boxes are optional. All entries in the Add Program dialog box are referred to collectively as the program item's *properties*.

3. Type a program-item title in the Program Title text box. (You can use up to 23 characters, including spaces.) This title will be the name, or menu option, that you select from the program group when you want to run the program. If you are creating a program item to start the database program Paradox, for example, you might type **Paradox** in the Program Title text box.

4. Type the program's start-up command in the Commands text box. A start-up command can be as simple as the program's name. For Paradox, for example, you would type **PARADOX**. (Refer to the sections that follow for discussion of more complex options available in the Commands text box, including multiple commands and replaceable parameters.)

5. Specify a start-up directory, if you choose, in the Startup Directory text box. The start-up directory is the name of the directory that must be active when the Shell issues the specified start-up command. If you are specifying a start-up directory for Paradox, you might type **C:\DATABASE\PDOX\P35DATA** in the Startup Directory text box. (The program file that the start-up command starts must be located in the start-up directory or listed in the PATH command.)

   If you don't specify a start-up directory, the currently selected directory on the logged disk is the start-up directory.

6. Specify a shortcut key for the program, if you choose, in the Application Shortcut Key text box. Press and hold down Ctrl, Alt, Shift, or any combination of these keys, and then press another key. The Shell displays the keystroke combination in the Application Shortcut Key text box. (For more information about shortcut keys, see the following section of this chapter.)

7. Type a password, if you choose, in the Password text box. (The password can be up to 20 characters long, including spaces.)

8. In addition to the five text boxes, the Add Program dialog box contains a Pause after Exit check box. When you leave a program that you started from the program-list area, the Pause after Exit check box determines whether the screen returns to the DOS Shell window immediately. By default, this check box is selected, directing the Shell to clear the screen and display the following message when you exit from a program:

```
Press any key to return to MS-DOS Shell.
```

The Shell window reappears on-screen after you press any key.

If you like this setting, leave the X in the check box. If you prefer that the Shell window reappear immediately when you leave a program, however, click the Pause after Exit check box to remove the X.

9. Click the Advanced command button to add a help message, to specify special memory or video requirements, or to select other advanced options. (For more information about this option, see "Specifying Advanced Program-Item Properties" later in this chapter.)

10. After you finish making selections in the Add Program dialog box, click OK or press Enter to save the settings and return to the DOS Shell window. The Shell adds the new program item to the program-list area.

Figure 16.9 lists Paradox as a program item in the Database Applications program group.

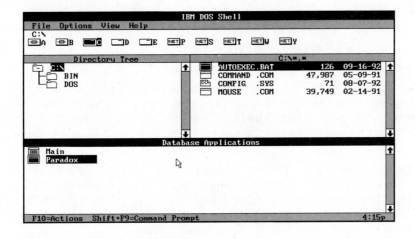

Fig. 16.9

The Database Applications program group with Paradox added.

Using Shortcut Keys

You can specify shortcut keys to start applications. When you specify these key combinations, the Shell displays them in the Application Shortcut Key text box. If you press and hold down Ctrl and Alt simultaneously and then press P, for example, the Shell displays *ALT+CTRL+P* in the text box.

A specified shortcut-key combination starts the program only if the following three conditions are met:

- The DOS 6.0 task swapper is enabled.

- You started the program through the DOS Shell's program-list area.

- You used one of the task-swapper keystrokes (Alt-Tab, Alt-Esc, or Ctrl-Esc) to switch to another program or back to the Shell.

Suppose that you first enable the DOS Shell task swapper and then start Paradox from the program item in the Database Applications program group. You then switch back to the Shell by pressing Alt-Tab, and start Microsoft Word. To return to Paradox quickly, you simply press the shortcut key you defined (for example, Ctrl-Alt-P). The task swapper quickly swaps Word to disk and displays the Paradox screen.

When you return to the DOS Shell window while the program you were using earlier is swapped out to disk, the Shell lists the shortcut in parentheses to the right of the program-item title in the active-task-list area.

Using Multiple Start-Up Commands

A single command often is sufficient to load a program, but sometimes you need to perform several operations before, after, or before *and* after running a program. The DOS Shell enables you to specify multiple DOS commands in the Commands text box of the Add Program dialog box.

Multiple commands in the Commands text box essentially resemble a batch file; you type all the commands on a single line, one after another. Separate each pair of commands with a semicolon. (Do not precede or follow the semicolon by spaces.) You can type up to 255 characters and spaces in the Commands text box.

Consider again the Paradox example. Suppose that you want the Shell to issue a PATH command before issuing the PARADOX command so that DOS can find the Paradox start-up command. In addition, you want the directory containing the Paradox program files to be the first directory listed in the path, to speed access to the Paradox program files. You would type the following text in the Commands text box:

PATH=C:\DATABASE\PDOX35;C:\DOS ; PARADOX

In the command, the first semicolon is part of the PATH command. The second semicolon, preceded and followed by spaces, separates the PATH command from the start-up command.

If you select Paradox in the Database Applications program group after entering the preceding commands, the Shell clears the screen and executes the two DOS commands in order.

In addition to including multiple commands in the Commands text box, you can call batch files from the Commands text box by using the CALL batch file command. For the preceding example, you could create a batch file named PDOX35.BAT that contains the following lines:

    PATH=C:\DATABASE\PDOX35;C:\DOS

    PARADOX

In the Commands text box, type only the command **CALL PDOX35**. The result is the same as placing the two preceding commands in the Commands text box.

Notes on Program Items

■ A batch file called from the Commands text box must be located either in the directory specified in the Startup Directory text box or in a directory that is in the current PATH statement. Otherwise, DOS may not be capable of finding the batch file, and the program item will fail to load the intended software program.

■ When you load a program through the DOS Shell, DOS loads a copy of COMMAND.COM, the command interpreter. DOS also loads a copy of the DOS environment, which includes the PATH statement (if any was issued). The PATH commands discussed in the preceding examples change the PATH value in the copy of the DOS environment but have no effect on the original environment.

After you exit from the program, DOS removes the copy of COMMAND.COM from memory and reverts to the original environment, including the original PATH statement.

Providing Information through Replaceable Parameters

Often, you may want to supply certain information to a program before loading and running it. You learned in Chapter 13, "Understanding Backups and the Care of Data," how to use replaceable parameters in batch files and macros. The DOS Shell provides a similar capability for use in program items. This section describes how to use replaceable parameters to provide additional start-up information.

You specify replaceable parameters in the Commands text box of the Add Program dialog box the same way that you specify them in batch files. Type a percent sign (%), followed by a number (1 through 9). You can have up to nine different replaceable parameters and can use any of the nine replaceable parameters multiple times in the same Commands text box.

If you want Paradox to run a specified Paradox Application Language (PAL) script at start-up, for example, add **%1** to the commands, making the full entry in the Commands text box read as follows:

PATH=C:\DATABASE\PDOX35;C:\DOS ; PARADOX %1

After making any other desired entries in the Add Program dialog box, click the OK command button or press Enter. The Shell displays a second Add Program dialog box (see fig. 16.10).

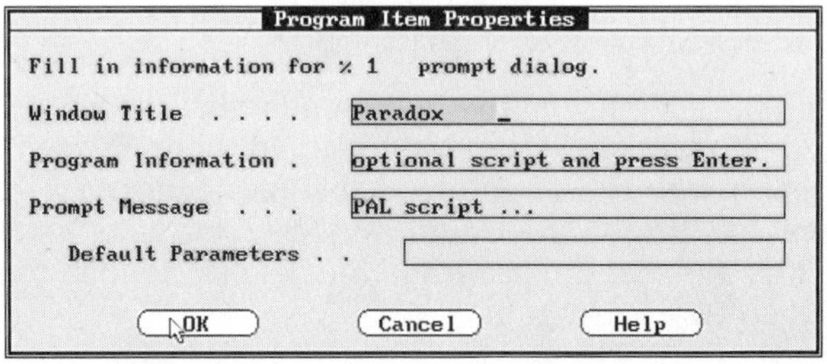

Fig. 16.10

The second Add Program dialog box.

A message at the top of this dialog box prompts you to *Fill in information for % 1 prompt dialog*. The information that you type in this dialog box determines what dialog box DOS displays when you execute the program item that you are defining.

In this second Add Program dialog box, you can define a custom dialog box that appears each time you start Paradox from the DOS Shell program list. The Shell enables you to create a custom dialog box for each replaceable parameter specified in the Commands text box. After adding the replaceable parameter in the preceding example, you can specify that the custom dialog box prompt the user to enter the name of a PAL script for Paradox to run at start-up.

The Add Program dialog box shown in figure 16.10 contains four text boxes: Window Title, Program Information, Prompt Message, and Default Parameters. Making entries in these text boxes is optional.

In the Window Title text box, you can enter the title you want to appear at the top of the custom dialog box. Continuing the Paradox example, you may type **Paradox** in this text box.

If you don't specify a window title, the Shell displays the first 25 characters in the Commands text box as the window title.

In the Program Information text box, you can type any general instructions that you want to appear below the title of the dialog box. Your message can be up to 106 characters long. For the Paradox example, you might type the following text:

Type the name of an optional script and press Enter.

If you choose to type a prompt in the Prompt Message text box, this prompt appears to the left of the text box in which the replaceable parameter appears. You can, for example, type the following prompt in the Prompt Message text box:

PAL script...

In the Default Parameters text box, you can type a value that you want the Shell to use when no entry is made in the dialog box that appears when you execute the program. You also can use either of the following two special parameters in the Default Parameters text box to provide a default parameter:

- *%F.* This replaceable parameter automatically is replaced by the file name that currently is selected in the Shell's file-list area.

- *%L.* This parameter automatically reverts the Shell to the preceding entry in the custom dialog box.

Use the %F parameter to instruct the Shell to use a selected file as the default entry. Use the %L parameter when you expect to use the same parameter value frequently. When you use the %L parameter, the replaceable parameter carries the value that you used the last time you selected this item from the program list. You can use the %L parameter, for example, to cause the Paradox program item to remember the last script name you entered.

 The Shell remembers only the parameters that you entered during the current DOS Shell session.

After you finish making selections in the second Add Program dialog box, click OK or press Enter to save your choices and return to the Shell window. The Shell adds the program item to the program group. When you execute the new program item, the Shell displays the custom dialog box that you defined for the purpose of entering a start-up parameter.

Figure 16.11 shows the custom Paradox dialog box that appears when you select Paradox in the Main program group.

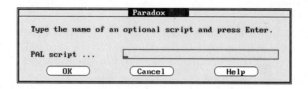

Specifying Advanced Program-Item Properties

In addition to the properties described in the preceding sections, the DOS Shell enables you to specify the following properties for a program item:

- A help message

- The amount of conventional memory that the program requires

- The amount of XMS (Lotus/Intel/Microsoft/AST Extended Memory Specification) memory that the program requires

- The video mode (text or graphics) that the program uses

- Reserved shortcut keys

- Task swapping (disabled or enabled)

When you want to specify any of these properties for a program item, click the Advanced command button in the Add Program dialog box. The Shell displays the Advanced dialog box (see fig. 16.12).

This dialog box contains four text boxes: Help Text, Conventional Memory KB Required, XMS Memory KB Required, and XMS Memory KB Limit. The dialog box also contains two Video Mode option buttons, three Reserve Shortcut Keys check boxes, and a Prevent Program Switch check box. All these fields are optional.

To specify properties in the Advanced dialog box, follow these steps:

1. Type a help message, if you choose, in the Help Text text box. (The message can be up to 255 characters long, but only 20 characters appear at any time; the text in the text box scrolls to the left as you type past the 20th character.)

   If you are using the Paradox program item, for example, you might type the following help message in the Help Text text box:

   > Starts the database program Paradox.

   You also can specify a script for Paradox to run at start-up.

   Afterward, you can display the help message by pressing F1 while the Paradox item is highlighted in the program-list area.

   The Shell displays help messages in its standard Shell Help dialog box and formats those messages to fit in that dialog box. If you want a line to break at a particular point, insert the characters **^m** (or **^M**) at that point. Any additional text starts on the next line when the help message is displayed in the Help dialog box. (Refer to the section "Adding a Program Group" earlier in this chapter for information on linking custom help messages to the built-in DOS Shell help messages.)

2. In the Conventional Memory KB Required text box, you can type the minimum number of kilobytes of conventional memory required to run the program. (Refer to the program's documentation for this number.)

   The Shell uses this information only when the task swapper is enabled. If insufficient conventional memory (less than 640K) is available when you attempt to execute the program item, the Shell does not attempt to run the program. This property does not limit the amount of memory that DOS makes available to the program; the property simply determines whether sufficient memory is available to run the program before the Shell instructs DOS to do so.

   If insufficient memory is available to run the program, the Shell displays a message to that effect. This property provides a much cleaner method of handling insufficient memory than merely waiting for the program to load and watching it "bomb out" for lack of memory.

3. In the XMS Memory KB Required text box, you can type the minimum amount (in kilobytes) of XMS memory that the program
requires. (For more information about XMS memory, refer to
Chapter 15, "Understanding Batch Files, DOSKey, and Macros.")

The Shell uses this information only when the task swapper is
enabled. If insufficient XMS memory is free when you attempt to
execute the program item, the Shell does not attempt to run the
program. By default, the Shell does not require any XMS memory
to be free before it attempts to run a program.

> **WARNING:** Using the XMS Memory KB Required text box
> can increase significantly the time required to swap between
> programs. Specify this property only if the program causes
> your system to freeze when insufficient XMS memory is
> available.

4. In the XMS Memory KB Limit text box, you can type the maximum
amount (in kilobytes) of XMS memory that you want DOS to allocate to the program, even if more XMS memory is available.

The Shell uses this information only when the task swapper is
enabled. By default, the Shell allocates a maximum of 384K of XMS
memory to a program. Some programs, however, need more or
less XMS memory. Specify a larger number if the program requires
more than 384K. You can type **-1** in the KB Limit text box to
instruct the Shell to allocate all available XMS memory to the
program.

5. Leave the Text option button (the default Video Mode setting)
selected for all program items if you have a VGA, EGA, or monochrome monitor.

Click the Graphics option button if you have a CGA monitor and
experience problems in switching to a program that uses graphics. The Graphics option reserves more memory for a program
that uses the Graphics mode of your display adapter. This option
is active only when the task swapper is active and is unnecessary
if you use a VGA or EGA monitor.

6. Check any Reserve Shortcut Keys check box to disable the specified task-swapper shortcut key. The DOS 6.0 task swapper (discussed in Chapter 9, "Managing Your Files"), uses the keystroke
combinations Alt-Tab, Alt-Esc, and Ctrl-Esc to switch between
programs and the DOS Shell window. If a program uses one or
more of these key combinations for some other purpose, click the

appropriate check box to disable DOSSHELL's handing of the key; otherwise, the task-swapper shortcuts override the program's shortcuts.

7. Click the Prevent Program Switch check box to prevent the Shell's task swapper from switching to another program without quitting the program you are using. When this option is active, you have to quit the program to return to the Shell and select another program.

8. Click OK or press Enter to close the Advanced dialog box and return to the Add Program dialog box.

Modifying Program-Item Properties

Now that you understand how to use the New command (File menu) to add a program item to a program group, modifying the properties of an existing program item should be easy.

To modify the properties of an existing program item, follow these steps:

1. Activate the program-list area. If the group that contains the program item that you want to modify is not included in the selected group, select the program group that includes that item.

2. Use the mouse or cursor-movement keys to move the selection bar to the name of the program item that contains the properties you want to modify.

3. Choose Properties from the File menu. The Program Item Properties dialog box appears.

4. Make the desired changes in the values in the text boxes—including changes in the values in any dialog boxes associated with replaceable parameters and changes in the values in the Advanced dialog box (if you are using advanced options). Then click OK or press Enter to confirm your choices.

   Alternatively, click Cancel to return to the Shell window without changing any of the program item's properties.

Deleting a Program Item

You may want to delete a program item that you no longer use. The program itself is not deleted—only the program item. To remove a program from your computer, you must delete that program's files from the disk.

To delete a program item, follow these steps:

1. Move the selection bar to the name of the item that you want to delete.

2. Choose Delete from the File menu or press Del. The Delete Item dialog box appears.

3. Select 1. Delete This Item. Then click OK or press Enter. The Shell deletes the program item from the selected program-group list.

Copying a Program Item

You also can place a copy of the current program item in the current program group or in a different program group.

> **CAUTION:** The DOS Shell has no prohibition against assigning the same name to two programs in the same group, but such an arrangement would be confusing to the user.

To copy a program item, follow these steps:

1. Select the program item that you want to copy.

2. Choose Copy from the File menu. The Shell displays the following message in the status bar:

```
Display Group to Copy To, then press F2. ESC to cancel.
```

3. Select the program group to which you want the Shell to copy the item.

4. Press the F2 key to copy the program item to the new group.

FROM HERE...

For Related Information

◄◄ "Using the Task Swapper," p. 309.

◄◄ "Understanding Replaceable Parameters," p. 560.

Chapter Summary

You now know how to customize the DOS Shell by changing its color settings and by adding and modifying program groups and program items. Important points covered in this chapter include the following:

■ You can change the colors of the screen in which the Shell appears.

■ You can add or change the program groups and program items that appear in the Shell's program-list area.

■ You can add custom help messages to program groups and program items in the program-list area.

Turn now to Chapter 17, "Configuring Your Computer," to learn how to fine-tune DOS 6.0 to get the most from your computer and its peripheral devices.

Configuring Your Computer

PCs on the market today have many similarities—they are based on the same family of computer chips, and they have similar components, such as memory, hard disks, and power supplies. Still, the differences between various makes and models of personal computers are greater today than ever before. DOS gives you the tools to fine-tune the operation of every element of your computer system, an exercise often called *configuring* your system. You can adjust a bewildering number of settings; how you manipulate these settings greatly affects how efficiently your PC works. Sadly, the people who do not understand how to configure their PCs greatly outnumber the people who do. By reading this chapter, you can become one who understands how to configure a computer.

Fortunately, the folks at Microsoft realize that configuring a modern PC can be challenging for most users, and perhaps the most important advance that Microsoft includes in DOS 6.0 is a tool—MemMaker—that performs the hardest part of the configuration automatically. If you want to call yourself a PC guru, you should understand the configuration process, but if you're a novice user, the worst part of working with MS-DOS just disappeared.

The default configuration of DOS, which may be adequate for many users, is designed as a "lowest-common-denominator," intended to work with the greatest number of systems. As PC technology advances, DOS also must enable users of the most up-to-date systems to take full advantage of their computers' most powerful features. This chapter describes how to use DOS to create the optimum configuration for your computer system, whether your system is a plain-vanilla PC or a banana split with all the toppings.

In this chapter, you learn how to use the files CONFIG.SYS and AUTOEXEC.BAT to configure your system. This chapter gives you an overview of how to customize your system configuration with DOS 6.0 and earlier versions. The remainder of the chapter explains how to optimize your system's memory resources, enhance disk performance, and use several other configuration commands and techniques. After you master the information presented in this chapter, you can fine-tune your PC so that it provides all the power you expected when you bought it.

Key Terms Used in This Chapter

CONFIG.SYS	A special text file that DOS reads during booting to find and execute configuration commands.
Device driver	A special program file, usually with a SYS extension, that DOS can load through a configuration command. Device drivers control how DOS and applications programs interact with specific items of hardware.
Expanded memory	Also referred to as EMS—Expanded Memory Specification; special RAM that DOS accesses as a device. Expanded memory conforms to the Lotus/Intel/Microsoft (LIM) EMS 3.2 or 4.0 standards.
Extended memory	Memory at addresses above 1M on 80286, 80386, and 80486 PCs. DOS 5.0 and 6.0 can load most of the operating system into the first 64K of extended memory.

High memory area	The first 64K of extended memory. DOS 5.0 and 6.0 can load a part of the operating system files into this area of memory.
Upper memory area	A 384K area of memory between 640K and 1M, usually reserved for use by certain system devices, such as your monitor. On a 80386 or 80486 PC, DOS 5.0 and 6.0 can use a portion of this upper memory area, referred to as *upper memory blocks*, for memory-resident programs and device drivers.
XMS	The Lotus/Intel/Microsoft/AST Extended Memory Specification, a standard that specifies a set of rules by which several programs can use extended memory cooperatively by means of a device driver.

Getting the Most from Your Computer Resources

Whether you use your own computer or a computer owned by your employer, someone has invested a significant sum of money in the system. This chapter helps you discover how to configure your computer to operate most efficiently—how to get the "most bang for the buck." You generally can improve the performance of software running on your PC in two ways: You can increase the amount of memory available to the software, and you can increase the speed at which your system or its components operate. You can tackle these efficiency-oriented goals in two general ways:

- Add or replace hardware.

- Use software to attain an optimal configuration for your existing hardware resources.

DOS fits into the software category. This chapter teaches you how to use DOS 6.0 and its CONFIG.SYS and AUTOEXEC.BAT files to increase the amount of memory available to applications. The chapter also explains how to use special device drivers and utility programs to enhance the performance of your hard disk, which in turn enhances software performance.

Reviewing **AUTOEXEC.BAT**

Chapter 15, "Understanding Batch Files, DOSKey, and Macros," introduces you to batch files and to the special batch file AUTOEXEC.BAT. Each time you turn on or reboot your computer, DOS executes AUTOEXEC.BAT (if it exists where DOS can find it on your computer's boot disk). AUTOEXEC.BAT is, therefore, a natural place to put configuration-related commands you want DOS to execute every time you start your system. Chapter 11, "Working with System Information," and Chapter 15, "Understanding Batch Files, DOSKey, and Macros," describe several examples of configuration-related commands, including TIME, DATE, PATH, and PROMPT.

This chapter introduces you to several more commands that are prime candidates for inclusion in your AUTOEXEC.BAT file. For example, the SET command is used often in AUTOEXEC.BAT to assign a value to an environment variable. This chapter also discusses the LOADHIGH command, which you can use in AUTOEXEC.BAT to load memory-resident applications programs into a special reserved memory area where they don't use up precious conventional (below 640K) memory.

FROM HERE...

For Related Information

◄◄ "Understanding the Contents of AUTOEXEC.BAT," p. 553.

◄◄ "Understanding Meta-Strings," p. 555.

◄◄ "Customizing Your Prompt," p. 556.

◄◄ "Understanding Replaceable Parameters," p. 560.

◄◄ "Using Batch-File Commands," p. 565.

Understanding **CONFIG.SYS**

After DOS starts but before it runs AUTOEXEC.BAT, DOS looks in the root directory of the boot disk for a file called CONFIG.SYS. If DOS finds CONFIG.SYS, DOS attempts to carry out the commands in the file. This file is intended specifically to *configure* your *system*, hence its name: CONFIG.SYS.

Similar in nature to AUTOEXEC.BAT, CONFIG.SYS is an ASCII text file consisting of a series of one-line commands. You can view the contents of CONFIG.SYS by issuing the following command at the DOS prompt:

TYPE CONFIG.SYS

Because CONFIG.SYS is an ASCII text file, you can create it by using the command COPY CON CONFIG.SYS. You also can create or edit CONFIG.SYS by using the DOS editor EDIT, a third-party text editor, or any word processing program that can output ASCII text files.

The commands you can include in CONFIG.SYS are not the same as the commands available in batch files. These commands are intended solely to configure your system at start-up and, therefore, in this book are referred to as *configuration commands*. (Some books refer to these commands as *directives*.) Table 17.1 lists the configuration commands you can use in your CONFIG.SYS file and describes the action each command performs.

Table 17.1 Configuration Commands

Command	Action
BREAK	Determines when DOS recognizes the Ctrl-C or Ctrl-Break key combination
BUFFERS	Sets the number of file buffers DOS reserves for transferring information to and from the disk
COUNTRY	Sets country-dependent information
DEVICE	Loads a driver that enables a particular device to be used with your system
DEVICEHIGH	Loads a device driver into an upper memory block, also called *reserved memory* (DOS 5.0 and 6.0 only)
DOS	Determines whether DOS is loaded into the high memory area and whether upper memory blocks are allocated (DOS 5.0 and 6.0 only)
DRIVPARM	Sets disk drive characteristics
FCBS	Determines the number of file control blocks that can be opened simultaneously
FILES	Sets the number of files that can be open at one time
INSTALL	Installs a memory-resident program
LASTDRIVE	Specifies the highest valid disk drive letter

continues

Table 17.1 Continued

Command	Action
NUMLOCK	Specifies the initial setting for the <Num Lock> key (DOS 6.0 only)
REM	Causes a line not to be executed so that you can insert a remark
SET	Sets the values of environment variables (DOS 6.0 only)
SHELL	Informs DOS what command processor should be used and where the processor is located
STACKS	Sets the number of stacks that DOS uses to process hardware interrupts
SWITCHES	Disables extended keyboard functions

This chapter discusses the most important configuration commands listed in table 17.1. The most frequently used configuration commands are probably FILES, BUFFERS, and DEVICE (and its relative DEVICEHIGH), which you may want to pay special attention to. Configuration commands not discussed in this chapter are explained in the Command Reference of this book.

NOTE   The documentation for most applications software packages and peripheral hardware devices recommends that you include particular commands in CONFIG.SYS. Read these recommendations carefully to determine whether you need to alter your CONFIG.SYS. Otherwise, a new software or hardware device you install may not operate the way you expect.

Understanding Device Drivers

MS-DOS provides certain features that every DOS user needs. Regardless of the type of computer you use or the software you run, you must be able to create directories, access files, and print to your printer. Many other features, however, may not be important to you, depending on the type of computer you have and how you use it. For example, DOS can work with a mouse, but this capability is not important to you if you don't own a mouse. If you plan to use a mouse with DOS, DOS must load the mouse-handling functions when your computer boots. If you don't plan to use a mouse, loading the mouse-handling functions ties up valuable memory, a sacrifice you don't want to make.

In order to allow you the flexibility of using only the parts of DOS that you need, DOS consists of a base portion (which contains the features that everybody needs) and a series of what you might think of as "plug-in modules" (pieces of programs that give DOS the instructions it needs to perform certain tasks). Because you can decide which of the optional modules to use, you don't waste memory loading features you don't need.

These plug-in modules are called *device drivers* because they generally give DOS the information needed to access various types of hardware devices. In addition to the device drivers that come with DOS, some add-on hardware comes with a device driver that enables your system to recognize and use the hardware. If, for example, you buy a mouse to use with your computer, you also must load the appropriate device driver so that DOS knows how to control the mouse.

One of the most important tasks you perform with the CONFIG.SYS file is telling DOS which device drivers to load when the computer boots. The DEVICE command tells DOS to load a device driver and uses the following syntax:

DEVICE = *d:path***filename.ext** */switches*

d: is the disk drive where the device driver file resides, *path* is the directory path to the device driver file, and **filename.ext** is the name of the device driver file. */switches* are any switches the device driver software needs.

If you buy a Microsoft mouse, for example, you also get a device driver called MOUSE.SYS that tells DOS how to use the mouse. If you place MOUSE.SYS in the root directory of your C drive, you can load MOUSE.SYS by adding the following command to CONFIG.SYS. (***Note:*** The spaces around the equal sign in this syntax are optional):

DEVICE = C:\MOUSE.SYS

You can load as many device drivers as you need, but you must use a separate DEVICE command for each driver you install.

Most users create a special subdirectory called \DRIVERS or \SYS and put the driver files in this directory so that they are out of the way of daily files. (You can give the directory containing your device drivers any valid file name.) If you put the driver files in a separate subdirectory, you must specify the path name as part of the name of the device driver, as shown in the following examples:

DEVICE = C:\DRIVERS\MOUSE.SYS

or

DEVICE = C:\SYS\MOUSE.SYS

Table 17.2 lists the device driver files included with DOS 6.0.

Table 17.2 DOS 6.0 Device Drivers

Device Driver	Description
ANSI.SYS	Enables control of display by using ANSI control sequences
DBLSPACE.SYS	Enables disk compression, greatly increasing the amount of data you can store on your hard disk (DOS 6.0 only)
DISPLAY.SYS	Provides support for code-page switching to the screen
DRIVER.SYS	Sets parameters for physical and logical disk drives
EGA.SYS	Saves and restores an EGA screen when using DOSSHELL and the task swapper
EMM386.EXE	Uses XMS memory in an 80386 or 80486 computer to emulate EMS memory and provide upper memory blocks
HIMEM.SYS	Manages extended memory
RAMDRIVE.SYS	Uses a portion of random-access memory (RAM) to simulate a hard disk—often called a *RAM disk*
SETVER.EXE	Establishes a version table that lists the version number DOS 6.0 reports to named programs
SMARTDRV.EXE	Uses extended or expanded memory to buffer disk reads

The most commonly used device drivers are discussed in this chapter. Refer to the Command Reference for the syntax of the drivers not covered here.

> **NOTE** When you install DOS 6.0, you may notice that DOS installs three files that appear to be device drivers because they end in the SYS extension: COUNTRY.SYS, KEYBOARD.SYS, and CHKSTATE.SYS. Despite their extension, these files are not device drivers; they are used internally by other DOS commands, and you cannot use them in your CONFIG.SYS file.

Understanding Types of Memory

All computer software needs memory (also known as RAM, or *random-access memory*) in which to store instructions and data. As software has become more powerful and complex, the amount of memory required to run much of the software available today has increased dramatically. In the early 1980s, users with 128K of memory wondered what use they'd ever find for so much memory. Ten years later, many PCs have a hundred times that much memory.

Many PC applications today require a minimum amount of memory, yet these applications usually run faster if more than the minimum amount of memory is available. You can make more memory available to your applications by purchasing more memory, but you can also increase available memory by carefully configuring DOS. Like application programs, DOS must use some of your computer's memory, too, and the less memory DOS uses, the more available for your applications.

In this section, you learn about the different areas of the PC's memory and the terms used to describe the PC's memory. Terms describing areas of memory are especially confusing because they are often similar and rather arbitrary. Many computer-literate users often confuse *extended memory* with *expanded memory* or *upper memory* with *high memory*. In fact, these terms are just now becoming standardized; in years past, even people who understood PC memory didn't always use identical terms.

In the next section, you learn how to configure your computer to make the most memory available to your applications.

Conventional Memory

In 1981, when the original IBM PC made its debut, the microprocessor at the heart of the PC was able to access up to 1 megabyte (1024K) memory locations. The designers needed to use some of those memory locations for internal purposes (such as video memory) and arbitrarily decided that the last 384K of those locations would be reserved for the hardware's use and unavailable to programs. The remaining memory, up to 640K, could be used for DOS and application programs. DOS required about 50K out of the 640K, and the remaining memory was available to application programs. The 640K was known as *conventional memory*. The remaining 384K locations, which were reserved and not available to programs, were known as the *upper memory area*, or UMA. Figure 17.1 illustrates this arrangement.

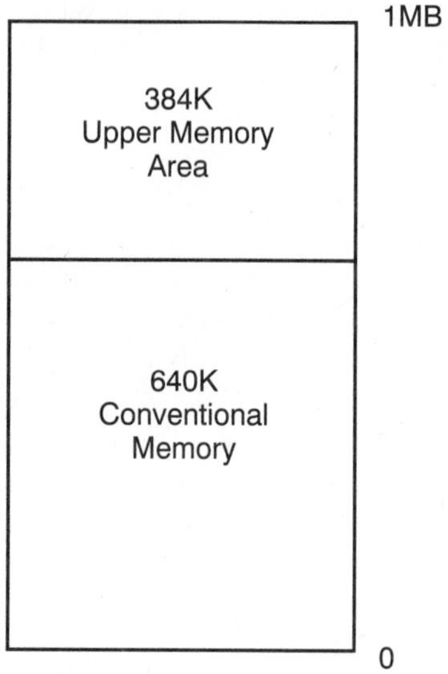

1MB

384K
Upper Memory
Area

640K
Conventional
Memory

0

Fig. 17.1

The relationship
between conven-
tional and upper
memory.

Most PCs at the time did not contain anywhere near the full 640K of
conventional memory, and it was not considered unreasonable to limit
the maximum memory available to applications at 640K. Because
memory was quite expensive in the early 1980s, few people believed
that anyone would soon be able to afford memory in excess of 640K.
Certainly no software vendors were selling programs that needed more
than 640K.

As PCs became more popular, however, memory prices plummeted. By
the mid- and late-1980s, more and more users could afford more than
640K—if only their PCs could use it. Analysts begin to talk about *the
640K barrier*, and some users began to wish that DOS could use more
than 640K. Since that time, two solutions have become widely used,
along with a couple of interesting tricks.

Expanded Memory

The first attempt to make more than 640K available to programs used a
technique that became known as *expanded memory*. In this scheme,
additional memory did not reside on the PC's main circuit board (the
motherboard) with the conventional memory; instead, the additional
memory sat on a plug-in board that could contain as much as 8M of
memory. DOS programs couldn't directly access the expanded memory
the way they could conventional memory, but programs could use the
expanded memory.

To understand how expanded memory works, consider an analogy. Suppose that you want take a look at old magazines in the library. Usually you're not allowed to search the shelves yourself; you tell the librarian which magazine you want to read. She finds and gives you the magazine. When you finish looking through the magazine, you return the magazine to the librarian, who returns it to the shelf.

Expanded memory works the same way. The memory on the expanded memory board is divided into equal-sized sections, each 64K, known as *pages*. The DOS programs themselves cannot access this memory, so they use the expanded memory board as a library. A special device driver supplied with the board, called an *expanded memory manager*, acts as librarian.

When a program needs something from expanded memory, the program communicates with the expanded memory manager and asks for a particular page of expanded memory. The expanded memory manager communicates with the board, and the board locates the requested page and makes a copy in a special 64K area within conventional memory. The program can access this copy and tells the memory manager when it is finished with the copy. The memory manager then copies the page from conventional memory back into expanded memory. Figure 17.2 illustrates this process.

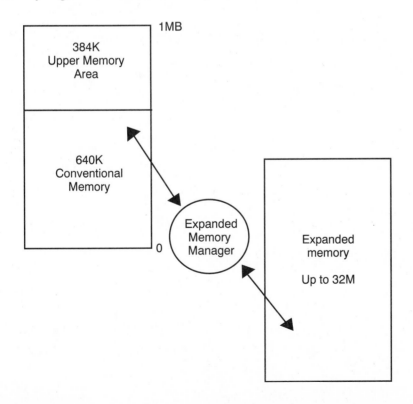

384K
Upper Memory
Area

1MB

640K
Conventional
Memory

0

Expanded
Memory
Manager

Expanded
memory

Up to 32M

Fig. 17.2

A diagram
showing how
DOS programs
access expanded
memory.

This scheme became known as the *Lotus-Intel-Microsoft Expanded Memory Specification, LIM/EMS,* or just *EMS.* The first version of the EMS specification, published in 1985, was numbered EMS Version 3.0 because it was compatible with DOS 3.0. The second revision was numbered EMS Version 3.2. Both EMS 3.0 and EMS 3.2 provide up to 8M of additional memory to applications written to take advantage of this specification. The most recent EMS revision, Version 4.0, announced in August 1987, can address up to 32M of expanded memory.

EMS was not a very elegant solution, however. It was slow and a programming nightmare to the programmers who had to write applications that used it.

Extended Memory

With the development of the 80286 microprocessor, PCs were capable of accessing more than 1M of memory without resorting to expanded memory boards. This additional memory, known as *extended memory,* is simply an extension of the computer's conventional memory and resides on the same board as the conventional memory. A special device driver, called an *extended memory manager,* controls the use of extended memory. (Development of the 80386 and 80486 greatly enhanced the usefulness of extended memory, providing access to even more memory.) Figure 17.3 illustrates this arrangement.

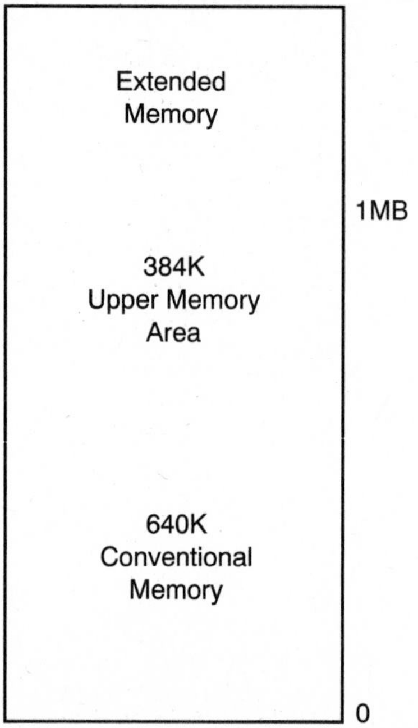

Extended Memory
1MB
384K Upper Memory Area
640K Conventional Memory
0

Fig. 17.3

Extended memory.

You may think that extended memory would at last enable you to run any size programs. The roadblock, however, was DOS. Although the computer hardware could access more than 1M, DOS could not. DOS could only access memory within the first 1M (conventional memory and upper memory). While programs could use extended memory to store data, the programs themselves (that is, the instructions) had to load within that the first 1M.

Upper Memory Blocks

Even though programs could store data in extended memory, DOS couldn't access extended memory. Programs, TSRs, and device drivers still had to squeeze into conventional memory. Software developers still longed for more memory within the 1M limit.

Somewhere along the way, a trick was discovered that allowed access to more memory. Even though the designers of DOS reserved 384K— the upper memory area—for system use, no PC actually uses all of that memory. Scattered throughout the 384K locations are areas of memory that aren't being used, some as large as 100K or more. The exact location and size of those unused areas varies from machine to machine, but they are always present.

Software vendors that wrote memory managers for PCs with a 80386 or 80486 found a way to trick the PC into thinking that some of its extended memory was relocated into the unused areas within the upper memory area. The trick involved a technique called *memory mapping*, the details of which are better left for a computer science textbook. These chunks of memory were called *upper memory blocks* or UMBs. Starting with DOS 5.0, you can load most DOS device drivers into these upper memory blocks, thus leaving more of your conventional memory available for programs.

Optimizing Your Computer's Memory

Now that you have an understanding of the different types of PC memory and how they interrelate, you can learn how to make the most of your PC's memory.

Using Extended Memory and HIMEM.SYS

Most computers today are sold with at least some extended memory. The most significant feature offered by DOS 5.0 and 6.0, in terms of optimizing the use of your computer, is the capacity to load most of the operating system software into extended memory. By loading most of the operating system software into extended memory, DOS 6.0 provides more conventional memory for applications, ultimately improving the performance of your system.

Before DOS or applications software can use extended memory, you must add to your CONFIG.SYS file a command to load an *extended memory manager*—a driver that provides a standard way for applications to address extended memory so that no two programs use the same portion of extended memory at the same time. DOS 4.0 and later versions include the extended memory manager HIMEM.SYS.

HIMEM.SYS manages memory according to the rules set out in the Extended Memory Specification (XMS) Version 2.0. According to this specification, three areas of memory above the conventional 640K barrier can be made available for programs to use:

- *Upper memory blocks* make up the memory within the 38K of reserved memory. Technically the term refers to all of the 384K, but people usually use the term to mean the unused portion of the 384K.

- *High memory area* (HMA) is the first 64K of extended memory, except that the first 16 bytes are actually within the upper memory area. A portion of the operating system can run in the HMA, and DOS 5.0 and 6.0 include the capability to load part of DOS into the HMA, freeing more conventional memory.

- *Extended memory blocks* (XMS memory) include all memory above 1,024K. When extended memory is managed by an extended memory manager, you refer to the memory as XMS memory.

NOTE   The terms used to describe DOS memory can be maddening. Try not to confuse high memory with upper memory:

- The upper memory area (UMA) consists of the 384K of memory above 640K up to 1M and is divided into many different sized blocks, called upper memory blocks (UMBs).

- The high memory area (HMA) is a single block essentially consisting of the first 64K of extended memory. However, the HMA slightly overlaps the upper memory area—the last 16 bytes of the upper memory area are the first 16 bytes of the high memory area. (Most people are not aware of this slight overlap, and it can be a good way to win bar bets.)

When used on an 80286, 80386, or 80486 PC, HIMEM.SYS provides HMA and XMS memory to programs that "know" how to use it. To access upper memory, however, the PC must contain an 80386 or 80486 CPU, and you must include one of the following device driver commands in CONFIG.SYS:

DEVICE=EMM386.EXE RAM

or

DEVICE=EMM386.EXE NOEMS

Refer to the next section for a full discussion of EMM386.EXE.

The syntax for using HIMEM.SYS is shown in the following:

DEVICE=*d:path***HIMEM.SYS** */A20CONTROL:ON\OFF /NUMHANDLES=n*
/EISA /HMAMIN=m /INT15=xxxx /MACHINE:xx
/SHADOWRAM:ON\OFF /CPUCLOCK:ON\OFF /QUIET

d: is the disk drive where the HIMEM.SYS resides, and *path*\ is the directory containing the device driver file. If HIMEM.SYS is contained in the \DOS directory on your C drive, for example, you include the following command in CONFIG.SYS:

DEVICE=C:\DOS\HIMEM.SYS

In most cases, you need only this command to activate the extended memory manager. In special cases, however, you may need to use one of the available switches described in the following paragraphs. The next section continues the discussion of loading DOS into upper memory.

According to the XMS specification, only one program at a time can use the high memory area. The switch */HMAMIN=n* sets the minimum amount of memory that must be requested by an application before the application is permitted to use HMA. If you load DOS into HMA, you can omit this switch, as explained in the section "Loading DOS into High Memory" later in this chapter.

When the extended memory manager assigns memory to a particular program, the extended memory manager assigns one or more extended memory block *handles* to the program. The */numhandles=n* switch indicates the maximum number of handles available. The number *n* must be from 1 through 128. The default is 32 handles, usually a sufficient number. Each reserved handle requires an additional 6 bytes of memory. Unless you are running software that complains that it does not have enough extended memory handles, you probably will not need this option.

Most current versions of commercial software support the XMS specification for addressing extended memory. Some older versions of programs, however, use a different method of addressing extended memory, known as the *Interrupt 15h* (*INT15h*) interface. If you work with software that uses the INT15h interface and you want to load DOS into HMA, add the */INT15=xxxx* switch. The number *xxxx* indicates the amount of extended memory you want HIMEM.SYS to assign to the INT15h interface. This number must be from 64 through 65,535 (kilobytes), and the default is 0. If you assign some of your extended memory to the Int15 interface, that memory is not available to programs that expect the XMS interface.

Internally DOS uses a wire called the *A20 memory address line* to access the high memory area. Explaining what the A20 address line is and how DOS uses it is not important here, but not all brands of PCs handle the A20 line in the same way. Normally, HIMEM.SYS can detect how your computer uses its A20 line, but if it guesses incorrectly, HIMEM.SYS displays the following error message:

```
Unable to control A20
```

If you see this message, use the */MACHINE:xx* switch in the HIMEM.SYS command to specify which type of A20 handler your machine uses. Insert for *xx* in the */MACHINE* switch the code that matches your computer. You can find the text codes in the Code column and the number codes in the Number column in table 17.3. If you see the error message but your computer is not listed in table 17.3, try the switch */MACHINE:1*.

Before DEVICE=HIMEM.SYS in CONFIG.SYS, you may have listed a device driver that also uses the A20 line. By default, HIMEM.SYS takes control of A20 even though the line is turned on when HIMEM.SYS loads. HIMEM.SYS warns you when this condition occurs by displaying the following message:

```
Warning: The A20 Line was already enabled!
```

Determine whether you really intend to have both drivers installed at one time. If so, you can prevent HIMEM.SYS from taking control of A20 by adding the switch */A20CONTROL:OFF* (the default setting is */A20CONTROL:ON*).

Table 17.3 A20 Handler Codes

Code	Number	Computer
at	1	IBM PC/AT
ps2	2	IBM PS/2
pt1cascade	3	Phoenix Cascade BIOS
hpvectra	4	HP Vectra (A and A+)
att6300plus	5	AT&T 6300 Plus
acer1100	6	Acer 1100
toshiba	7	Toshiba 1600 and 1200XE
wyse	8	Wyse 12.5 MHz 286
tulip	9	Tulip SX
zenith	10	Zenith ZBIOS
at1	11	IBM PC/AT (alternative delay)
at2	12	IBM PC/AT (alternative delay)
css	12	CSS Labs
at3	13	IBM PC/AT (alternative delay)
philips	13	Philips
fasthp	14	HP Vectra
IBM 7552	15	IBM 7552 Industrial Computer
Bull Mioral	16	Bull Mioral 60
DELL	17	DELL XBios

All PCs store some of their basic operating instructions in read-only memory (ROM); however, computers usually cannot access instructions from ROM as fast as they can access instructions from RAM. If you have plenty of memory and an 80386 (or better) computer, you usually can increase the performance of your computer by asking the computer to copy the instructions from ROM into an upper memory block (which is RAM). This technique is known as *shadow RAM*.

Shadow RAM uses some of your upper memory blocks. If you prefer to increase the amount of upper memory available for device drivers and memory-resident programs, use the */SHADOWRAM:OFF* switch. As HIMEM.SYS loads, the following message appears:

```
Shadow RAM disabled.
```

In some cases, DOS cannot turn off shadow RAM. Instead, DOS displays a message telling you that Shadow RAM is in use and cannot be disabled. (Check your hardware documentation for other methods of disabling shadow RAM.)

The */CPUCLOCK:ON* switch ensures that HIMEM.SYS does not slow your computer's *clock speed*, the speed at which your computer processes instructions. (Any change in clock speed does not affect your computer's real-time clock, which keeps time of day.) On the front panel of many PCs is an LED or other indicator that indicates the current clock speed. To prevent the clock speed from slowing, add the */CPUCLOCK:ON* switch to the DEVICE=HIMEM.SYS command in CONFIG.SYS.

If you are using a machine that uses an EISA (Extended Industry Standard Architecture) bus with more than 16M of memory, HIMEM will not normally allocate all the extended memory. Use the */EISA* switch to tell HIMEM to automatically allocate all available extended memory.

 NOTE   EISA buses are found mostly on high-end systems and cost several hundred dollars more than the older and more common ISA bus systems. If you don't know which bus you have, it's probably ISA.

When HIMEM.SYS loads, it usually prints status messages. If you want HIMEM.SYS to load without the usual status messages, add the */QUIET* switch.

Loading DOS into High Memory

DOS 5.0 and 6.0 enable you to load most of the operating system into an area of extended memory known as the high memory area (HMA), the first 64K of extended memory (except the first 16 bytes, which overlap the upper memory area). After the device driver HIMEM.SYS is loaded into the computer's memory, the command DOS=HIGH in CONFIG.SYS loads DOS into high memory.

The next time you boot the computer, DOS uses about 14K of space in conventional memory and loads the remainder of the operating system into the HMA. If, however, you don't use this command in CONFIG.SYS or don't have extended memory installed in your computer, DOS 6.0 occupies more than 62K of memory. By loading the operating system into high memory, DOS 6.0 can free about 48K of conventional memory.

Using Expanded Memory and EMM386.EXE

Because expanded memory was introduced before extended memory, many PC applications were written to take advantage of expanded memory, not extended memory. Unfortunately, extended memory is far less expensive and much more common today. The DOS device driver EMM386.EXE enables applications to use extended memory as though it were expanded memory, freeing you from the need for the special memory boards and device drivers that expanded memory requires. Thus EMM386.EXE emulates expanded memory by using extended memory.

> **NOTE** The device driver HIMEM.SYS, discussed must be loaded before EMM386.EXE. List DEVICE=HIMEM.SYS before DEVICE=EMM386.EXE in the CONFIG.SYS file. HIMEM.SYS makes extended memory available, and EMM386.EXE enables you to use some or all extended memory as though it were expanded memory. Do not use EMM386.EXE if you are using another driver from a third-party software vendor as an expanded memory manager.

> Some applications today can use either expanded memory or extended memory by accessing whichever is available. If you have a choice, use extended memory, which is faster.   **T I P**

In addition to its role as an expanded memory emulator, EMM386.EXE also is a *UMB provider*, working with HIMEM.SYS to provide upper memory blocks (UMBs) into which you can load device drivers and memory-resident programs. See the next section, "Loading Device Drivers and TSRs into Upper Memory," for further discussion of providing UMBs.

The syntax of the command for EMM386.EXE, used as a device driver, is shown in the following:

> **DEVICE=***c:\path***EMM386.EXE** *ON|OFF|AUTO MEMORY W=ON|OFF*
> *MIX|FRAME=address /Pmmmm Pn=address X=mmmm-nnn*
> *I=mmmm-nnn B=address L=minxms A=altregs H=handles*
> *D=nnn RAM NOEMS MIN=n /VERBOSE ROM=mmmm-nnnn NOVCPI*
> *WIN=mmmm-nnnn NOMOVEXBDA NOHIGHSCAN AUTBOOT NOHI*

In most cases, one of the following commands is sufficient:

DEVICE=EMM386.EXE RAM

or

DEVICE=EMM386.EXE NOEMS

The first command loads the expanded memory emulator and allocates 256K of extended memory to be used as expanded memory. The RAM switch enables upper memory. The second command also enables upper memory but tells EMM386 not to allocate extended memory for use as expanded memory.

You may sometimes need the remaining switches for the EMM386.EXE device driver to customize your computer for use with particularly demanding software or hardware. You can specify ON, OFF, or AUTO in the EMM386.EXE device driver command to indicate whether your computer starts in the EMM386.EXE active, inactive, or automatic mode, respectively. By default, the device driver is active, and EMM386.EXE makes extended memory available. However, some applications programs may not run properly when EMM386.EXE is active because EMM386.EXE places the computer in a mode known as Virtual 8086 mode. When you use EMM386.EXE as a device driver, the driver loads in memory and remains active (ON) unless you specify otherwise with the OFF switch.

The OFF switch starts the computer with EMM386.EXE loaded in memory but inactive. The XMS memory allocated as EMS memory is unavailable for any purpose. You can activate the driver with the following command at the DOS command prompt:

EMM386 ON

The OFF switch is not compatible, however, with the RAM or NOEMS switches, discussed later in this section.

Use AUTO if you want EMM386.EXE to activate only when an application requests EMS memory. This setting provides maximum compatibility with software that may not work properly in Virtual 8086 mode. Like the OFF switch, AUTO is not compatible with the *RAM* or *NOEMS* switches.

NOTE   Even though EMM386.EXE activates when an applications program requests EMS memory, the driver does not automatically deactivate when the applications program terminates. To turn off the driver, you must issue the following command at the command prompt:

EMM386 OFF

The *memory* parameter enables you to specify the amount of XMS memory you want EMM386.EXE to allocate as EMS memory. Type the number of kilobytes in the range 16 through 32,768. EMM386.EXE rounds any number you type down to the nearest multiple of 16. All unallocated memory remains available as XMS memory. The default EMS memory allocated is 256K.

> As a general rule, allocate only as much EMS memory as is required by your applications programs. Any memory allocated as EMS memory is no longer available as XMS memory. Some of the most powerful applications programs currently available, such as Microsoft Windows 3.1, work best with the maximum amount of XMS memory available. If none of your applications need expanded memory, use the NOEMS option so that no memory is allocated as expanded memory.

T I P

Use the *L=minxms* switch, in which *minxms* is the number of kilobytes, to indicate the minimum XMS memory that EMM386.EXE should allocate. This parameter overrides the *memory* parameter.

If you installed a Weitek math coprocessor chip—a special computer chip that improves the performance of computation-intensive software such as computer-aided design (CAD) software—use the *W=ON* switch. By default, the device driver does not support this type of coprocessor. You also can turn on or off support for the Weitek coprocessor with one of the following commands at the DOS prompt:

    EMM386 W=ON

    or

    EMM386 W=OFF

In some circumstances, you may want to use upper memory for device drivers and memory-resident programs, but you don't need EMS memory. Use the *NOEMS* switch with the EMM386.EXE driver to free the maximum amount of upper memory and to provide no EMS memory. For example, you may intend to run Windows 3.1 on your computer. Because Windows can use all your XMS memory, this software doesn't need EMS memory.

The */VERBOSE* switch causes EMM386 to print status and error messages when it loads. Normally EMM386 suppresses these messages. You can abbreviate /VERBOSE as /V.

EMM386 scans the upper memory area (UMA) for all available free memory. Unusual architectures may confuse EMM386, causing trouble when your computer boots or while you use the computer. The *NOHIGHSCAN* parameters limits EMM386's scanning of the UMA. If you experience problems when you use EMM386, adding the NOHIGHSCAN parameter may solve the problem.

EMM386 loads part of itself into the upper memory area. If one of your programs needs extra upper memory blocks, and you're willing to give up some of your conventional memory, the *NOHI* parameter causes EMM386 to load all of itself into conventional memory, and does not use any UMA.

The remaining switches available for use with EMM386.EXE are highly technical and beyond the scope of this book. Refer to Que's *DOS Programmer's Reference*, 3rd Edition, or to your DOS User's Guide or Technical Reference Manual for more information.

Loading Device Drivers and TSRs into Upper Memory

In addition to enabling you to run DOS in high memory, DOS 5.0 and 6.0 provide the capability of loading memory-resident programs and device drivers into upper memory blocks, freeing more conventional memory for other applications programs. DOS can access this area of memory in 80386 and 80486 PCs (including SXs) that have 1M or more of memory.

To load device drivers or memory-resident programs, also called *terminate-and-stay-resident (TSR) programs*, into upper memory, the following conditions must be met:

- Your computer has an 80386 or 80486 CPU.

- HIMEM.SYS is loaded as a device driver.

- EMM386.EXE is loaded as a device driver with the RAM or NOEMS switch.

- The command DOS=UMB appears in the CONFIG.SYS file.

    If you also want to use the command DOS=HIGH to load DOS into high memory, you can combine the two commands as shown in the following:

        DOS=HIGH, UMB

You can load two types of programs into upper memory: device drivers and memory-resident programs (TSRs). You already know that device drivers normally are loaded using the DEVICE command. When you want to load a device driver into upper memory, however, use the DEVICEHIGH command. The syntax for this configuration command is shown in the following:

> **DEVICEHIGH**=*c:path***filename.ext** */switches*

 NOTE The *switches* in the syntax for the preceding command are any switches you use for the file that you are loading, not for the DEVICEHIGH command itself.

To load into upper memory the screen driver ANSI.SYS, for example, you need the following command in CONFIG.SYS:

> DEVICEHIGH=C:\DOS\ANSI.SYS

When you boot the computer, DOS attempts to load ANSI.SYS into the upper memory area.

 NOTE DEVICEHIGH, as well as LOADHIGH (discussed later), recognizes two switches, /L and /S. When you use MemMaker to automatically configure your PC, MemMaker may use these switches in the commands it generates. These switches are not intended for use by users.

To load a memory-resident program into upper memory, precede the program's start-up command with LOADHIGH. (You can use the abbreviation LH in place of LOADHIGH.) The syntax for the command for LOADHIGH is shown in the following:

> **LOADHIGH** *c:path***programname** */switches*

To load DOSKEY (discussed in Chapter 15, "Understanding Batch Files, DOSKey, and Macros") into upper memory each time you start your computer, for example, add the following command to your AUTOEXEC.BAT file:

> LOADHIGH DOSKEY

The next time you reboot the computer, DOS attempts to load DOSKey into upper memory. DOS does not load a program into upper memory if the program requests that DOS allocate more memory during initialization than is available in the largest available upper memory block. If DOS is not successful when it tries to load device drivers or TSRs into the upper memory area, DOS loads the program into conventional memory instead.

Use the MEM command to determine whether a driver or program has loaded into upper memory.

Displaying the Amount of Free and Used Memory

To enable you to make the most efficient use of DOS 6.0's memory management utilities, DOS also enables you to display the amount of free and used memory at any point during a DOS session. Use DOS 6.0's MEM command for this purpose.

The syntax for the MEM command is shown in the following:

    MEM */CLASSIFY /DEBUG /FREE /MODULE modulename /PAGE*

Most of these options (/DEBUG, /FREE, and /MODULE) are primarily of interest to programmers. For any option, you can specify just the first letter, such as /C in place of /CLASSIFY, for example.

With no switches, MEM gives a basic report of how the memory on your machine is being used. The following provides a sample of a basic MEM report from a typical computer with 8M of memory:

```
Memory Type       Total =  Used  +  Free
- - - - - - - - -  - - - -  - - - -  - - - -
Conventional       640K      21K     619K
Upper              155K       6K     149K
Adapter RAM/ROM    229K     229K       0K
Extended (XMS)    7168K     104K    7064K
Expanded (EMS)       0K       0K       0K
- - - - - - - - -  - - - -  - - - -  - - - -
Total memory      8192K     360K    7832K

Total under 1 MB   795K      27K     768K

Largest executable program size       618K  (633328 bytes)
Largest free upper memory block       149K  (153056 bytes)
MS-DOS is resident in the high memory area.
```

Even this most basic report includes a wealth of information:

- This computer has 640K of conventional memory, of which 21K is currently in use (in this case, by DOS), leaving 619K free.

- This computer loaded EMM386, which found 155K available in upper memory blocks. 6K of the 155K is currently in use by a device driver that was loaded "high."

- This computer has 7168K of extended memory, 104K of which is in use.

- The computer has no expanded memory.

- The computer has 768K of memory available below 1M, representing the memory available for loading programs and device drivers on this machine.

- The largest program you can load into conventional memory is 618K.

- The largest free upper memory block is 149K. Consequently, you cannot load "high" any program or device driver that requires more memory than 149K.

- Most of DOS has been loaded into the high memory area because the command DOS=HIGH appeared in the CONFIG.SYS file.

With the /CLASSIFY switch, MEM lists all DOS programs and device drivers currently loaded. Along with the information shown above, MEM lists this additional information if you use /CLASSIFY:

```
Modules using memory below 1 MB:
  Name     Total      =    Conventional +   Upper Memory
  --------  ----------      ----------------  ----------------
  MSDOS     14877   (15K)   14877   (15K)         0    (0K)
  HIMEM      1104    (1K)    1104    (1K)         0    (0K)
  EMM386     3072    (3K)    3072    (3K)         0    (0K)
  ANSI       4208    (4K)    4208    (4K)         0    (0K)
  COMMAND    2912    (3K)    2912    (3K)         0    (0K)
  ALIAS      5744    (6K)       0    (0K)      5744    (6K)
  Free     782272  (764K  629216  (614K)    153056  (149K)
```

This sample report shows six programs and device drivers currently loaded and displays the amount of conventional and upper memory used by each:

■ *MSDOS* is the portion of MS-DOS that did not get loaded into the high memory area.

■ *HIMEM* is the HIMEM.SYS device driver.

■ *EMM386* is the EMM386.EXE device driver.

■ *ANSI* is the ANSI.SYS device driver, which this computer loads.

■ *COMMAND* is the DOS command interpreter.

■ *ALIAS* is a TSR program that was loaded into upper memory.

The *MEM /C* often displays more than a screenful of information. The */P* option tells MEM to pause after each screenful of data and wait for you to press a key before continuing.

After you identify a driver or memory-resident program that appears to be the right size to fit in the available UMB, edit CONFIG.SYS or AUTOEXEC.BAT to add DEVICEHIGH or LOADHIGH to the appropriate command. Reboot your computer, and issue the MEM /C command again to see whether the driver or program loaded.

T I P   Arriving at the optimal combination of device drivers and memory-resident programs loaded into upper memory may require some experimentation. DOS loads programs in the largest available UMB first, so try loading the largest drivers and programs first by placing their start-up commands earliest in CONFIG.SYS or AUTOEXEC.BAT.

General Tips for Optimizing Memory

Most computers sold today have at least a 386 microprocessor and come with some extended memory. If your computer meets these criteria, following these tips can enable you to use your memory most efficiently:

■ Your CONFIG.SYS file should load HIMEM.SYS first, then EMM386.EXE. Together these two drivers allow access to extended memory and upper memory blocks.

■ Unless you are running applications which need expanded memory, use the NOEMS option for EMM386.EXE so that all extended memory is available as XMS memory.

■ Load DOS into the high memory area and make upper memory available to DOS with the command DOS=HIGH,UMB.

- Use the DEVICEHIGH command for as many drivers as possible in your CONFIG.SYS file. You cannot use DEVICEHIGH for HIMEM.SYS or EMM386.EXE, and some other device drivers may not load properly with DEVICEHIGH. Experiment, and use MEM/C to determine whether the drivers loaded properly.

- Use LOADHIGH for any TSRs you load in your AUTOEXEC.BAT. Because some TSRs may not work correctly when loaded high, experiment until you determine what TSR you can load high.

- If you own a 386 computer or better, your CONFIG.SYS should begin with the following:

      DEVICE=C:\DOS\HIMEM.SYS
      DEVICE=C:\DOS\EMM386.EXE NOEMS
      DOS=HIGH,UMB

Configuring Memory with MemMaker

Understanding and configuring a PC's memory is one of the most challenging activities most users face. Because most users usually configure their computer's memory once, they never really get a chance to build any experience fiddling with the configuration. After nearly a dozen years of watching users stumble at configuring their PCs, Microsoft finally offers help. DOS 6.0 includes MemMaker, a utility that analyzes your PC and makes the appropriate changes to your CONFIG.SYS and AUTOEXEC.BAT so that your computer uses its memory most effectively.

MemMaker and Applications That Start Automatically

Some people use Windows or a particular application so often that they add a command to the end of their AUTOEXEC.BAT file to start the application automatically every time they boot. If you have added such a command that takes you automatically into Windows or any other program, read this warning carefully. If, on the other hand, you find yourself at the DOS prompt when your computer boots, you can skip this warning.

MemMaker does its work in three phases; between each phase, it reboots your computer. Each time MemMaker causes your computer to reboot, your AUTOEXEC.BAT starts your application as usual, preventing MemMaker from continuing its work. You must exit these programs for MemMaker perform the next phase.

continues

MemMaker and Applications That Start Automatically continued

Hint: If you start an application such as Windows in your AUTOEXEC.BAT file, place the word *REM* in front of the startup command (in this case, in front of WIN) before using MemMaker. REM causes DOS to ignore the rest of the command so that you don't have to exit your application during each MemMaker phase. When MemMaker has completed its work, remove REM so that your application again starts automatically each time you boot.

You can take two different paths to configure your memory with MemMaker. One is to follow the Express Setup. The other path you can choose is the Custom Setup.

Express Setup is the easier path to choose. You have little interaction with Express Setup, other than pressing Enter when MemMaker prompts you to do so. MemMaker searches through the upper memory area to find open memory addresses. MemMaker sorts device drivers and TSRs that you load in memory to see the optimum loading order. Finally, MemMaker updates your CONFIG.SYS and AUTOEXEC.BAT files for two reasons. MemMaker ensures that HIMEM.SYS and EMM386.EXE load to manage memory and that the DOS=UMB directive is in CONFIG.SYS to provide the link to upper memory blocks. In addition, MemMaker inserts DEVICEHIGH and LOADHIGH before the device drivers and TSRs that load in upper memory.

NOTE While MemMaker adds the device drivers HIMEM.SYS and EMM386.EXE and the upper memory block directive HIGH=UMB, it does not ensure that DOS loads into upper memory with the directive DOS=HIGH. Before using MemMaker, ensure that your system loads DOS in the high memory area by inserting DOS=HIGH in your CONFIG.SYS file and rebooting your computer. After you are running DOS in the high memory area (the MEM command tells you that DOS is in the high memory area), run MemMaker.

Custom Setup is very similar to Express Setup in that it scans the upper memory area for open address space, sorts device drivers and TSRs for optimum order, and updates your AUTOEXEC.BAT and CONFIG.SYS files. As you might expect, however, you may customize how MemMaker performs these tasks. The following list shows the elements you can customize using Custom Setup:

- Specify any TSRs that should not be included in optimization
- Aggressively scan the upper memory area

■ Set aside upper memory for Windows use

■ Use an area of upper memory set aside for the Monochrome Display Adapter (MDA) if you are using only an EGA or VGA display (but not SuperVGA)

■ Keep any special memory inclusions or exclusions that you specified with EMM386.EXE

■ Move the Extended BIOS data area in upper memory blocks

Now that you understand what MemMaker can do to optimize your computer's memory, you are ready to use MemMaker. The following two sections explain how to use MemMaker with Express Setup and with Custom Setup.

Using Express Setup

Follow these steps in order to run MemMaker using Express Setup:

1. At the DOS prompt, type **MEMMAKER** and press Enter.

2. MemMaker asks whether you want to continue. Assuming you didn't type MEMMAKER by accident, press Enter to continue.

3. MemMaker asks whether you want an Express or Custom setup, as shown in figure 17.4. For most users, an Express setup does an excellent job. Unless you are very knowledgeable about PCs and want to guide MemMaker's every step, press Enter to select an Express setup.

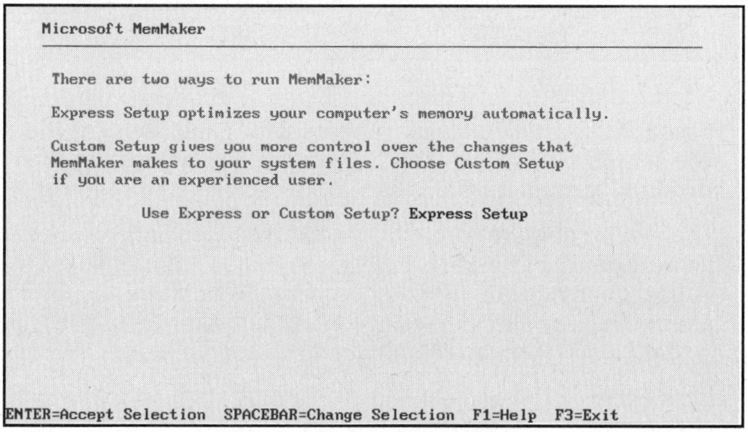

```
Microsoft MemMaker

   There are two ways to run MemMaker:

   Express Setup optimizes your computer's memory automatically.

   Custom Setup gives you more control over the changes that
   MemMaker makes to your system files. Choose Custom Setup
   if you are an experienced user.

        Use Express or Custom Setup? Express Setup




ENTER=Accept Selection  SPACEBAR=Change Selection  F1=Help  F3=Exit
```

Fig. 17.4

The MemMaker setup selection.

4. MemMaker asks whether you intend to use EMS (expanded) memory, as shown in figure 17.5. Answer Y or N, and press Enter. (If the answer you want is already showing, just press Enter.)

After completing the first phrase, MemMaker must reboot the computer. MemMaker displays the screen shown in figure 17.6.

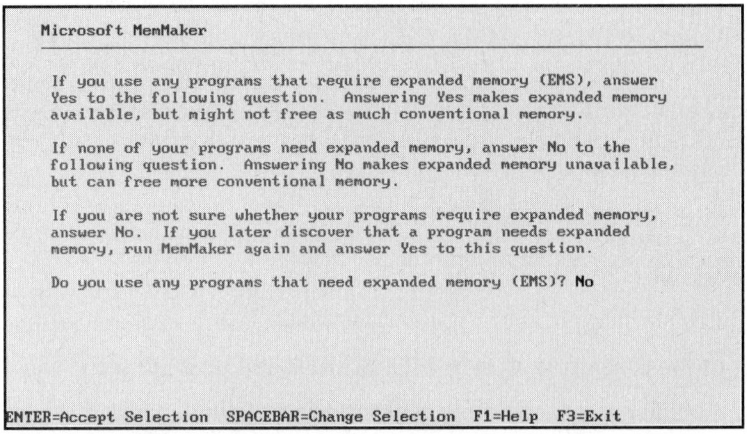

```
Microsoft MemMaker
─────────────────────────────────────────────────────────────

    If you use any programs that require expanded memory (EMS), answer
    Yes to the following question.  Answering Yes makes expanded memory
    available, but might not free as much conventional memory.

    If none of your programs need expanded memory, answer No to the
    following question.  Answering No makes expanded memory unavailable,
    but can free more conventional memory.

    If you are not sure whether your programs require expanded memory,
    answer No.  If you later discover that a program needs expanded
    memory, run MemMaker again and answer Yes to this question.

    Do you use any programs that need expanded memory (EMS)? No




ENTER=Accept Selection   SPACEBAR=Change Selection   F1=Help   F3=Exit
```

Fig. 17.5

The MemMaker EMS selection.

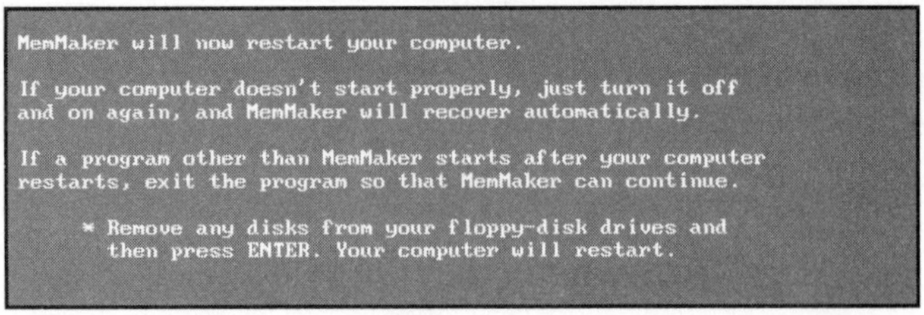

```
MemMaker will now restart your computer.

If your computer doesn't start properly, just turn it off
and on again, and MemMaker will recover automatically.

If a program other than MemMaker starts after your computer
restarts, exit the program so that MemMaker can continue.

     * Remove any disks from your floppy-disk drives and
       then press ENTER. Your computer will restart.
```

Fig. 17.6

The first MemMaker reboot notice.

5. Press Enter, and MemMaker reboots your computer. (As the screen in figure 17.6 explains, if your computer does not start correctly, turning it off and back on will cause it to reboot.)

When your computer reboots, MemMaker automatically begins the next phase of its work, telling you that it has calculated the optimal configuration for you computer. MemMaker displays another screen, as shown in figure 17.7, that asks you to press Enter so that MemMaker can reboot again.

6. Press Enter.

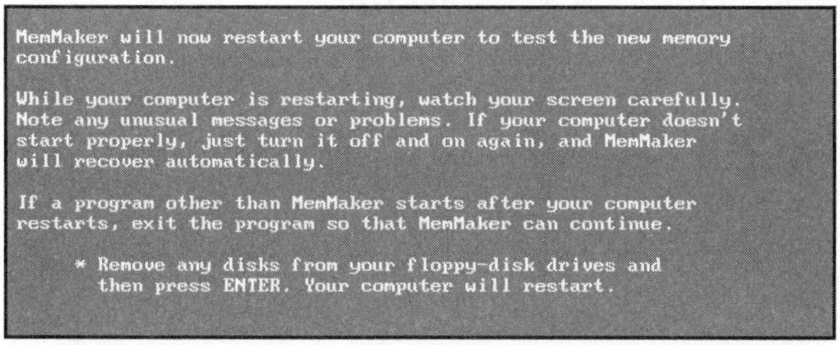

```
MemMaker will now restart your computer to test the new memory
configuration.

While your computer is restarting, watch your screen carefully.
Note any unusual messages or problems. If your computer doesn't
start properly, just turn it off and on again, and MemMaker
will recover automatically.

If a program other than MemMaker starts after your computer
restarts, exit the program so that MemMaker can continue.

     * Remove any disks from your floppy-disk drives and
       then press ENTER. Your computer will restart.
```

Fig. 17.7

The second
MemMaker
reboot notice.

During the reboot, your computer executes the CONFIG.SYS and AUTOEXEC.BAT files that MemMaker created. Although MemMaker should do an excellent job of configuring your computer for peak performance, there is always a chance that it will make a mistake. As your computer boots, watch carefully for any errors produced by the device drivers and programs that you load from your CONFIG.SYS and AUTOEXEC.BAT files.

After your computer completes its reboot, MemMaker begins its last phase. MemMaker displays the message shown in figure 17.8, asking whether you saw any errors during boot.

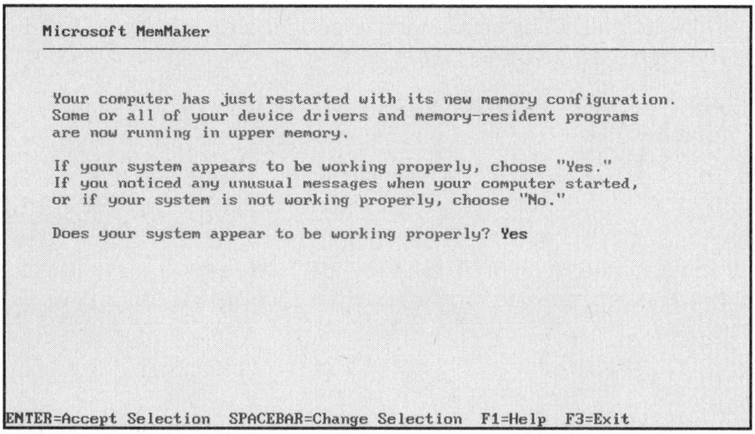

```
Microsoft MemMaker
_____

   Your computer has just restarted with its new memory configuration.
   Some or all of your device drivers and memory-resident programs
   are now running in upper memory.

   If your system appears to be working properly, choose "Yes."
   If you noticed any unusual messages when your computer started,
   or if your system is not working properly, choose "No."

   Does your system appear to be working properly? Yes




ENTER=Accept Selection   SPACEBAR=Change Selection   F1=Help   F3=Exit
```

Fig. 17.8

MemMaker
asking about
boot errors.

7. If your computer booted without errors, press Enter. If you noticed errors, read the sidebar "Fixing MemMaker Errors" for instruction on how to proceed.

MemMaker displays a table showing how the changes affect your available memory. A sample is shown in figure 17.9.

```
Microsoft MemMaker
─────────────────────────────────────────────────────────────────

MemMaker has finished optimizing your system's memory. The following
table summarizes the memory use (in bytes) on your system:

                            Before        After
   Memory Type              MemMaker      MemMaker      Change
   ─────────────            ────────      ────────

   Free conventional memory:  416,432      530,576      114,144

   Upper memory:
      Used by programs              0      114,160      114,160
      Reserved for Windows          0            0            0
      Reserved for EMS              0            0            0
      Free                    142,400       28,224

   Expanded memory:          Disabled     Disabled

   Your original CONFIG.SYS and AUTOEXEC.BAT files have been saved
   as CONFIG.UMB and AUTOEXEC.UMB.  If MemMaker changed your Windows
   SYSTEM.INI file, the original file was saved as SYSTEM.UMB.

ENTER=Exit   ESC=Undo changes
```

Fig. 17.9

A summary
report from
MemMaker.

This report tells you how much of each type of memory you had
available before and after MemMaker made its changes. In this
example, MemMaker adjusts commands in the AUTOEXEC.BAT
and CONFIG.SYS so that several device drivers and TSR programs
are loaded into upper memory, freeing up about 114K of conventional memory. MemMaker also tells you that it has saved your
original AUTOEXEC.BAT and CONFIG.SYS as AUTOEXEC.UMB and
CONFIG.UMB in case you later discover a problem and want to
return to using your original files.

8. When you finish examining this report, press Enter to exit
   MemMaker.

T I P   An easy way to run MemMaker is to use the /BATCH switch. From
the command line, type **MEMMAKER /BATCH**. This command runs
MemMaker in *automatic* mode, accepting all the default answers.

Using Custom Setup

Follow these steps in order to run MemMaker using Custom Setup:

1. At the DOS Prompt, type **MEMMAKER** and press Enter.

2. MemMaker asks whether you want to continue. Assuming you do,
   press Enter to continue.

3. MemMaker asks whether you want an Express or Custom setup (refer to figure 17.4). Press the space bar to select Custom Setup. Then, press Enter to continue.

4. MemMaker asks whether you intend to use EMS memory (refer to figure 17.5). Press the space bar to toggle between No and Yes. When you have made the correct selection, press Enter.

5. MemMaker now displays Advanced Options that enable you to customize the settings that MemMaker uses when optimizing memory. Each advanced option requires a Yes or No answer. Use the space bar to toggle between Yes and No for each option. Use the Down and Up arrow keys to move from one option to the next. The following list explains the options that you have to set:

   ■ *Specify which drivers and TSRs to include in optimization?* Answering Yes enables you to leave TSRs out of optimization that must be loaded into memory in a specific sequence or that give MemMaker trouble during optimization.

   ■ *Scan the upper memory area aggressively?* If you answer Yes, MemMaker includes the HIGHSCAN parameter in the EMM386.EXE line of CONFIG.SYS. Although EMM386.EXE normally scans the address range C600-EFFF for available upper memory, adding HIGHSCAN instructs EMM386.EXE to scan the address range C600-F7FF.

   ■ *Optimize upper memory for use with Windows?* If you answer Yes, EMM386.EXE sets aside upper memory for use by Windows. This provides more memory for DOS programs that you run from Windows. If you do not run DOS programs from Windows, choose No.

   ■ *Use monochrome region (B000-BFFF) for running programs?* Answer Yes if you have installed an EGA or VGA display adapter but not a monochrome or SuperVGA display adapter. The address range B000-BFFF can be used as upper memory if you have an EGA or VGA display adapter installed.

   ■ *Keep current EMM386 memory exclusions and inclusions?* If you currently are using EMM386.EXE and have specific ad-dresses specified to include or exclude, answer Yes to this question.

   ■ *Move Extended BIOS Data Area from conventional to upper memory?* Normally, EMM386.EXE moves the Extended Bios Data Area (EBDA) to upper memory. However, if any unusual problems occur while running MemMaker, answer No to this option.

6. After you answer all the Advanced Options correctly, press Enter to continue with MemMaker.

7. MemMaker searches your hard disk for a copy of Windows. If it finds Windows, MemMaker displays the directory in which the copy of Windows resides. If this directory is incorrect, type the correct directory. Press Enter to continue.

8. MemMaker now asks you to press Enter to restart your computer. MemMaker has inserted information in your start-up files to evaluate the way that your device drivers load into memory. MemMaker must reboot your computer for this evaluation. Ensure that you have no floppy diskettes in any drive; then press Enter to continue.

9. MemMaker restarts your computer, performs memory calculations, and prompts you to press Enter to restart your computer again. Press Enter to continue.

   When MemMaker restarts, it evaluates how much memory each device driver and TSR uses in memory. Then, MemMaker performs calculations to see the optimum loading order of your device drivers and TSRs to give you the most conventional memory. After MemMaker completes all calculations, it rewrites your CONFIG.SYS and AUTOEXEC.BAT files, including appropriate DEVICEHIGH and LOADHIGH statements.

10. MemMaker restarts your computer again and prompts you with the question Does your system appear to be working properly? If so, press Enter to accept the Yes default.

    If, however, you noticed any error messages as your computer started, press the space bar to toggle the answer to No and press Enter. If you answer No, your AUTOEXEC.BAT and CONFIG.SYS files are returned to their original form.

T   I   P   If you experience problems that you did not have before using MemMaker with programs, issue the MEMMAKER /UNDO command to remove any changes that MemMaker made.

11. MemMaker displays a report that shows how much memory you gained. Examine the report and press Enter to complete MemMaker and return to DOS. If you want to undo everything that MemMaker did, press Esc.

For Related Information

◀◀ "Loading DOSKey," p. 590.

◀◀ "Editing the Command Line," p. 592.

◀◀ "Reusing Commands," p. 594.

FROM HERE...

Increasing Hard Disk Performance

If your computer is typical, it spends a lot of its time accessing data and programs on hard disk. Speeding up your hard disk is probably the single most significant thing you can do to increase the speed of your system. Although you can increase the speed of your system by buying a faster hard disk, DOS gives you facilities to make better use of the disk you have.

The BUFFERS command in CONFIG.SYS tells DOS how much memory to reserve for file transfers. DOS sets aside an area of RAM called a *buffer* for temporary storage of data being transferred between the disk and an applications program.

When DOS is asked to retrieve information from a disk, DOS reads the information in increments of whole sectors (512 bytes). Excess data not required from that sector is left in the buffer. If this data is needed later, DOS does not need to perform another disk access to retrieve the data. Similarly, DOS tries to reduce disk activity when DOS writes information to the disk. If less than a full sector is to be written to the disk, DOS accumulates the information in a disk buffer. When the buffer is full, DOS writes the information to the disk. This action is called *flushing the buffer*. To make sure that all pertinent information is placed into a file, DOS also flushes the buffers when a program closes a disk file.

When a disk buffer becomes full or empty, DOS marks the buffer to indicate that it has been used recently. When DOS needs to reuse the buffers for new information, DOS takes the buffer that has not been used for the longest time.

The net effect of DOS's use of buffers is to reduce the number of disk accesses by reading and writing only full sectors. By reusing the least-recently used buffers, DOS retains information more likely to be needed next. Your programs and DOS run faster.

You can control the number of buffers available for DOS to use. Each buffer uses up some of your memory but results in faster disk access. The syntax for the BUFFERS command is shown in the following:

BUFFERS = n, *m*

The **n** parameter is the number of disk buffers you want DOS to allocate. A single buffer is about 512 bytes long (plus 16 bytes used by DOS). Use a number from 1 through 99. If you do not give the BUFFERS command, DOS uses a default value from 2 through 15, depending on the size of your disk drives, the amount of memory in your system, and the version of DOS you are using. Table 17.4 lists the different default buffer configurations.

The *m* parameter is a number in the range 1 through 8, that specifies the number of sectors DOS reads each time it is instructed to read a file. This feature is sometimes called a *secondary cache* or a *look-ahead buffer* and is available only in DOS 4.0 or later. When files most often are read sequentially, this type of buffer increases performance. Do not use this secondary cache feature if you are using or plan to use a disk caching program such as SMARTDRV.SYS, discussed in Chapter 18, "Getting the Most from Your Hard Drive."

Table 17.4 Default Number of Disk Buffers

DOS Version	Number of BUFFERS	Hardware
DOS pre-3.3	2	Floppy disk drives
	3	Hard disk
DOS 3.3 and later	2	360K floppy disk drive
	3	Any other hard or floppy disk drive
	5	More than 128K of RAM
	10	More than 256K of RAM
	15	More than 512K of RAM

Increasing the number of buffers generally improves disk performance, up to a point. The recommended number of buffers increases with the size of your hard disk. Consider the suggested buffer numbers listed in table 17.5 when adding a BUFFERS command to CONFIG.SYS. Using a number higher than the recommended number of buffers probably uses more memory without further improving speed.

Table 17.5 Suggested Number of Disk Buffers

Hard Disk	Number of Buffers
Less than 40M	20
40M to 79M	30
80M to 119M	40
120M or more	50

If you have an 85M hard disk and are not using a hard-disk caching program, for example, you may include the following BUFFERS command in CONFIG.SYS:

    BUFFERS=40,8

For Related Information

▶▶ "Using a Disk Cache (SMARTDRV)," p. 690.

▶▶ "Using FASTOPEN," p. 694.

▶▶ "Using a RAM Disk," p. 696.

FROM HERE...

Fine-Tuning Your Computer with CONFIG.SYS and AUTOEXEC.BAT

In addition to the commands covered earlier in this chapter, you can use many other commands in CONFIG.SYS or AUTOEXEC.BAT to customize your computer configuration. The following sections discuss other useful commands: SETVER, FCBS, FILES, LASTDRIVE, SHELL, INSTALL, REM, and SWITCHES.

Setting the Version with SETVER

Most programs in use today will not run under all versions of DOS, especially the older versions. Programs often ask DOS for DOS's version number; if DOS responds with a version that the program doesn't recognize, the program may refuse to continue, even though it can run under DOS 6.0. When a new version of DOS is introduced, some time passes before popular applications programs are upgraded to take full advantage of DOS's new features and to understand that they can run successfully under DOS 6.0. You can get a reluctant program to run in DOS 6.0 in two ways:

- Contact the software manufacturer or your vendor to obtain an upgrade, if necessary.

- Tell DOS to lie to the application program about the DOS version that you're using. Most programs that can run under any version of DOS can run under DOS 6.0 as well, if you fool the program into thinking you're using a version of DOS that the program knows. The SETVER command enables you to perpetrate the illusion of different versions of DOS.

If you use the SETVER device driver, DOS maintains a list, called the version table, which contains the names of programs that can run under DOS 6.0 but that refuse to do so. The table also contains the version of DOS that these programs are designed to use. With SETVER installed, whenever a program asks DOS for DOS's version number, SETVER searches its table for the program's name. If DOS finds the name in the table, it reports to the program that the DOS version is the version listed in the table rather than the real version (6.0).

The SETVER command operates as a device driver and an executable command. Before DOS can use the version table, you must load SETVER.EXE as a device driver. Use the following syntax:

DEVICE=d:path**SETVER.EXE**

The parameters d: and path\ are the disk and directory that contain the SETVER.EXE external program file.

After the device driver SETVER.EXE is loaded into memory, DOS uses the version table automatically to report the DOS version to listed applications programs.

You can use SETVER from the command line to display the current version table as well as add or delete program names. The syntax for using SETVER at the command line is shown in the following:

SETVER d:path\filename.ext n.nn /DELETE /QUIET

To display the version table, use SETVER with no switches or parameters. DOS displays a two-column listing with applications program names in the first column and the DOS version number in the second column. Microsoft has already tested the programs listed in the initial version table and determined that they operate properly in DOS 6.0. The version list that appears on-screen resembles the following:

```
WIN200.BIN      3.40
WIN100.BIN      3.40
WINWORD.EXE     4.10
EXCEL.EXE       4.10
HITACHI.SYS     4.00
MSCDEX.EXE      4.00
REDIR4.EXE      4.00
NET.EXE         4.00
NETWKSTA.EXE    4.00
DXMA0MOD.SYS    3.30
BAN.EXE         4.00
BAN.COM         4.00
MSREDIR.EXE     4.00
METRO.EXE       3.31
IBMCACHE.SYS    5.00
REDIR40.EXE     4.00
DD.EXE          4.01
DD.BIN          4.01
LL3.EXE         4.01
REDIR.EXE       4.00
SYQ55.SYS       4.00
SSTDRIVE.SYS    4.00
ZDRV.SYS        4.01
ZFMT.SYS        4.01
TOPSRDR.EXE     4.00
NETX.COM        5.00
EDLIN.EXE       5.00
BACKUP.EXE      5.00
ASSIGN.COM      5.00
EXE2BIN.EXE     5.00
JOIN.EXE        5.00
RECOVER.EXE     5.00
GRAFTABL.COM    5.00
NET5.COM        5.00
NETBEUI.DOS     5.00
LMSETUP.EXE     5.00
STACKER.COM     5.00
NCACHE.EXE      5.00
KERNEL.EXE      5.00
REDIR50.EXE     5.00
REDIR5.EXE      5.00
REDIRALL.EXE    5.00
IBMCACHE.SYS    5.00
DOSOAD.SYS      5.00
NET.COM         3.30
```

When you run one of the programs listed in the first column of the version table, DOS reports to the program the DOS version number listed in the second column.

If you have trouble running a program and the application displays an error message indicating that you are trying to execute the program with an incompatible version of DOS, you may want to try adding the program to the version table. Type the SETVER command as follows:

SETVER *c:path***filename.ext n.nn**

The *c:path* parameter indicates the disk and drive where the SETVER.EXE file is located on your system. The **filename.ext** parameter is the name and extension of the command that starts the applications program in question. The **n.nn** parameter is a DOS version number recognized by the applications program. Consult the program's documentation to determine which versions of DOS are supported.

Suppose, for example, that you want to run the program KILLERAP.EXE, but that the program supports only DOS Versions 3.0 to 3.3. To add KILLERAP.EXE to the version table, type the following command at the command prompt, and press Enter:

SETVER KILLERAP.EXE 3.30

DOS displays the message shown in figure 17.10.

```
C:\APPS>setver killerap.exe 3.30

WARNING - Contact your software vendor for information about whether a
specific program works with MS-DOS version 6.0. It is possible that
Microsoft has not verified whether the program will successfully run if
you use the SETVER command to change the program version number and
version table. If you run the program after changing the version table
in MS-DOS version 6.0, you may lose or corrupt data or introduce system
instabilities. Microsoft is not responsible for any loss or damage, or
for lost or corrupted data.

Version table successfully updated
The version change will take effect the next time you restart your system

C:\APPS>
```

Fig. 17.10

The SETVER
Warning
Message.

To verify that the application has been added to the version table, execute SETVER again without switches or parameters. The added application is listed at the end of the list. The modified table takes effect, however, only after you restart or reboot your computer.

If you later decide to delete a program from the version list, use the /DELETE (/D) switch and the *filename* parameter. To delete KILLERAP.EXE from the version table, for example, type one of the following commands at the command line, and press Enter:

> SETVER KILLERAP.EXE /DELETE

> or

> SETVER KILLERAP.EXE /D

DOS deletes the application name from the version table and displays the following message:

```
Version table successfully updated
```

The version change takes effect the next time you restart your system.

If you are using a batch file to delete an applications program name from the version table, you may want to suppress the preceding message. To prevent this message from appearing, add the /QUIET switch in addition to the /DELETE switch.

Accessing Files through FCBS

The FCBS configuration command enables you to use programs written for DOS 1.1; some DOS users find FCBS indispensable. FCB is an acronym for *file control block*. FCBS serves as one way a program can access a file. This method of file access was used by DOS 1.1 to communicate with programs. Later versions of DOS borrow a UNIX-like method for controlling files, called handles (discussed in "Using the FILES Command" in this chapter). Although FCBS can be used with any version of DOS, only DOS 2.0 and higher can use handles.

The syntax for the FCBS command in the CONFIG.SYS file is shown in the following:

> **FCBS = maxopen**

The **maxopen** parameter is a number from 1 through 255 that sets the maximum number of unique FCBs programs can open at one time. The default number is 4. You don't need to use this command in CONFIG.SYS unless you have a program that was designed to work with DOS 1.1 and the program cannot open all the required files (a message to this effect appears). In that case, use the FCBS command to increase the number of FCBs that can be open at one time.

You pay a small price in RAM to use the FCBS command. For each number above 4 that *maxopen* exceeds, DOS uses about 40 bytes.

Using the FILES Command

FILES is the configuration command used in DOS 2.0 and higher to enable UNIX-like file handling. UNIX and later versions of DOS use a *file handle* (a number corresponding to the file name) instead of file control blocks to access files. You never have to deal with file handles directly. Each applications program gives the operating system the name of the file or device you want to use. The operating system gives back to your program a handle and your program uses the handle to manipulate the file or device.

To include the FILES command in CONFIG.SYS, use the following syntax:

FILES = *n*

The *n* parameter is a number (8, which is the default, through 255) that determines the number of files that can be open at any time during a DOS session. Each additional file over 8 increases the size of DOS by 39 bytes.

If you do not specify the FILES command, DOS starts with eight file handles and immediately takes five handles for the standard devices, leaving only three handles for your programs. This number is almost never large enough for applications you are likely to run. On most systems, increase the number of handles to 20 or 30.

 NOTE Many installation programs for full-featured applications edit CONFIG.SYS for you and increase the number of files when necessary to run the software efficiently.

Using LASTDRIVE To Change the Number of Disk Drives

The LASTDRIVE configuration command informs DOS of the maximum number of disk drives on your system. Generally, LASTDRIVE is a command used with networked computers or with the pretender commands (such as SUBST).

If you do not use the LASTDRIVE command, DOS assumes that the last disk drive on your system is one more than the number of physical drives and RAM disks you are using. If your LASTDRIVE command specifies a letter corresponding to fewer drives than the number physically attached to your computer or created as RAM disks, DOS ignores the command. The LASTDRIVE command enables you to tell DOS how many disk drives, real or apparent, are on your system, including network drives and directories (if any) and drives created with the SUBST command, discussed later in this chapter (see the section "Substituting a Drive Name for a Path with SUBST" for more information).

If you want to use the LASTDRIVE command in CONFIG.SYS, use the following syntax:

LASTDRIVE = x

The x parameter is the letter for the last disk drive on your system. The letters A through Z in upper- or lowercase are acceptable.

A typical reason you may want to use LASTDRIVE is to establish logical disk drives. A *logical* disk drive can be a nickname for another disk drive, as explained in the section "Substituting a Drive Name for a Path with SUBST" in this chapter and in the Command Reference. A logical disk drive also may be another partition of the hard disk. A logical disk drive is just a name. DOS "thinks" that the logical disk drive is real.

Using the SHELL Command

The SHELL command was originally implemented to enable programmers to replace the DOS command interpreter (COMMAND.COM) with other command interpreters. The SHELL command is more commonly used, however, to perform the following two functions:

- Inform DOS that the command interpreter is in another directory, not in the boot disk's root directory.

- Expand the size of the *environment*—an area of RAM that stores named variables used by DOS and applications programs. Commands such as PATH and PROMPT store their current settings as environment variables. To display the contents of the environment, type **SET** at the command prompt, and press Enter.

> **WARNING:** SHELL is a tricky command; use it with caution. If used incorrectly, the SHELL command can lock up your system. Keep a bootable floppy disk handy for restarting your computer in case you run into a problem.

The syntax for the SHELL command is shown in the following:

SHELL = *d:path***filename.ext** *parameters*

The *d:path*\\ parameter specifies the disk drive and path that contain the command processor you want to use. **filename.ext** is the name of the command processor and should be COMMAND.COM if you are using the standard DOS command processor. The SHELL command doesn't take any other parameters or switches, but you can add command-line parameters or switches available for use with the command processor. The parameters for COMMAND.COM are explained in the next few paragraphs.

When used from the command line, COMMAND loads a copy of the command processor into memory. A common use of COMMAND is as a parameter of the SHELL command. The syntax for COMMAND is shown in the following:

COMMAND *d:path*\\ *device* */E:size* */P* */C string* */K:filename* */MSG*

The *d:path*\\ parameter specifies the disk drive and path that contain the command processor if it is not located in the root directory. Always use this parameter when including COMMAND in the SHELL configuration command. This parameter has the additional effect of setting an environment variable named *COMSPEC*, which informs DOS and other programs of the location and name of the current command processor.

/E:size is an optional switch that sets the environment space. The *size* parameter is a number from 160 through 32,768 that denotes the amount of memory reserved for the environment. (If you do not specify a multiple of 16, DOS rounds the size parameter up to the next highest multiple of 16.) By default, DOS 5.0 and 6.0 reserve 256 bytes for the environment (160 bytes in DOS 3.2 through 4.0).

The */P* switch instructs DOS to load the command processor permanently. Without the /P switch, DOS loads COMMAND.COM only temporarily into memory. When you are using COMMAND with the SHELL command in CONFIG.SYS, be sure to use the /P switch.

The */C* switch and *string* parameter work together. This combination causes DOS to load the command processor, execute any command represented by *string*, and then unload the command processor.

The */MSG* switch tells DOS to store all its error messages in memory rather than read them from the disk. This feature can speed operation. More importantly, when you are running a floppy disk system, you sometimes remove from the disk drive the disk that contains COMMAND.COM. Without the /MSG switch, DOS cannot access error messages contained on disk within the COMMAND.COM file itself. Use this switch only if you are running DOS from floppy disks. You also must use the /P switch any time you use the /MSG switch.

The /K parameter tells DOS to run a program or batch file. Use this switch only when running COMMAND from the DOS prompt and not as part of the SHELL command in CONFIG.SYS.

The DOS 6.0 Setup program adds the following command to the default CONFIG.SYS file:

SHELL=C:\DOS\COMMAND.COM C:\DOS\ /P

This configuration command tells DOS that COMMAND.COM is the command interpreter and that it is located in the \DOS directory on the C drive. The /P switch causes the command interpreter to be loaded permanently, not temporarily, in memory.

The preceding SHELL command enables you to place a copy of COMMAND.COM in C:\DOS and delete the copy in the root directory. This practice helps you maintain a clean root directory and protects COMMAND.COM from being replaced by an older version that may be on a floppy disk you are copying. If you accidentally copy the disk to the root directory, you don't overwrite the current version of COMMAND.COM.

Occasionally, you create such a long PATH command in AUTOEXEC.BAT that you fill the available environment space, causing DOS to display the message Out of environment space. If this message appears, use COMMAND with the SHELL command and the /E switch to specify a larger environment space. The following command used in CONFIG.SYS, for example, increases the environment to 384 bytes:

SHELL=C:\DOS\COMMAND.COM /E:384

If you already have a SHELL command in CONFIG.SYS, you can add the /E switch. Combining the two preceding SHELL commands, for example, you can include the following command in CONFIG.SYS:

SHELL=C:\DOS\COMMAND.COM C:\DOS\ /P /E:384

NOTE The SHELL command itself doesn't use any memory, but by increasing the environment space, you are reducing the amount of free conventional memory by an equal amount. In other words, increasing the environment space from 256 bytes to 384 bytes reduces free memory by 128 bytes.

Using the INSTALL Command

The INSTALL configuration command enables you to load certain utility programs that remain in memory from the CONFIG.SYS file. In versions of DOS before 4.0, you had to load these programs from the DOS prompt or through a batch file, such as AUTOEXEC.BAT. You can save several kilobytes of memory by loading a program from CONFIG.SYS with INSTALL rather than from the command line or a batch file as an executable program. DOS 4.0 and later versions support loading any of the following programs by using INSTALL:

FASTOPEN.EXE

KEYB.COM

NLSFUNC.EXE

SHARE.EXE

(The Command Reference provides more information about these programs.)

The syntax for using INSTALL in CONFIG.SYS is shown in the following:

INSTALL = *d:path***filename** *parameters*

The *d:path* parameter is the disk and path information, and **filename** is the name of the utility you want to load. The *parameters* parameter specifies parameters and switches that may be available for use with the utility you want DOS to load.

You may be able to use INSTALL with some memory-resident non-DOS programs. Do not use INSTALL to load a memory-resident program that uses environment variables or shortcut keys or that uses COMMAND.COM. The program you install with this command must have the extension COM or EXE.

Using the REM Command

The REM configuration command, which first appears in DOS 4.0, is equivalent to the REM batch file command. This command enables you to insert remarks into your CONFIG.SYS file. You can leave notes to yourself (or others) explaining what particular lines do. Such documentation in a CONFIG.SYS file is especially helpful if you use non-DOS device drivers for your hardware. You also can temporarily remove a CONFIG.SYS statement by prefacing the statement with a REM command. After you test the new configuration, you can return easily to the old configuration by simply removing the REM command.

The syntax for the REM command is shown in the following:

REM *remarks*

The *remarks* parameter can be any string of characters that fits on a single line in the CONFIG.SYS file.

Using the SWITCHES Command

The SWITCHES configuration command enables you to set any of four options that control how four of DOS's features operate. The syntax of the SWITCHES command is shown in the following:

SWITCHES = */K /W /N /F*

You can specify one or more of these four switches in a single SWITCHES command.

The */K* switch turns off the Enhanced Keyboard functions. This command works like the ANSI.SYS /K switch. Some software cannot work with the Enhanced Keyboard. Use this command to disable the Enhanced Keyboard so that the software functions properly. If you use the SWITCHES=/K command in CONFIG.SYS and also install ANSI.SYS as a device driver, add the /K switch to the DEVICE=ANSI.SYS line as well.

The */W* switch specifies that the WINA20.386 file has been moved to a directory other than the root directory. Use this switch if you moved WINA20.386 to another directory and are using Windows in enhanced mode.

Normally, you can use the F5 or F8 keys during the first two seconds of booting to bypass some or all of the commands in CONFIG.SYS or AUTOEXEC.BAT. The */N* switch tells DOS to ignore F5 or F8 during boot.

Normally DOS displays the message Starting MS-DOS at the beginning of the boot process and then pauses for two seconds before continuing. The */F* switch tells DOS to skip the 2-second pause.

Telling DOS When To Break

As mentioned earlier, Ctrl-Break and Ctrl-C are helpful but not foolproof panic buttons you can use to stop commands. The response to a Ctrl-Break or Ctrl-C is not instantaneous. Although only an "Oh, no" second may pass from the time you press the panic button until DOS responds, you still have time to wonder why DOS takes so long to respond. The reason is that DOS is busy doing other things most of the time and looks for Ctrl-Break only at intervals. You can use the BREAK command in CONFIG.SYS to tell DOS when to check for this key sequence. BREAK does not enable or disable the Break key; the BREAK command only controls when DOS checks for the Break key.

The syntax for the BREAK command is shown in the following:

> **BREAK=ON**
>
> or
>
> **BREAK=OFF**

The default setting for this command is OFF.

If you use the command BREAK=ON in CONFIG.SYS, DOS checks to see whether you pressed Ctrl-Break whenever a program requests some activity from DOS (performs a DOS *function call*). If you use the command BREAK=OFF, DOS checks for a Ctrl-Break only when DOS is working with the video display, keyboard, printer, or *asynchronous serial adapters* (the ports at the back of the computer).

If you use programs that do a great deal of disk accessing but little keyboard or screen work, you may want to set BREAK=ON. This setting enables you to break out of the program when something goes awry or when you simply want to stop DOS.

Using the DOS Pretender Commands

Because DOS manages disks in a logical rather than a strictly physical way, DOS can "pretend" that a disk's identity is different from the disk's name. DOS provides the following three commands that pretend that a disk's identity has changed:

- *ASSIGN* redirects disk operations from one disk to another.

- *JOIN* attaches an entire disk as a subdirectory to the directory structure of another disk.

- *SUBST* makes a directory of a disk appear to commands as a separate disk.

ASSIGN and JOIN are not built-in features of DOS 6.0; they are provided on the supplemental disks that come with DOS 6.0. SUBST, on the other hand, is a built-in DOS 6.0 function. The following sections examine these commands.

Reassigning Drive Names with the ASSIGN Command

Some older versions of software still expect files to be on floppy disk drives. Such assumptions by your software may not match your system's disk drive resources. Most users place their software on a hard disk, so software that wants to work from floppy disk drives sometimes does not work properly.

Installation programs for newer programs occasionally "insist" that you place the installation disk in drive A. But the new software you purchased may contain only 3 1/2-inch disks, and your 3 1/2-inch drive is drive B. You may not be able to install the program if its installation procedure requires you to insert the first disk into drive A.

You can use the external command ASSIGN to solve problems of this sort. This command redirects all DOS read and write requests from one drive designation to another. By using the ASSIGN command, DOS can work with a disk other than the one specified by an applications program or on the command line.

> The DOS 6.0 documentation indicates that future versions of DOS may not support the ASSIGN command. You may want to consider using the SUBST command instead of ASSIGN.

T I P

The syntax for the ASSIGN command is shown in the following:

ASSIGN d1=d2 ... */STATUS*

d1 is the drive letter from which you want to redirect read and write operations, the drive letter your software "thinks" it is working with.

d2 is the drive letter of the drive you actually want the program to use.

The ellipsis (...) indicates that more than one drive assignment can be made through a single ASSIGN command.

Use the /STATUS switch by itself to display a listing of current disk drive assignments (DOS 5.0 and 6.0 only).

When you issue the ASSIGN command, DOS redirects all read and write requests for d1 to d2. If you assign drive A to drive B, as shown in the following, all commands referring to drive A are sent to drive B:

ASSIGN A=B

If you later cannot remember what disk assignment you made, issue the following command:

ASSIGN /STATUS

DOS displays the following message:

```
Original A: set to B:
```

To revert to all original disk assignments, issue the ASSIGN command with no parameters, as follows:

ASSIGN

Use the ASSIGN command sparingly, and then only when required for a particular purpose. Certain programs may require disk information that is not available from the reassigned drive.

When using ASSIGN, consider the following guidelines:

- Do not assign the drive letter of a hard disk to another drive.

- Do not reassign a drive that is currently in use by a program.

- You can use an optional colon after the drive letter with DOS 4.0 and later.

- Remove any ASSIGN settings before running MSBACKUP, FDISK, LABEL, or RESTORE.

- Do not use ASSIGN if JOIN or SUBST is being used.

- Do not use ASSIGN before using the APPEND command.

- DISKCOPY, DISKCOMP, and FORMAT do not recognize any drive reassignments.

- d1 and d2 must physically exist in the computer.

Joining Two Disk Drives with JOIN

You use the JOIN command to add a disk drive to the directory structure of another disk. You can use this command from the command line or from within a batch file, including AUTOEXEC.BAT.

The external command JOIN enables you to have a floppy disk that appears to be part of a hard disk. The directory structure on the floppy disk is added to the directory structure of the hard disk. You also can use JOIN to attach one hard drive to a subdirectory on another hard drive.

The syntax for JOIN is shown in the following:

> **JOIN d1:** *d2:path /D*

The **d1:** parameter indicates the disk drive you want DOS to join to another drive. You can think of this drive as the *guest* disk drive.

The *d2:* parameter is the disk drive to which **d1:** is to be joined. You can think of this second drive as the *host* disk drive.

The *path* is the path of the directory to which you want to join the guest disk drive. You can think of this directory as the *host* directory.

Use the */D* switch to disconnect, or "unjoin," a specified guest disk drive from its host.

To show currently connected drives, use the JOIN command alone, as shown in the following:

> JOIN

To join drive B to the \DATA directory on your C drive, issue the following command:

> JOIN B: C:\DATA

If you later are not sure to which directory you assigned drive B, issue the JOIN command without parameters to display the following message:

```
B: => C:\DATA
```

Chapter 8, "Understanding and Managing Directories," discusses hierarchical directories and associated commands. The JOIN command connects or joins a guest drive to a directory position on a host disk drive. Any directory hierarchy on the guest drive becomes a part of the other disk drive's hierarchical structure.

Using the terminology of a directory tree, you can think of using the JOIN command as grafting a second tree onto the first. The second tree is positioned at least one level down the structure. The grafting point must be assigned a name so that DOS can refer to it. In this way, the root directory of the guest disk is given a new name. All directories below the root directory on this reassigned drive have this new name as part of their path.

DOS internally converts all read and write requests to this new subdirectory—and all layers below the subdirectory—into a drive assignment with the appropriate path.

When you use JOIN, consider the following guidelines:

- The directory specified by the path parameter must be empty or nonexistent.

- You cannot join a disk to the current directory.

- You cannot join a disk to the root directory of any drive.

- While a guest drive is joined to a host drive, you cannot access the guest drive by its original name.

- The entire guest drive is joined with the JOIN command.

- You cannot specify a networked drive as d1: or d2:.

- Do not use JOIN with SUBST or ASSIGN.

- Remove any JOIN settings before running DISKCOPY, DISKCOMP, FDISK, FORMAT, BACKUP, or RESTORE.

Substituting a Drive Name for a Path with SUBST

The external command SUBST is an opposite of the JOIN command. Instead of grafting a second disk onto the tree structure of another disk, the SUBST command splits a disk's directory structure in two. In effect, the SUBST command creates an alias disk drive name for a subdirectory—a *virtual drive*. You can use the SUBST command from the command line or from within a batch file, such as AUTOEXEC.BAT.

The syntax for the SUBST command is shown in the following:

SUBST d1: *d2:***path** */D*

The **d1:** parameter indicates the disk drive name you want DOS to assign as a virtual drive. d1 normally is not the name of a drive that exists in your system; however, d1 must be within the range specified by the LASTDRIVE command in CONFIG.SYS.

The *d2:* parameter is the disk drive that contains the path to which you want to assign the virtual drive, d1.

The **path** is the path of the directory you want to access as if it were a disk named d1.

Use the */D* switch to delete the virtual drive.

To see the current virtual drives created by SUBST, use the SUBST command without any parameters.

The SUBST command replaces a path name for a subdirectory with a drive letter. When a SUBST command is in effect, DOS translates all I/O requests to a particular drive letter to the correct path name.

The virtual drive created by the SUBST command inherits the directory tree structure of the subdirectory reassigned to a drive letter.

SUBST is commonly used in two different situations. If you are using a program that does not support path names, you can use the SUBST command to assign a drive letter to a directory. The program then refers to the drive letter, and DOS translates the request into a path. If, for example, the data for a program is stored in C:\WORDPROC, you can type the following:

> SUBST E: C:\WORDPROC

You tell the program that the data is stored in drive E.

When the substitution has been made, you can issue the following command:

> SUBST

The following message appears:

```
E: => C:\WORDPROC
```

To disconnect the substitution of drive E for the C:\WORDPROC directory, type the following command and press Enter:

> SUBST E: /D

The second common use for SUBST is to reduce typing long path names, which can be a tedious process when more than one person uses the same PC. Each user may have a separate section of the hard disk for storing data files, but common areas of the disk are used to store the programs. If the paths \USER1\WORDDATA and \USER1\SPREDATA exist on drive C, the typing needed to reach files in the directories can be reduced by entering the following command:

> SUBST E: C:\USER1

When using SUBST, consider the following guidelines:

- d1: and d2: must be different drive letters.
- You cannot specify a networked drive as d1: or d2:.
- d1: cannot be the current drive.

- d1: must have a designator smaller than the value in the LASTDRIVE statement of CONFIG.SYS.

- Do not use SUBST with ASSIGN or JOIN.

- Remove any SUBST settings before running BACKUP, CHKDSK, DISKCOPY, DISKCOMP, FDISK, FORMAT, LABEL, MIRROR, RECOVER, RESTORE, or SYS.

Using Other Device Control Commands

DOS provides other commands to control devices and report system information, which are briefly discussed in this section. These commands are explained in greater detail in the Command Reference.

The SET command displays the current environment settings and enables you to make new variable assignments.

The PRINT command enables you to print text files on your printer while you continue to do other PC work. This "background" printing can be a great time-saver if your applications programs don't have a similar feature.

The MODE command is a multifaceted device-control command. MODE can establish the height and width of your screen's lines and characters and control the speed of your serial ports. MODE can redirect the output from a parallel printer port to a serial port. MODE also can be used in association with code page support for international character sets on the PC. You may want to browse through the MODE section of the Command Reference.

FROM HERE...

For Related Information

◄◄ "Understanding the Hierarchical Directory System," p. 236.

◄◄ "Using PROMPT To Display a Full Path," p. 239.

◄◄ "Understanding the Directory Tree," p. 243.

◄◄ "Navigating the Directory Tree," p. 245.

Understanding DOS 6.0 Boot Options

In versions of DOS before 6.0, each time you booted your computer you had little control over what tasks DOS performed as it booted. DOS always executed the commands in your CONFIG.SYS, followed by the commands in your AUTOEXEC.BAT.

This lack of control can cause problems in several cases. Suppose, for example, that you had just added a command in your AUTOEXEC.BAT to load a TSR into memory and then discovered that the TSR caused your computer to hang immediately. You had no way to tell DOS to boot without executing the problem command. Your only option was to fish out a bootable DOS diskette, boot from it, and repair the problem.

DOS 6.0 contains a number of features that give you much greater control over what your computer does when it boots. Not only can you tell DOS to skip problem commands in situations like the errant TSR above, but you can also tell DOS to boot in any of several configurations which you define.

Booting DOS Cleanly

The CONFIG.SYS and AUTOEXEC.BAT files exist so that you can specify commands to be executed each time DOS boots. You may occasionally encounter a situation in which you do *not* want DOS to execute these commands, however. You may discover that changes you just made to your CONFIG.SYS are causing problems and your computer won't boot, or perhaps—because of some unusual circumstance—an automatic task you invoke within AUTOEXEC.BAT would have unfortunate consequences if it ran.

On such unusual occasions you can tell DOS 6.0 to skip the CONFIG.SYS and AUTOEXEC.BAT files. Upon booting your computer, DOS displays the message Starting MS-DOS and waits for two seconds before continuing. If you press F5 within the two-second period, the DOS prompt appears immediately, and none of your startup commands are executed.

Keep in mind the following information regarding this procedure:

- One of the lines in your CONFIG.SYS may be a SHELL= command, which tells DOS where to find the command interpreter, COMMAND.COM. Earlier versions of DOS cannot start without processing this line. However, if DOS 6.0 cannot locate COMMAND.COM—because it did not process the SHELL command or because you have an improper SHELL command—the program prompts you to enter the correct path to COMMAND.COM.

- Because DOS skips CONFIG.SYS, none of your device drivers are loaded. In particular, your mouse may not work, and any RAM disks, which are explained in Chapter 18, "Getting the Most from Your Hard Drive," will not be present.

- Because DOS skips your AUTOEXEC.BAT, no environment variables are set.

- Your path—usually set in AUTOEXEC.BAT—will be missing. You must type the full path name of commands you want to execute, or CD to the directory in which the commands reside.

Booting DOS Interactively

Rather than telling DOS to completely skip CONFIG.SYS and AUTOEXEC.BAT—as pressing F5 does—you might want to tell DOS to skip only certain lines. Suppose, for example, that you just added a new DEVICEHIGH command to your CONFIG.SYS, only to discover that this particular device driver hangs your computer when loaded high. Ideally, you want to tell DOS to skip only that one line.

When DOS displays the message Starting MS-DOS, press F8 so that DOS boots interactively. As DOS encounters each line in CONFIG.SYS, DOS asks you if you want to execute the command on that line. Consider the following message, for example:

```
DOS=HIGH [Y/N]?
```

DOS has encountered the **DOS=HIGH** command and is asking whether you want to execute that command. If you respond Y, DOS is loaded high; otherwise the command is skipped and DOS is loaded into conventional memory.

After DOS processes all commands in CONFIG.SYS (or at least, all the commands to which you responded Y), DOS displays the following message:

```
Process AUTOEXEC.BAT [Y/N]?
```

If you respond Y, DOS runs your AUTOEXEC.BAT file as usual; by responding N, you cause DOS to skip your AUTOEXEC.BAT completely.

When you press F8 during boot, you must decide whether to execute every command in CONFIG.SYS. Microsoft intended you to use F8 to test new configurations or to boot your computer when one of the commands in your CONFIG.SYS causes your computer to hang. However, you may encounter a situation in which you want to only occasionally execute a specific command in your CONFIG.SYS file. For example, when you use Microsoft Windows you probably want to make all of your extended memory available to Windows; when not running Windows, you might want to make some of that extended memory available for a RAM disk.

You can use the DEVICE? command to load a device driver, exactly as you would a DEVICE command. However, the question mark tells DOS to ask each time you boot the computer whether you want to load the device driver. Suppose, for example, that your CONFIG.SYS contains this command:

DEVICE? = C:\DOS\RAMDRIVE.SYS 2048 /E

Each time you boot your computer, DOS asks you whether you want to execute this command. Press Y and Enter if you do; N and Enter if you don't. Similarly, you can use DEVICEHIGH? in place of DEVICEHIGH if you want DOS to ask when you load a device into high memory.

Boot Menus

You probably perform many different tasks on your computer, and you may discover that a slightly different configuration is best for each type of task. At your desk during normal working hours, for example, you may need to load the network driver and mouse driver, but if you're playing games (outside of working hours, of course), you don't need these drivers and you want to save the extra memory they consume, but you do need the ANSI.SYS driver. With DOS 6.0, you can define which commands you want executed in each of many possible situations. Each time you boot, DOS displays a menu of choices.

Creating a Boot Menu

To create a boot menu, you divide your CONFIG.SYS into a series of blocks, each of which contains commands. Each block begins with a line that contains only a name in brackets, such as the following:

[games]

The first block must be called **[menu]**, and in it you explain to DOS what you want the menu to look like and what the possible choices should be. Using the preceding example, you might write a CONFIG.SYS that looks like this:

```
[menu]
menuitem=Work
menuitem=Games

[Work]
DEVICE=C:\DOS\HIMEM.SYS
DEVICE=C:\DOS\EMM386.EXE NOEMS
BUFFERS=20,0
FILES=30
DOS=UMB,HIGH
DEVICE=C:\DOS\NET.SYS
DEVICE=C:\DOS\MOUSE.SYS

[Games]
DEVICE=C:\DOS\HIMEM.SYS
DEVICE=C:\DOS\EMM386.EXE NOEMS
BUFFERS=20,0
FILES=30
DOS=UMB,HIGH
DEVICE=C:\DOS\ANSI.SYS
```

This CONFIG.SYS file is divided into three blocks. The first block, **[menu]**, tells DOS that the menu has two selections on it, Work and Games. When you boot the computer, DOS asks you to select one and then execute only the block with the name that corresponds to your selection.

In this example, you probably noticed that several lines are exactly the same in the **[Work]** block and the **[Games]** block. You can define one or more blocks called **[common]** which are always executed regardless of the selection you make from the menu. Thus you can shrink the CONFIG.SYS above by writing the following instead:

```
[menu]
menuitem=Work
menuitem=Games
```

```
[common]
DEVICE=C:\DOS\HIMEM.SYS
DEVICE=C:\DOS\EMM386.EXE NOEMS
BUFFERS=20,0
FILES=30
DOS=UMB,HIGH

[Work]
DEVICE=C:\DOS\NET.SYS
DEVICE=C:\DOS\MOUSE.SYS

[Games]
DEVICE=C:\DOS\ANSI.SYS
```

You can have more than one **[common]** block in your CONFIG.SYS; DOS executes these blocks in the order in which they appear.

Microsoft recommends that all CONFIG.SYS files end with a **[common]** block. When you install some software packages, they add commands to the CONFIG.SYS file, and you probably want those executed every time, regardless of the selection made from the menu at boot time. If you don't otherwise need a **[common]** block at the end, you can add an empty block simply by ending your CONFIG.SYS file with:

```
[common]
```

The **menuitem** command can contain a description as well as a block name, as shown in the following:

```
menuitem=Work1, Load Mouse and Network drivers
```

In this example, the name of the block to be executed is **Work1**, but the description that appears on the menu is "Load Mouse and Network drivers."

Setting Menu Colors

You can set the color scheme of the menu with the **menucolor** command, in which you specify the foreground and background colors of the menu. For example, if you want white characters on a red background, add this command:

```
menucolor=15,4
```

You can omit the second number, in which case DOS uses a black background. Table 17.6 shows the acceptable numbers and their associated colors.

Table 17.6 CONFIG.SYS Menu Colors

Number	Color	Number	Color
0	Black	8	Gray
1	Blue	9	Bright blue
2	Green	10	Bright green
3	Cyan	11	Bright cyan
4	Red	12	Bright red
5	Magenta	13	Bright magenta
6	Brown	14	Yellow
7	White	15	Bright white

Setting a Menu Default and Timeout Value

When DOS displays the boot menu, a *1* normally appears next to the prompt, indicating that pressing Enter is the same as selecting item 1 from the menu. If you want a different item as your default selection, add a command such as the following:

> menudefault=Games

This command tells DOS that the item corresponding to the block **[Games]** is the default selection.

You can also use **menudefault** to specify a timeout value. If the user doesn't make a selection within a specified number of seconds, DOS accepts the default and continues. Consider the following, for example:

> menudefault=Work, 20

This command tells DOS that the default selection is the item associated with the **[Work]** block and to accept this default automatically if the user doesn't make a selection with 20 seconds.

A complete sample **[menu]** block might resemble the following:

```
[menu]
menucolor=14
menuitem=WorkNet, Work configuration with Network
menuitem=WorkNoNet, Work configuration without Network
menuitem=Games
menuitem=Prog, Borland C++ programming environment
menudefault=WorkNoNet, 30
```

These commands tell DOS that the menu colors should be yellow on black. Four menu items are specified. For the third item, "Games" is both the name of the block and the description that appears on the menu; for the other three items, both a block name and a description are specified. The default selection is 2 (because the second item is WorkNoNet); DOS automatically accepts that selection if you don't select an item within 30 seconds.

Chapter Summary

In this chapter, you learned the following important points:

- DOS can alter your system's configuration through instructions in the CONFIG.SYS and AUTOEXEC.BAT files.

- The CONFIG.SYS file must be in the root directory of the boot disk. When you alter CONFIG.SYS, configuration changes do not occur until DOS is rebooted.

- Disk buffers make DOS work faster by placing requested information in RAM.

- DOS 6.0 provides several new memory management features that can free significant portions of conventional memory as well as speed the operation of your system.

- The FILES command sets the number of files DOS can open at any one time.

- The LASTDRIVE command specifies the last disk drive letter you want to use in your system.

- You can tell DOS when to look for the Ctrl-Break key sequence.

- You can cause DOS to pretend that a drive's identity is different than it really is through the JOIN, SUBST, and ASSIGN commands.

- You can use DOS menu commands to allow the selection of different configurations each time your computer boots.

In Chapter 18, "Getting the Most from Your Hard Drive," you discover additional ways to wring the greatest capabilities out of your hard disk.

Getting the Most from Your Hard Drive

Y our hard disk just may be the most important component of your computer. Many aspects of your computer's performance are strongly influenced by the characteristics of your disk. These characteristics include the following:

- *Speed.* The speed of your hard disk influences the speed of your system. Even if your computer's processor is super-fast, a slow disk can make your computer perform like a snail.

- *Space.* The amount of space on your disk determines what you can do with your computer. No matter how fast and powerful your processor is, if you have 20M of space on your disk, you will not be running much Windows software.

- *Safety.* The safety of your disk plays a large role in the amount of confidence you have in your system. If you are afraid that you may lose important data at any time because of mistakes or viruses, you will not think kindly of your computer.

The most dramatic way to increase your computer's performance is to purchase a larger, faster hard disk. Large, fast hard disks are expensive, however. As an alternative to buying another hard disk, you often can increase your computer's performance simply by making the best use of your current hard disk. In this chapter, you learn how to get the most from your hard disk: the most speed, the most space, and the most safety.

Getting the Most Speed from Your Hard Disk

The programs that you use on your computer frequently must access data on disk. The speed at which your computer can retrieve that information is one of the most significant factors that determine how fast the computer operates. You can buy faster disks (which are expensive), or you can use DOS, which provides several techniques you can use to increase the speed at which your programs get information without actually increasing the speed of your disk. The following sections explain those techniques.

Using a Disk Cache (SMARTDRV)

Perhaps the most significant way to enhance the performance of your hard disk is to use a *disk-caching program*. Disk caching takes advantage of the fact that during the course of normal work, most users access the same programs and data repeatedly within a short period. You might list the contents of a file, and then edit the file, and then print it; or you might run the same program several times in a row. Even if you don't access programs or data repeatedly, the programs you use probably do.

If you have a disk-caching program installed, that program allocates some of your memory for temporary data storage on disk. When you access data, the disk-caching program saves that data in its memory area, on the assumption that you are likely to use the same data—or related data stored with it—in the near future (within a few seconds, perhaps). If you or your program do try to read the same data again soon, the disk-caching program intercepts the disk access and gives the program the data stored in memory. You (or your program) receive the data immediately because DOS doesn't actually read the data from disk; instead, the disk-caching program found the data in its cache buffer. If your program never requests the same information again, the caching program eventually realizes that you are not likely to use that data soon and deletes the data from memory.

The disk-caching program that comes with DOS 6.0 is named SMARTDRV.EXE. SMARTDRV.EXE builds its buffer area in XMS or EMS memory, using very little conventional memory. When information is read from the disk, the information is placed in the cache, and re-quested information is sent to the program. SMARTDRV.EXE, however, reads more information than the program requests and stores this in-formation in memory. If the program later requests information that already is in memory, the cache can supply the information faster than DOS could if DOS had to read the disk again.

SMARTDRV.EXE eliminates redundant writes by putting information on disk only when the data differs from data already stored. The program also accumulates information, writing out data only when a certain amount has accumulated. *Write-caching* operations decrease the amount of time that your programs spend writing to disk, but write-caching also forces you to shut your computer down by issuing a spe-cial SMARTDRV command (explained later in this section).

> **CAUTION:** You may not want to use write-caching in an area with unreliable electrical power. If the power fails while SMARTDRV is accumulating data, you lose the data that has not yet been written to disk. This loss of data is of little concern if you own an uninter-ruptable power supply (UPS) which keeps your computer running during a power failure. Note that there is no equivalent danger in the case of read cache.

A disk-caching program like SMARTDRV.EXE remembers which sec-tions of the disk have been used most frequently. When the cache must be recycled, the program retains the data in the most frequently used areas and discards the data in the less frequently used areas. In a random disk-access operation in which program and data files are scat-tered uniformly across the disk, the cache method of recycling the l east frequently used area is more efficient than the buffer method of recycling the oldest area. A cache tends to keep in memory the most heavily used areas of the disk.

To start SMARTDRV, enter a command in your AUTOEXEC.BAT file that has the following syntax:

*d:path***SMARTDRV** *drive+* | *drive-... /E:elementsize initcachesize wincachesize /B:buffersize /C /R /L /Q /S* *d:path* represents the optional disk drive and path name for the SMARTDRV.EXE program. You then specify the drives for which you want SMARTDRV to use caching. This notation takes the form of a drive number, followed optionally by a plus (+) or minus (–) sign, as in the following examples:

C   Specifies that drive C will be cached for reads but not for writes

C+   Specifies that drive C will be cached for reads and writes

C–   Specifies that drive C will not be cached

If you don't specify any drive letters in your SMARTDRV command, floppy-disk drives are read-cached but not write-cached, and hard disks are read-cached and write-cached. Other kinds of drives—such as CD-ROM, network drives, and compressed drives—will not be cached.

The */E:elementsize* parameter specifies the number of bytes that SMARTDrive reads or writes at a time: 1024, 2048, 4096, or 8192 (the default value). The larger the value, the more conventional memory SMARTDRV uses, but the fewer disk accesses you are likely to need.

The *initcachesize* parameter is a number that specifies the size (in kilobytes) of the cache when SMARTDrive starts. The larger the cache, the more likely that SMARTDrive can find information required by programs in the cache. The larger the cache, however, the more memory SMARTDRV requires. If you do not specify initcachesize, SMARTDRV selects a value based on the amount of memory in your system.

The *wincachesize* parameter specifies the size (in kilobytes) to which the cache can be reduced when you start Windows so that Windows can use the memory for other purposes. The philosophy behind this parameter is that if SMARTDRV uses too much of your memory, Windows runs too slowly. Therefore, even though SMARTDRV will be less efficient by giving up some of its memory, Windows can run faster. When you exit Windows, SMARTDRV recovers the memory it gave up for Windows. (Table 18.1 shows the default values for initcachesize and wincachesize.)

The */B:buffersize* parameter tells SMARTDRV how much additional information to read when a disk read is executed. Because programs often read sequentially through files, SMARTDRV anticipates that the next data request will be for the area following the current area. The default size of the read-ahead buffer is 16K; this value can be any multiple of *elementsize*. The larger the value of *buffersize*, the more conventional memory SMARTDRV uses.

Table 18.1 Default SMARTDRV Memory Values

Size of Extended Memory	Default Value for Initcachesize	Default Value for Wincachesize
Up to 1M	All extended memory	Zero (no caching)
Up to 2M	1M	256K
Up to 4M	1M	512K
Up to 6M	2M	1M
6M or more	2M	2M

The /L switch prevents SMARTDRV from loading into your upper-memory area (UMA). This option may be useful if other programs need to use the UMA.

The /Q switch tells SMARTDRV to be "quiet" while installing itself rather than display the usual status messages.

You also can run SMARTDRV as a command from the DOS prompt. Two special switches—/S and /C—provide important features. You determine the status of SMARTDRV by using the /S switch. Following is an example of typical output:

```
Microsoft SMARTDrive Disk Cache version 4.1
Copyright 1991,1993 Microsoft Corp.

Room for    83 elements of   8,192 bytes each
There have been   1,481 cache hits
     and    361 cache misses
Cache size:  679,936 bytes
Cache size while running Windows:      0 bytes

           Disk Caching Status
drive   read cache   write cache   buffering
------------------------------------------------
   A:       yes           no           no
   B:       yes           no           no
   C:       yes           no           no

For help, type "Smartdrv /?".
```

Perhaps the most interesting information in this output is the speed that SMARTDRV achieves. In the preceding example (which was generated after a session with a word processing program), in 1,481 disk accesses, SMARTDRV already had the data in its cache. For only 361 attempted disk accesses did SMARTDRV actually have to access the disk. In other words, because of SMARTDRV, the computer didn't have to perform 80 percent of attempted disk accesses.

The /C switch is important if you use write-caching. Remember that write-caching causes SMARTDRV to accumulate data that is destined for the disk until a certain amount accumulates. If you are getting ready to turn your computer off, you must tell SMARTDRV that no more data will be written to disk and instruct the program to finish writing whatever data it has accumulated. You can perform this operation (called *flushing* in technical circles) by typing the following command:

SMARTDRV /C

You do not need to execute this command if you are rebooting by pressing Ctrl-Alt-Del. But if you have enabled write-caching, use this command when you reset or turn off your computer.

Using FASTOPEN

Another way to improve hard-disk performance is to use the FASTOPEN program. FASTOPEN is not a device driver per se, but an executable program that you can include in AUTOEXEC.BAT. You also can load the program through CONFIG.SYS, using the special INSTALL command (available in DOS 4.0 and covered in Chapter 17, "Configuring Your Computer and Managing Devices").

FASTOPEN, introduced with DOS 3.3, can be used only with hard drives. FASTOPEN caches directory information, holding in memory the locations of frequently used files and directories.

Directories are a type of file that users cannot access. DOS reads and writes directories in a manner similar to the way DOS handles other files. Part of the directory entry for a file or subdirectory holds the starting point for the file in the file-allocation table (FAT). Because DOS typically holds the FAT in the disk buffers, FASTOPEN was developed to hold directory entries in memory.

FASTOPEN is not a complex command, but you must do a little work before you can use it effectively. FASTOPEN's syntax is as follows:

INSTALL = *d:path***FASTOPEN.EXE d:** = *n* /X

or

d:path**FASTOPEN.EXE d:** = *n* /X

The first version of the FASTOPEN command uses INSTALL to load the program from CONFIG.SYS. If you issue the FASTOPEN command at the DOS prompt (or in your AUTOEXEC.BAT file), you must use the second version of the command.

> To load FASTOPEN into upper memory, use LOADHIGH in AUTOEXEC.BAT. The following command, for example, loads FASTOPEN into upper memory and tracks file names and directories on drive C:
>
> LOADHIGH C:\DOS\FASTOPEN C:

T I P

The *d:path*\ parameters represent the disk drive and path to the FASTOPEN.EXE file. The *d:* following the file name is the name of the first hard drive that you want FASTOPEN to track. (You can specify up to 24 hard disks or hard-disk partitions at one time.)

The */X* switch, which is similar to the */X* switches of other commands, enables FASTOPEN information to reside in EMS. By default, FASTOPEN uses conventional memory.

The *n* parameter is the number of directory entries that FASTOPEN should cache. Each file or subdirectory requires one directory entry. You can enter a value ranging from 10 through 999. If you do not specify a value for *n*, DOS uses the default value 48 (10 in DOS 3.3 and 4.0).

You can use FASTOPEN on as many disks as you want. Be aware, however, that the total number of directory entries or fragmented entries FASTOPEN can handle is 999. If you issue the command for several disk drives, the sum of the *n* values cannot exceed 999. The practical limit of *n* is between 100 and 200 per disk. If you specify a value much higher, DOS wades through the internal directory entries more slowly than it reads information from disk. Additionally, each directory entry stored in memory takes 48 bytes. Considering this trade-off of speed and memory, the 100-to-200-disks limit yields adequate performance.

Using too small a number for n also can be a disadvantage. When directory entries are recycled, the least recently used entry is discarded if a new entry is needed. If the n value is too small, DOS discards entries that it still may need. The objective is to have enough entries in memory so that FASTOPEN operates efficiently, but not so many entries that FASTOPEN wastes time wading through directory entries.

At minimum, n must exceed the number of subdirectories through which FASTOPEN must travel to reach the "deepest" subdirectory. The minimum value for n is 48; this value nearly always exceeds the number of levels in your directory organization. Suppose that you have a directory structure such as \DOS\BASIC\TEST. The deepest level is 3 down from the root—much less than DOS's default (48).

| **NOTE** | Keep in mind the following points regarding the use of FASTOPEN:

■ Do not use FASTOPEN if you are using Windows.

■ Do not run a disk defragmenting program, such as DEFRAG, while FASTOPEN is running. |

Using a RAM Disk

Another way to speed disk operation doesn't involve a disk at all. A *RAM disk* is a device driver that uses a portion of your computer's memory to emulate a disk drive. You use a RAM drive as you use any other disk drive, for example, following the same procedures for files and directories. Because this "imitation," or *virtual*, disk is located in RAM, a RAM disk is extremely fast compared with a real disk drive. You must, however, give up a significant amount of memory to create a useful RAM disk. Worse, you cannot store anything in that disk permanently—the contents of the RAM disk disappear when you turn off or reboot your computer.

As a general rule, a disk-caching program such as SMARTDRV.EXE provides more overall performance gains than a RAM disk can. You generally use RAM disks to enhance the performance of one or two specific programs that read and write to the disk frequently or that use overlays (see the "Overlays and RAM Disks" sidebar in this section). A disk cache, on the other hand, improves the performance of all programs that read and write to disk. If your computer's memory resources are limited, give more consideration to a disk cache than to a RAM disk.

Overlays and RAM Disks

Some programs are too large to fit in your PC's memory. These programs load a core part into memory and access additional parts from overlay files as necessary. When a new section of the program is needed, the appropriate overlay for that section is read from the disk into the area occupied by the current overlay.

The term *overlay* comes from this process of overlaying sections of program space in memory with new sections. RAM disks facilitate rapid switching of active overlays because the overlay disk files actually are in memory, not on disk. You must copy any needed overlay files to the RAM disk before starting the program. You also must configure the program to look for its overlays on the RAM disk.

The RAM disk driver that comes with DOS 6.0 (and with some earlier versions of DOS) is named RAMDRIVE.SYS. To install RAMDRIVE and create a virtual disk, include RAMDRIVE.SYS as a device driver in CONFIG.SYS. The syntax for including RAMDRIVE.SYS is shown in the following:

DEVICE = *d:path***RAMDRIVE.SYS** *disksize sectorsize*
    entries /E /A

d: is the disk drive, and *path*\ is the directory path for RAMDRIVE.SYS. The options for RAMDRIVE are described in the following paragraphs.

The *disksize* parameter indicates the size of the RAM disk (in kilobytes). This number can range from 16 to 32,767 (equivalent to 32M). The default value is 64.

The *sectorsize* parameter represents the size of the sectors used in the virtual disk. You can specify one of three sector sizes: 128, 256, or 512 bytes. The default sector size is 512 bytes in DOS 5.0 and 6.0, and 128 bytes in earlier versions. (DOS usually uses a sector size of 512 bytes for real disks.) Normally, you do not change this parameter; if you do, however, you also must specify the *disksize* parameter.

The *entries* parameter determines the maximum number of directory entries permitted in the RAM disk's root directory. This parameter can be a value ranging from 2 through 1,024. The default value is 64. You normally don't need to change this parameter. If you do specify the *entries* parameter, you also must enter the *disksize* and *sectorsize* parameters. Set the number of directories based on the size of the RAM disk and the number of files you are storing.

By default, DOS creates a RAM disk in conventional memory. You can, however, include the /E switch to cause the RAM disk to be created in XMS memory (the DEVICE=RAMDRIVE command must follow the DEVICE=HIMEM.SYS command). Even with this switch, however, RAMDRIVE uses some conventional memory, so you may want to try loading the RAMDRIVE.SYS device driver into upper memory. The following command creates a 1,024K RAM disk in XMS memory and loads the device driver into upper memory:

DEVICEHIGH=C:\DOS\RAMDRIVE.SYS 1024 /E

The /A switch, available in DOS 4.0 and later versions, creates the RAM disk in EMS memory. To use this switch, you must load an expanded memory manager (such as EMM386.EXE) before loading RAMDRIVE.SYS. You cannot use the /A and /E switches for the same RAM disk. You can create different RAM disks, however, some using EMS memory and others using XMS memory. Given a choice, use XMS memory.

After you insert the DEVICE=RAMDRIVE.SYS command into CONFIG.SYS and reboot your computer, DOS displays a message similar to the following during initialization of your computer:

```
Microsoft RAMDrive version 3.07 virtual disk D:
    Disk size: 1024
    Sector size: 512 bytes
    Allocation unit: 1 sectors
    Directory entries: 64
```

Most important, this message tells you that this RAM disk is accessed as drive D. The message also shows the disk size, sector size, allocation-unit (cluster) size, and maximum number of root-directory entries.

NOTE The logical disk drive names (the drive letters) that DOS assigns to disks created by RAMDRIVE.SYS and DRIVER.SYS (see the Command Reference) depend on the placement of the commands in the CONFIG.SYS file. You may try to use the wrong disk-drive name if you do not know how DOS assigns drive names. When DOS encounters a block device driver (that is, any device that transfers data in blocks rather than in bytes), DOS assigns the next-highest drive letter to that device. The order is first come, first assigned.

The potential for confusion comes when several block device drivers are loaded. The order of loading, determined by the order of the commands in the CONFIG.SYS file, determines the names assigned by DOS. If you load RAMDRIVE.SYS first and DRIVER.SYS second, the RAM disk may be named D and the DRIVER.SYS disk one letter higher. If you switch the lines so that DRIVER.SYS is loaded first, the disk-drive names also are switched; the DRIVER.SYS disk is named D, and the RAM disk is named E.

The amount of RAM in your computer, the programs you use, and the convenience of a RAM disk help determine what size RAM disk you use and even whether you should use a RAM disk.

> **WARNING:** Because RAM disks are memory-based devices, you lose their contents when you reboot or turn off your PC. To prevent data loss, you must copy the contents of a RAM disk to a conventional disk file before rebooting or turning off the power. If you (or your program) are creating or modifying RAM disk files, copy the files to an actual disk regularly in case a power failure occurs.

One excellent way to use a RAM disk is to assign the TEMP environment variable to this virtual drive. Certain programs use an environment variable named TEMP to determine where to create various temporary files. These temporary files usually are written and read frequently during the operation of the program; their temporary nature makes them good candidates for storage in a RAM disk. The DOS 6.0 Shell, for example, stores swap files in the directory specified by the TEMP environment variable.

To assign TEMP to a RAM disk, you first have to determine a name for the virtual disk and then use the SET command (see the Command Reference). Assign the TEMP variable to a subdirectory rather than to the RAM disk's root directory to avoid the 64-file-name limit. Assuming that the RAM disk becomes drive D, use the following commands in AUTOEXEC.BAT to create a directory on the virtual disk and to cause temporary files to be written to that directory:

```
MD D:\TEMPDATA

SET TEMP = D:\TEMPDATA
```

Some programs use an environment variable named TMP instead of TEMP for the same purpose. In such a case, substitute TMP for TEMP in the preceding command.

When you use a RAM disk and then run the DOS Shell in graphics display mode, a special RAM icon identifies the virtual disk.

Defragmenting Your Disk

If all you ever did with your hard disk was add files, the space available on your disk would be used very efficiently. DOS would add one file and then another to your disk, with each file being stored entirely within a contiguous area, followed by another contiguous file, an arrangement that enables DOS to access your files very efficiently.

Nobody, however, only adds new files to a disk. As you use your disk, you add new files, delete existing files, and add new data to existing files. Over time, data becomes scattered over the disk, and even the data within a single file may reside in chunks throughout the disk. This scattering of data is called *fragmentation*. The following sections discuss fragmentation in detail.

Understanding the Effects of Fragmentation

The more fragmented your disk, the slower your computer runs. Suppose that a third of your hard disk currently is full and that all the used space is at the front of the disk, so that you have no fragmentation. Whenever you request data from the disk, the disk heads do not have to move very far and can access your data quickly.

If the same data is spread across the disk, however, the disk head may have to move across the entire disk to access data. The longer movement requires more time, and you may notice the difference. Moreover, the disk may require more time to access each individual file. When you run a program (at least, a program that doesn't use overlays), DOS must read the program from disk into memory. That operation is much faster if the entire program is in successive locations on the disk and much slower if the disk heads must move to widely separated locations on the disk.

Fragmentation, which is almost inevitable, tends to increase the longer you use your disk. Programs that *defragment* your disk—that is, move all the data to the beginning of the disk and store each file's data in the same place—have long been available from third-party software vendors. The following section discusses DOS 6.0's built-in defragmenting program.

Understanding the Basic Operation of the DEFRAG Program

DOS 6.0 is the first version of DOS to come with a defragmenting program, called DEFRAG. You execute DEFRAG by typing **DEFRAG** at the DOS prompt. A dialog box appears, asking which drive you want to defragment (see fig. 18.1).

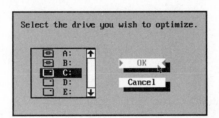

Fig. 18.1

The DEFRAG disk
selection dialog
box.

Select a drive by clicking a drive letter. Alternatively, use the arrow keys to move to the desired drive, and then press Enter. DEFRAG scans the selected drive and displays a map of the used and unused portions. You need not understand the map to use DEFRAG effectively, but if you're interested in understanding DEFRAG's analysis of your disk, study the legend at the bottom of the screen, which explains the symbols in the disk map.

After displaying the map, DEFRAG suggests one of the following courses of action:

- *Do nothing.* If the disk is not fragmented, DEFRAG tells you that you don't need to perform any operation.

- *Defragment files.* If most of the data in the used area of the disk is stored together but the individual files are scattered throughout that area, DEFRAG recommends that you defragment the files. After DEFRAG completes this operation, the same area of the disk will be in use, but the data in that area is rearranged so that the data for each file is stored together. DEFRAG usually recommends this operation for disks that are mostly full.

- *Defragment the disk.* If the used area of the disk is scattered across the disk, DEFRAG recommends that you defragment the disk. DEFRAG rearranges the used areas on the disk so that all the used portion of the disk is at the beginning of the disk and the data for each file is stored contiguously.

Figure 18.2 shows a typical recommendation from DEFRAG.

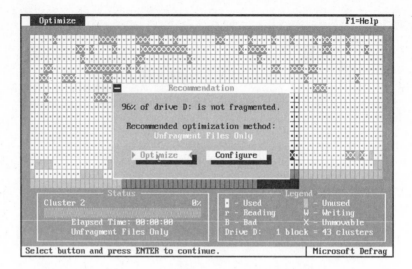

Fig. 18.2

DEFRAG
analysis and
recommendation.

If you click Optimize, DEFRAG reorganizes your disk, using the suggested method. Be prepared to wait. Although DEFRAG does its work quickly, it still may take a long time on a large, heavily fragmented disk.

When DEFRAG suggests a particular type of defragmentation, you do not have to accept its recommendation. When DEFRAG recommends that only the files be defragmented, for example, it is telling you that the extra efficiency you would gain by performing a disk defragmentation is not worth the time required by DEFRAG. However, you may be willing to let DEFRAG take the extra time to do the more complete disk defragmentation.

As figure 18.2 shows, when DEFRAG makes a recommendation, you can click Configure to select various options that control how DEFRAG works. When you click Configure, DEFRAG presents the Optimize menu, which includes more operations than just configuration—the first item tells DEFRAG to begin the defragmentation procedure. Table 18.2 lists the functions available in the Optimize menu.

If you want to change the type of defragmentation that DEFRAG performs, select Optimization Method. This selection presents a dialog box which enables you to specify whether DEFRAG defragments only files or completely defragments the disk. After you make a selection, you can select Begin Optimization from the Optimize menu; DEFRAG performs the optimization you selected.

Table 18.2 The DEFRAG Optimize (Configuration) Menu

Selection	Meaning
Begin Optimization	Begins optimization of your hard disk, using any configuration options you have selected.
Drive	Enables you to select the drive you want to optimize.
Optimization Method	Enables you to select disk optimization (full optimization) or file only (may leave empty space between files).
File Sort	Enables you to select how files will be sorted within directories, if at all.
Map Legend	Displays a legend of the symbols DEFRAG uses to show disk usage.
About Defrag	Displays information about the DEFRAG program.
Exit	Exits DEFRAG.

Sorting Directories

Normally DOS doesn't store file names in a directory in any particular order. As you create and delete files, DOS removes old names and inserts new names wherever empty space occurs. The result is that when you use DIR to list the contents of a directory, often the files appear to be listed in random order. (Some application programs, such as WordPerfect, sort this list by name each time they display the contents of a directory.)

While DEFRAG reorganizes your disk, you can tell it to organize the names of the files within the directories in one of five ways:

■ *Unsorted.* This selection, which is the default, tells DEFRAG to leave the names in their current order.

■ *Name.* DEFRAG organizes the directory alphabetically by file name. This option is probably the one you find most useful.

■ *Extension.* DEFRAG organizes the directory by extension name; for example, all the COM files appear together, all the EXE files together, and so on.

■ *Date & Time.* DEFRAG sorts the directory by the time and date the files were last modified. This option enables you to tell at a glance which files have and have not been modified recently.

■ *Size.* DEFRAG organizes files by the amount of disk space they consume.

You can also specify that the sort will be ascending or descending— that is, that values get larger or smaller as the directory listing proceeds. Usually you want an ascending sort for names so that the list starts with the beginning of the alphabet and proceeds through the end of the alphabet. If you're sorting by size, however, you may want a descending sort so that the biggest files are listed first and the smallest files last.

You can specify how DEFRAG sorts directories from the DEFRAG Optimize menu by selecting File Sort. Figure 18.3 shows the File Sort menu. Alternatively, you can provide command line arguments, discussed below, to specify file sort type.

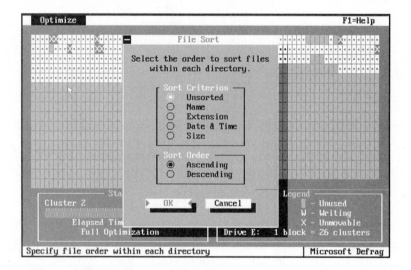

Fig. 18.3

The DEFRAG File Sort menu.

DEFRAG Startup Options

Most of the time you use DEFRAG, you will probably start it simply by typing DEFRAG. Like most DOS commands, however, DEFRAG has a number of startup options available. The complete syntax for DEFRAG is shown in the following:

DEFRAG *d: /F /U /S:order /B /SKIPHIGH /LCD /BW /G0/H*

Normally DEFRAG asks you which drive you want to defragment. If you specify the *d:* parameter, DEFRAG uses that as the drive you want to defragment.

Normally DEFRAG recommends the type of defragmentation you should perform. The */F* parameter tells DEFRAG to defragment the disk (leaving no empty spaces between files); the */U* parameter tells DEFRAG to defragment files (possibly leaving empty space between files). If you specify one of these parameters, DEFRAG does not make a recommendation, but will immediately carry out the type of defragmentation you specify.

You can control whether or not DEFRAG sorts directory entries with the */S* switch. */S* is optionally followed by a colon and one or more characters that specify how you want the entries sorted within each directory. Valid letters are listed in the following:

N	Alphabetical order by name
E	Alphabetical order by extension
D	By time and date, with the oldest dates (that is, files that were last modified farthest in the past) listed first
S	By size, with the smallest files listed first

For example, the following command defragments drive C: and sorts files in alphabetical order by name:

> DEFRAG C: /SN

You can also place a minus sign (–) after a sort letter to specify descending sort instead of ascending. Consider these two commands:

> DEFRAG C: /SS

> DEFRAG C: /SS-

The first (without the minus) lists the smallest files first; the second (with the minus) lists the largest files first.

The */B* switch tells DEFRAG to reboot your computer after the defragmentation process is complete.

The */SKIPHIGH* switch tells DEFRAG to load itself into conventional memory. Otherwise DEFRAG uses upper memory, if available.

The */LCD* switch uses a color scheme that is likely to be more readable if you are using a laptop or notebook computer with an LCD screen.

The */BW* switch tells DEFRAG to use a black-and-white color scheme, which is likely to be more pleasing if you have a monochrome monitor.

The /G0 switch disables the mouse and graphic character set. Use this switch if DEFRAG displays strange characters on your monitor.

Normally DEFRAG does not reorganize hidden files. Use the /H switch to tell DEFRAG to move hidden files.

> **NOTE** When you use DEFRAG, keep in mind the following restrictions:
>
> ■ You cannot use DEFRAG to defragment drives over a network.
>
> ■ You cannot run DEFRAG from Windows.
>
> ■ Disk statistics reported by DEFRAG and CHKDSK differ slightly. When listing the number of directories, for example, DEFRAG counts the root directory but CHKDSK does not.

FROM HERE...

For Related Information

◄◄ "Using the INSTALL Command," p. 672.

Getting the Most Space from Your Hard Disk

Since the introduction of PCs in 1981, the amount of disk storage space available to the average user has increased steadily. The original PCs used floppy diskettes with less than 1M of storage space. Today, many PCs are sold with hard disks that have several hundred times that amount of space; 100M and 200M hard disks are common.

You might think that if people managed to get by with less than 1M, they should be perfectly content with 200M or more. Of course, you would be wrong. If you buy a bigger briefcase, you simply find more things to put in it. The same is true of hard disks. As disk capacity has increased, so has the need for space.

A decade ago, few software vendors wrote software that required several megabytes of disk storage because they knew that few of their potential customers' systems had that kind of storage capability. Now few vendors think twice about releasing software that requires 5M or 10M of disk storage; they expect that most people will have that much space to spare.

Although you cannot increase the physical capacity of your disk without buying a larger disk, you may be able to increase the amount of data you can store on your disk by using the techniques discussed in this section.

Increasing Space by Deleting Unnecessary Files

Much of the software available today is very complex, offering many features that you probably will never use. As a result, many of the files that are copied to your hard disk when you install a software program are files that you never open. You may be able to find and delete some of these files, thereby freeing some of your hard-disk space.

Some programs, such as Microsoft Word for Windows, ask which features you expect to use and install only the files that are appropriate for you. If you later change your mind, you can install the missing pieces later.

When you install DOS, dozens of programs are installed on your hard disk. If you are short on disk space, you may want to browse through these programs and delete those that are not important to you. Consider the following examples:

- DOS 6.0 includes many files that enable DOS to work with foreign-language character sets, including German, Swedish, and French. If you expect to use your computer only in the United States, deleting these files can free disk space.

- Some DOS 6.0 utilities may duplicate functions that are available in other programs installed in your system. If you use a backup program (such as Norton Backup or FastBack), for example, you can delete the DOS backup program, MSBACKUP.

The manual that comes with DOS 6.0 lists some of the programs and files that you may not need and can delete to make more space available.

Using Disk Compression

If you were to examine the file that contains the text for this chapter, you would find that many words—such as *DOS* and *the*—are repeated frequently. Most data includes such repetition—patterns that occur over and over within a file, whether the file contains English text, customer data, or machine instructions.

Many programmers have written programs that analyze these patterns and squeeze a file's data into a smaller space by converting the data to a kind of shorthand notation. (PKZip and Arc are examples of such programs.) This process is known as *compression*. In special cases, the compressed data may require as little as 10 percent of the original space, although 50 percent is more typical.

Understanding DoubleSpace

DOS 6.0 includes a disk-compression program called DoubleSpace. DoubleSpace enables DOS to compress data automatically when you store the data on disk and to uncompress the data when you use it. DoubleSpace works transparently—you have no indication that your files are being compressed, except that your disk can hold more data than before.

You can select which drives use compression and which do not. You might decide, for example, to compress drive C but not drive D, which contains OS/2.

> **CAUTION:** Only DOS 6.0 can read a compressed drive. If you use another operating system in addition to DOS—such as OS/2, UNIX, Xenix, or Windows NT—you cannot access a compressed drive while you are running the other operating systems.

Using DoubleSpace provides one major advantage: the amount of data you can store on your hard disk is roughly doubled because DoubleSpace is analyzing your data and squeezing more information into less space. The exact amount of additional data you can store varies, depending on the characteristics of the data itself.

Using DoubleSpace also has the following minor disadvantages:

- DoubleSpace must perform extra work to compress and uncompress data each time you access your disk. This extra work takes time and slows your computer slightly. If you have a fast computer, such as a 386 or 486, the slowdown is so insignificant that you almost certainly will never notice the difference. On slower computers, however, you may notice that operations involving a lot of disk access seem to run a bit more slowly than before.

■ DoubleSpace requires some conventional memory—about 50K if you load DoubleSpace *high* (into upper memory) by using DEVICEHIGH.

■ A hard disk created with DoubleSpace cannot be used without the DoubleSpace device driver. This restriction is not likely to cause problems, but if your computer breaks, you would not be able to remove your hard disk and install it in a computer that uses an earlier version of DOS.

CAUTION: A drive may contain files that cannot or should not be compressed. Windows swap file, for example, must remain uncompressed.

When you apply compression to a drive, DoubleSpace makes the drive appear as though it were two drives, with two distinct drive letters. DoubleSpace divides the disk into a compressed drive and an uncompressed drive so that you still can store some of your files in an uncompressed format.

You can decide how much of the disk is allocated for each area. If you don't expect to store any files in an uncompressed format, make the uncompressed drive small (a fraction of a megabyte) and allocate the rest to the compressed drive. Conversely, if you expect to store the Windows swap file on the uncompressed drive, allocate several megabytes to that drive.

DOS assigns a new drive letter to one of the areas so that you can access either area by using the appropriate drive letter. If you apply compression to drive C, for example, DoubleSpace might tell you that from now on, C: refers to the compressed portion of the disk and J: refers to the uncompressed portion.

Installing DoubleSpace

To install DoubleSpace, type the following command at the DOS prompt:

DBLSPACE

You must not have any other programs running when you first issue this command. In particular, you must not be running the DOS Shell.

DoubleSpace first asks whether you want an Express or Custom Setup; the default is Express. If you select Express, DoubleSpace compresses the existing files on drive C. Select Custom setup if you want to select the drive to be compressed. DBLSPACE then installs the DoubleSpace driver in the DOS kernel and reboots your machine.

DoubleSpace also may add a line to your CONFIG.SYS file, such as the following:

    DEVICEHIGH=C:\DOS\DBLSPACE.SYS /MOVE

This line does *not* load the DoubleSpace device driver; the DOS kernel loads the driver automatically when you install DoubleSpace. Instead, the line moves the driver into upper memory (if you have upper memory blocks available). If you remove this line from your CONFIG.SYS, you still load the DoubleSpace driver—it just will not be moved into upper memory.

Controlling the Operation of DoubleSpace

You can run DoubleSpace at any time to get information about compression on your disks or to control various facets of DoubleSpace's operation.

You can run DoubleSpace simply by typing the following command:

    DBLSPACE

When DoubleSpace starts, it lists all the available drives that employ compression. For each drive, DoubleSpace shows the total amount of space and the current free space available.

Many DoubleSpace operations require you to select a drive, either by using the arrow keys to position the selection bar on one of the drives or by clicking a drive.

Estimating Space in a Compressed Drive

Important: The amount of total space and free space that DoubleSpace displays are *estimates* that depend on the type of data you store on the disk. In predicting free space, DoubleSpace assumes a 2-to-1 compression ratio, which is to say that if DoubleSpace has 10M of physical disk space free, the program predicts that it can compress 20M of your data into that space.

Its estimate may turn out to be far off, however. If you are storing files that contain nothing but tables of numbers, for example, you will do far better than 2-to-1. On the other hand, if you are storing GIF graphic files (which already are compressed), DoubleSpace cannot compress them at all; consequently, you cannot store nearly as much data as DoubleSpace predicted.

Displaying Compressed-Drive Information

To display information about a compressed drive, select the compressed drive, select Drive from the menu bar, and then select Info from the resulting menu. (If you do not have a mouse, press Alt-D, and then position the cursor on Info and press Enter.)

Figure 18.4 shows the information display for a small compressed drive. Notice that in this example, most of the disk is allocated for compressed files and is accessed as drive F; about 2M is uncompressed and is accessed as drive L.

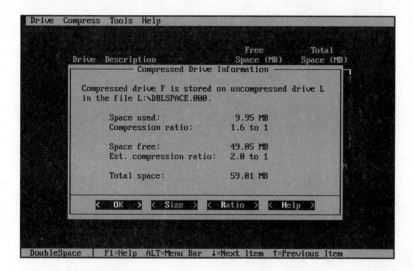

Fig. 18.4

DoubleSpace sample Drive Information.

This figure also tells you that the estimate of 49.05M free is based on a compression ratio of 2-to-1, but the compression ratio that DoubleSpace actually has achieved on the data stored so far is only 1.6-to-1. Therefore, if the rest of the drive is used for the same type of data, you will not be able to store as much data as DoubleSpace's estimate of 49M leads you to expect.

Clicking the Size and Ratio buttons enables you to change the size of the compressed area and the estimating ratio, respectively. The following sections discuss both methods.

Changing the Size of a Compressed Drive

On each compressed disk, DoubleSpace reserves some room for uncompressed files. To change the size of the uncompressed area (thereby changing the size of the compressed area correspondingly), perform one of the following actions:

■ While displaying the Compressed Drive Information dialog box click the Size button.

■ In the main screen, select Drive, then Change Size.

When you perform either action, the Change Size dialog box appears (see fig. 18.5).

```
┌──────────────────────── Change Size ────────────────────────┐
│                                                             │
│                           Compressed     Uncompressed       │
│                            Drive F         Drive L          │
│                                                             │
│     Current drive size:     59.01 MB       32.85 MB         │
│     Current free space:     49.85 MB        2.00 MB         │
│                                                             │
│     Minimum free space:      0.10 MB        0.13 MB         │
│     Maximum free space:     41.72 MB       26.24 MB         │
│                                                             │
│     New free space:         38.73 MB**    [2.00   ] MB      │
│                                                             │
│   ** based on estimated compression ratio of 2.0 to 1.     │
│                                                             │
│     To change the size of drive F, adjust the free space   │
│     on drive L.                                             │
│                                                             │
│          <   OK   >    < Cancel >    <  Help  >             │
└─────────────────────────────────────────────────────────────┘
```

Fig. 18.5

The Sample Change Size dialog box.

You can change the amount of space that DoubleSpace reserves for the uncompressed area. Remember that for every megabyte of uncompressed space you give up, you gain about 2M in the compressed drive.

Changing the Compression Ratio

By default, DoubleSpace uses a 2-to-1 compression ratio to predict the amount of free space left in a compressed drive. After you use a compressed drive for a time, however, you may discover that your ratio is different. You can ask DoubleSpace to use a different ratio to estimate free space by performing one of the following:

■ While displaying the Compressed Drive Information dialog box, click the Ratio button.

■ In the main screen, select Drive, then Change Ratio.

DoubleSpace displays the current ratio that it is using for estimates and the actual ratio that it has been able to achieve in compressing your files so far. If the files you previously stored in this drive are typical of the files that you expect to store in the future, you will want to change the new ratio to match the ratio for stored files.

In the Change Compression Ratio dialog box shown in figure 18.6, DoubleSpace is using a 2-to-1 ratio to estimate free space but has achieved a 1.6-to-1 ratio for existing files. If that pattern holds, DoubleSpace will overestimate the data you can store on the disk. Changing the compression ratio to 1.6 will bring DoubleSpace's estimate more in line with reality.

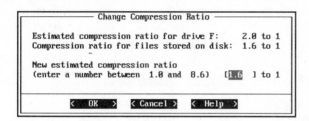

Fig. 18.6

The Change Compression Ratio dialog box.

Changing the compression ratio does not change the amount of compression that DoubleSpace can squeeze out of any specific file—only the ratio that DoubleSpace uses to estimate future compression.

Formatting a Compressed Drive

You do not need to format a compressed drive in the same sense that you format other drives to prepare them for use. When you use DoubleSpace to create a compressed drive, you must have already formatted that drive in the usual way. However, people often format an existing drive as a simple way of erasing all data on a drive, and you can format a compressed drive if you want to erase all the data stored on that drive. However, you cannot use the standard DOS format on a compressed drive.

To format a compressed drive, select the drive you want to format from the list of compressed drives, and then select Drive and Format. DoubleSpace displays an alert box that asks whether you're sure you want to format the drive. If you click OK, DoubleSpace erases all data stored in that drive.

> **WARNING:** You cannot unformat a compressed drive. After you select Format and click OK, your data is gone forever.

Deleting a Compressed Drive

If you no longer want to use a compressed drive, you can delete that drive. Select the drive you want to delete from the list of compressed drives. Select Drive and Delete. DoubleSpace displays a dialog box warning you that you will permanently destroy the contents of the compressed drive, and asks you for confirmation. If you click OK, DoubleSpace deletes the drive and all the data in the drive. The space that was allocated to the compressed drive is returned to the corresponding uncompressed drive.

Creating a New Uncompressed Drive

You can create a new compressed drive by selecting the Compress menu. DoubleSpace displays a menu in which you can select either of two ways of compressing the disk.

To compress an existing disk and all the data stored on it, follow this procedure:

1. From the Compress menu, select Existing drive. DoubleSpace displays a dialog box listing existing uncompressed drives, along with their current free space and projected free space.

2. Select the drive to which you want to apply compression. DoubleSpace displays a dialog box showing the drive letter that it will assign to the uncompressed drive and the amount of space it will allocate to that drive. The rest of the space will be allocated to the compressed drive.

   You must allocate at least 0.14M to the uncompressed drive; use this value if you do not expect to need any uncompressed space. If you want to change either of these values, select the value that you want to change.

   When you are ready to proceed, select Continue or press <Enter>.

3. DoubleSpace displays a dialog box warning you that after you compress a drive, you cannot uncompress it. DoubleSpace then prompts you to type C. If you type C, the program creates the compressed drive and compresses existing files in that drive. The new compressed drive uses the original drive letter, and the uncompressed drive receives the new drive letter.

If you want to leave existing files in the uncompressed drive and create a new compressed drive from the free portion of the existing drive, follow this procedure:

1. From the Compress menu, select Create new drive. DoubleSpace displays a dialog box listing existing uncompressed drives, along with their current free space and projected free space.

2. Select the drive to which you want to apply compression. DoubleSpace displays the drive letter it will assign to the compressed drive, the compression ratio it will use to estimate free space, and the amount of free space it will leave in the uncompressed drive, in addition to the space already used by existing files. The rest of the space will be allocated to the compressed drive.

   You must leave at least 0.14M of free space in the uncompressed drive; use this value if you do not expect to need any more uncompressed space. If you want to change any of these values, click the value you want to change.

   When you are ready to proceed, click Continue or press Enter.

3. DoubleSpace tells you how much time the program will require to create the drive and prompts you to type **C** to continue. The program then creates the compressed drive, which will be empty. All existing files remain in the uncompressed drive. The uncompressed drive retains the original drive letter, and the compressed drive receives the new drive letter.

Using Other DoubleSpace Features

You can choose two other useful features by selecting the Tools menu: Defragment and CHKDSK.

- *Defragment.* You cannot use the standard DOS DEFRAG command on a compressed drive; instead, select Tools, then Defrag. DoubleSpace displays a dialog box asking if you want to defragment the disk. If you select OK, DoubleSpace performs the defragmentation. Note that defragmenting a compressed disk does not significantly increase the speed with which you can access the disk (as DEFRAG does for a regular disk), but it does sometimes enable you to store a bit more on the compressed disk.

- *CHKDSK.* If a compressed drive becomes corrupted because of a power failure or hardware problem, you may need to use the CHKDSK program to repair the drive. You cannot use the DOS CHKDSK, which doesn't know how to fix a compressed drive. DoubleSpace includes its own CHKDSK routine.

Getting the Most Safety from Your Hard Disk

You depend on your hard disk to store valuable data and programs, which may represent thousands of dollars and many thousands of hours of hard work. DOS 6.0 includes features that help safeguard your investment against accidental erasure and malicious destruction.

Protecting Your Files with UNDELETE

The UNDELETE command protects you against accidentally deleting important files with the DEL command. With UNDELETE, you can usually recover files if you realize quickly that you have accidentally deleted them. The DOS 6.0 Setup program enables you to install both a DOS and a Windows version of UNDELETE.

Understanding the Undelete Levels of Protection

Whether you use the DOS or Windows version of UNDELETE, you can select one of three levels of protection against accidental loss of data:

■ *Delete Sentry* provides the most security against accidental deletion, at the cost of some of your memory and disk space. At this level, DOS creates a hidden directory called SENTRY. When you delete a file, DOS doesn't really delete it but instead moves the file to the SENTRY directory. If you later undelete the file, DOS simply moves the file back to its original location. DOS will not permit the SENTRY directory to grow beyond about seven percent of your disk space. If you delete a file that causes your SENTRY directory to grow beyond seven percent, DOS deletes the oldest file in your SENTRY directory to make room for the new file.

■ *Delete Tracker* is less secure than Delete Sentry. With this level of protection, DOS stores information about the deleted file in a hidden file called PCTRACKER.DEL. However, DOS marks the disk space used by your file as available for reuse. If you later want to undelete the file and DOS has not reused the space for a new file, DOS can restore the file with the information in PCTRACKER.DEL.

■ The standard level of protection is the least reliable, but it is always available and uses no extra disk space or memory. If you delete a file, DOS allows you to undelete it using information that may exist in the file's directory and in the File Allocation Table (FAT), provided that you have not created a new file that reuses the old file's disk space.

Table 18.3 shows the maximum amount of disk space and memory required by each level of protection.

Table 18.3 Requirements of UNDELETE Protection Levels		
Level of Protection	**Disk Space Required**	**Memory-Resident Portion**
Delete Sentry	significant	13.5K
Delete Tracker	minimal	13.5K
Standard	none	none

Starting Undelete

If you want to use the Standard level of protection, you don't need to take any action to start protection. Remember that the standard protection recovers files by using information that DOS leaves in the directory and FAT after it deletes a file.

If you are using a higher level, you must include an UNDELETE command in your AUTOEXEC.BAT to load the memory-resident portion of UNDELETE, and to specify the type of protection you want. To start UNDELETE, use this format:

UNDELETE */Sdrive /Tdrive-entries*

If you want to use Delete Sentry, specify the */S* switch followed by the drive letter you want to protect. If you don't specify a drive letter, UNDELETE protects the currently logged drive. If you want to protect several drives, you can specify several /S switches. To protect both drives C and D with Delete Sentry, for example, place the following command in your AUTOEXEC.BAT:

UNDELETE /SC /SD

This command causes UNDELETE to print the following message:

```
UNDELETE - A delete protection facility
Copyright  1987-1993 Central Point Software, Inc.
All rights reserved.

UNDELETE loaded.

Delete Protection Method is Delete Sentry.
Enabled for drives : C D

Initializing SENTRY control file on drive C.
```

To start UNDELETE with Delete Tracking, use the /T switch instead of /S. For example, to start Delete Tracking protection on drive C, use the following:

UNDELETE /TC

You can also specify the maximum number of files that Delete Tracking can track by following the drive letter with a dash and the number of files to track, which must be between 1 and 999. To begin Delete Tracking on drive D, for example, tracking a maximum of 500 files, add this command to your AUTOEXEC.BAT:

UNDELETE /TD-500

If you don't specify a maximum number of files to track, UNDELETE uses a default value based on the size of the hard disk. Table 18.4 shows the number of files tracked by UNDELETE for various size disks and how much disk space the PCTRACKER.DEL file created by UNDELETE will occupy.

Table 18.4 Default Files Tracked by UNDELETE

Disk Size	Files Tracked	Size of PCTRACKER.DEL
360K	25	5K
720K	50	9K
1.2M	75	14K
1.44M	75	14K
20M	101	18K
32M	202	36K
over 32MB	303	55K

> **NOTE** Do not use Delete Tracking on a drive that you have redirected by a JOIN or SUBST command. If you're using the ASSIGN command on a protected drive, you must issue the ASSIGN command before the UNDELETE command.
>
> Also, if you want to use UNDELETE on network drives, you must use Delete Sentry, and you must have permission to read, write, create files, and delete files from the drive's root directory.

Undeleting Files from DOS

If you discover that you have accidentally deleted a file, you may be able to use UNDELETE to restore the file. Your chances of restoring the file are best if Delete Sentry was enabled when you deleted the file, somewhat less if Delete Tracking was enabled, and still less if you are relying on standard protection.

Use the following format to recover one or more files:

   UNDELETE *d:path\filename /DT /DS /DOS /LIST /ALL*

The switches tell UNDELETE to recover only files that can be recovered using Delete Sentry (/DS), Delete Tracking (/DT), or standard protection (/DOS).

The simplest way to use UNDELETE is to change to the directory that contained the deleted files and type **UNDELETE** at the DOS prompt. UNDELETE looks for any files that can be recovered using any of the three protection methods, lists each file that can be recovered, and asks you if you want to recover each file. The example below shows a possible output generated by UNDELETE:

```
UNDELETE - A delete protection facility
Copyright  1987-1993 Central Point Software, Inc.
All rights reserved.

Directory: C:\QUICKEN\DATA
File Specifications: *.*

    Delete Sentry control file contains    5 deleted files.

    Deletion-tracking file not found.
```

```
    MS-DOS directory contains    2 deleted files.
    Of those,    0 files may be recovered.

Using the Delete Sentry method.

    GWC      QIF    15360  2-20-93  6:02p  ...A  Deleted:
2-21-93 11:28a
This file can be 100% undeleted. Undelete (Y/N)?
```

This output shows that you were currently in the \QUICKEN\DATA directory on drive C when you issued the UNDELETE command. UNDELETE found five files that had been deleted when Delete Sentry was in effect, none with Delete Tracking, and two with standard protection. However, neither of the files can be recovered that were deleted when standard protection was in effect.

UNDELETE then begins listing the files that it can recover and asking whether you want to recover each file. The first file, GWC.QIF, is 15,360 bytes in size and was deleted on 2/21/93 at 11:28 a.m. UNDELETE tells you that it can recover 100 percent of the file and prompts you to respond with Y or N, to indicate whether you would like UNDELETE to recover the file. Note that sometimes UNDELETE is able to recover only part of the file, and it indicates what percentage of the file it can recover for you.

NOTE   Because of a quirk in the way DOS deletes files, if you are using standard protection, UNDELETE is not able to determine the first character of each file's name. If you deleted a file originally called TEST.DOC, UNDELETE lists it as #EST.DOC, using the pound sign (#) in place of the missing first character. If you tell UNDELETE you want to recover the file, it asks you to supply the first letter. If you supply the wrong first letter (such as a "J" in this example), you simply wind up with the right file but the wrong name; the recovered file is called JEST.DOC.

If you specify the */LIST* switch, UNDELETE lists the files that can be recovered but does not attempt to recover them.

If you specify the */ALL* switch, UNDELETE recovers all available files without prompting for confirmation. For each file, it uses Delete Sentry if possible; otherwise, it uses Delete Tracking if possible; finally it uses standard protection.

If you use the */ALL* switch and UNDELETE uses standard protection to recover the file, UNDELETE supplies a pound sign (#) as the first character in the name. You will probably want to issue a RENAME command later to give the file its proper name.

If the pound sign would result in a file name identical to an existing file, UNDELETE uses a percent sign (%) instead. If necessary, it will continue through a list of characters until it finds a character that results in a name that doesn't already exist. The list of characters is as follows:

> #%&0123456789ABCDEFGHIJKLMNOPQRSTUVWXYZ.

Undeleting Files from Windows

The Windows version of UNDELETE works similarly to the DOS version. When you first invoke Undelete, you see in the Windows directory a list of all the deleted files that can be recovered. Since this is probably not the directory that interests you, your first action is to select the Drive/Directory button and enter the drive letter and directory that contains the file or files you want to recover.

Figure 18.7 shows a sample listing of a directory C:\DOS6. Undelete shows a short list of files that can be recovered and indicates the likelihood of recovering all the data intact. Most of the files are flagged as Perfect, indicating that Undelete is certain it can recover the entire file. One file is flagged as Excellent, indicating that UNDELETE believes it will be able to recover the entire file.

File	Condition	Size	Date	Time
C:\DOS6				
?EMP.TXT	Excellent	289 bytes	02/21/93	11:30AM
CH18TLB.BAK	Perfect	79KB	02/20/93	06:09PM
TEMP.TXT	Perfect	612 bytes	02/21/93	11:29AM
UNDEL.BAK	Perfect	18KB	02/21/93	11:52AM
UNDEL.BAK	Perfect	16KB	02/21/93	11:18AM
UNDEL.BAK	Perfect	15KB	02/20/93	06:02PM

Deleted Date: N/A   Deleted Time: N/A   Protected by: N/A
Path:

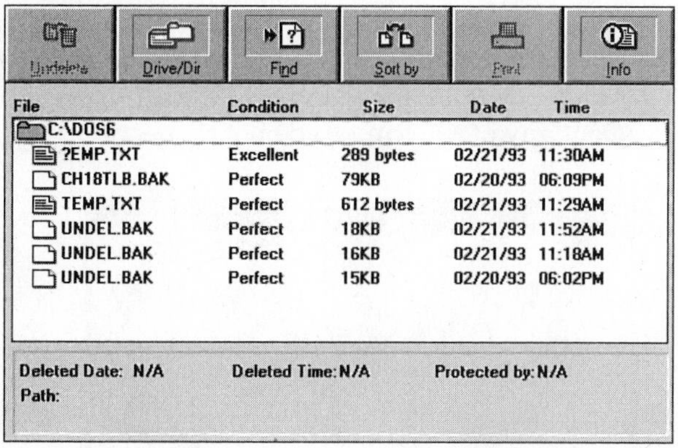

Fig. 18.7

Sample listing of deleted files.

To recover a file, select the file and then select Undelete. The file's status changes to Recovered.

Notice that the file listing in figure 18.8 shows one file with a question mark as the first character in its name. This file was deleted while standard protection was in effect, and as with the DOS version of Undelete, the Windows version cannot determine what the first character in the file's name is. If you ask to recover this file, Undelete asks you what the first character in the file's name should be. Undelete may tell you that certain characters are illegal as the first character of the file name, if that character causes a conflict with another existing file. If, for example, you try to undelete a file shown as ?ALES.WS1, Undelete tells you that "S" is an invalid first character if a file already exists called SALES.WS1.

If you want information on a file before you recover it, select the file and then select Info. Undelete displays a dialog box showing information about the file, including your chances of recovering the file intact. Figure 18.8 shows a sample information dialog box.

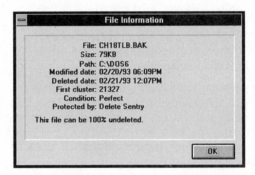

Fig. 18.8

Windows File Information dialog box.

From within Windows Undelete, you can select the type of protection you want by selecting the Options menu, and then Configure Delete Protection. Undelete displays the dialog box shown in figure 18.9 and allows you to select any of the three types of protection.

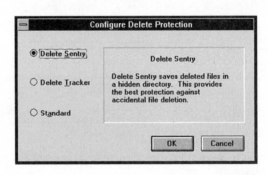

Fig. 18.9

Windows Configure Delete Protection dialog box.

Other Undelete Functions

The UNDELETE command can perform several miscellaneous functions, using this format:

UNDELETE */PURGEdrive /STATUS /LOAD /UNLOAD*

The */PURGE* switch causes UNDELETE to delete the contents of the SENTRY directory. Remember that if you use Delete Sentry, deleted files are moved to the SENTRY directory where they are available for recovery. They still occupy the same disk space. If you are deleting files in order to free up disk space and you use Delete Sentry, delete the files and then issue this command:

UNDELETE /PURGE

After you issue this command, however, you cannot recover the deleted files with Delete Sentry.

The */STATUS* switch causes UNDELETE to list information about the current status of UNDELETE. This switch displays the type of protection currently in effect, as well as the drives being protected.

The */UNLOAD* switch removes the memory-resident portion of UNDELETE, disabling Delete Sentry or Delete Tracking protection.

You can use the /LOAD command to start UNDELETE. UNDELETE examines the UNDELETE.INI initialization file, discussed in the next section, for information about the type of protection to provide.

The Undelete Initialization File UNDELETE.INI

When you first load UNDELETE with the /S or /T switch, UNDELETE creates an initialization file, UNDELETE.INI, in your DOS directory (usually /DOS). This file controls the operation of UNDELETE.

The exact content of the UNDELETE.INI file varies depending on the options you used to invoke UNDELETE, but a typical file might resemble the following:

```
[configuration]
archive=FALSE
days=7
percentage=20
[sentry.drives]
```

```
C=
D=
[mirror.drives]
[sentry.files]
sentry.files=*.* -*.TMP -*.VM? -*.WOA -*.SWP -*.SPL -
*.RMG -*.IMG -*.THM -*.DOV
[defaults]
d.sentry=TRUE
d.tracker=FALSE
```

The UNDELETE.INI file is made up of five sections: [configuration], [sentry.drives], [mirror.drives], [sentry.files], and [defaults].

The [configuration] section defines certain UNDELETE characteristics, including the following:

- The ARCHIVE command defines whether files with the archive bit set are protected by UNDELETE. A value of FALSE (as shown in the example above) specifies that they are not protected; a value of TRUE specifies that they are.

- The DAYS command specifies the number of days that files are to be saved. The default is 7, indicating that Delete Sentry will keep a file for seven days and then delete it if you haven't tried to recover it within that time. If you find yourself running low on disk space, you can decrease this time, causing Delete Sentry to keep files for a shorter period of time.

- The PERCENTAGE command specifies the percentage of the disk that Delete Sentry can use for deleted files. The default is 20 percent.

The [sentry.drives] section specifies which drives will be protected by the Delete Sentry method, if Delete Sentry is enabled. Note that all the drives specified in this section will be protected when you use Delete Sentry, even if the UNDELETE command you use does not specify all the drives listed in this section.

The [sentry.files] section contains a series of file specifications that determine which files will be protected by Delete Sentry or Delete Tracker. If a file specification is preceded by a minus sign (–), files matching that specification are not protected. The default, shown in the example above, specifies that UNDELETE will protect all files except those ending in .TMP, .VM?, .WOA, .SWP, .SPL, .RMG, .IMG, .THM, and

.DOV. These files tend to be temporary or work files, and the philosophy behind this choice of files is that if you accidentally deleted one of these files, you would not be terribly concerned if you couldn't recover it. If you regularly work with other types of files that you wouldn't be concerned about accidentally deleting, you can add them here by editing this file.

The [mirror.drives] section specifies which drives will be protected by the Delete Tracker, if Delete Tracker is enabled. As with the [sentry .drives] section, note that all the drives specified in this section will be protected when you use Delete Tracker, even if the UNDELETE command you use does not specify all the drives listed in this section.

The [defaults] section specifies which type of protection will be used. Either d.sentry or d.tracker should be set to TRUE; the other should be set to FALSE. In the example above, Delete Sentry will be used because d.sentry is set to TRUE.

Understanding Computer Viruses

In working with computers, you probably have encountered situations in which the computer didn't do what you wanted it to do. Frustrating as these situations can be, they simply represent a misunderstanding between you and your computer.

Computer viruses are quite different; viruses are supposed to do harm to your computer. Viruses are programs, written by unscrupulous programmers, that are designed to make copies of themselves and spread from one computer to another, just as a biological virus does in people. Usually, viruses also damage your computer by destroying legitimate data and programs. Creating a virus is against the law, but depraved programmers still spread viruses for the same reason that vandals throw bricks through windows: to cause senseless damage.

To protect yourself, you must understand how viruses work. The following sections explain computer viruses in detail.

Understanding How Viruses Spread

Computer viruses come in thousands of variations, each of which works a little differently. How viruses spread from one computer to another, and the damage they do, depends on how the virus is written.

A virus begins in the hands of an experienced but corrupt programmer who is either malicious or insensitive to the damage he or she causes. The programmer usually starts with an existing program (anything from a game to a word processing program) and adds a few carefully crafted instructions that modify the workings of the program. He or she then distributes the altered program to other users, either on a floppy disk or through an electronic bulletin board.

When the unsuspecting recipient runs the altered software, the program may appear to work correctly, but the added code—the virus—performs some type of operation that the victim doesn't want. This operation may delete important files or erase the hard disk entirely. The virus also may display a taunting message.

The most dangerous viruses, however, do no immediate damage; they may alter the operating system by planting a kind of time bomb. Days, weeks, or months after the original infected program ran, the operating system may suddenly go wild, deleting files and destroying data.

Worse, most viruses are designed to spread to other computers. Between the time when a virus infects a computer and the time when it begins to damage that computer, the virus may copy itself onto every floppy that the victim inserts into the computer. Because the victim is unaware that the computer is infected until the virus begins to do damage, he or she may unwittingly spread hundreds of copies to friends.

Strange as it may seem, more than 1,000 viruses exist today. You should be concerned about computer viruses, and you should be serious about protecting your system. However, you may derive some comfort from the knowledge that your computer can become infected in only one of two ways:

■ *Loading and running infected software.* Your chance of infecting your computer decreases greatly if you obtain software only from reputable software companies. When you load software from bulletin boards or from an illegal source, your chances of encountering a virus increase.

■ *Booting from an infected floppy.* Many viruses spread when a computer boots from a floppy that carries the virus. Beware of floppies that weren't formatted by you or by someone you trust.

Fighting Viruses

Your best defense against viruses is a virus-scanning program. Such a program can scan files and disks, looking for telltale sequences of instructions that have been identified as parts of known viruses. Used correctly, a good virus program can protect you against the vast majority of known viruses before they damage your computer.

DOS 6.0 includes two programs—Microsoft Anti-Virus (MSAV) and Microsoft Anti-Virus for Windows (MWAV)—that can scan your memory and disk for hundreds of known viruses. You can use these programs to detect and destroy viruses.

In its simplest use, you can start MSAV simply by typing **MSAV**. You can select the functions you want to perform from MSAV's menu. Figure 18.10 shows the main MSAV menu.

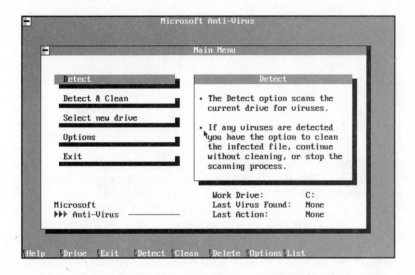

The following list describes the options in this menu:

- *Detect.* This option looks for viruses and tells you what it finds, but it does not destroy viruses.

- *Detect & Clean.* This option looks for viruses and destroys any that it finds.

■ *Select new drive.* This option enables you to specify the drive on which Detect or Detect & Clean runs.

■ *Options.* This option enables you to configure various options that determine how MSAV works.

■ *Exit* terminates MSAV.

The most common operation you will perform is scanning for viruses. To scan the currently logged drive for viruses, select Detect (or press <F2>). MSAV scans the current drive for viruses and reports on how many files it searched and how many viruses it found (none, you hope). Figure 18.11 shows a sample report after MSAV has done its work.

```
┌──────────────── Viruses Detected and Cleaned ────────────────┐
│                                                              │
│                       Checked        Infected       Cleaned  │
│                                                              │
│       Hard disks    :     1              0             0     │
│       Floppy disks  :     0              0             0     │
│       Total disks   :     1              0             0     │
│                                                              │
│       COM Files     :    25              0             0     │
│       EXE Files     :    49              0             0     │
│       Other Files   :    89              0             0     │
│       Total Files   :   163              0             0     │
│                                                              │
│       Scan Time     :  00:00:09                              │
│                                                  ▐ OK ▌      │
│                                                              │
└──────────────────────────────────────────────────────────────┘
```

Fig. 18.11

MSAV report after completing a scan.

With luck, you will never face the unpleasant prospect of finding a virus on your system. However, if MSAV finds a virus during its scan, it displays a dialog box telling you which virus it found, which file contained the virus, and asking what you want to do. If you select Continue, MSAV keeps looking for more viruses. If you select Clean, MSAV destroys the virus and then continues searching.

If you want to tell MSAV to scan your disk and clean any viruses it finds, select Detect and Clean. MSAV cleans any viruses it finds.

If you want to scan a different drive, select Select Drive (or press <F2>), and select the drive you want to scan.

The complete format of the DOS version of Microsoft Anti-Virus is shown below:

MSAV *drive: /S /C /R /A /L /N /P /F videoswitches /VIDEO*

If you specify the drive parameter, MSAV scans the indicated drive; otherwise, it scans the currently logged drive.

The /S switch tells MSAV to immediately invoke the Detect function, causing it to scan the specified drive. However, with this option, MSAV doesn't remove any viruses it finds. The /C switch tells it to scan and remove viruses it finds.

The /R switch tells MSAV to create a scan report. MSAV creates a file called MSAV.RPT, which lists the number of files MSAV scanned, the number of viruses detected, and the number of viruses removed. MSAV.RPT is always created in the drive's root directory.

The /A switch causes MSAV to scan all drives except A and B. The /L switch causes MSAV to scan all hard disks on your computer, but not drives on a network.

The /N switch causes MSAV to run without using the graphical user interface. If it detects a virus, it returns a special exit code (86). This switch is useful when scanning for viruses within a batch file.

The /P switch runs MSAV with a command-line interface instead of a graphical user interface. Normally, MSAV displays file names as it scans. The /F switch tells MSAV not to display file names. Use this switch only with the /N or /P switches.

MSAV also recognizes a large number of switches that control how it uses the screen. These switches are shown in table 18.5.

Table 18.5 MSAV Options for Controlling Display

Switch	Meaning
/25	Sets screen to 25 lines (default)
/28	Sets screen to 28 lines (VGA only)
/43	Sets screen to 43 lines (EGA or VGA)
/50	Sets screen to 50 lines (VGA only)
/60	Sets screen to 60 lines (Video 7 display adapters only)
/BF	Uses the computer's BIOS for video display
/BT	Enables graphics mouse in Windows
/BW	Uses black-and-white scheme
/FF	Uses screen updating that works especially fast on CGA displays
/IN	Uses color scheme
/LCD	Uses a scheme that works well on LCD screens

continues

Table 18.5 Continued	
Switch	**Meaning**
/LE	Reverses left and right mouse buttons
/MONO	Uses monochromatic color scheme
/NF	Disables alternate fonts
/NGM	Uses the default mouse character instead of graphic mouse pointer
/PS2	Resets the mouse if the mouse pointer disappears

The */VIDEO* switch displays all the options listed in table 18.5.

Understanding Checklists

After you have used MSAV to scan a drive, you may notice that each directory contains a file called CHKLIST.MS. This file contains identifying information (called checksums) about the files in that directory. Each time MSAV scans the files in that directory again, it can compare the current status of the file against information in the CHKLIST.MS file. If a file has become infected since the CHKLIST.MS file was created, the checksums indicates that a change has occurred.

The CHKLIST.MS files don't require much disk space, but if you want to free some disk space, you can start MSAV and press F7 to tell MSAV to delete all CHKLIST.MS files.

If you don't want MSAV to create CHKLIST.MS files in the future, start MSAV and select Options (or press F8), and turn off Create New Checksums.

Listing Virus

If you are interested in learning about the viruses known to MSAV, you can use MSAV's List feature to access its list of viruses. Start MSAV and press F9 to see MSAV's virus list.

You can use the scroll bars to scan through the list of known viruses, or you can search for a particular virus by entering its name in the blue box and selecting Find Next.

When you find a virus about which you would like more information, click the virus's name. MSAV displays information about the virus, such as the sample shown in figure 18.12.

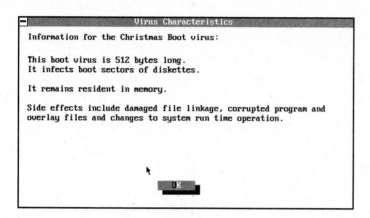

Using the Windows Version of Microsoft Anti-Virus

The Windows version of Microsoft Anti-Virus, MWAV, is almost identical in its operation to the DOS version. When you invoke MWAV, you see the dialog box shown in figure 18.13. Select the drive you want to scan, and then click Detect to scan without removing viruses or Detect and Clean to scan for viruses and remove any viruses found.

By selecting the Scan menu, you can access most of the other options described with MSAV in the previous section. This menu includes Delete CHKLIST Files, which deletes all the CHKLIST.MS files on your disk, and Virus List, which enables you to access MWAV's virus list.

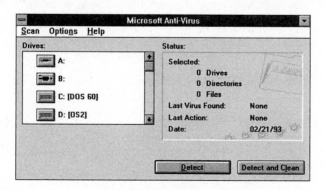

Guarding against Infection

Most users can protect themselves against viruses by following these steps:

1. Before you load any software from diskettes, scan all the diskettes with MSAV or MWAV. Click Select new drive, select your diskette drive, and execute Detect for each diskette.

2. After you install new software and *before* you run it, run MSAV or MWAV on your hard disk.

3. If you download software from bulletin boards, run MSAV or MWAV on your hard disk *before* you run that software.

4. Never boot from a floppy disk that you have not scanned for viruses (with MSAV or MWAV) or that you did not format yourself.

Chapter Summary

In this chapter, you discovered the utility programs that DOS 6.0 provides to enable you to use your hard disk most efficiently. You also learned the following:

■ You can increase the effective speed with which you can access data on your hard disk by creating a disk cache with SMARTDRV, by creating a RAM disk with RAMDRIVE, and by defragmenting your disk regularly with DEFRAG.

■ You can increase the amount of space available to you by using disk compression with DBLSPACE.

■ You can increase the security of your hard disk by insuring against accidental deletions with UNDELETE and by protecting your computer against viruses with Microsoft Anti-Virus (MSAV) and Microsoft Anti-Virus for Windows (MWAV).

The next chapter, "Understanding ANSI.SYS," begins Part IV, "Advancing Your DOS Capabilities," where you learn how to get the most out of DOS.

Advancing Your DOS Capabilities

PART

IV

OUTLINE

Understanding ANSI.SYS

The term *ANSI* refers to the American National Standards Institute. ANSI is one of several sets of computer standards established by the institute to specify the codes that computer manufacturers can use to control video displays and keyboard mapping.

ANSI.SYS is a *device driver*, meaning that it gives DOS additional control of the screen and keyboard devices beyond the control features built into the operating system. You use ANSI.SYS to enhance the functions of your video screen and keyboard. With ANSI.SYS, you can set screen colors, employ graphics, and specify other video attributes. You can provide that personal touch to your DOS prompt. You even can change the assignments of keys on your keyboard.

The ANSI.SYS file supplied with MS-DOS contains a subset of the ANSI standards. Third-party suppliers of other ANSI.SYS files may include more features in their versions of this file, but those features are not necessary for most users.

The method you use to add ANSI.SYS and other device drivers to DOS is to include it in the CONFIG.SYS file. The CONFIG.SYS file is a text or ASCII file that lists all device drivers and other configuration settings you use to customize your computer and its operation. DOS reads this file when your system boots and applies the configuration information contained in the file. This file must be in the root directory of the boot drive, whether that drive is a floppy or a hard drive. CONFIG.SYS is not absolutely necessary, but without the file, your computer may not properly operate or communicate with the peripheral devices in your system.

NOTE   You cannot dynamically change settings or devices installed in the CONFIG.SYS file. You can modify the file, and you then must reboot the computer for the changes to take effect.

When you turn off your computer, your system "forgets" the settings you used with the ANSI.SYS driver. To ensure that all ANSI features you want to use are permanently enabled, enter the ANSI.SYS instructions into your AUTOEXEC.BAT file. This procedure is fully discussed later in the section "Issuing ANSI.SYS Codes in Batch Files."

Installing ANSI.SYS

The only way you can install the ANSI.SYS driver is to include it in your CONFIG.SYS file. The format of the line must be as follows:

DEVICE=C:\DOS\ANSI.SYS */X /K /R*

or

DEVICEHIGH = C:\DOS\ANSI.SYS */X /K /R*

The */X* option enables you to remap extended keys if you are using a 101-key keyboard.

The */K* option treats 101-key keyboards as if they were 84-key keyboards, ignoring extended keys.

The */R* option slows screen scrolling for improved readability.

NOTE   The /X and /K switches are exclusive. You can use one of them, but you cannot use both.

When you install MS-DOS on your computer, DOS places the ANSI.SYS file in the \DOS subdirectory. If the ANSI.SYS actually is located in the root directory of your boot drive, you don't need to include the drive and directory names in the command line. If you placed the ANSI.SYS file in another directory or on another drive, however, make sure that you specify the exact location in the CONFIG.SYS statement.

You can use either of two basic methods to install ANSI.SYS. The first method is to use a text editor such as EDIT, which is provided with MS-DOS. (For information on how to use EDIT, see Chapter 14, "Using the DOS Editor.") If you want to use a word processing application such as WordPerfect or WordStar, make sure that you use the ASCII or non-document mode in saving the file.

The DOS setup utility creates a CONFIG.SYS file for you but, if your system does not yet have a CONFIG.SYS file, you can use the COPY command to create the file, copying the file from the keyboard to a disk file. Type the following command at the DOS prompt, pressing Enter at the end of each line:

COPY CON CONFIG.SYS

DEVICE=C:\DOS\ANSI.SYS<F6>

 NOTE Items in angle brackets (<>) indicate keys that you press. In the preceding command, for example, you press F6 after you type the command.

CAUTION: DOS does not warn you that a file already exists. Make sure that you do not overwrite an existing CONFIG.SYS file when you use the COPY CON procedure.

NOTE The F6 keystroke enters the end-of-file marker (Ctrl-Z) and ends the process of creating the file.

DOS responds with the message 1 file(s) copied.

Because MS-DOS 6.0 automatically creates a CONFIG.SYS file when you install the program, use EDIT or another text editor to modify the file before you add the ANSI.SYS device-driver command.   **T I P**

You may see other commands in your existing CONFIG.SYS file. If so, do not change those commands; simply add the new command to the list. The exact location of the statement is not critically important, but you must list it after the DBLSPACE driver if you have installed this utility and any memory statements. You may want to add the ANSI.SYS statement to the end of the existing file.

After you add ANSI.SYS to your CONFIG.SYS file, reboot your computer. DOS includes the ANSI.SYS driver in the operating-system configuration. In the following sections, you learn how to use this driver and take advantage of its features.

After you add the DEVICE=ANSI.SYS statement in the CONFIG.SYS file, you can run the MemMaker utility again if you have a 386 or higher computer.

 After you insert the DEVICE= command in CONFIG.SYS, you must reboot the computer to load ANSI.SYS in memory.

Using ANSI.SYS

After you place the ANSI.SYS command in the CONFIG.SYS file and reboot the system so that the new configuration takes effect, you must issue commands that tell DOS to use the ANSI features.

Because some software is written to use ANSI codes, one or more of your software programs may require that ANSI.SYS be loaded. The installation procedure for this type of software notifies you of this requirement. (In fact, the program may even install the command in the CONFIG.SYS file for you.)

You also can activate ANSI.SYS features by issuing the ANSI commands yourself. You must be aware, however, that you cannot simply type the commands at the DOS prompt; you must enter an Escape sequence.

All ANSI.SYS sequences begin with the Escape character, followed by a left bracket ([). If you attempt to type this sequence at the prompt, DOS understands the Escape character to be a command to cancel the current operation. If you press the Esc key at a DOS prompt, DOS responds by displaying a backslash (\) and moving the cursor down to the next line; the preceding line is canceled.

If ANSI.SYS codes are not included in a program, you can send these codes to DOS in three ways: by executing a batch file, by typing a text file (that is, by using the DOS TYPE command), or by including the codes in a PROMPT command. When you embed ANSI codes in Escape sequences, the ANSI.SYS device driver intercepts the codes and executes the appropriate commands, ignoring any characters that are not preceded by the proper codes.

You can create a text file or a batch file or set up your PROMPT format in the AUTOEXEC.BAT file by using the MS-DOS editor (EDIT) or another text editor. Whatever utility you use must be capable of entering the Escape character, which many word processing programs and older text editors cannot enter.

For information on using EDIT, see Chapter 14, "Using the DOS Editor."

> To enter the Escape character while using EDIT, hold down the Ctrl key, press P, and then press Esc.

T I P

NOTE Some text editors display the Escape character as ^[. The ANSI code sequence, however, requires a left bracket ([ ). Do not confuse the two characters. The ANSI sequence may thus look as though it starts with ^[[.

Issuing ANSI.SYS Codes in Batch Files

The key to using ANSI.SYS is to have the Escape sequences sent to the display screen. This procedure is the only way to ensure that the device driver properly intercepts and executes the commands. Batch files send these sequences to the screen through the ECHO command, which tells DOS to display all commands on-screen. (For more information on batch files, see Chapter 15, "Understanding Batch Files, DOSKey, and Macros.")

NOTE By default, ECHO is set ON unless you explicitly issue an ECHO OFF command. If you do use ECHO OFF, any ANSI code line you enter thereafter must begin with the ECHO command.

Suppose that you want to use a batch file to set up formatting for a double-density disk (360K) in a 5 1/4-inch high-density (1.2M) drive. Use EDIT to create the batch file containing the instruction for the special effect, such as changing the color of the screen. Follow these steps:

1. At the DOS prompt, type the following command:

   EDIT NEWDISK.BAT

   DOS responds by loading the text editor and displaying the main editing screen.

2. Type the following lines for the batch file:

   ```
   @ECHO OFF
   ECHO <CTRL>P<ESC>[37;41m
   ECHO THIS FUNCTION FORMATS DOUBLE DENSITY DISKETTES
       (360KB)IN DRIVE A:
   FORMAT A: /F:360
   ECHO <CTRL>P<ESC>[37;40m
   ```

The first line in the batch file tells DOS not to display any of the commands in the batch file unless specifically instructed to do so through the ECHO command, and the leading character (@) instructs DOS not to display the ECHO OFF command.

The second line is an ANSI.SYS code sequence that sets the color of the screen (red, with white characters). The ANSI code 37 produces a white foreground; 41 is the ANSI code for a red background. The character *m* indicates that screen-attribute codes are being issued. The last line of the batch file sets the screen back to white on black—the default setting. (Make sure that you use the lowercase character *m* in the ANSI.SYS Escape sequences.) To enter the Escape sequence, hold down the Ctrl key, press P, and then press Esc. EDIT displays a left-arrow character, which represents the Escape code.

T I P

If you have a monochrome monitor, you can substitute 7m for 35;41m in the second line of the batch file. The code 7 tells ANSI.SYS to set reverse video. If you use 7m instead of 35;41m, substitute 0m for 37;40m in the last line to set the screen back to normal.

After you create the batch file, save the file by typing the following sequence:

```
<ALT>F
S
<ALT>F
X
```

EDIT saves the file, and you return to the DOS command-line prompt.

3. Type the following command, pressing Enter at the end of the line:

NEWDISK

On a color monitor, the screen turns red, with *NEWDISK* displayed in white characters. On a monochrome monitor with the suggested substitutions, the screen is white with black characters (reverse video).

Press Ctrl-C to abort the format utility or Enter to format a double-density disk. After the batch file executes the abort or format command, it sends the final ANSI sequence to DOS, returning the screen to normal.

To see why you must use the ECHO command in the ANSI Escape sequence, remove the ECHO command from the last line of the batch

file and then run the file again. DOS 6.0 informs you that it received a
`Bad command or file name`, and the screen color does not change to
normal.

 NOTE To issue ANSI.SYS commands in a batch file, you must use
the ECHO command for each set of Escape sequences. Make
sure that each sequence starts with the Escape character
and a left bracket ([). The ANSI codes follow the bracket.

Issuing ANSI.SYS Codes in Text Files

Issuing ANSI codes in text files is similar to using the codes in batch
files. The difference is that you do not use an ECHO command in a text
file. Also, in order for the commands to take effect, you must use the
MS-DOS TYPE command to pass the codes to the display for DOS to
execute.

To create a text file, follow these steps:

1. Type the following EDIT command, pressing Enter at the end of
   the line:

       EDIT SCREEN.TXT

   DOS responds by loading the editor and displaying the main editing screen.

2. If you have a color monitor, type the following line for the text file:

       <CTRL>P<ESC>[37;41m

   If you do not have a color monitor, type the following line:

       <CTRL>P<ESC>[7m

3. Save the file and exit the editor by typing the following sequence:

       <ALT>F
       S
       <ALT>F
       X

To change the screen to red with white characters or to white with
black characters, type the following command after the DOS prompt,
pressing Enter at the end of the line:

       TYPE SCREEN.TXT

ANSI.SYS intercepts the characters of the file when being displayed to the screen with the TYPE command. The Escape sequence, followed by the bracket, causes the device driver to execute the ANSI commands instead of passing the characters through to DOS. Your screen now is red with white characters.

You can return your screen to normal by following this procedure. The same way you created SCREEN.TXT in the preceding example, create NORMAL.TXT with EDIT. Enter the following line, for example:

> <Ctrl>P<Esc>[37;40M

After you type this line, save the file. At the DOS prompt, type **TYPE NORMAL.TXT** to return your screen to normal.

Issuing ANSI.SYS Codes with the PROMPT Command

The third way to issue ANSI.SYS instructions is to include these instructions in a PROMPT command. You can enter a PROMPT command at the DOS command line or in a batch file (usually the AUTOEXEC.BAT file). The normal syntax of the command is shown in the following:

> **PROMPT <string>**

The alternative syntax, however, uses the SET command:

> **SET PROMPT=<string>**

 Make sure that you include an equal sign (=) when you use the SET command.

The *<string>* consists of a set of characters that may or may not include an ANSI Escape sequence. The characters you enter tell DOS how you want your DOS prompt to look.

Entering an Escape character in a PROMPT command is much easier than entering the character in a batch or text file. The characters *$e* represent Escape in this command. You don't have to enter the <Ctrl>P<Esc> sequence that you did in batch or text files, as shown in the preceding examples. $e is the escape character for PROMPT commands.

Table 19.1 lists the subcommand characters for the PROMPT command. The subcommands do not require ANSI.SYS.

Table 19.1 PROMPT Subcommand Characters

Characters	Subcommand
$$	Displays the $ character
$_	Moves the cursor to the next line, supplying a carriage return and line feed
$b	Displays the | character
$d	Displays the current system date
$e	Enters the Escape character used in ANSI.SYS commands
$g	Displays the > character
$h	Uses Backspace to erase the preceding character
$l	Displays the < character
$n	Displays the current drive letter
$p	Displays the current directory path and drive
$q	Displays the = character
$t	Displays the current system time
$v	Displays the operating system name and version

 NOTE You can enter all PROMPT subcommands, with the exception of ANSI.SYS commands that must be entered in lowercase, in uppercase or lowercase. See tables 19.2 through 19.5 later in this chapter for a list of the ANSI.SYS commands you can use with DOS.

PROMPT subcommands enable you to be creative in designing your own DOS prompt. If you decide to use the $t (system time) subcommand for your PROMPT format, for example, you may not want seconds and hundredths of seconds displayed. To suppress the display of seconds, for example, use the $h subcommand, which erases the preceding character, as shown in the following (note that the space character is included in the prompt):

    PROMPT THHHHH$H PG

DOS responds by displaying a prompt similar to 10:20 C:\>. The Backspace characters ($h) erase the seconds and hundredths of seconds that otherwise would appear.

NOTE   The time and/or date display is current at the time of display but is not updated until the prompt reappears.

The following command illustrates another PROMPT command that you might find appealing:

PROMPT Time: THHHHHH_Date: D_[DOS 6] PG

When you use this command, DOS displays a prompt similar to the following:

Time: 10:20

Date: Mon 5-11-1992

[DOS 6] C:\>

To add more pizzazz to your DOS prompt format, you can add color, as outlined in the following examples for using ANSI.SYS sequences:

- If you have a color monitor, enter the following command, using nine spaces for the nine periods:

  PROMPT $E[1;37;44mTime: THHHHH$H.........$E
  [40m$E[K$_$E[1;44mDate: DE[0;40m$E[K$_[DOS 6] PG

  NOTE   The *K* portion of *$E[K* must be uppercase.

  If you use this command, the display shows the time and date in bright white text on a blue background, returning to normal white on black for the prompt.

- If you have a monochrome monitor, enter the following command, using nine spaces for the nine periods:

  PROMPT $E[7mTime: THHHHH$H.........$E[0m$E
  [K$_$E[7mDate: DE[0m$E[K$_[DOS 6] PG

  The display now shows the time and date in black characters on a white background, returning to normal white on black for the prompt.

As the inclusion of [DOS 6] in the preceding examples indicates, you also can display a message in the DOS prompt. (The brackets are included for cosmetic purposes only. They are not required.) Be creative. *Beam me up, Scotty*; *The BRAIN*; *USA Forever*; and *BOOM!* are a few examples of DOS users' humor and imagination.

For Related Information

◄◄ "Mastering Fundamental Editing Techniques," p. 519.

◄◄ "Learning Special Editing Techniques," p. 522.

◄◄ "Using Batch-File Commands," p. 565.

FROM HERE...

Customizing Your Screen with ANSI.SYS

Now that you understand how to issue ANSI.SYS commands in batch files, in text files, and as part of a PROMPT command, you're ready to use ANSI.SYS commands to customize your screen display.

All ANSI screen commands begin with the normal Escape code and a left bracket ([) and end with a lowercase *m*. You can use as many screen-attribute codes as you require, as long as the codes are separated by semicolons (;) and providing that no code contradicts another code. The order of the codes is not important.

Table 19.2 lists the ANSI codes for setting the character mode. You can enter character mode codes and color codes, listed in tables 19.2 through 19.4, in any order. If you enter more than one code, be sure to separate the codes with a semicolon (;) and follow with *m* (lowercase).

Table 19.2 ANSI Screen-Character Codes

Code	Effect
0	Normal display (the default)
1	High-intensity text
4	Underlined text (monochrome)
5	Blinking text
7	Reverse video (black on white)
8	Hidden text (black on black)

NOTE Some screen effects depend on your hardware. Underlined text, for example, can be displayed only on a monochrome monitor.

Table 19.3 lists the ANSI screen-display codes that are available for use with DOS. These codes set the screen width or screen type. Only one code can be entered at a time and is followed by a lowercase H (*h*). You can reset the screen mode by using the lowercase L (*l*).

Table 19.3 ANSI Screen-Display Codes

Code	Screen Type
0	40 x 25 characters, monochrome
1	40 x 25 characters, color
2	80 x 25 characters, monochrome
3	80 x 25 characters, color
4	320 x 200 pixels, monochrome
5	320 x 200 pixels, color
6	640 x 200 pixels, monochrome
7	Turns word wrap on (set mode)
7	Turns word wrap off (reset mode)
14	640 X 200 pixels, color
15	640 X 350 pixels, monochrome
16	640 X 360 pixels, color
17	640 X 480 pixels, monochrome
18	640 X 480 pixels, color
19	320 X 200 pixels, color

Table 19.4 lists the foreground (text) and background (screen) colors that you can set with ANSI.SYS commands.

Table 19.4 ANSI Screen-Color Codes

Color	Foreground Code	Background Code
Black	30	40
Red	31	41
Green	32	42
Yellow	33	43
Blue	34	44

Color	Foreground Code	Background Code
Magenta	35	45
Cyan	36	46
White	37	47

NOTE Because all the ANSI codes listed in the preceding tables are in different sets, you can enter codes in any order in the Escape sequence.

You can use these codes to customize your system. You may, for example, use ANSI codes to set the default screen colors and prompt format in your AUTOEXEC.BAT file so that the desired settings are used whenever you boot your computer.

Another use for ANSI codes is in designing a menu for your computer. You can create a text file that displays a list of the applications installed in your system and the commands needed to run those applications, for example. (Often, these commands are batch files. You also can be creative with batch files.)

Table 19.5 lists additional ANSI.SYS commands you can use to customize your system.

Table 19.5 Additional ANSI.SYS Escape Sequences

ANSI code	Description
ESC[x;yH	Places cursor at a specific position
ESC[x;yf	Places cursor at a specific position
ESC[xA	Moves cursor up x rows
ESC[xB	Moves cursor down x rows
ESC[yC	Moves cursor right y columns
ESC[yD	Moves cursor left y columns
ESC[s	Saves current cursor position
ESC[u	Restores cursor position after a save
ESC[2J	Erases the screen and moves the cursor to home position
ESC[K	Erases from the cursor position to the end of the line

> **CAUTION:** Make sure that you use the uppercase and lowercase characters specified in Table 19.5; otherwise, the instructions to ANSI.SYS will not work.

The first two commands listed in table 19.5 are identical, causing the cursor to be placed at an absolute screen position. The commands that incorporate the characters *A*, *B*, *C*, and *D* move the cursor relative to the current cursor position. The last two sequences in the list erase the screen, fully and partially, respectively.

Customizing Your Keyboard with ANSI.SYS

Computers use a set of 256 codes that indicate specific characters. These codes make up the *ASCII character set*. (ASCII is an acronym for the American Standard Code for Information Interchange.) A space, for example, has ASCII code 48; the uppercase *A* has ASCII code 65; and the lowercase *a* has ASCII code 97. (See Appendix E, "ASCII and Extended ASCII Codes," for a list of ASCII codes.)

Every time you press a key on your keyboard, the system's circuits send a code to DOS; this code interprets the keystroke and displays the appropriate character. Not every code in the ASCII set, however, has a corresponding keyboard key. Moreover, some keys represent more than one character.

Keyboards actually send different codes to DOS for each key or key combination you press on the keyboard. These codes are known as *scan codes*. Many, but not all, scan codes correspond to ASCII codes; with the various key combinations that involve the Ctrl, Alt, Shift, and Num Lock keys, more than 256 keystrokes are possible. This problem is solved by the addition of a leading 0 to some scan codes.

When DOS receives a scan code from the keyboard, the program uses a built-in table to ascertain the proper character. When the ANSI.SYS device driver has been loaded through the CONFIG.SYS file, the ANSI driver takes over this chore. The driver also enables you to modify the table and to assign different characters to the scan codes.

Suppose, for example, that you have to prepare documents or data files that include fractions. You can assign ASCII codes for some fractions to keys that you normally don't use. ASCII code 171, for example, stands for ½, and code 172 stands for ¼. (See Appendix E, "ASCII and

Extended ASCII Codes," for a complete list of ASCII codes.) Using ANSI.SYS makes key reassignments easy.

To assign the ½ fraction (ASCII 171) to the Shift-6 key combination, which produces the character ^ (ASCII 94), for example, you can use either of the following commands:

ESC["^";"½"p

ESC[94;171p

The ANSI.SYS keyboard-assignment Escape sequence starts with the standard Escape character, followed by a left bracket ([). The next character is the ASCII code, the scan code, or the key representation within quotes. Then you specify the new ASCII code or the key representation within quotes. The two characters are separated by a semicolon (;). The sequence ends with the lowercase letter *p*. Thus in the above examples, scan code 171 replaces scan code 94, or the key representation ^ is entered with quote marks ("^") and is changed to "½".

CAUTION: Do not use spaces in the ANSI.SYS code sequence. If you use spaces, DOS may not interpret the sequence properly.

Remember that the first specification is for the key to be assigned. To restore the original key assignment, enter the code twice— ESC[94;94p, for example.

T I P

A key assignment does not need to be a single character. You also can assign a text message to a keystroke. This process is referred to as a *macro substitution*. If you often need to type the same sequence of characters, you easily can set up a macro substitution that enters those characters for you.

In the following example, the words *HiYo, Silver!* are assigned to the F7 key, which has the scan code 0;65:

ESC[0;65;"HiYo, Silver!"p

After you issue this ANSI.SYS instruction, either in a text file that you TYPE or in a batch file, DOS (through ANSI.SYS) displays the message *HiYo, Silver!* whenever you press F7.

Because no scan or ASCII code of 0 exists, ANSI.SYS understands that the first number indicates the extended scan code for the F7 key instead of the ASCII code for the uppercase *A*, which is 65. If you need to add a carriage return (ASCII code 13) after the message, include that code in the Escape sequence, as shown in the following:

ESC[0;65;"HiYo, Silver!";13p

> **CAUTION:** ANSI.SYS reassignment of normal character keys on your keyboard is not a good idea. Such a reassignment interferes with your normal operation of DOS and with many, if not all, of your software programs.

You can enter many of the ASCII character codes on your keyboard by holding down the Alt key while you type the ASCII code for the character you want to display. If you reassign keys, however, you no longer can enter certain key characters in this manner. Further, reassigned keys no longer function the same way. If you reassign the backslash key (\), for example, you no longer can use the backslash character to access subdirectories.

Table 19.6 lists the scan codes for the function keys and for other keys and key combinations that you may want to reassign. Extended codes appear in decimal format. Use all codes in the format 0;nn. Do not forget the leading 0.

Table 19.6 Selected Scan Codes for Function Keys and Other Keys

Key(s)	Codes
F1 to F10	59 to 68
Shift-F1 to Shift-F10	84 to 93
Ctrl-F1 to Ctrl-F10	94 to 103
Alt-F1 to Alt-F10	104 to 113
F11 to F12	133 to 134
Shift-F11 to Shift-F12	135 to 136
Ctrl-F11 to Ctrl-F12	137 to 138
Alt-F11 to Alt-F12	139 to 140
Ins	82
Del	83

Key(s)	Codes
Home	71
Ctrl-Home	119
End	79
Ctrl-End	117
PgUp	73
Ctrl-PgUp	132
PgDn	81
Ctrl-PgDn	118
←	75
Ctrl-←	115
→	77
Ctrl-→	116
↑	72
↓	80
Ctrl-PrtSc	114

CAUTION: When you use ANSI.SYS to reassign keys, keep in mind that DOS allows for a total of 200 characters. If your key re-assignments take more than 200 bytes, you overwrite part of the command processor in memory, and your system may lock up.

Chapter Summary

In this chapter, you learned that ANSI.SYS is a device driver that gives DOS increased screen- and keyboard-handling capability. You load the driver through a statement in the CONFIG.SYS file.

The key points covered in this chapter include the following:

■ You communicate with ANSI.SYS by issuing Escape sequences.

■ You cannot issue an Escape sequence from the command line.

■ You can issue an Escape sequence in a batch file, a prompt command, and a text file that you TYPE to the display.

■ You use MS-DOS EDIT to create the batch and text files for ANSI.SYS commands.

■ You can change screen attributes and colors through the ANSI.SYS commands.

■ You can change key definitions through the ANSI.SYS commands.

In Chapter 20, "Understanding the International Features of DOS," you learn another method of changing the characters on your screen display. The chapter discusses DOS support for international languages and for alternative time and date stamping.

Understanding the International Features of DOS

T he world is becoming progressively smaller and smaller. Today, frequent contact among people from many different countries is not at all unusual. You can use computers to prepare documents and other files to send to all parts of the world.

Anything you work on that has international implications can cause some inconvenience for you if you do not adapt your computer to handle various languages and national customs. Presumably, most people reading this book and using MS-DOS 6.0 as their operating system live in the United States and have computers that are built to operate in the United States. Fortunately, however, Microsoft has built in to DOS the capability to internationalize your computer. In fact, MS-DOS 6.0 provides three levels of internationalization. These levels involve the use of COUNTRY.SYS, KEYB.COM, and the feature known as *code page switching*.

You may consider your standard version of DOS as perfect for most uses. Suppose, however, that you must use a certain national format for expressing time, the date, and currency symbols. You can learn how to access these formats by reading this chapter and understanding the use of the COUNTRY.SYS configuration driver.

In Chapter 19, "Understanding ANSI.SYS," you learned how to reassign keyboard characters to any of the 256 available ASCII characters. In this chapter, you learn how to use the KEYB command to change keyboard-produced characters to those from another country or language.

You also learn how to change your system's default character set to that of another country. This procedure is called *code page switching*. (A *code page* is a complete national language character set.) With this feature of DOS, you can type on your keyboard, display on-screen, and—with the proper printer—print characters from other languages.

MS-DOS supports 24 national languages or country customs. Each country or language is identified by a country code that corresponds to the code given by international convention for telephone usage. Table 20.1 lists the countries and languages supported by DOS and their country codes. These country codes are referenced throughout this chapter.

Table 20.1 DOS-Supported Country Codes

Code	Country
001	USA
002	Canadian-French
003	Latin America
031	Netherlands
032	Belgium
033	France
034	Spain
036	Hungary
038	Croatia
038	Serbia/Yugoslavia
038	Slovenia
039	Italy
041	Switzerland (French)
041	Switzerland (German)
042	Czech Republic
042	Slovakia
044	United Kingdom

Code	Country
045	Denmark
046	Sweden
047	Norway
048	Poland
049	Germany
055	Brazil
061	International English
351	Portugal
358	Finland

NOTE When you use the country code or the code page number, you must use all three digits, including any leading zeros.

In addition to the American standard version that you can customize for the supported country codes, Microsoft produces special language versions in Arabic, Chinese, Israeli, Japanese, Korean, and Taiwanese.

Understanding COUNTRY.SYS

COUNTRY.SYS is a configuration file that you can use to display alternate currency, date, and time formats on your system without using other language characters. This file contains all the conventions for the supported countries and national formats. Of course, if you have no need to change the default formats for your version of MS-DOS 6.0, you have no need to use COUNTRY.SYS.

When you perform a disk directory command (DIR), the date and time stamps for disk files are displayed in the current national format. In the United States, the system date is normally displayed and stamped on files as MM-DD-YY. You can use alternate methods such as YY-MM-DD (French Canadian) or DD/MM/YY (United Kingdom), among others.

Time formats alternate between using colons to separate hours, minutes, seconds, and hundredths of a second (HH:MM:SS:HS, for example) and periods or commas (HH.MM.SS.HS and HH:MM:SS,HS, for example).

In addition to the variety of currency symbols, such as $, and £, differing customs dictate whether the decimal characters are periods (.) or commas (,)—likewise for the thousands separator. The placement of the currency symbol also can vary. In the United States, the dollar sign ($) precedes the amount, but some currency symbols are placed after the amount.

 NOTE COUNTRY.SYS contains information only for the video display and nothing for keyboards. To provide keyboard support, you must use the KEYB command in your AUTOEXEC.BAT file or from the DOS prompt. For more information, see the next section, "Understanding KEYB.COM."

You load COUNTRY.SYS by entering the COUNTRY command in the CONFIG.SYS file. Use the MS-DOS 6.0 text editor EDIT to enter a statement into the file. Enter the command in the following format:

COUNTRY=xxx,*yyy,C:\DOS\COUNTRY.SYS*

You must place the three-character numeric country code (refer to table 20.1) as the first parameter, as indicated by *xxx* in the example statements. You cannot omit this code.

The second parameter is the code page number for the country, as represented by the *yyy*. If you omit this code, DOS uses the default code page number for the country specified by the country code. See table 20.5 for specific country code page numbers.

NOTE The inclusion of the code page in the COUNTRY command is optional, even if you install code page switching. Make sure to include the code page, however, if you want an alternate code page—rather than the default code page—to be installed for the indicated country.

If the file COUNTRY.SYS is not located in the root directory of the boot drive, normally C:\, include the drive and directory location in the file specification. If you do not specify the second parameter (*yyy*), you still must include the second comma when you include the file specification, as in the following example:

COUNTRY=xxx,,*C:\DOS\COUNTRY.SYS*

NOTE The international country code is not the same code number as the country code page number. Table 20.1 lists supported country codes. Table 20.5 lists the supported country code page codes.

The default statement for the USA version is shown in the following:

COUNTRY=001

or

COUNTRY=001,,C:\DOS\COUNTRY.SYS

Figure 20.1 shows a standard directory listing that uses the American country code formats for the date (MM-DD-YY) and time (12-hour format with A.M./P.M. indicator).

```
Volume in drive C is DSK1_DRUC
Volume Serial Number is 11DA-3B69
Directory of C:\

C-ROOT        <DIR>      02-10-93    2:52p
CHAMPION      <DIR>      02-10-93    3:09p
CHAMPSTA      <DIR>      02-10-93    3:09p
COLLAGE       <DIR>      02-11-93    6:46p
DBASE         <DIR>      02-10-93    3:09p
DOS           <DIR>      02-10-93    1:58p
JOBCST        <DIR>      02-10-93    3:09p
TAPE          <DIR>      02-10-93    2:44p
TEMP          <DIR>      02-10-93    1:58p
UTILS         <DIR>      02-11-93    1:50p
WINA20     386      9349 01-28-93    6:00a
AUTOEXEC   BAT        58 02-11-93    1:47p
DATA       BAT        16 01-27-93    1:39p
NEWDISK    BAT       111 02-10-93    8:33p
COMMAND    COM     52841 01-28-93    6:00a
BEFSETUP   MSD     13996 02-10-93    5:28p
CONFIG     SYS       207 02-11-93    1:51p
        17 file(s)       76578 bytes
                     179462144 bytes free

C:\>
```

Fig. 20.1

Displaying a directory in the U.S. country code format.

If you want to use the United Kingdom currency, date, and time formats, use the following statement in your CONFIG.SYS:

COUNTRY=044,,C:\DOS\COUNTRY.SYS

After you use EDIT to modify your CONFIG.SYS file to contain this statement, save the file to disk and exit the editor. Then reboot your computer so that your change takes effect. When you next execute the DIR command, a directory listing shows the new format (see fig. 20.2).

Notice that the date format has changed to DD/MM/YY, and the time is displayed in 24-hour format.

```
Volume in drive C is DSK1_DRVC
Volume Serial Number is 11DA-3B69
Directory of C:\

C-ROOT        <DIR>     10/02/93    14:52
CHAMPION      <DIR>     10/02/93    15:09
CHAMPSTA      <DIR>     10/02/93    15:09
COLLAGE       <DIR>     11/02/93    18:46
DBASE         <DIR>     10/02/93    15:09
DOS           <DIR>     10/02/93    13:58
JOBCST        <DIR>     10/02/93    15:09
TAPE          <DIR>     10/02/93    14:44
TEMP          <DIR>     10/02/93    13:58
UTILS         <DIR>     11/02/93    13:50
WINA20   386       9349 28/01/93     6:00
AUTOEXEC BAT         58 11/02/93    13:47
DATA     BAT         16 27/01/93    13:39
NEWDISK  BAT        111 10/02/93    20:33
COMMAND  COM      52841 28/01/93     6:00
BEFSETUP MSD      13996 10/02/93    17:28
CONFIG   SYS        203 11/02/93    18:53
        17 file(s)        76574 bytes
                      179445760 bytes free

C:\>
```

Fig. 20.2

A directory in the country code format for the United Kingdom.

For Related Information

◄◄ "Understanding CONFIG.SYS," p. 630.

◄◄ "Understanding Device Drivers," p. 632.

Understanding KEYB.COM

Where the COUNTRY.SYS driver provides nondefault formats on the display screen, KEYB.COM provides compatible keyboard characters for the selected nationality. Table 20.2 lists the supported international keyboard codes.

Table 20.2 International Keyboard Codes

Code	Country
be	Belgium
br	Brazil
cf	Canadian French
cz	Czech Republic
dk	Denmark
fr	France

Code	Country
gr	Germany
hu	Hungary
it	Italy
la	Latin America
nl	Netherlands
no	Norway
pl	Poland
po	Portugal
sf	Switzerland (French)
sg	Switzerland (German)
sl	Slovakia
sp	Spain
su	Finland
sv	Sweden
uk	United Kingdom
us	USA
yu	Yugoslavia/Slovenia/Serbia

You normally place KEYB.COM in the AUTOEXEC.BAT file, although you can type the command at the DOS prompt. You also can load KEYB.COM through the CONFIG.SYS file when you use the command INSTALL=.

NOTE You can use the KEYB command even if you have not installed any country codes through COUNTRY.SYS.

Make sure that you have your DOS subdirectory (normally C:\DOS) in your system's search path. Then you do not need to specify the location of KEYB.COM unless you install the utility in the CONFIG.SYS file. The format of this command is shown in the following:

KEYB *xx,yyy,C:\DOS\KEYBOARD.SYS /E /ID:nnn*

The *xx* parameter is the two-letter code for the country or language (refer to table 20.2). The *yyy* parameter is the code page number, if used.

You also can add two options to the KEYB command: /E and /ID. Use /E to tell DOS that you are using an enhanced keyboard (101- or 102-key style) on a computer with an Intel 8086 or compatible processor. The second switch, /ID, tells DOS which keyboard you are physically using. You can use one of 20 keyboards especially designed for the supported countries. Three of those countries—France, Italy, and the United Kingdom—have two keyboard layouts available. Table 20.3 lists the countries with the alternate keyboards and the ID numbers you can use with KEYB.

Table 20.3 Alternate Keyboard Identification	
Country	**Keyboard ID**
France	120,189
Italy	141,142
United Kingdom	166,168

If you set your system to one of these three countries with COUNTRY.SYS and KEYB.COM and you use an alternate keyboard, you may find it useful to add the /ID:*nnn* switch to the KEYB command line, where *nnn* is one of the three-digit ID numbers, in order to make your keyboard work properly. This parameter is only valid with one of the 3 countries in table 20.3 and the listed ID numbers.

If you want to specify the code page to be used, you include it in the command line for KEYB. If the KEYBOARD.SYS file is not located in the root directory of the boot drive, you must include that file specification together with its path. The path is normally C:\DOS. If you include the location and name of KEYBOARD.SYS, you must include the second comma (KEYB xx,,C:\DOS\KEYBOARD.SYS) to hold the place for the code page parameter, even if you do not include the code page number.

If you enter the command KEYB without any parameters or switches and you have not yet installed the keyboard utility, DOS responds with the following message:

```
KEYB has not been installed

Active code page not available from CON device
```

At the DOS prompt, type **KEYB UK** and press Enter to load KEYB with the character set used for the United Kingdom. Again type **KEYB** and press Enter. DOS displays the following message:

```
Current keyboard code: UK  code page: 437

Active code page not available from CON device
```

As you can see, DOS assumes the default code page number for the United Kingdom, 437. Because at this point you are not concerned with code page switching, you can ignore the code page message. Later in this chapter (in the section "Understanding Code Page Switching"), this subject is discussed.

To install KEYB when MS-DOS boots and processes the CONFIG.SYS file, use the following format:

INSTALL=C:\DOS\KEYB.COM *xx,yyy,C:\DOS\KEYBOARD.SYS*

Because your system search path has not yet been set, you must include the location of the utility. You also must include the full name and extension of the program (C:\DOS\KEYB.COM) before continuing with the parameters for KEYB.

> DOS provides a way of switching between your hardware default keyboard layout and the layout you loaded with KEYB.COM. Press Ctrl-Alt-F1 (hold down the Ctrl and Alt keys and at the same time press F1) to switch to the USA keyboard layout. Press Ctrl-Alt-F2 to return to the keyboard layout installed with KEYB.

T I P

For Related Information

◄◄ "Understanding the AUTOEXEC.BAT File," p. 551.

FROM HERE...

Considering Keyboard Remappings

When you change the default country and keyboard codes on your computer system, you find that certain keys no longer work as labeled. The following information pertains to standard U.S. keyboards, but changing the country code also may affect systems with national keyboards.

Continuing with the previous examples for COUNTRY.SYS and KEYB.COM, set the country and keyboard codes to 044 and UK for the United Kingdom. Your CONFIG.SYS file should contain the following statement:

COUNTRY=044,,C:\DOS\COUNTRY.SYS

If necessary, reboot your computer so that this command takes effect. Then in your AUTOEXEC.BAT file or at the DOS prompt, type the following command and press Enter:

KEYB UK,,C:\DOS\KEYBOARD.SYS

After your system reboots and KEYB is installed, press the backslash key (\). Notice that instead of displaying the backslash character your system displays a pound sign, #. Pressing the pound sign key (Shift-3) produces the British currency symbol £. A few other key remappings occur when you use the United Kingdom country and keyboard codes on a standard American keyboard with the American default version of MS-DOS 6.0. Table 20.4 lists the remappings for this configuration.

Table 20.4 Remappings for the United Kingdom on a USA Keyboard

Standard Character	Remapped Character
~	⌐
@	"
#	£
|	~
\	#
"	@

T I P   If you require extensive use of an alternate language keyboard, you can save yourself the problem of remembering the key changes. Print the changed characters on address or disk labels, cut out the characters, and paste them to your keyboard in the remapped positions.

> **T I P**
>
> Because you lose the backslash key (\) with this remapping of your keyboard, you may have trouble working with subdirectories. To enter the backslash character, hold down the Alt key and, using the numeric keypad on the right side of your keyboard, type the numbers 9 and 2. You also can press Ctrl-Alt-F1 to switch to the USA layout and Ctrl-Alt-F2 to return to the country format you installed.

Understanding Code Page Switching

Certain areas of memory in your system store the character tables for your video screen and your keyboard. By switching tables, you can configure MS-DOS 6.0 to use alternate character tables to suit your national language and customs. These tables are called *code pages*.

NOTE Changing the character set used in your computer to support another language through code page switching does not change the language that DOS uses. All messages are displayed in the default (English) language in which DOS was written. No translation is made.

You can set your system to use an alternate code page permanently, or you can enable several code pages in memory and switch between them from the command line. These code pages are software prepared; your system's hardware is not changed. Your system already has a built-in hardware code page.

In the earlier section that discussed COUNTRY.SYS, you learned that each country or area of the world has a unique country code number borrowed from the international telephone convention. Each country or group of countries also has a code page number. (Many countries share a code page number with another country.) Table 20.5 lists the six code pages supported by MS-DOS 6.0.

Table 20.5 DOS-Supported National Code Pages	
Code	**Country/Language**
437	United States
850	Multilingual (Latin I)
852	Slavic (Latin II)
860	Portuguese
863	Canadian French
865	Nordic

Each DOS-supported code page includes support for several languages. This feature may simplify international communications so that documents prepared with the same character table may be processed by people in different countries using different languages, with all characters appearing the same to all concerned.

The international code page, code 850, has some graphic limitations in order to provide room for additional language characters required by some countries. A total of only 256 codes are available. If you normally use the USA code page, 437, for example, you may find that boxes under 850 lose their graphic corners and are replaced with other characters.

 NOTE When you install alternate code pages in your computer, the normal typewriter keys and their ASCII display characters do not change. Symbol keys are remapped, and by using special keystrokes, you can enter national language characters with your keyboard.

Checking Your Hardware for Code Page Switching

You do need the proper hardware to utilize software code page switching. All code page information required for loading alternate character sets is contained in disk files with the extension CPI. Two screen device code page information files are supplied with DOS. EGA.CPI provides support for EGA and VGA displays, and LCD.CPI provides support for LCD screens. You must have an EGA, VGA, or LCD video display. Hercules-type monographic and CGA screens do not support this feature.

NOTE The files LCD.CPI, 4201.CPI, 4208.CPI, and 5202.CPI as well as PRINTER.SYS are no longer automatically supplied as part of MS-DOS 6.0. However, these files and others are available from Microsoft on a Supplemental Diskette. Call or write Microsoft to request this disk or download the information from CompuServe, MSDOS6 forum.

If you have an EGA or a VGA screen, you can have up to six software code pages. If you have an LCD display, you can have only one software code page. If you have a monographic or CGA video adapter and monitor, you can utilize only the built-in hardware code page.

Certain printers and 100 percent compatibles also support code page switching. Three code page information files are provided with MS-DOS 6.0: 4201.CPI, 4208.CPI, and 5202.CPI. Table 20.6 lists the printers supported by these files. Even if your printer emulates one of these printers, it also must have the capability of accepting code page switching. (Some printers provide emulation but not code page support.)

Table 20.6 National Code Page Printer Files

Printer	Code Page File
IBM Proprinter II, III	4201.CPI
IBM Proprinter XL	4201.CPI
IBM Proprinter X24E	4208.CPI
IBM Proprinter XL24E	4208.CPI
IBM Quietwriter III	5202.CPI

Installing Code Page Switching

Assuming that you have the appropriate hardware, you need to take a number of steps and load programs to enable code page switching, both for your video screen and for your printer. (You use MS-DOS EDIT to make the changes you must make to both the CONFIG.SYS file and the AUTOEXEC.BAT file.)

To enable code page switching for your video display, you add to the CONFIG.SYS file a statement for the DISPLAY.SYS device driver. To enable code page switching for your printer, you add a statement for the PRINTER.SYS device driver. If you want code page switching enabled for both devices, you simply include both statements. (You also must use the COUNTRY.SYS device driver to handle the screen formats for currency, the date, and the time.) Then, to provide the national language support, you add the NLSFUNC.EXE command to your AUTOEXEC.BAT file.

The following sections explain in detail how you set up code page switching on your system, including how to use DISPLAY.SYS, PRINTER.SYS, and NLSFUNC.EXE to enable the feature; how to use MODE PREPARE to load the code page tables; and how to use CHCP and MODE SELECT to switch the code page.

Using DISPLAY.SYS

Use the device driver DISPLAY.SYS to enable code page switching for your video display. You can use DISPLAY.SYS only if you have an EGA, VGA, or LCD monitor and adapter.

The format of the command is shown in the following:

DEVICE=C:\DOS\DISPLAY.SYS CON=(monitor,_hardware,xx_**)**

or

DEVICE=C:\DOS\DISPLAY.SYS CON=(monitor,_hardware,_
_(xx,yy)_**)**

NOTE   You can also use the DEVICEHIGH= command.

Unless you move the DISPLAY.SYS file to the root directory of your boot drive, you must specify the location of the file, normally C:\DOS. Enter the monitor type as the first parameter for the CONsole device (monitor). EGA is the typical **monitor** entry and stands for both EGA and VGA monitors. Use LCD for LCD screens. No other values are possible.

The second parameter, _hardware_, refers to the built-in hardware code page. In the U.S., this code page is 437, but do not specify it if you are not certain of your system.

The variable _xx_ refers to the number of code pages you want enabled in your system. This parameter tells DOS to set aside memory for the number of additional character tables to be installed in the AUTOEXEC.BAT file or at the DOS prompt.

Enter a number for the variable _yy_ to represent the number of subfonts you want. You can specify the number of fonts that DOS should store in memory. The number of subfonts available for EGA/VGA displays is two, and only one is available for LCD displays. Normally all are stored;

however, you can lower the number stored and, thus, reduce the amount of memory used. If you use this variable, you must place a pair of parentheses around the number of code pages and the number of fonts, as shown in the second example.

To enable code page switching for your display for French Canada and also to allow for the use of the international code, for example, enter the following statement in your CONFIG.SYS file:

DEVICE=C:\DOS\DISPLAY.SYS CON=(EGA,,2)

No default hardware code page is declared, and DOS is instructed to set aside memory for two code pages for an EGA or VGA adapter and monitor. Do not omit the commas.

You can specify up to six code page tables to be prepared in memory in addition to the hardware code page. Just remember that code pages take up RAM and may lower the amount of conventional memory available for your applications. Do not set aside more memory than is required. Each code page takes up 5,632 bytes of RAM for EGA/VGA.

Using PRINTER.SYS

Use the device driver PRINTER.SYS to enable code page switching for your printer if you have one of the supported printers or a compatible. A supported printer can be attached to any or all of the three allowed parallel printer ports: LPT1, LPT2, or LPT3.

The format of the command is shown in the following:

DEVICE=C:\DOS\PRINTER.SYS LPTx=(printer,*hardware,yy***)**

Unless you move the PRINTER.SYS file to the root directory of your boot drive, you must specify the location of the file, normally C:\DOS. Replace the *x* with the proper parallel port number: 1, 2, or 3.

Replace **printer** with 4201, 4208, or 5202, whichever is appropriate for your printer. The next parameter, *hardware*, refers to the built-in hardware code page. In the U.S., this code page is 437, but do not specify it if you are not certain of your printer.

The variable *yy* refers to the number of additional code pages that your hardware can support and you want prepared. This parameter tells DOS to set aside memory for the number of additional character tables to be installed in the AUTOEXEC.BAT file or at the DOS prompt.

To instruct DOS to set aside memory for two code pages for an IBM Quietwriter III or compatible printer attached to LPT1, for example, enter the following statement in your CONFIG.SYS file:

DEVICE=C:\DOS\PRINTER.SYS LPT1=(5202,,2)

No default hardware code page is declared.

You can specify up to six code page tables to be prepared in memory. The maximum, however, depends on the printer you are using. Do not set aside more memory than is required because these tables consume memory.

 NOTE To enable code page switching on your printer, make sure that your printer is turned on and on-line when your system is booted. Otherwise, the control signals cannot be downloaded into the printer.

Using NLSFUNC.EXE

After you take care of the required statements in your CONFIG.SYS file for COUNTRY.SYS and DISPLAY.SYS, move your attention to the AUTOEXEC.BAT file. As discussed in this chapter's section "Understanding KEYB.COM" make sure that your keyboard is specified for the appropriate national keyboard and code page number. The following command, for example, specifies code page 863 for French Canada:

KEYB cf,863,C:\DOS\KEYBOARD.SYS

You then must include NLSFUNC as the next command to provide the National Language Support (NLS) for code page switching. You can type this command at the DOS prompt or place the command in your AUTOEXEC.BAT or CONFIG.SYS file for automatic loading whenever you boot your computer. To enter the NLSFUNC command in your CONFIG.SYS file, use the following format:

INSTALL=C:\DOS\NLSFUNC.EXE

Because a path has not yet been established when the command is in your CONFIG.SYS file, you must specify the location of the NLSFUNC file.

Up to this point, you have specified your country code of choice and have prepared your system to utilize code page switching. The following sections explain how to use the commands that load the specified code pages into the prepared memory areas.

Loading the Code Page Tables

You include the MODE command in the AUTOEXEC.BAT file to load code page information, specifying the code pages to be prepared and the code page file to use for the tables. Use MODE CON: to load the code page information for your video display, the console. Use MODE LPT1: to load the code page information for your printer and to download the information to the printer. (Make sure that your printer is turned on and is on-line to receive the downloaded data.)

In the command, you can list as many code pages as you specified in the CONFIG.SYS file as additional code pages to be used. Do not specify the hardware default code page number because this table is already built in. The format of the command is shown in the following (the parentheses are required):

MODE device CP PREPARE=((xxx,yyy) filename)

device indicates that you want to load a character set into your console, keyboard, or parallel printers.

xxx and **yyy** indicate the code page numbers to be prepared.

filename refers to the CPI file where the table is stored on disk for the device.

Consider the following example:

MODE CON: CP PREPARE=((863,850) C:\DOS\EGA.CPI)

In this command, MODE is used to PREPARE (or PREP) the console (CON:) for code pages (CP), with code pages 863 for French Canada and the international 850. EGA.CPI is listed as the table file for EGA and VGA monitors. The location of this file is in the C:\DOS subdirectory.

For your printer, use the MODE command for each parallel printer port listed in the CONFIG.SYS file's PRINTER.SYS statement. The following examples prepare the printers at the LPT1 and LPT2 ports:

MODE LPT1: CP PREP=((863,850) C:\DOS\5202.CPI)

MODE LPT2: CP PREP=((863,850) C:\DOS\4201.CPI)

As with the other AUTOEXEC.BAT commands for code page switching, you also can enter the MODE commands at the DOS prompt.

Switching the Code Page

After you complete all the preparation work—specifying the nationality and code page codes to be used, setting aside the memory for the language tables, and loading the character tables—you are ready to use the new code pages.

In the previous examples, you prepared your system to use the French Canada character set. To have this character set take effect, you must issue the CHCP command, for *CH*anging the *C*ode *P*age. Type **CHCP**, press the space bar, type the code page number, and press Enter, as shown in the following:

CHCP 863

Enter this command in your AUTOEXEC.BAT file or at the DOS prompt. The instruction tells DOS to change the current code page to the new code page specified in the command on all devices prepared, including the printer if you have included it in the CONFIG.SYS and AUTOEXEC.BAT files. Make certain that the printer is turned on and is on-line so that the new code page can take effect.

You also can selectively change code pages of individual devices by using the MODE SELECT command and pressing Enter. The full format of the command is shown in the following:

MODE device CODEPAGE SELECT = xxx

For **device**, use CON for console; PRN, which is the same as LPT1; or LPT*y*, where *y* is 1, 2, or 3. After the equal sign (=), enter the code page number (**xxx**).

NOTE   You can abbreviate CODEPAGE as CP and SELECT as SEL.

Suppose, for example, that you want to change the code page in your IBM Quietwriter III printer, but you don't want to affect the monitor display. If your printer is attached to LPT1 and you want to print with the French Canada character set, issue the following command and press Enter:

MODE LPT1 CP SEL=863

Exploring More Uses for MODE and CODEPAGE

To ascertain the currently active code page for any device, issue the following command and press Enter:

MODE device CODEPAGE */STATUS*

This command works the same with or without the /STATUS option on the command tail. DOS returns the status of the active and all prepared code pages for the specified device, including the hardware code page, as shown in figure 20.3.

```
C:\>MODE CON CODEPAGE /STATUS

Active code page for device CON is 863
Hardware code pages:
    code page 437
Prepared code pages:
    code page 863
    code page 850

MODE status code page function completed

C:\>
```

Fig. 20.3

Viewing the code
page status.

To check the code page for the display monitor, for example, type this
command at the DOS prompt and press Enter:

MODE CON CP

At times, you may need to refresh the code page for a particular device,
especially code page printers. The printers do not store the code page
fonts when they are turned off and on again. Also, use the following
command if the printer was not turned on and on-line when you enabled code page switching on the printer:

MODE device CODEPAGE REFRESH

NOTE   You can abbreviate CODEPAGE as CP and REFRESH as REF.

To refresh the code page for the printer hooked up to LPT1, for
example, type the following command at the DOS prompt and
press Enter:

MODE LPT1 CP REF

If you issue a code page command for your printer through CHCP,
MODE SELECT, or MODE REFRESH, and your printer does not accept
code pages or is not turned on and on-line, an error message appears
when you try to print. You may notice a delay before receiving the
error message, depending on the length of the time-out period.

Using Dead Keys To Cope with the Changed Keyboard

When you tell DOS to use a different keyboard or character set, your keyboard keys produce different results. In addition to the remapped keyboard, a new device enables you to enter special language characters. This device is called a *dead key*.

Normally when you type an alphabetic character on your keyboard, the letter appears without any accents. The use of a dead key enables you to enter an acute accent (´), a grave accent (`), or a circumflex accent (^) with certain vowels and other keys. These marks are used in certain languages but are not provided on a standard American keyboard.

When you press the dead key, nothing appears on-screen. When you press the next appropriate letter key, the accented character appears. If you press an inappropriate key, DOS beeps and displays nothing.

Table 20.7 lists the keys on the U.S. keyboard that are remapped when you enable code page 863 (for French Canada).

Table 20.7 Language Support for French Canada on U.S. Keyboard	
Standard Character	**Remapped Character**
'	#
~	|
@	"
#	/
^	?
\	<
|	>
/	e´
?	E´

Table 20.8 lists the dead key keyboard mappings for French Canada.

Table 20.8 French Canada Language Support Using Dead Keys

Dead Key	Standard Character	Remapped Character
]	c	ç
Shift-]	C	Ç
Shift-]	e	ë
Shift-]	i	ï
Shift-]	u	ü
Shift-]	E	Ë
Shift-]	I	Ï
Shift-]	U	Ü
[	a	â
[	e	ê
[	i	î
[	o	ô
[	u	û
Shift-[	A	Á
Shift-[	E	Ê
Shift-[	I	Î
Shift-[	O	Ô
Shift-[	U	Û
'	a	à
'	e	è
'	u	ù
'	A	À
'	E	È
'	U	Ù
'	'	`

For other national languages on a U.S. or other keyboard, a little testing should give you the ability to use the language-specific characters that you may require. The four keys you should test as dead keys are the apostrophe ('), question mark (?), left square bracket ([), and right square bracket (]).

As an alternative to using code page switching to access special language-specific characters, you can load the support for the required language table with the KEYB command and then use the Alt-*nnn* technique. The *nnn* stands for the ASCII code for the specific character and is typed on the numeric keypad of your keyboard (not on the numbers above the typewriter keys of your keyboard).

FROM HERE...

For Related Information

◄◄ "Optimizing Your Computer's Memory," p. 639.

Chapter Summary

In this chapter, you learned how you can customize your computer system with national language support. This chapter included the following important points:

- You use COUNTRY.SYS to provide national formats for currency, the date, and the time.

- You use KEYB.COM to nationalize your keyboard for certain characters. You can load this command in the AUTOEXEC.BAT file, the CONFIG.SYS file, or at the DOS prompt.

- You enable code page switching to utilize foreign language character sets on your EGA, VGA, or LCD monitor, your keyboard, and a supported printer.

- You can place the device driver COUNTRY.SYS in your CONFIG.SYS file with the international country code and may include the appropriate code page number.

- To enable code page switching, you first must set aside memory for the language tables by using DISPLAY.SYS and PRINTER.SYS statements in the CONFIG.SYS file. Then you enter the command to enable national language support, NLSFUNC, specifying the COUNTRY.SYS file.

- To load the code page tables, you use the MODE device CODEPAGE PREPARE command, once for your video display and once for your printer.

- You use the new language character set by issuing the CHCP command for the appropriate code page number or by selectively using the MODE device CODEPAGE SELECT command.

Command Reference

DOS 6.0 provides extensive on-line help in three forms:

- The HELP command (described later in this Command Reference) provides syntax, notes, and examples for all DOS commands.

- Every DOS command supports the /? switch, which provides a short description of the command and its syntax.

- The FASTHELP command (described later in this Command Reference) provides the same short description and syntax for every DOS command as the /? switch.

The commands in this reference are divided into three groups: Batch Commands, Configuration Commands, and DOS Utilities Commands. The commands are listed alphabetically within each group.

Batch Commands

Batch Command   V1, V2, V3, V4, V5, V6-Internal

Executes one or more commands contained in an ASCII disk file that has a BAT extension.

Syntax

> *dc:pathc***filename** *parameters*

dc: is the disk drive that holds the batch file.

pathc is the path to the batch file.

filename is the root name of the batch file.

parameters are the parameters to be used by the batch file.

Reference

See Chapter 15, "Understanding Batch Files, DOSKey, and Macros."

Rules for Batch Files

1. A batch file must use the extension BAT.

2. To invoke a batch file, simply type the root name. To invoke the batch file OFTEN.BAT, for example, type **OFTEN** and press Enter.

3. DOS executes each command one line at a time. The specified parameters are substituted for the markers when the command is used.

4. DOS recognizes a maximum of 10 parameters. You can use the SHIFT subcommand to get around this limitation.

5. You can stop a running batch file by pressing Ctrl-Break. DOS displays the following message:

```
Terminate batch job (Y/N)?
```

If you type **Y**, DOS ignores all subsequent commands, and the system prompt appears. If you type **N**, DOS skips the current command but continues to process the other commands in the file.

6. You can make DOS execute a second batch file immediately after the first by typing the name of the second batch file as the last command in the first file. You also can execute a second batch file within the first and return to the first file by using the CALL subcommand.

Rules for the AUTOEXEC.BAT File

1. AUTOEXEC.BAT must reside in the boot disk's root directory.

2. DOS, when booted, automatically executes the AUTOEXEC.BAT file.

   DOS 6.0 does not execute AUTOEXEC.BAT (or CONFIG.SYS) if you press F5 or hold down the Shift key when the Starting MS-DOS… message appears during the boot process. You also can skip executing AUTOEXEC.BAT if you press F8 when the Starting MS-DOS… message appears, and then type **N** in response to the message Process AUTOEXEC.BAT [Y,N]?.

3. When DOS executes the AUTOEXEC.BAT file after the computer boots, the system does not automatically request date and time. You must place DATE and TIME commands in the AUTOEXEC.BAT file to change the system date and time.

Rules for Creating Batch Files

1. A batch file contains ASCII text.

2. You can include any valid DOS system-level command.

3. You can enter any valid batch subcommand. (The batch subcommands are included in this Command Reference.) You also can use replaceable parameters (%0–9%). You can use environmental variables by enclosing the name of the variable in percent signs (for example, %COMSPEC%).

4. To designate a file name that contains a percent symbol, type the percent symbol twice. To use a file called A100%.TXT, for example, you type **A100%%.TXT**. This rule differs from the one for parameter markers, in which percent symbols precede the parameter markers, and from the rule for environmental variables, which are enclosed in percent symbols.

5. Beginning with DOS 3.3, you can prevent the display of any line from the batch file by typing @ as the first character in the line.

CALL   V3.3, V4, V5, V6-Internal

Runs a second batch file and returns control to the first batch file.

Syntax

CALL *dc:pathc***filename** *parameters*

dc: is the disk drive that holds the called batch file.

pathc is the path to the called batch file.

filename is the root name of the called batch file.

parameters are the parameters to be used by the batch file.

Reference

See Chapter 15, "Understanding Batch Files, DOSKey, and Macros."

Rule

DOS runs the named batch file as though you invoked the file from the keyboard. Parameters are passed to the called batch file as though you used the keyboard.

Notes

You can duplicate this procedure in versions of DOS before 3.3 by using COMMAND in the following format:

COMMAND /C *dc:pathc***filename** *parameters*

filename is the root name of the second batch file.

Do not use pipes (|) and redirection symbols (<<, <, >, and >>) with CALL.

A batch file can call itself; however, to avoid recursion, such a file needs to explicitly end, for example, by including an EXIT command or by instructing the user to press Ctrl-Break.

CHOICE   V6-External

Suspends batch file processing and prompts the user to make a choice before processing resumes.

Syntax

> dc:pathc**CHOICE** /C:keys /N /S /T:c,ss text

dc: is the disk drive that holds the called batch file.

pathc is the path to the called batch file.

text, which is displayed just before the "prompt" of the keys the user can press, tells the user about the choice that has to be made. Quotation marks (") may be used around *text* but do not have to be used unless *text* contains a switch character (/) or a trailing blank.

Switches

/C:keys   Specifies the keys that will be displayed in the prompt. The colon (:) is optional. If /C is not specified, CHOICE acts as though you specified /C:YN.

/N   Suppresses the prompt (see below).

/S   Enables case sensitivity for the *keys*. That is, if /S is specified, the uppercase key represents a different response from the lowercase key. If /S is not specified, the uppercase key is the same as the lowercase key.

/T:c,ss   Specifies a default key and the number of seconds to wait for the user to press a key before the default is used. The colon (:) is optional. *C* must be one of the keys specified by */C:keys*. *ss* must be from 0 to 99 (0 means no pause before *c* is used).

Reference

See Chapter 15, "Understanding Batch Files, DOSKey, and Macros."

Rules

1. When a CHOICE command is executed, the user sees the command's *text*, followed by a prompt. The prompt is a left bracket ([), followed by the first key in */C:keys*, followed by a comma, followed by the other *keys* (separated by commas), followed by a right bracket (]), followed by a question mark (?). /C:YN, for example, produces the prompt [Y,N]?

2. CHOICE returns different values in ERRORLEVEL to the batch file, depending on which of the */C:keys* is pressed in response to the prompt. Pressing the first key returns 1, pressing the second returns 2, and so on.

   If the user presses Ctrl-Break and then does not terminate the batch job, a value of 0 is returned. If DOS detects an error, a value of 255 is returned.

3. If the user presses a key that is not one of */C:keys*, the computer beeps.

Examples

To ask the user whether to continue with the batch file:

CHOICE /C:YN "Yes to continue and No to exit "
IF ERRORLEVEL 2 GOTO EXIT

You see the following:

```
Yes to continue and No to exit [Y,N]?
```

To load the mouse driver from your AUTOEXEC.BAT file unless told otherwise within 3 seconds:

CHOICE /C:YN /T:3,Y "Load the mouse driver "
IF ERRORLEVEL 2 GOTO NOMOUSE

To provide a menu of choices:

@ECHO OFF
CLS
ECHO.
ECHO F First action
ECHO S Second action
ECHO T Third action
ECHO.
CHOICE /C:FST "Choose an action "
IF ERRORLEVEL 255 GOTO ERROR
IF ERRORLEVEL 3 GOTO THIRD

```
IF ERRORLEVEL 2 GOTO SECOND
IF ERRORLEVEL 1 GOTO FIRST

:ERROR
ECHO GOT AN ERROR OR BREAK
GOTO END

:THIRD
ECHO PRESSED T
GOTO END

:SECOND
ECHO PRESSED S
GOTO END

:FIRST
ECHO PRESSED F
GOTO END

:END
```

ECHO   *V2, V3, V4, V5, V6-Internal*

Displays a message, and enables or prevents the display of batch commands and other messages as DOS executes batch subcommands.

Syntax

To display a message, use the following format:

ECHO *message*

message is the text of the message to be displayed on-screen.

To turn off the display of commands and other batch-command messages, use the following format:

ECHO OFF

To turn on the display of commands and messages, use the following format:

ECHO ON

To see the status of ECHO, use the following format:

ECHO

Reference

See Chapter 15, "Understanding Batch Files, DOSKey, and Macros."

Rules

1. For unconditional display of a message on-screen, use the command ECHO MESSAGE. The MESSAGE you designate is displayed whether ECHO is on or off.

2. You cannot display a pipe (|) or redirection character (< or >) when you use ECHO.

3. When ECHO is on, the batch file displays commands as DOS executes each line. The batch file also displays any messages from the batch subcommands.

4. When ECHO is off, the batch file does not display the commands as DOS executes them. Additionally, the batch file displays no messages produced by other batch subcommands. Exceptions to this rule are the Strike a key when ready message (which is generated by the PAUSE subcommand) and any ECHO message command.

5. DOS starts the system with ECHO on.

6. An ECHO OFF command is active until DOS completes batch processing or encounters an ECHO ON command. If one batch file invokes another, ECHO OFF remains in effect until the final batch file is processed.

7. ECHO affects only messages produced by batch subcommands. The command does not affect messages from other DOS commands or programs.

Notes

You can suppress the display of a single batch file line by typing @ as the first character in a line. When you type the line **@ECHO OFF**, for example, the command ECHO OFF is not displayed.

To display a blank line of the screen, type **ECHO.** (Do not use a space between the O and the period.)

To suppress the output of a command, use I/O redirection to the null device (NUL). To suppress a copied-file message when you are using COPY, for example, use the following format:

COPY file1.ext file2.ext >NUL

The command output is sent to the null device and is not displayed on the screen.

FOR..IN..DO

V2, V3, V4, V5, V6-Internal

Enables iterative (repeated) processing of a DOS command.

Syntax

Used in a batch program, the syntax is as follows:

FOR %%*variable* **IN (***set***) DO** *command*

Used from a command prompt, the syntax is as follows:

FOR %*variable* **IN (***set***) DO** *command*

variable is a single character (except 0 through 9).

set is one or more words or file specifications separated by blanks. The file specification is in the form *d:path\filename.ext*. Wild cards are allowed. The parentheses are required.

command represents the DOS command and command parameters to be performed for each word or file in the set.

Reference

See Chapter 15, "Understanding Batch Files, DOSKey, and Macros."

Rules

1. You can use more than one word or a full file specification in the set. You must use spaces or commas to separate words or file specifications.

2. %%variable becomes each literal word or full file specification in the set. If you use wild-card characters, FOR..IN..DO executes once for each file that matches the wild-card file specification.

3. You can use path names with FOR..IN..DO.

4. You cannot nest FOR..IN..DO subcommands (put two of these commands in the same line). You can use other batch

subcommands with FOR..IN..DO, and you can have a batch file be the command executed by the FOR.

Example

To delete all the temporary files in the current directory:

FOR %%a IN (*.tmp temp????.*) DO del %%a

Note

If you omit IN, parentheses, or DO, or use a variable name that is more than one character long, DOS displays the message Syntax error.

GOTO   V2, V3, V4, V5, V6-Internal

Jumps (transfers control) to the line following the label in the batch file and continues batch-file execution from that line.

Syntax

GOTO label

label is a name of one or more characters, preceded by a colon. When specifying a label on a separate line, precede the label with a colon. Only the first eight characters of the label name are significant. It identifies the next line of a batch file to be executed.

Reference

See Chapter 15, "Understanding Batch Files, DOSKey, and Macros."

Rules

1. The label must be the first item in a line of a batch file and must start with a colon (:).

2. When the command GOTO label is executed, DOS jumps to the line following the label and continues executing the batch file.

3. If a batch file does not contain the label specified by a GOTO, the batch file stops and DOS displays the following message:

Label not found

Note

Adding a colon as the first character of a line in a batch file *comments out* the line by causing DOS to treat it as a label rather than as a line to be executed.

IF   V2, V3, V4, V5, V6-Internal

Enables conditional execution of a DOS command.

Syntax

IF *NOT* condition command

NOT tests for the opposite of the condition (executes the command if the condition is false).

condition is what is being tested. Condition can be one of the following entries:

ERRORLEVEL number	DOS tests the exit code (0 to 255) of the program. If the exit code is greater than or equal to the number, the condition is true.
string1 == string2	DOS compares these two alphanumeric strings to determine whether they are identical. The strings can be literals (which do not require quotation marks), batch variables (for example, %1), and environment variables (for example, %COMSPEC%).
EXIST *d:path***filename**.*ext*	DOS tests whether *d:path* **\filename**.*ext* is in the specified drive or path (if you provide a drive name or path name) or is in the current drive and directory.

command is any valid DOS batch file command.

Reference

See Chapter 15, "Understanding Batch Files, DOSKey, and Macros."

Rules

1. For the IF subcommand, if **condition** is true, **command** is executed. If **condition** is false, DOS skips **command** and immediately executes the next line of the batch file.

2. For the IF NOT subcommand, if **condition** is false, **command** is executed. If **condition** is true, DOS skips **command** and immediately executes the next line of the batch file.

3. The only DOS commands that produce exit codes are BACKUP, CHOICE, CHKDSK, DEFRAG, DELTREE, DISKCOMP, DISKCOPY, FIND, FORMAT, GRAFTABL, KEYB, MOVE, MSAV, REPLACE, RESTORE, SETVER, and XCOPY. Using an ERRORLEVEL condition with a program that does not leave an exit code is meaningless.

4. For **string1** == **string2**, DOS makes a literal, character-by-character comparison of the two strings. The comparison is based on the ASCII character set, and uppercase and lowercase letters are distinguished.

5. When you are using **string1** == **string2** with parameter markers (%0 through %9), neither string can be null (empty, or nonexistent). If either string is null, DOS displays the message Syntax error and aborts the batch file.

Note

When testing an ERRORLEVEL number, be sure to test for the highest possible number first. Consider the following example:

```
IF ERRORLEVEL 1 GOTO VALUE 1
IF ERRORLEVEL 2 GOTO VALUE 2
```

This example always goes to value 1, even if an ERRORLEVEL of 2 is returned.

Example

To jump around part of a batch file if the network menu choice was not chosen from a DOS 6.0 multiconfiguration CONFIG.SYS was not a [common]:

IF NOT .%CONFIG%==.NETWORK GOTO FINISH

PAUSE
V1, V2, V3, V4, V5, V6-Internal

Suspends batch-file processing until a key is pressed and (optionally) displays a message.

Syntax

PAUSE

Reference

See Chapter 15, "Understanding Batch Files, DOSKey, and Macros."

Rules

1. If ECHO is on, DOS displays the characters PAUSE and any others that follow PAUSE on the same line. This can be used to give the user information about how they are to respond.

2. Regardless of the ECHO setting, DOS displays the following message:

   Press any key to continue…

   To terminate the batch job rather than continue, press Ctrl-C. DOS displays the message Terminate batch job (Y/N)? Type **Y**.

REM
V1, V2, V3, V4, V5, V6-Internal

Places a comment within a batch file or within the CONFIG.SYS file. DOS ignores lines that begin with REM.

Syntax

REM *message*

message is a string of up to 123 characters that cannot contain pipe (|) or redirection (< or >) characters.

Reference

See Chapter 15, "Understanding Batch Files, DOSKey, and Macros."

Rules

1. REM must be the last batch-file command in the line when used with the subcommands IF or FOR..IN..DO.

2. When DOS encounters a REM subcommand in a batch file, DOS displays the message if ECHO is on. If ECHO is off, DOS does not display the message.

SHIFT   V2, V3, V4, V5, V6-Internal

Shifts command-line parameters one position to the left when a batch file is invoked.

Syntax

SHIFT

Reference

See Chapter 15, "Understanding Batch Files, DOSKey, and Macros."

Rules

1. When you use SHIFT, DOS moves the command-line parameters one position to the left.

2. DOS discards the former first parameter (%0).

3. DOS shifts parameter 10, if it exists, into 9, parameter 11 into parameter 10, and so on.

Configuration Commands

Configuration Commands

V1, V2, V3, V4, V5, V6-Internal

These commands can appear in your CONFIG.SYS file. With several minor and four major exceptions, DOS executes the commands in the order in which they appear in the file. The major exceptions are as follows:

- When your computer is booting and you press F5 or hold down the Shift key immediately after the `Starting MS-DOS...` message appears, all of CONFIG.SYS is skipped.

- When your computer is booting and you press F8 immediately after the `Starting MS-DOS...` message appears, DOS asks which commands you want to be executed.

- If you type a question mark (?) between the command name and the equal sign, DOS asks during the boot whether you want the command to be executed.

- Using a menu, the menu commands described later, and configuration blocks, you can partition CONFIG.SYS into blocks of commands. This procedure enables you to control, during the boot process, which blocks are executed.

See Chapter 17, "Configuring Your Computer," for details.

BREAK

V3, V4, V5, V6-Internal

Determines when DOS looks for a Ctrl-Break or Ctrl-C to stop a program.

Syntax

To turn on BREAK, use the following format:

BREAK = ON

To turn off BREAK, use the following format:

BREAK = OFF

Reference

See Chapter 17, "Configuring Your Computer."

Note

The setting for BREAK in the CONFIG.SYS file works in the same manner as setting BREAK from the DOS prompt.

BUFFERS   *V2, V3, V4, V5, V6-Internal*

Sets the number of disk buffers that DOS sets aside in memory.

Syntax

If you have a DOS version prior to 4.0, use the following format:

BUFFERS = nn

If you have DOS 4.0, use the following format:

BUFFERS = nn,*mm* /X

If you have DOS 5.0, use the following format:

BUFFERS = nn,*mmm*

If you have DOS 6.0, use the following format:

BUFFERS = nn,*mmmm*

nn is the number of buffers to be set, in the range of 1 to 99. If you have DOS 4.0, you can set a maximum 10,000 buffers by using the /X switch.

mm is the number of sectors, from 1 to 8, that can be read or written at a time. The default is 1.

mmm is the number of buffers, from 1 to 8, in the secondary buffer cache. The default is 1.

mmmm is the number of buffers, from 0 to 8, in the secondary buffer cache. The default is 0.

Switch

/X   Uses expanded memory for buffer storage (DOS 4.0 only).

Reference

See Chapter 17, "Configuring Your Computer."

Notes

Do not set more buffers than you need. One buffer occupies 532 bytes, so a setting of 50 buffers requires more than 26K of RAM. You may find that a setting of 15 to 25 is adequate. Many software programs recommend specific buffer settings; set the buffers accordingly.

DOS 5.0 and 6.0 load themselves into HMA. If DOS is in HMA, the buffers also will be placed there. Enough room for approximately 48 buffers exists.

To find out how much RAM is being used for disk buffers, type **MEM /D /P**.

If your computer has an 8086 or 8088 processor, buffers in the secondary cache can speed up certain disk operations. If you have a faster processor, however, using SMARTDRV is a better procedure.

COUNTRY   *V3, V4, V5, V6-Internal*

Instructs DOS to modify the input and display of date, time, and field divider information, the order in which characters are sorted, and which characters can be used in file names to match the formats of different countries.

Syntax

COUNTRY = nnn

If you have DOS 3.3 or a later version, use the following format:

COUNTRY = nnn,*mmm,d:path\filename.ext*

nnn is the country code.

mmm is the code page for the country.

d: is the drive that contains *filenamef.extf.*

path is the path that contains *filenamef.extf.*

filename.ext is the default file that contains the country information (for example, COUNTRY.SYS).

Following is a list of country codes and code pages:

Language	Country Code	Code Pages
Belgium	032	850, 437
Canadian-French	002	863, 850
Croatian	038	852, 850
Czech	042	852, 850
Danish	045	850, 865
(Dutch) Netherlands	031	850, 437
English (International)	061	437, 850
English (U.K.)	044	437, 850
English (U.S.)	001	437, 850
Finnish	358	850, 437
French (France)	033	850, 437
French (Switzerland)	041	850, 437
German (Germany)	049	850, 437
German (Switzerland)	041	850, 437
Hungarian	036	852, 850
Italian	039	850, 437
Latin America	003	850, 437
Norwegian	047	850, 865
Polish	048	852, 850
Portuguese (Brazil)	055	850, 437
Portuguese (Portugal)	351	850, 860
Serbian	038	852, 850
Slovak	042	852, 850

Language	Country Code	Code Pages
Slovenian	038	852, 850
Spanish (Latin American)	003	850, 437
Spanish (Spain)	034	850, 437
Swedish	046	850, 437

References

See Chapter 17, "Configuring Your Computer," and Chapter 20, "Understanding the International Features of DOS."

Rules

1. For a particular country code, you can use only one of the two-page codes in the preceding list. If you use the country code 001 (United States), for example, you can use the code-page code 437 or 850. You cannot use the code-page code 863 (Canadian-French).

2. The default country code is 001 (United States).

3. If you do not specify *d:\path\filenamef.extf*, DOS looks for COUNTRY.SYS in the root directory of your startup drive.

4. You can override *d:\path\filenamef.extf* by issuing the NLSFUNC command.

5. Code pages for the following countries and languages also are available in special versions of DOS: Arabic, Israel, Japan, Korea, People's Republic of China, and Taiwan.

DEVICE   *V2, V3, V4, V5, V6-Internal*

Instructs DOS to load, link, and use a special device driver.

Syntax

DEVICE = *d:path***filename.ext** *options*

d: is the drive where DOS can find the device driver to be used.

path is the DOS path to the device driver.

filename.ext represents the root file name and optional extension of the device driver. (There is no default extension.)

options are any parameters or switches that you can use with a device driver.

Reference

See Chapter 17, "Configuring Your Computer."

Notes

DOS 6.0 supplies the following drivers: ANSI.SYS, DISPLAY.SYS, DRIVER.SYS, DBLSPACE.SYS, EGA.SYS, EMM386.EXE, HIMEM.SYS, INTERLNK.EXE, POWER.EXE, RAMDRIVE.SYS, SETVER.EXE, and SMARTDRV.EXE.

Some drivers must be loaded in a particular order (for example, HIMEM.SYS before EMM386.EXE).

DEVICEHIGH   V5, V6-Internal

Loads device drivers into upper-memory blocks (UMBs), which frees conventional memory for programs and other uses.

Syntax

In DOS 5.0, use the following format:

DEVICEHIGH *SIZE=hexbyte d:path***filename.ext** *options*

In DOS 6.0, use the following format:

DEVICEHIGH */L:region1,minsize1;region2,minsize2 /S=*
*d:path***filename.ext** *options*

d: is the drive where DOS can find the device driver.

path is the DOS path to the device driver.

filename.ext represents the file name and extension of the device driver.

options represents any parameters or switches that you can use with the device driver.

SIZE = *hexbyte* is the amount of reserved memory that must be available for the device driver to be loaded into memory. *hexbyte* is the size in bytes, expressed as a hexadecimal value.

Switches

/L:region1,minsize1; region2,minsize2	Tells DOS to load the driver into one or more particular blocks (regions) of upper memory.
Region1, region2...	UMB region numbers. (Use the MEM /F command to determine what regions are available and their sizes.)
Minsize1, minsize2...	Minimum sizes (in kilobytes) of the UMBs into which the driver should be loaded.
/S	Shrinks the UMB to its minimum size while the driver is loading. /S is used only with the /L switch and affects only UMBs for which a minimum size has been specified. (/S normally is used only by MemMaker, which analyzes a driver's memory usage to determine whether the /S switch can be used safely.)

Reference

See Chapter 17, "Configuring Your Computer."

Notes

Before using the DEVICEHIGH command, you must install HIMEM.SYS and a UMB provider, and then execute a DOS=UMB command. If your computer has an Intel 80386, 80486, or equivalent processor, you can install EMM386.EXE with the DEVICE command as the UMB provider. (For more information, see the DOS Utilities command section later in this Command Reference.)

If your system does not have enough high memory to hold a driver, DEVICEHIGH loads the driver into conventional memory.

By default, DOS loads a driver into the largest free UMB and makes the other UMBs available to that driver. Use the /L switch to fine-tune your configuration by forcing small drivers into small UMBs. Loading a driver with a /L switch, however, gives the driver access only to that UMB. Therefore, if the driver needs access to more than one UMB, you need to specify multiple regions with the /L switch. (To see how a driver uses upper memory, use the **MEM /M** *driver-name* command.)

DOS does not load a driver into a UMB if the UMB is smaller than the driver's load size. If the driver needs more memory when it runs than when it is loaded, you need to specify one or more *minsize* parameters, which are the size(s) of the UMB(s) that the driver needs when it runs. This procedure forces DOS to load the driver into a larger-than-normal UMB.

Examples

To load the device driver YOURDRV.SYS into the largest UMB:

> **DEVICE=C:\DOS\HIMEM.SYS**
> **DEVICE=C:\DOS\EMM386.EXE NOEMS**
> **DOS=UMB**
> **DEVICEHIGH=C:\YOURDRV.SYS**

To load the driver into region 1:

> **DEVICEHIGH=/L:1 C:\YOURDRV.SYS**

To load a different driver into regions 1 and 2:

> **DEVICEHIGH=/L:1;2 C:\YOURDRV2.SYS**

To load that driver into regions 1 and 2 (but only if region 1 is at least 15K and region 2 is at least 20K):

> **DEVICEHIGH=/L:1,15;2,20 C:\YOURDRV2.SYS**

DOS   V5, V6-External

Tells DOS to manage the upper-memory area and/or to load itself into the high-memory area. The latter procedure frees conventional memory.

Syntax

> **DOS** = *UMB|NOUMB, HIGH|LOW*

Switches

UMB   Tells DOS to maintain a link between conventional
            memory and reserved memory (upper-memory
            blocks), enabling you to load some device drivers
            and memory-resident programs into reserved
            memory.

NOUMB   Disconnects the link established by UMB (the de-
            fault).

HIGH   Loads part of DOS into the first 64K of extended
            memory—the high-memory area (HMA).

LOW   Keeps all of DOS in conventional memory (the de-
            fault).

Reference

See Chapter 17, "Configuring Your Computer."

Rules

1. HIMEM.SYS, or some other extended memory manager, must
   be loaded before DOS can run in extended memory (HMA).

2. For DOS=UMB to be effective, you must install a UMB provider. If your computer has an 80386SX or higher CPU,
   EMM386.EXE can be used with the RAM or the NOEMS
   switch.

3. If you want to load DOS into extended memory, the DOS
   command must come after the DEVICE=HIMEM.SYS command in your CONFIG.SYS file.

Notes

If you are using DOS on an 80286, 80386SX, or higher computer
with more than 1M of RAM, DOS=HIGH enables DOS to relocate a
portion of itself into the high-memory area (HMA). Doing so frees
up conventional memory for your programs' use.

If you are using an 80386SX or higher computer with at least 1M
of RAM, you can enable DOS to remap memory into the reserved
area between 640K and 1M by using HIMEM.SYS, EMM386.EXE,
and the DOS=UMB command. This procedure enables DOS to load
device drivers and memory-resident programs into the reserved
area, freeing conventional memory for use by programs.

Message

```
HMA not available: loading DOS low
```

Information: Your CONFIG.SYS contains the line DOS=HIGH, but DOS cannot load into high memory because no memory is available. This error can occur because no DEVICE=HIMEM.SYS command exists in your CONFIG.SYS file.

DRIVPARM   V3, V4, V5, V6-Internal

Defines or changes the parameters of an existing block device, such as a disk drive.

Syntax

DRIVPARM = **/D:num** */C /F:type /H:hds /I /N /S:sec /T:trk*

Switches

/D:num   Specifies the physical drive number (**num**) ranging from 0 to 255. Drive A=0, drive B=1, drive C=2, and so on.

/C   Specifies that the drive supports *change-line*, meaning that the drive has sensor support to determine when the drive door is open. When the drive door is open, DOS considers the drive to be empty.

/F:type   Determines the type of drive. *type* is one of the following numbers:

Type	Drive specification
0	160K/320K/180K/360K
1	1.2M
2	720K (2 is the default if you do not specify /F)
3	Single-density 8-inch disk (not available in DOS 5.0 or 6.0; see SETVER later in this Command Reference)
4	Double-density 8-inch disk (not available in DOS 5.0 or 6; see SETVER later in this Command Reference)

Type	Drive specification
5	Hard disk
6	Tape drive
7	1.44M
8	Read-write optical disk
9	2.88M

/H:hds   Specifies the total number of drive heads. *hds* is a number from 1 to 99. The default value of *hds* depends on the value of /F.

/I   Used if you have a 3 1/2-inch drive connected internally to your floppy-drive controller but your ROM BIOS does not support a 3 1/2-inch drive.

/N   Specifies that your drive or other block device is not removable (in other words, a hard disk). The default value of /N depends on the value of /F.

/S:sec   Specifies the total number of sectors per track in the drive. *sec* can be a number from 1 to 99. The default value of *sec* depends on the value of /F.

/T:trk   Specifies the number of tracks per side of a disk or the total number of tracks per tape. The default value of *trk* depends on the value of /F.

Reference

See Chapter 17, "Configuring Your Computer."

FCBS   *V2, V3, V4, V5, V6-Internal*

Specifies the number of DOS file-control blocks that can be open simultaneously and how many always are kept open.

Syntax

FCBS = maxopen, *neverclose*

maxopen is the number of file-control blocks (FCBs) that can be open at any given time. The value can be from 1 to 255. The default is 4.

neverclose is the number of FCBs that always are open. The default value is 0. This variable is not used in DOS 5.0 and 6.0.

Reference

See Chapter 17, "Configuring Your Computer."

Note

FCBS is rarely used. DOS began to use file handles rather than FCBs starting with Version 2.0. The number of programs available that use FCBs is diminishing. All major commercial programs available as of this printing use file handles. If you find a DOS 1 program that uses FCBs and if you find that program helpful, use the FCBS setting.

FILES   *V2, V3, V4, V5, V6-Internal*

Specifies the number of file handles that can be open at any given time (generally, one file handle per file).

Syntax

FILES = nnn

nnn is the number of file handles that can be open at any given time. The value can be from 8 to 255. The default is 8.

Reference

See Chapter 17, "Configuring Your Computer."

Rules

1. If you use several programs that require FILES settings, set your FILES statement to the maximum required value.

2. Microsoft Windows 3.1 recommends a setting of at least 30.

3. Each file handle above the default (8) takes approximately 39 bytes of memory.

INCLUDE   *V6-Internal*

Tells DOS to execute the contents of a configuration block as though a copy of that block were substituted for the include command.

Syntax

INCLUDE = blockname

blockname is the name of the configuration block to be included.

Rule

INCLUDE commands are not legal in menu blocks.

Note

In a multiconfiguration CONFIG.SYS, you can put into its own block a group of configuration commands used in several configuration blocks. Using INCLUDE to include these commands avoids possible mistyping and makes the CONFIG.SYS easier to maintain.

INSTALL   *V4, V5, V6-Internal*

Starts a memory-resident program from CONFIG.SYS. Examples of valid programs that you can start with INSTALL are FASTOPEN, KEYB, NLSFUNC, and SHARE.

Syntax

INSTALL = *dc:pathc***filename.ext** *options*

dc: is the drive that contains **filename.ext**.

pathc is the subdirectory where **filename.ext** is located.

filename.ext is the name of the file (for example, FASTOPEN.EXE, KEYB.COM, NLSFUNC.EXE, or SHARE.EXE).

options represents any parameter(s) that **filename.ext** requires to function.

Reference

See Chapter 17, "Configuring Your Computer."

Rules

1. INSTALL does not create an environment for the program that is loaded. Therefore, do not use INSTALL to load programs that use environment variables or shortcut keys or that require COMMAND.COM (for example, to handle critical drops).

2. All INSTALL commands are executed after all the DEVICE commands in a CONFIG.SYS and before the command-line interpreter is loaded.

LASTDRIVE   *V3, V4, V5, V6-Internal*

Sets the last valid drive letter.

Syntax

LASTDRIVE = x

x represents the highest system drive. By default, the drive letter is one higher than the last physical device in your system.

Reference

See Chapter 17, "Configuring Your Computer."

Notes

If you use the SUBST command to assign drive letters to subdirectories, use the LASTDRIVE statement to increase the usable drive letters. If you use a local-area network, you can use the LASTDRIVE statement to identify the highest letter that can be assigned as a drive letter to a subdirectory.

DOS allocates a structure in memory for each drive letter, so you should not specify unnecessary letters.

MENUCOLOR   *V6-Internal*

Specifies the text and background colors for the startup menu and is only valid within menu block.

Syntax

> **MENUCOLOR = textcolor**,*backcolor*

textcolor is a number from 0 to 15 that specifies the color of the menu text.

backcolor is a number from 0 to 15 that specifies the color of the screen behind the text. The default is 0 (black).

Reference

See Chapter 17, "Configuring Your Computer."

Rules

1. The relationships between the color numbers and the colors are as follows:

Code	Color	Code	Color
0	Black	8	Gray
1	Blue	9	Bright blue
2	Green	10	Bright green
3	Cyan	11	Bright cyan
4	Red	12	Bright red
5	Magenta	13	Bright magenta
6	Brown	14	Yellow
7	White	15	Bright white

2. The color choices made by MENUCOLOR are intended only for the configuration menu. They remain in effect only until the screen mode is changed or reset (by loading ANSI.SYS, for example) or until a CLS command is executed.

Notes

If you specify the same color for the text and the background, the text will not be visible.

If you specify white as a background color, the highlighting of the default menu item will not be visible.

MENUDEFAULT   V6-Internal

Specifies the default menu item and timeout for the start-up menu and is valid only within a menu block.

Syntax

MENUDEFAULT = blockname,*timeout*

blockname is the name of the menu block that DOS will execute if you do not respond to the message Enter a choice.

timeout is the number of seconds (from 0 to 90) that DOS will wait for you to respond to the message Enter a choice before using the default and continuing to execute CONFIG.SYS. If *timeout* is omitted, DOS waits until you press Enter. If *timeout* is 0, the startup menu doesn't appear, and the default is immediately selected. You don't have an opportunity to make a choice.

Reference

See Chapter 17, "Configuring Your Computer."

Rules

1. When the start-up menu is displayed, the default menu item is highlighted, its number appears after the Enter a choice prompt, and a time remaining countdown timer at the right edge of the screen is started at *timeout* seconds.

2. If a startup menu is defined without a MENUDEFAULT, its default is item 1.

MENUITEM   *V6-Internal*

Defines an item in the start-up menu and is only valid within a
menu block.

Syntax

> **MENUITEM = blockname,***menutext*

blockname is the name of the configuration block that DOS will
execute if this menu item is selected. **blockname** can be up to 70
characters long and can contain most printable characters except
spaces, backslashes (\), forward slashes (/), commas (,), semicolons (;), equal signs (=), and brackets ([and]).

menutext is the text displayed for this menu item. *menutext* can be
up to 70 characters long. The default is the configuration block
name.

Reference

See Chapter 17, "Configuring Your Computer."

Rules

1. The maximum number of menu items is nine. (If you need
   to define more than nine menu items, use the SUBMENU
   command.)

2. If DOS cannot find the specified configuration block name,
   the menu item is not displayed.

Example

The following CONFIG.SYS fragment displays two choices to the
user when the computer boots: a normal configuration and a
network configuration.

```
[menu]
NUMLOCK=OFF
MENUCOLOR=4,6
MENUITEM=normal, Normal config (no network)
MENUITEM=network, Network config (normal + network)
MENUDEFAULT=normal,5
```

[normal]
DEVICE=C:\DOS\HIMENM.SYS
DEVICE=C:\DOS\EMM386.EXE NOEMS
DEVICEHIGH /L:1=C:\DOS\ANSI.SYS
SHELL=C:\DOS=COMMAND.COM C:\DOS\/P

[network]
INCLUDE=normal
DEVICEHIGH=c:\net\network.sys
LASTDRIVE=I

[common]

NUMLOCK   *V6-Internal*

Turns your keyboard NumLock on or off when you start the computer. This command is only valid in a menu block.

Syntax

NUMLOCK = *ON|OFF*

ON|OFF is the state in which you want your keyboard NumLock set.

Reference

See Chapter 17, "Configuring Your Computer."

REM   *V4, V5, V6-Internal*

Places remarks or hides statements in the CONFIG.SYS file.

Syntax

REM *message*

message is a string of up to 123 characters.

Reference

See Chapter 17, "Configuring Your Computer."

SHELL   V3, V4, V5, V6-Internal

Changes the default DOS command processor or modifies some command-processor defaults (for example, the size of the environment).

Syntax

SHELL = *d:path***filename.ext** *parameters*

d: is the name of the drive where DOS can find the command processor to be used.

path\\ is the DOS path to the command processor.

filename.ext represents the root file name and extension of the command processor.

parameters represents the optional parameters that the command processor uses.

References

See Chapter 15, "Understanding Batch Files, DOSKey, and Macros." Also refer to the COMMAND section in this Command Reference.

Rule

If CONFIG.SYS does not contain a SHELL command, DOS tries to use COMMAND.COM from the root directory of the boot device. If that file does not exist, DOS displays the following message:

```
Bad or missing Command Interpreter
```

Enter correct name of Command Interpreter (e.g., C:COMMAND.COM).

Note

You must use this command if you want your command processor to have a nondefault amount of environment.

STACKS   V3.2, V3.3, V4.0, V4.01, V5, V6-Internal

Allots memory used to store information when a hardware interrupt occurs.

Syntax

STACKS = n,m

n is the number of stacks to be allotted. Valid numbers are 0 and 8 through 64. The default for computers that use the 8088/8086 microprocessor is 0; the default for computers that use 80286, 80386SX, and higher microprocessors is 9.

m is the size (in bytes) of each stack. Valid numbers are 0 and 32 through 512. The default for computers that use the 8088/8086 microprocessor is 0; the default for computers that use 80286, 80386SX, and higher microprocessors is 128.

Reference

See Chapter 17, "Configuring Your Computer."

Rule

Increasing the number or size of stacks decreases available conventional memory.

Notes

You may find that the default stacks are adequate for normal usage. If you regularly see the message Fatal: Internal Stack Failure, System Halted, however, increase the stacks. First, increase the number of stacks. If the error persists, increase the size of each stack.

Other error messages that indicate the need for additional stack space are Stack overflow and Exception error 12.

Although many systems work fine with STACKS=0,0, Windows 3.1 recommends STACKS=9,256 for DOS 3.3 and above if you get stack overflow errors.

SUBMENU   V6-Internal

Defines an item in the startup menu that, when selected, displays another menu. This command is only valid in a menu block.

Syntax

SUBMENU = blockname,*menutext*

blockname is the configuration block name of a menu that will be displayed if this menu item is selected. **blockname** can be up to 70 characters long and can contain most printable characters except spaces, backslashes (\), forward slashes (/), commas (,), semi-colons (;), equals signs (=), and brackets ([and]).

menutext is the text displayed for this menu item. *menutext* can be up to 70 characters long. The default is the configuration block name.

Rules

1. A SUBMENU configuration block can have any name that is legal for a configuration block.

2. If DOS cannot find the specified configuration block name, the submenu item is not displayed.

Note

Use SUBMENU if you need more than nine choices in a configuration menu.

SWITCHES   V6-Internal

Defines DOS startup options.

Syntax

SWITCHES = */F /K /N /W*

Switches

/F	No delay occurs after `Starting MS-DOS...` appears at the beginning of startup.
/K	Causes an enhanced keyboard to function as a conventional keyboard.
/N	Prevents startup from being interrupted by pressing F5 or F8.
/W	Specifies that the WINA20.386 file required by MS Windows 3.0 in enhanced mode has been moved out of the root directory.

Rule

If you use /W, you must also add a DEVICE command to the [386Enh] heading in your Windows 3.0 SYSTEM.INI file that gives the path to WINA20.386.

DOS Utilities Commands

APPEND   *V3.3, V4, V5, V6-External*

Instructs DOS to search the specified directories on the specified disks for data (nonprogram and nonbatch) files. In recent versions of DOS, you can also search for executable files.

Syntax

To establish the data-file search path the first time, use the following format:

>*dc:pathc***APPEND** *d1:path1;d2:path2;d3:path3;...*

dc: is the name of the disk drive that holds the command.

pathc is the path to the command.

d1:, d2:, d3: are valid drive names.

path1, path2, path3 are valid paths to the directories that you want DOS to search for data (nonprogram and nonbatch) files. The ellipsis (...) represents additional drive and path names, and can include network drives.

To use either of the APPEND switches, use the following format:

>*dc:pathc***APPEND** */X /E*

In DOS 4.0, 5, and 6, you also can use the following syntax for the */X* switch:

>*dc:pathc***APPEND** */X:OFF*
>*dc:pathc***APPEND** */X:ON*

To change the data-file search path, use the following format:

>**APPEND** *d1:path1,d2:path2;d3:path3;...*

In DOS 4.0, 5.0, and 6.0, the default state of a search for files for which the drive or path is specified as follows:

>**APPEND** */PATH:ON*

To turn off a search for files for which the drive or path is specified (in DOS 4.0, 5.0, and 6.0), use the following format:

APPEND */PATH:OFF*

To see the search path, use the following format:

APPEND

To disconnect the data-file search, use the following format:

APPEND ;

Switches

/X	Directs DOS to search the appended directories for program files, not just data files.
/X:ON	Same as /X (DOS 4.0, 5.0, and 6.0).
/X:OFF	Turns this feature off (DOS 4.0, 5.0, and 6.0).
/E	Places the drive paths in the environment variable APPEND.
/PATH:ON	Turns on search for files for which the drive or path has been explicitly specified (DOS 4.0, 5.0, and 6.0).
/PATH:OFF	Turns off search for files for which the drive or path has been explicitly specified (DOS 4.0, 5.0, and 6.0).

Rules

1. The first time you execute APPEND, the program loads from the disk and installs itself in DOS. APPEND then becomes an internal command and is not reloaded from the disk until you restart DOS.

2. You can use the /X and /E switches only when you first invoke APPEND. You cannot use any path names with these two switches. If you use /E a second time, DOS says that it is an invalid switch.

3. If you specify more than one set of paths, the following rules apply:

   ■ The path sets must be separated by semicolons.

   ■ The search for the nonprogram files is conducted in the order in which you listed the path sets. First, the command searches the specified directory (or current directory, if no other directory is specified). Then the command searches *d1:path1*, followed by *d2:path2*, and so on, until APPEND finds the file or exhausts the list of directory paths.

4. The length of the paths provided for APPEND cannot exceed 127 characters. This limit includes the APPEND command name.

5. If DOS encounters an invalid path, such as a misspelled path or a path that no longer exists, DOS skips the path and does not display a message.

6. If you use the /X switch, programs that use the following DOS Interrupt 21h functions automatically search the appended list:

   Find First Entry (11h)

   Find First File (4Eh)

   Execute Program (EXEC) (4Bh)

7. In DOS 4.0, 5.0, and 6.0, you can disable the /X switch by using /X:OFF.

8. Do not use RESTORE while you are using the /X switch.

9. To disable APPEND, type the command, followed by a semicolon (;). APPEND remains resident but inactive until you issue another APPEND command with path names.

10. If you use the /E switch, DOS establishes an environmental variable named APPEND. The variable holds the current paths that APPEND uses.

11. The file that APPEND finds can be safely read by the program. Any changes you make in the file are saved in a copy of the file placed in the current directory; the original file remains intact.

12. If you are using the ASSIGN command with APPEND, you must issue the APPEND command first.

13. Do not use APPEND with Microsoft Windows or the Windows Setup program.

Examples

To enable the searching of the append path list for executable files as well as for data files and set the environment variable APPEND to the path list, assuming that APPEND is in the current directory or in the PATH:

   APPEND /X /E

To instruct APPEND to search the specified or current directory for nonprogram files and then to search the directories C:\BIN and C:\BIN\OVR:

APPEND C:\BIN;C:\BIN\OVR

To instruct APPEND to ignore invalid drive or path designations and to search the APPEND path for the file. (If you type **TYPE C:\TEMP\DOCUMENT.TXT** but the directory C:\TEMP does not exist, APPEND searches the APPEND paths for DOCUMENT.TXT):

APPEND /PATH:ON

To disable the APPEND command, which stays in memory until you restart DOS. (To reactivate APPEND, simply add a set of path names to the command):

APPEND ;

Notes

APPEND is the counterpart of the PATH command, which works with program files. APPEND is the PATH command for data and other nonprogram files. The command is especially useful if you run programs that do not support hierarchical directories.

You can use APPEND /X to trick programs at three levels. First, when a program attempts to open a file to read, APPEND enables the program to find the file. Second, when a program searches for a file name, APPEND enables the program to find the file name. Third, when a program attempts to execute another program, APPEND helps the first program find and then execute the second program.

The /E switch places the paths fed to APPEND in the environment, under the variable named APPEND. If you use /E, programs can examine the environment for the APPEND variable and use the contents to find their files. However, do not use the APPEND command from within a program if you use /E. The changes that APPEND makes in the environment are temporary; the copy of COMMAND.COM used to run APPEND is temporary. When you return to the program, you lose the changes made by APPEND.

Be cautious if you write to files that APPEND finds. APPEND tricks programs into reading files from any location. APPEND does not trick programs when the programs write files. DOS saves changes you make to a file in a copy of that file, which DOS then places in the current directory. The original file in the directory in which you used APPEND remains unchanged. This file duplication can be confusing when you use a file in one directory, save the new version, and then move to another directory and attempt to reuse the file. You are working with the original file without the changes; the altered file remains in the directory from which you made the changes.

If you use APPEND with the ASSIGN command, you must start APPEND before you use the ASSIGN command. Reversing the order produces an error message, and the command does not load.

Messages

1. `APPEND/ASSIGN Conflict`
   `APPEND/TopView Conflict`

   Error: You tried to use APPEND after you loaded ASSIGN, TopView, or DESQview. If you are using TopView or DESQview, exit the program, issue the APPEND command, and then restart your program. If you are using ASSIGN, break the assignment, issue the APPEND command, and then reissue ASSIGN.

2. `APPEND already installed`

   Warning: You attempted to load APPEND a second time. Give the command again by entering APPEND and its parameters rather than APPEND.EXE and its parameters.

3. `Incorrect APPEND version`

   Error: You used a version of APPEND from a different version of DOS. Make sure that you do not use an APPEND version from the IBM Local Area Network (LAN) program. The problem may be that the wrong version of APPEND is loading first from a PATHed directory.

4. `No Append`

   Information: You typed APPEND to see the current path, and APPEND currently is inactive.

ASSIGN   V2, V3, V4, V5-External

Instructs DOS to use a drive other than the one specified by a program or command.

ASSIGN is included on the DOS Supplementary Program disk, not in the standard DOS 6.0 package.

Syntax

To reroute drive activity, use the following format:

*dc:pathc***ASSIGN d1***:=***d2***:.../STATUS*

To clear the reassignment, use the following format:

*dc:pathc***ASSIGN**

dc: is the name of the drive that holds the command.

pathc is the path to the command.

d1*:* is the letter of the drive that the program or DOS normally uses.

d2*:* is the letter of the drive that you want the program or DOS to use instead of the usual drive.

The ellipsis (...) represents additional drive assignments.

Switch

/STATUS   Displays all current drive assignments.

Reference

See Chapter 12, "Controlling Devices."

Rules

1. You can use a space on either side of the equal sign.

2. You can give more than one assignment on the same line. Use a space between each set of assignments, as in the following example:

   ASSIGN B=C A=C

3. Use ASSIGN only when necessary.

4. Do not ASSIGN a drive to a drive that is not on your system. If you make this mistake, DOS displays the following error message:

```
Invalid parameter
```

Examples

To make DOS reroute to drive C any activity for drive A. (You can use a space on either side of the equals sign):

ASSIGN A = C or ASSIGN A=C

To make DOS reroute to drive C any activity for drives A and B:

ASSIGN A=C B=C

To display the current drive assignments:

ASSIGN */STATUS*

or

ASSIGN */S*

To clear any previous drive reassignment:

ASSIGN

Note

In DOS 3.1 and more recent versions, an alternative to ASSIGN is SUBST, which assigns a drive letter to a subdirectory (see the section in this Command Reference on the SUBST command). For compatibility with later versions of DOS, consider using SUBST rather than ASSIGN.

ATTRIB   V3, V4, V5, V6-External

Displays, sets, or clears a file's read-only, archive, system, or hidden attributes.

Syntax

To set the file's attributes on, use the following format:

*dc:pathc***ATTRIB** *+R +A +S +H d:path***filename.ext***/S*

To clear the file's attributes, use the following format:

*dc:pathc***ATTRIB** *–R –A –S –H d:path***filename.ext***/S*

To display a file's attribute status, use the following format:

*dc:pathc***ATTRIB** *d:path***filename.ext***/s*

dc: is the name of the drive that holds the command.

pathc is the path to the command.

+R/–R sets a file's read-only attribute on and off.

+A/–A sets a file's archive attribute on and off.

+S/–S sets the file's system attribute on and off (versions 5.0 and 6.0 only).

+H/–H sets a file's hidden attribute on and off (versions 5.0 and 6.0 only).

d: is the name of the drive that holds the files for which the attributes are displayed or changed.

path is the path to the files for which the attributes will be displayed or changed.

filename.ext is the name of the file(s) for which the attributes will be displayed or changed. Wild cards are permitted.

Switch

/S   Sets or clears the attributes of the specified files in the specified directory and all subdirectories to that directory.

Reference

See Chapter 8, "Understanding and Managing Directories."

Rules

1. If you do not provide a file name (**filename.ext**), DOS acts as though you used the file name *.*.

2. If you provide an incorrect file name, DOS displays the following error message:

   ```
   File not found
   ```

3. If you provide an incorrect parameter, DOS displays the following error message:

   `Parameter format not correct`

4. You can use the R, A, S, and H characters together or individually in the command. You can mix the plus and minus attributes of the commands (for example, +R –A), but you cannot use plus and minus attributes for the same character in the command (for example, +R –R).

5. If a file has both the hidden and system attributes set, you cannot clear each attribute individually with separate ATTRIB commands (or DOS displays the message `Not resetting hidden file` or `Not resetting system file`. You must reset both attributes by using one command such as ATTRIB -H -S.

6. If you use ATTRIB to set the attributes of directories, you must explicitly name the directory (that is, you cannot use wild cards).

Message

`Access denied`

Error: You are attempting to delete a read-only file. To delete the file, use ATTRIB with the –R parameter to remove the read-only attribute. Then use DEL to delete the file.

BACKUP   *V2, V3, V4, V5-External*

Backs up one or more files from a hard disk or a floppy disk to another disk.

BACKUP is included on the DOS Supplemental Program disk, not in the standard DOS 6.0 package. However, see MSBACKUP in this Command Reference and refer to Chapter 13, "Understanding Backups and the Care of Data."

Syntax

*dc:pathc***BACKUP** **d1:***path\\filename.ext* **d2:** */S /M /A*
/D:date /T:time /F /L:dl:filenamel.extl

dc: is the drive that holds the command.

pathc is the path to the command.

d1: is the hard disk or floppy disk drive to be backed up.

path is the starting directory path for backup.

filename.ext specifies the name(s) of the file(s) you want to back up. Wild cards are allowed.

d2: is the hard disk or floppy disk drive that receives the backup files.

Switches

/S	Backs up all *subdirectories*, starting with the specified or current directory on the source disk and working downward.
/M	Backs up all files *modified* since the last backup.
/A	*Adds* the file(s) to be backed up to the files already on the specified floppy disk drive. If /A is omitted, the files are deleted.
/D:date	Backs up any file that you create or change on or after the specified *date*.
/T:time	Backs up any file that you create or change at or after the specified *time* on the specified date (used with the */D* switch).
/F	*Formats* the destination floppy disk if the disk is not formatted. (DOS 4.0 and 5.0 format the target floppy disks automatically without the use of this switch.)
/F:size	In DOS 4.0 and 5.0, *formats* the destination floppy disk according to the *size* specified. (If you have a 1.2M disk drive but only 360K disks, you can specify /F:360 to format the 360K disk in the 1.2M drive.)
/L:dl:pathl\\ filenamel.ext	Creates a *log* file.

Exit Codes

Code	Explanation
0	Successful backup
1	No files found to be backed up

Code	Explanation
2	Some files not backed up because of sharing problems
3	Aborted by the user (Ctrl-Break or Ctrl-C)
4	Aborted because of an error

Rules

1. Give both a source and a destination for BACKUP. Neither disk can be used in an ASSIGN, SUBST, or JOIN command.

2. The source name must specify the valid name of the disk drive to be backed up. The source name also can include either or both of the following entries:

   ■ A valid directory path that contains the files to be backed up

   ■ A file name with appropriate extensions, if desired (wild cards are allowed)

3. The destination is any valid name for a floppy or hard disk drive.

4. To keep the files on a previously backed-up disk, use the /A option. If you do not use this switch, all files previously stored on the receiving disk are destroyed, or all files in the \BACKUP subdirectory of the hard disk are destroyed.

   To use the /A option with floppy disks, you must start with a disk that contains the special files created by BACKUP, named CONTROL.*xxx* and BACKUP.*xxx* (*xxx* is the number of the disk). Otherwise, BACKUP displays the message Last backup diskette not inserted and aborts the process.

5. If you back up onto floppy disks, all files are placed in the root directory. If you back up onto another hard disk, the files are stored in the subdirectory \BACKUP.

6. To create a log of the files that BACKUP processed, use the /L switch. If you do not specify a full file name, BACKUP creates the log file under the name BACKUP.LOG in the source disk's root directory.

7. If you do not specify a file name (*filenamel.extl*) for the log file, BACKUP names it BACKUP.LOG. If you do not specify a location (*dl:path1*) for the log file, BACKUP puts it in the root directory of the disk that is being backed up.

8. If you use a log file name, you must use a colon between the *L* and the first character in the name. Do not use spaces from the beginning of the switch to the end of the log file name. If you do not use a log file name, do not use a colon after the *L*.

9. If a log file already exists, BACKUP adds to the log file. If a file does not exist, a new file is created. You cannot place the log file on the destination disk (the disk used to store the backup files).

Examples

For the following examples, assume that the hard disk is C and that the following subdirectories exist:

```
C:\
C:\DOS
C:\WP
C:\DATA
C:\DATA\LETTERS
C:\DATA\MEMOS
```

1. To back up the entire hard disk:

   BACKUP C:\ A: /S

   Here, the source to be backed up is specified as C:\. The /S switch instructs BACKUP to back up all subdirectories of the source—that is, all subdirectories of the root directory.

2. To back up a specific subdirectory:

   BACKUP C:\DATA\LETTERS A:

   This example shows how to back up a single subdirectory. In this case, the subdirectory LETTERS is backed up. You do not need to use any switches.

3. To back up several subdirectories:

   BACKUP C:\DATA A: /S

   In this example, \DATA is the source to be backed up. Because of the /S switch, all subdirectories of \DATA are backed up.

4. To back up all files as of a specified date:

   BACKUP C:\ A: /S /D:08/21/89

   In this example, all files that were created or modified on or after August 21, 1989, are backed up. Notice that the root directory is the source and that the /S switch is used to back up all subdirectories of the source directory.

5. To back up only modified files:

    BACKUP C:\ A: /S /M

    The /M switch tells BACKUP to back up all files with the archive bit set on. When you create or modify a file, the archive bit is set on. When you back up a file, BACKUP turns off the archive bit.

6. To add modified files to the current backup disks:

    BACKUP C:\ A: /S /M /A

    As in the preceding example, only modified files are backed up. But here, BACKUP does not overwrite files on the backup disk. Instead, you see the following message:

    ```
    Insert last backup diskette in drive A:
    Press any key to continue…
    ```

    BACKUP begins to add modified files to the backup disks because of the /A switch.

Notes

Depending on the DOS version, the features of BACKUP vary. In DOS versions before 3.3, BACKUP creates a heading file called BACKUPID.@@@ on each floppy disk. This file holds the date, time, and disk number of the backup. BACKUP stores each backed-up file individually on the disk. Each file contains a 128-byte heading that identifies the path, file name, the file's original directory attributes, and whether the file is complete or partial.

In 3.3 and more recent versions, BACKUP uses a different approach for the floppy disk that holds the backup files. A file called CONTROL.*nnn* holds the directory, file names, and other housekeeping information. All backed-up files are placed in one large file called BACKUP.*nnn*. (For both files, *nnn* represents the number of the backup disk.) The two files are marked as read-only, so that you do not inadvertently erase or alter them.

In 3.3 and more recent versions, BACKUP places all the files in a larger file, thereby achieving a speed gain over its predecessors. The backup process is reduced to less than half the time required by previous versions of DOS. You cannot, however, determine which disk holds a given file. The log file is the only method of locating a file in DOS 3.3 and more recent versions.

Although BACKUP automatically creates space on the disk that receives the backups by deleting files on the disk (unless you specify /A), it does not remove any directories and their files from the receiving disk. If you back up onto such a disk, you will need many more disks than usual.

Messages

1. Cannot find FORMAT.EXE

   Error: While running BACKUP, you provided an unformatted floppy disk, and BACKUP could not find the FORMAT command.

2. Cannot FORMAT nonremovable drive *d*:

   Error: The destination disk is a hard disk or networked disk drive, and you used the /F switch to request formatting.

   When you see this message, BACKUP aborts. To recover from this error, issue the BACKUP command again without the /F switch, or use a floppy disk drive as the destination.

3. Insert backup diskette *nn* in drive *d*:

   Warning! Files in the target drive
   d:\ root directory will be erased
   Press any key to continue

   Information and warning: This message appears during the backup process when you back up to floppy disks. When you use the /A switch, the message does not appear for the first target disk but does appear for subsequent disks. This message appears for all disks when you do not use /A.

   The message instructs you to put the first or next backup disk (disk number *nn* in the series) into drive *d*: and to press any key to continue. The message also warns that BACKUP deletes all existing files in the root directory of the receiving disk before files are transferred. Make sure that the proper disk is in the drive, and then press any key to start the backup operation.

4. Insert last backup diskette in drive *d*:
   Strike any key when ready

   Information: This message appears only when you use the /A switch and invoke BACKUP without placing the final disk for the backup set in the correct disk drive. Insert the proper disk into the drive, and then press any key to start the backup operation.

5. `Insert backup source diskette in drive` *d*`:`
   `Strike any key when ready`

   Information: You specified a floppy disk drive as the source for BACKUP. BACKUP is instructing you to insert the source disk and to press any key when you are ready to begin the backup process.

6. `Last backup diskette not inserted`

   Warning or error: This message appears when you use the /A switch and when the disk in the drive is not the last disk of a previous series. If you used a disk previously processed by BACKUP, this message appears with the `Insert last backup disk in drive` *d:* message. If the disk was not previously processed by BACKUP, BACKUP aborts.

BREAK　　　*V2, V3, V4, V5, V6-Internal*

Determines when DOS looks for a Ctrl-Break sequence to stop a program.

Syntax

To turn on BREAK, use the following format:

BREAK ON

To turn off BREAK, use the following format:

BREAK OFF

To determine whether BREAK is on or off, use the following format:

BREAK

You also can use BREAK in your CONFIG.SYS file (see the BREAK section of Configuration Commands later in this Command Reference).

Note

Normally, DOS only checks for CTRL-Break while it reads from the keyboard or writes to the screen or a printer. If you set BREAK to ON, you extend CTRL-Break checking to other functions, such as disk read and write operations.

CHCP   V3.3, V4, V5, V6-Internal

Changes or displays the code page (character set) used by DOS.

Syntax

To change the current code page, use the following format:

CHCP codepage

To display the current code page, use the following format:

CHCP

codepage is a valid three-digit code-page number. Following is a list of acceptable code pages:

Codepage	Name
437	English (U.S)
850	Multilingual (Latin I)
852	Slavic (Latin II)
860	Portuguese
863	Canadian-French
865	Nordic

Reference

See Chapter 20, "Understanding the International Features of DOS."

Rules

1. Before using CHCP, you must use the COUNTRY command (to specify the location of the country-information file, normally COUNTRY.SYS), or use the NLSFUNC command (to specify a location that overrides that of the COUNTRY command), or place COUNTRY.SYS in the root directory of the current disk. Otherwise, DOS returns the message `Cannot open specified country information file.`

2. Before using CHCP, you must use the NLSFUNC command.

Notes

CHCP is a system-wide code-page (character-set) changer. CHCP simultaneously resets all affected devices to the changed font. MODE works similarly but changes only one device at a time.

When you select a code page, the new code page becomes the specified code page. If you include CONFIG.SYS directives for devices that use code pages, such as DEVICE=DISPLAY.SYS, CHCP loads the correct code pages for the devices.

You can access the COUNTRY.SYS file to get country information. If you do not specify the location of COUNTRY.SYS when you invoke NLSFUNC, COUNTRY.SYS must exist in the current disk's root directory. Otherwise, DOS returns the message `Cannot open specified country information file`.

Messages

1. `Code page nnn not prepared for device ddd`

   Error: CHCP could not select the code page *nnn* because of one of the following errors:

   - You did not use MODE to prepare a code page for this device.

   - An I/O error occurred while DOS was sending the new font information to the device.

   - The device is busy (for example, a printer is in use or off-line).

   - The device does not support code-page switching.

   Check to make sure that the command MODE CODEPAGE PREPARE was issued for the appropriate devices and that the devices are on-line and ready. Then try CHCP again.

2. `Invalid code page`

   Error: CHCP could not select the code page because of one of the following errors:

   - You specified an invalid code page for the country.

   - You did not use the MODE command to prepare a code page.

   Be sure that you run NLSFUNC and that you use the command MODE CODEPAGE PREPARE to prepare the code page for the appropriate devices.

3. NLSFUNC not installed

   Error: You attempted to change the code page but did not initiate NLSFUNC before using CHCP. If you plan to use code pages and have the correct directives in CONFIG.SYS, add NLSFUNC to your AUTOEXEC.BAT file so that the command is executed when you boot the computer.

CHDIR or CD *V2, V3, V4, V5, V6–Internal*

Changes or shows the path of the current directory.

Syntax

To change the current directory, use either of these formats:

CHDIR *d:***path**

or

CD *d:***path**

To change the current directory to its parent directory, use either of these formats:

CHDIR ..

or

CD ..

To show the current directory path in a disk drive, use either of these formats:

CHDIR *d:*

or

CD *d:*

d: is a valid disk drive name.

path is a valid directory path.

Reference

See Chapter 8, "Understanding and Managing Directories."

Rule

To start the move with the disk's root directory, use the backslash (\) as the path's first character. Otherwise, DOS assumes that the path starts with the current directory.

Notes

To move through more than one directory at a time, use the path character (\) to separate each directory name. You can chain together as many directories as you want, provided that the total number of characters for the path does not exceed 63.

You are not restricted to changing directories in the current disk. If the current drive is drive A and the disk with the sample directory is in drive B, for example, you can type B: before each path name, and your commands work the same way.

CHKDSK

V1, V2, V3, V4, V5, V6-External

Checks the directory and the File Allocation Table (FAT) of the disk, and reports disk and memory status. CHKDSK also can repair errors in the directories or the FAT.

Syntax

*dc:pathc***CHKDSK** *d:path\filename.ext /F/V*

dc: is the drive that holds the command.

pathc is the path to the command.

d: is the disk drive to be analyzed.

path is the directory path to the files to be analyzed.

filename.ext is a valid DOS file name. Wild cards are permitted.

Switches

/F Fixes the FAT and other problems if errors are found. (Do not use this switch when you are running under Microsoft Windows or the DOS Task Swapper.)

/V Shows CHKDSK's progress and displays more detailed information about the errors that the program finds. (This switch is known as the *verbose switch*.)

Reference

See Chapter 7, "Preparing and Maintaining Disks."

Rules

1. You must direct CHKDSK to repair the disk by using the /F switch. CHKDSK asks you to confirm that you want the repairs made before it proceeds.

2. CHKDSK cannot process a directory in which you used the JOIN command—that is, a second disk joined to a subdirectory.

3. CHKDSK does not process a disk on which you used a SUBST command.

4. CHKDSK cannot process a disk drive on which you used the ASSIGN command.

5. CHKDSK cannot process a networked (shared) disk.

6. Do not use CHKDSK on disks that contain open files.

7. After completing its normal checks on a DoubleSpace drive, CHKDSK automatically runs DBLSPACE /CHKDSK on the drive.

Notes

CHKDSK shows you the following information:

- Volume name and creation date (only disks with volume labels)
- Volume serial number (if it exists)
- Total disk space
- Number of files and bytes used for hidden or system files

■ Number of files and bytes used for directories

■ Number of files and bytes used for user (normal) files

■ Bytes used by bad sectors (flawed disk space)

■ Bytes available (free space) on disk

■ Bytes of total conventional memory (RAM)

■ Bytes of available conventional memory

In DOS 4.0 and later versions, CHKDSK also reports the following information:

■ Total bytes in each allocation unit

■ Total allocation units on the disk

■ Available allocation units on the disk

An allocation unit equates to a cluster.

CHKDSK checks a disk's directories and the FAT. The command also checks the amount of memory in the system and determines how much of that memory is free. If errors are found, CHKDSK reports them on-screen before making a status report.

If lost clusters are found, CHKDSK asks whether you want to repair them. You must type **Y** or **N**. If you type **Y**, CHKDSK shows a report on-screen as if the lost clusters were repaired. This report is only a simulation, however. To actually reclaim the lost clusters, you must issue a second command: CHKDSK /F.

The CHKDSK file name checks to see whether the specified file(s) are stored contiguously on the disk. DOS reports any noncontiguously stored files and how many different sections store the file(s). If CHKDSK reports many noncontiguous files, you may want to run DEFRAG on the disk.

CHKDSK does not check to see whether your files can be read. Neither does CHKDSK test your disk to determine whether new bad spots have appeared.

Messages

1. `All specified file(s) are contiguous`

   Information: The files you specified are stored in contiguous sectors on the disk. Disk performance for the files should be optimal.

2. *filename*
   ```
   Allocation error, size adjusted
   ```

   Warning: The file name has an invalid sector number in the FAT. The file was truncated by CHKDSK at the end of the last valid sector.

   Check this file to verify that all information in the file is correct. If you find a problem, use your backup copy of the file. This message usually appears when the problem is in the FAT, not in the file. Your file probably is still good.

3. *filename*
   ```
   Contains xxx non-contiguous blocks
   ```

   Information: *filename* is not stored contiguously on the disk but in *xxx* number of pieces. This arrangement can decrease the performance of the disk. If you find that many files on a disk are stored in noncontiguous pieces, you may want to run DEFRAG.

4. *directoryname*
   ```
   Convert directory to file (Y/N)?
   ```

   Warning: *directoryname* contains so much bad information that the directory no longer is usable. If you type **Y**, CHKDSK converts the directory into a file so that you can use DEBUG or another tool to repair the directory. If you type **N**, no action is taken.

   The first time you see this message, type **N**. Try to copy files from this directory to another disk, and check the copied files to see whether they are usable. Then rerun CHKDSK to convert the directory into a file and try to recover the rest of the files.

5. *directoryname*
   ```
   is joined,
   tree past this point not processed
   ```

   Warning: CHKDSK encountered a directory that actually is a disk joined to the currently processed disk. CHKDSK does not process this subdirectory but continues to process the remaining portion of the real disk.

6. ```
   Errors found, F parameter not specified
   Corrections will not be written to the disk
   ```

   Information: CHDSK found an error. This message tells you that CHKDSK will go through the motions of repairing the disk but will not actually change the file because you did not use the /F switch.
   ```

7. `filename`
   `First allocation unit is invalid, entry truncated`

   Warning: `filename`'s first entry in the FAT refers to a nonexistent portion of the disk. If you used the /F switch, the file becomes a zero-length file (truncated).

   Try to copy this file to another floppy disk before CHKDSK truncates the file. You may not get a useful copy, however, and the original file will be lost.

8. `. or ..`
   `Entry has a bad attribute`
   or `Entry has a bad size or`
   `Entry has a bad link`

   Warning: The link to the parent directory (..) or the current directory (.) has a problem. If you used the /F switch, CHKDSK attempts to repair the problem. Normally, this procedure is safe, and you do not risk losing files.

9. `filename`
   `Has invalid allocation unit, file truncated`

   Information and warning: Part of the chain of FAT entries for `filename` points to a nonexistent part of the disk. The /F switch truncates the file at its last valid sector. If you did not use the /F switch, DOS takes no corrective action. Try to copy this file to a different disk, and then rerun CHKDSK with the /F switch. (You may lose part of the file.)

10. `filename1`
    `Is cross linked on allocation unit x`
    `filename2`
    `Is cross linked on allocation unit x`

    Warning: Two files—`filename1` and `filename2`—had an entry in the FAT that points to the same area (cluster) of the disk. In other words, the two files believe that they own the same piece of the disk.

    CHKDSK takes no action. To handle the problem, copy both files to another floppy disk, delete the files from the original disk, and edit the files as necessary. (The files may contain garbage.)

11. `Insufficient room in root directory`
    `Erase files from root and repeat CHKDSK`

    Error: CHKDSK recovered so many "lost" clusters from the disk that the root directory is full. CHKDSK aborts at this point.

Examine the FILE*xxxx*.CHK files. If you find nothing useful, delete them. Rerun CHKDSK with the /F switch to continue recovering lost clusters.

12. *xxxxxxxxxx* bytes disk space freed

Information: CHKDSK regained some disk space that was improperly marked as "in use." *xxxxxxxxx* tells you how many additional bytes are now available. To free this disk space, review and delete any FILE*xxxx*.CHK file that does not contain useful information.

13. *xxx* lost allocation units found in *yyy* chains
Convert lost chains to files (Y/N)?

Information: Although CHKDSK found *xxx* blocks of data allocated in the FAT, no file on the disk is using these blocks. The blocks are lost clusters, which CHKDSK normally can free if no other error or warning message appears.

If you use the /F switch and type **Y**, CHKDSK joins each set of lost chains into a file placed in the root directory of the disk. That file is called FILE*xxxx*.CHK, in which *xxxx* is a consecutive number between 0000 and 9999. Examine this file, and delete any clusters that contain no useful information.

If you use the /F switch and type **N**, CHKDSK simply frees the lost chains so that other files can reuse the disk space. No files are created. If you type **Y** and omit /F, CHKDSK displays the actions that you can take but takes no action itself.

CLS (Clear Screen)   *V2, V3, V4, V5, V6-Internal*

Erases the screen.

Syntax

CLS

Reference

See Chapter 12, "Controlling Devices."

Notes

This command clears all information from the screen and places the cursor at the home position in the upper left corner.

This command affects only the active video display, not memory.

If you used the ANSI control codes to set the foreground and background, the color settings remain in effect.

If you did not set the foreground/background color, the screen reverts to light characters on a dark background.

COMMAND *V2, V3, V4, V5, V6-External*

Invokes another copy of COMMAND.COM, the command processor.

Syntax

*dc:pathc***COMMAND** *d:path\\ cttydevice /E:size /K filename /P /MSG /C string*

In your CONFIG.SYS, use the following format:

SHELL=*dc:pathc***COMMAND** *d:path\\ cttydevice /E:size /P /MSG*

dc: is the drive where DOS can find a copy of COMMAND.COM.

pathc is the DOS path to the copy of COMMAND.COM.

d:path is the drive and directory location of COMMAND.COM. This path is assigned to the COMSPEC environment variable.

cttydevice is the device used for input and output. The default is CON:.

Switches

/E:size	Sets the *size* of the environment. Size is a decimal number from 160 to 32,768 bytes, rounded up to the nearest multiple of 16 (refer to the SHELL command). The default is 256.
/K filename	Runs *filename* (a program or batch file) and then displays the DOS command prompt.
/P	Keeps this copy permanently in memory (until the next system reset). Generally used only as part of the SHELL command.
/MSG	Loads all error messages into memory. Must be used with /P. Generally useful only if you are running DOS from diskettes.
/C string	Passes the command and parameters represented by *string* to the new copy of COMMAND.COM and returns to the primary command processor.

Reference

See Chapter 11, "Working with System Information."

Rules

1. The string in the /C option is interpreted by the additional copy of COMMAND.COM, just as though you typed the string at the system level. /C must be the last switch used in the line. Do not use the form **COMMAND**/C *string* /P.

2. You can exit from the second copy of the command processor by issuing the command EXIT, unless you used the /P option (permanent).

3. If you issue the /P and /C switches together, /P is ignored.

4. Do not use the /K switch in the SHELL command line in your CONFIG.SYS. This switch may cause problems with applications and installation programs that alter your AUTOEXEC.BAT file.

Notes

COMMAND often is used with the SHELL directive to enable COMMAND.COM to reside in a subdirectory, rather than the root directory.

You can use COMMAND with all versions of DOS to call a second batch file from an originating batch file. Suppose that a batch file called BATCH1.BAT contains the following line:

COMMAND /C BATCH2

BATCH1 calls BATCH2.BAT. BATCH2.BAT executes and, after completing the last line of the batch file, returns to BATCH1 to complete the originating batch file. This method of calling a batch file is similar to the CALL batch subcommand available in DOS 3.3 and later versions.

If you use DOS 5.0 or 6.0 with a floppy-disk-only system, you can specify the /MSG switch in the SHELL directive of CONFIG.SYS. This switch loads all error messages in memory. If an error occurs, you do not need a disk with COMMAND.COM in the drive. (The switch uses an additional 1K of RAM.)

You can use the /K *filename* switch to specify that the DOS prompt in Microsoft Windows should use a startup file other than AUTOEXEC.BAT. Open the DOSPRMPT.PIF file (using the PIF Editor), and type **/K *filename*** in the Optional Parameters box.

COMP   *V1, V2, V3, V4, V5-External*

Compares two sets of disk files of the same name and length. COMP is included on the DOS 6 Supplemental Programs disk, not in the standard DOS 6.0 package. The FC command, which is discussed later in this Command Reference, provides much the same capabilities as COMP.

Syntax

*dc:pathc***COMP** *d1:path1\\filename1.ext1*
d2:path2\\filename2.ext2

In Version 5.0, use the following format:

*dc:pathc***COMP** *d1:path1\\filename1.ext1*
d2:path2\\filename2.ext2 /D/A/L/N=x/C

dc: is the drive that holds the command.

pathc is the path to the command.

d1: is the drive that contains the first set of files to be compared.

path1 is the path to the first set of files.

filename1.ext1 is the file name for the first set of files. Wild cards are allowed.

d2: is the drive that contains the second set of files to be compared.

path2 is the path to the second set of files.

filename2.ext2 is the file name for the second set of files. Wild cards are allowed.

d1 and *d2* may be the same.

path1 and *path2* may be the same.

filename1.ext and *filename2.ext2* may be the same.

Special Terms

d1:path1\filename1.ext1 is the *primary* file set.

d2:path2\filename2.ext2 is the *secondary* file set.

Switches

The following switches are available only in Version 5.0:

/D	Displays differences in hex format.
/A	Displays differences as characters.
/L	Displays the number of the line in which the difference occurred.
/N=x	Compares the first *x* number of lines of a file.
/C	Performs a comparison of files that is not case-sensitive.

Reference

See Chapter 13, "Understanding Backups and the Care of Data."

Rules

1. If you do not enter a file name, all files for that set, whether primary or secondary, are compared (which is the same as typing ***.***). However, only the files in the secondary set with names that match file names in the primary set are compared.

2. If you do not enter a drive, path, or file name, COMP prompts you for the primary and secondary file sets to compare. Otherwise, the correct disks must be in the correct drive if you are comparing files on disks. COMP does not wait for you to insert disks if you use both primary and secondary file names.

3. After 10 mismatches (unequal comparisons) between the contents of two compared files, COMP ends the comparison and aborts.

Note

A more versatile utility for file comparison is FC, discussed later in this Command Reference.

Messages

1. `Compare error at offset xxxxxxxx`

   Information: The files that you are comparing are not the same. The difference occurs at *xxxxxxxx* bytes from the start of the file. The number provided is in hexadecimal format, base 16. The values of the differing bytes in the files also are displayed in hexadecimal format.

2. `Files are different sizes`

   Warning: You asked COMP to compare two files of different lengths. Because COMP compares only files of the same size, COMP skips the comparison.

3. `10 Mismatches - ending compare`

   Warning: COMP found 10 mismatches between the two files you compared. COMP, therefore, assumes that no reason exists to continue, and the comparison is aborted.

COPY V1, V2, V3, V4, V5, V6-Internal

Copies files between disk drives or between drives and devices, and enables you to keep or change the file names or to join files.

Syntax

To copy a file, use either of the following formats:

> **COPY***/A/B d1:path1***filename1.ext1***/A/B*
> *d0:path0***filename0.ext0***/A/B/V*

or

> **COPY** */A/B d1:path1***filename1.ext1***/A/B/V*

To join several files into one, use the following format:

> **COPY** */A/B d1:path1***filename1.ext1***/A/B*
> *+ d2:path2***filename2.ext2***/A/B +...*

d1:, *d2:*, and *d0:* are valid drive names.

path1, *path2*, and *path0* are valid path names.

filename1.ext1 and **filename2.ext2** are valid file names. Wild cards are allowed.

The ellipsis (...) represents additional files in the format *dx:pathx***filenamex.extx**.

Special Terms

The file copied *from* is the *source file*. The names that contain 1 and 2 are the source files.

The file copied *to* is the *destination file*. This file is represented by a 0.

Switches

/V   Verifies that the copy was recorded correctly.

The following switches create different effects on the source and the destination.

For the source file:

/A   Treats the file as an ASCII (text) file. The command copies all the information in the file up to, but not including, the end-of-file marker (Ctrl-Z). Data after the end-of-file marker is ignored.

/B   Copies the entire file (based on size, as listed in the directory) as if the file were a program file *(binary1)*. All end-of-file markers (Ctrl-Z) are treated as normal characters, and EOF characters are copied.

For the destination file:

/A	Adds an end-of-file marker (Ctrl-Z) to the end of the ASCII text file at the conclusion of the copying process.
/B	Does not add the end-of-file marker to this binary file.

Reference

See Chapter 9, "Managing Your Files."

Rules

To copy files with both source and destination given:

1. The following rules apply to the file name:

   ■ You must provide either a path name or a file name. Wild cards are allowed in the source file name. If you do not provide a file name but provide a path name for the source, DOS assumes *.*.

   ■ If you do not provide a destination file name, the copied file has the same name, creation date, and creation time as the source file.

2. You can substitute a device name for the complete source or destination name.

3. When you copy between disk drives, COPY assumes that binary files are copied (as though you used the /B switch).

4. When you copy to or from a device other than a disk drive, COPY assumes that ASCII files are copied (as though you used the /A switch).

5. An /A or /B switch overrides the default settings for COPY.

To copy files with only one file specified:

1. The file specification you use (*d1:path1***filename1.ext1**) is the source. This specification needs one or both of the following items:

   ■ A valid file name. Wild cards are allowed.

   ■ A drive name, a path name, or both. If you provide only one name, that name must differ from the current drive name or path name. If you provide both names, at least one name must differ from the current drive name or path name.

2. The source cannot be a device name.

3. The destination is the current drive and current directory.

4. The copied file(s) use the same name as the source file(s).

5. COPY assumes that binary files are copied (as though you used the /B switch).

To concatenate files:

1. The destination file is the last file in the list unless you add a plus sign (+) before that file name. If you do not specify a destination file name, the first source name becomes the destination name.

2. If you do not provide a drive name, DOS uses the current drive.

3. If you do not provide a path, DOS uses the current directory.

4. The following rules apply to source files:

   ■ You must provide a valid file name. Wild cards are allowed, but using them can be dangerous. If you do not provide a destination file name, DOS uses the first file name as the destination file name.

   ■ After the first file name, any additional source file specifications must be preceded by a plus sign (+).

5. The following rules apply to the destination file:

   ■ You can use only one destination file specification. If you provide a destination without wild cards, DOS uses only one destination file. If you provide a destination file name with wild cards, DOS uses one or more destination files.

   ■ If you do not provide a destination, DOS uses the first source file as the destination. The first file that matches the wild-card file name is used as the destination file if you used a wild card as part of the first source file name, and the files to be joined are appended to the first source file.

Notes

The meanings of the /A and /B switches depend on their positions in the line. The /A or /B switch affects the file that immediately precedes the switch and all files that follow the switch until DOS encounters another /A or /B switch. When you use one of these switches before a file name, the switch affects all following files until DOS encounters another /A or /B that contradicts the earlier switch.

Use XCOPY to copy zero-length files and all of a directory's files and subdirectories.

To change the time and date of a file to the current time and date:

COPY /B *filename.ext+,,*

You can create a text file by copying what you type to the file. Use the following format:

COPY CON *filename.ext*

What you type will be copied to the file until you press Ctrl-Z or F6.

Messages

1. Content of destination lost before copy

    Warning: A destination file was not the first source file. The previous contents were destroyed. COPY continues to concatenate any remaining files.

2. File cannot be copied onto itself

    Error: You attempted to copy a file back to the same disk and directory that contains the same file name. This error usually occurs when you misspell or omit parts of the source or destination drive, path, or file name. Check your spelling and the source and destination names, and then try the command again.

CTTY   V2, V3, V4, V5, V6-Internal

Changes the standard input and output device to an auxiliary console, or changes the input and output device back from an auxiliary console to the keyboard and video display.

Syntax

CTTY device

device is the device that you want to use as the new standard input and output device. This name must be a valid DOS device name.

Reference

See Chapter 12, "Controlling Devices."

Rules

1. The device must be a character-oriented device capable of both input and output. DOS supplies several such devices, including AUX, COM1, COM2, COM3, COM4, CON, LPT1, LPT2, LPT3, and PRN.

2. Typing a colon (:) after the device name is optional.

3. CTTY does not affect any other form of redirected I/O or piping. For example, the < (redirect from), the > (redirect to), and the | (pipe between programs) work as usual.

Notes

The CTTY command is designed so that you can use a terminal or teleprinter, rather than the normal keyboard and video display, for console input and output. This versatility has little effect on most PC users.

To return control to the standard console, type **CTTY CON** on the auxiliary console. If you cannot, you must reboot to reenable the standard console.

The CTTY command does not affect programs that input and output directly to hardware.

COMMAND also can change the device.

DATE   *V1, V2, V3, V4, V5, V6-Internal*

Displays and/or changes the system date.

Syntax

To find out the system's date and be prompted for a new one, type the following command:

DATE

To set the system's date, use this format:

>   **DATE** *date_string*

date_string represents the day (*dd*), month (*mm*), and year(*yy* or *yyyy*), separated by periods (.), hyphens (-), or forward slashes (/). The format depends on the COUNTRY setting in CONFIG.SYS. In the United States, for example, the date format is *dd-mm-yy* or *dd-mm-yyyy* (any of the other legal separators can be substituted for the hyphens).

mm is a one- or two-digit number that represents the month (1 to 12).

dd is a one- or two-digit number that represents the day (1 to 31).

yy is a two-digit number that represents the year (80 to 99, which represent 1980 to 1999).

yyyy is a four-digit number that represents the year (1980 to 2099).

Reference

See Chapter 11, "Working with System Information."

Rule

The date entry and display correspond to the COUNTRY setting in your CONFIG.SYS file.

Notes

When you boot the computer, DOS issues the DATE and TIME commands to set the system clock. If you placed an AUTOEXEC.BAT file on the boot disk, DOS does not display a prompt for the date or time. You can include the DATE or TIME commands in the AUTOEXEC.BAT file to have these functions set when DOS boots.

Some computers, such as the IBM Personal Computer AT and compatibles, use battery-operated clocks. After you set the clock when you install the system, you need not enter the date or time again until the battery wears out.

When you create or update a file, DOS updates the directory, using the date you entered. This date shows which copy is the latest revision of the file. Several DOS commands (such as XCOPY) can use the date in selecting files.

The day-of-year calendar uses the time-of-day clock. If you leave your system on overnight, the day advances by one at midnight. DOS also makes appropriate calendar adjustments for leap years.

DBLSPACE   *V6-External*

Starts the full-screen interface to the DoubleSpace disk-compression capability. DoubleSpace automatically compresses information on hard disks or floppy disks and configures many aspects of the compression. Automatic compression enables you to put more programs and information on a disk than you can without compression. The general target is to double the amount of information.

With switches and parameters, you can control each aspect of DoubleSpace from the DOS command line. The many possible combinations are covered in the sections of this Command Reference that deal with specific DoubleSpace commands.

Syntax

DBLSPACE

Reference

See Chapter 18, "Getting the Most from Your Hard Drive."

Notes

The first time you use the DBLSPACE command, DoubleSpace Setup starts. The setup program enables you to compress one or more hard disks and loads DBLSPACE.BIN into memory. DBLSPACE.BIN is the device driver that provides access to compressed drives.

Subsequent uses of the DBLSPACE command start the full-screen interface. The full-screen interface and the DBLSPACE switches and parameters give you control of all DoubleSpace operations.

DoubleSpace works by creating a large hidden file, called a compressed volume file (CVF), on one of your drives, called the *host drive*, and presenting that drive as a new drive, called a *compressed drive*. For example, you might make a CVF on your D drive that results in a compressed drive E; you and your programs then can use the files on the compressed drive without taking any special action.

CVF names use the format DBLSPACE.*xxx*, in which *xxx* is a number (such as 000 or 001).

As you must whenever you create anything that results in a new disk-drive letter (for example, a network connection or INTERLNK), you need to use the LASTDRIV command to make the new drive letter available to DOS.

DBLSPACE /CHKDSK   V6-External

Checks the structure of a compressed drive. The command reports errors (such as lost clusters and cross-linked files) and can correct some errors.

Syntax

*dc:pathc***DBLSPACE /CHKDSK** */F drive:*

dc:pathc represents the drive and directory that hold the command.

drive: is the letter of the compressed drive that you want to check. The default is the current drive.

Switch

/F   Specifies that errors be fixed and not just reported.

Reference

See Chapter 18, "Getting the Most from Your Hard Drive."

Note

Running CHKDSK on a compressed drive automatically invokes **DBLSPACE /CHKDSK** on the drive after CHKDSK finishes checking the integrity of the drive's file-allocation table (FAT).

DBLSPACE /COMPRESS   V6-External

Compresses the files on an existing hard disk, floppy disk, or other removable disk, making more space available.

Syntax

dc:pathc**DBLSPACE /COMPRESS drive:** */NEWDRIVE=driven: /RESERVE=size*

dc:pathc**DBLSPACE /COM drive:** */NEW=driven: /RES=size*

dc:pathc\\ represents the drive and directory that hold the command.

drive: is the letter of the uncompressed (host) drive that you want to compress.

Switches

/NEWDRIVE=driven: Specifies the letter of the uncompressed (host) drive after compression. If you omit */NEWDRIVE=driven:*, DOS uses the next available drive letter.

/RESERVE=size Specifies the amount of space (in M) to be left uncompressed on the host drive. The default is 2M.

Reference

See Chapter 18, "Getting the Most from Your Hard Drive."

Rules

1. A drive must contain some free space before DoubleSpace can compress it. If you want to compress your boot drive, for example, that drive must have at least 1.2M of free space. Other hard disks and floppy disks must have at least 0.65M of free space.

2. DoubleSpace cannot compress 360K floppy disks.

3. You must mount a compressed floppy disk before you can use it. (For more information, see the section on the DBLSPACE /MOUNT command later in this Command Reference.)

4. If you want to read a compressed floppy disk on another computer, you must use a computer that also uses DoubleSpace.

Note

Your system probably needs some uncompressed disk space, because some files (such as Windows permanent swap files) do not work properly if you store them on a compressed drive.

Example

To compress drive D so that the compressed part is known as D and the uncompressed (host) part, known as E, contains 3M of uncompressed free space:

DBLSPACE /COMPRESS D: /NEWDRIVE=E: /RESERVE=3

DBLSPACE /CREATE   V6-External

Creates a new compressed drive by using free space on an uncompressed drive.

Syntax

*dc:pathc***DBLSPACE /CREATE drive:** */NEWDRIVE=driven: /SIZE=size /RESERVE=size*

*dc:pathc***DBLSPACE /CR drive:** */N=driven: /SI=size /RE=size*

dc:pathc represents the drive and directory that hold the command.

drive: is the letter of the uncompressed (host) drive that contains the free space from which the new compressed drive will be created.

Switches

/NEWDRIVE=driven:	Specifies the letter of the new compressed drive. The default is the next available drive letter.
/SIZE=size	Specifies the size (in M) of the compressed volume file (CVF) on the host drive. Depending on how well your files compress, the CVF will occupy approximately half as much space on the new compressed drive. You cannot specify */SIZE* if you specify */RESERVE*.

| /RESERVE=size | Specifies the amount of space (in M) to be left uncompressed on the host drive. To make the compressed drive as large as possible, specify *size* as 0 (zero). The default is 1M. You cannot specify /RE-SERVE if you specify /SIZE. |

Reference

See Chapter 18, "Getting the Most from Your Hard Drive."

Rules

1. A drive must contain some free space before DoubleSpace can compress it. If you want to compress your boot drive, for example, that drive must have at least 1.2M of free space. Other hard disks and floppy disks must have at least 0.65M of free space.

2. DoubleSpace cannot compress 360K floppy disks.

3. You must mount a compressed floppy disk before you can use it. (For more information, see the section on the DBLSPACE / MOUNT command later in this Command Reference.)

4. If you want to read a compressed floppy disk on another computer, you must use a computer that also uses DoubleSpace.

Note

Your system probably needs some uncompressed disk space, because some files (such as Windows permanent swap files) do not work properly when you store them on a compressed drive.

Examples

To create a new compressed drive that has the next available drive letter as its name and that uses all the available free space on the uncompressed drive D:

DBLSPACE /CREATE D: /RESERVE=0

To create a new compressed drive F that uses 20M of free space on the uncompressed drive D:

DBLSPACE /CREATE D: /NEWDRIVE=F: /SIZE=20

DBLSPACE /DEFRAGMENT   *V6-External*

Defragments a compressed drive by moving all the drive's free space to the end of the drive. This command enables you to get the maximum reduction in the size of the drive when you issue the DBLSPACE /SIZE command.

Syntax

*dc:pathc***DBLSPACE /DEFRAGMENT** *drive:*

*dc:pathc***DBLSPACE /DEF** *drive:*

dc:pathc represents the drive and directory that hold the command.

drive: is the letter of the compressed drive that you want to defragment. The default is the current drive.

Reference

See Chapter 18, "Getting the Most from Your Hard Drive."

Notes

Unlike defragmenting an uncompressed hard disk, defragmenting a DoubleSpace disk does not improve the disk's performance. Defragmenting only moves the free space to the end of the compressed drive so that DBLSPACE /SIZE will be most effective.

You cannot tell how badly fragmented a compressed drive is before you decide to defragment it.

How long defragmenting takes depends on many factors, including the speed of your computer, the size of your compressed drive, and the speed of your disk drive. The process can take a long time, however—perhaps several hours.

You can stop the defragmentation process at any time by pressing Esc.

DBLSPACE /DELETE   *V6-External*

Deletes a compressed drive and its associated compressed volume file (CVF).

Syntax

*dc:pathc***DBLSPACE /DELETE drive:**

*dc:pathc***DBLSPACE /DEL drive:**

dc:pathc represents the drive and directory that hold the command.

drive: is the letter of the compressed drive that you want to delete.

Reference

See Chapter 18, "Getting the Most from Your Hard Drive."

Rules

1. Deleting a compressed drive deletes all the files in that drive.

2. You cannot delete drive C.

Note

If you accidentally delete a compressed drive, you may be able to restore it with UNDELETE, because a compressed drive is a file on one of your uncompressed disks. The files corresponding to compressed drives are hidden and have names in the format DBLSPACE.*xxx*, in which *xxx* is a number (such as 000 or 001). If you can undelete the associated file, you can remount it with DBLSPACE /MOUNT.

DBLSPACE /FORMAT   *V6-External*

Formats a compressed drive.

Syntax

>*dc:pathc***DBLSPACE /FORMAT drive:**
>
>*dc:pathc***DBLSPACE /F drive:**

dc:pathc\ represents the drive and directory that hold the command.

drive: is the letter of the compressed drive that you want to format.

Reference

See Chapter 18, "Getting the Most from Your Hard Drive."

Rule

You cannot format drive C.

Notes

Formatting a compressed drive deletes all the files on that drive.

You cannot unformat a compressed drive after performing a /FORMAT operation on that drive.

DBLSPACE /INFO   V6-External

Displays information about a compressed drive.

Syntax

>*dc:pathc***DBLSPACE /INFO drive:**
>
>*dc:pathc***DBLSPACE drive:**

dc:pathc\ represents the drive and directory that hold the command.

drive: is the letter of the compressed drive about which you want information.

Reference

See Chapter 18, "Getting the Most from Your Hard Drive."

Note

The command displays the following information: the drive, path, and name of the drive's CVF; the drive's available and free space; and the drive's actual and estimated compression ratios.

DBLSPACE /LIST   V6-External

Displays information about your computer's local drives.

Syntax

> *dc:pathc***DBLSPACE /LIST**
>
> *dc:pathc***DBLSPACE /L**

dc:pathc represents the drive and directory that hold the command.

Reference

See Chapter 18, "Getting the Most from Your Hard Drive."

Note

The command displays the following information: the drive letters; the types of drives (for example, removable, local hard, and compressed hard); the drives' total size and amount of free space; and, for compressed drives, the drive, path, and name of the associated CVF.

DBLSPACE /MOUNT   V6-External

Associates a drive letter with a compressed volume file (CVF) so that you can access the files in the CVF as though they were on a disk. Normally, DoubleSpace mounts CVFs for you, so you need to mount a CVF only if you have explicitly unmounted it or if the CVF is on a floppy disk.

Syntax

*dc:pathc***DBLSPACE** /**MOUNT**=*nnn* **drive:**
/*NEWDRIVE*=*driven:*

*dc:pathc***DBLSPACE** /**MO**=*nnn* **drive:** /*NEW*=*driven:*

dc:pathc represents the drive and directory that hold the command.

drive: is the letter of the uncompressed (host) drive containing the CVF that you want to mount.

Switches

/**MOUNT**=*nnn*   Specifies that the CVF named DBLSPACE.*nnn* on **drive** be mounted. The default is DBLSPACE.000.

/*NEWDRIVE*=*driven:*   Specifies the letter of **drive:**DBLSPACE.*nnn*. The default is the next available drive letter.

Reference

See Chapter 18, "Getting the Most from Your Hard Drive."

Examples

To mount the CVF D:\\DBLSPACE.001 as the next available drive letter:

DBLSPACE /MOUNT=001 D:

To mount a DoubleSpace compressed floppy disk in A as the next available drive letter:

DBLSPACE /MOUNT A:

DBLSPACE /RATIO   V6-External

Changes the estimated compression ratio of a compressed drive.

DoubleSpace uses the estimated compression ratio to estimate how much free space the compressed drive will contain. You may want to change the estimated ratio if you are about to copy to the compressed drive files that differ significantly from those that already are on the drive.

Syntax

> *dc:pathc***DBLSPACE /RATIO**=*n.m drive: /ALL*
>
> *dc:pathc***DBLSPACE /RA** =*n.m drive: /ALL*

dc:pathc represents the drive and directory that hold the command.

drive: is the letter of the compressed drive for which you want to change the estimated compression ratio. DOS uses the current drive unless you specify */ALL.* You cannot specify both *drive:* and */ALL.*

Switches

/RATIO=*n.m*   Specifies the new estimated compression ratio. The range is from 1.0 to 16.0. The default is the actual compression ratio for the drive.

/ALL   Specifies that the estimated compression ratios be changed for all mounted compressed drives. You cannot specify both *drive:* and */ALL.*

Reference

See Chapter 18, "Getting the Most from Your Hard Drive."

Examples

To change all your mounted compressed drives so that their estimated compression ratios equal their actual compression ratios:

> **DBLSPACE /RATIO D: /ALL**

To change the estimated compression ratio of compressed drive E to 1.7:

> **DBLSPACE /RATIO=1.7 E:**

DBLSPACE /SIZE   V6-External

Changes the size of a compressed drive.

You may want to make a compressed drive smaller if you need more free space on its host drive. You may want to make a compressed drive larger if its host drive has a great deal of free space.

Syntax

> *dc:pathc***DBLSPACE** */SIZE*=*size* */RESERVE*=*size2* **drive:**

> *dc:pathc***DBLSPACE** */SI*=*size* */RES*=*size2* **drive:**

dc:pathc represents the drive and directory that hold the command.

drive: is the letter of the compressed drive that you want to make larger or smaller.

Switches

/SIZE=size	Specifies the space (in M) that **drive:**'s CVF should take up on its host (uncompressed) drive. You cannot specify both =*size* and */RESERVE*=*size2*. The default is to make the host drive as small as possible.
/RESERVE=size2	Specifies the space (in M) to be left free on the host (uncompressed) drive after **drive:** is resized. You cannot specify both =*size* and */RESERVE*=*size2*. The default is to make the host drive as small as possible.

Reference

See Chapter 18, "Getting the Most from Your Hard Drive."

Examples

To change the size of compressed drive E so its CVF takes up 30M on its host (uncompressed) drive:

> **DBLSPACE /SIZE=30 E:**

To make compressed drive E as large as possible so that its host drive contains no uncompressed free space:

> **DBLSPACE /SIZE /RESERVE=0 E:**

DBLSPACE /UNMOUNT   *V6-External*

Breaks the association between a drive letter and a compressed volume file (CVF), temporarily making a compressed drive unavailable.

Syntax

*dc:pathc***DBLSPACE /UNMOUNT** *drive:*

*dc:pathc***DBLSPACE /U** *drive:*

dc:pathc represents the drive and directory that hold the command.

drive: is the letter of the compressed drive that you want to unmount. The default is the current drive.

Reference

See Chapter 18, "Getting the Most from Your Hard Drive."

Rule

You cannot unmount drive C.

Note

Use DBLSPACE /MOUNT to regain access to the compressed drive.

DBLSPACE.SYS   *V6-External*

Specifies whether the DoubleSpace driver, DBLSPACE.BIN, ends up in conventional or upper memory.

Syntax

DEVICE=*dc:pathc***DBLSPACE.SYS** */MOVE*

DEVICEHIGH=*dc:pathc***DBLSPACE.SYS** */MOVE*

dc:pathc represents the drive and directory that hold DBLSPACE.SYS.

Switch

    /MOVE   Specifies that DBLSPACE.BIN be moved from the top of conventional memory to the bottom of available conventional memory (if **DEVICE=** was used) or to upper memory (if **DEVICEHIGH=** was used and if a sufficient amount of upper memory is available). Moving DBLSPACE.BIN can prevent conflicts with the few programs that require access to the top of conventional memory. Moving this driver to upper memory also frees conventional memory.

Reference

See Chapter 18, "Getting the Most from Your Hard Drive."

Rules

1. DBLSPACE.BIN provides access to compressed drives.

2. When your computer is booted and you have compressed drives, DBLSPACE.BIN is loaded before commands in CONFIG.SYS and AUTOEXEC.BAT are executed so that the commands can access compressed drives. At that time, DBLSPACE.BIN resides in upper conventional memory.

DEBUG   *V2, V3, V4, V5, V6-External*

A utility that tests and edits programs. DEBUG also assembles the machine code from assembly-language mnemonics, unassembles bytes into source statements, and allocates EMS (expanded memory).

Syntax

    *dc:pathc***DEBUG** *de:pathe\\filenamee.exte parameters*

dc:pathc represents the drive and directory that hold the command.

de:pathe represents the drive and directory that hold the file to be edited.

filenamee.exte is the file to be loaded into memory for editing.

parameters represents whatever parameters the file needs.

Rules

1. If DEBUG.EXE is not in the search path, you must specify the drive and directory where DEBUG is located.

2. You can create small assembly-language programs with DEBUG, using 8088/8086/8087 op codes only.

Examples

To start DEBUG:

DEBUG

To start DEBUG, loading PROGRAM.EXE from C:\UTILS for editing:

DEBUG C:\UTILS\PROGRAM.EXE

Note

The DEBUG utility enables you to load a program into memory and then edit, test, and save the edited program back to the disk. You also can use DEBUG to create small machine-language programs. See the on-line help for DEBUG commands.

DEFRAG   V6-External

Moves files and clusters within files to optimize disk performance.

Syntax

*dc:pathc***DEFRAG** *drive: /F /S:sortorder /B /SKIPHIGH /LCD /BW /G0 /H*

*dc:pathc***DEFRAG** *drive: /U /B /SKIPHIGH /LCD /BW /G0 /H*

dc:pathc represents the drive and directory that hold the command.

drive: is the drive to be optimized.

Switches

/F	Provides the best optimization but takes the most time. Defragments files, moves them to the front of the disk, and puts all the empty space at the end of the disk.
/U	Takes the least amount of time. Defragments files but does not rearrange them. The empty space is left spread over the disk.
/S	Controls the order of files in their directories. If you omit this switch, the current order is unchanged. The colon (:) is optional. Use any combination of the following values without separating them with spaces:

N	Sorts in alphabetical order by name (A to Z).
N–	Sorts in reverse alphabetical order by name (Z to A).
E	Sorts in alphabetical order by extension (A to Z).
E–	Sorts in reverse alphabetical order by extension (Z to A).
D	Sorts by date and time (newest to oldest).
D–	Sorts by date and time (oldest to newest).
S	Sorts by size (smallest to largest).
S–	Sorts by size (largest to smallest).

/B	Restarts your computer after the files have been reorganized.
/SKIPHIGH	Loads DEFRAG into conventional memory.
/LCD	Uses colors suited to a liquid-crystal display.
/BW	Uses colors suited to a monochrome display.
/G0	Disables the graphic mouse and graphic character set.
/H	Moves hidden files.

Rules

1. DOS starts DEFRAG in interactive mode if you omit one or more required parameters from the command line.

2. DEFRAG takes over the entire screen to show what it is doing.

3. By default, DEFRAG is loaded into upper memory if enough memory is free.

4. Do not use DEFRAG to optimize network drives or drives created with Interlnk.

5. If you are using FASTOPEN when you defragment, specify DEFRAG /B so that the out-of-date buffers kept by FASTOPEN will not be used after the defragmenting operation.

6. Start DEFRAG only from DOS, not from the Microsoft Windows DOS prompt. Otherwise, you may lose data.

Exit Codes

Code	Explanation
0	Defragmentation was successful
1	Internal error
2	No free clusters (DEFRAG needs one free cluster on the target disk)
3	Ctrl-C stopped DEFRAG
4	General error
5	Error while reading a cluster on the target disk
6	Error while writing a cluster on the target disk
7	Allocation error (use the CHKDSK command with the /F switch to try to correct the problem on the target disk)
8	Memory error
9	Insufficient memory to defragment the target disk

DEL

V1, V2, V3, V4, V5, V6-Internal

Deletes files from the disk.

DEL is an alternative command for ERASE and performs the same functions. See the ERASE section later in this Command Reference for a complete description.

DELOLDOS

V5, V6-External

Deletes from the hard disk all files from a previous version of DOS after a DOS 5.0 or 6.0 installation.

Syntax

*dc:pathc***DELOLDOS** */B*

dc:pathc represents the drive and directory that hold the command.

Switch

/B   Forces black-and-white screen mode.

Rules

1. After you start DELOLDOS, you can exit without deleting the old version of DOS by pressing any key except Y.

2. Be sure that all your programs are compatible with the new DOS before you delete the old version.

3. After doing a DELOLDOS, you cannot use the uninstall disk created by DOS 5.0 or 6.0 Setup to restore your previous DOS version.

Note

When you upgrade to DOS 5.0 or 6.0, the old version of DOS is preserved in part on your hard disk in the directory OLD_DOS.1 and on the Uninstall disks that the DOS Setup program creates. After you are sure that the upgrade works correctly and is compatible with the programs that you normally use, you can delete the old DOS from the hard disk, thereby freeing additional storage space.

DELTREE   V6-External

Deletes a directory and all of its files and subdirectories.

Syntax

*dc:pathc***DELTREE** */Y drive:***path**

dc:pathc represents the drive and directory that hold the command.

drive: is the drive of the directory that you want to delete.

path is the directory where the deletion is to start. (You can use wild cards.)

Switch

/Y   Suppresses prompting for permission to delete each directory specified by **path**.

Reference

See Chapter 8, "Understanding and Managing Directories."

Rules

1. This command deletes all files—even hidden, read-only, and system files.

2. DOS prompts you for permission to delete each directory specified by **path**, unless you specify **/Y**.

3. If DELTREE is successful, the command exits with an ERRORLEVEL value of 0.

Note

Exercise great caution with this command, particularly if you specify wild cards. You easily can delete more files than you intend.

DIR

V1, V2, V3, V4, V5, V6-Internal

Lists any or all files and subdirectories in a disk directory.

By default, the list includes the following information:

- Volume label and serial number
- One directory or file name per line
- File size (in bytes)
- Date and time of the last modification
- Number of files listed
- Total bytes listed
- Number of available bytes remaining on the disk

Syntax

In versions of DOS prior to Version 5.0, use the following syntax:

DIR *d:path\filename.ext /P/W*

In DOS 5.0, use the following format:

DIR *d:path\filename.ext/P/W /A:attributes/O:sortorder/S/B/L*

In DOS 6.0, use the following format:

DIR *d:path\filename.ext/P/W /A:attributes/O:sortorder/S/B /L/C/CH*

d: is the drive holding the disk that you want to examine.

path is the path to the directory that you want to examine.

filename.ext is a valid file name. Wild cards are permitted.

Switches

/P	Pauses when the screen is full and waits for you to press any key.
/W	Generates a wide (80-column) display of the file names; file size, date, and time are not displayed.

The following switches are valid in DOS 5.0 and 6.0 only:

/A:attributes	Displays only files with the attributes you specify. If the *attributes* parameter is omitted, DOS displays all files (the colon is optional):
no switch	Displays all files except system and hidden files.
H	Displays hidden files.
–H	Displays all files that are not hidden.
S	Displays only system files.
–S	Displays all files except system files.
D	Displays only directories (no files).
–D	Displays only files (no directories).
A	Displays files that are ready for archiving (backup).
–A	Displays files that have not changed since the last backup.
R	Displays read-only files.
–R	Displays files that are not read-only.
/O:sortorder	Controls the order in which DOS displays the information about the files and directories. If you omit *sortorder*, DIR displays directories and files in alphabetical order (the colon is optional):
no switch	No sorting. Directories and files are displayed in the order in which they occur in the directory.
N	Sorts alphabetically by name (A to Z).
–N	Sorts by name in reverse alphabetical order (Z to A).
E	Sorts alphabetically by extension (A to Z).
–E	Sorts by extension in reverse alphabetical order (Z to A).

D	Sorts by date and time (earliest to latest).
–D	Sorts by date and time in reverse order (latest to earliest).
S	Sorts by size (smallest to largest).
–S	Sorts by size (largest to smallest).
C	Sorts by DoubleSpace compression ratio (lowest to highest). DOS 6.0 only.
–C	Sorts by DoubleSpace compression ratio (highest to lowest). DOS 6.0 only.
G	Groups directories before files.
–G	Groups directories after files.
/S	Lists all occurrences of the specified file name in the specified directory and all subdirectories.
/B	Lists only file names with no header or trailer information. This switch overrides /W.
/L	Displays all information in lowercase.

The following switches are valid for DOS 6.0 only:

/C	Displays the compression ratios of files on a DoubleSpace volume, assuming an 8K cluster size. Suppressed by /W or /B.
/CH	Displays the compression ratios of files on a DoubleSpace volume, assuming the cluster size of the last drive. Supresses by /W or /B.

Reference

See Chapter 9, "Managing Your Files."

Rules

1. You cannot use the DIR command for a drive in which you used the ASSIGN or JOIN command. You must break the assignment before you view the directory for a drive in which you used ASSIGN. Use the path name of the disk that you used in the JOIN command. You can use the DIR command on the host disk drive involved in a JOIN command.

2. When more than one *sortorder* value is specified, the file names are sorted from the leftmost value to the rightmost value.

Notes

DIR does not report statistics for disk drives in which you used the ASSIGN or JOIN command. For disk drives in which you used JOIN, DIR reports the free space of the host disk drive (the disk drive to which the second disk drive is joined). DIR does not, however, report the total of the two disk drives in which you use JOIN. First remove ASSIGN or JOIN from the drive to find its amount of free space.

In DOS 5.0 or 6.0, you can use SET DIRCMD to set DIR switches in the AUTOEXEC.BAT file. If you want DIR to display files and directories a page at a time, enter the following command into your AUTOEXEC.BAT file:

SET DIRCMD=/P

To override the preset switch, use the following format:

DIR /-P

To view the options set with the DIRCMD variable, type the following command:

SET

DISKCOMP

V1, V2, V3, V4, V5, V6-External

Compares two floppy disks on a track-for-track, sector-for-sector basis to see whether their contents are identical.

Syntax

*dc:pathc***DISKCOMP** *d1: d2: /1 /8*

dc: is the drive that holds the command.

pathc is the path to the command.

d1: and *d2:* are the drives that hold the disks to be compared. These drives can be the same.

Switches

/1   Compares only the first side of the floppy disk, even if the disk or disk drive is double-sided.

/8   Compares only eight sectors per track, even if the first disk has a different number of sectors per track.

Exit Codes

Code	Explanation
0	Compared OK
1	Did not compare
2	CTRL-C error
3	Hard (uncorrectable or critical) error
4	Initialization error

Reference

See Chapter 6, "Understanding Disks and Files."

Rules

1. If you provide only one valid floppy-drive name, DOS uses the current drive for the comparison.

2. If *d1:* and *d2:* are the same, DISKCOMP prompts you when diskettes need to be swapped.

3. Compare only compatible floppy disks formatted with the same number of tracks, sectors, and sides.

4. Do not use DISKCOMP for a drive in which you used the ASSIGN, JOIN, or SUBST command or for a network drive.

5. Two disks that contain the same files will not compare the same with DISKCOMP if the information in the files is arranged differently on the two disks.

Note

Remember to compare only floppy disks that were duplicated with DISKCOPY.

Messages

1. `Compare error on`
   `Track tt, side s`

   Warning: The disks you are comparing are different at track number *tt*, side *s*. DISKCOMP does not specify which sectors are different—only that one or more sectors differ. If you just used DISKCOPY on these disks and DOS reported no problem, the second disk probably has a flaw. Reformat the disk and try DISKCOPY again. Otherwise, assume that the disks are different.

2. `Compare OK`

   Information: DISKCOMP compared the two floppy disks and found that they match.

3. `Drive types or diskette types not compatible`

   or

   `Incompatible disks`

   Error: The disk drives are of different types (3 1/2 or 5 1/4 inch) or the floppy disks are different. The first disk was successfully read on both sides. DOS noticed the discrepancy when it tried to read the second disk.

4. `Unrecoverable read error on drive x`
   `Track tt, side s`

   Warning: DOS made four attempts to read the data from the floppy disk in the specified drive. The error is in track *tt*, side *s*. If drive *x* is the disk that holds the destination (copied) disk, the copy probably is bad. (The disk has a *hard*— unrecoverable—read error.) If drive *x* holds the original disk, a flaw existed when the disk was formatted, or a flaw developed during use.

   Run CHKDSK on the original disk and look for the line `bytes in bad sectors`. Even if this line is displayed, the original disk and the copy may be good (the bad sectors may not be used by any of the files on the disk). When you format a disk, FORMAT detects bad sectors and "hides" them. DISKCOMP, however, does not check for bad sectors; it attempts to compare the tracks, even if bad sectors exist. For safety's sake, retire the original disk soon.

5. Invalid drive specification
   Specified drive does not exist
   or is non-removable

   Error: One (or both) of the specified drives does not exist or is a hard disk. This can result from specifying only one drive to DISKCOMP and having the current drive be a hard disk.

DISKCOPY *V1, V2, V3, V4, V5, V6-External*

Copies the contents of one floppy disk to another on a track-for-track basis, making an exact copy. DISKCOPY works only with floppy disks.

Syntax

> *dc:pathc***DISKCOPY** *d1: d2: /1 /V*

dc: is the disk drive that holds the command.

pathc is the path to the command.

d1: is the floppy disk drive that holds the source (original) disk.

d2: is the floppy disk drive that holds the destination disk (disk to be copied to).

Switches

/1   Copies only the first side of the disk. (This switch is not available in the Epson Equity version of DOS.)

/V   Verifies that the copy is correct (DOS 4.0 and later versions). This switch slows the copy process.

Special Terms

The floppy disk you are copying *from* is the *source*, or first floppy disk.

The floppy disk you are copying *to* is the *destination*, or second disk.

Exit Codes

Code	Explanation
0	Successful Copy.
1	Nonfatal error, read/write error.
2	CTRL-C used to stop DISKCOPY.
3	Fatal hard error.
4	Initialization error.

Reference

See Chapter 6, "Understanding Disks and Files."

Rules

1. The source and destination disk drives must be real floppy disk drives—not hard or networked disk drives, RAM disks, or disk drives in which you used the JOIN or SUBST command. Defaulting to or specifying a nonreal source or destination disk drive causes DOS to return an error message and abort the copy operation.

2. If you do not provide a source disk drive name, DISKCOPY uses the default disk drive. If you provide an improper source disk drive, DISKCOPY issues an error message and aborts.

3. If your system has a single floppy disk drive and if you provide only one valid floppy disk drive name, DOS uses that drive as both the source and destination disk drive for the copy. If your system uses two floppy disk drives and you provide only one valid disk drive name, DOS displays the message Invalid drive specification error.

4. DISKCOPY destroys any information recorded on the destination disk. Do not use as the destination disk one that contains information you want to keep.

5. To ensure that the copy is correct, run DISKCOMP on the two disks.

6. DISKCOPY ignores the effects of an ASSIGN command.

7. DISKCOPY recognizes unformatted destination disks and automatically formats them as part of the copying process.

Notes

Write-protecting the source disk is important when you use only one floppy disk drive to make a copy of a disk. DOS periodically prompts you to change the disk. You cannot damage a write-protected source disk if you inadvertently insert that disk when DOS asks for the destination disk.

When you use DISKCOPY, DOS reads into memory as much information as possible from the source disk. DOS then copies this information to the destination disk and reads the next batch of information from the source disk. The more free memory is available, the less time you need to copy a disk.

DISKCOPY copies whatever level of file fragmentation is on the source disk to the destination disk. To avert this problem, you may want to DEFRAG the source disk before copying it or FORMAT the destination disk and then XCOPY files to it.

Messages

1. Drive types or diskette types not compatible

   Error: The drive types or disk capacities that you tried to use are different and cannot handle the operation, or the destination disk is the wrong capacity. DOS read the first disk, but the drive specified as the destination is not the right type. You cannot DISKCOPY high-density disks in non-high-density disk drives or copy double-sided disks in single-sided disk drives.

2. Read error on drive *d*:
   Write error on drive *d*:

   Warning: DISKCOPY cannot accurately read or write the disk in drive *d*:. The disk is not properly inserted, the source disk is not formatted (or is a non-DOS disk), or the drive door is open. Check these possibilities.

3. SOURCE diskette bad or incompatible TARGET diskette bad or incompatible

   Warning: DISKCOPY detected errors while reading the source disk (first message) or writing the destination (target) disk (second message). Bad sectors may exist on either disk, or the disk may be in the wrong type of drive.

Determine whether either floppy disk has bad sectors. If so, do not use DISKCOPY on either disk. If the source disk is bad, use COPY *. to copy files from the source disk. If the destination disk is bad, try a different disk, or try to reformat the disk and then use DISKCOPY.

4. Invalid drive specification
   Specified drive does not exist
   or is non-removable

Error: One or both of the two specified drives does not exist or is a hard disk.

DOSKEY   V5, V6-External

Enables you to repeat and edit DOS commands and to create macros.

Syntax

*dc:pathc***DOSKEY** */REINSTALL /BUFSIZE=size /MACROS /HISTORY /INSERT /OVERSTRIKE macroname=text*

dc: is the drive that holds the command.

pathc is the path to the command.

macroname is the name of the macro that you want to define.

text represents the commands that you want DOS to execute when you type the macro name at a DOS command prompt. If *text* is null, the definition of *macroname* is deleted.

Switches

/REINSTALL	Installs a new copy of DOSKey even if a copy already is installed. This clears the DOSKey buffer.
/BUFSIZE=size	Specifies the buffer size. The default is 512. The minimum is 256. Increasing or decreasing this value affects how much conventional memory is available if DOSKey is loaded into conventional memory.
/MACROS	Displays a listing of DOSKey-created macros. You can redirect output by using the redirection symbol (>). This switch can be abbreviated as */M*.

/HISTORY	Displays a list of all commands stored by DOSKey. You can redirect output by using the redirection symbol (>). This switch can be abbreviated as */H*.
/INSERT	Inserts new text into the file (as if the Insert key had been pressed). The default is /OVERSTRIKE. Pressing the Insert key toggles between Insert and Overstrike modes.
/OVERSTRIKE	New text overwrites old text (as if the Insert key had been pressed).

Reference

See Chapter 15, "Understanding Batch Files, DOSKey, and Macros."

Notes

Ordinarily, DOS remembers the last command you typed at the command line. With DOSKey, however, DOS can store a history of commands in memory. The number of commands retained in memory depends on the size of the buffer (normally 512 bytes). When the buffer is full, DOS eliminates the oldest command to make room for the new command. The buffer contains macros and the history of commands.

You can press several keys to recall a command in the history. Those keys and their functions are as follows:

Key	Function
↑	Displays the last command in history
↓	Displays the next command in history; when the last command is reached, DOS redisplays the first command
PgUp	Displays the first command in history
PgDn	Displays the last command in history

In addition to the standard DOS editing keys, you can use several keys and key combinations to edit a command in the command line. These additional keys are as follows:

Key	Function
←	Moves cursor one character to the left
Ctrl-←	Moves cursor one word to the left
→	Moves cursor one character to the right
Ctrl-→	Moves cursor one word to the right
Home	Moves cursor to the first character in command line
End	Moves cursor to the final position in command line
Esc	Erases current command line
F7	Numbers and lists all commands in history and indicates which is the current command
Alt-F7	Erases all commands from history
F8	Retrieves the most recent command from history that matches what you typed in the command line before pressing F8 (repeated pressing of F8 retrieves older matching commands)
F9	Enables you to specify, by number, which command in history to make current (to see command numbers, press F7)
Alt-F10	Erases all macros from memory

DOSKey enables you to create macros. A macro, like a batch file, performs one or more DOS commands assigned to a specific name. After you type the name of a macro and press Enter, the macro executes the commands assigned to the macro name. When you create a macro, you can use the following special symbols:

Code	Description
$g or $G	Used for redirecting output; use instead of >
gg or GG	Used for adding to an output file; use instead of >>
$l or $L	Used for redirecting input; use instead of <
$b or $B	Used for piping; use instead of |
$t or $T	Separates macro commands
$$	Places the dollar sign in the command line
$1 through $9	Replaceable parameters; same as %1 through %9 in a batch file

Code	Description
$*	Replaceable parameter that represents everything typed in the command line after the macro name

When you create a macro, you can include any valid DOS command, including the name of a batch file. You can start a batch file from a macro, but you cannot start a macro from a batch file.

Examples

To copy the most recent DOS commands to the batch file MYHIST.BAT (DOSKey enables you to save DOS commands that you then can execute at any time):

DOSKEY /HISTORY > MYHIST.BAT

Invoked as **CDD D \MYSTUFF** to change the current directory to \MYSTUFF on disk D:

DOSKEY CDD=$1: $T CD $2

Messages

1. Cannot change BUFSIZE

   Error: You cannot change the DOSKey buffer unless you also use the REINSTALL switch, which clears the buffer.

2. Insufficient memory to store macro. Use the DOSKEY command with the /BUFSIZE switch to increase available memory.

   Warning: Your DOSKey macros have filled the total space set aside for them. You must enlarge the memory area for macros (the default is 512 bytes) by using the BUFSIZE switch (and the REINSTALL switch) before you can enter any new macros. Using REINSTALL clears the buffer.

3. Invalid macro definition

   Error: You entered an illegal character or command with DOSKey or attempted to create a DOSKey macro with an illegal definition. This message appears, for example, if you use a GOTO command in a DOSKey macro. Correct any errors and carefully retype the macro.

DOSSHELL   V4, V5, V6-External

Starts the Shell (a graphical user interface) that accompanies DOS.

Syntax

To start DOS Shell in text mode, use the following format:

   *dc:pathc***DOSSHELL** */T:screen /B*

To start DOS Shell in graphics mode, use the following format:

   *dc:pathc***DOSSHELL** */G:screen /B*

To start DOS Shell in the default screen mode, use the following format:

   *dc:pathc***DOSSHELL**

dc:pathc represents the drive and subdirectory where DOSSHELL is located.

Switches

/T:screen   Displays DOS Shell in text mode, using the resolution described by *screen*.

/G:screen   Displays DOS Shell in graphics mode, using the resolution described by *screen*, as follows:

Switch	Monochrome /CGA	EGA	VGA
/T:L	25 lines	25 lines	25 lines
/T:M	x	43 lines	43 lines
/T:M1	x	43 lines	43 lines
/T:M2	x	43 lines	50 lines
/T:H	x	43 lines	43 lines
/T:H1	x	43 lines	43 lines
/T:H2	x	43 lines	50 lines
/G:L	25 lines	25 lines	25 lines
/G:M	x	43 lines	30 lines

Switch	Monochrome /CGA	EGA	VGA
/G:M1	x	43 lines	30 lines
/G:M2	x	43 lines	34 lines
/G:H	x	43 lines	43 lines
/G:H1	x	43 lines	43 lines
/G:H2	x	43 lines	60 lines

/B Starts DOS Shell in black-and-white rather than in color.

Reference

See Chapter 15, "Understanding Batch Files, DOSKey, and Macros."

Rules

1. When you start the DOS Shell without switches, the display is based on the default display and color settings.

2. To start the DOS Shell with a screen display other than the default, you must use the /G or /T switch.

3. Each time you start the DOS Shell, the Shell searches the disk for directories and files.

4. Do not start Microsoft Windows from the DOS Shell.

5. You need at least 384K of free conventional memory to start the DOS Shell.

Examples

To start the DOS Shell in the default screen mode:

DOSSHELL

To start the DOS Shell in black-and-white mode (use this command if you use a black-and-white monitor or if you use a laptop or notebook computer with an LCD screen):

DOSSHELL /B

Notes

In DOS 4.0, DOSSHELL was a batch file that started the Shell and held all the switches needed to start the Shell in the correct configuration for your computer. In DOS 5.0 and later versions, DOSSHELL is a program. When you install DOS, DOSSHELL is configured for your computer system.

Your DOSSHELL settings are preserved in your DOSSHELL.INI file. The DOS 6.0 installation does not overwrite or modify that file, which may produce inconsistencies on your system (references to BACKUP rather than to MSBACKUP, for example). You can avoid these inconsistencies by renaming DOSSHELL.INI before you install DOS 6.0 and then manually editing changes from your renamed DOSSHELL.INI into your new DOSSHELL.INI, by using EDIT or by using EXPAND to uncompress EGA.IN_ (for EGA and VGA systems) from the DOS 6.0 installation disks and then using EDIT to update DOSSHELL.INI.

Messages

1. Not enough memory to run DOSSHELL

   Error: Not enough conventional memory is available to start DOSSHELL. You may have too many TSRs loaded into memory, or you may be trying to start DOSSHELL while you jumped to DOS from a program without first exiting the program. Remove TSRs from memory, or exit the program loaded into memory and then try to restart DOSSHELL.

2. Not enough free conventional memory to run program

   or

   Not enough free extended memory to run program

   Either of these messages can appear when you try to start a program from the DOS Shell without sufficient available memory. Remove the TSRs from memory to free conventional memory.

3. Unable to run specified program.
   Too many tasks running.

   Error: You have already opened the maximum number of tasks for your configuration. Close one or more of the tasks that are open.

4. Unable to run specified program.

Error: The program that you tried to start cannot be started correctly. You may have specified the program name incorrectly.

5. You cannot quit MS-DOS Shell with programs in the Active Task List; quit those programs first.

Error: You tried to exit the DOS Shell while at least one program was switched. Exit the switched program, and then quit DOS Shell.

EDIT   V5, V6-External

Activates the DOS full-screen ASCII text-file editor.

Syntax

dc:pathc**EDIT** *d:path\\filename /B /G /H /NOHI*

dc: is the drive that holds the command.

pathc is the path to the command.

filename is the name of the ASCII text file that you want to edit.

Switches

/B	EDIT uses colors appropriate for a black-and-white (monochrome) display.
/G	EDIT uses the fastest screen-updating method for a CGA monitor.
/H	EDIT uses the maximum number of lines available on your monitor.
/NOHI	EDIT uses 8 colors rather than 16.

Reference

See Chapter 14, "Using the DOS Editor."

Rule

For EDIT to work, QBASIC.EXE must be in the current directory, in your PATH, or in the same directory as EDIT.COM.

EMM386.EXE   V5, V6-External

Enables an 80386, 80386SX, or higher CPU to convert extended memory into EMS 4.0 expanded memory and to control that expanded memory; also remaps extended memory to upper-memory blocks.

Syntax

As a device driver in CONFIG.SYS:

> **DEVICE** = *dc:pathc***EMM386.EXE** *ON\|OFF\|AUTO ramval*
> *MIN=size W=ON\|OFF Ms \|FRAME=xxxx \|/Pyyyy /Pn=yyyy*
> *X=mmmm-nnnn I=mmmm-nnnn B=zzzz L=xmsmem A=regs*
> *H=hhh D=nnn RAM=mmmm-nnnn NOEMS NOVCPI*
> *NOHIGHSCAN VERBOSE WIN=mmmm-nnnn NOHI*
> *ROM=mmmm-nnnn NOMOVEXBDA ALTBOOT*

As a command:

> *dc:pathc***EMM386** *ON\|OFF\|AUTO W=ON\|OFF*

dc: is the drive that holds the EMM386.EXE.

pathc is the path to EMM386.EXE.

ON\|OFF\|AUTO enables EMM386.EXE, disables it, or enables it to provide expanded-memory and upper-memory-block support only when a program requests it. The default is ON.

ramval represents the maximum amount of RAM in 1K bytes to be assigned as EMS 4.0/Virtual Control Program Interface memory. Enter a value ranging from 64 to the smaller of 32768 or the amount of extended memory available when EMM386.EXE is loaded. Any number that you enter is rounded down to the nearest multiple of 16. The default is 0 if NOEMS is specified. Otherwise, all available extended memory is used as EMS/VCPI.

Switches

MIN=size is the minimum amount of RAM (in 1K bytes) that EMM386 is guaranteed to provide. Enter a value ranging from 0 to the value of *ramval*. The default is 0 if *NOEMS* is specified and 256 otherwise. If *size* is greater than *ramval*, *size* is used.

W=ON|OFF enables or disables support for the Weitek coprocessor. The default is *W=OFF*.

Ms|FRAME=xxxx|Pyyyy specifies the beginning address of the EMS page frame. *s* is a number that represents the beginning address. The numbers and associated hexadecimal addresses are as follows:

s	Address
1	C000
2	C400
3	C800
4	CC00
5	D000
6	D400
7	D800
8	DC00
9	E000
10*	8000
11*	8400
12*	8800
13*	8C00
14*	9000

* Use only in computers with at least 512K of memory.

xxxx specifies a hexadecimal address from 8000 through 9000 and C000 through E000 in increments of 400 hexadecimal or *NONE*. The latter disables the page frame and may cause programs that require expanded memory to fail.

yyyy specifies a hexadecimal address from 8000 through 9000 and C000 through E000 in increments of 400 hexadecimal.

Pn=yyyy defines an address for a page segment. *n* represents the page and can have a value of 0 through 255. *yyyy* is a hexadecimal address from 8000 through 9000 and C000 through E000 in increments of 400 hexadecimal. To remain compatible with EMS 3.2, P0 through P3 must be contiguous addresses. You cannot specify P0 through P3 with this option if you use *Ms*, *FRAME=xxxx*, or */Pyyyy*.

X=mmmm-nnnn specifies a range of memory that should not be used for an EMS page frame or UMB. *mmmm* and *nnnn* can have values ranging from A000H through FFFFH and are rounded down to the nearest 4K boundary. The *X* switch overrides the *I* switch if their ranges overlap.

I=mmmm-nnnn specifies a range of memory that should be used for an EMS page frame or UMB. *mmmm* and *nnnn* can have values ranging from A000H through FFFFH and are rounded down to the nearest 4K boundary. The *X* switch overrides the *I* switch if their ranges overlap.

B=zzzz specifies the lowest address to use for bank switching (swapping of 16K pages). *zzzz* can have a value from 1000H through 4000H. The default is 4000H.

L=xmsmem specifies the number of 1K bytes that must remain as extended memory instead of being converted to EMS memory. The default is 0. For 1M bytes to remain as extended memory, use L=1024.

A=regs is used to allocate the number of fast alternative register sets that EMM386 may use (for multitasking). *regs* can have a value from 0 through 254. The default is 7. Each alternative register set adds about 200 bytes to the size of EMM386.

H=hhh enables you to change the number of handles EMM386.EXE can use. *hhh* can have a value from 2 to 255. The default is 64.

D=nnn specifies the amount of memory (in 1K bytes) reserved for DMA (buffered direct memory access). This value should cover the largest non-floppy transfer. *nnn* can be from 16 through 256. The default is 16.

RAM=mmmm-nnnn specifies a range of memory to be used for UMBs. If simply *RAM* is specified, all extended memory is used and enables EMS support for UMBs and an EMS page frame.

NOEMS specifies that access to UMBs is to be provided, but not for expanded memory—that is, an EMS page frame is prohibited.

NOVCPI disables support for VCPI applications and must be used with NOEMS, in which case *ramval* and *MIN* are ignored.

NOHIGHSCAN causes EMM386 to be less aggressive in scanning upper memory for UMBs. Use this switch only if you are having trouble with EMM386.

VERBOSE specifies that EMM386 display status and error messages when DOS boots. This switch can be abbreviated as *V*. (You also can get status and error messages by holding down the Alt key while DOS boots.

WIN=mmmm-nnnn specifies a range of memory for Microsoft Windows instead of EMM386. *mmmm* and *nnnn* can have values ranging from A000H through FFFFH and are rounded down to the nearest 4K boundary. The *X* switch overrides the *WIN* switch if their ranges overlap. The *WIN* switch overrides the *RAM*, *ROM*, and *I* switches if their ranges overlap.

NOHI specifies that EMM386 should not load any part of itself into upper memory.

ROM=mmmm-nnnn specifies a range of memory for shadow RAM, which is read-only memory (ROM) copied into faster RAM. *mmmm* and *nnnn* can have values ranging from A000H through FFFFH and are rounded down to the nearest 4K boundary.

NOMOVEXBDA prevents EMM386 from moving the extended BIOS data from conventional memory to upper memory.

ALTBOOT specifies that EMM386 use an alternative method of rebooting your computer when you press Ctrl-Alt-Del. Use this switch only if you are having trouble.

Reference

See Chapter 17, "Configuring Your Computer."

Rules

1. Works only on 80386, 80386SX, and higher systems.

2. HIMEM.SYS must be installed as a device driver in CONFIG.SYS before EMM386.EXE.

3. To create UMBs, you must include the *RAM* or *NOEMS* parameters, and you must include at least DOS=UMB in CONFIG.SYS.

4. Before you can use EMM386.EXE from the command line, you must install EMM386 as a device driver in CONFIG.SYS.

5. Any DEVICEHIGH commands in CONFIG.SYS must come after the DEVICE=HIMEM.SYS and DEVICE=EMM386.EXE RAM (or NOEMS) commands.

6. When EMM386 is used with Microsoft Windows 3.1, the *I*, *X*, *NOEMS*, *Ms*, *FRAME*, and *Pyyyy* switches override the EMMINCLUDE, EMMEXCLUDE, and EMMPAGEFRAME settings in the Windows SYSTEM.INI file.

7. SMARTDRV double-buffering may be required before DEVICEHIGH commands that load installable device drivers that use expanded memory.

8. When EMM386 is not supplying expanded memory, non-VCPI compliant programs can run (for example, Microsoft Windows 3.0 in Standard mode).

9. The high-memory area (HMA) must be available to enable a Weitek coprocessor. If DOS is loaded into HMA by a DOS=HIGH in your CONFIG.SYS file, you may not be able to enable the Weitek coprocessor.

ERASE   V1, V2, V3, V4, V5, V6-Internal

Removes one or more files from a directory.

Syntax

ERASE *d:path***filename.ext**

or

DEL *d:path***filename.ext**

In DOS 4.0, 5.0, and 6.0, you can add the /P switch, as in the following examples:

ERASE *d:path***filename.ext** */P*

or

DEL *d:path***filename.ext** */P*

d: is the name of the drive that holds the file(s) to be erased.

path is the directory of the file(s) to be erased.

filename.ext is the name of the file(s) to be erased. Wild cards are allowed.

Switch

/P   DOS 4.0 and later versions prompt you before eras-
            ing the file with the message `filename.ext, De-`
            `lete (Y/N)?` Responses are Y for yes, N for no, and
            Ctrl-C to return to the command prompt.

Reference

See Chapter 8, "Understanding and Managing Directories."

Rules

1. If you do not provide a drive name, the current drive is used.

2. If you do not provide a path name, the current directory is
   used.

3. If you provide a drive name, a path name, or both, but no file
   name, DOS assumes that the file name is *.* (all files).

4. If you provide a drive name, a path name, or both, and
   specify either *.* or no name for the file name, DOS displays
   the following message:

   ```
   All files in directory will be deleted
   Are you sure (Y/N)?
   ```

   If you type **Y**, DOS erases all files in the specified directory
   (but not in the subdirectories). If you type **N**, no files are
   erased.

Notes

You may be able to recover the erased file by using the special
DOS 5.0 and 6.0 utility program UNDELETE. Use UNDELETE
immediately after accidentally erasing a file.

DOS's RECOVER utility does not recover erased files, as you might
expect. RECOVER is designed only to repair a file that contains
bad sectors or that has a bad directory entry.

Message

```
Access denied
```

Error: You attempted to erase a file that is marked as read-only or that is being used by another program or computer and is temporarily marked as read-only.

If the file that you intend to erase has the read-only, system, or hidden attributes set, use the ATTRIB command to turn off those attributes before attempting to erase the file again.

EXE2BIN   *V1.1, V2, V3, V5-External*

Changes suitably formatted EXE files to BIN or COM files. EXE2BIN is included with the DOS 6.0 Supplemental Programs disk, not in the standard DOS 6.0 package.

Syntax

*dc:pathc***EXE2BIN** *d1:path1/***filename1.ext1**
d2:path2/filename2.ext2

dc: is the drive that holds the command.

pathc is the path to the command.

d1: is the drive that holds the file to be converted.

path1/ is the directory of the file to be converted.

filename1 is the root name of the file to be converted.

d2: is the drive for the output file.

path2/ is the directory of the output file.

filename2 is the root name of the output file.

Special Terms

The file to be converted is the *source* file.

The output file is the *destination* file.

Rules

1. You must specify a name for the source file (the file to be converted).

2. If you do not specify a name for the destination file, EXE2BIN uses the name of the source file.

3. If you do not specify an extension for the source file, EXE2BIN uses the extension EXE.

4. If you do not specify an extension for the destination file, EXE2BIN uses the extension BIN.

5. The EXE file must be in the correct format (following the Microsoft conventions).

Note

EXE2BIN is a programming utility that converts EXE (executable) program files to COM or BIN (binary image) files. The resulting program takes less disk space and loads faster. Unless you use a compiler-based programming language, you probably won't use this command.

EXIT   V2, V3, V4, V5, V6-Internal

Quits COMMAND.COM and returns to the program that started COMMAND.COM.

Syntax

EXIT

References

See Chapter 11, "Working with System Information"; also refer to the COMMAND section earlier in this Command Reference.

Rule

This command has no effect if COMMAND.COM is loaded with the /P switch.

EXPAND   V5, V6-External

Copies a compressed, unusable file from the DOS distribution disks to uncompressed, usable form.

Syntax

> *dc:pathc***EXPAND** *d1:path1\\filename.ext…*
>   *dd:pathd\\filenamed.extd*

dc:pathc represents the drive and directory that hold the command.

d1:path1 represents the letter of the drive and path where the compressed file is located.

filename.ext is the name of the compressed file.

The ellipsis (…) represents additional compressed-file specifications.

dd:pathd\\filenamed.extd represents the drive, path, or new file name to which the compressed file is expanded.

Rule

1. You can use EXPAND only to decompress files from the DOS distribution disks.

2. If you specify more than one compressed file, you can only specify a destination drive or path (not a file name).

3. If you don't specify a compressed file or a destination, EXPAND prompts you for the missing information.

Example

To expand FORMAT.COM from a DOS distribution disk to C:\DOS:

EXPAND A:FORMAT.CO_ C:\DOS\FORMAT.COM

Notes

Files stored on the original DOS 5.0 and 6.0 disks are compressed files. This compression enables more data to be stored on fewer disks than files that are not compressed. Before you can use a file on these disks, however, you must decompress the file.

When you use SETUP to install DOS, the files are decompressed as they are transferred to the correct disks. But suppose that you delete a file accidentally or that for some reason, a file becomes corrupted. You must transfer the file from the original DOS disk. EXPAND transfers and decompresses the file as it transfers. Consider EXPAND to be a form of COPY. EXPAND, however, is a "one-way" copy.

See the file PACKING.LST in your DOS directory on your DOS distribution disks for a list of which compressed files are on which DOS distribution disks.

Messages

1. `Input file 'filename' already in expanded format`

   Error: You attempted to expand an uncompressed file. Verify that you specified the correct compressed file.

2. `Error in compressed input file format: filename`

   Error: The compressed file was corrupted. Use a different copy of the compressed file.

FASTHELP   V6-External

Provides a brief description and the syntax of a DOS command.

Syntax

> *dc:pathc***FASTHELP** *command*

dc: is the drive that holds FASTHELP.

pathc is the path to FASTHELP.

command is the DOS command for which you want help. If you do not provide a command name, DOS provides one-line descriptions of all DOS commands.

Note

The information provided for a *command* is the same as that provided by the following:

> *command* /**?**

For more extensive information on DOS commands, type **HELP command**.

FASTOPEN   *V3.3, V4, V5, V6-External*

Keeps directory information in memory so that DOS can find and use frequently needed files quickly.

Syntax

*dc:pathc***FASTOPEN d:**=*nnn…*

The following syntax is available in DOS 4.0:

*dc:pathc***FASTOPEN d:**=*(nnn,mmm)…/X*

In DOS 5.0 and later versions, use the following syntax:

*dc:pathc***FASTOPEN d:**=*nnn…/X*

dc: is the name of the drive that holds the command.

pathc is the path to the command.

d: is the name of the drive whose directory information should be held in memory.

nnn is the number of directory entries to be held in memory (10 to 999). The default is 48.

mmm is the number of fragmented entries for the drive (1 to 999).

Switch

/X   Tells DOS to use expanded memory to store the information buffered by FASTOPEN.

Reference

See Chapter 17, "Configuring Your Computer."

Rules

1. You must specify the name of the drive whose entries are in memory. The drive cannot be a floppy drive.

2. You can use FASTOPEN for up to 24 nonfloppy drives for a total of 999 files. Simply type the additional drives, separated by spaces, in the same command line.

3. Do not use FASTOPEN from the DOS Shell or if you are run-ning MS Windows or a disk defragmention program such as DEFRAG.

4. If you provide *nnn*, the value must be between 10 and 999, inclusive. FASTOPEN's minimum value is 10 or the maximum level of your deepest directory plus 1, whichever is greater.

5. You cannot run more than one copy of FASTOPEN. If you want to change FASTOPEN settings, you must reboot your computer.

6. Each FASTOPEN entry you specify increases FASTOPEN's size by approximately 48 bytes.

Notes

FASTOPEN works by keeping directory information in memory. Because disk buffers already hold FAT information, FASTOPEN enables DOS to search memory for a file or a subdirectory entry, to locate the corresponding FAT entry quickly, and to open the file. If you have many files and use FASTOPEN effectively, you can increase DOS's performance.

As is true of BUFFERS, no predetermined best number exists. The default value of 48 works well in many installations. If your subdirectories run many levels deep or if you use many files, specifying a larger number can improve performance. Using too large a value for *nnn* (greater than 200), however, slows the system. DOS spends more time examining in-memory directory entries than rereading the entries from the disk.

You can use the INSTALL command to put FASTOPEN in your CONFIG.SYS file.

FC   V2, V3, V4, V5, V6-External

Compares two disk files or two sets of disk files.

Syntax

For an ASCII comparison:

> *dc:pathc***FC** */A /C /L /LBn /N /T /W /x*
> *d1:path1***filename1.ext1** *d2:path2***filename2.ext2**

For a binary comparison:

>*dc:pathc***FC** */B d1:path1***filename1.ext1**
>*d2:path2*filename2.ext2

dc: is the drive that holds the command.

pathc is the path to the command.

d1: is the drive that holds the first file.

path1 is the path to the first file.

filename1.ext1 is the name of the first file. Wild cards are allowed, enabling you to specify a set of files.

d2: is the drive that holds the second file.

path2 is the path to the second file.

filename2.ext2 is the name of the second file. Wild cards are allowed, enabling you to specify a set of files.

Switches

/A	Abbreviates the display of an ASCII comparison to the first and last line of each group of differences.
/B	Forces a binary file comparison, which involves a byte-by-byte comparison with no synchronization after a mismatch. This switch is the default for files with EXE, COM, SYS, OBJ, LIB, and BIN extensions.
/C	Causes DOS to ignore the case of letters.
/L	Compares files in ASCII mode, which involves a line-by-line comparison with resynchronization attempted after a mismatch. This switch is the default for files without EXE, COM, SYS, OBJ, LIB, and BIN extensions.
/LBn	Sets the internal buffer to *n* lines. A comparison is terminated if the files have more than this number of consecutive differing lines.
/N	Displays line numbers for ASCII comparisons.
/T	Suppresses expansion of tabs to spaces.
/W	Compresses tabs and spaces to a single space and causes tabs and spaces to be ignored if those characters are at the beginning or end of a line.
/x	Sets the number of lines (1 through 9) that must match before the files are considered to be resynchronized. The default is 2.

Reference

See Chapter 13, "Understanding Backups and the Care of Data."

Rules

1. A difference in a binary file comparison is displayed as follows:

   aaaaaaaa: *xx yy*

   aaaaaaaa represents the hexadecimal address of a mismatching pair of bytes; *xx* is the mismatching hexadecimal byte from the first file; and *yy* is the mismatching hexadecimal byte from the second file.

2. If you use a wild card in the first file name, DOS compares all the specified files with the second file name. If you use a wild card in the second file name, DOS uses the corresponding value from the first file name in the second file name.

Examples

To compare every text file in the current directory with C:\README.TXT:

FC *.TXT C:\README.TXT

To compare README.TXT in the current directory with C:\README.TXT:

FC README.TXT C:*.TXT

To compare every text file in the current directory with the file of the same name in C:\:

FC *.TXT C:*.TXT

FDISK   V2, V3, V4, V5, V6-External

Prepares a hard disk to accept an operating system such as DOS.

Syntax

*dc:pathc***FDISK** */STATUS*

dc:pathc represents the drive and directory that hold the command.

Switch

/STATUS   Displays some partition information without starting FDISK (DOS 6.0 only).

Reference

See Chapter 7, "Preparing and Maintaining Disks."

Rules

1. You must use FDISK to create a partition on a hard disk before you can use FORMAT to format the hard disk.

2. You may change the size of a partition only by removing existing partitions. (You lose all data in the partitions.)

3. FDISK does not work in SUBST, Interlnk, and network drives.

Notes

In versions of DOS earlier than 4.0, DOS can recognize only a hard disk of 32M or less. Starting with DOS 3.3, DOS can create multiple logical partitions. A 40M hard disk can be partitioned into two drives (C and D, for example). Starting with DOS 4.0, however, FDISK can partition a disk larger than 32M into one drive.

If you plan to use more than one operating system, use FDISK to partition part of the hard disk for DOS and another part of the hard disk for the other operating system.

> **CAUTION:** Do not use FDISK to remove or change a partition unless you have backed up all data in the partition. When you remove or change a partition, you lose all data in that partition.

FIND   V2, V3, V4, V5, V6-External

Displays all the lines of the designated files that match (or do not match, depending on the switches used) the specified string.

Syntax

> *dc:pathc***FIND***/V/C/N/I* **"string"** *d:path\\filename.ext...*

dc: is the drive that holds the command.

pathc is the path to the command.

"string" represents the characters you want to find. The characters must be enclosed in quotation marks.

d: is the drive for the file.

path is the directory that holds the file.

filename.ext is the file that you want to search. If you omit *filename.ext*, FIND acts as a filter, searching input that has been redirected to it.

The ellipsis (...) indicates optional *d:path***filename.ext** specifications.

Switches

/C	Displays only a count of the total number of lines that contain "**string**".
/I	Specifies that the search is case-insensitive (DOS 5.0 and later versions).
/N	Displays lines that contain "**string**", preceded by the file line number.
/V	Displays lines that do not contain "**string**".

Exit Codes

Code	Explanation
0	FIND operated without error and found at least one match
1	FIND operated without error and found no matches
2	FIND had an error and cannot report whether any matches were found

Reference

See Chapter 9, "Managing Your Files."

Rules

1. You can use more than one file specification. All file specifications must appear after the string and must be separated by spaces.

2. If you do not provide any file specifications, FIND expects information from the keyboard (standard input).

3. If you use switches with FIND, you must place them between FIND and the string. Most DOS commands require that you place switches at the end of the command line.

4. You must enclose the string in double quotation marks. To use the double-quote character itself in the string, use two double-quote characters in a row.

5. Wild cards are not allowed in file specifications. You can get the effect of wild cards by using FIND in a FOR command.

Notes

FIND is one of several filters provided with DOS 3.0 and later versions. The command can find lines that contain strings and those that do not. FIND also can number and count lines of text, rather than simply display them.

This filter is useful when combined with DOS I/O redirection. You can redirect FIND's output to a file by using the > redirection symbol. Because FIND accepts a sequence of files to search, you do not need to redirect the input to FIND.

Examples

To search README.TXT for "Microsoft":

FIND "Microsoft" C:\DOS\README.TXT

To search all batch files in the current directory for "default":

FOR %%A IN (*.BAT) DO FIND "default" %%A

To determine the path and file names for all batch files on the current disk:

DIR \ /S/B | FIND ".BAT"

FORMAT

V1, V2, V3, V4, V5, V6-External

Initializes a disk to accept DOS information and files. FORMAT also checks the disk for defective tracks and (optionally) places DOS on the floppy disk or hard disk.

Syntax

> *dc:pathc***FORMAT d:** */S/1/8/V/B/4/N:ss/T:tt*

In DOS 4.0 and later versions, you can add the /V:label and /F:size switches, as follows:

> *dc:pathc***FORMAT d:** */S/1/8/V/B/4/N:ss/T:tt /V:label/F:size*

In DOS 5.0 and later versions, you can add the /U and /Q switches, as follows:

> *dc:pathc***FORMAT d:** */S/1/8/V/B/4/N:ss/T:tt /V:label/F:size/ U/Q*

dc: is the drive that holds the command.

pathc is the path to the command.

d: is a valid drive name to be formatted.

Switches

/S   Places copies of the operating-system files on the disk so that DOS can boot from the disk. For MS-DOS, those files are the command line interpreter printed to by the environment variable COMSPEC (generally COMMAND.COM), the hidden files IO.SYS and MSDOS.SYS, and, if necessary, DBLSPACE.BIN (DOS 6.0 only).

/1   Formats only the first side of the floppy disk.

/8   Formats an eight-sector floppy disk (for compatibility with DOS 1.0).

/V   Prompts for a volume label for the disk.

/B   Leaves space for the system version, but does not place the operating-system files on the disk. (See the section on the SYS command later in this Command Reference.) This switch is not necessary in DOS 6.0.

/4	Formats a floppy disk in a 1.2M drive for double-density (320K/360K) use. Some systems, however, cannot read the resulting disk reliably.
/N:ss	Formats the disk with *ss* number of sectors (*ss* ranges from 1 to 99). Must be used with */T*. Generally, use */F* in preference to this switch.
/T:ttt	Formats the disk with *ttt* number of tracks per side (*ttt* ranges from 1 to 999). Must be used with */N*. Generally, use */F* in preference to this switch.
/F:size	Specifies the size to which a disk should be formatted, which can be less than the drive's maximum. Generally, use this switch in preference to a combination of */N* and */T*. The following table lists the possible values of *size*:

Drive Capacity	Allowable Values for *size*
160K, 180K	160, 160K, 160KB, 180, 180K, and 180KB
320K, 360K	All of preceding, plus 320, 320K, 320KB, 360, 360K, and 360KB
1.2M	All of preceding, plus 1200, 1200K, 1200KB, 1.2, 1.2M, and 1.2MB
720K	720, 720K, and 720KB
1.44M	All for 720K, plus 1440, 1440K, 1440KB, 1.44, 1.44M, and 1.44MB
2.88M	All for 1.44M, plus 2880, 2880K, 2880KB, 2.88, 2.88M, and 2.88MB

/V:label	Makes *label* (which can be up to 11 characters) the disk's label.
/U	Specifies an *unconditional* format for a floppy disk. Unconditional formatting destroys all data on a floppy disk, so you cannot unformat the disk. (For more information on unformatting, see the section on the UNFORMAT command later in this Command Reference.)
/Q	FORMAT performs a *quick* format by clearing only the FAT and root directory on the disk; this switch does not check the disk for bad sectors.

Exit Codes

Code	Explanation
0	Successful completion of last format
3	Aborted by user (Ctrl-Break or Ctrl-C)
4	Aborted due to an unspecified error
5	Aborted due to an N response on a hard disk format

Reference

See Chapter 7, "Preparing and Maintaining Disks."

Rules

1. If you do not provide a drive name, DOS uses the current drive.

2. Unless otherwise directed through a switch, DOS formats the disk to the DOS maximum capacity for the drive.

3. Some switches do not work together. For example, you cannot use the following switch combinations:

   - */V* with */8*

   - */1*, */4*, */8*, or */B* with the hard disk

   - */F* with */N* and */T*

4. In DOS 5.0 and later versions, if you do not specify /U, format performs a "safe" format. DOS creates a file containing file information and saves the file to a safe place on disk where the UNFORMAT command can find it if you need to unformat the disk. FORMAT then clears the FAT and root directory of the disk but does not erase any data. Therefore, the UNFORMAT command enables you to restore a disk if you did not intend to format the disk.

5. If you are formatting a hard disk, FORMAT displays the following message:

```
WARNING, ALL DATA ON NON-REMOVABLE DISK
DRIVE d: WILL BE LOST!
Proceed with Format (Y/N)?
```

Type **Y** to format the hard disk or **N** to abort the formatting operation.

Notes

Do not try to format any type of virtual disk; a disk that is part of an ASSIGN, SUBST, or JOIN command; or a networked or Interlnk disk.

Never try to format a RAM disk. Under some circumstances, FORMAT acts erratically when you use it to format a RAM disk, particularly RAMDRIVE (the DOS RAM disk program). The responses can range from a `Divide overflow` message to a lockup of your computer. If the computer locks up, turn the system off, and then turn it on again. Obviously, you lose the RAM disk's contents, but no hard or floppy disks are damaged.

In pre-5.0 versions of DOS, FORMAT destroys the information recorded on a floppy or hard disk. Do not use the command on any disk—floppy or hard—that contains useful information.

In DOS 5.0 and later versions, FORMAT performs a safe format. When you use the command to format a previously formatted disk, DOS copies the FAT and root directory before clearing them and then checks the disk. The existing data is not cleared. If you accidentally format a safely formatted disk, you can unformat the disk. To erase all data from a previously used floppy disk, use the /U switch. An unconditional format takes about 27 percent longer than the default safe format.

The /Q switch, another feature of DOS 5.0 and later versions, enables you to format a disk quickly. The /Q switch clears the FAT and root directory but does not check the disk for bad sectors. To reuse a disk that you know is good, use the /Q switch. The quick format is nearly 80 percent faster than the default safe format.

160K and 180K disks are known as single-sided, double-density, 5 1/4-inch disks.

320K and 360K disks are known as double-sided, double-density, 5 1/4-inch disks.

1.2M disks are known as double-sided, quadruple-density, 5 1/4-inch disks.

720K disks are known as double-sided, double-density, 3 1/2-inch disks.

1.44M disks are known as double-sided, quadruple-density, 3 1/2-inch disks.

2.88M disks are known as double-sided, extra-high-density, 3 1/2-inch disks.

Messages

1. `Checking existing disk format.`

   Information: FORMAT is checking the disk to see whether it has been formatted previously.

2. `Saving UNFORMAT information.`

   Information: If the disk has been formatted, the directory and FAT are saved on the disk, and a safe format is performed. A safely formatted disk can be unformatted.

3. `Drive A error. Insufficient space for the MIRROR image`
   `file.`
   `There was an error creating the format recovery file.`

   Warning: The previously formatted disk doesn't have room for the mirror-image file (the file that contains a copy of the FAT and root directory). The disk doesn't have enough room to save a copy of the root directory and FAT. Be sure that you want to format the disk that is located in the drive.

4. `This disk cannot be unformatted.`

   Warning: You cannot unformat this disk after it has been formatted. Either your system does not have enough room to save a copy of the root directory and FAT, or you are changing the contents of the disk by using the /B and /S switches.

5. `Invalid media or track 0 bad`
   `disk unusable`

   Warning: Track 0 holds the boot record, the FAT, and the directory. This track is bad, and the floppy disk is unusable. Try reformatting the floppy disk. If the error recurs, you cannot use the floppy disk.

   This error can occur when you format 720K floppy disks as 1.44M floppy disks (if you forget to use the /N:9 or /F:720 switch when you formatted the disk in a 1.44M drive), or when you format 360K floppy disks as 1.2M floppy disks (if you forget the /4 or /F:360 switch).

   This error also can occur when you format 1.2M floppy disks at lower capacities (such as 360K) and use the /4 switch. In this case, try using a floppy disk rated for double-sided, double-density use.

6. WARNING, ALL DATA ON NON-REMOVABLE DISK
   DRIVE *d*: WILL BE LOST!
   Proceed with Format (Y/N)?

Warning: FORMAT is warning you that you are about to format a hard disk. To format the hard disk, type **Y** and press Enter. If you do not want to format the hard disk, type **N** and press Enter.

GRAFTABL   V3, V4, V5-External

Loads into memory the tables of additional character sets to be displayed on the Color/Graphics Adapter (CGA). GRAFTABL is included on the DOS 6.0 Supplemental Program disk, not in the standard DOS 6.0 package.

Syntax

To install or change the table that the CGA uses, use the following format:

dc:pathc**GRAFTABL** *codepage*

To display the number of the current table, use the following format:

dc:pathc**GRAFTABL** **/STATUS**

dc: is the drive that holds the command.

pathc\\ is the path to the command.

codepage represents the three-digit number of the code page for the display.

Exit Codes

Code	Explanation
0	GRAFTABL installed successfully for the first time.
1	The code page used for GRAFTABL was successfully changed, or if no new code page was specified, an existing code page exists.
2	GRAFTABL is installed, no previous code page was installed or is installed.

Code	Explanation
3	Incorrect parameter, no change in GRAFTABL.
4	Incorrect version of DOS.

Rules

1. To display legible characters in the ASCII range 128 to 255 when you are in APA (all-points-addressable) mode on the Color/Graphics Adapter (CGA), load GRAFTABL.

2. GRAFTABL increases the size of DOS by 1,360 bytes.

3. *codepage* represents the appropriate code page and can be any of the following codes:

Code	Country or language
437	United States
850	Multilingual (Latin I)
852	Slavic (Latin II)
860	Portuguese
863	Canadian-French
865	Nordic

If you do not specify a page, DOS uses the code 437.

4. After you invoke GRAFTABL, the only way to deactivate the command is to restart DOS.

Notes

The IBM Color Graphics Adapter (CGA) in graphics mode produces low-quality ASCII characters in the 128-to-255 range.

GRAFTABL is useful only when your system is equipped with the CGA and when you use the CGA in medium- or high-resolution graphics mode.

GRAPHICS   *V2, V3, V4, V5, V6-External*

Prints the contents of the graphics screen on a suitable printer.

Syntax

    *dc:pathc***GRAPHICS** *printer /R /B /LCD*

In DOS 4.0 and later versions, you can add the name of a file that contains printer information, as follows:

    *dc:pathc***GRAPHICS** *printer d:path\\filename.ext /R /B /LCD /PRINTBOX:x*

dc: is the drive that holds the command.

pathc is the path to the command.

printer is the type of IBM Personal Computer printer you are using. The printer can be one of the following:

COLOR1	IBM Personal Color Printer with a black ribbon
COLOR4	IBM Personal Color Printer with an RGB (red, green, blue, and black) ribbon, which produces four colors
COLOR8	IBM Personal Color Printer with a CMY (cyan, magenta, yellow, and black) ribbon, which produces eight colors
COMPACT	Compact printer (not an option in DOS 4.0 and later versions)
GRAPHICS	IBM Personal Graphics Printer, IBM ProPrinter, or IBM Quietwriter
THERMAL	IBM PC-Convertible thermal printer

In DOS 4.0 and later versions, you also can specify the following printer:

GRAPHICSWIDE	IBM Personal Graphics Printer with 11-inch-wide carriage

In DOS 5.0 and later versions, you also can specify the following printers:

Printer	Description
DESKJET	A Hewlett-Packard DeskJet printer
HPDEFAULT	Any Hewlett-Packard PCL printer

Printer	Description
LASERJET	A Hewlett-Packard PCL printer
LASERJETII	A Hewlett-Packard LaserJet II printer
PAINTJET	A Hewlett-Packard PaintJet printer
QUIETJET	A Hewlett-Packard QuietJet printer
QUIETJETPLUS	A Hewlett-Packard QuietJet Plus printer
RUGGEDWRITER	A Hewlett-Packard RuggedWriter printer
RUGGEDWRITERWIDE	A Hewlett-Packard RuggedWriterwide printer
THINKJET	A Hewlett-Packard ThinkJet printer

filename is the file name that contains printer information (DOS 4.0 and later versions). If you do not specify a file name, DOS uses the name GRAPHICS.PRO in the current directory or *dc:pathc*.

Switches

/B	Prints the background color of the screen. You can use this switch only when the printer type is COLOR4 or COLOR8.
/LCD	Prints the image as displayed on the PC Convertible's LCD display. This switch is the equivalent of /PRINTBOX:LCD.
/PRINTBOX:x	Prints the image and uses the print-box size *id* represented by *x*. This value must match the first entry of a Printbox statement in the printer profile (DOS 4.0 and later versions), such as *lcd* or *std*.
/R	Reverses colors so that the image on the paper matches the screen (a white image on a black background).

Reference

See Chapter 12, "Controlling Devices."

HELP   V5, V6-External

Displays syntax, notes, and examples for a DOS command.

Syntax

To display Help's table of contents, use the following format:

    *dc:pathc***HELP**

To display the syntax of *command*, use the following format:

    *dc:pathc***HELP** *command*

dc: is the drive that contains the command.

pathc is the directory where the command is located.

Rule

For HELP to work, QBASIC.EXE must be in the current directory, in your search path, or in the same directory as HELP.COM.

Notes

Help is available for many topics other than DOS commands (for example, CONFIG.SYS commands). See Help's table of contents for a complete list.

In addition to extensive syntax help, Help displays usage notes and examples, and links related material by hypertext links.

Simple syntax help for DOS commands is available from DOSHELP or by typing the following command:

    command **/?**

INTERLNK.EXE   V6-External

Establishes or breaks the relationship (redirection) between a drive letter or a printer port on a client (generally a laptop computer) and a drive or printer on a server (generally a desktop computer).

Syntax

As a command:

*dc:pathc***INTERLNK** *client:=server:*

As a device driver in CONFIG.SYS:

DEVICE = *dc:pathc***INTERLNK.EXE** */DRIVES:n /NOPRINTER
/COM:n\addr /LPT:n\addr /AUTO /NOSCAN /LOW /BAUD:rate /V*

dc: is the drive that holds the driver.

pathc is the path to the driver.

client is the client drive letter that is redirected to the server. The drive letter must be one established by the INTERLNK.EXE in your CONFIG.SYS file.

server is the server driver letter to which *client* is being redirected and must be a letter listed in the `This Computer (Server)` column of the Interlnk server screen.

Switches

/DRIVES:n	Specifies that *n* client drives be redirected to the server. By default, *n* is 3. If *n* is 0, only printers are redirected.
/NOPRINTER	Specifies that client printer ports are not redirected to the server. By default, all printer ports are redirected.
/COM:n\addr	Specifies which client serial port to use for connecting to the server. The colon (:) is optional. *n* is the number of the port. *addr* is the hexadecimal address of the port. By default, DOS uses the first serial port that is connected to a server.
/LPT:n\addr	Specifies which client parallel port to use for connecting to the server. The colon (:) is optional. *n* is the number of the port. *addr* is the hexadecimal address of the port. By default, DOS uses the first parallel port that is connected to a server.
/AUTO	Specifies that the INTERLNK.EXE device driver be removed from the client's memory if a connection cannot be established to a server when the client is booted. By default, INTERLNK.EXE remains in memory even if a connection cannot be established.

/NOSCAN	Specifies that a connection between the client and a server should not be attempted when the client is booted. The default is to try to connect when INTERLNK.EXE is loaded.
/LOW	Loads INTERLNK.EXE into conventional memory even if there is room in upper memory. By default, INTERLNK.EXE is loaded into upper memory if room exists.
/BAUD:rate	Specifies maximum bits per second (bps) for serial communication. Values are 9600, 19200, 38400, 57600, and 115200. The default is 115200.
/V	Should be used if one of your computers stops running when using a serial connection. This switch prevents conflicts with a computer's timer.

Reference

See Chapter 9, "Managing Your Files."

Rules

1. INTERLNK.EXE must be installed as a device driver before you use the INTERLNK command.

2. The drive letters created in the client by the INTERLNK.EXE device statement are the next sequential *n* letters available when INTERLNK.EXE is executed.

3. To display Interlnk's status, type **INTERLNK** at a DOS command prompt.

4. If INTERLNK.EXE is used to connect to a computer that is not running INTERSVR, the new drives in the client will be empty.

5. By default, all the client serial ports and then all the client parallel ports are scanned for a connection to a server. Only the serial ports are scanned if */COM* is specified and */LPT* is not. Only the parallel ports are scanned if */LPT* is specified and */COM* is not.

6. Because INTERLNK.EXE adds disk letters to your system, parts of your current system that use specific device letters

(for example, CONFIG.SYS and AUTOEXEC.BAT) may have to be modified if you add an INTERLNK.EXE statement to your CONFIG.SYS. To avoid those possible modifications, you may want to put the INTERLNK.EXE line last in your CONFIG.SYS file.

7. You can reduce INTERLNK.EXE's size by using the */NOPRINTER*, */LPT*, and */COM* switches to indicate that you do not require the inclusion of code to support all types of devices.

8. If you use a serial mouse, use the */LPT* or */COM* switch to prevent INTERLNK.EXE from scanning and possibly trying to use the mouse's serial port.

9. If you are using Microsoft Windows on the client to print to a redirected LPT1 or LPT2, first use the Control Panel to assign the printer to LPT1.DOS or LPT2.DOS, respectively.

10. Some DOS features may not be available on the client if its version of DOS differs from the server's version. For example, a client that runs a version of DOS that does not support partitions that are larger than 32M will not be able to use large partitions on the server.

11. INTERLNK.EXE does not work with CHKDSK, DEFRAG, DISKCOMP, DISKCOPY, FDISK, FORMAT, SYS, UNDELETE, and UNFORMAT.

Examples

1. In CONFIG.SYS, to specify an INTERLNK connection for three drives using a non-standard serial port that has a hexadecimal address of 3F8. (To use the first available port, specify /COM rather than /COM:3F8.) Printers are not redirected:

    **DEVICE=C:\DOS\INTERLNK.EXE /COM:3F8
    /NOPRINTER**

    If the system doing the INTERLNK.EXE has a diskette drive (A:) and a hard disk drive (C:), and if the server has two diskette drives (A: and B:) and a hard disk drive (C:), when the first system reads or writes to its newly created D drive, that system is reading or writing to the server's C drive.

2. To break the relationship (cancel the redirection) between the client's D drive and a server drive:

    INTERLNK D=

INTERSVR   V6-External

Starts the Interlnk server that cooperates with an INTERLNK.EXE
in a client system to enable the client to use the server's drives
and printers.

Syntax

> *dc:pathc***INTERSVR** *dr:... /X=dnr:... /COM:n \\addr*
> */LPT:n \\addr /BAUD:rate /B /V*

To copy the Interlnk files to a connected computer that is not
running Interlnk, use the following format:

> *dc:pathc***INTERSVR /RCOPY**

dc: is the drive that holds the command.

pathc\\ is the path to the command.

dr:... is the letter of a drive that can be redirected. The ellipsis
(...) indicates that more than one drive can be redirected by a
single INTERSVR command. By default, all drives are redirected.

Switches

/X=dnr:...	Specifies *dnr* as a drive letter that will not be redirected. The ellipsis (...) indicates that more than one drive can be excluded by a single INTERSVR command. By default, no drives are excluded.
/COM:n \\addr	Specifies which server serial port to use for connecting to the client. The colon (:) is optional. *n* is the number of the port. *addr* is the hexadecimal address of the port. By default, DOS uses the first serial port that is connected to a client.
/LPT:n \\addr	Specifies which server parallel port to use for connecting to the client. The colon (:) is optional. *n* is the number of the port. *addr* is the hexadecimal address of the port. By default, DOS uses the first parallel port that is connected to a client.
/BAUD:rate	Specifies maximum bits per second (bps) for serial communication. Values are 9600, 19200, 38400, 57600, and 115200. The default is 115200.

/B	Forces the use of a color scheme appropriate for a black-and-white (monochrome) monitor.
/V	Prevents conflicts with a computer's timer. Should be used if one of your computers stops running when using a serial connection.
/RCOPY	Copies the Interlnk files from your computer to another (more convenient than copying the files to a diskette and taking the diskette to the target computer). The computers must be connected by a seven-wire, null-modem serial cable, and the target system must support the MODE command.

Rules

1. INTERSVR redirects drives in the order in which you specify them.

2. INTERSVR does not redirect network drives, CD-ROM drives, or any other device that already uses a redirection interface.

3. When it is running in a task-switching or multitasking environment, INTERSVR disables task switching and key combinations that switch to other tasks.

4. By default, all the server serial ports and then all the server parallel ports are scanned for a connection to a client. Only the serial ports are scanned if */COM* is specified and */LPT* is not. Only the parallel ports are scanned if */LPT* is specified and */COM* is not.

5. INTERSVR does not work with CHKDSK, DEFRAG, DISKCOMP, DISKCOPY, FDISK, FORMAT, MIRROR, SYS, UNDELETE, and UNFORMAT.

JOIN *V3.1, V3.2, V3.3, V4, V5-External*

Produces a directory structure by connecting one drive to a subdirectory of another drive. JOIN is included on the DOS 6.0 Supplemental Program disk, not in the standard DOS 6.0 package.

Syntax

To connect disk drives, use the following format:

*dc:pathc***JOIN d1:** *d2:***dirname**

To disconnect disk drives, use the following format:

*dc:pathc***JOIN d1:** **/D**

To show currently connected drives, use the following format:

*dc:pathc***JOIN**

dc: is the drive that holds the command.

pathc is the path to the command.

d1: is the drive to be connected. DOS calls **d1:** the *guest disk drive*.

d2: is the drive to which **d1:** is to be connected. DOS calls *d2:* the *host disk drive*.

\\dirname is a subdirectory in the root directory of *d2:* (the host drive). DOS calls **\\dirname** the *host subdirectory*. **\\dirname** holds the connection to **d1:** (the guest drive).

Switch

/D   Disconnects the specified guest drive from the host drive.

Reference

See Chapter 12, "Controlling Devices."

Rules

1. You must specify the guest-drive name.
2. If you do not name a host drive, DOS uses the current drive.
3. You must specify the host subdirectory, which must be a Level 1 subdirectory.
4. In DOS 3.1 and 3.2, you cannot use the host drive's current directory as the host subdirectory.
5. The host and guest drives must not be networked drives.
6. The host and guest drives must not be part of a SUBST or ASSIGN command.

7. You cannot use the current drive as the guest drive.

8. If the host subdirectory does not exist, JOIN creates one. The subdirectory, if it exists, must be empty (DIR must show only the . and .. entries).

9. When the drives are joined, the guest drive's root directory and entire directory tree are added to the host subdirectory. All subdirectories of the guest's root directory become subdirectories of the host subdirectory.

10. A guest drive, when joined to the host drive, appears to be part of the host subdirectory. You can access this drive only through the host drive and subdirectory.

11. To break the connection, specify the guest drive's normal name with the /D switch. You can use the guest drive's normal name only when you disconnect the drives.

12. To see all the current drive connections, type **JOIN** with no parameters. If no connections exist, JOIN does not display any message, and the system prompt appears.

13. Do not use the BACKUP, CHKDSK, DISKCOMP, DISKCOPY, FDISK, RESTORE, or FORMAT commands in the guest or host drive.

14. When JOIN is in effect, the DIR command works normally but reports the bytes free only for the host drive.

15. While JOIN is in effect, CHKDSK processes the host drive but does not process or report information on the guest portion of the drive. To run CHKDSK on the guest drive, you first must disconnect the guest drive from the host drive.

Notes

You can use JOIN to connect a RAM disk to a real disk so that you can use the RAM disk as though it were part of a floppy disk or hard disk drive. You also can use JOIN to connect two hard drives.

Some programs allow only one drive to hold data or certain parts of the program. Programs written for DOS 2.0 and later versions, however, enable you to specify subdirectory names. If you use such a program, you can invoke the JOIN command to trick the program into using multiple drives as though the drives were one large drive.

JOIN does not affect the guest drive. Rather, JOIN affects only the way you access the files in that drive. You cannot exceed the maximum number of files in the guest drive's root directory. In the host subdirectory, a file's size cannot exceed the guest drive's size.

Message

```
Directory not empty
```

Error: You tried to use a host subdirectory that is not empty—that is, the subdirectory contains files other than the . and .. entries. Perform any of the following actions before you try the command again:

- Delete all files in the host subdirectory.

- Specify an empty subdirectory.

- Create a new subdirectory.

- Name a nonexistent host subdirectory.

KEYB   V2, V3, V4, V5, V6-External

Changes the keyboard layout and characters from American English to another language/country.

Syntax

To change the current keyboard layout, use the following format:

*dc:pathc***KEYB** *keycode, codepage, d:path\\KEYBOARD.SYS*

To specify a keyboard identification code:

*dc:pathc***KEYB** *keycode, codepage, d:path\\KEYBOARD.SYS*
/ID:*code*

DOS 5.0 and later versions support the following format:

*dc:pathc***KEYB** *keycode, codepage, d:path\\KEYBOARD.SYS*
/ID:*code* **/E**

To display the current values for KEYB, use the following format:

*dc:pathc***KEYB**

dc: is the drive that holds the command.

pathc is the path to the command.

keycode is the two-character keyboard code.

codepage is the three-digit code page that you want to use. The default is the current code page.

d:path\\KEYBOARD.SYS represents the drive and path to KEYBOARD.SYS or an equivalent file.

Switches

/E	Assumes that an Enhanced Keyboard is installed (DOS 5.0 and later versions). This switch is only necessary on 8088 and 8086 based systems.
/ID:*code*	Specifies the type of Enhanced Keyboard that you want to use. This switch is only for countries that have more than one keyboard for the same language (for example, France, Italy, and the United Kingdom). The following table lists the values for *keycode*, *codepage*, and *code*:

Language (Country)	Keycode	Code Page	Code
Belgium	be	850, 437	(none)
Canadian-French	cf	850, 863	(none)
Croatian	yu	852, 850	(none)
Czech	cz	852, 850	(none)
Danish	dk	850, 865	(none)
Dutch	nl	850, 437	(none)
English (International)	+	437, 850	(none)
English (U.K.)	uk	437, 850	166, 168
English (U.S.)	us	437, 850	(none)
Finnish	su	850, 437	(none)
French (France)	fr	850, 437	129, 189
French (Switzerland)	sf	850, 437	(none)
German (Germany)	gr	850, 437	(none)

continues

Language (Country)	Keycode	Code Page	Code
German (Switzerland)	sg	850, 437	(none)
Hungarian	hu	852, 850	(none)
Italian	it	850, 437	141, 142
Norwegian	no	850, 865	(none)
Polish	pl	852, 850	(none)
Portuguese (Brazil)	br	850, 437	(none)
Portuguese (Portugal)	po	850, 860	(none)
Serbian/ Yugoslavian	yu	852, 850	(none)
Slovak	sl	852, 850	(none)
Slovenian	yu	852, 850	(none)
Spanish (Latin American)	la	850, 437	(none)
Spanish (Spain)	sp	850, 437	(none)
Swedish	sv	850, 437	(none)

Exit Codes

Code	Explanation
0	KEYB ran successfully.
1	Invalid keycode type, code page, or other syntax error.
2	Bad or missing KEYBOARD.SYS file.
3	KEYB could not create a keyboard table in memory (not available in DOS 5.0 and later versions).
4	KEYB could not communicate successfully with CON (the console).
5	The specified code page was not prepared.
6	The internal translation table for the selected code page could not be found; *keycode* and *codepage* are incompatible (not available in DOS 5.0 and later versions).
7	Incorrect version of DOS (available only in DOS 4.0).

Reference

See Chapter 20, "Understanding the International Features of DOS."

Rules

1. To use one of the foreign-language character sets, load the KEYB program and type the appropriate two-letter code for your country.

2. If you do not specify a code page, DOS uses the default code page for your country. The default code page is established by the COUNTRY directive in CONFIG.SYS or, if the COUNTRY directive is not used, by the DOS default code page.

3. You must specify a code page that is compatible with your keyboard code selection.

4. If you do not specify the keyboard definition file, it defaults to KEYBOARD.SYS. DOS looks for this file in the current disk's root directory. Otherwise, DOS uses the full file name to search for the file. If you do not specify a disk drive, DOS searches the current disk drive. If you do not specify a path, DOS searches the current directory.

5. After loading, the program reconfigures the keyboard into the appropriate layout for the specified language.

6. To use the American English layout after you issue the KEYB command, press Ctrl-Alt-F1. To return to the foreign-language layout, press Ctrl-Alt-F2. To switch to "typewriter mode," press Ctrl-Alt-F7.

7. When you use it for the first time, the KEYB command increases the size of DOS by approximately 2K. After that, you can use KEYB as often as you want without further enlarging DOS.

8. To display the active keyboard and the code pages, type **KEYB** without any parameters.

9. You can use KEYB with INSTALL in your CONFIG.SYS file.

Messages

1. `Active code page not available from CON device`

   Information: You issued the KEYB command to display the current setting, but the command could not determine what code page is in use. The DEVICE=DISPLAY.SYS directive was not provided in CONFIG.SYS, or no currently loaded CON code page is active.

If the DISPLAY.SYS line was included in your CONFIG.SYS file, you must give the MODE CON CODEPAGE PREPARE command to load the font files into memory.

2. `Bad or missing Keyboard Definition File`

Error: The keyboard definition file (usually KEYBOARD.SYS) is corrupted, or KEYB cannot find the file. If you did not specify a drive and path name, KEYB looks for the file in the current drive's root directory.

Copy the file to the root directory, or provide the full drive and path name for the file to KEYB.

3. `Code page requested (codepage) is not valid`
   `for given keyboard code`

Error: You provided a keyboard code but not a code page, or the specified keyboard code does not match the currently active code page for the console. KEYB does not alter the current keyboard or code page. Choose a new console code page that matches the keyboard code (by using the MODE CON CODEPAGE SELECT command), or specify the appropriate matching code page when you reissue the KEYB command.

4. `Code page specified is inconsistent with the`
   `selected code page`

Warning: You specified a keyboard code and a code page, but a different code page was active for the console (CON). The code page specified to KEYB is now active for the keyboard but not for the video display.

Use the MODE CON CODEPAGE SELECT command to activate the correct code page (the one specified to KEYB) for the video screen.

5. `Code page specified has not been prepared`

Error: The DEVICE=DISPLAY.SYS directive was included in your CONFIG.SYS file, but your KEYB command specified a keyboard code that needs a code page that is not prepared. Use the MODE CON CODEPAGE PREPARE command to prepare the code page for the keyboard code that you want to use.

6. `Current CON code page: codepage`

Information: The console's current code page is designated by the number *codepage*.

7. Current keyboard code: `keycode`
   code page: `codepage`

   Information: The current keyboard code is a two-character *keycode*, and the code page used by the keyboard is a three-digit *codepage*.

8. One or more CON code pages invalid for given keyboard code

   Warning: You used the MODE command to prepare several code pages for the console (CON), but you specified a keyboard code that is not compatible with one or more console code pages. KEYB creates the necessary information to work with those keyboard and code pages that are compatible. DOS ignores the incompatible keyboard and code page combinations.

LABEL   V3, V4, V5, V6-External

Creates, changes, or deletes a disk's volume label.

Syntax

> *dc:pathc***LABEL** *d:volume_label*

dc: is the drive that holds the command.

pathc is the path to the command.

d: is the disk whose label you want to change. (The colon is required.)

volume_label is the disk's new volume label.

Reference

See Chapter 7, "Preparing and Maintaining Disks."

Rules

1. A valid volume label immediately becomes the volume label for the specified drive.

2. If you do not specify a volume label, DOS prompts you to enter a new volume label. You can perform one of the following actions:

- Type a valid volume name, and then press Enter. DOS makes this name the new volume label. If a volume label already exists, DOS replaces the old volume label with the new.

- Press Enter to delete the current label without specifying a replacement label. DOS asks you to confirm the deletion.

3. If you enter an invalid volume label, DOS responds with a warning message and asks again for the new volume label.

4. Do not use LABEL in a networked disk drive (one that belongs to another computer). If you try to label a networked drive, DOS displays an error message and ignores the command.

5. Do not use LABEL on a disk in any drive that is affected by the SUBST, JOIN, or ASSIGN commands, because DOS labels the "real" disk in the drive instead.

   Suppose that you use the command ASSIGN A=C. If you then enter the command LABEL A:, DOS actually changes the volume label of the disk in drive C.

6. A label consists of up to 11 printing characters and may include spaces but not tabs or any of the following characters: * ? / \ | . , ; : + = [ ] ( ) & ^ < >. Lowercase ASCII characters are mapped to uppercase.

Notes

When you format a disk in DOS 4.0 and later versions, you are prompted to enter a volume label. Whether or not you assign a label, DOS gives the disk a serial number. The serial number is not part of the volume label. Remember that a space is a valid character in a volume label.

Spaces and underscores can increase the readability of a volume label. DOS 3.0 and 3.1, however, reject a space in a volume name when the name is typed in the command line (for example, LABEL MY DISK). To put a space in a volume label, type LABEL, press the space bar, type the drive name (if needed), and then press Enter. Do not type a volume label in the command line. When LABEL asks for a new volume label, you can type the label with spaces.

Message

```
Delete current volume label (Y/N)?
```

Information and Warning: You did not enter a volume label when DOS prompted you. DOS is asking whether to delete the current label or to leave it unaltered. To delete the current label, type **Y**; to keep the label intact, type **N**.

LOADFIX   *V5, V6-External*

Loads and executes a program above the first 64K of conventional memory.

Syntax

*dc:pathc***LOADFIX** *d:path***filename.ext** *parameters*

dc:pathc represents the drive and directory that hold the command.

filename.ext is the name of the file to be executed.

parameters represents whatever parameters are needed by **filename.ext**.

Rule

Use LOADFIX only to start a program when DOS displays the message `Packed file corrupt`.

Note

If you are using DOS 5.0 or a later version to load DOS into the HMA, a packed file may be loaded into the first 64K of RAM and may fail to work. In such a case, DOS may display the error message `Packed file corrupt`, and the computer will return to the DOS prompt.

LOADHIGH   *V5, V6-Internal*

Loads device drivers or memory-resident programs into upper
memory, beyond conventional memory.

Syntax

To load a program into the largest free block of upper memory,
use the following format:

LOADHIGH *d:pathc***filename.ext** *prog_options*

or

LH *d:path***filename.ext** *prog_options*

To load a program into a specific region of memory, use the
following format:

LOADHIGH */L:region1,minsize1;region2:minsize2... /S*
*d:pathc***filename.ext** *prog_options*

or

LH */L:region1,minsize1;region2:minsize2... /S*
*d:path***filename.ext** *prog_options*

d:path is the location of the device driver or memory-resident
program to be loaded high.

filename.ext is the name of the device driver or memory-resident
program to be loaded high.

prog_options are any options that are required by **filename.ext**.

Switches

/L:region1,minsize1; region2:minsize2...	Specifies one or more regions of upper memory into which the program is to be loaded. *minsize* specifies the minimum size of the UMB.
/S	Specifies that the UMB be shrunk to its minimum size while the program loads.

Reference

See Chapter 17, "Configuring Your Computer."

Rules

1. You must use an upper-memory manager. For a computer equipped with an 80386SX or higher microprocessor and at least 1M of RAM, DOS provides EMM386.EXE.

2. Your CONFIG.SYS file must contain at least the following statements (or the equivalent third-party memory-management routines):

   DEVICE=HIMEM.SYS
   DEVICE=EMM386.EXE RAM (or DEVICE=EMM386.EXE NOEMS)
   DOS=UMB

3. If enough upper memory is not available to accommodate a program, DOS loads the program into conventional memory without warning.

4. When a program is loaded by default into the largest free UMB, that program automatically gains access to all other UMBs. If you use /L, you have to explicitly grant the program access to other upper-memory regions by specifying other /L parameters.

5. /S normally is used only by MemMaker, which analyzes a program's memory usage to determine whether /S is safe.

6. /S must be used only with an /L switch that specifies a minimum size.

7. Use *minsize* when a program is larger when it runs than when it loads.

Example

To load the driver, MYDRV.COM, into upper-memory regions 1 and 3:

LOADHIGH /L:1;3 C:\BIN\MYDRV.COM

Note

Use MEM /F to determine the size of free regions.

MEM   V4, V5, V6-External

Displays the amount of used and unused memory, allocated and
open memory areas, and all programs currently in the system.

Syntax

For DOS 4.0:

> *dc:pathc***MEM** */PROGRAM /DEBUG*

For DOS 5.0:

> *dc:pathc***MEM** */PROGRAM /DEBUG /CLASSIFY*

For DOS 6.0:

> *dc:pathc***MEM** */CLASSIFY /DEBUG /FREE /MODULE name
> /PAGE*

dc: is the drive that contains the command.

pathc is the subdirectory where the command is located.

Switches

/CLASSIFY (or */C*)	Displays programs that are in conventional and upper memory, their location in memory, and their size. Also displays a summary of the total free bytes of conventional and upper memory and the size of the largest executable program. You can use this switch with */PAGE*.
/DEBUG (or */D*)	Displays detailed information about the programs and driver in memory, including the address, name, size, and type of each segment for every program. Also displays a summary of the total free bytes of conventional and upper memory and the size of the largest executable program. You can use this switch with */PAGE*.
/FREE (or */F*)	Displays the free areas of conventional and upper memory in decimal and hexadecimal format. You can use this switch with */PAGE*.

/MODULE name (or /M)	Displays the memory usage of the *name* module, including the segment address, UMB region number, name, and type of each segment. You can use this switch with */PAGE*.
/PAGE (or /P)	Pauses after each screen of output (DOS 6.0 only). You can use this switch with any of the other switches.
/PROGRAM	Displays the status of programs that are loaded into memory (DOS 4.0 and 5.0 only).

Reference

See Chapter 11, "Working with System Information."

Rules

1. You can specify */CLASSIFY*, */DEBUG*, */FREE*, and */MODULE* one a time.

2. DOS displays the status of extended memory only if you have more than 1M of extended memory in your computer.

3. The status of expanded memory is displayed only if you have expanded memory that confirms to Version 4.0 of the Lotus/Intel/Microsoft Expanded Memory Specification (LIM EMS).

4. DOS displays the status of upper memory only if a UMB provider (for example, EMM386) is installed and DOS=UMB is included in your CONFIG.SYS file.

5. DOS does not display the status of upper memory if you are running DOS under Microsoft Windows 3.0.

Notes

A good way to determine a module name for **MEM** */MODULE name* is first to issue the command **MEM /C**.

If your PC has UMBs, you can use **MEM /C** or **MEM /D** extensively as you begin to load device drivers and TSRs into upper memory. MEM displays the location and size of each program in memory. This information can help you determine the order in which device drivers and TSRs load so that you can determine how best to use UMBs.

MEMMAKER   V6-External

Attempts to optimize your computer's conventional memory by moving device drivers and memory-resident programs (TSRs) to upper memory. (You must have an 80386SX or above computer and extended memory to use this command.)

Syntax

*dc:pathc***MEMMAKER** */B /BATCH /SESSION /SWAP:drive /T /UNDO /W:n,m*

dc: is the optional drive that contains the command.

pathc is the optional subdirectory where the command is located.

Switches

/B	Causes MemMaker to display correctly on a monochrome (black-and-white) monitor.
/BATCH	Runs MemMaker in batch (unattended) mode. When you use this switch, DOS takes only the default actions and, if an error occurs, restores your CONFIG.SYS, AUTOEXEC.BAT, and (if necessary) Microsoft Windows SYSTEM.INI files. You can determine what was done by looking in the MEMMAKER.STS file.
/SESSION	Used by MemMaker during its optimization process.
/SWAP:drive	Specifies your boot drive's new disk letter. You need this switch only in rare cases (for example, when disk-compression software, such as Stacker 1.0, swaps drive letters.) Unless MemMaker knows your boot disk drive, it cannot find your start-up files.
/T	Disables IBM Token Ring detection.
/UNDO	Undoes changes in the CONFIG.SYS, AUTOEXEC.BAT, and (if necessary) Microsoft Windows SYSTEM.INI files from a previous use of MemMaker. Use this switch if your system does

not work after you run MemMaker or if you are dissatisfied with the new configuration.

/W:n,m   Specifies how much upper memory (in K) to reserve for Microsoft Windows translation buffers. Windows needs two such buffers in either upper or conventional memory. *n* is the size of the first, and *m* is the size of the second. The default is /W:0,0.

Reference

See Chapter 17, "Configuring Your Computer."

Notes

You do not have to use */SWAP:drive* if you are using Microsoft DoubleSpace, SuperStar, or Stacker 2.0 or 3.0.

MIRROR   *V5-External*

Records information about the file-allocation table (FAT) and the root directory to enable you to use the UNFORMAT and UNDELETE commands.

MIRROR is included on the DOS 6.0 Supplemental Program disk but not in the standard DOS 6.0 package. For information about similar capabilities in DOS 6.0, see the section on the UNDELETE command later in this Command Reference.

Syntax

*dc:pathc***MIRROR** *d1: d2: dn: /Tdrive-entries /1*

To save information about a drive partition, use the following format:

*dc:pathc***MIRROR** *d1: d2: dn:* **/PARTN**

To quit tracking deleted files, use the following format:

*dc:pathc***MIRROR/U**

dc:pathc represents the optional drive and subdirectory where MIRROR is located.

d1:, *d2:*, and *dn:* are the disk drives that you track with MIRROR.

Switches

/Tdrive-entries	Loads a memory-resident tracking program that records information about deleted files. The *drive* specifies the drive where MIRROR saves information about deleted files. *-entries* is an optional value (ranging from 1 to 999) that specifies the maximum number of deleted files to be tracked.
/1	Keeps MIRROR from creating a backup of the mirror file when the file is updated.
/PARTN	Makes a copy of the drive's partition table.
/U	Removes the tracking program from the part of memory that keeps track of deleted files.

Reference

See Chapter 7, "Preparing and Maintaining Disks."

Rules

1. Do not use the /U switch in drives that use JOIN or SUBST.

2. If you use ASSIGN, you must place this command before the MIRROR command.

3. DOS saves information about deleted files in the file PCTRACKR.DEL. The UNDELETE command uses this file.

4. DOS saves system information, the FAT, and the root directory in the file MIRROR.FIL. The UNFORMAT command uses this file.

5. DOS saves information about the hard-drive partition in the file PARTNSAV.FIL. The UNFORMAT command uses this file.

Notes

When you track deleted files, you can specify how many files are contained in the PCTRACKR.DEL file (1 to 999). The default values, however, probably are satisfactory. Those values are as follows:

Size of disk	Entries stored
360K	25
720K	50

Size of disk	Entries stored
1.2M/1.44M	75
20M	101
32M	202
Larger than 32M	303

Using the /PARTN switch with MIRROR creates the file
PARTNSAV.FIL. This file contains information from the drive's
partition table. The partition initially is created with FDISK. You
are instructed to place a floppy disk in drive A, rather than save
PARTNSAV.FIL on the hard disk. The file is saved on the disk.
Label and store the disk in a safe place.

UNFORMAT, a companion command to MIRROR, uses these files.
If you lose information, if you accidentally format a disk, or if the
partition table is damaged, you can recover the lost information
by using UNFORMAT if you previously used MIRROR.

> **CAUTION:** The MIRROR and UNFORMAT commands are not
> replacements for proper backups of your hard disk.

Messages

1. Creates an image of the system area.
   Drive C being processed.
   The MIRROR process was successful.

   Information: These messages appear when you issue the
   command MIRROR while drive C is the current drive. The
   messages indicate that MIRROR performed successfully.

2. Deletion-tracking software being installed.
   The following drives are supported:

   Drive C - Default files saved.
   Installation complete.

   Information: These messages appear when you install MIR-
   ROR with delete tracking. The messages indicate that delete
   tracking for drive C is installed correctly.

3. WARNING! Unrecognized DOS INT 25h/26h handler.
   Some other TSR programs may behave erratically while
   deletion-tracking software is resident!

Warning: Some other TSR conflicted with delete tracking. Experiment with loading TSRs and delete tracking in a different order. When you find the correct order, modify AUTOEXEC.BAT so that the TSRs and delete tracking are loaded in the correct sequence.

Try installing the MIRROR program before other resident programs.

MKDIR or MD   *V2, V3, V4, V5, V6-Internal*

Creates a subdirectory.

Syntax

MKDIR *d:path***dirname**

or

MD *d:path***dirname**

d: is the drive for the subdirectory.

path\ indicates the path to the directory that will hold the subdirectory.

dirname is the subdirectory that you are creating.

Reference

See Chapter 8, "Understanding and Managing Directories."

Rules

1. If you do not specify a path name but provide a drive name, DOS establishes the subdirectory in the current directory of the specified drive. If you do not specify a path name or a drive name, DOS establishes the subdirectory in the current directory of the current drive.

2. If you use a path name, use the path character (\) to separate the path name from the directory name.

3. You must specify the new subdirectory name (1 to 8 characters); specifying an extension is optional. The name must conform to the rules for creating directory names.

4. You cannot use a directory name that is identical to a file name in the parent directory. If you have a file named MYFILE in the current directory, for example, you cannot create the subdirectory MYFILE in this directory. If the file is named MYFILE.TXT, however, the names do not conflict, and you can create the MYFILE subdirectory.

5. The maximum length of a path (from the root directory to the final directory) is 63 characters, including the backslashes.

Note

You are not restricted to creating subdirectories in the current directory. If you add a path name, DOS establishes a new subdirectory in the directory that you specify.

Message

```
Unable to create directory
```

Error: One of the following errors occurred:

■ You tried to create a directory that already exists.

■ You provided an incorrect path name.

■ The disk's directory is full.

■ The disk is full.

■ A file with the same name already exists.

Check the directory in which the new subdirectory was to be created. If a conflicting name exists, either change the file name or use a new directory name. If the disk or the root directory is full, delete some files, create the subdirectory in a different directory, or use a different disk.

MODE Commands   *V1, V2, V3, V4, V5, V6-External*

The MODE command generally configures system devices. The details of the command's functions, however, are so varied that the syntax is complex. Therefore, the following sections cover each of the MODE command's functions separately.

MODE   *V3.3, V4.0, V4.01,*
CODEPAGE PREP   *V5, V6-External*

Prepares (chooses) the code pages to be used with a device.

Syntax

*dc:pathc***MODE device CODEPAGE PREPARE =
((codepage**, *codepage,...)dp:pathp***pagefile.ext)**

or

*dc:pathc***MODE device CP PREP = ((codepage**, *codepage,...)*
*dp:pathp***pagefile.ext)**

dc: is the drive that holds the command.

pathc is the path to the command.

device is the device for which you are choosing code pages.
You can select one of the following devices:

CON*:*   The console

LPTx*:*   The first, second, or third parallel printer
(**x** is 1, 2, or 3)

PRN*:*   The first parallel printer

codepage is the number of the code page(s) to be used with the
device. The ellipsis (...) represents additional code pages.

Following are the choices for **codepage**:

codepage	Country/language
437	United States
850	Multilingual (Latin 1)
852	Slavic (Latin 2)
860	Portuguese
863	Canadian-French
865	Nordic

dp: is the drive that holds the code-page (font) information.

pathp is the path to the file that holds the code-page (font)
information.

pagefile.ext is the file that holds the code-page (font) information:

pagefile.ext	Description
EGA.CPI	Enhanced Graphics Adapter (EGA) and IBM PS/2
4201.CPI	IBM Proprinter II and III Model 4201, Proprinter XL Model 4202, and compatibles
4208.CPI	IBM Proprinter X24E Model 4207, Proprinter XL24E Model 4208, and compatibles
5202.CPI	IBM Quietwriter III printer
LCD.CPI	IBM PC-convertible liquid crystal display/screen

Reference

See Chapter 20, "Understanding the International Features of DOS."

Rules

1. You must specify a valid device. The options are CON:, PRN:, LPT1:, LPT2:, and LPT3:. (The colon after the device name is optional.)

2. You must use the formats CODEPAGE or CP and PREPARE or PREP.

3. You must specify one or more code pages, using commas to separate the numbers if you specify more than one. You must enclose the entire list of code pages in parentheses.

4. When you add or replace code pages, enter a comma for any code page that you do not want to change.

Example

To prepare the first parallel port with the multilingual (Latin 1) code page found in the file C:\DOS\4201.CPI:

MODE LPT1 CP PREP=((850),C:\DOS\4201.CPI)

Note

MODE CODEPAGE PREPARE is used to prepare code pages (fonts) for the console (keyboard and display) and the printers. Issue this subcommand before issuing the MODE CODEPAGE SELECT subcommand, unless you use the IBM Quietwriter III printer, whose font information is contained in cartridges. If the code page that you need is in a cartridge, you do not need to use the PREPARE command.

MODE CODEPAGE REFRESH — V3.3, V4.0, V4.01, V5, V6-External

Reloads and reactivates the code page used with a device.

Syntax

> *dc:pathc***MODE device CODEPAGE REFRESH**
>
> or
>
> *dc:pathc***MODE device CP REF**

dc: is the drive that holds the command.

pathc is the path to the command.

device is the device for which you are choosing code pages. You can select one of the following devices:

CON:	The console
LPTx:	The first, second, or third parallel printer (**x** is 1, 2, or 3)
PRN:	The first parallel printer

Reference

See Chapter 20, "Understanding the International Features of DOS."

Rules

1. You must specify a valid device. The options are CON:, PRN:, LPT1:, LPT2:, and LPT3:. (The colon after the device name is optional.)

2. You must use the formats CODEPAGE or CP and REFRESH or REF.

Note

MODE CODEPAGE REFRESH downloads, if necessary, and reactivates the currently selected code page on a device. Use this command after you turn on your printer or after a program changes the video display and leaves the console code page in ruins.

MODE
CODEPAGE SELECT

V3.3, V4.0, V4.01,
V5, V6-External

Activates the code page used with a device.

Syntax

*dc:pathc***MODE device CODEPAGE SELECT = codepage**

or

*dc:pathc***MODE device CP SEL = codepage**

dc: is the drive that holds the command.

pathc is the path to the command.

device is the device for which you are choosing code pages. You can select one of the following devices:

CON: The console

LPTx: The first, second, or third parallel printer
       (**x** is 1, 2, or 3)

PRN: The first parallel printer

codepage represents the numbers of the code pages to be used with the device. (For a table of values, refer to the section on CODEPAGE PREPARE earlier in this Command Reference.)

Reference

See Chapter 20, "Understanding the International Features of DOS."

Rules

1. You must specify a valid device. The options are CON:, PRN:, LPT1:, LPT2:, and LPT3:. (The colon after the device name is optional.)

2. You must use the formats CODEPAGE or CP and SELECT or SEL.

3. You must specify a code page. The code page must be either part of a MODE CODEPAGE PREPARE command for the device or the hardware code page specified to the appropriate device driver.

Notes

MODE CODEPAGE SELECT activates a currently prepared code page or reactivates a hardware code page. You can use MODE CODEPAGE SELECT only on these two types of code pages.

MODE CODEPAGE SELECT usually completes a downloading of any software font to the device, except for the Quietwriter III printer, which uses cartridges.

MODE CODEPAGE SELECT activates code pages for individual devices. You can use the CHCP command to activate the code pages for all available devices.

Reference

See Chapter 20, "Understanding the International Features of DOS."

MODE CODEPAGE STATUS   V3.3, V4.0, V4.01, V5, V6-External

Displays a device's code-page status.

Syntax

*dc:pathc***MODE device CODEPAGE** */STATUS*

or

*dc:pathc***MODE device CP** */STA*

dc: is the drive that holds the command.

pathc is the path to the command.

device is the device for which you are choosing code pages. You can select one of the following devices:

CON: The console

LPTx: The first, second, or third parallel printer (**x** is 1, 2, or 3)

PRN: The first parallel printer

Switch

/STATUS or /STA   Displays the status of the device's code pages. This switch is the default.

Reference

See Chapter 20, "Understanding the International Features of DOS."

Rules

1. You must specify a valid device. The options are CON:, PRN:, LPT1:, LPT2:, and LPT3:. (The colon after the device name is optional.)

2. You must use the format CODEPAGE or CP.

3. You can use the /STATUS or /STA switch.

4. MODE /STATUS displays the following information about the device:

   ■ The selected (active) code page, if one is selected

   ■ The hardware code page(s)

   ■ Any prepared code page(s)

   ■ Any available positions for additional prepared code pages

MODE COM PORT   V1.1, V2, V3, V3.3, V4, V5, V6-External

Controls the protocol characteristics of the Asynchronous Communications Adapter.

Syntax

*dc:pathc***MODE COMy***: **baud**, parity, databits, stopbits, P*

If you have DOS 4.0, 5.0, or 6.0, you can use the following format:

*dc:pathc***MODE COMy***: BAUD=baud PARITY=parity*
DATA=databits STOP=stopbits RETRY=ret

y*:* is the adapter number (1, 2, 3, or 4); the colon after the number is optional.

baud is the baud rate (110, 150, 300, 600, 1200, 2400, 4800, 9600, or 19200); this parameter actually is bits per second for rates higher than 300. Not all computers support 19200 baud.

parity represents the parity-checking setting (None, Odd, Even, Mark, or Space). In versions of DOS before 4.0, use N, O, or E. Not all computers support Mark and Space.

databits is the number of data bits (5 to 8). The default is 7. Not all computers support 5 and 6 data bits.

stopbits is the number of stop bits (1, 1.5, or 2). If baud is 110, the default is 2; otherwise, the default is 1. Not all computers support 1.5 stop bits.

P represents continuous retries on time-out errors.

ret tells DOS what to do when a time-out error occurs. This parameter causes part of MODE to remain resident in memory. You can choose one of the following options:

ret	Action
B	Return busy when the port is busy
E	Return error when the port is busy
P	Retry until output is accepted
R	Return ready when the port is busy (infinite retry)
NONE	Take no action (the default)

Reference

See Chapter 12, "Controlling Devices."

Rules

1. For DOS versions before 5.0, you must enter the adapter's number, followed by a space and a baud rate. If you type the optional colon, you must type the adapter number immediately before the colon. All other parameters are optional.

2. If you do not want to change a parameter, enter a comma for that value.

3. If you enter an invalid parameter, DOS responds with an invalid-parameter message and takes no further action.

4. You can enter only the first two digits of the baud rate (for example, 11 for 110 baud and 96 for 9600 baud).

5. If you want continuous retries after a time-out, you must enter P or RETRY=B whenever you use the MODE COMn: command.

6. If the adapter is set for continuous retries (P or RETRY=B) and the device is not ready, the computer is looping. You can abort this loop by pressing Ctrl-Break.

7. If you use a networked printer, do not use any of the RETRY values.

MODE DISPLAY   V2, V3, V4-External

Switches the active display adapter between the monochrome display and a graphics adapter/array (Color Graphics Adapter, Enhanced Color Graphics Adapter, or Video Graphics Array) on a two-display system, and sets the graphics adapter/array's characteristics.

Syntax

       *dc:pathc***MODE dt**

       or

       *dc:pathc***MODE** *dt,* **s***, T*

If you are using DOS 4.0 or a later version, you can use the following formats:

*dc:pathc***MODE CON: COLS=***x* **LINES=***y*

or

*dc:pathc***MODE dt***,y*

dc: is the name of the drive that holds the command.

pathc is the path to the command.

dt is the display type, which may be any of the following:

40	Sets the graphics display to 40 characters per line
80	Sets the graphics display to 80 characters per line
BW40	Makes the graphics display the active display and sets the mode to 40 characters per line, black-and-white (color disabled)
BW80	Makes the graphics display the active display and sets the mode to 80 characters per line, black-and-white (color disabled)
CO40	Makes the graphics display the active display and sets the mode to 40 characters per line (color enabled)
CO80	Makes the graphics display the active display and sets the mode to 80 characters per line (color enabled)
MONO	Makes the monochrome display the active display

s shifts the CGA display right (R) or left (L) one character.

T requests alignment of the graphics display with a one-line test pattern.

x specifies the number of columns to be displayed (40 or 80).

y specifies the number of lines on the display and can have the value 25, 43, or 50. (Your display adapter may not support all three values.)

Reference

See Chapter 11, "Working with System Information."

Rules

1. For the first form of the command, you must enter the display type (dt); all other parameters are optional.

2. For the second form of the command, you must enter the shift parameter (R or L, for shifting right or left). The display type (*dt*) and test pattern (*T*) are optional.

3. The **s** (R or L) parameter works only with the Color Graphics Adapter; the display does not shift if you use this command with any other adapter. The *T* parameter displays the test pattern only on a Color Graphics Adapter.

4. Changing the number of lines requires you to load ANSI.SYS in your CONFIG.SYS file.

Note

Several DOS commands, such as DIR /P and MODE, act on the setting for the number of lines.

MODE   V4, V5, V6-External
KEY REPEAT

Adjusts the rate at which the keyboard repeats a character.

Syntax

*dc:pathc***MODE CON RATE** = *x* **DELAY** = *y*

dc is the drive containing the MODE command.

pathc is the optional path containing the MODE command.

x is a value that specifies the character-repeat rate (1 to 32). Those values represent approximately 2 to 30 characters per second. The default is 20 for IBM AT-compatibles and 21 for IBM PS/2-compatibles.

y specifies the length of delay between the initial pressing of the key and the start of automatic character repetition. This value can be 1, 2, 3, or 4, which represent delays of 1/4 second, 1/2 second, 3/4 second, and one full second, respectively. The default is 2.

Reference

See Chapter 11, "Working with System Information."

Rule

RATE and DELAY must be set together (in the same command).

MODE PRINTER PORT
V1, V2, V3, V4, V5, V6-EXTERNAL

Sets the parallel-printer characteristics.

Syntax

*dc:pathc***MODE LPTx**:*cpl,lpi,P*

If you have DOS 4.0, 5.0, or 6.0, you can use the following format:

*dc:pathc***MODE LPTx**: *COLS=cpl LINES=lpi RETRY=ret*

dc: is the drive that holds the command.

pathc is the path to the command.

x: is the printer number (1, 2, or 3). The colon is optional.

cpl is the number of characters per line (80, 132). The default is 80.

lpi is the number of lines per inch (six or eight). The default is 8.

P specifies continuous retries on time-out errors.

ret tells DOS what to do when a time-out error occurs. This parameter causes part of MODE to remain resident in memory. You can choose one of the following options:

ret	Action
B	Return busy when the port is busy.
E	Return error when the port is busy.
P	Retry until the printer is not busy.
R	Return ready when the port is busy (infinite retry).
N or NONE	Take no action (the default).

Reference

See Chapter 12, "Controlling Devices."

Rules

1. You must specify a printer number, but all other parameters are optional, including the colon after the printer number.

2. If you do not want to change a parameter, enter a comma for that parameter.

3. The COMy: command cancels the effect of MODE LPTx:.

4. A parameter does not change if you skip that parameter or use an invalid parameter. The printer number, however, must be entered correctly.

5. In DOS 3.3 and earlier versions, if you specify P for continuous retries, you can cancel P only by reentering the MODE command without P. In later versions of DOS, the RETRY=B option has the same effect as the P option of previous DOS versions.

6. If you use a networked printer, do not use any of the RETRY values.

7. The characters-per-line and lines-per-inch portions of the command affect only IBM printers, Epson printers, and other printers that use Epson-compatible control codes.

Notes

This command controls IBM matrix and graphics printers, all Epson printers, and Epson-compatible printers. The command may work partially or not at all on other printers.

When you change the column width, MODE sends the special printer-control code that specifies the normal font (80) or the condensed font (132). When you change the lines-per-inch setting, MODE sends the correct printer-control code for printing 6 or 8 lines per inch. MODE also sets the printer to 88 lines per page for an 8-lines-per-inch setting and to 66 lines per page for a 6-lines-per-inch setting.

If you use the P option of DOS 3.3 or earlier versions or the B retry option of later versions of DOS and attempt to print on a deselected printer, the computer does not issue a time-out error. Rather, the computer internally loops until the printer is ready (turned on, connected to the PC, and selected). For about a minute, the computer appears to be locked up. To abort the continuous retry, press Ctrl-Break.

MODE REDIRECTION

V2, V3, V4, V5, V6-External

Forces DOS to print to a serial printer instead of a parallel printer.

Syntax

*dc:pathc***MODE LPTx: = COMy:**

dc: is the drive that holds the command.

pathc is the path to the command.

x: is the parallel-printer number (1, 2, or 3). The colon is optional.

y: is the Asynchronous Communications Adapter number (1, 2, 3, or 4).

Reference

See Chapter 12, "Controlling Devices."

Rules

1. You must provide a valid number for both the parallel printer and the serial printer.

2. After you issue the command, all printing that normally goes to the parallel printer goes to the designated serial printer.

3. You can cancel or undo this command by issuing the MODE LPTx: command.

Notes

This form of MODE is useful for systems that are connected to a serial printer. When you type the following command, the serial printer receives all the output that usually is sent to the system printer (assuming that the serial printer is connected to the first Asynchronous Communications Adapter):

MODE LPT1: = COM1:

This output includes the print-screen (Shift-PrtSc) function. Before you issue the MODE LPT=COMy command, use the MODE COMn: command to set up the serial adapter used for the serial printer.

MODE STATUS

V4, V5, V6-External

Displays the status of a specified device or of all devices that can be set by MODE.

Syntax

> *dc:pathc***MODE** *device /STATUS*

dc: is the drive that holds the command.

pathc is the path to the command.

device is the optional device to be checked by MODE.

Switch

/STATUS   Checks the status of a device or devices. If you prefer, you can enter /STA rather than the complete /STATUS.

Reference

See Chapter 7, "Preparing and Maintaining Disks."

Notes

This command enables you to see the status of any device that you normally set with MODE. When you type **MODE LPT1 /STA**, for example, DOS displays the status of the first parallel port.

MODE is the equivalent of MODE /STATUS.

MORE

V2, V3, V4, V5, V6-External

Displays one screen of information from the standard input device, pauses, and then displays the message -More-. When you press any key, MORE displays the next screen of information.

Syntax

*dm:pathm***MORE** *< d:path***filename**.*ext*

or

command | *dm:pathm***MORE**

dm: is the drive that holds the command.

pathm is the path to the command.

d: is the drive that holds the file to be displayed.

path is the path to the file to be displayed.

filename.*ext* is the name of the file to be displayed.

command is the DOS command whose output is to be displayed (for example, TYPE).

Reference

See Chapter 12, "Controlling Devices."

Rules

1. MORE displays one screen of information on a standard screen.

2. After displaying a screen of information, MORE waits for a keystroke before filling the screen with new information. This process repeats until all output is displayed.

3. MORE is useful with I/O redirection and piping.

Notes

MORE is a DOS filter that enables you to display information without manually pausing the screen.

MORE, when used with redirection or piping, is similar to the TYPE command, but MORE pauses after each screen of information.

MORE intelligently handles two aspects of displaying text. The command pauses after displaying a screenful of lines, as defined by you with the MODE command. The command also wraps lines that are longer than the width of your screen and reduces the number of lines that are displayed so that unread lines do not scroll off the screen.

MOVE   *V6-External*

Moves one or more files to another directory, or renames one or more directories.

Syntax

To move one or more files, use the following format:

> *dc:pathc***MOVE** *d1:path1***filename1** *d2:path2\\filename2...*
> *dd:pathd***name**

To rename a directory, use the following format:

> *dc:pathc***MOVE** *d:path***dirname** *d:path***dirname2**

dc: is the drive that holds the command.

pathc is the path to the command.

d1: is the disk that holds the file to be moved and the new name or directory.

path1 is the path that holds the file to be moved.

filename1 represents the name of the file to be moved. Wild cards are allowed.

path2\\filename2... represents the disks, paths, and file names of other files to be moved to the same directory as **filename1**.

dd:pathd represents the drive and path of the directory to which the files are to be moved.

name generally is the name of the directory to which the files are to be moved. If you are moving only one file, this parameter can be a new name for **filename1**—that is, you can rename and move a file at the same time. If you are moving more than one file and **name** is a nonexistent directory, MOVE asks permission to create the directory and to move the file into that directory.

d:path represents the disk and path of the file to be renamed.

dirname is the name of the directory to be renamed.

dirname2 is the new name for the directory.

Switch

/Y	Specifies that you not be prompted if a destination directory has to be created for a move.

Examples

To move the file README.TXT in the current directory and the file C:\BIN\SETUP.EXE to the directory C:\TEMP (the files are not renamed):

MOVE README.TXT, C:\BIN\SETUP.EXE C:\TEMP

To change the name of the file README.TXT in the current directory to README.1ST:

MOVE README.TXT README.1ST

To move and rename C:\INFO\README.TXT to C:\TEMP\README.BAK:

MOVE C:\INFO\README.TXT C:\TEMP\README.BAK

To change the name of the directory C:\BIN to C:\OLDBIN:

MOVE C:\BIN C:\OLDBIN

Reference

See Chapter 8, "Understanding and Managing Directories."

Rules

1. If you move a file to a directory that already includes a file with that name, DOS overwrites the file in the destination directory without warning.

2. You cannot rename a directory that you are moving to a different disk or to a different relative position on a disk. The disk and path in front of both **dirname** and **dirname2** have to be the same.

3. If the destination directory does not exist, DOS can create it automatically.

Notes

If you specify several files to be moved and a file name, rather than a directory, as the destination, DOS displays the message Cannot move multiple files to a single file.

If a MOVE operation is successful, DOS returns an ERRORLEVEL of 0. If an error occurs, DOS returns a value of 1.

MSAV   V6-External

Scans your computer's memory and disks for viruses and (optionally) deletes viruses.

Syntax

To interact with MSAV's full-screen display and then start scanning, use the following format:

*dc:\pathc***MSAV** */R /video /mouse*

To immediately start scanning one or more disks, directories, and/or files with MSAV's full-screen display to show progress, use the following format:

*dc:pathc***MSAV** *d1:... d2:path2\filename2 /S /C /R /A /L /video /mouse*

To immediately start scanning one or more disks, directories, and/or files with a command-line interface to show progress, use the following format:

*dc:pathc***MSAV** */S /C /R /A /L /N /P /F /video /mouse*

To get on-line help on the video and mouse options, use the following format:

*dc:pathc***MSAV /VIDEO**

dc: is the drive that holds the command.

pathc is the path to the command.

d1:... represents one or more drives that you want to scan. If you specify a disk, you should not specify *path*.

d2:path2\filename2 represents one or more directories and/or files that you want to scan. If you specify a directory, all the files in that directory and in its subdirectories are scanned.

path is the absolute directory that you want to scan, along with all of its subdirectories. If you specify *path*, do not specify a disk.

Switches

/S	Scans for viruses but does not remove them (the default).
/C	Scans for and removes viruses.

/R	Creates a summary report of MSAV's activity in the file MSAV.RPT in the root directory of the boot drive, listing the number of files checked, the number of viruses found, and the number of viruses removed. By default, a report is not created.
/A	Scans all drives except A and B.
/L	Scans all drives except network drives.
/N	Turns off full-screen display of information during the scan.
/P	Shows the scanning process in the command line and displays the equivalent of MSAV.RPT.
/F	Turns off the display of file names that are being scanned. (Use only with /N or /P.)
/VIDEO	Displays command-line help on video and mouse options.
/video	*video* can be any of the following:

25	Sets the display to 25 lines (the default)
28	Sets the display to 28 lines (VGA)
43	Sets the display to 43 lines (EGA and VGA)
50	Sets the display to 50 lines (VGA)
60	Sets the display to 60 lines (Video 7 video adapters only)
IN	Forces the display to use color
BW	Forces the display to use black-and-white
MONO	Forces the display to use monochrome (IBM monochrome)
LCD	Forces the display to use a liquid-crystal-display color scheme
FF	Uses the fastest screen updating for CGA (may cause "snow")
BF	Uses your computer's BIOS fonts (use only if the default graphics characters in the full-screen display do not display properly)

	NF	No fonts (no graphics characters should be used in the full-screen display)
	BT	Allows the use of a graphics mouse in Microsoft Windows and graphics fonts in DESQview and Ultravision
/mouse	*mouse* can be any of the following:	
	NGM	No graphics mouse, which uses the default mouse character rather than a graphics cursor in the full-screen display
	LE	Switches the left and right mouse buttons
	PS2	Resets the mouse if the cursor disappears or freezes

Reference

See Chapter 18, "Getting the Most from Your Hard Drive."

Different options are available from the full-screen display and from the command line.

DOS 6.0 includes a Microsoft Windows version of MSAV.

The options you choose while in full-screen mode are recorded in the file MSAV.INI.

MSBACKUP   V6-External

Backs up one or more files from a hard disk or floppy disk to another disk.

Syntax

    *dc:pathc***MSBACKUP** *d:path\\setupfile /BW /LCD /MDA*

dc: is the drive that holds the command.

pathc is the path to the command.

d: is the drive that holds the setup file.

path is the path to the setup file.

setupfile represents the file that holds your saved settings, the names of the files to be backed up, and the type of backup you want. This file must have a SET extension. The default is DEFAULT.SET.

Switches

/BW	DOSBACK uses colors appropriate for a black-and-white display.
/LCD	DOSBACK uses colors appropriate for a liquid-crystal display.
/MDA	DOSBACK uses colors appropriate for a mono-chrome display adapter.

Reference

See Chapter 13, "Understanding Backups and the Care of Data."

Rules

1. You do not explicitly create a setup file. MSBACKUP creates a setup file (or updates it, if you specified one in the MSBACKUP command line) when you save your program settings and file selections.

2. You cannot start MSBACKUP from a floppy disk. This utility and its other program files must be on your hard disk.

3. When looking for its configuration information, backup sets, and catalogs, MSBACKUP first looks in the directory specified by the MSDOSDATA environment variable, then in the directory from which it was started, and then in the current directory. You can use MSDOSDATA to point at your own configuration if you share MSBACKUP with other people.

Notes

DOS 6.0 includes a Microsoft Windows version of MSBACKUP.

When it performs a backup, MSBACKUP creates a catalog file that contains information about the files that were backed up. When you need to restore a file, you can search the catalog files to determine which one contains the files you want.

Catalog files encode information in their names. Decoding CD30401A.FUL, for example, yields the following characters:

Character	Meaning
C	The first drive backed up in this set.
D	The last drive backed up in this set. (Had C been the only drive, the catalog file's name would have been CC30401A.FUL.)
3	The last digit of the year of the backup (here, 1993).
04	The month of the backup (here, April).
01	The day of the backup (here, the first).
A	The ID of the backup on that day. If more than one backup of the same drive(s) is performed on the same day and the Keep Old Backup Catalogs options is set, a letter from A through Z is assigned to indicate the order in which the otherwise identically named catalog files were created. A is the first, B is the second, and so on. If the Keep Old Backup Catalogs option is not set, the ID alternates between A and B.
FUL	The backup type (here, FULL). The other possibilities are INC (incremental) and DIF (differential).

When you perform a full backup, MSBACKUP creates a master catalog file, which keeps track of all the backup catalogs that will be made during a backup cycle. When you need to restore a file, loading the master catalog automatically merges all the catalogs of the backup cycle, so you can select the latest version of a file easily (although you can choose to restore an earlier version).

MSBACKUP puts one copy of the backup catalog on your hard disk and a second copy on the disk or network drive that contains your backup set.

If DOS displays the message Insufficient memory while you use MSBACKUP, follow these steps:

1. Make sure that your computer has at least 512K of conventional memory.

2. Quit MSBACKUP, remove all memory-resident programs (TSRs) from memory, and try again.

3. In MSBACKUP, turn off the Compress Backup Data option (in the Disk Backup Options dialog box).

MSCDEX   V6-External

Provides access to CD-ROM drives.

Syntax

> *dc:pathc***MSCDEX** */D:drvsig* */D:drvsig2... /E /K /S /V*
> */L:letter /M:number*

dc: is the drive that holds the command.

pathc is the path to the command.

Switches

/D:drvsig */D:drvsig2...*	Specifies the driver signature of your CD-ROM and the driver signatures of your other CD-ROMs. Each signature must match the parameter of the /D switch in CONFIG.SYS that starts the corresponding CD-ROM device driver.
/E	Enables the CD-ROM driver to use available expanded memory to store sector buffers.
/K	Enables recognition of Kanji CD-ROM labels.
/S	Enables sharing of CD-ROM drives on a server.
/V	Displays memory statistics when MSCDEX starts.
/L:letter	Specifies the drive letter to be assigned to the first CD-ROM. Additional CD-ROMs are assigned letters in sequence.
/M:number	Specifies the number of sector buffers.

Rules

1. Your CD-ROM's device driver must be loaded by your CONFIG.SYS file. It should include a /D parameter to assign a driver signature (also called a driver name) to the driver.

2. Your CONFIG.SYS file must include a LASTDRIVE command that provides enough device letters for your network, DoubleSpace, and MSCDEX needs.

3. MSCDEX can be invoked by your AUTOEXEC.BAT file or from the DOS command line.

4. Invoke MSCDEX before you start Microsoft Windows.

Example

Following is a typical CONFIG.SYS line and corresponding MSCDEX line for enabling a single CD-ROM as drive E:

> **DEVICE=C:\DEVICES\CDROMDRV.SYS /D:MSCD000**
>
> **C:\DOS\MSCDEX /D:MSCD000 /L:E**

MSD   *V6-External*

Activates Microsoft Diagnostics, which reports detailed information about your computer.

Syntax

To use MSD interactively with a full-screen display, use the following format:

> *dc:pathc***MSD** */B /I*

To use MSD to generate a report to a file, use the following format:

> *dc:pathc***MSD** */I /F d:path\name /P d:path\name /S d:path\name*

dc: is the drive that holds the command.

pathc is the path to the command.

d: is the drive that receives the report file.

path is the directory that receives the report file.

name is the name of the report file.

Switches

/B   Forces the display to black-and-white.

/F   Prompts you for certain information (your name, company, address, country, telephone number, and comments), and then incorporates that information into the complete report that is written to the specified file.

/I	Prevents MSD from detecting hardware when the utility starts (use this switch if MSD does not start or run properly).
/P	Writes a complete report to the specified file.
/S	Write a summary report to the specified file.

Note

MSD provides information about your computer (for example, its manufacturer, bus type, and ROM BIOS manufacturer) and about its upper-memory use, video display, network, operating system, mouse, other adapters, disk drives, LPT ports, COM ports, IRQ stations, TSR programs, and device drivers. This information can be valuable when you are correcting problems and installing new hardware.

NLSFUNC　　V3.3, V4, V5, V6-External

Supports extended country information (national-language support, or NLS) in DOS and enables the CHCP command.

Syntax

*dc:pathc***NLSFUNC** *d:path\filename.ext*

dc: is the drive that holds the command.

pathc is the path to the command.

d: is the drive that holds the country-information file.

path is the path to the country-information file.

filename.ext is the country-information file (usually COUNTRY.SYS). This file overrides the default specified by the COUNTRY command.

Reference

See Chapter 20, "Understanding the International Features of DOS."

Rules

1. If you provide a drive or path name, you also must provide the name of the information file (usually COUNTRY.SYS).

2. If you omit the full file name, DOS searches for the file COUNTRY.SYS in the current disk's root directory.

3. Once loaded, NLSFUNC remains active until you restart DOS.

Note

You can use the INSTALL command in DOS 4.0 or later versions to activate the NLSFUNC command from CONFIG.SYS. After specifying the COUNTRY line in CONFIG.SYS, use the following format:

INSTALL=*dc:path***NLSFUNC** *d:path**filename.ext*

This procedure uses less memory than starting NLSFUNC from the DOS prompt.

PATH   V2, V3, V4, V5, V6-Internal

Tells DOS to search the specific directories in the specified drives if a program or batch file is not found in the current directory.

Syntax

PATH *d1:path1;d2:path2;d3:path3;...*

To display the current PATH, use the following format:

PATH

To clear the current PATH (to the current directory), use the following format:

PATH ;

d1:, *d2:*, and *d3:* are valid drive names.

path1, *path2*, and *path3* are valid path names to the commands that you want to run in any directory.

The ellipsis (...) represents additional drives and path names.

Reference

See Chapter 15, "Understanding Batch Files, DOSKey, and Macros."

Rules

1. If you specify more than one set of paths, the following rules apply:

   ■ The path sets must be separated by semicolons.

   ■ The search for the programs or batch files is made in the order in which you list the path sets. First, DOS searches the current directory; then DOS searches d1:path1, d2:path2, d3:path3, and so on until the command or batch file is found.

2. The maximum length of PATH is 127 characters.

3. The PATH command establishes the value of an environment variable named PATH.

Notes

When you type the name of a program or batch file, DOS searches the current directory. If the program or batch file is not found, DOS searches each path in sequence. If the program or batch file is not found in any of the paths, DOS displays the error message `Bad command or file name`.

You can shorten PATH by using the SUBST command to substitute drive letters for deeply nested paths. Another technique is to remove a path that is included only to start one program, make a batch file that performs a CD to that path and invokes that program, and put the batch file in a directory that still is included in PATH.

Message

`Invalid drive in search path`

Warning: You specified a nonexistent drive name in one of the paths. This message appears when DOS searches for a program or batch file, not when you give the PATH command.

Use PATH or SET to see the current path. If the drive temporarily is invalid because of a JOIN or SUBST command, you can ignore this message. If you specified the wrong disk drive, issue the PATH command again and provide the complete set of directory paths that you want to use.

POWER.EXE   V6-External

Allows some control of your computer's power consumption when applications and devices are idle, if your computer conforms to the Advanced Power Management (APM) specification. Battery-powered PCs are the likeliest candidates to support that specification.

Syntax

For use in CONFIG.SYS, use the following format:

DEVICE=*dc:pathc***POWER** *ADV:MAX ADV:REG ADV:MIN STD OFF /LOW*

For use from the DOS command line, use the following format:

*dc:pathc***POWER** *ADV:MAX ADV:REG ADV:MIN STD OFF*

To display the current power setting, use the following format:

*dc:pathc***POWER**

dc: is the drive that holds the command.

pathc is the path to the command.

ADV:MAX specifies the maximum level of power conservation.

ADV:REG specifies a balance between conservation and performance. This parameter is the default.

ADV:MIN specifies minimum conservation. Use this parameter if *ADV:MAX* and *ADV:REG* provide unsatisfactory performance.

STD conserves power by using only the power-management features of your computer's hardware, if the hardware supports the APM specification. If not, *STD* turns off power management.

OFF turns off power management.

Switch

/LOW   Forces POWER.EXE to load into low (conventional) memory rather than upper memory (the default).

Rule

Before using the POWER command, you must load POWER.EXE with a DEVICE statement in your CONFIG.SYS file.

Note

Power conservation generally reduces the performance of programs and devices.

PRINT   *V2, V3, V4, V5, V6-External*

Causes the printer to print a list of files while the computer performs other tasks.

Syntax

> *dc:pathc***PRINT** */D:device /B:bufsiz*
> */M:maxtick /Q:maxfiles*
> */S:timeslice /U:busytick /T*
> *d1:path1\\filename1.ext1 /P /C*
> *d2:path2\\filename2.ext2/P /C...*

d1: and *d2:* are valid drive names.

path1 and *path2* are valid path names to the files to be printed.

filename1.ext1 and *filename2.ext2* are the files that you want to print. Wild cards are allowed.

The ellipsis (...) represents additional file names in the format *dx:pathx\\filenamex.extx.*

Switches

You can specify any of the following switches, but only the first time you start PRINT:

/B:bufsiz	Specifies the size of the memory buffer to be used while the files are printing. *bufsiz* can be any number from 512 to 16,384. The default is 512 bytes.
/D:device	Specifies the device to be used for printing. *device* is any valid DOS device name. (You must list this switch first whenever you use */D:device*.)
/M:maxtick	Specifies, in clock ticks, the maximum amount of time that PRINT uses to send characters to the printer every time PRINT gets a turn. *maxtick* can be any number from 1 to 255. The default is 2.
/Q:maxfiles	Specifies the number of files that can be in the queue for printing. *maxfiles* can be any number from 4 to 32. The default is 10.
/S:timeslice	Specifies the number of clock ticks allocated for PRINT. *timeslice* can be a number from 1 to 255. The default is 8. Increasing *timeslice* speeds printing and slows other tasks.
/U:busytick	Specifies, in clock ticks, the maximum amount of time for the program to wait for a busy or unavailable printer. *busytick* can be any number from 1 to 255. The default is 1.

You can specify any of the following switches whenever you use PRINT:

/C	*Cancels* the background printing of the file(s). (See the following Notes section.)
/P	Queues up the file(s) for printing. (See the following Notes section.)
/T	*Terminates* the background printing of all files, including any file that currently is printing.

Reference

See Chapter 12, "Controlling Devices."

Rules

1. If you do not provide a file name, DOS displays the background printing status.

2. You can specify the switches /B, /D, /M, /Q, /S, and /U only when you first use PRINT. If you use the /D switch, you must type this switch first in the line. You can list the remaining five switches in any order before you specify a file name.

3. The /D switch specifies the print device that you want to use (LPT1, LPT2, LPT3, COM1, COM2, COM3, or COM4). If you omit /D the first time you use PRINT, DOS displays the following prompt: `Name of list device [PRN]:`. You can respond in either of two ways:

   ■ Press Enter to send the files to PRN (normally LPT1:). If LPT1: is redirected (refer to the sections on MODE commands earlier in this Command Reference), the files are rerouted.

   ■ Enter a valid DOS device name. Printing is directed to this device. If you enter a device that is not connected to your system, PRINT accepts files in the queue. The files are not processed, however, and you lose processing speed.

   You cannot change the assignment for background printing until you restart DOS.

4. If you name a file with no switch, DOS assumes that you want to use the /P (print) switch.

5. Files print in the order in which you list their names. If you use wild cards, the files are printed in the order in which they are listed in the directory.

6. The command PRINT /C has no effect if you do not specify a file name.

7. The first time you invoke PRINT, DOS increases in size by approximately 5,500 bytes. When you increase or decrease certain default settings, you proportionally change the size of DOS. To regain this memory space, however, you must restart DOS.

Notes

The /B switch acts like a disk buffer. PRINT reads into memory a portion of the document to be printed. As you increase the value of *bufsiz*, you decrease the number of times that PRINT must read the file from the disk, thereby increasing printing speed. Always use a multiple of 512 (1,024, 2,048, and so on) as the value of *bufsiz*. The default size (512 bytes) is adequate for most purposes, but using /B:4096 increases printing speed for most one- and two-page documents.

When the default values are assumed, PRINT gets 22 percent of the computer's time.

The positions of the /P, /C, and /T switches in the command line are important. Each switch affects the file immediately preceding it in the command line, and all subsequent files until DOS encounters another switch. The following command, for example, places the files LETTER.TXT and PROGRAM.DOC in the queue to be background-printed:

> PRINT LETTER.TXT /P PROGRAM.DOC MYFILE.TXT /C TEST.DOC

The /C switch, however, cancels the background printing of MYFILE.TXT and TEST.DOC.

In this example, the /P switch affects the preceding file (LETTER.TXT) and the following file (PROGRAM.DOC). Similarly, the /C switch affects the preceding file (MYFILE.TXT) and the following file (TEXT.DOC).

If you use the /T switch, background printing is canceled for all files in the queue, including the file that currently is printing. You do not need to use /T with a file name because the switch terminates printing for all files, including files listed in the command line.

If a disk error occurs during background printing, DOS cancels the current print job and places a disk-error message on the printout. The printer then performs a form feed, the bell rings, and DOS prints all remaining files in the queue.

Messages

1. `filename` is currently being printed
   `filename` is in queue

   Information: This message tells you which file is printing and names the files that are in line to be printed. This message appears when you use PRINT with no parameters or when you queue additional files.

2. `PRINT queue is empty`

   Information: No files are in line to be printed by PRINT.

3. `PRINT queue is full`

   Warning: You attempted to place too many files in the PRINT queue. The request to add more files fails for each file past the limit. You must wait until PRINT processes a file before you can add another file to the queue.

4. Resident part of PRINT installed

Information: The first time you use PRINT, this message indicates that PRINT installed itself in DOS and increased the size of DOS by about 5,500 bytes.

PROMPT   *V2, V3, V4, V5, V6-Internal*

Customizes the DOS system prompt (A>, the A prompt).

Syntax

PROMPT *promptstring*

promptstring is the text to be used for the new system prompt.

References

See Chapters 8, "Understanding and Managing Directories," and 11, "Working with System Information."

Rules

1. If you do not enter the *promptstring*, the standard system prompt reappears (A>).

2. The new system prompt stays in effect until you restart DOS or reissue the PROMPT command.

3. The PROMPT command creates an environment variable named PROMPT. You can use the SET command to display the value of the PROMPT variable.

4. Any text you type for *promptstring* becomes the new system prompt. You can type special characters by using the meta-strings (see the list following these rules).

A *meta-string* is a group of characters that is transformed into another character or group of characters. All meta-strings begin with the dollar-sign symbol ($) and have two characters, including the $. The following list contains meta-string characters and their meanings:

Meta-string	Character produced
$$	$ (dollar sign)
$_ (underscore)	Carriage return and line feed (moves to the first position of the following line)
$b	| (vertical bar)
$d	The date (similar to the DATE command)
$e	The Escape character (CHR$(27))
$g	> (greater-than symbol)
$h	The Backspace character (CHR$(8)), which erases the preceding character
$l	< (less-than symbol)
$n	The current drive
$p	The current drive and path, including the current directory
$q	= (equal sign)
$t	The time (similar to the TIME command)
$v	The DOS version number
$(any other)	Nothing or null; DOS ignores the character

Note

When DOS runs in Microsoft Windows, the prompt string is kept in the WINPMT environment variable, so you can make your DOS prompt in Windows different from your normal DOS prompt.

Examples

To make the prompt be the current drive and path, followed by >, use the following command:

PROMPT PG

Assuming that your CONFIG.SYS loads ANSI.SYS and that you have white text (foreground) on a blue background, the following command changes the prompt to a blinking red *HI*, followed by >:

PROMPT &E[5; 3/mHI$E[0; 37; 44m$G

QBASIC
V5, V6-External

Loads the BASIC interpreter.

Syntax

*dc:pathc***QBASIC** */H /NOHI /B /EDITOR   /G /MBF /RUN*
d:path\\filename.ext

dc:pathc represents the drive and subdirectory where QBasic is located.

d:path is the optional location of the QBasic program to be loaded into memory.

filename.ext is the name of the QBasic program.

Switches

/B	Switches QBasic to black-and-white mode.
/EDITOR	Starts DOS Edit.
/G	Enables CGA monitors to update quickly (do not use this switch if "snow" appears on-screen).
/H	Changes the display mode to display QBasic with the maximum number of lines.
/MBF	Enables the QBasic statements CVS, CVD, MKS$, and MKD$ to use the Microsoft Binary Format for numbers (that is, converts them to MKSMBF$, MKDMBF$, CVSMBI, and CVDMBF, respectively).
/NOHI	Enables QBasic to work with monitors that do not support high-intensity video (do not use with COMPAQ laptop computers).
/RUN d:path\\filename.ext	Loads *filename.ext* into memory and starts execution.

Rule

The file that you specify when starting QBasic is loaded into memory for editing. You must start execution manually unless you use the /RUN switch.

Notes

QBasic is a comprehensive development environment for inter-preted BASIC and a subset of Microsoft QuickBASIC. BASIC and BASICA are provided with IBM DOS 5.0 and are not provided in MS-DOS 6.0. GWBASIC no longer is provided.

QBASIC.EXE is necessary to run EDIT and HELP.

RECOVER   V2, V3, V4, V5-External

Recovers a file with bad sectors or a file from a disk with a dam-aged directory. RECOVER is not included in the standard DOS 6.0 package or the DOS 6.0 Supplemental Program disk.

Syntax

To recover a file, use the following format:

*dc:pathc***RECOVER** *d:path\\filename.ext*

To recover a disk with a damaged directory, use the following format:

*dc:pathc***RECOVER d:**

dc: is the drive that holds the command.

pathc is the path to the command.

d: is the drive that holds the damaged file or floppy disk.

path is the path to the directory that holds the file to be recovered.

filename.ext is the file that you want to recover.

Reference

See Chapter 8, "Understanding and Managing Directories."

Rules

1. If you provide only a drive name, DOS attempts to recover the disk's directory. (This rule applies to the second syntax line shown in the Syntax section.)

2. RECOVER does not restore erased files.

3. Do not use RECOVER with the ASSIGN, SUBST, or JOIN command. The results are unpredictable.

Notes

RECOVER attempts to recover either a file with a bad sector or a disk with a directory that contains a bad sector. To recover a file that contains one or more bad sectors, type **RECOVER d:filename.ext**. (DOS tells you when a file has bad sectors by displaying a disk-error message when you try to use the file.)

When RECOVER works on a file, DOS attempts to read the file's sectors one at a time. After RECOVER reads a sector, the information is placed in a temporary file. RECOVER skips any sectors that cannot be read, but the FAT is marked so that no other program can use the bad sector. This process continues until the entire file is read. RECOVER then erases the old file and gives the old file's name to the temporary file, which becomes a new replacement file. This new file is placed in the directory where the old file resided.

If the damaged file is a program file, you probably cannot use the program. If the file is a data or text file, you can recover some information. Because RECOVER reads the entire file, make sure that you use a text editor or word processing program to eliminate any garbage at the end of the file.

Do not use RECOVER to recover an entire disk. DOS creates a new root directory and then recovers each file and subdirectory. The system names the recovered files FILE *nnnn*.REC (*nnnn* is a four-digit number). Even good files are placed in FILE *nnnn*.REC files. To determine which original file corresponds to a FILE *nnnn*.REC file, you must use the TYPE command to view each file, print each file and use the last printed directory of the disk, or have a good memory.

RECOVER does not recover erased files. Use the UNDELETE command for that purpose.

RENAME
or REN

V1, V2, V3, V4,
V5, V6-Internal

Changes the names of disk files.

Syntax

RENAME *d:path***filename1**.*ext1* **filename2**.*ext2*

or

REN *d:path***filename1**.*ext1* **filename2**.*ext2*

d: is the drive that holds the file(s) to be renamed.

path\ is the path to the file(s) to be renamed.

filename1.*ext1* is the file's current name. Wild cards are allowed.

filename2.*ext2* is the file's new name. Wild cards are allowed.

Reference

See Chapter 9, "Managing Your Files."

Rules

1. You can provide a disk name and path name for only the first file.

2. You must provide both the old and the new file names and all appropriate extensions. Wild-card characters are permitted in the file names.

Notes

RENAME (or the short form, REN) changes the name of a file on the disk. The command does not rename directories; use the MOVE command to rename a directory.

Because you are renaming an established disk file, the file's drive or path designation goes with the old name so that DOS knows which file to rename.

Wild-card characters are acceptable in either the old or the new name.

Message

```
Duplicate filename or File not found
```

Error: You attempted to change a file name to a name that already exists, or you asked DOS to rename a file that does not exist in the directory. Check the directory for conflicting names, make sure that the file name exists and that you spelled the name correctly, and then reissue the command.

REPLACE   V3.2, V3.3, V4, V5, V6-External

Selectively replaces files on one disk with files of the same name from another disk; selectively adds files to a disk by copying the files from another disk.

Syntax

*dc:pathc***REPLACE** *ds:paths***filenames.***exts dd:pathd /A /P /R /S /W*

In DOS 4.0 and later versions, you can add a */U* switch, as follows:

*dc:pathc***REPLACE** *ds:paths***filenames.***exts dd:pathd /A /P /R /S /W /U*

dc: is the drive that holds the command.

pathc is the path to the command.

ds: is the drive that holds the replacement file(s).

paths is the path to the replacement file(s).

filenames.*exts* represents the name of the replacement file(s). Wild cards are permitted.

dd: is the drive whose file(s) you want to replace.

pathd is the directory to receive the replacement file(s).

Switches

/A	Adds files from the source disk that do not exist on the destination disk. (Does not work with the /S and /U switches.)
/P	Prompts you as each file is replaced on or added to the destination disk.
/R	Replaces read-only files on the destination disk.
/S	Replaces all files with matching names in the current directory and subdirectories. (/S does not work with the /A switch.)
/U	In DOS 4.0 and later versions, updates (replaces) only files whose date and time are older than the source file's date and time. (Does not work with the /A switch.)
/W	Instructs REPLACE to prompt you and wait for the source floppy disk to be inserted.

Exit Codes

REPLACE returns the DOS exit codes. A zero exit code indicates successful completion; nonzero exit codes indicate various types of errors. Following are some common exit codes:

Code	Explanation
0	Successful operation.
1	Version of DOS incompatible with REPLACE.
2	No source files were found.
3	Source or target path is invalid.
5	Access denied to the file or directory.
8	Out of memory.
11	Invalid parameter or incorrect number of parameters.
15	Invalid disk drive (not in DOS 5.0 and later versions).
22	Incorrect version of DOS (not in DOS 5.0 and later versions).

Reference

See Chapter 9, "Managing Your Files."

Rules

1. If you do not name the source drive, DOS uses the current drive.

2. If you do not name the source path, DOS uses the current directory.

3. You must specify a source file name. Wild cards are allowed.

4. If you do not name the destination drive, DOS adds files to—or replaces files in—the current drive.

5. If you do not name the destination path, DOS adds files to—or replaces files in—the current directory.

Notes

If you do not use REPLACE with caution, this command's speedy find-and-replace capability can have the effect of an unrelenting search-and-destroy mission on your data. Be careful when you unleash REPLACE on several subdirectories at a time, particularly when you use REPLACE /S on the entire disk. You could replace a file that you want to save somewhere on the disk, because REPLACE updates the file based on file name alone.

To prevent such unwanted replacements, limit the destination path name to cover only the directories that hold the files you want replaced. Check the source and destination directories for matching file names. If you find conflicts or have doubts, use the /P switch; REPLACE asks for approval before replacing files.

If you use DOS 4.0 or a later version, the /U switch can help you avoid replacing wrong files. /U compares the files' date and time stamps. The destination file is replaced only if the file is older than the source file.

Messages

1. `File cannot be copied onto itself` *filename*

   Warning: The source and destination disk and directories are identical. You probably did not specify a destination, so the source disk and directory are the current disk and directory. Otherwise, you specified the same drive and directory twice. REPLACE does not process *filename*.

Check the command line to ensure that you specified the correct source and destination for REPLACE, and then try the command again.

2. *nnn* `file(s) added`

   or

   nnn `file(s) replaced`

   Information: REPLACE indicates how many files are added or replaced. The first message appears when you use the /A switch; the second message appears if you do not use the /A switch. The message does not indicate that potential files are added or replaced; rather, the message appears when at least one file is added or replaced, regardless of errors that occur later.

3. `No files found` *filename*

   Error: REPLACE could not find any files that matched the source file name *filename*. One of the following errors probably occurred:

   - You misspelled the source file name.

   - You provided the drive and directory names but omitted the file name.

   - You provided the wrong drive or directory name for the source.

   - You inserted the wrong floppy disk into the drive.

   Check the command line to ensure that the correct disk is in the drive, and then retry the command.

4. `Invalid parameter combination`

   Error: You used both the /A and /S switches or the /A and /U switches, which you cannot use together in a REPLACE command. To replace files, omit /A. Because you cannot add files to more than one directory at a time, you cannot use /S with /A. To add files to more than one directory, issue separate REPLACE commands, each time specifying a different directory to which files are to be added.

RESTORE   *V2, V3, V4, V5, V6-External*

Restores one or more backup files created by BACKUP from one disk to another disk. If your backup file was created by MSBACKUP, you need to use MSBACKUP to restore data from that file.

Syntax

> *dc:pathc***RESTORE d1:** *d2:path***filename.ext** */S /P /M /N*
> */B:date /A:date /L:time /E:time /D*

dc: is the drive that holds the command.

pathc is the path to the command.

d1: is the drive that holds the backup files.

d2: is the drive that is to receive the restored files.

path is the path to the directory that is to receive the restored files. (This parameter must be the same as the directory from which the files were backed up.)

filename.ext is the file that you want to restore. Wild cards are allowed.

Switches

/A:date	Restores all files that were created or modified on or after the date you specify. The format of *date* depends on the COUNTRY in your CONFIG.SYS file.
/B:date	Restores all files that were created or modified on or before the date you specify. The format of *date* depends on the COUNTRY in your CONFIG.SYS file.
/D	Lists files to be restored without actually performing the restoration (DOS 5.0 and later versions). You must specify *d2:*.
/E:time	Restores all files that were created or modified at or before the time you specify. The format of *time* depends on the COUNTRY in your CONFIG.SYS file.
/L:time	Restores all files that were created or modified at or before the time you specify. The format of *time* depends on the COUNTRY in your CONFIG.SYS file.

/M	Restores all files that were modified or deleted since the backup set was made.
/N	Restores all files that no longer exist in the destination directory.
/P	Prompts you before restoring a file that was changed since the last backup or before restoring a file marked as read-only.
/S	Restores files in the current directory and all subdirectories. When you use this switch, RESTORE re-creates all necessary subdirectories that were removed and then restores the files in the re-created subdirectories.

Exit Codes

Code	Explanation
0	Normal completion
1	No files were found to restore
3	Terminated by the operator (through Ctrl-Break or Esc)
4	Terminated by an encountered error

Reference

See Chapter 13, "Understanding Backups and the Care of Data."

Rules

1. You must provide the name of the drive that holds the backup files. If the current disk is the disk that is to receive the restored files, you do not need to specify the destination drive.

2. If you do not name a path, RESTORE uses the current directory of the receiving disk.

3. If you do not provide a file name, RESTORE restores all backup files from the directory. Omitting the file name is the same as using *.*.

4. RESTORE prompts you to insert the backup disks in order. If you insert a disk out of order, RESTORE prompts you to insert the correct disk.

5. Do not combine the /B, /A, and /N switches in the same RESTORE command.

6. Be cautious when you restore files that were backed up while an ASSIGN, SUBST, or JOIN command was in effect. When you use RESTORE, clear any existing APPEND, ASSIGN, SUBST, or JOIN commands. Do not use RESTORE /M or RESTORE /N while APPEND /X is in effect. RESTORE attempts to search the directories for modified or missing files. APPEND tricks RESTORE into finding files in the paths specified to the APPEND command. RESTORE then may restore files that should not be restored and not restore files that should be restored. To disable APPEND, issue the APPEND ; command.

7. RESTORE cannot restore DOS system files (for example, IO.SYS and MSDOS.SYS) to the positions in the file structure necessary to make a disk bootable.

Notes

BACKUP and RESTORE in DOS 3.3 and later versions are radically different from the corresponding commands in previous versions. These commands place all backed-up files in one larger file and maintain a separate information file on the same disk. In DOS 3.3 and later versions, RESTORE handles the new and old backup-file formats, which means that these newer versions of RESTORE can restore backups created by any version of BACKUP.

Messages

1. `Insert backup diskette nn in drive d:`
   `Strike any key when ready`

   Information: RESTORE wants the next disk in sequence. This message appears when you are restoring files that were backed up onto floppy disks. Insert the next floppy disk (in the proper sequence) into drive D, and then press any key.

2. `Insert restore target in drive d:`
   `Strike any key when ready`

   Information: RESTORE is asking you to insert the floppy disk that is to receive the restored files. This message appears only when you restore files onto floppy disks. Insert the target disk into drive D, and then press any key.

3. `*** Listing files on drive A: ***`

   Information: You used the /D switch with RESTORE, and the files that *would be* restored are listed. The listed files follow the file specification that you used for restoration.

4. `Source does not contain backup files`

   Error: RESTORE found no files that were backed up with the BACKUP command. BACKUP may have malfunctioned when backing up files, or you may have inserted the wrong disk.

5. `Source and target drives are the same`

   Error: RESTORE determined that the drive that holds the backup files is the same as the drive that you designated to receive the restored files. You may have forgotten to specify the drive that holds the backup files or the target disk. If your system has one floppy drive and you tried to restore files onto a floppy disk, specify drives A and B.

6. `System files restored`
   `Target disk may not be bootable`

   Warning: You restored the three system files (IO.SYS, MSDOS.SYS, and COMMAND.COM) from the backup floppy disks. These files may not have been restored to the proper location on the disk, and you cannot use them to start DOS.

7. `Warning! Diskette is out of sequence`
   `Replace the diskette or continue if okay`
   `Strike any key when ready`

   Warning: You inserted a backup floppy disk out of order. Place the correct disk in the drive and continue.

8. `Warning! File` *filename*
   `was changed after it was backed up`
   `or is a read-only file`
   `Replace the file (Y/N)?`

   Warning: This message appears when you use the /P switch. Either the file *filename* already exists on the hard disk and is marked as read-only, or the date of the file on the target disk is later than that of the backup copy (which may mean that the backup copy is obsolete). Type **Y** to replace the existing file with the backup copy or **N** to skip the file.

9. `Warning! No files were found to restore`

   Warning: The files you wanted to restore are not on the disk from which you tried to restore them. Try again with another disk or another file specification. If you did not create a log file when you created the BACKUP floppy disk, you can determine the directories and files that are on the floppy disk by TYPEing the binary CONTROL file that is on the floppy disk and interpreting what you see.

RMDIR or RD   *V2, V3, V4, V5, V6-Internal*

Removes a directory or subdirectory.

Syntax

RMDIR *d:***path**

or

RD *d:***path**

d: is the drive that holds the subdirectory.

path is the path to the subdirectory. The last path name is the subdirectory that you want to delete.

Reference

See Chapter 8, "Understanding and Managing Directories."

Rules

1. You must name the subdirectory that you want to delete.

2. The subdirectory to be deleted must be empty of all files, including hidden files.

3. You cannot delete the current directory of any drive.

Messages

1. `Invalid path, not directory`

   `or directory not empty`

   Error: RMDIR did not remove the specified directory because one of the following errors occurred:

   ■ You listed an invalid directory in the path.

   ■ Files other than the . and .. entries still exist.

■ You misspelled the path or directory name.

Check each possibility and try again.

You can delete all the files in a directory and remove the directory with DELTREE.

2. `Attempt to remove current directory - drive:path`

Error: RMDIR did not remove the specified directory for one of the following reasons:

■ The directory is the current directory of the current drive.

■ The directory was the current directory of another drive.

■ The directory was redirected with the SUBST command.

In the first two cases, perform a CHDIR operation on a directory that is not a subdirectory of the directory that you want to delete, and attempt the RMDIR operation again. In the third case, perform a RMDIR operation on the actual directory affected by the SUBST command.

SELECT   *V3, V4-External*

Prepares a disk with the DOS files and configures the CONFIG.SYS and AUTOEXEC.BAT files for your country. In DOS 4.0, SELECT was expanded to a full-featured, menu-oriented DOS installation utility. SELECT is not included in DOS 5.0 and later versions.

Syntax

In DOS 3.0 through 3.3, use the following format:

*dc:pathc***SELECT** *ds: dd:pathd* **countrycode keycode**

dc: is the drive that holds the command.

pathc is the path to the command.

ds: is the source disk.

dd:pathd represents the destination disk and subdirectory.

SET   V2, V3, V4, V5, V6-Internal

Sets, shows, or removes a system environment variable.

Syntax

To display the environment, use the following format:

SET

To add to or alter the environment, use the following format:

SET name=_string_

name is the string that you want to add to the environment.

string is the information that you want to store in the environment.

The _environment_ is the portion of RAM reserved for alphanumeric information that DOS commands and user programs can examine and use. For example, the environment usually contains COMSPEC, which is the location of COMMAND.COM; PATH, which contains the additional paths for finding programs and batch files; and PROMPT, the string that defines the DOS system prompt.

Reference

See Chapter 11, "Working with System Information."

Rules

1. To delete a name, use SET name= without specifying a string.

2. Any lowercase letters in the name parameter change to uppercase letters in the environment. The characters in the string parameter do not change.

3. You can use the SET command instead of PROMPT or PATH to set the system prompt and the information for the PATH command.

Message

`Out of environment space`

Error: You see this message if the environment is not large enough to hold the string you want to add. (Refer to the

/E-switch information in the COMMAND section earlier in this Command Reference.)

SETVER.EXE   V5, V6-External

When used as a device driver, SETVER.EXE loads into memory the DOS version table, which contains the names of applications and drivers and the DOS version number that should be reported to each if they ask DOS its version number.

From the command line, you use SETVER.EXE to add, delete, and display entries in the DOS version table.

Syntax

To load the DOS version table into memory in CONFIG.SYS, use the following format:

  DEVICE=dc:$pathc$**SETVER.EXE**

  or

  DEVICEHIGH=dc:$pathc$**SETVER.EXE**

To add a program to the version table, use the following format:

  dc:$pathc$**SETVER** d:$path$ **filename.ext n.nn**

To remove a program from the version table, use the following format:

  dc:$pathc$**SETVER** d:$path$ **filename.ext** */DELETE /QUIET*

To view the version table, use the following format:

  dc:$pathc$**SETVER** d:$path$

dc:$pathc$\\ represents the drive and subdirectory path that holds the command.

d:$path$ represents the drive and path that holds the copy of SETVER.EXE containing the version table. (This parameter, which generally is the same as dc:$pathc$, generally is omitted.)

filename.ext is the name of the application or device driver to which a particular DOS version number should be reported. Wild cards are not permitted.

n.nn is the DOS version number to be reported (for example, 3.31 or 5.0).

Switches

/DELETE (or /D)   Deletes the entry for the specified program.

/QUIET (or /Q)   Displays no messages; works only with DELETE.

Exit Codes

Code	Explanation
0	Successful completion.
1	Invalid command switch.
2	Invalid file name.
3	Insufficient memory.
4	Invalid version number format.
5	Specified entry was not found in table.
6	Could not find SETVER.EXE file.
7	Invalid drive specifier.
8	Too many command line parameters.
9	Missing parameters.
10	Error reading the SETVER.EXE file.
11	SETVER.EXE file is corrupt.
12	Specified SETVER.EXE file does not support a version table.
13	Insufficient space in version table for new entry.
14	Error writing SETVER.EXE file.

Reference

See Chapter 11, "Working with System Information."

Rules

1. You must include SETVER.EXE in CONFIG.SYS as a device driver to load the version table into memory.

2. If you want to affect a driver, the SETVER.EXE entry in CONFIG.SYS must precede the loading of the driver.

3. You must reboot the computer to affect any changes made in the version table.

4. If you specify a program that already is in the version table, the new entry overwrites the old entry.

Notes

The basic idea of SETVER is that some applications and device drivers do not work with a new version of DOS only because they ask DOS for its version number and find out that the number is higher than the number for which their manufacturers have certified them. If these applications and drivers would only try to execute, the general upward compatibility among versions of DOS might allow them to work.

WARNING: When possible, contact your software dealer or the software manufacturer to verify compatibility of an existing application or device driver with a new version of DOS. Fooling an application or driver into running may result in corruption or loss of data.

Having the correct match of program and DOS version is particularly important for disk optimizers and disk-caching programs, which can cause serious, widespread file damage if they operate incorrectly.

Message

```
Version table successfully updated
The version change will take effect the next time you
restart your system
```

Information: You updated the version table but must restart the computer system for the changes to take place. In a long message that is not shown here, you also are reminded of the risks of using SETVER.

SHARE   V3, V4, V5, V6-External

Enables DOS support for file and record locking. In DOS 4.0, the command also is used to support large disk partitions.

Syntax

*dc:pathc***SHARE** */F:name_space /L:numlocks*

dc: is the drive that holds the command.

pathc is the path to the command.

Switches

/F:name_space	Sets the amount of memory space (*name_space* bytes large) used for file sharing. The default is 2,048.
/L:numlocks	Sets the maximum number (*numlocks*) of file/record locks to be used. The default is 20.

Rules

1. When SHARE is loaded, DOS checks for file and record locks as each file is opened, read, and written.

2. SHARE normally enlarges DOS by approximately 6,192 bytes in DOS 5.0 and 5,248 bytes in DOS 6.0. If the number of locks (/L switch) or memory space (/F switch) increases or decreases, DOS also increases or decreases proportionately. SHARE can be loaded into upper memory.

3. The only way to remove SHARE is to restart DOS.

4. In DOS 4.0, use SHARE if your hard disk is formatted with partitions larger than 32M. SHARE is not required to use large partitions in DOS 5.0 and later versions.

5. You can load SHARE with INSTALL in your CONFIG.SYS file (DOS 4.0 and later versions).

6. You may need SHARE to run some programs with the Microsoft Flash File System.

Notes

You use SHARE when two or more programs or processes share a computer's files. After SHARE is loaded, DOS checks each file for locks whenever the file is opened, read, or written. If a file is open for exclusive use, an error message results from subsequent attempts to open the file. If one program locks a portion of a file, an error message results if another program tries to read or write the locked portion.

SHARE is most effective when all file-sharing programs can handle the DOS functions for locking files and records (DOS 3.0 and later versions). SHARE is either partially or completely ineffective with programs that do not use the DOS file- and record-locking features.

SHARE affects two or more programs running on the same computer, not two or more computers using the same file (networked computers). For networks, record and file locking are made possible by software provided with the network.

You must use SHARE if you use DOS 4.0 or 4.01 and if your hard disk is formatted larger than 32M. For convenience, you can use INSTALL in the CONFIG.SYS file to activate SHARE. In the CONFIG.SYS file, for example, the following command activates SHARE if SHARE.EXE is located in the \DOS subdirectory of drive C:

    INSTALL = C:\DOS\SHARE.EXE

SMARTDRV.EXE   *V5, V6-External*

When used as a device driver, SMARTDRV.EXE enables double buffering, which is required by hard-disk controllers that cannot work with memory provided by EMM386.EXE or by Windows running in 386-Enhanced mode.

When used from the command line, SMARTDRV.EXE starts or configures SMARTDrive, a disk-caching utility that can speed disk operations significantly.

Syntax

To turn on double buffering, add the following command to your CONFIG.SYS file:

DEVICE=_dc:pathc_**\SMARTDRV.EXE /DOUBLE_BUFFER**

To start SMARTDrive from your AUTOEXEC.BAT file or from a command prompt, use the following format:

dc:pathc**\SMARTDRV** _drive+_ |-... _/E:esize initsize winsize /B:bsize /C /R /L /Q /N /S_

After SMARTDrive is running, use the following format:

dc:pathc**\SMARTDRV** _drive+_ |–... _/C /R /S_

dc:pathc represents the drive and subdirectory path where SMARTDRV.EXE is located.

drive+ |–... represents the letters of one or more drives for which you want to enable or disable caching. *drive* enables read-caching and disables write-caching. *drive+* enables read- and write-caching. *drive–* disables caching.

If you start SMARTDrive but do not specify a drive, floppy and Interlnk drives are read-cached only; hard drives are read- and write-cached; and CD-ROM, network, compressed, and Microsoft Flash memory-card drives are not cached.

initsize is the size (in K) of the cache when SMARTDrive starts. Following are the default values for this parameter:

Extended memory	initsize	winsize
Up to 1M	All	0 (no caching)
Up to 2M	1M	256K
Up to 4M	1M	512K
Up to 6M	2M	1M
More than 6M	2M	2M

winsize is the size (in K) by which SMARTDrive will reduce its cache when Microsoft Windows starts, freeing that memory for Windows to use. When you quit Windows, that memory is returned to SMARTDrive and defaults to the values listed in the preceding table. If *winsize* is larger than *initsize*, SMARTDrive acts as though the two parameters were the same.

Switches

/B:bsize	Specifies (in bytes that are a multiple of *esize*) the size of the read-ahead buffer— that is, how much SMARTDrive reads beyond a disk request. The default is 16384. The smaller the number, the less conventional memory SMARTDrive takes and the slower the performance.
/C	Forces SMARTDrive to write all of its write buffers to the disks.

/DOUBLE_BUFFER	Enables double buffering. Inserting this switch into your CONFIG.SYS file does not hurt if your system does not need it, but it does take up memory. You can remove the switch if all the entries in the buffering column of the SMARTDRV /S display are no. (It may take a while for – entries to turn into no entries.)
/E:esize	Specifies (in bytes) element size, which is the amount of cache that SMARTDrive moves at once. Values can be 1024, 2048, 4096, and 8192. The default is 8192. The smaller the number, the less conventional memory SMARTDrive takes and the slower the performance.
/L	Forces SMARTDrive to load into low (conventional) memory even if room exists in upper memory.
/N	Forces "verbose" mode, so that status messages appear when SMARTDrive starts. You cannot use this switch with /Q.
/Q	Forces "quiet" mode, so that status messages do not appear when SMARTDrive starts. (Error messages always appear.) /Q is the default. You cannot use this switch with /N.
/R	Resets SMARTDrive by clearing its caches and restarting it.
/S	Displays SMARTDrive's status, including what and how drives are cached and a cache hit statistic.

Reference

See Chapter 18, "Getting the Most from Your Hard Drive."

Rules

1. Before you turn off or reset your computer, you must perform a SMARTDRV /C operation to guarantee that no data is lost from SMARTDrive's write buffers. SMARTDrive performs the operation automatically if you press Ctrl-Alt-Del.

2. For SMARTDrive to use extended memory, you must load HIMEM.SYS or some other extended-memory manager.

3. By default, SMARTDRV.EXE tries to load into upper memory.

Notes

If you are using double-buffering and your system runs slowly, try loading SMARTDrive with the /L switch.

Double buffering is needed only by some ESDI and SCSI hard disk interfaces.

If you have a compressed disk drive, use SMARTDrive on the underlying uncompressed drive.

If you are using a third-party CONFIG.SYS and AUTOEXEC.BAT file manager, that utility needs to be set up to perform a SMARTDRV /C operation before it reboots your computer.

DOS 6.0 comes with SMARTMON.EXE, a Windows program for monitoring and adjusting SMARTDrive.

Examples

To start SMARTDrive with all the defaults (a good fit for most systems):

C:\DOS\SMARTDRV

To enable read-caching for the C drive and read- and write-caching for the D drive, using a 4M cache for DOS that can get no smaller than 2M when Microsoft Windows is running:

C:\DOS\SMARTDRV c d+ 4096 2048

SORT   V2, V3, V4, V5, V6-External

Reads lines from the standard input device, performs an ASCII sort of the lines, and then writes the lines to the standard output device. The sort can be in ascending or descending order and can start at any column in the line.

Syntax

*dc:pathc***SORT** */R /+c*

dc: is the drive holding the command.

pathc is the path to the command.

Switches

/+c   Starts sorting with column number *c*. *c* is a positive integer. The default is 1.

/R   Sorts in descending order. Thus, the letter Z comes first and the letter A comes last, followed by the numbers 9 to 0. (The default sort order is ascending.)

Reference

See Chapter 12, "Controlling Devices."

Rules

1. If you do not redirect the input or output, all input is from the keyboard (standard input), and all output is to the video display (standard output). If you redirect input and output, use different names for the input and output files.

2. SORT can handle a maximum file size of 64K (65,535 characters).

3. SORT sorts text files and discards any information after, and including, the end-of-file marker.

4. SORT uses the collating sequence appropriate to your country code and code-page settings. (Refer to the section on the COUNTRY command earlier in this Command Reference.)

5. SORT is case-insensitive—that is, the command treats *b* and *B* alike.

Examples

1. To sort the lines in the file WORDS.TXT and display the sorted lines on-screen:

    SORT <WORDS.TXT

2. To sort, in reverse order, the lines in the file WORDS.TXT and display the lines on-screen:

    SORT <WORDS.TXT /R

3. To start sorting at the eighth character of each line in WORDS.TXT and display the output on-screen:

    SORT /+8 <WORDS.TXT

4. To display directory information, sorted by file size:

    DIR | SORT /+14

    (The file size starts in the 14th column.) Unfortunately, other lines, such as the volume label, also are sorted, starting in the 14th column. DIR /O provides a more direct and elaborate way of sorting directory information.

SUBST   V3.1, V3.2, V3.3, V4, V5, V6-External

Creates an alias drive name for a subdirectory; used principally with programs that do not use path names.

Syntax

To establish an alias, use the following format:

   *dc:pathc***SUBST d1:** *d2:***pathname**

To delete an alias, use the following format:

   *dc:pathc***SUBST d1: /D**

To display the current aliases, use the following format:

   *dc:pathc***SUBST**

dc: is the drive holding the command.

pathc is the path to the command.

d1: is a valid drive name that becomes the alias, or nickname. **d1:** may be a nonexistent drive, but it must be less than or equal to the value specified by the LASTDRIVE command in your CONFIG.SYS file.

*d2:***pathname** represents the valid drive name and directory path that will be nicknamed **d1:**. The default for *d2* is the current drive.

Switch

   /D   Deletes the alias.

Reference

See Chapter 12, "Controlling Devices."

Notes

Do not use ASSIGN, BACKUP, CHKDSK, DEFRAG, DISKCOPY, DISKCOMP, FDISK, FORMAT, JOIN, LABEL, MIRROR, RECOVER, RESTORE, or SYS with the SUBST drive name.

Do not perform a SUBST operation during a DOS session in Microsoft Windows.

Messages

1. `Cannot SUBST a network drive`

   Error: You tried to use another computer's drive (that is, a networked drive) as the alias drive. You cannot use a networked drive with SUBST.

2. `Invalid parameter`

   Error: The value that you specified for the alias drive (d1:) exceeded the value specified by the LASTDRIVE command in your CONFIG.SYS file.

SYS   *V1, V2, V3, V4, V5, V6-External*

Places a copy of DOS (the hidden system files IO.SYS and MSDOS.SYS, and COMMAND.COM for MS-DOS; the files IBMBIO.COM, IBMDOS.COM, and COMMAND.COM for IBM DOS) on the specified disk. In DOS 6.0, DBLSPACE.BIN also can be copied.

Syntax

   *dc:pathc***SYS d2:**

dc: is the drive that holds the command.

pathc is the path to the command.

d2: is the drive that is to receive the copies of the DOS files from the root directory of the current drive.

In DOS 4.0 and later versions, you also may specify a source drive and path for the system files, as follows:

   *dc:pathc***SYS** *d1:path1* **d2:**

d1:path1 represents the source drive and path for the system files. This parameter defaults to the root directory of the current drive for the system files and to the file pointed to by the environment variable COMSPEC for the command-line interpreter (generally, COMMAND.COM).

Reference

See Chapter 7, "Preparing and Maintaining Disks."

Rules

1. You must specify the drive that will receive a copy of DOS.

2. To receive a copy of a version of DOS before 4.0, the disk must meet one of the following criteria:

   - The disk was formatted with the /S option.

   - The disk was formatted with the /B option.

   - This disk is formatted but empty.

   If you attempt to put the system on a disk that does not meet one of these conditions, the message No room for system on destination disk appears, and DOS does not perform the operation.

3. In pre-4.0 versions of DOS, the disk that was to receive the DOS operating-system files was required to have sufficient contiguous free space for the files IO.SYS and MSDOS.SYS (IBMBIO.COM and IBMDOS.COM in IBM DOS). Subsequent versions of DOS require only that enough free space exist, not that the space be contiguous.

4. A copy of DOS (the IO.SYS and MSDOS.SYS files) should reside on the current disk; if not, you need to specify a source disk and path for the file. Otherwise, you are prompted to insert a floppy disk containing these files into the disk drive.

5. You cannot use SYS in a networked drive; in a drive formed by ASSIGN, JOIN, or SUBST; or in an Interlnk drive.

6. In pre-5.0 versions of DOS, you have to copy COMMAND.COM to the target disk in a separate step.

7. DOS copies the file indicated by the environment variable COMSPEC to the target disk and names the file COMMAND.COM, even if it is not COMMAND.COM (for example, if you are using a third-party replacement for COMMAND.COM).

Messages

1. `No system on default disk drive`
   `Insert system disk in drive d:`
   `and strike any key when ready`

   Information: SYS could not find IO.SYS, MSDOS.SYS, or
   COMMAND.COM. You must perform one of the following
   steps:

   - Enter a SYS command that correctly specifies the
     locations of those files.

   - Reenter the SYS command after making the drive that
     holds those files the current disk drive.

   - Enter a SYS command specifying that the files are on a
     floppy disk that you have loaded.

2. `System transferred`

   Information: SYS has placed IO.SYS and MSDOS.SYS on the
   target disk.

3. `Could not copy COMMAND.COM onto target disk`

   Warning: The root directory of your boot disk does not contain a COMMAND.COM file to copy to the target disk. (The
   environment variable COMSPEC probably is pointing to a
   different directory.) Copy COMMAND.COM to the root directory of your hard disk and reissue the SYS command, or use
   a SYS command that specifies a directory where the system
   files and COMMAND.COM exist.

TIME   *V1, V2, V3, V4, V5, V6-Internal*

Sets and shows the system time.

Syntax

To enter the time, use the following format:

   TIME *hh:mm:ss.xx*

In DOS 4.0 and later versions, use the following format:

   TIME *hh:mm:ss.xx A |P*

To display the time and then be prompted to enter a new time, use the following format:

TIME

If you press Enter after the time prompt, DOS does not change the current time.

hh is the one- or two-digit number that represents hours (0 to 23).

mm is the one- or two-digit number that represents minutes (0 to 59).

ss is the one- or two-digit number that represents seconds (0 to 59).

xx is the one- or two-digit number that represents hundredths of a second (0 to 99).

A | *P* can designate A.M. or P.M. If you do not use *A* or *P*, you must enter the time in 24-hour (military) format.

 NOTE   Depending on the country-code setting in your CONFIG.SYS file (refer to the section on the COUNTRY command earlier in this Command Reference), a comma may be the separator between seconds and hundredths of seconds.

Reference

See Chapter 11, "Working with System Information."

Notes

The TIME command sets the computer's internal 24-hour clock. The time and date are recorded in the directory when you create or change a file. This information can help you find the most recent version of a file when you check your directory.

Most PCs use an internal clock, backed up by a battery, that is accurate to about one minute a month, so you rarely have to set the time after you set it initially. If your system does not retain the time after you turn off your computer, however, put TIME and DATE commands in your AUTOEXEC.BAT file so that DOS does not default to a nonsense time and date when you turn on your computer.

TREE   *V2, V3, V4, V5, V6-External*

Displays all the subdirectories on a disk and (optionally) displays all the files in each directory.

Syntax

*dc:pathc***TREE** *d:path /F /A*

dc: is the drive that holds the command.

pathc is the path to the command.

d: is the drive that holds the disk that you want to examine.

path is the subdirectory in which you want the examination to start.

Switches

/A   Uses ASCII characters to display the connection of subdirectories, rather than the default graphics characters.

/F   Displays all files in the directories.

Reference

See Chapter 8, "Understanding and Managing Directories."

TYPE   *V1, V2, V3, V4, V5, V6-Internal*

Displays a file's contents on the monitor.

Syntax

TYPE *d:path***filename**.*ext*

d: is the drive that holds the file to be displayed on-screen.

path is the path to the file.

filename.*ext* is the file to be displayed. Wild cards are not permitted.

Reference

See Chapter 9, "Managing Your Files."

Notes

The TYPE command displays a file's characters on-screen. You can use TYPE to see a file's contents.

Strange characters appear on-screen when you use TYPE for some data files and most program files, because TYPE tries to display the machine-language instructions as ASCII characters.

As you can with most other DOS commands, you can redirect the output of TYPE to the printer by adding >PRN to the command line or by pressing Ctrl-PrtSc. (Don't forget to press Ctrl-PrtSc again to turn off the printing instruction.)

To keep the contents of a long file from scrolling off the screen before you can read them, you can pipe the output of TYPE through MORE. Alternatively, you can press Ctrl-S to stop the display and Ctrl-Q to restart it.

Example

To display the contents of the DOS README.TXT file one screen at a time:

TYPE C:\DOS\README.TXT | MORE

UNDELETE   V5, V6-External

Recovers files that were deleted with the DEL command.

In DOS 5.0, UNDELETE uses MIRROR's delete-tracking file (if available) to restore a deleted file.

In DOS 6.0, UNDELETE uses a delete-sentry file or a delete-tracking file (if either exists) to restore a deleted file.

Either version may be able to restore a deleted file without any special files if the file was deleted recently and little disk activity has occurred since the deletion.

Syntax

In DOS 5.0, use the following format:

> *dc:pathc***UNDELETE** *d:path\\filename.ext /LIST /DT /DOS /ALL*

In DOS 6.0, to load the memory-resident program that UNDELETE uses for delete-sentry and delete-tracking protection, use the following format:

> *dc:pathc***UNDELETE** */LOAD /Sdrive /Tdrive-entries*

In DOS 6.0, to manipulate UNDELETE, use the following format:

> *dc:pathc***UNDELETE** */LIST /ALL /PURGEdrive /STATUS /U*

In DOS 6.0, to undelete one or more files, use the following format:

> *dc:pathc***UNDELETE** *d:path\\filename.ext /DT /DS /DOS /LIST*

dc: is the drive that holds the command.

pathc is the path to the command.

d: is the drive where the deleted file resides.

path is the directory path to the file.

filename.ext is the name of the file that you want to undelete. Wild cards are permitted.

Switches

/ALL	Restores files without prompting. The Delete Sentry method is used, if it is available. Otherwise, the Delete Tracking method is used, if it is available. If neither method is available, the normal DOS directory method is used (see the Notes section for this command). You can use /ALL with any of the other switches.
/DOS	Restores files that DOS lists as deleted. UNDELETE prompts you before each file is restored.
/DS	Recovers only the files listed in the SENTRY directory. UNDELETE prompts you before each file is restored.

/DT	Restores only the files listed in the delete-tracking file. UNDELETE prompts you before each file is restored.
/LIST	Provides a list of deleted files but does not undelete them. The type of list produced varies with the use of the /DT, /DS, and /DOS switches.
/LOAD	Loads the Undelete memory-resident program into conventional memory, using the UNDELETE.INI file. If that file does not exist, UNDELETE creates a default UNDELETE.INI file.
/PURGEdrive	Deletes the contents of the SENTRY directory created by Delete Sentry protection. *drive* defaults to the current drive.
/Sdrive	Enables Delete Sentry protection and loads the Undelete memory-resident program into memory, using the UNDELETE.INI file. *drive* defaults to the current drive.
/STATUS	Displays the type of protection in effect for each drive.
/Tdrive-entries	Enables Delete Tracker protection and loads the Undelete memory-resident program into memory, using the UNDELETE.INI file. The *drive* parameter is the drive for which you want Delete Tracker protection. *entries* is a number (ranging from 1 through 999) that specifies the maximum number of entries in the deletion-tracking file, PCTRACKR.DEL. The default value is determined by the following table:

Disk Size	Entries	PCTRACKR.DEL Size
360K	25	5K
720K	50	9K
1.2M	75	14K
1.44M	75	14K
20M	101	18K
32M	202	36K
Larger than 32M	303	55K

/U   Unloads the Undelete memory-resident pro-
                                 gram from memory, disabling Delete Tracking
                                 or Delete Sentry protection if either was active.

Rules

1. UNDELETE cannot restore deleted subdirectories.

2. UNDELETE cannot restore a file if you deleted the
   subdirectory that contained the file.

3. Do not use delete tracking for any drive that has been redirected with JOIN or SUBST. You can, however, install delete
   tracking by using ASSIGN before UNDELETE.

Notes

UNDELETE restores deleted files, using the delete-tracking or
delete-sentry file (if either exists), or the standard DOS directory.

Delete Sentry provides the highest level of protection by saving
deleted files in a SENTRY directory. The size of the SENTRY directory (including the files that it contains) is limited to approximately seven percent of your disk. Old files are purged to make
room for new ones.

Delete Tracking provides an intermediate level of protection by
maintaining a hidden file called PCTRACKR.DEL that records the
locations of a file's allocation units (clusters). You can recover a
deleted file until its freed allocation units are allocated to a new
file. Delete Tracking takes the same amount of memory as Delete
Sentry.

When a file is deleted, DOS removes the first character in the
file name. If you use UNDELETE with the /DOS switch, you are
prompted for a character to replace the missing first character. If
you use the /ALL switch, and if a delete-tracking or delete-sentry
file does not exist, UNDELETE restores each deleted file without
prompts, using the character # as the first character of the
file name. A deleted file named BETTER.TXT, for example, is
undeleted as #ETTER.TXT.

If BETTER.TXT and LETTER.TXT are deleted, BETTER.TXT
is restored as #ETTER.TXT, and LETTER.TXT is restored as
%ETTER.TXT. UNDELETE uses the following replacement characters in the order listed:

    # % & - 0 1 2 3 4 5 6 7 8 9 A B through Z

Although UNDELETE enables you to recover files that you deleted accidentally, do not use this command as a substitute for backing up data. Be sure to keep up-to-date backups of your data.

Examples

For the following examples, assume that the DOS commands are stored in a directory that is in your PATH.

To restore all deleted files in the root directory of drive C without prompting for confirmation on each file:

C:\UNDELETE /ALL

To provide a list of all currently deleted files:

UNDELETE /LIST

To create C:\PCTRACKR.DEL to track up to 200 deleted files on drive C and load the memory-resident portion of UNDELETE:

UNDELETE /TC-200

UNFORMAT   *V5, V6-External*

Recovers disks that were inadvertently reformatted.

In DOS 5.0, UNFORMAT uses the files produced by the MIRROR command (if those files are available) to restore the disk to its condition before reformatting. In DOS 5.0 and 6.0, you probably can unformat disks if they were not formatted with FORMAT /U.

The UNFORMAT command works on both hard disks and floppy disks.

Syntax

In DOS 5.0, use the following format:

*dc:pathc***UNFORMAT** *d: /J /P /L /U /TEST /PARTN*

In DOS 6.0, use the following format:

*dc:pathc***UNFORMAT** *d: /P /L /TEST*

dc: is the drive that holds the command.

pathc is the path to the command.

d: is the drive where the deleted file resides.

Switches

/J	Confirms that the MIRROR command contains the necessary information to restore the disk. (This switch does not unformat the disk.) Available only in DOS 5.0.
/L	Lists all files and directory names found. If used with the PARTN switch, */L* displays current partition tables. The default (no */L*) is to list only subdirectories and fragmented files.
/P	Directs all output to the printer connected to LPT1.
/PARTN	Restores the partition table of a hard disk. You must use the PARTNSAV.FIL file created by the MIRROR /PARTN command. Available only in DOS 5.0.
/TEST	Shows how UNFORMAT will re-create the information on the disk. (Like the */J* switch, this switch does not actually unformat the disk.)
/U	Unformats without using the MIRROR files. Available only in DOS 5.0.

Reference

See Chapter 7, "Preparing and Maintaining Disks."

Rules

1. To unformat your hard disk, you first must reboot from drive A, using a specially prepared floppy disk (see the Notes section for this command).

2. If you format a floppy disk by using the FORMAT /U switch, UNFORMAT cannot restore the disk.

3. UNFORMAT works only on disks that have sectors of 512, 1024, or 2048 bytes.

Notes

UNFORMAT attempts to recover a formatted disk by using the MIRROR image files created by the MIRROR command or by using information in the disk's root directory and file-allocation table. The second process is slower and less reliable than the first.

To prepare for the eventuality that you may need to use UNFORMAT, format a floppy disk (using the /S switch to make the disk bootable), and then transfer the UNFORMAT.EXE file to that disk. Also transfer the CONFIG.SYS files, the AUTOEXEC.BAT files, and any device drivers needed for the computer's operation. Thereafter, if you accidentally format the hard disk, you can boot from the floppy disk and perform an UNFORMAT operation.

Before you use UNFORMAT to recover the disk, use the command with the /J or /TEST switches to determine whether your MIRROR files are up-to-date or whether the UNFORMAT command can recover files in the way that you want.

In DOS 6.0, UNFORMAT cannot recover fragmented files. You will be asked if you want to recover such files by truncating them at the end of their contiguous sectors.

VER　　*V2, V3, V4, V5, V6-Internal*

Shows the DOS version number on-screen.

Syntax

VER

Reference

See Chapter 11, "Working with System Information."

Note

The VER command displays a one-digit DOS version number, followed by a two-digit revision number, reminding you which DOS version (Version 2.0 through 5.0) the computer is using.

VERIFY　　*V2, V3, V4, V5, V6-Internal*

Sets the computer to check the accuracy of data written to a disk to ensure that information was recorded properly, and then shows whether the data was checked.

Syntax

To show the verify status, use the following format:

VERIFY

To set the verify status, use the following format:

VERIFY ON

or

VERIFY OFF

By default, VERIFY is off.

Reference

See Chapter 9, "Managing Your Files."

Rules

1. VERIFY accepts only the parameters ON and OFF.

2. When on, VERIFY remains on until one of the following events occurs:

   ■ A VERIFY OFF command is issued.

   ■ A SET VERIFY system call turns off the command.

   ■ DOS is restarted.

Notes

If VERIFY is on, data integrity is increased. If VERIFY is off, you can write to the disk faster. You usually are wise to leave VERIFY off if you are not working with critical information, such as a company's accounting figures. You are wise to turn VERIFY on, however, when you are backing up your hard disk or making important copies on floppy disks.

COPY /V turns VERIFY on for the duration of the command and then turns it off.

VOL   V2, V3, V4, V5, V6-Internal

Displays the disk's volume label and serial number (if they exist).

Syntax

> **VOL** *d:*

d: is the drive whose label you want to display. The default is the current drive.

Reference

See Chapter 7, "Preparing and Maintaining Disks."

VSAFE   V6-External

Monitors your computer for viruses and displays a warning when it finds one.

Syntax

> *dc:pathc***VSAFE** */option+* | *–... /NE /NX /Ax /Cx /N /D /U*

dc: is the drive that holds the command.

pathc is the path to the command.

Switches

/Ax	Sets the hot key as Alt plus the key specified by *x*.
/Cx	Sets the hot key as Ctrl plus the key specified by *x*.
/D	Turns off checksumming.
/N	Instructs VSafe to monitor network drives.
/NE	Prevents VSafe from loading into expanded memory.

/NX	Prevents VSafe from loading into extended memory.
/option+ | –...	Specifies how VSafe checks for viruses. Use a plus sign (+) after *option* to enable the switch; use a minus sign (–) after *option* to disable it. Choose *option* from the following list:

1	Warns of formatting that could erase the hard disk (default: on)
2	Warns of a program's attempt to stay in memory (default: off)
3	Prevents programs from writing to disks (default: off)
4	Checks executable files that DOS opens (default: on)
5	Checks all disks for boot-sector viruses (default: on)
6	Warns of attempts to write to the boot sector or to the partition table of the hard disk (default: on)
7	Warns of attempts to write to the boot sector of a floppy disk (default: off)
8	Warns of attempts to modify executable files (default: on)

/U	Unloads VSafe from memory.

Rules

1. Turn off VSafe before you install Microsoft Windows.

2. Do not use VSafe after you start Microsoft Windows.

3. If you use VSafe with Microsoft Windows, run the MWAVTSR.EXE memory-resident program by adding the following line to your WIN.INI file:

   ```
   load=mwavtsr.exe
   ```

   MWAVTSR.EXE enables VSafe messages to be displayed in Windows.

4. The default hot key is Alt-V.

Note

VSafe is a memory-resident program that takes up a varying amount of conventional, extended, and expanded memory. In DOS 6.0, VSafe takes up 44K of conventional memory, 23K of conventional and 23K of extended memory, or 7K of conventional and 64K of expanded memory.

Example

To turn on warnings about programs' attempts to stay in memory, to turn off checks for boot-sector viruses, and to make Alt-Q the hot key:

VSAFE /2+ /5– /AQ

XCOPY   V3.2, V3.3, V4, V5, V6-External

Selectively copies groups of files from one or more subdirectories. In DOS 6.0, hidden and system files are not copied.

Syntax

dc:pathc**XCOPY ds:paths\\filenames.exts**
dd:pathd*filenamed.extd /A /D:date /E /M /P /S /V /W*

dc: is the drive that holds the command.

pathc\\ is the path to the command.

ds: is the source drive, which holds the files that you want to copy.

paths\\ is the starting directory path to the files that you want to copy.

filenames.exts represents a file that you want to copy. Wild cards are allowed.

dd: is the destination drive, which receives the copied files. DOS refers to the destination drive as the *target*.

pathd\\ is the starting directory that is to receive the copied files.

filenamed.extd represents the new name of a copied file. Wild cards are allowed.

Switches

/A	Copies only files whose archive attribute is on; does not turn off the archive attribute. /A is similar to /M, except that /A does not reset the archive attribute.
/D:date	Copies only files that were changed or created on or after the date you specify. The date's form depends on the setting of the COUNTRY directive in CONFIG.SYS.
/E	Creates parallel subdirectories on the destination disk, even if the original subdirectory is empty.
/M	Copies only files whose archive attribute is on (modified files) and turns off the archive attribute. /M is similar to /A, except /M does reset the archive attribute.
/P	Causes XCOPY to prompt you for approval before copying a file.
/S	Copies all directories and subdirectories that contain files.
/V	Verifies that the copy was recorded correctly.
/W	Causes XCOPY to prompt you and wait for your response before starting the copy operation. (You can use this switch to give you time to insert the source floppy disk, for example.)

Exit Codes

Code	Explanation
0	Successful copy.
1	No files were found to copy.
2	Terminated by a Ctrl-C.
4	Initialization error, for example, not enough memory or disk space or invalid disk drive name or other syntax error.
5	Disk write error.

Reference

See Chapter 13, "Understanding Backups and the Care of Data."

Rules

1. You must specify the source drive, path, and file name first, and then the destination drive, path, and file name.

2. Do not use a device name other than a drive for the source or destination name. For example, you cannot use LPT1: or COM1:.

3. The source-file specification (**ds:paths\filenames.exts**) must include one or both of the following parameters:

   ■ A valid file name. Wild cards are permitted.

   ■ A drive name, a path name, or both.

4. If you do not specify the source drive name, DOS uses the current drive.

5. If you do not specify the source path, DOS uses the drive's current directory.

6. If you specify a drive or path for the source but do not specify a source file name (**filenames.exts**), DOS assumes *.*.

7. If you omit a new name for the destination file, the copied file has the same name as the source file.

8. If you do not specify the destination file, the source file specification must include one or both of the following parameters:

   ■ A drive name other than the current drive.

   ■ A path name other than the current disk's current directory.

9. Do not use the source disk in an APPEND /X command. If the source disk is part of an APPEND command, disconnect the command by using APPEND ; before you use XCOPY.

10. XCOPY sets the archive bit on created files.

Notes

To use XCOPY to copy more files than will fit on one destination disk, make sure that the files' archive attribute is on. You can use the ATTRIB command to perform this step. Then use the XCOPY command repeatedly with the /M or /M /S switch.

When the destination floppy disk is full, change floppy disks and reissue the command. The files that were copied now have their archive attribute turned off, so XCOPY skips these files. XCOPY copies the files that were not yet copied—those files that have the archive attribute turned on.

XCOPY and APPEND /X are a troublesome combination. To use XCOPY on a disk that is involved in an APPEND command, disconnect APPEND before you execute the XCOPY command.

Use XCOPY, rather than DISKCOPY, to copy files to a device that is not the same format as the source.

Messages

1. Cannot perform a cyclic copy

   Error: You used the /S switch, and at least one of the destination directories is a subdirectory of the source directories. When you use /S, XCOPY cannot copy files to destination directories that are part of the source directories. If you must copy files from more than one directory, issue individual XCOPY commands to copy the directories one at a time.

2. Cannot XCOPY from a reserved device

   Error: You specified one of DOS's reserved device names (for example, LPT1) as the source of the files to be copied. Reissue XCOPY, using a disk path and directory.

3. Does %s specify a file name
   or directory name on the target
   (F = file, D = directory)?

   Information: You specified a destination file name in which the final name does not exist as a directory. XCOPY does not know whether the final name in the destination is a file name or a directory.

If the destination name is a directory name, type **D**. XCOPY creates the needed directory and begins copying files. If the destination name is a file name, type **F**. XCOPY copies files to this file.

4. `nnn File(s) copied`

Information: XCOPY copied *nnn* files to the destination disk. This message appears regardless of any errors that occur.

5. `Insufficient disk space`

Error: The destination disk ran out of space. The file that you were copying when the error occurred was erased from the destination. Either delete any unneeded files from the destination disk or use a different disk and then retry the command.

6. `Reading source file(s)…`

Information: XCOPY is reading the source directories for file names.

7. `Unable to create directory`

Error: XCOPY could not create a subdirectory on the destination disk for one of the following reasons:

- Part of the destination path name is wrong or misspelled.

- The disk's root directory is full.

- The disk is full.

- A file with the same name as the created directory already exists.

- You used a directory name that actually is a device name.

Be sure that the destination name is correct. Use the DIR command to check the destination disk. If the disk or the root directory is full, erase files or use another destination disk. If a file exists that uses the same name as the intended directory, rename the file or change the directory's name when you reissue the XCOPY command.

■ If you are installing DOS on a hard disk, you must assign a DOS partition to the hard disk and then prepare the partition by formatting.

As installation proceeds, you are prompted to insert floppy disks. Place the requested disk in the drive and press Enter. If you are installing DOS on floppy disks rather than a hard disk, be sure to label each floppy disk, following the on-screen instructions.

When installation is complete, Setup restarts the computer.

Upgrading to Version 6.0

This section explains how to install the upgrade version of DOS Version 6.0. The Setup program in the upgrade version installs the operating system on a computer that already contains an earlier version of DOS. You do not have to reformat your hard disk. Existing data is untouched, but you should back up the system before beginning installation.

If you decide to uninstall DOS Version 6.0 and revert to the earlier version of DOS, an UNINSTALL program enables you to do so.

Before you can use the Setup program, your system must meet the following minimum requirements:

■ DOS Version 2.11 or later

■ At least 256K of memory

■ If you have a hard disk, at least 4M of available space

If you have an OS/2 partition on your hard disk, Setup warns you. If you have any non-DOS partitions on your hard disk, refer to the documentation that accompanies MS-DOS 6.0.

Versions of DOS before 4.0 did not recognize hard disk partitions larger than 32M. If you have been using one of these versions of DOS and have a hard disk larger than 32M, you may want to repartition and reformat the hard disk by using DOS Version 6.0 before running Setup. (For more information, see "Repartitioning the Hard Disk" at the end of this appendix.)

CAUTION: Some non-Microsoft disk-caching, anti-virus, and delete protection programs conflict with DOS 6.0 Setup. If you are using any of these programs, disable them before upgrading to DOS 6.0. Simply edit your CONFIG.SYS or AUTOEXEC.BAT files, and add REM to the line that starts the utility.

For example, if a line in AUTOEXEC.BAT that starts a disk cache reads C:\UTILS\DISKCASH, alter the line to read REM C:\UTILS\DISKCASH. Save the file and then reboot your computer before upgrading to DOS 6.0. After you complete the installation, you can remove REM from AUTOEXEC.BAT so that you can again use the utility that you temporarily disabled, or use one of the utilities that come with DOS 6.0.

Starting Setup

To install the upgrade version of DOS 6.0, follow these steps:

1. Remove from memory any TSRs or device drivers used for disk caching, virus protection, and delete protection, and reboot your computer.

2. Insert the DOS Version 6.0 distribution disk marked Disk 1 into floppy disk drive A.

3. Access the DOS prompt and change to the drive containing Disk 1. To start Setup, type **SETUP** and press Enter.

   To force Setup to install to floppy disks, even if your system has a hard disk, type **SETUP /F** at the DOS prompt and press Enter.

 To create the DOS floppy disks, follow the procedure described in "Upgrading Version 6.0 to Floppy Disks" later in this appendix. (You may want to create a complete set of disks as a backup copy.)

You can use any of the following switches when starting Setup:

Switch	Description
/B	Runs Setup in black and white rather than color
/E	Installs the Windows and MS-DOS versions of Anti-Virus, Backup, and Undelete

Switch	Description
/F	Creates a minimal floppy disk version of DOS 6.0
/G	Runs Setup without creating an UNINSTALL disk or prompting to update network drivers
/H	Selects all default DOS 6.0 Setup options
/I	Does not attempt to detect hardware
/M	Performs a minimal DOS 6.0 installation on your hard disk
/Q	Copies DOS utilities and files to a hard disk (use this switch after naming Setup with the /M switch)
/U	Installs DOS 6.0 even if your computer contains partitions that are incompatible with DOS 6.0

When Setup begins, the program briefly displays the following message:

```
Please wait.
Setup is checking your system configuration.
```

Setup attempts to determine the type of system you have, the current date and time settings, the country setting, whether the system has a hard disk, the display type, the CPU type, and the amount of memory.

If you have a hard disk, Setup displays the following message:

```
Welcome to Setup.

Setup prepares MS-DOS 6 to run on your
computer.


    To set up MS-DOS now, press ENTER.

    To learn more about Setup before continuing, press F1.

    To quit Setup without installing MS-DOS, press F3.
```

T I P   If you have difficulty reading the screen, you can make the screen more readable by pressing F5 to remove color information.

If you are installing to floppy disks, your screen will appear as follows:

```
Welcome to Setup.

You have chosen to perform a minimal installation of
MS-DOS 6 on a floppy disk. You must provide a formatted
or unformatted floppy disk that works in your computer's
drive A. Label the disk as follows:

        STARTUP

Setup copies the MS-DOS system files and a few important
utilities to this disk. You can use this disk to run
MS-DOS 6.

    For more information about Setup, press F1.

    To exit Setup without installing MS-DOS, press F3.

    To set up MS-DOS on a floppy disk, press ENTER.
```

DOS Version 6.0 upgrading procedures vary depending on whether you are upgrading the operating system to a hard disk or to floppy disks. Follow the upgrade procedure described in one of the following sections.

Upgrading Version 6.0 to a Hard Disk

To continue upgrading DOS Version 6.0 to a hard disk, make sure that you started Setup by following the steps in the section "Starting Setup," and then follow these steps:

1. Press Enter to continue Setup. The following message appears on-screen:

During Setup, you will need to provide and label one
or two floppy disks. Each disk can be unformatted
or newly formatted and must work in drive A. (If you
use 360K disks, you may need two disks; otherwise,
you need only one disk.)

Label the disk(s) as follows:

        UNINSTALL #1
        UNINSTALL #2 (if needed)

Setup saves some of your original DOS files on the
UNINSTALL disk(s), and others on your hard disk in a
directory named OLD_DOS.x. With these files, you can
restore your original DOS if necessary.
When you finish labeling your UNINSTALL disk(s),
press ENTER to continue Setup.

        When you finish labeling your UNINSTALL disk(s)
        press ENTER to continue Setup.

2. Label a floppy disk UNINSTALL, and then press Enter to continue.

3. Setup next displays a system settings box. Make any changes to
   the options in this box. The options are listed in the following:

   ■ *DOS Type.* Indicates the manufacturer of the version of DOS
     currently installed on your system—for example, IBM PC DOS.
     If Setup cannot determine the manufacturer, the program
     displays MS-DOS.

   ■ *DOS Path.* Indicates the directory in which DOS files currently
     are installed.

   ■ *Display Type.* Denotes the display type that Setup expects
     the system to have, based on Setup's initial analysis of the
     system.

   Select DOS Type, DOS Path, or Display Type, and then press Enter
   to make any changes (see the following note and tip).

NOTE If the DOS Type that Setup displays is MS-DOS, rather than a specific manufacturer, you may need to modify this setting; your version of DOS may contain files that are unique to your brand of computer. Use the up-arrow key to highlight the DOS Type line and then press Enter. Setup displays a list of companies that are licensed to produce the version of DOS installed on your system. (If necessary, you can scroll this list by pressing the up- and down-arrow keys.)

Highlight the name of the company that manufactured your current DOS version. Making this selection causes Setup to maintain in the DOS directory any files that your hardware needs. If you cannot determine which company produced the version of DOS that currently is on your system, select MS-DOS or OTHER.

After you make a selection and press Enter, Setup returns to the system settings box.

T I P If you don't want DOS installed on the same disk and directory in which the current version of DOS is stored, use the up-arrow key to highlight the DOS Path line and press Enter. Setup displays the current path—for example, `C:\DOS`. Edit the path to indicate the drive and directory to which you want Setup to copy DOS files, and then press Enter. Setup returns to the system settings box.

4. Select The Settings Are Correct in the system settings box and press Enter to continue.

5. Setup next displays a list of the programs that it can install. For each program, you can choose the DOS version, the Windows version, both versions, or neither version. The list also shows the disk sizes that the programs need. If you need to change any of the selections, edit them in the same manner as in the system settings box.

6. Select Install the Listed Programs and press Enter to continue.

7. Setup displays the directory on your hard disk containing Windows, if you have Windows on your hard disk. If this directory is not where Windows is installed, edit the path. Then press Enter.

8. Setup displays the following message:

```
Setup is ready to upgrade your system to MS-DOS 6.
Do not interrupt Setup during the upgrade process.

    To install MS-DOS 6 files now, press Y.

    To exit Setup without installing MS-DOS, press F3.
```

Press **Y** to continue, or press F3 to cancel the installation procedure.

9. If you confirm that you want Setup to continue, Setup begins copying files. Then the program prompts you to label a disk UNINSTALL #1 and to insert that disk into the floppy disk drive.

10. Place the UNINSTALL #1 disk in the indicated floppy drive and press Enter. Any data on the disk is erased.

11. Setup copies files from the hard disk to the UNINSTALL disk and copies other files to a new directory on the hard disk named \OLD_DOS.1.

    You may be prompted for the disk capacity. If so, select the appropriate option and press Enter. If you are instructed to do so, label a disk UNINSTALL #2, place this disk in the floppy disk drive, and press Enter.

 The files on the UNINSTALL disk(s) and in the \OLD_DOS.1 directory are used later only if you decide to remove DOS Version 6.0 from the system and return to the preceding version.

12. After Setup finishes creating the UNINSTALL disk(s), Setup instructs you to insert the DOS Version 6.0 disk labeled Disk 1 into the floppy disk drive.

    Insert Disk 1 into the specified drive and press Enter.

13. Setup begins copying files to the hard disk. As Setup continues, you will be asked to remove and insert additional disks. When prompted to do so, insert the disks and press Enter to continue.

 During the installation procedure, Setup displays the percentage of installation completed. Setup also displays a horizontal bar graph that expands according to the number of files copied to the hard disk.

14. When Setup finishes, remove the last disk from the floppy drive and press Enter, as prompted on-screen.

Setup reboots the computer. If you indicated that you want the Shell to run at startup, the DOS Shell screen appears. Otherwise, you see the following prompt:

```
C:\>
```

The installation process is complete.

> **CAUTION:** When you use Setup to install DOS Version 6.0 on the hard disk, Setup modifies any existing CONFIG.SYS and AUTOEXEC.BAT files (configuration files are discussed in Chapter 17). Setup renames the original files CONFIG.DAT and AUTOEXEC.DAT and saves them on the UNINSTALL disk. If you need to return to your original version of DOS, follow the instructions in "Using UNINSTALL" later in this appendix.

Upgrading Version 6.0 to Floppy Disks

Make sure that you started Setup as described in the section "Starting Setup." Use the following instructions to upgrade DOS Version 6.0 to floppy disks or to create a bootable DOS 6.0 disk:

1. Press Enter to continue with installation. Setup displays a system settings box containing the following options:

    ■ *Install on Drive.* Indicates the drive to which Setup installs DOS files, unless you specify otherwise. The default drive may be A: or B:.

    ■ *Display Type.* Denotes the display type Setup expects the system to have, based on Setup's initial analysis of the system.

2. If necessary, select either Install on Drive or Display Type, and then press Enter to make any changes. Follow the on-screen instructions to make changes. When you finish making changes, press Enter again. Setup returns to the preceding dialog box.

3. Select The Settings Are Correct and press Enter.

    Setup begins reading files into memory.

As Setup proceeds, remove and insert disks only when you are prompted to do so. Be particularly careful to note which disk and drive Setup specifies when you remove and insert disks. Ensure that you label disks as instructed.

> **NOTE** Not all DOS 6.0 files are expanded and copied. The STARTUP floppy disk contains enough files for a minimum system; others may be expanded with the EXPAND program, located on the STARTUP disk. The STARTUP disk contains the following files: COMMAND.COM, ATTRIB.EXE, DEBUG.EXE, EXPAND.EXE, FDISK.EXE, FORMAT.COM, RESTORE.EXE, SYS.COM, CHKDSK.EXE, EDIT.COM, QBASIC.EXE, and MSAV.EXE.

4. You may be asked to select from a menu the capacity of your disk. You must select the size of the floppy disk you are creating, not the ones that came with DOS and Setup. Then press Enter.

5. Setup begins reading files from the DOS 6.0 disks and copies these files to your STARTUP disk. As Setup progresses, it prompts you to switch disks. Switch disks as prompted, pressing Enter to continue.

> **NOTE** During the installation procedure, Setup displays the percentage of installation completed. Setup also displays a horizontal bar graph that expands according to the number of files copied to the disks.

The installation process is complete. Use the Startup disk each time you need to start the computer.

> To ensure that you do not delete or modify files accidentally, write-protect the floppy disks on which you installed DOS 6.0 using UNINSTALL.
>
> **T I P**

When you use the upgrade version of DOS Version 6.0 to install the operating system to a hard disk, Setup creates an UNINSTALL disk, or two disks called UNINSTALL #1 and UNINSTALL #2. An UNINSTALL disk contains files that enable you to remove DOS Version 6.0 from the system and to return to the preceding version of DOS. Returning to the old version of DOS is not possible, however, if you have repartitioned the hard disk. Additionally, files saved on a DoubleSpace partition will be inaccessible after an UNINSTALL operation, so you must carefully back up these files first.

To uninstall DOS Version 6.0, follow these steps:

1. Place the disk labeled UNINSTALL or UNINSTALL #1 in drive A and reboot the computer by pressing Ctrl-Alt-Del.

2. After the computer finishes its self-test procedures, DOS begins the UNINSTALL procedure and displays the following message:

```
YOUR HARD DISK INSTALLATION WAS SUCCESSFULLY COMPLETED.
Continuing with the UNINSTALL program will remove MS-DOS 6
files from the hard disk and will replace them with your
original DOS.

To restore your original DOS, press R.

To exit, remove the UNINSTALL disk from drive A and
press E.
```

To continue with UNINSTALL, press R.

 NOTE   To exit and return to DOS, remove the UNINSTALL disk from the floppy disk drive and press E. The UNINSTALL program reboots the computer.

3. Replace the disk labeled UNINSTALL #1 with UNINSTALL #2 when you are prompted to do so. (Skip this step if Setup created only one UNINSTALL disk.)

4. The UNINSTALL program deletes the DOS Version 6.0 files, copies necessary files from the UNINSTALL disk(s) to the hard disk, and copies the old DOS files from the \OLD_DOS.1 directory to the original DOS directory on the hard disk.

5. When the UNINSTALL procedure is complete, the following message appears on-screen:

```
Uninstall is now complete
Please remove any disks from your floppy disk drives and
press any key to restart your original DOS.
```

6. Remove the UNINSTALL disk from the floppy drive and press any key. The UNINSTALL program reboots the computer. DOS Version 6.0 is gone, and the original version of DOS is installed in its place.

Deleting Old DOS Files

After you determine that DOS Version 6.0 meets your needs and that you don't want to return to the preceding version of DOS, you may want to delete the old version of DOS from the hard disk to free disk space. After you perform this cleanup, however, you no longer can run the UNINSTALL procedure described in the preceding section; the files that the UNINSTALL program needs are erased along with the old DOS files.

To delete the old version of DOS from your hard disk, follow these steps:

1. Type the following command at the DOS prompt, and then press Enter:

   DELOLDOS

2. The program displays the following warning message:

   ```
   Running DELOLDOS removes all old DOS files from
   the system, making it impossible to recover the
   previous DOS. To continue with DELOLDOS, press Y.
   To exit, press any other key.
   ```

   To continue with DELOLDOS, press Y. Press any other key to return to the DOS prompt without deleting the old DOS files.

3. After you confirm that you want to delete all old DOS files, DELOLDOS displays a message that it is DELETING OLD_DOS.1 as it deletes the files from the hard disk.

4. When all files have been erased, the program displays a message indicating that the old DOS files have been deleted. Press Enter to return to the DOS prompt.

Repartitioning the Hard Disk

If your hard drive is larger than 32M, and if you have been using a version of DOS earlier than Version 4.0, you may want to use Version 6.0 to repartition the hard disk, because pre-4.0 versions of DOS do not recognize hard disk drives larger than 32M.

To use larger hard disks with pre-4.0 versions of DOS, you have to use FDISK to create several *logical* partitions. (DOS Version 3.3 enabled users to divide a hard disk into multiple partitions, each of which was 32M or smaller; DOS then treated each partition as though it were a separate physical disk drive, referred to as a *logical* drive.) Alternatively, you must use a special partitioning program supplied by the manufacturer of the hard disk. DOS 4.0 and later versions enable you to create a primary DOS partition up to 2 gigabytes (2,000M).

 NOTE In DOS 4.0, you had to run the program SHARE.EXE to use a partition larger than 32M. DOS 5.0 and 6.0 do not use the program SHARE.EXE in this manner and do not require you to load any other special utility to take advantage of a large hard disk.

To repartition the hard disk so that you have a partition larger than 32M, follow these steps:

1. Back up all programs and data on the hard disk.

    NOTE Repartitioning the hard disk deletes all data. You need the backup to restore all files to the hard disk after you repartition and reformat the disk.

2. Create a set of DOS 6.0 floppy disks, following the instructions in "Upgrading Version 6.0 to Floppy Disks" earlier in this appendix.

3. Remove all DOS partitions, using the partitioning program that created the current partitions if that program is available. The FDISK command in DOS 6.0 usually can do this job, even when the partition was created by another program, but using the original program generally is a better idea.

    NOTE Before you can use the DOS Version 6.0 partitioning program, you need to boot the computer by using the DOS 6.0 STARTUP disk.

4. Place the disk labeled STARTUP in drive A and reboot the computer. DOS Version 6.0 starts, displaying the following prompt:

```
A:\>
```

You finally are ready to repartition the disk.

5. Type the following command, and then press Enter:

   FDISK

6. FDISK starts, displaying a menu that contains the following options:

   ```
   1. Create DOS partition or Logical DOS Drive
   2. Set active partition
   3. Delete partition or Logical DOS Drive
   4. Display partition information
   ```

7. FDISK prompts you to enter a choice and suggests option 1 (Create DOS Partition or Logical DOS Drive). Press Enter to select that option.

 NOTE If you are removing the current partitions with DOS 6.0, select option 3 (Delete Partition or Logical DOS Drive), and then press Enter. Follow the prompts to remove the partitions. After you remove the partitions, reboot the computer and start FDISK again.

8. FDISK displays a menu containing the following options:

   ```
   1. Create Primary DOS Partition
   2. Create Extended DOS Partition
   3. Create Logical DOS Drive(s) in the Extended DOS Partition
   ```

9. FDISK again suggests option 1 (Create Primary DOS Partition). Press Enter to select that option.

10. FDISK asks whether you want to use the maximum available size for the primary DOS partition. The default answer is Yes, which creates a partition equal in size to the entire hard disk. To create a partition that includes the entire hard disk, press Y.

11. FDISK indicates that the system will now restart. The program further instructs you to insert a system disk into drive A and then press any key.

12. Make sure that the STARTUP disk still is in drive A, and then press a key on the keyboard. The computer restarts, displaying the A:\> prompt.

13. The next step is to format the primary hard disk partition. With the Startup disk in drive A, type the following command and then press Enter:

    FORMAT C: /S

14. FORMAT warns you that all data on drive C will be lost and asks whether you want to proceed with formatting. Press Y, and then press Enter to proceed.

15. FORMAT displays a message indicating the size of the disk that begins the formatting process.

16. When the process is complete, FORMAT prompts you to enter a volume label. Type a label of up to 11 characters (including spaces), and then press Enter.

17. FORMAT informs you of the total number of bytes on the disk, the space used by the operating system, and the number of bytes free for storage of programs and data. You now are ready to restore to the hard disk the backup copy of the data that originally was on the disk.

    If you used the DOS command BACKUP to create the copy, use RESTORE from the Startup disk to copy the files back to the hard disk.

    If you used a third-party backup program to create the copy, install the backup program on your hard disk and then follow that program's instructions for restoring the files to your hard disk.

18. After you restore the programs and data files, you are ready to install DOS Version 6.0 on the hard disk. Insert the DOS Version 6.0 distribution disk labeled Disk 1 into drive A or drive B, and then follow the instructions in "Upgrading Version 6.0 to a Hard Disk" earlier in this appendix.

DOS Messages

DOS messages can be divided into two groups: general and device error messages. The larger group of general messages is listed first, followed by the device error messages. Both lists are organized alphabetically.

General DOS Messages

General DOS messages fall into three groups: error messages, warning messages, and information messages. *Error messages* indicate that DOS has encountered a problem with a command or with the syntax you used. Execution stops when DOS displays an error message. *Warning messages* tell you in advance that the next action you take may cause unwanted changes to files or to your system and often include a prompt, which enables you to select an action. *Information messages* display needed information about your system's operation or your DOS version's performance. Like warning messages, these messages also often include a prompt.

The following messages may appear at any time during a work session: from the time you start your computer until you turn your computer off. In this appendix, messages that occur only when you start DOS are indicated by "start-up." With most start-up errors, DOS did not start; you must reboot the system.

Other error messages occur when DOS aborts a program and returns to the system prompt, such as A> or C>.

A BAD UMB number has been specified

ERROR: You have attempted a LOADHIGH (or LH) with the /L parameter referring to a nonexistent UMB area. The best way to correct this is to rerun MEMMAKER.

Access denied

ERROR: You or a program attempted to change or erase a file that is marked as read-only or that is in use. If the file is marked as read-only, you can change the read-only attribute with the ATTRIB command.

Active Code Page: *xxx*

INFORMATION: You issued CHCP, which displayed *xxx*, the code page currently in use by the system.

Active Code Page for device *ddd* is *xxx*

INFORMATION: You issued MODE, which lists the code page currently in use for device *ddd*. To display a single screen at a time, pipe this command into MORE (MODE|MORE).

Active Code Page not available from CON device

ERROR: You used KEYB with a code page not supported on the CON device (screen).

Add filename? (Y/N)

PROMPT: You issued REPLACE /P; DOS asks whether you want to add the file to the disk.

Adding filename

INFORMATION: REPLACE displays this message while adding filename to your disk.

All available space in the Extended DOS Partition is assigned to logical drives.

ERROR: No room remains for logical drives in the extended partition. Use FDISK to change the size of the extended partition.

All files canceled by operator

INFORMATION: You issued PRINT /T, which removes all files from the print queue.

```
All files in directory will be deleted!
Are you sure (Y/N)?
```
> WARNING: You issued DEL or ERASE with the *.* wild card. To
> continue, press Y; to cancel, press N. Then press the Enter key.

```
All logical drives deleted in the Extended DOS Partition
```
> INFORMATION: While using FDISK, you removed all logical drives
> associated with the extended DOS partition.

```
Allocation error, size adjusted
```
> WARNING: The contents of a file have been truncated because the
> size indicated in the directory is not consistent with the amount
> of data allocated to the file. Use CHKDSK /F to correct the
> discrepancy.

```
All specified file(s) are contiguous
```
> INFORMATION: None of the files you specified (to CHKDSK) is
> fragmented.

```
A program was run that took memory that Backup requires.
The program must be removed from memory before Backup can
continue
```
> ERROR: You have installed a TSR (resident program) that leaves
> insufficient memory for BACKUP. Examples of this would be
> PRINT or some forms of MODE. The resident program must be
> unloaded before you can continue backup. Use MEM to see which
> TSR was loaded last.

```
ANSI.SYS must be installed to perform requested function
```
> WARNING: While using MODE, you requested a screen function
> that cannot be performed until you load ANSI.SYS.

```
An incompatible DOSKey is already installed.
```
> ERROR: The version of DOSKey you're trying to run is not compat-
> ible with the one already in memory. Make sure you don't mix the
> DOSKEY.COM that comes with DOS 6.0 with another vendor's
> command line editor.

```
APPEND already installed
```
> INFORMATION: You tried to issue APPEND with /X or /E after
> previously using APPEND. You can use the /E switch only the first
> time you type APPEND after starting your system. You can use the
> /X switch only if it was used during initialization.

APPEND/ASSIGN Conflict

WARNING: You cannot use APPEND on an assigned drive. Cancel the drive assignment before using APPEND with this drive.

ATTENTION: A serious disk error has occurred while writing to drive

ERROR: Smartdrv has detected a hard disk error when write caching was enabled. Since the application may have already continued to something else, the usual corrections don't apply. Write caching must only be enabled for reliable media.

/B invalid with a black and white printer

ERROR: You tried to print the background color by using GRAPHICS /B, but you do not have a color printer connected to your computer.

Backing up files to drive x:

INFORMATION: This message appears while you back up files to the specified drive.

Bad Command or file name

ERROR: You entered an invalid name for invoking a command, program, or batch file. The most frequent causes are the following: you misspelled a name, you omitted a required disk drive or path name, or you omitted the command name when giving parameters (for example, omitting the WordStar command, WS, by typing MYFILE instead of WS MYFILE).

Check the spelling on the command line and make sure that the command, program, or batch file is in the location specified. Then try the command again.

Bad or Missing Command Interpreter

ERROR (start-up): DOS does not start because it cannot find COMMAND.COM, the command interpreter.

If this message appears during start-up, COMMAND.COM is not on the start-up disk, or a COMMAND.COM file from a previous version of DOS is on the disk. If you used the SHELL command in CONFIG.SYS, the message means that the SHELL command is improperly phrased or that COMMAND.COM is not where you specified.

With DOS 6.0 you can override CONFIG.SYS using the F8 or F5 keys during boot. This solution works if the correct COMMAND.COM is in the root directory. Otherwise, place another disk that contains the operating system (IO.SYS, MSDOS.SYS, and COMMAND.COM) in the floppy disk drive and reset the system. After DOS starts, copy COMMAND.COM to the original start-up disk so that you can boot DOS in the future.

If this message appears while you are running DOS, several explanations are possible. COMMAND.COM has been erased from the disk and directory you used when starting DOS; a version of COMMAND.COM from a previous version of DOS has overwritten the good version; or the COMSPEC entry in the environment has been changed. You must restart DOS by resetting the system.

If resetting the system does not solve your problem, restart the computer from a copy of your DOS master disk. Copy COMMAND.COM from this disk to the offending disk.

Bad or missing filename

WARNING (start-up): This message means that the device driver file name was not found, that an error occurred when the device driver was loaded, that a break address for the device driver was beyond the RAM available to the computer, or that DOS detected an error while loading the driver into memory. DOS continues booting without the device driver filename.

If DOS loads, check your CONFIG.SYS file for the line DEVICE=filename. Make sure that the line is typed correctly and that the device driver is at the specified location; then reboot the system. If the message reappears, copy the file from its original disk to the boot disk and try starting DOS again. If the error persists, the device driver is bad; contact the dealer or publisher who sold the driver to you.

Bad or Missing Keyboard definition file

WARNING: DOS cannot find KEYBOARD.SYS as specified by the KEYB command. Solving this problem may take several steps. First, check to make sure that KEYBOARD.SYS exists and is in the correct path; then retype the KEYB command. If you get the same message, KEYB.COM or KEYBOARD.SYS may be corrupted.

Bad Partition Table

ERROR: While using FORMAT, DOS was unable to find a DOS partition on the fixed disk you specified. Run FDISK and create a DOS partition on this fixed-disk drive.

`Batch file missing`

ERROR: DOS could not find the batch file it was processing. The batch file may have been erased or renamed. With DOS 3.0 only, the disk containing the batch file may have been changed, causing DOS to abort processing the batch file.

If you are using DOS 3.0 and you changed the disk that contains the batch file, restart the batch file without changing the disk. You may need to edit the batch file so that you do not need to change disks. This procedure applies only to DOS 3.0.

If the batch file includes a RENAME command that causes the originating batch file name to change, edit the batch file to prevent renaming when the batch file is processed again. If the file was erased, re-create the batch file from its backup file if possible. Edit the file to ensure that the batch file does not erase itself.

`Baud rate required`

ERROR: When using MODE COMx commands to set any COM port parameters, you must at least indicate the baud rate.

`BREAK is off`

or

`BREAK is on`

INFORMATION: When you use BREAK by itself, one of these messages displays the current BREAK setting. You can set BREAK at the command line or in CONFIG.SYS.

`Cannot change BUFSIZE`

ERROR: You cannot change the DOSKey buffer size, once loaded.

`Cannot CHDIR to path - tree past this point not processed`

ERROR: CHKDSK was unable to go to the specified directory. No subdirectories below this directory are verified. Run CHKDSK /F to correct this error.

`Cannot CHDIR to root`

ERROR: CHKDSK was checking the tree structure of the directory and was unable to return to the root directory. Remaining subdirectories were not checked. Restart DOS. If the message continues to display, the disk is unusable and must be reformatted.

`Cannot CHKDSK a network drive`

WARNING: You cannot use CHKDSK to check drives that are redirected over the network.

`Cannot Chkdsk a SUBSTed or ASSIGNed drive`

WARNING: You cannot use CHKDSK to check substituted or assigned drives.

`Cannot create a zero size partition`

ERROR: While using FDISK, you tried to create a partition of zero percent (0 megabytes). To correct this error, you must allocate one percent (or a minimum of 1M) of hard disk space to any partition you create.

`Cannot create extended DOS partition without primary DOS partition on disk x`

ERROR: While using FDISK, you tried to create an extended DOS partition before giving your first fixed-disk drive a primary DOS partition. To correct this problem, simply create a DOS partition on your first fixed-disk drive. When this operation is complete, you can create an extended DOS partition if you have room on this disk or if you have a second fixed disk.

`Cannot create Logical DOS drive without an Extended DOS Partition on the current drive`

ERROR: When using FDISK, you must create an extended DOS partition before you can create a logical drive.

`Cannot DISKCOMP to or from a network drive`

ERROR: You cannot compare disks on any disk drive that has been reassigned to a network.

`Cannot delete Extended DOS Partition while logical drives exist`

ERROR: When using FDISK to delete an extended DOS partition, you first must remove any logical drives.

`Cannot DISKCOPY to or from a network drive`

ERROR: You attempted to copy a floppy disk to a drive that was redirected to a computer network. DISKCOPY does not copy disks directly to a networked disk drive. Use COPY to copy the disk.

Cannot do binary reads from a device

ERROR: You tried to copy from a device by using the /B switch. To complete the copy process, use the ASCII (/A) switch to create an ASCII copy, or you can use the COPY command without the /B switch.

Cannot edit .BAK file—rename file

ERROR: Files that have a BAK extension cannot be altered in Edlin. Rename the file by changing the extension to any name other than BAK.

Cannot find file QBASIC.EXE

ERROR: EDIT.COM cannot find the QBASIC program. The editor is really a part of the QBASIC system, so both must be available to edit a file with EDIT.

Cannot find GRAPHICS profile

ERROR: You did not give the path of the GRAPHICS.PRO file; DOS could not find it in the current directory.

Cannot find System Files

ERROR: While running FORMAT, you specified a drive that did not have the system files in the root directory.

Cannot format an ASSIGNed or SUBSTed drive.

ERROR: You attempted to format a drive that was mapped to another drive with ASSIGN or SUBST. To perform a successful format, you must run ASSIGN or SUBST again to clear the drive assignments.

Cannot FORMAT a network drive

ERROR: You tried to format a disk in a drive being used by a network.

Cannot LABEL a Network drive

ERROR: You cannot use LABEL with drives redirected over the network.

Cannot LABEL a JOINed, SUBSTed or ASSIGNed drive

ERROR: You attempted to label a drive created with JOIN, SUBST, or ASSIGN.

`Cannot load COMMAND, system halted`

> ERROR: DOS attempted to reload COMMAND.COM, but the area where DOS keeps track of memory was destroyed, or the command processor was not found in the directory specified by the COMSPEC= entry. The system halts.
>
> This message may indicate that COMMAND.COM was erased from the disk and directory you used when starting DOS, or that the COMSPEC= entry in the environment has been changed. Restart DOS from your usual start-up disk. If DOS does not start, the copy of COMMAND.COM has been erased. Restart DOS from the DOS start-up or master disk, and copy COMMAND.COM onto your usual start-up disk.
>
> Alternatively, an errant program may have corrupted the memory allocation table where DOS tracks available memory. Try running the same program that was in the computer when the system halted. If the problem occurs again, the program is defective. Contact the dealer or publisher who sold you the program.

`Cannot loadhigh batch file`

> WARNING: The LOADHIGH (or LH) command is used only for TSR (resident) programs. Batch files may not be run this way.

`Cannot move multiple files to a single file`

> ERROR: When using MOVE with wildcards for the source file specification, you must specify a directory for the destination. The most common cause for this error is a misspelled name.

`Cannot perform a cyclic copy`

> ERROR: When using XCOPY /S, you cannot specify a target that is a subdirectory of the source. You may use a temporary disk or file to bypass this limitation if the directory tree structure allows a temporary disk or file.

`Cannot recover .. entry,`
`Entry has a bad attribute (or link or size)`

> ERROR, WARNING: The .. entry (the parent directory) is defective and cannot be recovered. If you have specified the /F switch, CHKDSK tries to correct the error.

`Cannot setup expanded memory`

> ERROR: FASTOPEN cannot correctly access your expanded memory (EMS).

Cannot specify default drive

> ERROR: You specified the default drive as a SYS destination. Switch to another drive before issuing the SYS command.

Cannot start COMMAND, exiting

> ERROR: You or one of your programs directed DOS to load another copy of COMMAND.COM, but DOS could not load it. Your CONFIG.SYS FILES command is set too low, or you do not have enough free memory for another copy of COMMAND.COM.

> If your system has 256K or more and FILES is less than 10, edit the CONFIG.SYS file on your start-up disk, using FILES=15 or FILES=20. Then restart DOS.

> If the problem recurs, you do not have enough memory in your computer, or you have too many resident or background programs competing for memory space. Restart DOS, loading only the essential programs. If necessary, eliminate unneeded device drivers or RAM disk software. You also can obtain additional RAM for your system.

Cannot SUBST a Network drive

> ERROR: You cannot substitute drives redirected over the network.

Cannot SYS a Network drive

> ERROR: You cannot transfer system files to drives that are redirected over the network.

Cannot use FASTOPEN for drive x

> ERROR: You attempted to use FASTOPEN over a network, with a floppy disk drive, or with more than four disks at one time.

Cannot use PRINT - Use NET PRINT

> ERROR: You tried to use PRINT over the network. Use NET PRINT, or consult your system administrator for the correct procedure for printing files over the network.

Cannot XCOPY from a reserved device

Cannot XCOPY to a reserved device

> ERROR: The specified XCOPY source/target is a character device (printer), an asynchronous communication device, or NULL. You must specify a file or block device as your source and your target.

`CHDIR .. failed, trying alternate method`

WARNING: CHKDSK was unable to return to a parent directory while checking the tree structure. CHKDSK attempts to return to the parent directory by starting over at the root and repeating the search.

`Code page not prepared`

ERROR: While using MODE, you selected a code page not yet prepared for the system or without the correct font to support the current video mode. To correct this error, prepare a code page using the MODE PREPARE command. If you have installed the DISPLAY.SYS installable device driver, make sure that the DEVICE command line in your CONFIG.SYS file allows for additional subfonts.

`Code page xxx not prepared for all devices`

ERROR: While using CHCP, you selected a code page not currently supported by a device. To correct this error, first make sure that your device supports code-page switching and that it is on-line. Then issue the MODE PREPARE command to ready the device for the code page. You are ready to retry CHCP.

`Code page xxx not prepared for system`

ERROR: CHCP is unable to select a code page for the system. If NLSFUNC is installed and your CONFIG.SYS file does not install device drivers, you can retry CHCP. If CONFIG.SYS installs device drivers, you must issue the MODE PREPARE command to prepare the specific code page for each device before retrying the CHCP command.

`Code page operation not supported on this device`

ERROR: While using MODE, you selected a device and code page combination not recognized by DOS. Make sure that you specified a valid device and code page and that the code page you selected is supported on the device.

`Code page requested (xxx) is not valid for given keyboard code`

ERROR: You selected an incompatible keyboard code and code page combination. Reenter the KEYB command with a valid keyboard code and code page.

Code page specified has not been prepared

> ERROR: You issued the KEYB command with an unrecognized code page. Prepare the code page for your CON (your console screen device) by using the MODE PREPARE command; then retry KEYB.

Code page specified is inconsistent with selected code page

> WARNING: You used KEYB with an option not compatible with the code page for your console screen device. Specify a compatible option, or issue the MODE select command to change the code page for your console screen device.

Code page *xxx*

> INFORMATION: This message displays the code page currently in use by the specified device. If you type MODE CON, for example, the message returns the code page in use for your screen.

Code pages cannot be prepared

> ERROR: You attempted to use a duplicate code page for the specified device; or with MODE PREPARE, you specified more code pages than DOS supports for that device. Check CONFIG.SYS to see how many prepared code pages your device command line allows, or issue MODE /STATUS at the command line (for example, MODE /STATUS CON) to view the code pages already prepared for the device.

Compare error at offset *xxxxxxxx*

> INFORMATION: The files you are comparing are not the same. The difference occurs at *xxxxxxxx* bytes from the beginning of the file. The number of bytes as well as the values for the differing bytes are given in hexadecimal format (base 16).

Compare error on side *s*, track *t*

> INFORMATION: DISKCOMP has located a difference on the disk in the specified drive on side *s*, at track *t*.

Compare process ended

> ERROR: A fatal error occurred during the comparison operation.

Comparing *t* tracks *n* sectors per track, *s* side(s)

> INFORMATION: This message confirms the format of the disks you are comparing.

X contains *n* non-contiguous blocks

>WARNING: CHKDSK found noncontiguous blocks on drive *X*. If you like, you can use a defragmenter to eliminate the fragmentation, or use COPY or XCOPY to transfer the fragmented files to a freshly formatted floppy disk in a sequential form.

Configuration too large for memory

>ERROR (start-up): DOS could not load because you set too many FILES or BUFFERS in your CONFIG.SYS file or specified too large an environment area (/E) with the SHELL command. This problem occurs only on systems with less than 256K.

>Restart DOS with a different configuration; then edit the CONFIG.SYS file on your boot disk, lowering the number of FILES, BUFFERS, or both. You also can edit CONFIG.SYS to reduce the size of the environment in addition to or as an alternative to lowering the number of FILES and BUFFERS. Restart DOS with the edited disk.

>Another alternative is to increase the RAM in your system.

Content of destination lost before copy

>ERROR: The original contents of the destination file for the COPY (concatenation) operation were overwritten because the destination and one of the source files had the same name. You may be able to recover the file with UNDELETE; if not, you can restore the destination file from your backup disk.

Copy process ended

>ERROR: The DISKCOPY process ended before completion. Test with CHKDSK, then copy the remaining files onto the disk with COPY or XCOPY.

Current code page settings:

>INFORMATION: You issued the MODE command with a specified device. If you want to see code settings for all devices, type MODE without listing a device.

Current CON code page: *xxx*

>INFORMATION: This message displays the current keyboard code and code page along with the current code page used by the console screen device (CON).

`Current drive is no longer valid`

WARNING: The system prompt includes the meta-symbol $p, to display current directory, or $n, to display current drive. You tried to change the default drive to a drive that isn't valid (for example, you tried to make floppy drive current without a floppy present). DOS presented you with an error message, `Abort`, `Retry, Fail?`. When you responded *Fail*, DOS temporarily changed the prompt to the above message.

The invalid drive error also occurs when a current networked or SUBST disk drive is deleted or disconnected. Simply change the current drive to a valid disk drive.

`Current keyboard does not support this code page`

ERROR: You selected a code page incompatible with the current keyboard code. First, check the selected code page. If the code page is correct, change the keyboard code with KEYB.

`Device ddd not prepared`

ERROR: No code page is present for this device.

`Disk boot failure`

ERROR (start-up): An error occurred when DOS tried to load into memory. The disk contained IO.SYS and MSDOS.SYS, but one of the two files could not be loaded.

Try starting DOS from the disk again. If the error recurs, try starting DOS from a disk you know is good, such as a copy of your DOS start-up or master disk. If DOS still fails to boot, you have a disk drive problem. Contact your dealer.

`Disk full. Edits lost.`

ERROR: Edlin cannot save your work to disk because the designated disk is full. Always make sure that you have a disk with plenty of room to save your files.

`Disk unsuitable for system disk`

WARNING: FORMAT detected one or more bad sectors on the floppy disk in the area where DOS normally resides. Because the portion of the disk where DOS must reside is unusable, you cannot boot DOS from this disk.

Try reformatting the disk. Some floppy disks format successfully the second time. If FORMAT gives this message again, you cannot boot from the disk.

Divide overflow

ERROR: DOS aborted a program that attempted to divide by zero. The program was incorrectly entered or contains a logic flaw. If you wrote the program, correct the error and try the program again. If you purchased the program, report the problem to the dealer or publisher.

This message also may appear when you attempt to format a RAM disk with DOS 3.0 or 3.1. Make sure that you are formatting the correct disk and try again.

Do not specify filename(s) Command format: DISKCOMP [drive1: [drive2:]] [/1] [/8]

ERROR: You typed an incorrect switch or added one or more file names with the DISKCOMP command. DISKCOMP syntax does not accept file names on the command line.

Do not specify filename(s) Command Format: DISKCOPY [drive1: [drive2:]] [/1] [/V]

ERROR: You added an incorrect switch to the command or placed a file name in the command string. Retype the command, and press Enter.

DOS is in HMA

DOS is in low memory

INFORMATION: Most of the DOS system can be optionally loaded above the first megabyte in the HMA (High Memory Area), if you have at least a 286, have some available extended memory, and use the DOS=HIGH parameter in CONFIG.SYS. These messages tell you whether DOS is in the HMA or not.

DOS memory-arena error

ERROR: When you are using the DOS Editor, this message indicates a serious memory error. If possible, save your work to a different file and reboot your computer.

Drive assignment syntax error

ERROR: INTERLNK found a syntax error in its command line. Double-check the syntax with HELP INTERLNK.

Drive types or diskette types not compatible

ERROR: When using DISKCOMP or DISKCOPY, you specified two drives of different capacities. You cannot, for example, DISKCOMP or DISKCOPY from a 1.2M drive to a 360K drive. Retype the command using compatible drives.

`Duplicate filename or File not found`

> ERROR: While using RENAME (or REN), you attempted to change a file name to a name that already exists, or the file to be renamed did not exist in the directory. Check the directory to make sure that the file name exists and that you have spelled it correctly. Then try again.

`Enter current Volume Label for drive `*`d`*`:`

> WARNING: You are attempting to format a hard disk that has a volume label. Enter the exact volume label to proceed with the format; if you do not want to enter a volume label, press Enter, and FORMAT will quit.

`Error in COUNTRY command`

> WARNING (start-up): The COUNTRY command in CONFIG.SYS is improperly phrased or has an incorrect country code or code page number. DOS continues to load but uses the default information for the COUNTRY command.

> After DOS has started, check the COUNTRY line in your CONFIG.SYS file. Make sure that the command is correctly phrased (with commas between country code, code page, and COUNTRY.SYS file) and that any given information is correct. If you detect an error in the line, edit the line, save the file, and restart DOS.

> If you do not find an error, restart DOS. If the same message appears, edit CONFIG.SYS. Reenter the COUNTRY command and delete the old COUNTRY line. The old line may contain some nonsense characters that DOS can see but that are not apparent to your text-editing program.

`Error in EXE file`

> ERROR: DOS detected an error while attempting to load a program stored in an EXE file. The problem, which is in the relocation information DOS needs to load the program, may occur if the EXE file has been altered.

> Restart DOS and try the program again, this time using a backup copy of the program. If the message appears again, the program is flawed. If you are using a purchased program, contact the dealer or publisher. If you wrote the program, issue LINK to produce another copy of the program.

`Error loading operating system`

> ERROR (start-up): A disk error occurred when DOS was loading from the hard disk. DOS does not start.

Restart the computer. If the error occurs after several tries, restart DOS from the floppy disk drive. If the hard disk does not respond (that is, you cannot run DIR or CHKDSK without getting an error), you have a problem with the hard disk. Contact your dealer. If the hard disk does respond, place another copy of DOS on your hard disk by using SYS. You also may need to copy COMMAND.COM to the hard disk.

Increase to 15 or 20 the number of FILES in the CONFIG.SYS file of your start-up disk. Restart DOS. If the error recurs, you may have a problem with the disk. Try a backup copy of the program. If the backup works, copy the backup over the offending file.

If an error occurs in the copying process, you have a flawed disk. If the problem is a floppy disk, copy the files from the flawed disk to another disk and reformat or discard the original disk. If the problem is the hard disk, immediately back up your files and run RECOVER on the offending file. If the problem persists, your hard disk may be damaged.

Error reading directory

ERROR: During a FORMAT procedure, DOS was unable to read the directory; bad sectors may have developed in the file allocation table (FAT) structure.

If the message occurs when DOS is reading a floppy disk, the disk is unusable and should be thrown away. If DOS cannot read your hard disk, however, the problem is more serious, and you may have to reformat your disk. Remember to back up your data files regularly in order to prevent major losses.

Error reading (or writing) partition table

ERROR: DOS could not read from (or write to) the disk's partition table during the FORMAT operation because the partition table is corrupted. Run FDISK on the disk and reformat the disk.

Error writing to file on remote system

ERROR: INTERSVR has detected that the remote system (the one running INTERLNK) has a write error. The most likely reason is that the remote disk is full.

Extended Error

ERROR: COMMAND.COM has detected an error but cannot tell you the normal error message because the diskette containing COMMAND.COM is missing. (This error doesn't generally occur on a hard disk system.) To avoid these "anonymous" errors, use the /MSG switch on the SHELL= line of CONFIG.SYS.

```
File allocation table bad, drive d
Abort, Retry, Fail?
```

WARNING: DOS encountered a problem in the file allocation table of the disk in drive *d*. Press R to retry several times; if the message recurs, press A to abort.

If you are using a floppy disk, try to copy all the files to another disk, and then reformat or discard the original disk. If you are using a hard disk, back up files on the disk, and then reformat it. You cannot use the disk until you have reformatted it.

```
File cannot be copied onto itself
```

ERROR: You attempted to copy a file to a disk and directory containing the same file name. This error often occurs when you misspell or omit parts of the source or destination drive, path, or file name; this error also may occur when you are using wild-card characters for file names, or when you used SUBST. Check your spelling and the source and destination names, and then try the command again.

```
File creation error
```

ERROR: A program or DOS failed to add a new file to the directory or to replace an existing file.

If the file already exists, issue the ATTRIB command to check whether the file is marked as read-only. If the read-only flag is set and you want to change or erase the file, remove the read-only flag with ATTRIB; then try again. If the problem occurs when the read-only flag is not set, run CHKDSK without the /F switch to determine whether the directory is full, the disk is full, or some other problem exists with the disk.

```
File not found
```

ERROR: DOS could not find the specified file. The file is not on the current disk or directory, or you specified the disk drive name, path name, or file name incorrectly. Check these possibilities and try the command again.

```
filename device driver cannot be initialized
```

WARNING (start-up): In CONFIG.SYS, the parameters in the device driver file name or the syntax of the DEVICE line is incorrect. Check for incorrect parameters and phrasing errors in the DEVICE line. Edit the DEVICE line in the CONFIG.SYS file, save the file, and restart DOS.

FIRST diskette bad or incompatible

> or

SECOND diskette bad or incompatible

> ERROR: One of these messages may appear when you issue
> DISKCOMP. The messages indicate that the FIRST (source) or the
> SECOND (target) floppy disk is unreadable, or that the disks you
> are attempting to compare have different format densities.

Format not supported on drive *x*:

> ERROR: You cannot use the FORMAT command on the specified
> drive. If you entered device driver parameters that your computer
> cannot support, DOS displays this message. Check CONFIG.SYS
> for bad DEVICE or DRIVPARM commands.

Formatting while copying

> INFORMATION: DISKCOPY displays this message as it copies data
> to an unformatted disk.

Illegal device name

> ERROR: DOS does not recognize the device name you entered
> with the MODE command.

Incorrect DOS Version

> ERROR: The copy of the file holding the command you just
> entered is from a different version of DOS.
>
> Get a copy of the command from the correct version of DOS
> (usually from your copy of the DOS start-up or master disk), and
> try the command again. If the disk you are using has been updated
> to hold new versions of DOS, copy the new versions over the old
> ones.

Insert disk with batch file
and strike any key when ready

> PROMPT: DOS attempted to execute the next command from a
> batch file, but the disk holding the batch file is not in the disk
> drive. This message occurs for DOS 3.1 and later versions. DOS 3.0
> gives a fatal error when the disk is changed.

`Insert the disk with the batch file into the disk drive, and press a key to continue.`

`Insert disk with \COMMAND.COM in drive` *d*
`and strike any key when ready`

> PROMPT: DOS needs to reload COMMAND.COM but cannot find it on the start-up disk. If you are using floppy disks, the disk in drive *d* (usually A) has probably been changed. Place a disk with a good copy of COMMAND.COM in drive *d*, and press a key.

`Insert diskette for drive` *x* `and press`
`any key when ready`

> PROMPT: On a system with one floppy disk drive or a system in which DRIVER.SYS creates more than one logical disk drive from a physical disk drive, you or one of your programs specified a tandem disk drive *x* (such as A or B) that is different from the current disk drive.

> If the correct disk is in the disk drive, press a key. Otherwise, insert the correct disk into the floppy disk drive, and then press a key.

`Insufficient disk space`

> WARNING, ERROR: The disk does not have enough free space to hold the file being written. All DOS programs terminate when this problem occurs, but some non-DOS programs continue.

> If you think that the disk should have enough room to hold the file, run CHKDSK to determine whether the disk has a problem. When you terminate programs early by pressing Ctrl-Break, DOS may not be able to do the necessary clean-up work, leaving some disk space temporarily trapped. CHKDSK can free these areas.

> If you have simply run out of disk space, free some disk space or insert a different disk; then try the command again.

`Insufficient memory to store macro. Use the DOSKEY command`
`with the /BUFSIZE switch to increase available memory.`

> WARNING: Your DOSKey macros have filled the total space set aside for them. You must enlarge the memory area for macros (the default is 512 bytes) by using the BUFSIZE switch before you can enter any new macros.

`Intermediate file error during pipe`

> ERROR: DOS cannot create or write to one or both of the intermediate files it uses when piping information between programs because the disk is full, the root directory of the current disk is full,

or the TEMP environment variable points to an illegal path. The most frequent cause is insufficient disk space.

Run DIR on the root directory of the current disk drive to make sure that you have enough room in the root directory for two additional files. If you do not have enough room, make room by deleting or copying and deleting files. You also can copy the necessary files to a different disk with sufficient room.

This error also may occur if a program is deleting files, including the temporary files DOS creates. In this case, correct the program, contact the dealer or program publisher, or avoid using the program with piping.

Internal stack overflow
System halted

ERROR: Your programs and DOS have exhausted the stack, the memory space reserved for temporary use. This problem is usually caused by a rapid succession of hardware devices demanding attention. DOS stops, and the system must be turned off and on again to restart DOS.

The circumstances that cause this message are generally infrequent and erratic, and they may not recur. If you want to prevent this error from occurring, add the STACKS command to your CONFIG.SYS file. If the command is already in your CONFIG.SYS file, increase the number of stacks specified.

Invalid /BAUD parameter

WARNING: You have selected an illegal baud rate for either INTERLNK or INTERSVR. For example, you have /BAUD:9200 instead of /BAUD:9600.

Invalid characters in volume label

ERROR: You attempted to enter more than 11 alphanumeric characters, or you entered illegal characters (+, =, /, \ , and |, for example) when you typed the disk's volume label (the disk name). Retype the volume label with valid characters.

Invalid COMMAND.COM in drive *d*:

WARNING: DOS tried to reload COMMAND.COM from the disk in drive *d* and found that the file was from a different version of DOS. Follow the instructions for inserting a disk with the correct version.

If you frequently use the disk that generated this warning message, copy the correct version of COMMAND.COM to that disk.

`Invalid COMMAND.COM, system halted`

ERROR: DOS could not find COMMAND.COM on the hard disk. DOS halts and must be restarted.

COMMAND.COM may have been erased, or the COMSPEC variable in the environment may have been changed. Restart the computer from the hard disk. If a message indicates that COMMAND.COM is missing, the file was erased. Restart DOS from a floppy disk, and copy COMMAND.COM to the root directory of the hard disk or to the location your SHELL command indicates, if you have placed this command in your CONFIG.SYS file.

If you restart DOS and this message appears later, a program or batch file is erasing COMMAND.COM or altering the COMSPEC variable. If a program is erasing COMMAND.COM, contact the dealer or publisher who sold you the program. If a batch file is erasing COMMAND.COM, edit the batch file. If COMSPEC is being altered, edit the offending batch file or program, or place COMMAND.COM in the subdirectory your program or batch file expects.

`Invalid COUNTRY code or code page`

WARNING (start-up): The COUNTRY code number or the code page number given to the COUNTRY command in CONFIG.SYS is incorrect or incompatible. DOS ignores the COUNTRY command and continues the start-up process.

Check the COUNTRY command in your CONFIG.SYS file (see Chapter 20, "Understanding the International Features of DOS") to determine whether the correct and compatible country code and code page numbers are specified. If you detect an error, edit and save the file. Then restart DOS.

`Invalid date`

ERROR: You gave an impossible date or an invalid character to separate the month, day, and year. This message also appears if you enter the date from the keypad when it is not in numeric mode.

`Invalid device parameters from device driver`

ERROR: The partition did not fall on a track boundary. You may have set the DEVICE drivers incorrectly in CONFIG.SYS or attempted to format a hard disk formatted with DOS 2.x so that the total number of hidden sectors is not evenly divisible by the number of sectors on a track. Therefore, the partition may not start on a track boundary.

To correct the error, run FDISK before performing a format, or check CONFIG.SYS for a bad DEVICE or DRIVPARM command.

Invalid directory

ERROR: One of the following occurred: you specified a directory name that does not exist, you misspelled the directory name, the directory path is on a different disk, you did not give the path character (\ ) at the beginning of the name, or you did not separate the directory names with the path character. Check your directory names to make sure that the directory exists, and try the command again.

Invalid disk change
Abort, Retry, Fail?

WARNING: A diskette was changed while a program had open files to be written to the diskette. Place the correct disk in the disk drive, and press R to retry. Typically this check is supported on drives bigger than 360K.

Invalid drive in search path

WARNING: You specified an invalid disk drive name in the PATH command, or a disk drive you named is nonexistent or hidden temporarily by a SUBST or JOIN command.

Use PATH to check the paths you instructed DOS to search. If you gave a nonexistent disk drive name, issue the PATH command again with the correct search paths. If the problem is temporary because of a SUBST or JOIN command, you can run PATH, leaving out or correcting the wrong entry. Or you can just ignore the warning message.

Invalid drive or file name

ERROR: You gave the name of a nonexistent disk drive, or you mistyped the disk drive or file name.

Remember that certain DOS commands (such as SUBST and JOIN) temporarily hide disk drive names while the command is in effect. Check the disk drive name you gave, and try the command again.

Invalid drive specification

ERROR: One of the following occurred: you entered an invalid or nonexistent disk drive as a parameter to a command; you specified the same disk drive for the source and destination; or by not giving a parameter, you defaulted to the same disk drive for the source and the destination.

Remember that some DOS commands (such as SUBST and JOIN) temporarily hide disk drive names while the command is in effect. Check the disk drive names. If the command is objecting to a missing parameter and defaulting to the wrong disk drive, name the correct disk drive explicitly.

```
Invalid drive specification
Specified drive does not exist
or is non-removable
```

ERROR: One of the following occurred: you gave the name of a nonexistent disk drive, you named the hard disk drive when using commands for floppy disks only, you did not give a disk drive name and defaulted to the hard disk when using commands for floppy disks only, or you named or defaulted to a RAM disk drive when using commands for an actual floppy disk.

Remember that certain DOS commands (such as SUBST and JOIN) temporarily hide disk drive names while the command is in effect. Check the disk drive name you gave, and try the command again.

```
Invalid keyboard code specified
```

ERROR: You selected an invalid code. Enter the KEYB command again with the correct keyboard code.

```
Invalid macro definition
```

ERROR: You entered an illegal character or command with DOSKey or attempted to create a DOSKey macro with an illegal definition. This message appears, for example, if you use a GOTO command in a DOSKey macro. Correct any errors, and carefully retype the macro.

```
Invalid media or Track 0 bad - disk unusable
```

ERROR: A disk you are trying to format may be damaged. A disk may not format the first time. Try to format again; if the same message appears, the disk is bad and should be discarded. With some versions of FORMAT, this same symptom can be caused by memory boundary problems. If the symptom occurs for multiple diskettes, try changing the number or sizes of TSRs to see whether the symptoms change.

```
Invalid number of parameters
```

ERROR: You have given too few or too many parameters to a command. One of the following occurred: you omitted required information, you omitted a colon immediately after the disk drive name, you inserted an extra space, you omitted a required space, or you omitted a slash (/) in front of a switch.

Invalid parameter

ERROR: At least one parameter you entered for the command is not valid. One of the following occurred: you omitted required information, you omitted a colon immediately after the disk drive name, you inserted an extra space, you omitted a required space, you omitted a slash (/) in front of a switch, or you used a switch the command does not recognize. For more information, check the explanation of this message in the Command Reference for the command you issued.

Invalid parameter combination

You typed conflicting parameters with a DOS command. Retype the command with only one of the conflicting switches.

Invalid partition table

ERROR (start-up): DOS has detected a problem in the hard disk's partition information. Restart DOS from a floppy disk. Back up all files from the hard disk, if possible, and run FDISK to correct the problem. If you change the partition information, you must reformat the hard disk and restore all its files.

Invalid path

ERROR: One of the following problems exists: the path name contains illegal characters, the name has more than 63 characters, or a directory name within the path is misspelled or does not exist.

Check the spelling of the path name. If necessary, check the disk directory with DIR to make sure that the directory you have specified exists and that you have specified the correct path name. Make sure that the path name contains no more than 63 characters. If necessary, change the current directory to a directory "closer" to the file to shorten the path name.

Invalid path or file name

ERROR: You gave a directory name or file name that does not exist, specified the wrong directory name (a directory not on the path), or mistyped a name. COPY aborts when it encounters an invalid path or file name. If you specified a wild card for a file name, COPY transfers all valid files before it issues the error message.

Check to see which files have been transferred. Determine whether the directory and file names are spelled correctly and whether the path is correct. Then try again.

`Invalid STACK parameters`

WARNING (start-up): One of the following problems exists with the STACKS command in your CONFIG.SYS file: a comma is missing between the number of stacks and the size of the stack, the number of stack frames is not in the range of 8 through 64, the stack size is not in the range of 32 through 512, you have omitted the number of stack frames or the stack size, or the stack frame or the stack size (but not both) is 0. DOS continues to start but ignores the STACKS command.

Check the STACKS command in your CONFIG.SYS file. Edit and save the file; then restart DOS.

`Invalid time`

ERROR: You gave an impossible time or invalid character to separate the hour, minute, and second. This message also appears if you enter the time from the keypad when it is not in numeric mode.

`Invalid Volume ID`

ERROR: When formatting a fixed (or hard) disk, you entered an incorrect volume label, and DOS aborted the format attempt. Type **VOL** at the C prompt and press Enter to view the volume label of the disk, and try the command again.

`Memory allocation error`
`Cannot load COMMAND, system halted`

ERROR: A program destroyed the area where DOS keeps track of memory. You must restart DOS. If this error occurs again with the same program, the program has a flaw. Try a backup copy of the program. If the problem persists, contact the dealer or program publisher.

`Missing operating system`

ERROR (start-up): The DOS hard disk partition entry is marked as bootable (capable of starting DOS), but the DOS partition does not contain a copy of DOS. DOS does not start.

Start DOS from a floppy disk. Issue the SYS C: command to place DOS on the hard disk, and then copy COMMAND.COM to the disk. If this command fails to solve the problem, you must back up the existing files, if any, from the hard disk; then issue FORMAT /S to place a copy of the operating system on the hard disk. If necessary, restore the files you backed up.

`MSBACKUP program files must be located on your hard disk.`
`You cannot start MSBACKUP from a floppy disk.`

> ERROR: MSBACKUP relies on being able to repeatedly access its
> program files during the backup operation. You must start it from
> a hard disk so that the program files will be available throughout
> the process. Change the default drive to the hard disk before
> starting MSBACKUP.

`Must enter both /T and /N parameters`

> ERROR: On FORMAT, you must specify /T (number of tracks per
> side) and /N (number of sectors per disk) on the same command
> line. If you include the one, you must include the other.

`No drive letters redirected`

> INFORMATION: INTERLNK isn't currently redirecting any drive
> letters to the remote system.

`No free file handles`
`Cannot start COMMAND, exiting`

> ERROR: DOS could not load an additional copy of COMMAND.COM
> because no file handles were available. Edit the CONFIG.SYS file
> on your start-up disk to increase by five the number of file handles
> (using the FILES command). Restart DOS, and try the command
> again.

`No printer ports letters redirected`

> INFORMATION: INTERLNK isn't currently redirecting any printer
> ports to the remote system.

`No room for system on destination disk`

> ERROR: This error isn't nearly so prevalent in DOS 6.0. SYS rear-
> ranges the files as needed to make a system bootable, but issues
> this error if there is insufficient room or if the root directory is
> full.

`Non-System disk or disk error`
`Replace and strike any key when ready`

> ERROR (start-up): Your disk does not contain IO.SYS and
> MSDOS.SYS, or a read error occurred when you started the sys-
> tem. DOS does not start.

> If you are using a floppy disk system, insert a bootable disk into
> drive A, and press a key. The most frequent cause of this message
> on hard disk systems is leaving a nonbootable disk in drive A with
> the door closed. Open the door to disk drive A, and press a key.
> DOS boots from the hard disk.

No serial ports were found

> ERROR: You specified the /COM switch on INTERSVR, but no serial ports are available. This could happen if a TSR (resident program) has taken control of the available port, or if the hardware is configured to an invalid address.

No system on default drive

> ERROR: SYS cannot find the system files. Insert a disk containing the system files, such as the DOS disk, and type the command again. If the system files are available on another drive, issue the other form of the SYS command, indicating the location of the system files.

Not enough memory

> or

Insufficient memory

> ERROR: The computer does not have enough free RAM to execute the program or command. If you loaded a resident program, such as PRINT, GRAPHICS, SideKick, or ProKey, restart DOS, and try the command again before loading any resident program. If this method fails to solve the problem, remove any nonessential device drivers or RAM disk software from CONFIG.SYS and restart DOS. If this option also fails, your computer does not have enough memory for this command. You must increase your RAM memory to run the command.

Out of environment space

> WARNING: DOS cannot add additional strings to the environment from the SET command because the environment cannot be expanded. This error occurs when you are loading a resident program, such as MODE, PRINT, GRAPHICS, SideKick, or ProKey.

> If you are running DOS 3.1 or later, refer to the SHELL command in Chapter 15, "Understanding Batch Files, DOSKey, and Macros," (on customizing DOS) for information about expanding the default space for the environment. DOS 3.0 has no method for expanding the environment.

Out of memory

> ERROR: The amount of memory is insufficient to perform the operation you requested. This error occurs in the DOS 5.0 Editor.

`Packed File Corrupt`

> ERROR: The program appears to be damaged. A common cause
> for this symptom is older format packed executables, which could
> not load into the first 64K of conventional memory. With older
> operating system versions, the resident portion of the system
> generally used enough memory that this wasn't a problem. In DOS
> 5.0 and DOS 6.0, the DOS=HIGH, DEVICEHIGH, and LOADHIGH fea-
> tures can reduce memory usage enough that this problem occurs
> with certain programs. Use the LOADFIX command to temporarily
> use up enough memory that the program is loaded at a location it
> can manage.

`Parameters not supported`

> or

`Parameters not supported by drive`

> ERROR: You entered parameters that do not exist, that are not
> supported by the DOS version you are running, or that are in-
> compatible with the specified disk drive. Run VER to determine
> whether the current DOS version supports the parameters
> (or switches) you specified.

`Parameters not compatible`
`with fixed disk`

> ERROR: A device driver for a hard disk does not support generic
> IOCtl functions.

`Parse Error`

> ERROR: COMMAND.COM has detected an error but cannot tell
> you the normal error message because the diskette containing
> COMMAND.COM is missing. (This error doesn't generally occur
> on a hard disk system.) To avoid these "anonymous" errors, use
> the /MSG switch on the SHELL= line of CONFIG.SYS.

`Path not found`

> ERROR: A specified file or directory path does not exist. You may
> have misspelled the file name or directory name, or you may have
> omitted a path character (\) between directory names or between
> the final directory name and the file name. Another possibility is
> that the file or directory does not exist in the place specified.
> Check these possibilities, and try again.

`Path too long`

> ERROR: You have given a path name that exceeds the DOS 63-character limit, or you omitted a space between file names. Check the command line. If the phrasing is correct, you must change to a directory "closer" to the file you want and try the command again.

`Program too big to fit in memory`

> ERROR: The computer does not have enough memory to load the program or the command you invoked. If you have any resident programs loaded (such as PRINT, GRAPHICS, or SideKick), restart DOS, and try the command again without loading the resident programs. If this message appears again, reduce the number of buffers (BUFFERS) in the CONFIG.SYS file, eliminate nonessential device drivers or RAM disk software, and restart DOS. If the problem persists, your computer does not have enough RAM for the program or command. You must increase the amount of RAM in your computer to run the program.

`Required parameter missing`

> ERROR: Many DOS commands give this error when you omit part of the parameter list. You may have specified only a single name with the MOVE command, for example.

`Same parameter entered twice`

> ERROR: You duplicated a switch when you typed a command. Retype the command using the parameter only once.

`Sector size too large in file filename`

> WARNING: The device driver *filename* is inconsistent. The device driver defined a particular sector size for DOS but attempted to use a different size. The copy of the device driver is bad, or the device driver is incorrect. Make a fresh copy of the device driver from its master copy, and then reboot DOS. If the message appears again, the device driver is incorrect. If you wrote the driver, correct the error. If you purchased the program, contact the dealer or software publisher.

`SOURCE diskette bad or incompatible`

> ERROR: The disk you attempted to read during a copy process was damaged or in the wrong format (for example, a high-density disk in a double-density disk drive). DOS cannot read the disk.

`Specified COM port number not recognized by BIOS`

ERROR: The port number is legal, but your ROM BIOS doesn't support it. Generally, this can happen with older BIOS that only support two COM ports. Either replace the BIOS or use a different port.

`Syntax error`

ERROR: You phrased a command improperly by omitting needed information, giving extraneous information, inserting an extra space into a file or path name, or using an incorrect switch. Check the command line for these possibilities, and try the command again.

`TARGET diskette bad or incompatible`

or

`Target diskette may be unusable`

or

`Target diskette unusable`

ERROR: A problem exists with the target disk. DOS does not recognize the format of the target disk in the drive, or the disk is defective. Make sure that the target disk is the same density as the source disk, run CHKDSK on the target disk to determine the problem, or try to reformat the disk before proceeding with the disk copy operation.

`TARGET media has lower capacity than SOURCE`
`Continue anyway (Y/N)?`

WARNING: The target disk can hold fewer bytes of data than the source disk. The most likely cause is bad sectors on the target disk. If you press Y, some data on the source disk may not fit onto the target disk.

To avoid the possibility of an incomplete transfer of data, type **N**, and insert a disk with the same capacity as the source disk. If you are not copying "hidden" files, you also can issue the COPY *.* command to transfer files.

`This program requires Microsoft Windows`

ERROR: You tried to run a program at the DOS prompt that needs Microsoft Windows to execute. If you're already running Windows, use Alt-Tab to switch to the Program Manager, and start it from there. If you haven't started Windows, use WIN to do so.

There are no serial ports or parallel ports available for
communication

> ERROR: INTRSVR cannot find any serial ports or any parallel ports
> that are not already in use. Without such a port, INTRSVR cannot
> communicate with INTRLNK.

Too many block devices

> WARNING (start-up): Your CONFIG.SYS file contains too many
> DEVICE commands. DOS continues to start but does not install
> additional device drivers.

> DOS can handle only 26 block devices. The block devices created
> by the DEVICE commands plus the number of block devices auto-
> matically created by DOS exceed this number. Remove any unnec-
> essary DEVICE commands from your CONFIG.SYS file and restart
> DOS.

Too many parallel ports, port ignored

> WARNING: INTERLNK cannot automatically scan this many
> parallel ports. The earlier ones will be used.

Too many serial ports, port ignored

> WARNING: INTERLNK cannot automatically scan this many serial
> ports. The earlier ones will be used.

Top level process aborted, cannot continue

> ERROR (start-up): COMMAND.COM or another DOS command
> detected a disk error, and you chose the A (Abort) option. DOS
> cannot finish starting itself, and the system halts.

> Try to start DOS again. If the error recurs, start DOS from a floppy
> disk (if starting from the hard disk) or from a different floppy disk
> (if starting from a floppy disk). After DOS has started, issue the
> SYS command to place another copy of the operating system on
> the disk, and copy COMMAND.COM to the disk. If DOS reports an
> error while copying, the disk is bad. Reformat or discard the
> floppy disk or back up and reformat the hard disk.

There is not enough room to create a restore file
You will not be able to use the unformat utility
Proceed with Format (Y/N)?

> WARNING: The disk lacks sufficient room to create a restore file.
> Without this file, you cannot use UNFORMAT to reverse the for-
> mat you are attempting.

Trying to recover allocation unit *nnn*

> INFORMATION, WARNING: A bad allocation unit was found when the FORMAT command executed.

Unable to create destination

> ERROR: MOVE was unable to create the destination file. Possible reasons are that the destination drive is full or that the destination is the root directory, which lacks room.

Unable to create directory

> ERROR: You or a program could not create a directory for one of the following reasons: a directory by the same name already exists; a file by the same name already exists; you are adding a directory to the root directory, and the root directory is full; or the directory name has illegal characters or is a device name.

> Issue DIR to make sure that no file or directory already exists with the same name. If you are adding the directory to the root directory, remove or move (copy, then erase) any nonessential files or directories. Check the spelling of the directory name, and make sure that the command is properly phrased.

Unable to initialize serial port COM*n*

> ERROR: INTRSVR was unable to initialize the specified serial port. The most common reason is that two devices in the system have the same port address.

Unable to load MS-DOS Shell, Retry (y/n)?

> ERROR, PROMPT: DOS could not load the Shell. You may be using a DOS command-line feature of a program, and the Shell does not fit into memory. The DOS Shell program also may be corrupted.

> Exit the program, and try to load the Shell. If the Shell still doesn't load, it probably is corrupt. Reboot your system and load the Shell. If the same error message appears, copy the Shell from a backup disk to your hard disk.

[Unable to open source]

> ERROR: MOVE was unable to open the specified source file. This could be due to an illegal character in the file name, but the more common cause is trying to move a directory to a different place in the disk hierarchy. You may rename a directory with the MOVE command but not actually move it.

Unable to read source

> ERROR: A disk problem occurred while transferring the data from source file to destination. Use COPY to copy the file, compare it, and then delete the original.

Unable to write BOOT

> ERROR: FORMAT cannot write to the BOOT track or DOS partition of the disk that is being formatted because one of these areas is bad. Discard the bad disk, insert another unformatted disk, and try the FORMAT command again.

Unable to write destination

> ERROR: A disk problem occurred while transferring the data from source file to destination. Double-check that the destination disk has sufficient room for the file. If the error still occurs, use COPY.

Unrecognized command in CONFIG.SYS

Error in CONFIG.SYS line *nnn*

> WARNING (start-up): DOS detected an improperly phrased command in CONFIG.SYS. The command is ignored, and DOS continues to start. Examine the indicated line in the CONFIG.SYS file, looking for an improperly phrased or incorrect command. Edit the line, save the file, and restart DOS.

Unrecognized switch

> ERROR: You have tried to use a switch that was illegal for the particular internal command. Type the command followed by /? to find out what options are permitted.

Unrecoverable read error on drive *x* side *n*, track *n*

> ERROR: DOS was unable to read the data at the specified location on the disk. DOS makes four attempts before generating this message. Copy all files on the questionable disk to another disk, and try the command again, first with a new disk and then with the backup disk. If the original disk cannot be reformatted, discard it.

Unrecoverable transmission errors, maximum retries exceeded

> ERROR: INTRSVR is getting excessive errors on the communication cable to INTERLNK. Check that the connections are screwed in tightly, and that the cable is not routed too close to electrical interference, such as an arc welder.

Unrecoverable write error on drive *x* side *n*, track *n*

> ERROR: DOS was unable to write to a disk at the location specified. Try the command again; if the error recurs, the target disk is damaged at that location. If the damaged disk contains important data, copy the files to an empty, freshly formatted disk, and try to reformat the damaged disk. If the disk is bad, discard it.

WARNING: Unable to use a disk cache on the specified drive

> WARNING: You specified a drive to Smartdrv that isn't a normal block device. Neither network devices nor CD-ROM drives can normally be cached. Smartdrv ignores this drive letter.

Write failure, diskette unusable

> ERROR: DOS found bad sectors in the boot or FAT areas of the target disk. Discard the disk, and use another to create a System disk.

You have started the Interlnk server in a task-switching environment. Task-switching, key combinations, and some disk-writing operations are disabled

To restore these functions, exit the server

> WARNING: INTERLNK cannot permit certain things to happen while it is in control. One of these is DOSSHELL's capability to switch tasks. If INTERLNK got swapped while communicating with the INTERSVR, it could mean loss of data. So INTERLNK inhibits these operations until it completes.

You must specify the host drive for a DoubleSpace drive

> ERROR: SMARTDRV must be given the host drive letter to cache; the compressed drive will also be cached, and the effective cache size is increased because of the compression. You cannot separately cache the compressed drive.

DOS Device Error Messages

When DOS detects an error while reading or writing to disk drives or other devices, one of the following messages appears, usually followed by Abort, Retry, Fail? or Abort,Retry,Ignore?:

type error reading *device*

type error writing *device*

> *type* is the type of error, and *device* is the device at fault. If the device is a floppy disk drive, do not remove the disk from the drive. Refer to the possible causes and corrective actions described in this section, which lists the types of error messages that may appear.

/B invalid with a black and white printer

> You issued the GRAPHICS command with the /B switch, which indicates a background color. You cannot print a background color on a black-and-white printer.

Bad call format

> A device driver was given a requested header with an incorrect length. The problem is the applications software making the call.

Bad command

> The device driver issued an invalid or unsupported command to the device. The problem may be with the device driver software or with other software trying to use the device driver. If you wrote the program, correct it. If you purchased the program, contact the dealer or publisher who sold you the program.

Bad unit

> An invalid subunit number was passed to the device driver. The problem may be with the device driver software or with other software trying to use the device driver. Contact the dealer who sold you the device driver.

Data

> DOS could not correctly read or write the data. The disk has probably developed a defective spot.

Drive not ready

> An error occurred when DOS tried to read or write to the disk drive. For floppy disk drives, the drive door may be open, the floppy disk may not have been inserted, or the disk may not be formatted. For hard disk drives, the drive may not be prepared properly; that is, you may have a hardware problem.

FCB unavailable

With the file-sharing program (SHARE.EXE) loaded, a program using the DOS 1 method of file handling attempted to open concurrently more file control blocks than were specified with the FCBS command.

Select the Abort option (see the end of this section). Increase the value of the FCBS CONFIG.SYS command (usually by four), and reboot the system. If the message appears again, increase the value again, and reboot.

General failure

This message is a catchall for errors not covered elsewhere. The error usually occurs for one of the following reasons: you are using an unformatted disk; the disk drive door is open; the floppy disk is not seated properly; or you are using the wrong type of disk in a disk drive, such as a 360K disk in a 1.2M disk drive.

Lock violation

With the file-sharing program (SHARE.EXE) or the network software loaded, a program attempted to access a locked file. Your best choice is Retry. Then try Abort. If you press A, however, any data in memory is probably lost.

Must specify COM1, COM2, COM3 or COM4

You must specify the COM port in this form of the MODE command.

No paper

The printer is out of paper or not turned on.

Non-DOS disk

The FAT has invalid information, making the disk unstable. You can abort and run CHKDSK to determine whether corrective action is possible. If CHKDSK fails, you can reformat the disk. Reformatting, however, destroys any remaining information on the disk. If the disk seems to be working correctly, do an extra backup before reformatting.

If you use more than one operating system, the disk has probably been formatted under the other operating system and should not be reformatted.

Not ready

> The device is not ready and cannot receive or transmit data. Check the connections, making sure that the power is on and the device is ready. For floppy disk drives, make sure that the disk is formatted and properly seated in the disk drive.

Read fault

> DOS was unable to read the data, probably from a disk. Check the disk drive doors to make sure that the disk is inserted properly.

Sector not found

> The disk drive was unable to find the sector on the disk. This error is usually the result of a defective spot on the disk or of defective drive electronics. Some copy-protection schemes also use a defective spot to prevent unauthorized duplication of the disk.

Seek

> The disk drive could not find the proper track on the disk. This error is usually the result of a defective spot on the disk, an unformatted disk, or drive electronics problems.

Write fault

> DOS could not write the data to this device. You may have inserted the disk improperly or left the disk drive door open. Another possibility is an electronics failure in the floppy or hard disk drive. The most frequent cause is a bad spot on the disk.

Write protect

> The disk is write-protected. DOS is attempting to write to this disk. If the disk is a floppy, and if the write is intentional, the disk may be removed, the write-protect tab adjusted, and the same disk replaced. Don't ever switch diskettes at this prompt, unless you know for sure that the program can handle it. Normally, you should either use A for abort, or R for retry (after fixing the write-protect on the same diskette).

Responding to Error Messages

One of the previously listed messages (usually Data, Read fault, or Write fault) appears when you are using a double-sided disk in a single-sided disk drive or a 9-sector disk (DOS 2 and later) with a version of DOS 1.

DOS displays one of these error messages and the Abort, Retry, Fail? prompt for DOS 3.3 and higher, or Abort,Retry,Ignore? for versions of DOS before 3.3.

If you press A for Abort, DOS ends the program that requested the read or write condition. Pressing R for Retry causes DOS to try the operation again. If you press F for Fail or I for Ignore, DOS skips the operation, and the program continues. Some data may be lost, however, when you select Fail or Ignore.

The order of preference, unless stated differently under the message, is R, A, and F or I. Retry the operation at least twice. If the condition persists, you must decide whether to abort the program or ignore the error. If you ignore the error, data may be lost. If you abort, data still being processed by the program and not yet written to the disk is lost.

Changes between Versions of DOS

T his appendix briefly describes all the changes in the seven versions between DOS 2.0 and DOS 6.0.

Changes between DOS 2.0 and DOS 3.0

DOS 3.0 offers several new commands, changed commands, and changed features.

New Configuration Commands

The following CONFIG.SYS commands are new in DOS 3.0:

COUNTRY	Enables you to change the way DOS displays the date, the time, and other information for international use
FCBS	Controls DOS's reactions to a program's use of DOS 1 file handling
LASTDRIVE	Sets the last disk-drive letter that DOS uses
VDISK.SYS	Provides a RAM (virtual) disk

Other New Commands

The following commands also are new in DOS 3.0:

ATTRIB	Enables you to set the read-only attribute of a file
GRAFTABL	Provides legible display of some graphics characters when you use the Color/Graphics Adapter in medium-resolution graphics mode
KEYB*xx*	Changes the keyboard layout for international character sets
LABEL	Enables you to add, change, or delete a disk's volume label
SELECT	Enables you to customize the start-up disk for use with international character sets other than English
SHARE	Provides file sharing (file and record locking)

Changed Commands

The following commands were changed between DOS 2.0 and DOS 3.0:

BACKUP/RESTORE	Backs up floppy disks; enables you to place backups on another hard disk
DATE/TIME	Supports international date and time formats
FORMAT	Includes the /4 switch to format 360K floppy disks on 1.2M disk drives; warns you when you are about to format a hard disk
GRAPHICS	Enables you to print graphics screens on some dot-matrix and color printers

Changed Features

With DOS 3.0, you can specify drive and path names before an external command or program name. Using this command format enables you to run programs that do not reside in the current directory or in a directory specified in the PATH command.

Changes between DOS 3.0 and DOS 3.1

The following changes were made between DOS 3.0 and 3.1.

New Commands

The following commands are new in DOS 3.1:

JOIN	Enables the user to connect the directory structures of two disk drives, creating "one" disk drive
SUBST	Enables you to use a subdirectory as a disk drive

New Feature

DOS 3.1 supports the IBM PC Network.

Changed Commands

The following commands were changed between DOS 3.0 and DOS 3.1:

LABEL	Prompts before deleting a volume label
TREE	/F displays file names with the directory tree

Changes between DOS 3.1 and DOS 3.2

The following changes were made between DOS 3.1 and DOS 3.2.

New Configuration Commands

The following CONFIG.SYS commands are new in DOS 3.2:

DRIVER.SYS	Supports different sizes of floppy disks, particularly 720K microfloppy drives on PCs
STACKS	Sets the number and size of DOS's internal stacks

Other New Commands

The following commands also were added in DOS 3.2:

REPLACE	Selectively updates files in one or many directories; adds missing files to a directory
XCOPY	Copies files from one or more directories to another; selectively copies files

Changed Commands

The following commands were changed between DOS 3.1 and DOS 3.2:

ATTRIB	+A/-A switch controls the archive attribute
COMMAND	/E supports the environment size (often used with the SHELL configuration command)
DISKCOMP	Supports 720K floppy disks
DISKCOPY	Supports 720K floppy disks
FORMAT	Supports formatting of 720K floppy disks; requests verification before you format a nonremovable disk that has a volume label; disk-drive name required
SELECT	Formats the hard disk and copies DOS files

New Feature

DOS 3.2 supports the IBM Token Ring.

Changes between DOS 3.2 and DOS 3.3

The following changes were made between DOS 3.2 and DOS 3.3.

New Configuration Commands

The following device drivers for use with the DEVICE configuration command are new in DOS 3.3:

DISPLAY.SYS	Supports code pages (multiple fonts) on EGA, VGA, and PC Convertible monitors
PRINTER.SYS	Supports code pages (multiple fonts) on the IBM ProPrinter and Quietwriter III

Other New Commands

The following commands also are new in DOS 3.3:

APPEND	Performs PATH-like function for data files
CHCP	Provides code-page changing
FASTOPEN	Provides a directory-caching program for hard disks
NLSFUNC	Provides support for additional international character sets (code pages)

Changed Commands

The following commands were changed between DOS 3.2 and DOS 3.3:

ATTRIB	/S changes the attributes of files in subdirectories
BACKUP	Places all backed-up files into a single file on each backup disk; /F formats floppy disks; /T backs up files based on their time; /L produces a log file

BUFFERS	Bases default buffers on the computer's RAM
COMMAND	Changes default environment size from 128 bytes to 160 bytes
COUNTRY	Supports code pages and a separate country-information file (COUNTRY.SYS)
DATE/TIME	Sets the computer's clock and calendar
DISKCOMP	Supports 1.44M floppy disks
DISKCOPY	Supports 1.44M floppy disks
FDISK	Supports multiple logical disks on a large hard disk
FORMAT	Adds the /N switch for number of sectors and the /T switch for number of tracks; supports 1.44M microfloppy disks
GRAFTABL	Supports code pages as well as additional devices and higher baud rates
KEYB	Replaces KEYBxx programs; supports additional layouts
MODE	Supports code pages as well as additional devices (COM4) and higher baud rates (19,200)
RESTORE	/N restores erased or modified files; /B restores files modified before a given date; /L and /E restore files modified after or before a given time

Batch File Enhancements

Batch files	Supports environment variables
@	Suppresses the display of a line
CALL	Runs a second batch file, returning control to the first batch file

Changes between DOS 3.3 and DOS 4.0

The following changes were made between DOS 3.3 and DOS 4.0.

New Configuration Commands

The following CONFIG.SYS commands are new in DOS 4.0:

INSTALL — Enables loading of terminate-and-stay-resident (TSR) programs previously loaded from the DOS command prompt or in the AUTOEXEC.BAT file; installable programs include FASTOPEN.EXE, KEYB.COM, NLSFUNC.EXE, and SHARE.EXE

REM — Enables you to insert remarks into a CONFIG.SYS file; DOS ignores REM lines

SWITCHES — Disables Enhanced Keyboard functions for compatibility with software that does not recognize the Enhanced Keyboard

XMA2EMS.SYS — Creates and manages expanded memory from certain types of extended memory

XMAEM.SYS — Uses extended memory to emulate an expanded memory adapter on 80386 machines

Other New Commands

The following commands also are new in DOS 4.0:

MEM — Provides a report on available conventional, extended, and expanded memory; lists how much of each is unused

TRUENAME — Lists the actual name of a drive or directory that is affected by a JOIN or SUBST command

Changed Commands

The following commands were changed between DOS 3.3 and DOS 4.0:

ANSI.SYS — /X redefines keys added to Enhanced Keyboards; /L overrides programs that reset the number of screen rows to 25; /K turns off Enhanced Keyboard functions for compatibility with older software

APPEND — Ignores file operations that already include a drive or path in the original specification

BACKUP	Formats destination floppy disks automatically, if necessary
BUFFERS	/X tells DOS to use expanded memory; specifies up to 10,000 buffers and 1 to 8 look-ahead buffers
CHKDSK	Shows the disk's serial number and lists the size and number of allocation units
COUNTRY	Provides support for Japanese, Korean, and Chinese characters (on special Asian hardware only)
DEL/ERASE	/P prompts for confirmation before each file is deleted
DIR	Shows the disk's serial number
DISPLAY.SYS	Checks hardware and chooses the most appropriate type of active display if you don't specify an adapter type
FASTOPEN	/X tells DOS to use expanded memory
FDISK	Supports larger disk partitions and has easier-to-use menus and displays
FORMAT	/V:*label* specifies the volume label; /F:*size* indicates the size of a floppy disk
GRAFTABL	Supports code page 850
GRAPHICS	Supports EGA and VGA adapters; can support more printers
KEYB	/ID.nnn chooses a specific keyboard for countries (such as France, Italy, and Great Britain) that have more than one Enhanced Keyboard
MODE	Specifies the keyboard rate and number of lines displayed on-screen; has parameters for COM ports
PRINTER.SYS	Supports additional features of the IBM ProPrinter
REPLACE	/U updates files that have a more recent date and time
SELECT	Installs DOS
SYS	Enables specification of an optional source drive
TIME	Enables a 12- or 24-hour clock, depending on the country code in use
TREE	Creates a graphic depiction of the directory tree
VDISK.SYS	/X tells DOS to use expanded memory; /E tells DOS to use extended memory

New User Interface

A new user interface, the DOS Shell, enables you to run programs and manage files through a visually oriented menu system. Many error messages are different, and error checking is refined.

Changes between DOS 4.0 and DOS 5.0

The following changes were made between DOS 4.0 and DOS 5.0.

New Configuration Commands

The following CONFIG.SYS commands are new in DOS 5.0:

DEVICEHIGH	Loads device drivers into upper-memory blocks (UMB)
DOS	Loads the operating system into the high-memory area (HMA); supports loading of device drivers into upper-memory blocks (UMB)
EMM386.EXE	Provides expanded memory management; uses XMS memory to emulate expanded memory in 80386 and 80486 PCs; supports upper-memory block (UMB) in 80386 and 80486 PCs; includes VCPI and busmaster support
HIMEM.SYS	Manages extended memory in compliance with the extended-memory specification (XMS); enables the HMA
SETVER	Enables you to control the DOS version reported to a program

Other New Commands

The following commands also are new in DOS 5.0:

DOSKEY	Stores command-line statements in memory for later editing and use

EDIT	Invokes a full-screen, mouse-compatible ASCII-file editor that has on-line documentation with hypertext links
LOADHIGH (LH)	Loads programs into upper (reserved) memory
MIRROR	Saves file-allocation-table (FAT) information; loads delete-tracking memory-resident program
QBASIC	Invokes an improved BASIC programming language interpreter and a full-screen programming environment
SETUP	Installs DOS 5.0
UNDELETE	Recovers a deleted file
UNFORMAT	Recovers data after an accidental format

Changed Commands

The following commands were changed between DOS 4.0 and DOS 5.0:

ATTRIB	+S/-S sets and clears the system attribute; +H/-H sets and clears the hidden attribute
DIR	/S searches multiple subdirectories for files; /O sorts the directory listing by file size, file name, type of file, and date and time of file creation; /A displays file attributes; the DIRCMD environment variable stores DIR settings; /B displays file name only; /L displays file names in lowercase
DOSSHELL	Enables you to view the file-list area and program-list area simultaneously, rename directories, search for files, and switch among active programs; provides full mouse support
FDISK	Creates a single partition up to 2G (gigabytes); SHARE no longer is needed to access partitions larger than 32M
FIND	Ignores case during a search for a character string
FORMAT	Runs MIRROR automatically in anticipation of a possible need to unformat a disk; /Q quick-formats a previously formatted disk; /U performs unconditional formatting; supports 2.88M 3.5-inch floppy disks
MEM	/Program and /Debug display the status of programs and drivers as well as information on RAM availability; /Classify lists program size, summarizes memory in use, and lists the largest blocks of RAM available in conventional and upper memory

| MODE | Sets typematic rate and delay, which controls the rate at which keys repeat |
| On-line help | /? after or HELP before any command-line command displays the command syntax, along with a short description of the command's purpose |

Changes between DOS 5.0 and DOS 6.0

The following changes were made between DOS 5.0 and DOS 6.0.

New Configuration Commands

The following CONFIG.SYS commands are new in DOS 6.0:

[COMMON]	Provides a special block of configuration lines that are processed for all menu blocks
DBLSPACE.SYS	Provides access to compressed drives
INCLUDE	Interprets another block of configuration lines as though that block were copied into this place in the CONFIG.SYS file
INTERLNK.EXE	Enables you to use drives and printers from another PC, connected through a serial or parallel cable
MENUCOLOR	Enables you to choose color selections for menu display during boot process
MENUDEFAULT	Defines which menu item is initially highlighted as the default and determines the amount of time that should pass before the default is automatically executed
MENUITEM	Generates a menu display during boot process
NUMLOCK	Enables you to specify whether the NUMLOCK key is initially in the locked or unlocked state
POWER.EXE	Provides a device driver to control power-saving features in laptops
SET	Enables you to create and modify environment variables from CONFIG.SYS

SUBMENU	Generates subsidiary menus during boot process
SWITCHES	Restricts use of Enhanced Keyboard functions; controls where WINA20.386 file is placed; prevents use of F5 and F8 keys to bypass CONFIG.SYS commands

Other New Commands

The following commands also are new in DOS 6.0:

CHOICE	Enables a batch file to check for user keystrokes
DBLSPACE	Customizes drives compressed by DBLSPACE.SYS
DEFRAG	Rearranges files in a disk partition for improved performance
DELTREE	Deletes a directory and all the files contained within it
EXPAND	Copies and decompresses files from original MS-DOS 6.0 disks
FASTHELP	Displays brief help information about commands; less detailed than HELP
HELP	Displays the complete reference information for all DOS commands
INTERLNK	Provides a client-side utility for connecting two PCs via serial or parallel cable
INTERSVR	Provides a server utility for connecting two PCs via serial or parallel cable
MEMMAKER	Optimizes use of upper-memory blocks (UMB) by device drivers and terminate-and-stay-resident (TSR) programs
MOVE	Moves one or more files from one location to another; can also rename a directory
MSAV	Tests a disk for viruses and (optionally) removes them
MSBACKUP	Backs up or restores files; archives files to floppies
MSD	Displays detailed technical information about computer hardware and resident software
MWAV	Tests a disk for viruses and (optionally) removes them (Windows version of MSAV)

MWAVTSR	Allows messages from the VSAFE program to be visible in Windows
MWBACKUP	Backs up or restores files; archives files to floppies (Windows version of MSBACKUP)
MWUNDEL	Recovers a deleted file (Windows version of UNDELETE)
POWER	Provides a power-control utility for laptops; used with POWER.EXE device driver
SMARTMON	Monitors and controls efficiency of SMARTDRV cache (Windows utility)
VSAFE	Provides a TSR for active protection against viruses

If your PC is connected to a LAN manager network or to a network where other computers are running Microsoft Windows for Workgroups, the following commands also are available in DOS 6.0:

NET	Provides network access
MAIL	Handles workgroup mail
MICRO	Provides a resident program for user notification of incoming mail

Changed Commands

The following commands were changed between DOS 5.0 and 6.0:

COMMAND	/K switch runs a batch file and doesn't exit afterward
DEVICE	Optional question mark causes user query during boot, enabling user to choose whether to load the driver
EMM386	Offers the following new switches: AUTO, MIN. L, NOVCPI. HIGHSCAN, WIN, NOHI, ROM, NOMOVEXBDA, ALTBOOT
HIMEM	Offers the following new switches: /A20CONTROL, /EISA, and /VERBOSE
MEM	Offers the following new switches: /FREE, /MODULE, /PAGE; the old switch /PROGRAM was deleted
SET	Is now legal in CONFIG.SYS
UNDELETE	Offers new TSR form that saves whole files as they are deleted

NOTE The following commands were moved to the supplemental disk. Although no longer part of MS-DOS, these commands can be ordered from Microsoft by using the order form provided in the MS-DOS manual (RECOVER is no longer available):

ASSIGN

BACKUP

COMP

EDLIN

EXE2BIN

GORILLA

GRAFTABL

JOIN

MIRROR

New Features

The following table summarizes the new features of DOS 6.0:

Anti-Virus	New programs for DOS and Windows that detect and remove viruses
Backup	New backup programs for DOS and Windows that have greater speed and offer data compression
CONFIG.SYS	Enables you to display menus at boot time so that you can choose between alternative configurations
DBLSPACE	Provides real-time compression of hard and floppy disks
DEFRAG	Improves disk performance by eliminating file fragmentation
EMM386	Uses a single pool of memory for both EMS and XMS, eliminating the need for pre-allocation
F5	Pressing this key during the boot process bypasses CONFIG.SYS and AUTOEXEC.BAT entirely
F8	Pressing this key during boots enables you to determine—line by line—whether you want to process each line of CONFIG.SYS
HELP	Provides help for all DOS and Windows commands

Installation	Easier and more flexible installation process
MEMMAKER	Automatically optimizes loading of TSRs and device drivers in upper-memory blocks
Workgroup	Several new applications for communicating with users of Windows for Workgroups

DOS Control and Editing Keys

This appendix lists the functions of various control and editing keys used at the command line and in the DOS Shell.

Command-Line Control Keys

Backspace-←	Moves left and deletes one character from the line
Ctrl-Alt-Del	Restarts (reboots) DOS
Ctrl-Break Ctrl-C	Stops a command; generates a new prompt
Ctrl-Num Lock Ctrl-S	Freezes the video display; pressing any other key restarts the display
Ctrl-PrtSc Ctrl-PrintScreen Ctrl-P	Echoes lines sent to the screen to the printer, giving this sequence
Enter	Tells DOS to act on the line you just typed
Shift-PrtSc Shift-PrintScreen	Prints the contents of the video display

Command-Line Editing Keys without DOSKey

When you type a line at the DOS prompt and press Enter, DOS copies the line into an input buffer. When you press certain keys, you can use the same line over and over.

The following keys enable you to edit the input-buffer line. When you press Enter, the new line is placed in the primary input buffer as DOS executes the line. These editing keys are effective when editing the input-buffer, if DOSKey is not loaded.

Tab	Moves the cursor to the next tab stop and puts the tab character in the input buffer
Del	Deletes a character from the line
Esc	Cancels the current line without changing the buffer
F1 or →	Copies one character from the preceding command line
F2	Copies all characters from the preceding command line up to, but not including, the next character you type
F3	Copies all remaining characters from the preceding command line
F4	Deletes all characters from the preceding command line up to, but not including, the next character you type (opposite of F2)
F5	Moves the current line into the buffer but does not enable DOS to execute the line
F6	Puts an end-of-file marker (^Z) in the command buffer
Ins	Enables you to insert characters into the command line

Command-Line Editing Keys with DOSKey

If you have DOSKey loaded, the following keys are available:

←	Moves the cursor one character to the left
→	Moves the cursor one character to the right

↑	Displays the preceding DOS command
↓	Displays the DOS command issued after the one currently displayed, or displays a blank line when you are at the end of the list
Alt-F7	Clears the command-history buffer
Alt-F10	Clears macro definitions
Backspace	Moves the cursor one column to the left, deleting the character that was there
Ctrl-←	Moves the cursor one word to the left
Ctrl-→	Moves the cursor one word to the right
Ctrl-End	Removes all characters from the cursor to the end of the line
Ctrl-Home	Removes all characters from the cursor to the beginning of the line
Del	Deletes the character at the cursor
End	Moves the cursor to the space after the last character in the command line
Esc	Erases the contents of the command line
F7	Displays the contents of the command-history buffer in a numbered list
F8	Searches for the command(s) that most closely match characters typed at the command line
F9	Prompts for a line number, where *line number* refers to the number displayed next to a command in the command-history listing generated by pressing F7; press the number to display the corresponding command
Home	Moves the cursor to the left end of the command line
Ins	Toggles between Replace mode (the default) and Insert mode (notice that the cursor changes shape)
PgDn	Displays the last command stored in the DOSKey command buffer
PgUp	Displays the earliest command issued that still is stored in the DOSKey command buffer

Keystroke Commands

DOS 6.0 assigns special functions to some keys when you use them within the DOS Shell:

+	Expands current branch of the directory tree by one level
*	Expands all levels of current branch of the directory tree
-	Collapses current branch of the directory tree
↑ or ↓	Moves selection cursor in the direction of the arrow
Alt	Activates the menu bar (same as F10)
Alt-F4	Exits from the DOS Shell to the command line and removes the DOS Shell from memory (same as F3)
Ctrl-*	Expands all branches of the directory tree
Ctrl-/	Selects all files in the selected directory
Ctrl-\	Deselects all files in the selected directory
Ctrl-End	Moves to the end of the list
Ctrl-F5	Refreshes the file list for current directory
Ctrl-Home	Moves to the beginning of a list
Ctrl-letter key	Selects drive and displays directories
↓	In the directory tree, moves cursor to the following directory
↑	In the directory tree, moves cursor to the preceding directory
Del	Deletes the selected file(s); in the program list, deletes the selected item
End	Moves to the bottom of the selected area
Esc	Cancels the current function
F1	Displays context-sensitive help
F2	In the program list, copies the selected program
F3	Exits from the DOS Shell to the command line and removes the DOS Shell from memory (same as Alt-F4)
F5	Refreshes the file list(s)
F7	Moves the selected file(s)
F8	Copies the selected file(s)

F9	Displays contents of the selected file; illegal if more than one file is selected
F10	Activates the menu bar (same as Alt)
Home	Moves to the top of the selected area
Letter key	Moves to the next file beginning with that letter
PgDn	Scrolls down through the selected area one screen at a time
PgUp	Scrolls up through the selected area one screen at a time
Shift-↑ or Shift-↓	In the file-list area, extends the selection in the direction of the arrow
Shift-F5	Repaints the screen
Shift-F8	Toggles Add mode for extending the selection of nonconsecutive files; select files by pressing the space bar
Shift-F9	Accesses the command line without removing the DOS Shell from memory; use EXIT to get back to the DOS Shell
Shift-PgDn	Extends the selection to include all files in the following window
Shift-PgUp	Extends the selection to include all files in the preceding window
Shift-space bar	Adds all files between the cursor position and the preceding selected file
Shift-Tab	Cycles counterclockwise through the DOS Shell window
Space bar	In Add mode, adds this file to the selection at the location of the cursor
Tab	Cycles clockwise through the DOS Shell window

The following key commands are available in the DOS Shell if task swapping is enabled:

Alt-Tab	Cycles through list of programs
Ctrl-Esc	Suspends program and moves to the DOS Shell window
Shift-Enter	Starts a program and adds it to the task list

When the console is used like an input file in commands (COPYCON, *filename* for example), certain keystrokes have the following special meanings:

Backspace	Backs up one column and removes the character
Ctrl-Break or Ctrl-C	Aborts the command
F6	Puts an end-of-file marker (^Z) in the buffer and terminates the copy operation when you press Enter; any data following the marker is not copied to the destination file

ASCII and Extended ASCII Codes

T his appendix presents the ASCII, Extended ASCII, and Extended Function ASCII codes.

Dec X_{10}	Hex X_{16}	Binary X_2	ASCII Character
000	00	0000 0000	null
001	01	0000 0001	☺
002	02	0000 0010	☻
003	03	0000 0011	♥
004	04	0000 0100	◆
005	05	0000 0101	♣
006	06	0000 0110	♠

Dec X_{10}	Hex X_{16}	Binary X_2	ASCII Character
007	07	0000 0111	●
008	08	0000 1000	■
009	09	0000 1001	○
010	0A	0000 1010	■
011	0B	0000 1011	♂
012	0C	0000 1100	♀
013	0D	0000 1101	♪
014	0E	0000 1110	♪♪
015	0F	0000 1111	☼
016	10	0001 0000	►
017	11	0001 0001	◄
018	12	0001 0010	↕
019	13	0001 0011	‼
020	14	0001 0100	¶
021	15	0001 0101	§
022	16	0001 0110	▬
023	17	0001 0111	↨
024	18	0001 1000	↑
025	19	0001 1001	↓
026	1A	0001 1010	→
027	1B	0001 1011	←
028	1C	0001 1100	FS
029	1D	0001 1101	GS
030	1E	0001 1110	RS
031	1F	0001 1111	US
032	20	0010 0000	SP
033	21	0010 0001	!
034	22	0010 0010	"
035	23	0010 0011	#
036	24	0010 0100	$
037	25	0010 0101	%

Dec X_{10}	Hex X_{16}	Binary X_2	ASCII Character
038	26	0010 0110	&
039	27	0010 0111	'
040	28	0010 1000	(
041	29	0010 1001	)
042	2A	0010 1010	*
043	2B	0010 1011	+
044	2C	0010 1100	,
045	2D	0010 1101	-
046	2E	0010 1110	.
047	2F	0010 1111	/
048	30	0011 0000	0
049	31	0011 0001	1
050	32	0011 0010	2
051	33	0011 0011	3
052	34	0011 0100	4
053	35	0011 0101	5
054	36	0011 0110	6
055	37	0011 0111	7
056	38	0011 1000	8
057	39	0011 1001	9
058	3A	0011 1010	:
059	3B	0011 1011	;
060	3C	0011 1100	<
061	3D	0011 1101	=
062	3E	0011 1110	>
063	3F	0011 1111	?
064	40	0100 0000	@
065	41	0100 0001	A
066	42	0100 0010	B
067	43	0100 0011	C
068	44	0100 0100	D
069	45	0100 0101	E
070	46	0100 0110	F

Dec X_{10}	Hex X_{16}	Binary X_2	ASCII Character
071	47	0100 0111	G
072	48	0100 1000	H
073	49	0100 1001	I
074	4A	0100 1010	J
075	4B	0100 1011	K
076	4C	0100 1100	L
077	4D	0100 1101	M
078	4E	0100 1110	N
079	4F	0100 1111	O
080	50	0101 0000	P
081	51	0101 0001	Q
082	52	0101 0010	R
083	53	0101 0011	S
084	54	0101 0100	T
085	55	0101 0101	U
086	56	0101 0110	V
087	57	0101 0111	W
088	58	0101 1000	X
089	59	0101 1001	Y
090	5A	0101 1010	Z
091	5B	0101 1011	[
092	5C	0101 1100	\
093	5D	0101 1101	]
094	5E	0101 1110	^
095	5F	0101 1111	–
096	60	0110 0000	`
097	61	0110 0001	a
098	62	0110 0010	b
099	63	0110 0011	c
100	64	0110 0100	d
101	65	0110 0101	e
102	66	0110 0110	f
103	67	0110 0111	g

Dec X_{10}	Hex X_{16}	Binary X_2	ASCII Character
104	68	0110 1000	h
105	69	0110 1001	i
106	6A	0110 1010	j
107	6B	0110 1011	k
108	6C	0110 1100	l
109	6D	0110 1101	m
110	6E	0110 1110	n
111	6F	0110 1111	o
112	70	0111 0000	p
113	71	0111 0001	q
114	72	0111 0010	r
115	73	0111 0011	s
116	74	0111 0100	t
117	75	0111 0101	u
118	76	0111 0110	v
119	77	0111 0111	w
120	78	0111 1000	x
121	79	0111 1001	y
122	7A	0111 1010	z
123	7B	0111 1011	{
124	7C	0111 1100	¦
125	7D	0111 1101	}
126	7E	0111 1110	~
127	7F	0111 1111	DEL
128	80	1000 0000	Ç
129	81	1000 0001	ü
130	82	1000 0010	é
131	83	1000 0011	â
132	84	1000 0100	ä
133	85	1000 0101	à
134	86	1000 0110	å
135	87	1000 0111	ç
136	88	1000 1000	ê

Dec X_{10}	Hex X_{16}	Binary X_2	ASCII Character
137	89	1000 1001	ë
138	8A	1000 1010	è
139	8B	1000 1011	ï
140	8C	1000 1100	î
141	8D	1000 1101	ì
142	8E	1000 1110	Ä
143	8F	1000 1111	Å
144	90	1001 0000	É
145	91	1001 0001	æ
146	92	1001 0010	Æ
147	93	1001 0011	ô
148	94	1001 0100	ö
149	95	1001 0101	ò
150	96	1001 0110	û
151	97	1001 0111	ù
152	98	1001 1000	ÿ
153	99	1001 1001	Ö
154	9A	1001 1010	Ü
155	9B	1001 1011	¢
156	9C	1001 1100	£
157	9D	1001 1101	¥
158	9E	1001 1110	Pt
159	9F	1001 1111	ƒ
160	A0	1010 0000	á
161	A1	1010 0001	í
162	A2	1010 0010	ó
163	A3	1010 0011	ú
164	A4	1010 0100	ñ
165	A5	1010 0101	Ñ
166	A6	1010 0110	ª
167	A7	1010 0111	º
168	A8	1010 1000	¿
169	A9	1010 1001	⌐

Dec X₁₀	Hex X₁₆	Binary X₂	ASCII Character
170	AA	1010 1010	⌐
171	AB	1010 1011	½
172	AC	1010 1100	¼
173	AD	1010 1101	¡
174	AE	1010 1110	«
175	AF	1010 1111	»
176	B0	1011 0000	░
177	B1	1011 0001	▒
178	B2	1011 0010	▓
179	B3	1011 0011	│
180	B4	1011 0100	┤
181	B5	1011 0101	╡
182	B6	1011 0110	╢
183	B7	1011 0111	╖
184	B8	1011 1000	╕
185	B9	1011 1001	╣
186	BA	1011 1010	║
187	BB	1011 1011	╗
188	BC	1011 1100	╝
189	BD	1011 1101	╜
190	BE	1011 1110	╛
191	BF	1011 1111	┐
192	C0	1100 0000	└
193	C1	1100 0001	┴
194	C2	1100 0010	┬
195	C3	1100 0011	├
196	C4	1100 0100	─
197	C5	1100 0101	┼
198	C6	1100 0110	
199	C7	1100 0111	╟
200	C8	1100 1000	╚
201	C9	1100 1001	╔
202	CA	1100 1010	╩

Dec X_{10}	Hex X_{16}	Binary X_2	ASCII Character
203	CB	1100 1011	⊤⊤
204	CC	1100 1100	╠
205	CD	1100 1101	=
206	CE	1100 1110	╬
207	CF	1100 1111	⊥
208	D0	1101 0000	╨
209	D1	1101 0001	╤
210	D2	1101 0010	╥
211	D3	1101 0011	╙
212	D4	1101 0100	╘
213	D5	1101 0101	╒
214	D6	1101 0110	╓
215	D7	1101 0111	╫
216	D8	1101 1000	╪
217	D9	1101 1001	┘
218	DA	1101 1010	┌
219	DB	1101 1011	█
220	DC	1101 1100	▄
221	DD	1101 1101	▌
222	DE	1101 1110	▐
223	DF	1101 1111	▀
224	E0	1110 0000	α
225	E1	1110 0001	β
226	E2	1110 0010	Γ
227	E3	1110 0011	π
228	E4	1110 0100	Σ
229	E5	1110 0101	σ
230	E6	1110 0110	μ
231	E7	1110 0111	τ
232	E8	1110 1000	Φ
233	E9	1110 1001	θ
234	EA	1110 1010	Ω

Dec X_{10}	Hex X_{16}	Binary X_2	ASCII Character
235	EB	1110 1011	δ
236	EC	1110 1100	∞
237	ED	1110 1101	ø
238	EE	1110 1110	∈
239	EF	1110 1111	∩
240	F0	1110 0000	≡
241	F1	1111 0001	±
242	F2	1111 0010	≥
243	F3	1111 0011	≤
244	F4	1111 0100	⌠
245	F5	1111 0101	⌡
246	F6	1111 0110	÷
247	F7	1111 0111	≈
248	F8	1111 1000	°
249	F9	1111 1001	•
250	FA	1111 1010	·
251	FB	1111 1011	√
252	FC	1111 1100	η
253	FD	1111 1101	2
254	FE	1111 1110	■
255	FF	1111 1111	

Symbols

A

Q-R

W

X–Y–Z